Cheap Sleep Guide to Europe 1993

KATIE WOOD was born and educated in Edinburgh. She read Communications then English at university, and worked as a freelance journalist before specializing in travel in 1981. Author of many guidebooks, she has made a name for herself both in Britain and internationally for her practical, down-to-earth approach, and the quality of her research.

Katie Wood continues to write freelance for, among others, the *Observer*, the *Independent*, the *Guardian*, the *Scotsman* and several national magazines. She also regularly contributes to television and radio travel programmes. She is a fellow of the Royal Geographical Society, undertakes specialist travel consultancy work for airlines and tourist boards, and is acknowledged as an expert on the impact of travel on the environment.

Married with two children, Katie Wood lives in Perth, Scotland.

GU00760710

Available by Katie Wood
Europe By Train
The Best of British Country House Hotels
The 100 Greatest Holidays in the World
The 1992 Business Travel Guide
The Good Tourist
The Good Tourist in France
The Good Tourist in the UK
The Good Tourist in Turkey
Scotland

Cheap Sleep Guide to Europe 1993

KATIE WOOD

**Editorial Assistant and
1992–3 Head Researcher: Craig Aitken**

Fontana

An Imprint of HarperCollins*Publishers*

An Imprint of HarperCollinsPublishers,
77–85 Fulham Palace Road,
Hammersmith, London W6 8JB

A FONTANA ORIGINAL 1993

9 8 7 6 5 4 3 2 1

Copyright © Katie Wood 1992, 1993

The Author asserts the moral right to
be identified as the author of this work

A catalogue record for this book is
available from the British Library

ISBN 0 00 637728 9

Set in Palacio by
Avocet Typesetters, Bicester, Oxon

Printed in Great Britain by
HarperCollinsManufacturing Glasgow

All rights reserved. No part of this publication may be
reproduced, stored in a retrieval system, or transmitted,
in any form or by any means, electronic, mechanical,
photocopying, recording or otherwise, without the prior
permission of the publishers.

This book is sold subject to the condition that it shall not,
by way of trade or otherwise, be lent, re-sold, hired out or
otherwise circulated without the publisher's prior consent
in any form of binding or cover other than that in which it
is published and without a similar condition including this
condition being imposed on the subsequent purchaser.

Contents

To Craig Aitken, editorial assistant and 1992–3 head researcher, a large debt is owed for his last-minute burning of the midnight oil. Also for his checking, double-checking and checking again. Sorry about the fleas in the various pits, Craig. By the time you stop scratching, you'll be on the road again.

Introduction

The single most difficult thing when travelling round Europe on a budget is to find a clean, safe and comfortable place to lay your head come nightfall. Whether you're Inter Railing, hitching, cycling, bussing or driving round the continent, unless you want to follow a strict timetable and book beds ahead (and you can rarely book the real budget ones anyway), your main headache is going to be getting accommodation sorted out.

In the main cities and resorts in high season, you'll soon begin to feel as if you're back in the school nativity play again – the Mary and Joseph 'no room at the inn' syndrome really gets to you after a while, as you trail round the streets looking for a suitable pensione, hostel or campsite. Rather than being 'great with child', of course, you're great with rucksack – almost as uncomfortable after a few miles in high temperatures. It's not much to ask, you grumble to anyone who'll listen, a bed for under £10 a night, preferably nearer £5. But the trouble these days is that so many people are 'doing Europe' using the same guidebooks, that supply never meets the demand. Or does it? Well, there actually *are* enough places, it's all a matter of knowing where to look. In your home town, you could probably find beds for £5–8 without a problem. But that's because you would *know* where to look, whereas a tourist in your town would never find it so simple. And that's the position, a stranger, that you will be in many times in Europe.

This book can be your guide to the 'inside knowledge' that a local has. I've stayed in more than my fair share of dives, from a house of ill-repute in Casablanca (not a lot of sleep that night!) to what turned out to be a hippy commune in Denmark (you thought no one said 'far-out, man' any longer?). Neither were experiences I'd repeat, but as the wrinklies say, 'If I'd known then what I know now . . .' So as I slap on the vitamin E cream, you might as well have the benefit of my good and bad experiences now.

This guide is written as a reaction to the literally hundreds of letters I receive each year from readers of my *Europe by Train* guide. You asked for more accommodation suggestions – well, now you've got them, in a book dedicated exclusively to this subject. And as I've listed so many, it should spread *Cheap Sleep* readers more thinly and at least give each of you a chance of getting that pack off your back and putting your feet up, after a long day's travelling. I know, after a couple of hours searching, in true biblical style, you'd even settle for a stable.

This guide covers all types of cheap accommodation: pensiones; hostels – both IYHF and independent; campsites; sleep-ins; student hostels; campus accommodation; private accommodation with families; and, if all else fails, 'safe' places to sleep rough. The recommendations will obviously vary in quality and price, but they are all the cheapest around in that country – it's just a fact that a 'cheap sleep' in Norway will cost you three times what it will in Turkey.

In terms of hierarchy and which type of accommodation suits who, basically, **hotels**, **pensiones** and **B&Bs** are usually the most expensive, but they are also one of the most comfortable options. About the same price, and an excellent way of finding out more about the locals is to stay with them direct: **private accommodation** is generally arranged through Tourist Offices. Effectively you become a paying guest, mixing with the family and getting the opportunity to ask all the questions about their lifestyle and culture that you otherwise might not have had the chance to. **Private** and **IYHF hostels** are pretty much on a par in terms of price. If a private hostel is offering rates half that of the local IYHF, it's generally because standards are extremely low.

Sleep-Ins and **YMCA/YWCA Interpoints** are fairly recent developments. Very reasonably priced, and an excellent way to meet other travellers, the only problem is that they're limited to certain locations in Europe. **Camping** is fine if you're the outdoor type and are experienced in pitching a tent and cooking over a camping stove. An International Camping Carnet is a good idea if you plan doing a good deal of camping and these Carnets can be bought at most sites. Official camping is obviously more regimented than 'freelance' camping, but as the latter is illegal in some countries (I state which in the guide), the choice is often made for you. Always clean up after yourself and seek permission from the landowner, wherever you are. Using **student halls of residence** is a good way to get round Europe. It's cheap, they're well equipped, and you meet other travellers. Tourist Offices have details.

If you want further information to that provided in this book, and if you're very organized, you could write ahead to the individual country's Tourist Boards, located in your capital city (London in our case).

If you come across a place suggested in this guide that has dropped standards, upped prices or is definitely not worth recommending any longer, please drop me a line and let me know. Likewise, if you find a little gem, pass on the info so we can all benefit. Particularly in Eastern Europe, where the demand for cheap beds now exceeds supply ten times over, we could all do with other travellers' hints and help.

However you do it, wherever you get to, I sincerely hope this much-requested guide will help you.

KATIE WOOD
Perth, Scotland
December 1992

Be a Good Tourist

As this edition of *Cheap Sleep* goes to press the second edition of my latest project is about to be published; it's something very close to my heart; something I believe in very strongly, and not since the launch of *Europe by Train* have I felt that there was such a great need for a book like this. It should be of interest to many of *Cheap Sleep*'s and *Europe by Train*'s intrepid types, and the theory behind the book is of relevance to all of us who travel, in any way, at any time. Called *The Good Tourist – A Guide to Green Travel Worldwide* – the book addresses the issues of the impact of tourism on the environment and society. It's about what you are on the point of doing – travelling to a foreign country; any country. What you do; where you go; how you go; where you sleep; what you eat – it all has a great impact on that country. You can make this a positive or negative experience. For too many countries, for too many years now, the impact has been increasingly negative, and it's up to every one of us to take account of our actions.

Traditionally, travel has been seen as a good thing. Tourism generates valuable income for a country (indeed, more money is made through tourism and its related services than any other industry in the world!), and broadening the horizons and experiencing other cultures can only do good, can't it? Well, it can be good for the guest, but what of the host in this relationship? How much income goes back into the pockets of the waiters and taxi drivers in Third World countries such as Thailand and Gambia from all the mass tourism in their country? How much land is given over to developments for wealthy tourists? What control do any of us as individuals have on the mass developments going on the world over in the name of tourism?

We are destroying the very things we set out to see. Europe is a classic case, and travelling through it is a good way to discover the truth about the tourist industry. Venice is sinking under the weight of tourists' feet; the Acropolis is being eroded by pollution and over-visiting; the once-beautiful beaches of the Spanish costas and the Med are polluted and ugly; the Alps are crumbling under the pressure of skiing.

Fortunately, the current wave of 'green thinking' is also percolating into tourism and travel. But is enough being done? Where is the mass industry going? Are you leaving your conscience at home when you travel? Have you really questioned why you are making this trip? Do you truly respect the country you are visiting? What do you hope to gain from this trip? Do you make an effort to meet the locals and to get to know the real culture of the place? Are you staying in appropriate accommodation; are you adding to the litter and pollution? The chances are, you, like most educated independent travellers, are among the few who try to be as 'green' as possible in your travel. Staying in locals' houses, or hostels or camping makes sense, and having a caring and aware attitude, you will probably be contributing as little as possible to the deterioration of our world.

My husband (an ecologist) and I have written a book which looks in detail at how to be a good tourist; it looks at the impact of all different types of holidays; it tells you which companies to travel with (and which not to). Now that being green is so trendy, it's good to separate the wheat from the chaff. Reading this may make your European wanderings all the more pertinent and give you more of an idea of the overall plan of things. The book aims to take a balanced approach between tourism and related development, and the need to conserve the very things that most of us as tourists want to enjoy. Knowing so many of you from your letters as I do, I feel sure it's the sort of read you'll enjoy. I welcome your comments.

The Good Tourist Guide is reissued in 1992 along with the first two in a new series, *The Good Tourist in the UK* and *The Good Tourist in France*.

Note to readers

The exchange rate used in this guide is £1 = $1.75.

AUSTRIA (Österreich)

Despite being widely regarded as one of the most expensive countries to visit, accommodation prices in Austria are reasonable, especially when the quality of the places to stay is taken into account. The standard of all types of accommodation in Austria is high, with impeccable levels of cleanliness almost guaranteed. With only a few exceptions, finding moderately priced accommodation on arrival is relatively easy in most places throughout the year. As the student hostels and IYHF hostels do not open until July, late June can be a particularly bad time for those looking for inexpensive accommodation in the cities. Finding somewhere cheap to stay in Vienna can be tricky at any time of the year, while Salzburg becomes very crowded during its summer festival (late July–August). However, as there are reasonably cheap rooms available in the cities, and plenty of hostel beds, you can save yourself frustration on arrival (and probably money as well) by taking the trouble to book ahead. If you have not booked in advance, it might be advisable to take a tent, even if only for use in emergencies.

Hotels are graded from one star up to five stars. In general, hotel prices are higher in the cities (especially Vienna) and in the Alpine resorts, so unless you are travelling extensively, hotels are likely to be beyond your budget in most places you visit. Away from the main tourist towns and resorts, a double in a one-star hotel generally costs from 400AS upwards per person (£20; $35), but in the more popular tourist areas prices for a similar room start around 700AS p.p. (£35; $61). As hoteliers try to fill their rooms outside the peak-season months of July to August, prices may be reduced: in May, June and September by 15–25 per cent, and by up to 40 per cent for the rest of the year. Pensions, seasonal hotels and *gasthaüser* are cheaper than hotels. These are graded from one star up to four stars, with a two-star pension being the rough equivalent of a one-star hotel. Outside Vienna, prices for doubles are normally under 400AS (£20; $35). Unfortunately, these tend to fill up quickly during the busy periods.

Private rooms and **gasthäuser** can be booked through Tourist Offices, or through private organizations which control a number of rooms. Alternatively, simply approach the owner of any house or farmhouse displaying a sign saying '*Zimmer frei*', or showing a stylized white bed on a green background. In the cities and resorts expect to pay from 300–400AS (£15–20; $26–35) for doubles. Elsewhere, 100–160AS for a single (£5–8; $9–14), 150–260AS (£7.50–13.00; $13–23) for doubles is the normal price range. Travellers staying only one night may be liable to a small surcharge. The overnight price usually includes a continental breakfast.

At some **farms** it is possible to rent apartments. Most sleep from three to five people, but occasionally larger apartments are available. Assuming you fill all the bed space, you can expect to pay from 60–130AS each per night (£3–7.50; $5.00–13) in the summer. During the winter months prices rise slightly, adding perhaps another 20AS (£1; $1.75) per night to the bill. The minimum length of stay permissible in farm accommodation seems to vary between regions. In the Tyrol it is only possible to pre-book for a week at a time, but in other areas stays of one night seem quite acceptable. If there is a train station nearby, farm accommodation can make a good base for exploring the surrounding area.

There are about a hundred **IYHF** hostels spread over the country, covering all the main places of interest. Many are only open for the period between April/May and September/October, while some open only during July and August. Providing there is space, stays of longer than three days are allowed. The large city hostels can be very institutional, but in the rural areas hostels can be a bit more easygoing, although the 10 p.m. curfew will probably be strictly enforced. In city hostels there is usually a midnight curfew. In general, prices vary from 100–160AS (£5–8; $9–14), usually with breakfast. Higher prices are sometimes charged at the large city hostels, which seek to attract groups by providing a range of facilities that may be of little interest to the budget traveller. As a result, they tend to be monopolized by these groups. It is advisable to have an IYHF card. While some hostels may let you stay for a 25AS surcharge (£1.25; $2), the hostels in Vienna are for members only, as is the main hostel in Innsbruck.

You will also find a few **independent hostels** in the main towns. These are mainly seasonal (May/June to September/October). Unfortunately, curfews are usually just as restrictive as those of their IYHF counterparts. Prices for dormitory accommodation are similar to the IYHF hostels, but some of the independent hostels also offer singles and doubles, with prices ranging from 130–220AS (£6.50–11; $11.50–19.50) per person. Similar prices are charged for accommodation in the various **student residences** that are let out for periods between July and September. Some are run by students themselves, and a much more relaxed atmosphere usually prevails in these establishments.

It is easy to recommend **camping** in Austria, as the campsites are among the best in Europe. Charges at the 450 sites are reasonable, given that they are immaculately maintained and have all the necessary facilities. Pitching a tent costs 35–50AS (£1.75–2.50; $3.00–4.50) and there is a similar fee per occupant. The International Camping Carnet is not obligatory, but holders qualify for reductions at most sites. All the main towns have at least one campsite, and there are plenty of sites in the countryside. Except in Vienna and Linz, the city sites are all within walking distance of the centre. One site in Vienna stays open all year round, but elsewhere even the city sites only open for a period between Easter/May and September/October.

Freelance camping is allowed, but you must first obtain the consent of the local *Bürgermeister*, or the landowner. Avoid lighting fires in or around woodland. Camping rough is a useful option for those planning to do a bit of walking along the excellent network of hiking trails. Be sure to have a good quality sleeping bag, as it gets very cold at night. For anyone planning to hike extensively in the Alps, there are about seven hundred mountain huts, with 25,000 sleeping places (beds, or mattresses on the floor to put your sleeping bag on). Even if all the places are filled, it is unlikely that you will be turned away. All the huts have at least rudimentary kitchen facilities, and many serve meals. Joining one of the clubs might save you money in the long run. The largest is the Österreichischer Alpenverein, which offers its members discounts of 30–60 per cent on the normal overnight prices of 60–180AS (£3–9; $5–16), plus reduced prices on various cable-car trips and organized outings. Membership costs about 300AS (£15; $26) for under 26s, 400AS (£20; $35) otherwise. If you are going hiking in the east of the country, it might be better to get in touch with the Österreichischer Touristenklub.

ADDRESSES

Austrian National Tourist Office	30 Saint George Street, London, W1R 0AL (tel. 071 629 0461)
Austrian YHA Österreichische Jugendherbergsverband	Schottenring 28, 1010 Wien (tel. 0222 5335353). List from the Austrian National Tourist Office.
Camping Österreichischer Camping Club	Johannesgasse 20, 1010 Wien. List from the Austrian National Tourist Office.
Farm accommodation	Various regional lists available from the Austrian National Tourist Office.
Mountain huts	Österreichischer Alpenverein, Wilhelm-Greil-strasse 15, Innsbruck 6020 (tel. 05222 584107).
	Austrian Alpine Club, Getreidemarkt 3, 1060 Wien (tel. 0222 5638673). The UK branch is at Longcroft House, Fretherne Road, Welwyn Garden City, Herts., AL8 6PQ (tel. 0707 324835).

Mountain huts
(continued)

Österreichischer Touristenklub (ÖTK),
1 Backerstrasse 16, Wien
(tel. 0222 523844).

Graz   (tel. code 0316)

Tourist Office
Grazer Tourismus, Herrengasse 16, A-8010 Graz (tel. 835241).
A 10–15 minute walk from the train station. Go right from
the station, left along Annenstrasse, straight through
Südtirolerplatz and over the River Mur. Murgasse leads into
the Hauptplatz, from which you go right after about 250m.
Alternatively, take tram 3 from Europaplatz to the right of the
train station.

HOTELS

Cheapest doubles around 290AS (£14.50; $25.50)

Frühstückspension Kügerl-Lukas, Waagner-Biro-Strasse 8
(tel. 52590). Go right from Graz Hbf, right through the
underpass, then right again. A few minutes' walk.
Gasthof Dorrer, Steinberstrasse 41 (tel. 52647). Well out from
the centre, in the north-western part of the city.

Cheapest doubles around 440AS (£22; $38.50)

Gasthof Schmid Greiner, Grabenstrasse 64 (tel. 681482). A
15–20 minute walk from Graz Hbf. Go down
Keplerstrasse, across the river and straight on until you
see Grabenstrasse on the left.
Gasthof Dokterbauer, Krottendorferstrasse 91 (tel. 284235).
In Graz-West, far from the town centre.
Gasthof Saringer, Gaisbergweg 7 (tel. 53514). In the north-
west of the city, well out from the centre.

Cheapest doubles around 470AS (£23.50; $41)

Gasthof Kokol, Thalstrasse 3 (tel. 53329). In Graz-Nord, far
from the centre.
Gasthof 'Kehlberghof', Kehlbergstrasse 83 (tel. 284125). In
Graz-West, far from the city centre.

Cheapest doubles around 500AS (£25; $44)

Frühstückspension Rückert, Rückertgasse 4 (tel. 33031). Head
right from Graz Hbf to the crossroads. Take tram 1 heading
left down Annenstrasse to junction of Hartenaugasse and
Leechgasse. Rückertgasse is on the right.

'Alt Eggenberg' Wagenhofer, Baiernstrasse 3 (tel. 56615). In
the north-west of the city, well out from the centre. From
the train station head right to the crossroads. Take tram
1 along Eggenbergerstrasse to the terminus on Georgigasse
in Eggenberg. Baiernstrasse is at the top of Georgigasse.

Hotel Strasser, Eggenberger Gurtel 11 (tel. 913977). A
5-minute walk from Graz Hbf, right, then straight over the
crossroads.

PRIVATE ROOMS

Rooms around 130AS (£6.50; $11.50) per person

Geiger, Waltendorfer Hauptstrasse 199a, Waltendorf (tel.
464160). tram 3 from Graz Hbf to Krenngasse.

Puchleitner, Kainbach 155, Ries (tel. 3016685). From the
crossroads right of Graz Hbf take tram 7 heading down
Annenstrasse to the terminus in St Leonhard.

Cheapest rooms around 160AS (£8; $14) per person

Prugger, Riesstrasse 96c, Ries (tel. 378642). Same direction
as Puchleitner above. Walk up Riesstrasse from the tram
terminus.

Stampfl, Mühl 27, Stattegg (tel. 691956). From Hauptplatz
(see Tourist Office above) take tram 4 or 5 to Andritz.

Sagmeister, Purgleitnerstrasse 17, Jakomini (tel. 440225).
Local train to Graz Ostbahnhof, or tram 6 from Graz Hbf
to the junction of Munzgrabenstrasse and Möserhofgasse.
Purgleitnerstrasse is parallel to the right of Brucknerstrasse,
which runs off Munzgrabenstrasse.

Cheapest rooms around 180AS (£9; $16) per person

Maier, Zinsdorfgasse 16, Geidorf (tel. 348353). Bus 31 to Zinsendorfgasse, or bus 63 to Universität.

Hofer, Richard Wagnerstrasse 13 (tel. 383408). Bus 31 to Kreuzgasse.

Rooms around 200AS (£10; $17.50) per person

Weinzettl, Drosselweg 7 (tel. 432752). Tram 3 from Graz Hbf to Krenngasse.

IYHF HOSTEL

Idlhofgasse 74 (tel. 914876). 110AS (£5.50; $9.50) in 8-bedded dorms, 170AS (£8.50; $15) in 4-bedded rooms. Five minutes' walk from the train station. On leaving the station turn right along Bahnhofgurtel, left up Josef-Huber-Gasse, then right into Idlhofgasse.

CAMPING

Graz-Nord (tel. 627622). Open May–Sept. From the crossroads to the right of Graz Hbf take tram 7 heading down Eggenbergerstrasse to the terminus on Burenstrasse in Baiersdorf. Go down Burgenlandstrasse, and straight on until you see the camping area.

Central, Graz-Strassgang (tel. 281831). Open April–Oct. From Hauptplatz (see Tourist Office above) take tram 4 or 5 to the junction of Theodor-Körner-Strasse and Robert-Stolz-Gasse. Go to the right up Stolz-Gasse. The campsite is on the other side of Grabenstrasse, a short walk to the right.

Innsbruck (tel. code 0512)

Tourist Offices
Tourismusverband Innsbruck-Igls, Burggraben 3, 6021
Innsbruck. Contact this office in advance for information, or
to book hotels or private rooms. On arrival, you can book
accommodation or obtain information at the Stadtverkehrsbüro
at the same address (tel. 5356). Open daily 8 a.m. to 7 p.m.
Another branch operates at the main train station (Innsbruck
Hbf) (tel. 583766). Open daily 9 a.m. to 10 p.m. If you are
arriving by car or motorbike, there are offices providing
information and accommodation services on all the main routes
into Innsbruck. The commission for booking rooms at any of
the offices above is 25AS.

Basic Directions
Innsbruck Hbf is just under 10-minutes' walk from the town
centre. From Südtiroler Platz in front of the station take
Brixnerstrasse leading away from the station at the right end
of the square, across Boznerplatz and Wilhelm-Greil-Strasse
and down Meranerstrasse into Maria-Theresien-Strasse.
Turning right at this point, you can follow the street past the
St Anne column to the junction of Marktgraben (left) and
Burggraben (right). Straight ahead Kaiser-Friedrich-Strasse
leads to the Golden Roof in the heart of the Old Town before
turning left towards the River Inn and the Innbrücke.
Alternatively, you can head right from Südtiroler Platz along
Bruneckerstrasse, turn left along Museumstrasse, and then left
again at the junction with Burggraben to the start of Kaiser-
Friedrich-Strasse. Instead of turning left along Museumstrasse
at the end of Bruneckerstrasse, you can turn right under the
railway line to the start of König-Laurin-Strasse (left) and
Amraserstrasse (right). About 15-minutes' walk down
Amraserstrasse is the start of Amraser Seestrasse.
Amraserstrasse itself continues on towards Schlossstrasse (on
the other side of the motorway, at the end of Amraserstrasse),
which leads to Schloss Ambras, a half-hour's walk from

Innsbruck Hbf. A third possibility at the end of Bruneckerstrasse is to follow Ing.-Etzel-Strasse along the side of the railway. Turning left off this street at Claudiastrasse, you reach Claudiaplatz, from which Conradstrasse leads into Falkstrasse. Going right on Falkstrasse you arrive at the junction of the street with Rennweg and Erzherzog-Eugen-Strasse, a short walk from the Mühlauer Brücke. Going left from Südtiroler Platz Sterzingerstrasse leads into Südbahnstrasse, which crosses Karmelitengasse before joining Leopoldstrasse. Going right, Leopoldstrasse leads into Maria-Theresien-Strasse, going left, the street runs into Brennerstrasse near the foot of the Bergisel with the famous ski-jump.

HOTELS

Prices quoted are per person. However, solo travellers can usually expect a supplement to be added to these prices.

Cheapest prices 180–200AS (£9–10; $16–17.50)

Ferrarihof, Brennerstrasse 8 (tel. 580968). Tram 1 to the Bergisel terminus or a 15-minute walk from Innsbruck Hbf.

Riese Haymon, Haymongasse 4 (tel. 599837). About 12 minutes' walk from Innsbruck Hbf. At the junction of Südbahnstrasse and Leopoldstrasse, Rotes Gassl is diagonally opposite. Haymongasse is left off Rotes Gassl.

Menghini, Beda-Weber-Gasse 29 (tel. 41243). Bus S or K to Dr Glatz-Strasse. Follow the street right from the direction the bus was travelling, right along Kaufmannstrasse, then first left into Beda-Weber-Gasse. A 20-minute walk from Innsbruck Hbf: left off Südbahnstrasse along Karmelitengasse, left over the Olympiabrücke and straight on to Burgenlandstrasse, then right down Wetterherrenweg, before going left at Beda-Weber-Gasse.

Möslheim, Oberkoflerweg 8 (tel. 67134). Bus C, D or E to Anton-Rauch-Strasse, or a 25-minute walk from Innsbruck

Hbf. Over the Mühlauer Brücke, up Anton-Rauch-Strasse, and then left at Oberkoflerweg.

Rimmi, Harterhofweg 82 (tel. 84726). Far from the centre, off the main road to Seefeld in the suburb of Kranebitten. Bus LK to Kranebitten.

Cheapest prices 210–230AS (£10.50–11.50; $18.50–20)

Gartenhotel Putzker, Layrstrasse 2 (tel. 281912). Bus F to Fischnalerstrasse (across Fürstenweg from Layrstrasse) or a 15–20-minute walk from Innsbruck Hbf. Near the St Anne column go down Anichstrasse, and then follow Blasius-Hueber-Strasse across the Inn. Turn left along Fürstenweg, and then right at Layrstrasse.

Goldenes Brünnl, St Nikolaus-Gasse 1 (tel. 283519). Bus K to Innstrasse, or a 15-minute walk from Innsbruck Hbf. Cross the river by the Innbrücke and head right along Innstrasse until you see St Nicholas-Gasse on the left.

Laurin, Gumppstrasse 19 (tel. 41104). Tram 3 from Innsbruck Hbf to Gumppstrasse, or a 10-minute walk, left off Amraserstrasse shortly after crossing the Sill.

Heis, Dorfgasse 11 (tel. 285345). Bus A to Daxgasse, then a short walk up that street into Dorfgasse, or a 20-minute walk from Innsbruck Hbf. Cross the Inn by the Innbrücke, head away from the river up Höttingergasse, left at the top of the street, and then right at Dorfgasse.

Paula, Weiherburggasse 15 (tel. 292262). See Glockenhaus IYHF hostel below for directions.

Ölberg, Höhenstrasse 52 (tel. 286125). A long walk from the station in the hills above the suburb of Hötting. Bus N to Ölberg from Innsbruck Hbf.

Neuhauser, Exlgasse 49 (tel. 284185). Bus B to Exlgasse from Innsbruck Hbf, bus F to Angergasse then a short walk back to Exlgasse. A long way from Innsbruck Hbf, but only a few minutes' walk from the Höttinger Bahnhof.

Innrain, Innrain 38 (tel. 588981). A 10-minute walk from Innsbruck Hbf. Follow Marktgraben to the start of Innrain.

Lisbeth, Dr Glatz-Strasse 24 (tel. 41107). Bus S or K to Dr

Glatz-Strasse then left down the street from the way the bus was travelling, or tram 3 to the Dr Glatz-Strasse stop on Amraserstrasse. The tram stop is slightly further away. A 15–20-minute walk from Innsbruck Hbf, right off Amraserstrasse, or left off Burgenlandstrasse (see Hotel Menghini above).

Bergisel, Bergisel 2 (tel. 581912). A three-star hotel with only a few rooms at these prices. A 15-minute walk from Innsbruck Hbf or tram 1 to the Bergisel terminus.

Cheapest prices around 235–250AS (£11.75–12.50; $20.50–22)

Bistro, Pradlerstrasse 2 (tel. 46319). Bus R to Pradlerstrasse or a 10-minute walk from Innsbruck Hbf. Left off Amraserstrasse down Defreggerstrasse shortly after crossing the Sill, then left along Pradlerstrasse.

Hotel-Pension Binder, Dr Glatz-Strasse 20 (tel. 42236). See Lisbeth for directions.

Oberrauch, Leopoldstrasse 35 (tel. 587881). Just over 5 minutes' walk from the station. Head off Sudbahnstrasse down Mentlgasse on to Leopoldstrasse, then a short walk right.

Glockenhaus, Weiherburggasse 3 (tel. 85563). See Glockenhaus IYHF hostel for directions.

Cheapest doubles around 260AS (£13; $23)

Stoi, Salurnerstrasse 7 (tel. 585434). A few minutes' walk from Innsbruck Hbf. The street leads away from the station at the left hand end of Südtiroler Platz.

Goldener Winkel, Reichenauerstrasse 16 (tel. 46368). Bus R to Pradlerstrasse, or a 12-minute walk from Innsbruck Hbf (see Jugendherberge Innsbruck IYHF hostel for directions).

PRIVATE ROOMS

Cheapest prices around 140AS (£7; $12.50) per person

Elisabeth Mayr, Pradler Saggen 3 (tel. 449243). Bus R to

Pauluskirche, or a 15–20 minute-walk from the station. At the end of König-Laurin-Strasse turn right along Dreiheiligenstrasse, across the Sill then left along Kärnterstrasse beside the river. Pradler Saggen is in from the river, just beyond Prinz-Eugen-Strasse.

Cheapest prices around 160AS (£8; $14) per person

Maria Grabner, Col-di-Lana-Strasse 14 (No telephone). Well out from the centre. Bus S to Dörrstrasse (other side of Hallerstrasse from Col-di-Lana-Strasse).

Agnes Lechtaler, Luigenstrasse 39 (tel. 439103). Near Schloss Amras. Bus K to Amras, or a 30-minute walk from Innsbruck Hbf. Right off Amraser Seestrasse down Geyrstrasse into Luigenstrasse.

Cheapest prices around 175-190AS (£8.75–9.50; $15.50–16.50) per person

Josefine Egger, Gumppstrasse 57 (tel. 416075). A 10–15-minute walk from Innsbruck Hbf, left off Amraserstrasse shortly after crossing the Sill, or tram 3 to Gumppstrasse.

Anny Gastl, Prinz-Eugen-Strasse 81 (tel. 447962). Bus R to Pauluskirche or about 20 minutes' walk from Innsbruck Hbf. Follow Reichenauerstrasse until you see Prinz-Eugen-Strasse on the left. See Jugendherberge Innsbruck IYHF hostel for directions.

Anna Hueber, Oberkoflerweg 16 (tel 676555). See hotel Möslheim, above, for directions.

Trude Mader, Schlossstrasse 10 (tel. 428504). Near Schloss Ambras. Tram 3 to the Amras terminus or a half-hour walk from Innsbruck Hbf.

Friedl Mair, Arzlerstrasse 89 (tel. 61246). Well out from the centre but buses C, D and E all run along the street.

Maria Rauschgatt, Karwendelstrasse 6 (tel. 571410). Bus C or W to Karwendelstrasse or a 20-minute walk from Innsbruck Hbf. At the junction of Südbahnstrasse and Leopoldstrasse cross over and take Anton-Melzer-Strasse into Egger-Lienz-Strasse from which you turn left down Fritz-Pregl-Strasse into Karwendelstrasse.

Hermine Rofner, Plonergasse 10 (tel. 437935). Bus S or K to Dr Glatz-Strasse. Walk down the street to the right of the direction the bus was travelling, left at Kaufmannstrasse then left almost immediately into Plonergasse. A 20-minute walk from Innsbruck Hbf. Follow directions for Hotel Menghini to Wetterherrenweg but turn left along Kaufmannstrasse and then right at Plonergasse.

STUDENT RESIDENCES

Technikerhaus, Fischnalerstrasse 26 (tel. 282110). Open July–Sept. Prices start around 225AS (£11.25; $19.50). Bus B to Technikerheim or a 20-minute walk from Innsbruck Hbf. Near the St Anne column take Anichstrasse. Follow Blasius-Hueber-Strasse across the Inn then turn left on Prandtauer Ufer along the river. Go right at Hutterweg then left along Santifallerstrasse into Fischnalerstrasse.

Internationales Studentenhaus, Rechengasse 7 (tel. 59477). Open July–Sept. Prices start around 235AS (£11.75; $20.50). Follow directions for Technikerhaus to Blasius-Hueber-Strasse, turn left along Innrain, then right at Rechengasse.

IYHF HOSTELS

Jugendherberge Innsbruck, Reichenauerstrasse 147 (tel. 46179/46180). Open all year. From 10 July–31 Aug. a temporary hostel operates at the same address in a student dormitory. Both charge around 160AS (£8; $14) for the first night, 130AS (£6.50; $11.50) per night thereafter. The overnight price includes breakfast and bed linen. Open to IYHF members only. Bus O or R to Campingplatz-Jugendherberge from Innsbruck Hbf or a 20-minute walk. At the end of König-Laurin-Strasse go right down Dreiheiligenstrasse, across the Sill and on to the start of Reichenauerstrasse. Head left to the hostel.

Torsten-Arneus-Schwedenhaus, Rennweg 17b (tel. 585814).
Open July–Aug. Curfew 10 p.m. Members only. 100AS
(£5; $9). Breakfast and sheets cost extra. Bus C to
Handelsakademie from Innsbruck Hbf or a 15–20-minute
walk. Turn right off Museumstrasse along Sillgasse, cross
Universitätstrasse and then follow Kaiserjägerstrasse to its
junction with Rennweg by the Inn. The hostel is near the
junction of the two streets.

Glockenhaus, Weiherburggasse 3 (tel. 286515). Open year
round. Doubles and quads around 150AS (£7.50; $13) per
person. Anyone looking for dormitory accommodation is
referred to the St Nikolaus hostel, below. Bus K to
Schmelzergasse. Walk up Schmelzergasse to the start of
Weiherburggasse. A 15–20-minute walk from Innsbruck
Hbf. From Museumstrasse head right along Burggraben
into Rennweg. Cross the river by the Innsteg, walk right
a little along Innstrasse then go left up Schmelzergasse.

Jugendherberge St Nikolaus, Innstrasse 95 (tel. 286515).
Open all year. Same management as the Glockenhaus
hostel. 130AS (£6.50; $11.50). See the Glockenhaus hostel
above for directions.

Volkshaus Innsbruck, Radetzkystrasse 41 (tel. 466682). Open
all year. 110AS (£5.50; $9.50) without breakfast. Bus O or
R to Radetzkystrasse or a 15–20-minute walk from
Innsbruck Hbf. Left off Reichenauerstrasse (see
Jugendherberge IYHF hostel above).

HOSTELS

St Paulus, Reichenauerstrasse 72 (tel. 44291). Open mid-
June–mid-Aug. Curfew 10 p.m. Dorms 100AS (£5; $9)
without breakfast. Bus R to Pauluskirche or about 15
minutes' walk from Innsbruck Hbf. See Jugendherberge
IYHF hostel above for directions.

MK-Jugendzentrum, Sillgasse 8a (tel. 571311). Open
July–mid-Sept. Curfew 11 p.m. 140AS (£7; $12.50) for B&B
in dorms. Price falls by about a quarter after the first night.

A 5-minute walk from Innsbruck Hbf, right of Museumstrasse.

CAMPING

Reichenau, Reichenauerstrasse 147 (tel. 46252). Open Apr.–Oct. 70AS (£3.50; $6) per person, tent included. Small reduction for students. The closest site to the town centre. See Jugendherberge IYHF hostel above for directions.

Seewirt, Geyrstrasse 25 (tel. 46153). Open all year. 40AS (£2; $3.50) per tent, 55AS (£2.75; $5) per person. Bus K to Geyrstrasse or a 20–25-minute walk from Innsbruck Hbf. Left along Amraser Seestrasse from Amraserstrasse then right down Geyrstrasse.

Innsbruck Kranebitten, Kranebitten Allee 214 (tel. 284180). Open May–Sept. Far from the centre in the suburb of Kranebitten, just off the main road to Seefeld. Bus LK to Kranebitten.

Kitzbühel (tel. code 05356)

Tourist Office
Tourismusverband, Hinterstadt 18, 6370 Kitzbühel (tel. 2155/2272). Open Mon. to Sat. 8.30 a.m. to 7.30 p.m., Sun. 9 a.m. to 5 p.m. The Tourist Office charges no commission for finding rooms. Just outside the door is a free telephone you can use to make reservations for local accommodation. From Kitzbühel Hbf go straight down Bahnhofstrasse, left along Josef-Pirchl-Strasse and then right at Hinterstadt. From the other train station, Hahnenkamm, walk down Josef-Herold-Strasse into Vorderstadt, go left, then left again into Hinterstadt. Of the two train stations, Hahnenkamm is the closest to the town centre but not all trains stop at the station. Arriving from Innsbruck or Wörgl the train reaches

Hahnenkamm before Kitzbühel Hbf; coming from Salzburg the train reaches Kitzbühel Hbf first.

Accommodation
The prices quoted below are for the summer high season (July–Aug.) and are based on two people sharing a room. Supplements for single rooms are shown where applicable. All prices below are only valid for stays of three days and upwards. The vast majority of the establishments listed below are either in the town centre or on the fringes of the town (exceptions are noted). As the town is small you will have no trouble getting to accommodation just outside on foot. Try to reserve these accommodation suggestions in advance as their location ensures their popularity. Even if you cannot find a bed in one of these places you should still be able to find accommodation relatively easily outside the winter season, as there are literally thousands of rooms available in and around Kitzbühel, though you will either have to pay higher prices to stay in the town itself or stay a fair distance outside the town if you want similarly priced accommodation.

PENSIONS

Cheapest price for B&B around 130AS (£6.50; $11.50) per person

Schmidinger, Ehrenbachgasse 13 (tel. 3134).

Cheapest price for B&B around 160AS (£8; $14) per person

Burgstallhof, Burgstallstrasse 41 (tel. 2529/4092). Just outside the town in Ecking, beyond Pulverturmweg.

Cheapest price for B&B around 170AS (£8.50; $15) per person

Arnika, St Johannesstrasse 31a (tel. 2338). Single supplement 20AS (£1; $1.75). Out from the town on the road to St Johanne. An easy walk from Kitzbühel Hbf. Turn right at the end of Bahnhofstrasse.

Astlingerhof, Bichinweg 11 (tel. 2775). Single supplement 30AS (£1.50; $2.50). Out from the centre, off Jochbergerstrasse (main road to Aurach and Jochberg).

Eugenie, Pulverturmweg 3 (tel. 2820). See Burgstallhof, above.

Jodlhof, Aschbachweg 17 (tel. 3004). Just outside the town, near the hospital (Krankenhaus).

Karlberger, Hahnenkammstrasse 9 (tel. 4003). Just outside the town in Ecking, near the Schischule Total.

Cheapest price for B&B around 180AS (£9; $16) per person

Reiwag, Josef-Pirchl-Strasse 54 (tel. 2601). Single supplement 25AS (£1.25; $2.25). See Tourist Office above.

Cheapest price for B&B around 190AS (£9.50; $16.75) per person

Caroline, Schulgasse 7 (tel. 2274/71971). Off Josef-Herold-Strasse. See Tourist Office above.

Erlenhof, Burgstallstrasse 27 (tel.2828). See Karlberger hostel, above.

Hörl, Josef-Pirchl-Strasse 60 (tel. 3144). Single supplement 20AS (£1; $1.75). See Tourist Office above.

Maria, Malernweg 3 (tel. 3174). Single supplement 25AS (£1.25; $2.25). Just outside the town, on the road to Högl.

Cheapest price for B&B around 200AS (£10; $17.50) per person

Entstrasser, Jochbergerstrasse 97 (tel. 4884). Single supplement 20AS (£1; $1.75). Out from the town on the road to Aurach and Jochberg.

Hauser, Ehrenbachgasse 29 (tel. 2852). Single supplement 50AS (£2.50; $4.50).

Hebenstreit, Jodlfeld 1 (tel. 3022). Single supplement 50AS (£2.50; $4.50). Just outside the town, near the junction of Unterleitenweg and Aschbachweg.

PRIVATE ROOMS

Cheapest price around 140AS (£7; $12) per person

Haus Wibmer, Webergasse 6 (tel. 3950). Single supplement 20AS (£1; $1.75).

Cheapest price around 150AS (£7.50; $13) per person

Haus Gasteiger, Pfarrau 16 (tel. 2148). Just outside the town.
Haus Schmidl, Im Gries 15 (tel. 2748). Single supplement 10AS (£0.50; $1).

Cheapest price around 160AS (£8; $14) per person

Restaurant Glockenspiel, Hinterstadt 13 (2nd floor) (tel. 2516).
Haus Kasparek, Ehrenbachgasse 15 (tel. 4219). Single supplement 80AS (£1.50; $2.75).

Cheapest price around 170AS (£8.50; $15) per person

Haus Koller, Knappengasse 16 (tel. 3165).
Wetti Schmidinger, Ehrenbachgasse 13 (tel. 3134). Single supplement 20AS (£1; $1.75).

Cheapest price around 180AS (£9; $15.75) per person

Haus Gantschnigg, Kirchgasse 25 (tel. 4358). Single supplement 30AS (£1.50; $2.50).
Marienheim, Hornweg 8 (tel. 2092).
Haus Hain, Ehrenbachgasse 20 (tel. 2546).
Haus Reiter, Hornweg 24 (tel. 53542).
Landhaus Resch, Alfons-Petzold-Weg 2a (tel. 41652). Single supplement 15AS (£0.75; $1.25).

Cheapest price around 190AS (£9.50; $16.50) per person

Gasthaus Reiter, Hammerschmiedstrasse 5b (tel. 3124).
Haus Hagenmüller, Josef-Herold-Strasse 3 (tel. 4610/2709). See **Tourist Office** above.

Cheapest price around 200AS (£10; $17.50) per person

Anna-Maria Hechenberger, Webergasse 3 (tel. 2487).

FARMHOUSE ACCOMMODATION

Cheapest price around 160AS (£8; $14) per person

Eckinghof, Schwarzseestrasse 5 (tel. 53263). Single supplement 20AS (£1; $1.75). Just outside the town in Ecking.

Cheapest price around 170AS (£8.50; $15) per person

Reiterhof, Malernweg 14 (tel. 4209). Single supplement 10AS (£0.50; $1). Just outside the town on the road to Högl.

IYHF HOSTEL

Oberndorf 64, Niederstrasseerhof (tel. 3651).

CAMPING

Schwarzsee (tel. 2806/4479). Open all year round. As the name suggests, the site is near the Schwarzsee, a fair distance from the town centre. The site is an easy walk from the Schwarzsee train station.

Salzburg   (tel. code 0662)

Tourist Offices
Fremdenverkehrsbetriebe der Stadt Salzburg, Auerspergstrasse 7, A-5020 Salzburg (tel. 88987). Head office of the city tourist board. Contact this office for information in advance. The tourist board run six information centres in the city. A list of hotels and a list of private rooms are available from these offices.

Information Mozartplatz, Mozartplatz 5 (tel. 847568). In the centre of the Old Town. Open Mon. to Sat. 9 a.m. to 6 p.m., Sun. 9 a.m. to 8 p.m. throughout the year.

Information Hauptbahnhof (tel. 871712/873638). In the train station. Open daily 8.30 a.m. to 8 p.m. all year round.

Information Salzburg-Mitte, Münchner Bundesstrasse 1 (tel. 432228/433110). Open all year round for traffic arriving from Munich.

Information Salzburg Süd, Park & Ride Parkplatz, Alpenstrasse (tel. 20966). Open throughout the year for traffic arriving from Carinthia and Steiermark.

Information Salzburg-Nord, Autobahnstation Kaserne (tel. 663220). Open Apr. to Oct. for traffic arriving from Vienna and Linz.

Information Salzburg-West, Flughafen, Innsbrucker Bundesstrasse 95 (BP filling station). Open Apr. to Oct. Serves the airport, and traffic arriving from Innsbruck.

Public Transport

Salzburg's public transport system consists mainly of buses and trolleybuses (there is no duplication of route numbers so for convenience all are referred to as buses below). Single fares cost around 20AS (£1; $1.75). Passes are available for 24 and 72 hours. As well as the bus network these passes cover the railway to the castle, the lift to the Mönchsberg terrace, and the Salzburg-Bergheim railway. The 24-hour pass pays for itself after three trips, the 72-hour pass after six trips. If you find accommodation within walking distance of the centre you will hardly need to use public transport as all the sights except Schloss Hellbrunn and Schloss Leopoldskron are easily reached on foot.

Basic Directions

Salzburg Hbf and the bus station are right next to each other. From the stations Rainerstrasse heads down to Mirbellplatz, another important bus terminal. Continuing straight on down Dreifaltigkeitsgasse you arrive at the junction with Linzer Gasse just before the Staatsbrücke crosses over the River

Salzach. Crossing the bridge and heading left along the riverside you can turn right at the next bridge (Mozartsteg) into Mozartplatz. The walk from the train station to Mirbellplatz takes about ten minutes, from the station to the Salzach about fifteen minutes, and from the station to Mozartplatz about twenty minutes. Buses 1, 2, 5, 6, 51 and 55 all run from Salzburg Hbf to the Staatsbrücke, buses 5, 51 and 55 continue on to Mozartsteg.

Finding Accommodation in Salzburg

Despite the fact that the city often seems very crowded during the day you can usually find suitable accommodation without too much trouble, as many people visit the city as part of a coach tour and do not spend the night in Salzburg. However, accommodation can be very difficult to find during the city's summer festival (late July–Aug.). All the hostels fill rapidly at this time. Unless you have a tent you may have to spend around 200AS (£10; $17.50) on a private room (assuming there are any available), or even more on a hotel. Prices in some hotels fall slightly outside the peak season (May–Oct.).

HOTELS

Cheapest doubles around 360AS (£18; $31.50)

Junger Fuchs, Linzer Gasse 54 (tel. (875496). Singles start around 200AS (£10; $17.50). Prices fall slightly off-season. Left off Mirbellplatz at Schrannengasse, then right down Wolf-Dietrich-Strasse into Linzer Gasse, or a bus to the Staatsbrücke and walk up Linzer Gasse.

Cheapest doubles around 400AS (£20; $35)

Noisternig, Innsbrucker Bundesstrasse 57 (tel. 827646). Singles start at the same price. Bus 77 from Salzburg Hbf runs along the street, stopping 300m from the hotel. Buses 1 and 2 run around the town before stopping near the Post Office on Maxglaner Hauptstrasse. Continue in the direction the bus was going and then turn left at Innsbrucker Bundesstrasse, about 150m away.

Elisabeth, Vogelweiderstrasse 52 (tel. 871664). Take the rear exit from the train station on to Lastenstrasse, left, then sharp right at Weiserhofstrasse, then left along Breitenfelderstrasse into Vogelweiderstrasse. Just under 10 minutes' walk. Bus 15 runs to the town centre from Vogelweiderstrasse.

Sandwirt, Lastenstrasse 6a (tel. 874351). Take the rear exit from the train station on to Lastenstrasse and head right. A few minutes' walk.

Merian, Merianstrasse 40 (tel. 8740060). Take the rear exit from the train station on to Lastenstrasse, head right, then left down Merianstrasse. About 8 minutes' walk. Bus 15 runs from the stop on Bayerhamerstrasse to the town centre.

Hämmerle, Innsbrucker Bundesstrasse 57a (tel. 827647). Singles start at 200AS (£10; $17.50). See Hotel Noisternig, above, for directions.

Cheapest doubles around 420AS (£21; $37)

Winkler, Linzer Bundesstrasse 92 (tel. 660924). Singles start at 240AS (£12; $21). Near the terminal for bus 29 on Linzer Bundesstrasse. The bus runs from Mirbellplatz, not Salzburg Hbf.

Cheapest doubles around 440AS (£22; $39)

Wastlwirt, Rochusgasse 15 (tel. 845483). Singles start around 240AS (£12; $21). Bus 27 from Mirbellplatz runs along Rochusgasse, stopping about 300m past the hotel.

Lilienhof, Siezenheimerstrasse 62 (tel. (433630). Take bus 77 from Salzburg Hbf to Innsbrucker Bundesstrasse, then change to bus 80 which runs down Otto-von-Lilienthal-Strasse. The hotel is on the corner of the junction with Siezenheimerstrasse, a short walk from the bus stop.

Haus Wartenberg, Riedenburgerstrasse 2 (tel. 844284). Bus 1 or 2 from Salzburg Hbf to the stop on Neutorstrasse after passing Leopoldskronstrasse on the left. Then a 300m walk, on along Neutorstrasse, right at Bayernstrasse, then right again.

Cheapest doubles around 460AS (£23; $40)

Samhof, Negrellisstrasse 19 (tel. (874622). Singles start around 230AS (£11.50; $20). Bus 33 from Salzburg Hbf stops by the junction of Samstrasse, Negrellisstrasse and Maxstrasse. The hotel is a short walk away.

Cheapest doubles around 480AS (£24; $42)

Wegscheider, Thumeggerstrasse 4 (tel. 820385). Singles around 260AS (£13; $23). Bus 5 from Salzburg Hbf or bus 15 from Mirbellplatz to the first stop on Berchtesgadenerstrasse, then a short walk. Thumeggerstrasse is off Neukomgasse.

Uberfuhr, Ignaz-Rieder-Kai 43 (tel. 23010). Bus 5 from Salzburg Hbf to Mozartsteg then bus 49 along Aignerstrasse to the stop at the junction with Uberfuhrstrasse, followed by a short walk, down Uberfuhrstrasse to the Salzach, then right.

Salzburger Motel, Friedenstrasse 6 (tel. 20871). Bus 51 from Salzburg Hbf to the stop by the junction of Alpenstrasse and Friedenstrasse (after Michael-Pacher-Strasse crosses Alpenstrasse).

Dietmann, Ignaz-Harrer-Strasse 13 (tel. 431364). Prices fall slightly off-season. Bus 77 from Salzburg Hbf runs along the street but the hotel is only 10 minutes' walk from the station. Head left down Rainerstrasse, then right at St Julien Strasse which runs into Ignaz-Harrer-Strasse.

Bergland, Rupertgasse 15 (tel. 872318). About 15 minutes' walk from the train station. Rupertgasse is left of Bayerhamerstrasse (see Jugendherberge Glockengasse IYHF hostel below for directions). A 10–15-minute-walk from the centre.

Cheapest doubles around 500AS (£25; $44)

Teufl-Überfuhr, Franz-Hinterholzer-Kai 38 (tel. 21213). Bus
51 from Salzburg Hbf to the first stop on Alpenstrasse (after
the bus passes Aspergasse on the right), then a 5-minute
walk, on along Alpenstrasse, left down Falstauergasse to
the Salzach, then right along Franz-Hinterholzer-Kai.

Hinterbruhl, Schanzlgasse 12 (tel. 846798). Buses 5 and 55
stop at the end of Schanzlgasse shortly after crossing the
Salzach by the Nonntaler Brücke.

Wallner, Aiglhofstrasse 15 (tel. 845023). Bus 29 from
Mirbellplatz runs along the street, stopping about 200m
beyond the hotel.

Itzlinger Hof, Itzlinger Hauptstrasse 11 (tel. 51210). About
8-minutes' walk from Salzburg Hbf. Follow Kaiserschützenstrasse away from the station, right down Fanny-
von-Lehnert-Strasse to the end, left, then right at Itzlinger
Hauptstrasse. Bus 51 runs along the street to the town
centre.

Eisl, Itzlinger Hauptstrasse 13 (tel. 50105). See Itzlinger Hof,
above, for directions.

Edelweiss, Kendlerstrasse 57 (tel. 824883). Bus 27 from
Mirbellplatz stops almost outside the hotel.

Cheapest doubles around 520AS (£26; $46)

Salzburg International Hotel, Moosstrasse 106 (tel.
824617/824618). Price is for doubles with a shower/bath.
Bus 15 from Mirbellplatz to Moosstrasse, then change to
bus 60. Bus 60 stops almost at the door of the hotel.

Zur Post, Maxglaner Hauptstrasse 45 (tel. 845772). Buses 1
and 2 from Salzburg Hbf run along the street stopping a
short distance beyond the hotel.

Römerwirt, Nonntaler Hauptstrasse 47 (tel. 843391). Bus 5
from Salzburg Hbf to the first stop on Nonntaler
Hauptstrasse, just along the street from the hotel.

Noppinger, Maxglaner Hauptstrasse 29 (tel. 846235). See Zur
Post, above, for directions. Close to the bus stop.

Mayburgerkai, Mayburgerkai 48 (tel. 876579). A 5-minute

walk from Salzburg Hbf. Head away from the train station down Kaiserschützenstrasse, straight on down Jahnstrasse to the river, then right.

Junior, Innsbrucker Bundesstrasse 49 (tel. 827648). See Hotel Noisternig, above, for directions.

Ganshof, Ganshofstrasse 13 (tel. 846628). Bus 27 from Mirbellplatz to the first stop on the street, then a short walk in the direction the bus was going.

Jahn, Elisabethstrasse 31 (tel. 871405). A few minutes' walk from Salzburg Hbf. Follow Kaiserschützenstrasse away from the station, on down Jahnstrasse, then right.

Billroth, Billrothstrasse 10-18 (tel. 20596). Bus 51 from Salzburg Hbf to the stop on Alpenstrasse just past the junction with Billrothstrasse. Under 5-minutes' walk from the bus stop.

Helmhof, Kirchengasse 29 (tel. 433079). Bus 29 from Mirbellplatz to the stop after Münchener Bundesstrasse crosses the motorway. Down to the end of Fischergasse, then left down Lieferinger Hauptstrasse, over the motorway and right at Kirchengasse.

PRIVATE ROOMS

Prices for private rooms start around 200AS (£10; $17.50) per person. Prices are set according to the location of the house, and the facilities available in the room. All the owners below offer basic rooms with the use of the shower/bath in the house.

Maria Bamberger, Gerhart-Hauptmann-Strasse 10 (tel. 8429653/821474). Doubles and triples. Bus 5 from Salzburg Hbf.

Josefa Fagerer, Moosstrasse 68d (tel. 824978). Singles and doubles. Bus 15 from Mirbellplatz along Moosstrasse until the stop just around the corner on Firmianstrasse. Then a few minutes' walk, back on to Moosstrasse, then left.

Helga Bankhammer, Moosstrasse 77 (tel. 830067). Doubles only. See Josefa Fagerer, above, for directions. A 5-minute walk from the bus stop.

Elfriede Feichtner, Hildebrandtgasse 17 (tel. 22814). Singles
only. Open July–Sept. Bus 51 from Salzburg Hbf.

Georg Gandolf, Moosstrasse 170 (tel. 8428485/826364).
Doubles and triples. Bus 15 from Mirbellplatz to the start
of Moosstrasse, then change to bus 60.

Adele Gellner, Samergasse 10a (tel. 798833). Open July–Aug.
Doubles only. Bus 15 from Mirbellplatz.

Hilda Hollbacher, Lieferinger Hauptstrasse 101 (tel. 356283).
Open June–Sept. Singles and doubles. See Hotel Helmhof,
above, for directions.

Anna Sommerauer, Moosstrasse 100 (tel. 824877). Singles
only. See Georg Gandolf, above, for directions.

Maria Schweiger, Gerhart-Hauptmann-Strasse 9 (tel.
8419785/820824). Open June–Aug. Doubles only. Bus 5
from Salzburg Hbf.

Maria Langwieder, Törringstrasse 41 (tel. 433129). Singles,
doubles and triples. Bus 29 from Mirbellplatz.

Elisabeth Mayerhofer, Moosstrasse 68c (tel. 8428394). See
Josefa Fagerer, above, for directions.

Theresia Nussbaumer, Moosstrasse 164 (tel. 830229). Singles,
doubles and triples. See Georg Gandolf, above, for
directions.

Karoline Oberholzner, Gerhart-Hauptmann-Strasse 38 (tel.
8429630/821465). Bus 5 from Salzburg Hbf.

IYHF HOSTELS

Jugendgästehaus Salzburg, Josef-Preis-Allee 18 (tel.
8426700/846857). Midnight curfew. Dorms 150AS (£7.50;
$13). Quads 195AS (£9.75; $17) per person. Doubles 250AS
(£12.50; $22) per person. With breakfast. Very popular with
school groups. Advance reservations by letter advised.
Otherwise arrive between 7 a.m. and 9 a.m., or as soon
as possible after 11 a.m. when the reception re-opens. Bus
5 or 51 to Justizgebäude (the first stop on Petersbrunnstrasse after crossing the river), then a 5-minute walk on
along Petersbrunnstrasse, then left down Josef-Preis-Allee.

Jugendherberge Aigen, Aignerstrasse 34 (tel. 23248). B&B in

dorms 130AS (£6.50; $11.50). Bus 5 from Salzburg Hbf to Mozartsteg, then bus 49 along Aignerstrasse. The bus stops about 350m beyond the hostel.

Jugendherberge Glockengasse, Glockengasse 8 (tel. 876241). Open Apr.–mid-Oct. Midnight curfew. B&B in dorms 130AS (£6.50; $11.50). Cooking facilities available. A 15-minute walk from Salzburg Hbf, 10 minutes' walk from the town centre. From the station head left down Rainerstrasse, left through the underpass into Gabelsbergerstrasse. Straight on into Bayernhamerstrasse, right down Bayernhamerstrasse until it joins Schallmooser Hauptstrasse. The small alley across the street leads into Glockengasse. Bus 29 runs from Schallmooser Hauptstrasse to the town centre.

Jugendherberge Eduard-Heinrich-Haus, Eduard-Heinrich-Strasse 2 (tel. 25976). B&B in dorms 140AS (£7; $12.50). Bus 51 from Salzburg Hbf to the third stop on Alpenstrasse, at the junction with Hans-Sperl-Strasse and Egger-Lienz-Gasse. About 6 minutes' walk from the bus stop, down Egger-Lienz-Gasse, right at Henri-Dunant-Strasse, and then left.

Jugendherberge Haunspergstrasse, Haunspergstrasse 27 (tel. 875030). Curfew 11 p.m. Open 4 July–31 Aug. B&B in dorms 140AS (£7; $12.50). A 5-minute walk from Salzburg Hbf. Left a short distance from the station, then right along Porschestrasse, right again at Elisabethstrasse, then left at Stauffenstrasse into Haunspergstrasse.

St Elisabeth, Plainstrasse 83 (tel. 50728). Open 11 July–31 Aug. B&B in dorms 130AS (£6.50; $11.50). A 5-minute walk from the train station. Take Kaiserschützenstrasse heading away from Salzburg Hbf, on down Jahnstrasse, then right.

Salzburg-Walserfeld, Schulstrasse 18 (tel. 851377). Open 1 July–25 Aug. B&B in dorms 120AS (£6; $10.50). 11 p.m. curfew. Bus 77 from Salzburg Hbf.

CAMPING

Stadt-Camping, Bayerhamerstrasse 14a (tel. (871169). Open

May–Sept. 60AS (£3; $5) per person, (tent included). About 700m from the rear exit of Salzburg Hbf. See Hotel Merian, above, for directions. Right at Bayerhamerstrasse.

Schloss Aigen, Weberbartlweg 20 (tel. 22079/272243). Open May–Sept. 50AS (£2.50; $4.50) per tent, 38AS (£1.90; $3.50) per person. Bus 5 from Salzburg Hbf to Mozartsteg, then bus 49 along Aignerstrasse to the stop Glaserstrasse. From the stop, a 10-minute walk along Glaserstrasse, then left up Weberbartlweg. The closest train station is Bahnhof Aigen, on Aigenerstrasse, a 20-minute walk from the campsite.

Gnigl (Ost), Parscherstrasse 4 (tel. 644143/644144). Open May– Sept. 20AS (£1; $1.75) per tent, 30AS (£1.50; $2.50) per person. Bus 29 from Mirbellplatz along Linzer Bundesstrasse to the stop near the junction with Parscherstrasse (after the bus crosses over the railway) then a 200m walk. Bus 27 from Mirbellplatz to the first stop on Eichstrasse (again over the railway) is 400m from the site.

Stadtblick, Rauchenbichlerstrasse 21 (tel. 50652). Open Apr.–Oct. 30AS (£1.50; $2.50) per tent, 50AS (£2.50; $4.50) per person. Bus 51 from Salzburg Hbf to the stop on Kirchenstrasse by the junction with Rauchenbichlerstrasse, then a 5-minute walk to the site.

'Nord-Sam', Samstrasse 22a (tel. 660494/660611). Open Apr.–Oct. 60AS (£3; $5) per tent, 35–50AS (£1.75–2.50; $3.00–4.50) per person. Bus 33 from Salzburg Hbf to the first stop after Samstrasse passes under the railway lines.

ASK, Flughafen (West), Karolingerstrasse 4 (tel. 845602). Open May–mid-Sept. 30AS (£1.50; $2.50) per tent, 40AS (£2; $3.50) per person. About 10-minutes' walk from the airport, right off Innsbrucker Bundesstrasse. Bus 77 from the train station stops by the junction of Innsbrucker Bundesstrasse and Karolingerstrasse, leaving a short walk to the site.

Kasern (Jägerwirt), Carl-Zuckmayer-Strasse 26 (tel. 50576). Open Apr.–Oct. 20AS (£1; $1.75) per tent, 55AS (£2.75; $5) per person.

IYHF HOSTELS NEARBY

Traunerstrasse 22, Traunstein (tel. 861 4742). Open only to visitors aged 26 and under. DM15 (£5.25; $9.50). In Germany, on the line from Munich to Salzburg. About 40 minutes from Salzburg by local train. If you are leaving Munich in the late afternoon during the summer you might want to consider staying here, then getting into Salzburg early next morning.

Vienna (Wien) (tel. code 01)

Tourist Offices

Wiener Fremdenverkehrsamt, Obere Augartenstrasse 40, 1025 Wien (tel. 21114). Contact this office if you want to obtain information in advance. On arrival, information and room-finding services are available at the nine offices operated by the Vienna Tourist Board throughout the city.

Main office, Kärntnerstrasse 38 (tel. 5138852). Open daily 9 a.m. to 7 p.m. U-bahn lines U1, U2 and U4: Karlsplatz. From the Westbahnhof trams 52 and 58 run down Mariahilferstrasse to Burgring/Opernring. Kärntnerstrasse is to the right, along Opernring.

Westbahnhof. Open daily 8 a.m.–6.30 p.m.

Südbahnhof. Open daily July–Sept. 8 a.m.–10 p.m., Easter–June and Oct. 9 a.m.–7 p.m.

Flughafen Wien-Schwechat. In the airport arrivals hall. Open daily June–Sept. 8.30 a.m.–11 p.m., Oct.–May 8.30 a.m.–10 p.m.

Reichsbrücke landing stage. If arriving by boat go to the DDSG information counter. Open Apr.–Oct. 7 a.m.–6 p.m.

Autobahn A1 (west motorway). At the Wien-Auhof services. Open Apr.–Oct. 8 a.m.–10 p.m., Nov. 9 a.m.–7 p.m., Dec.–Mar. 10 a.m.–6 p.m. For traffic from Innsbruck,

Salzburg, Prague and České Budějovice (via Linz) and Germany.

Autobahn A2 (south motorway). Exit: Zentrum, Triesterstrasse. Open July–Sept. 8 a.m.–10 p.m., mid-Mar.–June and Oct. 9 a.m.–7 p.m. For traffic arriving from Graz, Klagenfurt, Llubljana and Italy.

Autobahn A4 (east motorway). Exit: Simmeringer Haide, Landwehrstrasse. Open late Mar.–Sept. 8 a.m.–6 p.m. For traffic arriving from Bratislava, Slovakia and from Budapest.

Florisdorfer Brücke/Donauinsel. Open late Mar.–Sept. 8 a.m.–6 p.m. For traffic arriving from Brno, Moravia and from Prague (via Moravia).

Vienna's Stations
The vast majority of people travelling to Vienna by train arrive at one of the two main stations, either the Westbahnhof, or the Südbahnhof. Any train passing through Salzburg, Innsbruck, Switzerland, or what was formerly West Germany, arrives at the Westbahnhof. Trains from Budapest and Romania going on to these places stop at the Westbahnhof. Of the two daily trains running from Budapest to Vienna, one (via Gyor) goes to the Westbahnhof, the other (via Sopron) goes to the Südbahnhof. Trains from Graz, Klagenfurt, Poland, Brno, Bratislava, Italy, Greece, Sofia, Belgrade and Zagreb stop at the Südbahnhof, as do trains from Budapest continuing on to any of these destinations. The only other railway station you are likely to arrive at is Franz-Josefs Bahnhof. This station receives international trains from Berlin, Leipzig, Dresden, Prague and České Budějovice, as well as local services from Krems-an-der-Donau. Wien-Nord and Wien-Mitte deal with local commuter trains only, but Wien-Mitte is the main bus station and the city air terminal. While all the stations are served by the U-bahn, only when the U3 is complete will it become possible to travel between them all by underground. Until then, getting between the stations may appear a daunting prospect to those unfamiliar with the city. In fact, it is easy. From the Westbahnhof, tram 5 runs to the Franz-Josefs Bhf,

tram 18 to the Südbahnhof. From the Südbahnhof, the Schnellbahn runs to Wien-Mitte and Wien-Nord. To get between the Südbahnhof and Franz-Josefs Bhf, take tram D from station to station, or take the U2 to Karlsplatz and change to the U4 to Friedensbrücke, a few minutes' walk from Franz-Josefs Bhf (from Wien-Mitte take U4 direct).

City Transport

Vienna has an integrated public transport system comprising Schnellbahn, U-bahn, tram and bus services. Of these only the Schnellbahn is free to railpass holders. A single trip costs around 20AS (£1; $1.75), with the ticket remaining valid if you have to transfer between different forms of transport. Visitors can buy cheap 24-hour, 72-hour and eight-day passes (passport photo required), which pay for themselves after three, six and twelve journeys respectively. Wherever you are staying in Vienna you will probably want to buy a pass, and they are almost essential if you are camping or hostelling as most of the sites and hostels are well out from the centre. The system shuts down around midnight (not much of a problem for hostellers as this coincides with curfews, but effectively imposing a curfew on anyone staying in a hotel, private room or campsite outside walking distance of the city centre), except at weekends when night buses run on a number of routes between Schwedenplatz in the city centre and the suburbs between 12.30–4.00 a.m. A special fare of 25AS (£1.25; $2) applies on these buses.

Finding Accommodation in Summer

Finding a cheap bed can be a problem during the summer months. Late June is particularly bad. By this time, large numbers of independent travellers are arriving in town but the extra bed space created by the conversion of student accommodation into temporary hotels and hostels is available only from July to September. It is advisable to reserve accommodation in writing well in advance of your date of arrival throughout the summer. Failing this, try to phone ahead at least twenty-four hours in advance.

HOTELS

A continental breakfast is included in the overnight price at all the hotels below, unless indicated otherwise. At a few hotels a buffet breakfast is provided.

Cheapest doubles around 380AS (£19; $33)

Rosen-Hotel Europahaus, Linzerstrasse 429 (tel. 922538). A student residence run as a hotel during the summer vacation (usually July–Sept). Tram 52 from the Mariahilferstrasse stop by the Westbahnhof runs along Linzerstrasse.

Cheapest doubles around 420AS (£21; $37)

Don Bosco, Hagenmüllergasse 33 (tel. 71184/711555). Tram 18 from the Westbahnhof or Südbahnhof dir: Stadionbrücke to L.-Koessler Platz near the Donaukanal. Take Dietrichgasse from the square, left on Lechnerstrasse, then right.

Cyrus, Laxenburgerstrasse 14 (tel. 6044288/622578). Singles start at the same price. Near the Südbahnhof. Schnellbahn/U1: Südtirolerplatz is slightly closer. From the Südbahnhof walk left to Südtirolerplatz, from which you can follow Laxenburgerstrasse.

Auhof, Auhofstrasse 205 (tel. 825289). Without breakfast. Far out in the west of the city.

Jägerwald, Karl Bekehrtystrasse 66 (tel. 946266). Singles start around 230AS (£11.50; $20). Out in the western suburbs.

Cheapest doubles around 440AS (£22; $39)

Auer, Lazarettgasse 3 (tel. 432121). U6: Alserstrasse, or tram 8 heading left from the Westbahnhof passes the end of Lazarettgasse/Jörgerstrasse, just after Hernalser Hauptstrasse on the left.

Cheapest doubles around 460AS (£23; $40)

Matauschek, Breitenseerstrasse 14 (tel. 923532).

Schnellbahn: Breitensee (change at Penzing). From Hüttelsdorferstrasse take Kendlergasse, then right along Spallartgasse. From U4: Hietzing tram 10 runs along Breitenseerstrasse.

Reimer, Kirchengasse 18 (tel. 936162). A 10–15-minute walk from the Westbahnhof, left off Mariahilferstrasse as you walk towards the centre, or take tram 52 or 58 down Mariahilferstrasse.

Esterhazy, Nelkengasse 3 (tel. 5875159). Without breakfast. A 10-minute walk from the Westbahnhof, right off Mariahilferstrasse as you walk towards the centre, or take tram 52 or 58 down Mariahilferstrasse.

Goldenes Einhorn, Am Hundsturm 5 (tel. 554755). Without breakfast. U4: Margaretengürtel, then down Margaretengürtel and left at the end of the St Johann-Park. Am Hundsturm is to the right. A 15-minute walk from the Westbahnhof. Walk right around Margaretengürtel and Gumpendorfergürtel to the U-bahn station.

Cheapest doubles around 480AS (£24; $42)

Auersperg, Auerspergstrasse 9 (tel. 4325490/5127493). Buffet breakfast. U2: Lerchenfelderstrasse. The street begins at the U-bahn stop.

Falstaff, Müllnergasse 5 (tel. 349127/349186). U4: Rossauer Lane. From Rossauer Lande by the Donaukanal Pramergasse or Grünentorgasse lead away from the canal into Müllnergasse.

Hargita, Andreasgasse 1 (tel. 961928/9328564). Without breakfast. A 5–10-minute walk from the Westbahnhof, to the left off Mariahilferstrasse heading towards the town centre.

Quisiana, Windmühlgasse 6 (tel. 5873341). Windmühlgasse runs between Mariahilferstrasse and Gumpendorfer-strasse. Tram 52 or 58 from the Westbahnhof (or a 15-minute walk, going right at Berngasse). U4: Kettenbrückengasse. Stiegengasse leads into

Gumpendorferstrasse. Go left to the junction with Windmühlgasse.

Kagranerhof, Wagramerstrasse 141 (tel. 231187). U1: Zentrum Kagran. Cross Czernetzplatz into Wagramerstrasse. The hotel is just a short distance from the U-bahn stop.

Praterstern, Mayergasse 6 (tel. 240123). Without breakfast. Near Wien-Nord station. Schnellbahn/U1: Praterstern (Wien-Nord). A short walk down Praterstrasse, then left.

Cheapest doubles around 500AS (£25; $44)

Alsergrund, Alserstrasse 33 (tel. 4332317/5127493). U6: Alserstrasse, or from the Westbahnhof tram 5 to Alserstrasse, or tram 8 to the junction of Hernalser Gürtel and Alsterstrasse (trams heading left from the front of the station).

Kreiner, Hadersdorf Hauptstrasse 31 (tel. 971131). Out in the western suburb of Hadersdorf. Schnellbahn: Hadersdorf Weidlingau.

Stadt Bamberg, Mariahilferstrasse 167 (tel. 837608). A short walk from the Westbahnhof. Right on leaving the station, then right down Mariahilferstrasse along the side of the station.

Auge Gottes, Nussdorferstrasse 75 (tel. 342585). A student residence run as a hotel during the summer vacation (usually July–Sept.). Near the Franz-Josefs train station (Schnellbahn: Franz-Josefs Bhf.). Trams 5 and 8 heading left from the Westbahnhof run to opposite ends of Nussdorferstrasse.

Cheapest doubles around 520AS (£26; $46)

Wild, Langegasse 10 (tel. 435174). U2: Lerchenfelder-strasse. A short walk up Lerchenfelderstrasse, then right.

Baltic, Skodagasse 15 (tel. 420173). Tram 5 from the Westbahnhof or Franz-Josefs Bhf to Skodagasse.

Caroline, Gudrunstrasse 138 (tel. 6048070). U1: Keplerplatz. The hotel is about 500m from the U-bahn

stop, across Laxenburgerstrasse. Schnellbahn:
Matzleinsdorfer Platz is at the end of Gudrunstrasse, a
10-minute walk away. The hotel is a 15-minute walk from
the Südbahnhof. Go left to Südtiroler Platz, left again
down Laxenburgerstrasse, then right at Gudrunstrasse.

Fünfhaus, Sperrgasse 9 (tel. 839253). A 5-minute walk from
the Westbahnhof to the junction of Hernalsergürtel and
Alserstrasse. Hörlgasse is to the left, a short distance
down Alserstrasse.

Strandhotel Alte Donau, Wagramerstrasse 51 (tel. 236730).
U1: Alte Donau. Cross the Alte Donau by the bridge,
then along Wagramerstrasse.

Kraml, Brauergasse 5 (tel. 5878588). U4: Pilgramgasse, then
a short walk up Hofmühlgasse, right along Gumpendorferstrasse into Brauergasse. A 10-minute walk from
the Westbahnhof, down Mariahilferstrasse towards the
centre, right into Otto-Bauer-Strasse, first left, then right.

Stalehner, Ranftlgasse 11 (tel. 4082505). U6: Alserstrasse,
or tram 8 heading left from the Westbahnhof to the
junction of Hernalsergürtel and Jörgerstrasse. Ranftlgasse is to the right, a short distance down Jörgerstrasse.

Stasta, Lehmanngasse 11 (tel. 8697880).

Adlon, Hofenedergasse 4 (tel. 266788). Near Wien-Nord.
Schnellbahn/U1: Praterstern (Wien-Nord). The street is
to the right off Franzensbrückestrasse.

Kugel, Siebensterngasse 43 (tel. 933355). U2: Volkstheater,
then a short walk up Burggasse and left along Kirchengasse into Siebensterngasse. A 15-minute walk from the
Westbahnhof. Go left, then right at U.-Loritz Platz and
down Westbahnstrasse, left at Neubaugasse, then almost
immediately to the right.

Pani, Erlaerstrasse 37 (tel. 671697). Schnellbahn: Liesing,
then bus 64A or 66A along Erlaerstrasse.

Cheapest doubles around 540AS (£27; $47)

Minu, Alserstrasse 43 (tel. 426196). U6: Alserstrasse, or

tram 5 from the Westbahnhof or Franz-Josefs Bhf to Alserstrasse.

Koper, Bennogasse 21 (tel. 486443). Bennogasse runs between Josefstadterstrasse and Alserstrasse, a short walk down either from the Lerchenfeldergürtel/ Hernalsergürtel ring road. U6: Josefstadterstrasse or Alserstrasse, or tram 8 heading left from the Westbahnhof along the ring road to the appropriate junctions.

Lindenhof, Lindengasse 4 (tel. 930498). A 5–10-minute walk from the Westbahnhof, down Mariahilferstrasse towards the centre, left along Schottenfeldgasse, then right.

Steindl, Triesterstrasse 67 (tel. 6041278). Schnellbahn: Matzleinsdorfer Platz, then bus 65A along Triesterstrasse.

Cheapest doubles around 560AS (£28; $49)

Goldener Bär, Türkenstrasse 27 (tel. 345111). Buffet breakfast. U2: Schottentor. From Maria Theresien-Strasse a short walk along Wahringerstrasse or Liechtensteinstrasse takes you into Türkenstrasse.

PRIVATE ROOMS AND APARTMENTS

Neither private rooms nor apartments are available through the offices of the Vienna Tourist Board. Apply instead to:

Mitwohnzentrale, Laudongasse 7 (tel. 4026061). Open Mon.–Fri. 10 a.m.–6 p.m. This private accommodation agency finds rooms and apartments for those staying at least three days. Room prices start at 150AS (£7.50; $13) per day, while apartments cost from 500AS (£25; $44) per day. On top of the cost of your accommodation the agency levies a commission, which varies according to the length of your stay. Tram 8 heading left from the Westbahnhof to the junction of Hernalsergürtel and

Laudongasse. Tram 5 from Franz-Josefs Bhf. to Laudongasse.

ÖKISTA, Türkenstrasse 4–6 (tel. 3475260). Open Mon.–Fri. 9 a.m.–5 p.m. KISTA (the student travel agency) find slightly cheaper rooms than Mitwohnzentrale, and charge no commission for doing so. U2: Schottentor. From Maria Theresien-Strasse a short walk along Wahringerstrasse or Liechtensteinstrasse takes you into Türkenstrasse.

Österreichisches Verkehrsbüro, Friedrichstrasse 7, 1043 Wien (tel. 588000). Write or phone in advance for information.

Reisebüro Hippesroither, Neustiftsgasse 66, 1070 Wien (tel. 939219). Write or phone in advance for information.

Hedwig Gally, Arnsteingasse 25/10 (tel. 8129073/8304244). Not far from the Westbahnhof. Prices for doubles start around 380AS (£19; $33).

Irmgard Lauria, Kaiserstrasse 77, Apartment 8 (tel. 934152). About 220AS (£11; $19) per person in quads with cooking facilities. Dorms cost around 180AS (£9; $16). A 5–10-minute walk from the Westbahnhof. Go diagonally left across Europa Platz, down Stollgasse into Kaiserstrasse.

IYHF HOSTELS

Expect to pay 130–150AS (£6.50–7.50; $12.25–18.75; DM14.25–21.75) for B&B

Jugendgästehaus Wien-Brigittenau, Friedrich-Engelsplatz 24 (tel. 338294/3300598). Curfew 12.30 a.m. 170AS (£8.50; $15). U1 U4 to Schwedenplatz, then tram N to Florisdorfer Brücke Friedrich-Engelsplatz.

Myrthengasse, Myrthengasse 7/Neustiftgasse 85 (tel. 936316/939429/937462). Curfew 12.30 a.m. 170AS (£8.50; $15). U6 to Burggasse, bus 48A to Neubaug. Walk back a short distance then right. Fifteen minutes on foot from the centre and the Westbahnhof. Left as you leave the station along Neubaugürtel, right down Burggasse, crossed by Myrthengasse.

Jugendgästehaus Hütteldorf-Hacking, Schlossbergasse 8 (tel. 8770263). Curfew 11.45 p.m. 170AS (£8.50; $15). Schnellbahn from Westbahnhof to Hütteldorf (last train 10.15 p.m.) or U4 to the same stop. Across the footbridge, then a clearly signposted 5-minute walk.

Schlossherberge am Wilhelminenberg, Savoyenstrasse 2 (tel. 458503). Curfew midnight. 200AS (£10; $17.50). U6 to Thaliastrasse (or tram 5 from the Westbahnhof). Then bus 46B or 146B from here to the hostel. Check these buses with the Tourist Office, or with the hostel.

Ruthensteiner, Robert Hamerlinggasse 24 (tel. 834693). 24-hr reception. Singles 230AS (£11.50; $20), doubles 390AS (£19.50; $34); triples 500AS (£25; $44). Dorms 140AS (£7; $12.50). Five-minute walk from the Westbahnhof. Follow Mariahilferstrasse along the side of the station, left on Palmgasse, then first right.

Turmherberge 'Don Bosco', Lechnerstrasse 12 (tel. 7131494). Open 1 Mar.–30 Nov. 11.30 p.m. curfew. Roman Catholic-run hostel in an old church bell tower. Very cheap. Bed only 65AS (£3.25; $6). Over the years this hotel has sometimes enforced a men-only policy, sometimes not. Women should ring ahead before heading out to the hostel. From the Westbahnhof and the Südbahnhof tram 18 direction Stadionbrücke to the terminus. From l.-Koessler Platz follow Dietrichgasse into Lechnerstrasse.

HOSTELS/UNIVERSITY DORMS

Hostel Zöhrer, Skodagasse 26 (tel. 430730). Open all year. Cooking facilities. B&B 170AS (£8.50; $15). Off Alserstrasse (U6: Alserstrasse). Tram 5 from the Westbahnhof or Franz-Josefs Bhf to Skodagasse.

City-Hostel, Seilerstätte 30 (tel. 5128463/5127923). Open July–Sept. B&B. Singles 290AS (£14.50; $25), doubles 400AS (£20; $35). U1, U2 and U4: Karlsplatz. From the

Opera walk down Kärntnerstrasse, right at Krügerstrasse, then left. From the Westbahnhof tram 52 or 58 run down Mariahilferstrasse to Burgring/ Opernring, a short walk from the Opera.

Kolpingfamilie Wien-Meidling, Bendlgasse 10-12 (tel. 835487). Open all year. Cooking facilities. Bed only 110–170AS (£5.50–8.50; $9.50–15). Breakfast and dinner available. U6: Niederhofstrasse. Following Niederhofstrasse away from Miedlinger Hauptstrasse leads you into Bendlgasse. U4/U6: Langenfeldgasse, is slightly longer: down Langenfeldgasse, right at Arndtstrasse, then fourth left.

YMCA Inter Rail Point, Kenyongasse 25 (tel. 936304). Open mid-July–mid-Aug. Slightly cheaper than the main IYHF hostels. Reluctant to take phone reservations. A 5–10-minute walk from the Westbahnhof. Diagonally left across Europa Platz, right down Stollgasse until it is crossed by Kenyongasse.

Believe-It-Or-Not, Myrthengasse 10 (tel. 5264658/964658). 190AS (£9.50; $16.50). See directions for the IYHF Hostel in Myrthengasse.

Pfeilheim Jugendgästehaus, Pfeilgasse 6 (tel. 431661/431646). Open July–Sept. Singles 250AS (£12.50; $22), doubles 430AS (£21.50; $38). From the Westbahnhof and Franz-Josefs Bhf tram 5 to Thaliastrasse/ Lerchenfelderstrasse. Down the latter, left Blindengasse, then first right. From the Südbahnhof, bus 13A to Strozzigasse. Pfeilgasse runs off Strozzigasse.

Rudolfinum Jugendgästehaus, Mayerhofgasse 3 (tel. 5055384). Open July–Sept. Singles 240AS (£12; $21), doubles 420AS (£21; $37). U1: Taubstummengasse. Mayerhofgasse is off Favoritenstrasse on the right as you walk towards the Südbahnhof. A 10-minute walk from the Südbahnhof. Left to Südtiroler Platz, right up Favoritenstrasse, then left.

Porzellaneum der Wiener Universität, Porzellangasse 30 (tel. 347282). Singles and doubles around 170AS (£8.50; $15) per person. About 10 per cent extra for one-night stays. A 5-minute walk from Franz-Josefs Bhf. Porzellangasse begins at J.-Tandler-Platz on Alserbachstrasse by the station. From the Südbahnhof take tram D along Porzellangasse to the junction with Fürstengasse. Tram 5 will get you to Franz-Josefs Bhf from the Westbahnhof.

Katholisches Studentenhaus, Peter-Jordan-Strasse 29 (tel. 349264). Singles and doubles around 165AS (£8.25; $14.50) per person. Tram 38 from the Westbahnhof to Hardtgasse. From the Südbahnhof tram D to Schottentor (U2: Schottentor) to join tram 38.

Katholisches Studentenhaus, Zaunschertgasse 4 (tel. 382197). An affiliate of the dormitory above. Doubles only.

CAMPING

Expect to pay around 55AS (£2.75; $5) per tent and per person

Aktiv Camping Neue Donau, Am Kleehaufel (tel. 942314). Open late Apr.–Sept. Near the Praterbrücke, 3 3/4 miles from the centre. U1: Kaisermühlen, then bus 91A to the site, or Schnellbahn: Lobau (from the Südbahnhof), followed by a 500m walk to the campsite.

Wien-Sud, Breitenfurterstrasse 269 (tel. 869218). Open July–Aug. 4½ miles from the centre. U6: Philadelphia-brücke, then bus 62A, or Schnellbahn: Atzgersdorf Mauer, then an easy walk or bus 66A to the site.

Wien-West I, Hüttelbergstrasse 40 (tel. 941449). Open 15 July–15 Sept. 3 3/4 miles from the centre. Schnellbahn (from Westbahnhof) or U4 to Hütteldorf, then bus 152 to the site.

Wien-West II, Hüttelbergstrasse 80 (tel. 942314). Open all year. 4-bed bungalows available, 100AS (£5; $9.50; DM14.50) p.p. Just up the road from Wien-West I.

Schwimmbad Camping Rodaun, An der Au 2 (tel. 884154). Open 17 March–16 Nov. About 6 1/2 miles from the town centre. U4 to Hietzing (tram 58 from the Westbhf.) then tram 60 to the end.

Schloss Laxenburg, Münchendorferstrasse, Laxenburg (tel. 02236-71333). Open late Mar.–early Oct. Ten miles from the centre, in the grounds of an old Habsburg hunting lodge. Until 9.40 p.m. you can catch a bus from Wien-Mitte to the site.

SLEEPING OUT

Although not really recommended the Prater Park is the most obvious. Schnellbahn/U1: Praterstern (Wien-Nord), or Schnellbahn: Stadtlauer Brücke Lusthaus at the other end of the park.

BELGIUM
(België/Belgique)

On the whole, Belgium poses no serious problems for the
budget traveller but, unless you can afford to stay in hotels
all the time, you will have to stay in different types of
accommodation as you travel around since some of the main
places of interest lack hostels and/or campsites. However, as
Belgium is a small country with a very efficient rail network,
those with railpasses have the option of choosing one or two
bases and visiting other places on daytrips; e.g. from Ghent
or Bruges you can easily visit all of Flanders, from Namur all
of Wallonia.

Unlike in neighbouring France, there are no really cheap
hotel rooms in Belgium. You will do well to find a double for
under 1100BF (£18.50; $32) in the main towns, where the
cheapest hotels normally charge around 1200BF (£20; $35) for
doubles. Considering the number of other possibilities open
to budget travellers in Belgium, it is unlikely you will ever have
to take a hotel room unless you want to, but if you do have
to spend a night or two in a cheap hotel you should have little
cause for complaint about the standard of cleanliness or
comfort.

Hostelling is a cheap and, usually, convenient way of seeing
the country. With the exception of Ghent, Leuven, Lier and
Ieper, all the main towns of interest have a hostel. Ghent has
been devoid of hostels since its IYHF hostel closed in the
mid-1980s. The IYHF hostel in Liège closed around the same
time, but luckily travellers have the option of the excellent Tilff-
Liège IYHF hostel on the outskirts of the city, just a short train
trip away. Elsewhere, problems are only likely to arise around
Easter and during the period July–August, when it can be
difficult to find a hostel bed in Brussels, Bruges and Ostend.

There are two IYHF-affiliated hostel associations in Belgium. The Flemish Association operates around twenty hostels; its Walloon counterpart half that number. The normal overnight charge is 300–350BF (£5.00–5.80; $9–10.50), which includes breakfast. The exceptions are the Flemish YHA-operated hostels in Bruges and Ostend, and the hostels of both associations in Brussels, where prices range from 350–630BF (£5.80–10.50; $10.50–18.50). Where space is available most hostels admit non-members on the payment of a 100BF (£1.70; $3) supplement. Curfews are normally 11 p.m. but the hostels in the cities tend to stay open later.

As well as IYHF hostels, Antwerp, Bruges and Brussels offer a number of independent hostels. Generally free of the organized groups who head for the main IYHF hostels, the prices and standards of the independent hostels tend to be on a par with those of the official establishments, while curfews are normally more relaxed. Wallonia is littered with 'gîtes d'étapes' which can provide very cheap lodgings in places not served by hostels. An organization called 'Friends of Nature' (Natuurvrienden/Amis de la Nature) also operates a network of hostels throughout the country. Ask the local Tourist Office for details of any such hostels in the locality.

Despite there being over 500 **campsites** in this small country, camping is not an ideal way to see Belgium unless you have a railpass or a car. Sites are heavily concentrated in the rural parts of Wallonia and along the Flemish coast, and the rest of the country is more sparsely served. Major tourist attractions such as Ieper, Kortrijk, Mechelen, Leuven, Lier and Diest all lack campsites, though a short rail trip will invariably find you one in a neighbouring town. Visitors to Liège should head for the site at Tilff, just outside the city. Sites range in quality, and are priced accordingly. Compared to other western European countries, camping in Belgium is very cheap. Prices for a solo traveller can be as low as 60BF (£1; $1.75) per night, but 100–150BF (£1.70–2.50; $3–4.50) is more normal. However, prices at some of the coastal sites can be as high as 250BF (£4.20; $7.50) per night.

You should only end up on the street by design, or

unforeseen disaster. If you do, vagrancy charges can only be pressed if you are penniless. Late arrivals hoping to sleep in train station waiting rooms should note that only Ostend station stays open all night. The rest close for anything between two to five hours. If you are desperate, your best chance to avoid being thrown on to the street in the early hours is to try the little waiting rooms on the platforms (there are none in Antwerpen Centraal, but you can try Antwerpen-Berchem).

ADDRESSES

Belgian Tourist Office	Premier House, 2 Gayton Road, Harrow, Middlesex,HA1 2XU (tel. 081 427 6760).
Flemish YHA	Vlaamse Jeugdherbergcentrale, Van Stralenstraat 40, 2060 Antwerpen (tel. 03 2327218).
Walloon YHA	Centrale Wallone des Auberges de la Jeunesse, rue van Oost 52, 1030 Bruxelles (tel. 02 2153100).
Gîtes d'étapes	Gîte d'étape du CBTJ, rue Montoyer 31/8, 1040 Bruxelles (tel. 02 5125417). Étapes de la Route, rue Traversière 9, 1030 Bruxelles (tel. 02 2186025).
Friends of Nature	Natuurvrienden (Flanders) (tel. 03 361862). Amis de la Nature (Wallonia) (tel. 041 522875).
Camping	Map available from the Belgian Tourist Office.

Antwerp (Antwerpen) (tel. code 03)

Tourist Offices
Dienst voor Toerisme, Grote Markt 15, 2000 Antwerpen (tel.
2320103). Open Mon.–Fri. 8.30 a.m.–6 p.m., weekends
and public holidays 9 a.m.–5 p.m. Town plan 20BF (£0.34;
$0.57). Hotel lists and free hotel reservations.
Dienst voor Toerisme, Pavilion, Koningin Astridplein (tel.
2330570). Open Mon.–Fri. 8.30 a.m.–8 p.m., Sat. 9 a.m.–7
p.m., Sun. and public holidays 9 a.m.–5 p.m. Same
services as the office on the Grote Markt. Opposite the
main exit of Antwerpen-Centraal.

Basic Directions
Paris–Amsterdam trains stop at Antwerpen-Berchem from
which you can catch a connecting train to the main station at
Antwerpen-Centraal. The main exit of Antwerpen-Centraal is
on Koningin Astridplein, a 15–20-minute walk from the
Cathedral of Our Lady and the Grote Markt in the heart of the
old city. To walk there, head left from the main exit of the train
station in De Keyserlei. This street runs into Leysstraat which
subsequently becomes Meir. At the fork in the road either
Eiermarkt (right) or Schoermarkt (left and slightly longer) will
take you on to Groenplaats. To reach the Grote Markt walk
round the cathedral, keeping the building on your right hand
side. Trams 2 and 15 run from Antwerpen-Centraal to the
Groenplaats for around 35BF (£0.60; $1).

HOTELS

Cheapest doubles around 950BF (£15.75; $28)
Vredehof, De Keyzerhoeve 14 (tel. 5689900). Singles around
550BF (£9.25; $16). In the suburb of Antwerpen-Zandvliet.

Cheapest doubles around 1200BF (£20; $35)
Billard Palace, Koningin Astridplein 40 (tel. 2334455). On the

left-hand side of the square as you emerge from
Antwerpen-Centraal.
Rubenshof, Amerikalei 115–117 (tel. 2370789). About 25–30
minutes' walk from the main train station, close to the Fine
Arts Museum (Kon. Museum voor Schone Kunsten). Walk
down De Keyserlei, then turn left at the junction with
Frankrijklei and keep going. Tram 12, 23 or 24.

Cheapest doubles around 1300BF (£21.75; $38)

Oud Dijksterhuis, Koningin Astridplein 22 (tel. 2340866).

Cheapest doubles around 1450BF (£24; $42)

Florida, De Keyserlei 59 (tel. 2321443).

Cheapest doubles around 1600BF (£27; $47)

Monico, Koningin Astridplein 34 (tel. 2250093).
Harmonie, Harmoniestraat 25 (tel. 2380298).

IYHF HOSTEL

Op-Sinjoorke, Eric Sasselaan 2 (tel. 2380273). Midnight
curfew. B&B in dorms around 375BF (£6.25; $11) for IYHF
members. From Central Station bus 27 to Camille
Huysmanslaan. From there the hostel is signposted.
Alternatively, tram 2 dir. Hoboken to the Bouwcentrum
stop.

HOSTELS

New International Youth Home, Provinciestraat 256 (tel.
2300522). Curfew 11 p.m. B&B in dorms around 400BF
(£6.75; $11.50). Singles 700BF (£11.75; $21), doubles around
550BF (£9.25; $16) per person, triples 500BF (£8.25; $14.50)
per person, quads 460BF (£7.50; $13) per person. Tram 11
from Antwerpen-Centraal, or a 10-minute walk. Follow
Pelikaanstraat down the left hand side of the station into

Simonstraat and then Mercatorstraat. Turn left off Mercatorstraat down Provinciestraat.

Boomerang, Volkstraat 58 (tel. 2384782). B&B in dorms around 400BF (£6.75; $11.50). Small rooms are slightly cheaper than at the New International Youth Home. Near the Kon. Museum voor Schone Kunsten. From Antwerpen-Centraal take tram 23 to the Museum stop; from Antwerpen-Berchem take tram 8. The hostel is a 25-minute walk from Antwerpen-Centraal. Turn left off De Keyserlei along Frankrijklei and continue along Britselei to the start of Amerikalei. Head right down Tolstraat and keep on going straight ahead until you reach Volkstraat.

Square Sleep-Inn, Bolivarplaats 1 (tel. 2373748). One–four-bedded rooms. Singles are about 550BF (£9.25; $16). Otherwise rooms are much the same in price as those at the New International Youth Home.

Scoutel-VVKSM, Stoomstraat 3–7 (tel. 2264606). Slightly more expensive one-, two-, and three-bed rooms than at the hostels above. Five minutes from Antwerpen-Centraal.

International Seamen's House, Falconrui 21 (tel. 2321609). Compared to the other hostels singles are cheap, doubles more expensive.

CAMPING

Both of the following municipal sites charge the same, about 50BF (£0.85; $1.50) per person and per tent, and are open 1 Apr.–30 Sept.

'De Molen', Thonetlaan, St Annastrand (tel. 2196090). Across the River Schelde from the city centre.

'Vogelzang', Vogelzanglaan (behind the Bouwcentrum) (tel. 2385717). Tram 2 dir. Hoboken from Central Station takes you to the Bouwcentrum.

Bruges (Brugge) (tel. code 050)

Tourist Offices
Dienst voor Toerisme, Burg 11, 8000 Brugge (tel. 448686).
Apr.–Sept. open Mon.–Fri. 9.30 a.m.–6.30 p.m., weekends
10 a.m.–noon and 2.00–6.30 p.m.; Oct.–Mar. open Mon.–Fri.
9.30 a.m.–12.45 p.m., and 2.00–5.45 p.m., Sat. 10.00
a.m.–12.45 p.m. and 2.00–5.45 p.m. Accommodation service.
Excellent map of the city with the sights and suggested walking
tours 20BF (£0.34; $0.57). Wide range of information on the
city and its surroundings. The branch office in the train station
has a restricted range of information but also offers an
accommodation service. Mar.–Oct. open 2.45–9.00 p.m.;
Nov.–Feb. open 1.45–8.00 p.m.

Basic Directions
Bruges' train station is a 15–20 minute-walk from the city
centre. After crossing Stationsplein in front of the station, the
main road leading away to the left passes the equestrian statue
of King Albert I, before arriving at the wide expanse of 't Zand.
From the right hand side of the square, Zuidzandstraat runs
past Sint-Salvators Kerk into Steenstraat, which leads in turn
to the Markt. From the far left corner of the Markt,
Philipstockstraat leads into Burg. As you enter this square the
Town Hall is on your right-hand side. Across the square is the
former palace of the 'Brugse Vrije', now the seat of the Tourist
Office.
  Going straight across the road from the left-hand side of
Stationsplein takes you into Oostmeers. Heading right from
Stationsplein round the main road takes you up past the coach
park to the junction with the road to Lille (Rijsel) and Kortrijk.
Going right from this junction is Baron Ruzettelaan. Heading
left along Katelijnestraat and continuing straight ahead takes
you past the end of Heilige-Geeststraat into Simon Stevinplein.
Crossing the square and turning right takes you down
Steenstraat into the Markt.

HOTELS

Cheapest doubles around 1120BF (£18.75; $33)

De Royal, 't Zand 5 (tel. 343284).

Cheapest doubles around 1220BF (£20.25; $36)

't Keizerhof, Oostmeers 126 (tel. 338728).
Ensor, Speelmansrei 10 (tel. 342589).

Cheapest doubles around 1260BF (£21; $37)

't Speelmanshuys, 't Zand 3 (tel. 339552).

Cheapest doubles around 1320BF (£22; $38.50)

Leopold, 't Zand 26 (tel. 335129).
Central, Markt 30 (tel. 331805).
De Gulden Kogge, Damse Vaart Zuid 12, Damme (tel. 354217). Damme is a picturesque and historic village about four miles from Bruges. Buses run to Damme from the train station in Bruges.

Cheapest doubles around 1380BF (£23; $40)

Imperial, Dweerstraat 24 (tel. 339014). Dweerstraat runs left off Zuidzandstraat.
Rembrandt-Rubens, Walplein 38 (tel. 336439). From Oostmeers turn right along Zonnekemeers into Walplein or turn left off Katelijnestraat down Walstraat into the square.
Jacobs, Baliestraat 1 (tel. 339831). A ten-minute walk from the Markt, by St. Giles' Church (Sint-Gillis-Kerk).
Het Geestelijk Hof, Heilige Geeststraat 2 (tel. 342594). From Zuidzandstraat go right around Sint-Salvators-Kerk to the start of Heilige Geeststraat.

Cheapest doubles around 1480BF (£24.75; $43)

Gasthof De Krakele, St Pieterskaai 63 (tel. 315643).

Cheapest doubles around 1540BF (£25.75; $45)

Singe d'Or, 't Zand 18 (tel. 334848).
De Pauw, St Gilliskerkhof 8 (tel. 337118). By the St. Giles'
church. A ten-minute walk from the Markt.

Cheapest doubles around 1650BF (£27.50; $48)

Le Panier d'Or, Markt 28 (tel. 343234).
Cordoeanier, Cordoeanierstraat 16-18 (tel. 339051). Off
Philipstockstraat.
Graaf Van Vlaanderen, 't Zand 19 (tel. 333150).

BED & BREAKFAST

Cheapest doubles around 1250BF (£20.75; $36.50)

K. & A. Dieltjens-Debruyne, St Walburgastraat 14 (tel.
334294). Well located, about 5 minutes' walk from the
Markt.
José Claerhout, St Pieterskaai 66 (tel. 313246).

Cheapest doubles around 1350BF (£22.50; $40)

Catherine Nijssen, Moerstraat 50 (tel. 343171).
Robert Van Nevel, Carmersstraat 13 (tel. 316860).

IYHF HOSTEL

Baron Ruzettelaan 143 (tel. 352679). B&B in dorms around
375BF (£6.25; $11). Quads with showers around 475BF (£8;
$14) per person. Non-members pay a supplement of
around 100BF (£1.70; $3) if space is available. Excellent for
an IYHF hostel. The bar serves cheap beer from 6
p.m.–midnight. Reserve in advance. A 20-minute walk
from the train station or the centre, or bus 2 to
Steenbrugge.

HOSTELS

All the hostels advertise in the train station. Some will pick you up if you give them a phone call. See the adverts for details. Prices for dorms at all the hostels are roughly the same as at the IYHF hostel. All the hostels include breakfast in the overnight price.

> Kilroy's Garden, Singel 12 (tel. 389382). The most recently opened. Only a few minutes' walk from the station. Also offers two-, three-and four-bed rooms.
>
> Bruno's Passage, Dweerstraat 26 (tel. 340232). Dorms from around 350–420BF (£5.75–7.00; $10–12) depending on the size of the dorm. Dweerstraat runs left off Zuidzandstraat

The two hostels below were the original independent hostels in Bruges. Both are located about ten minutes from the town centre, but a considerable distance from the station. When Bruno's Passage opened it began to draw a disproportionate share of the trade because of its proximity to the train station. Hence the development of free pick-up schemes.

> Snuffel Travellers' Inn, Ezelstraat 49 (tel. 333133). Doubles around 500BF (£8.25; $15) per person. Dorms around 375BF (£6.25; $11). From the Markt follow Sint-Jakobsstraat which runs into Ezelstraat. Bus 3, 8, 9 or 13 from the train station.
>
> Bauhaus International Youth Hotel, Langestraat 135–137 (tel. 336175). Mixed dorms around 340BF (£5.75; $10), singles around 600BF (£10; $17.50), doubles around 500BF (£8.25; $15) per person, triples around 420BF (£7; $12) per person, quads around 380BF (£6.50; $11) per person.

CAMPING

> 'St Michiel', Tillegemstraat 55 (tel. 059 806824 or Bruges 380819). Open all year. Around 120BF (£2; $3.59) per tent, 100BF (£1.70; $3) per person. In the Sint-Michiels area of the city. Bus 7 from the train station.
>
> 'Memling', Veltemweg 109 (tel. 355845). Open Mar.–Dec.

Around 85BF (£1.40; $2.50) per tent and per person. The smaller of the two sites, in the Sint-Kruis area of the city. There is a large supermarket nearby.

Brussels (Brussel/Bruxelles)

(tel. code 02)

Tourist Offices

TIB, Hôtel de Ville, Grand Place (tel. 5138940). June–Sept. open daily 9 a.m.–6 p.m., Oct.–May same hours but closed Sun. The office sells the useful *Brussels Guide & Map* 50BF (£0.85; $1.50). Free hotel reservations and information on public transport.

National Tourist Office, rue Marché-aux-Herbes 61 (tel. 5123030). June–Sept. open Mon.–Fri. 9 a.m.–8 p.m., weekends 9 a.m.–7 p.m.; Mar.–May and Oct. 9 a.m.–6 p.m. daily; Nov.–Feb. Mon.–Sat. 9 a.m.–6 p.m., Sun. 1–5 p.m. Information on the whole of the country. The office makes hotel reservations in Brussels.

Tourist Information, Zaventem International Airport. Accommodation service and information on public transport.

Acotra, rue de la Montagne 38 (tel. 5134480/5134489). Youth tourism office. Good source of information on cheap accommodation for young travellers. Acotra also has an office at the airport.

BTR, P.O.B. 41, 1000 Brussels 23 (tel. 2305029). For advance reservation of hotels.

Street Signs

Historically Brussels is a Flemish city, but the majority of its inhabitants today (around 70 per cent) are French speakers. It is only in comparatively recent times that the city was declared bilingual, and street names given in their Flemish as well as French forms. The section below uses a mixture of

Flemish and French street names. Hopefully the directions given will get you right to where you want to go, but do not worry about approaching someone if you get lost. The people of Brussels are generally friendly and few Flemish speakers will object to you using the French version of a street name (or vice versa).

Arriving in Brussels

There are three main train stations of interest to tourists: Gare du Nord, Gare du Midi and Gare Centrale. The latter is most convenient for the sights and for the Tourist Offices, but not all through-trains stop at this station. There are frequent connections from Gare du Nord and Gare du Midi to Gare Centrale, so it is no problem if your train does not stop at Gare Centrale, as long as you get off at one of the other stations. Gare Centrale lies between Gare du Nord and Gare du Midi, so if your train travels straight from Midi to Nord (or vice versa) make sure you get off at the second station. There is a half-hourly train service between Zaventem International Airport and Gare Centrale and Gare du Nord until 11.45 p.m. (a 20-minute trip, free with railpasses).

Running along the front of Gare Centrale is the busy Keizerinlaan. Towards the left hand end of this road, rue de l'Infante Isabella runs away from the station. Follow this street down past the Chapel of Mary Magdalene and continue straight ahead, passing the restaurants to arrive at the start of rue Marché-aux-Herbes, just beyond the entrance to the Galeries Royales St Hubert on your right. Continuing down this street takes you to the National Tourist Office. Turning left takes you into Grand Place. TIB is located in the Town Hall on the opposite side of the square.

The two main coach companies operating from the UK both drop passengers a short distance from the Grand Place. Hoverspeed coaches stop at Place de la Bourse, from which Boterstraat leads into Grand Place. Eurolines stop a little further away at Place de Brouckere. From this square follow Anspachlaan to Place de la Bourse, then turn left along

Beurstraat down the side of the Stock Exchange to the start
of Boterstraat.

HOTELS

Cheapest doubles around 1000BF (£16.50; $29)

Ragheno, Fonsnylaan 11 (tel. 5382221). Fonsnylaan runs
alongside Gare du Midi on the other side of the station
from the main entrance. The hotel is about 150m right from
the rear exit on to Fonsnylaan.

Bosquet, rue Bosquet 70 (tel. 5385230). A 10–15-minute walk
from Gare du Midi. Walk down Boulevard de l'Europe and
turn right onto Hallepoortlaan. Follow this road round into
Jasparlaan and keep on going until you see rue Bosquet
on your right. Metro: Place Louise is under 5 minutes' walk
away. Follow Av. de la Toison until you see rue Bosquet
on the left.

New Galaxy, rue du Progrès 7A (tel. 2194776). Rue du
Progrès runs between Gare du Nord and the Rogier metro
stop (about 500m separates the two). Leave Gare du Nord
by the side exit on to Place du Nord, or head left from the
main exit around the station.

Cheapest doubles around 1100BF (£18.50; $32)

La Potinière, Fr. Jos. Navezstraat 165 (tel. 2152030). A
10–15-minute walk from Gare du Nord. Head right from
the main exit and take the first right under the tracks. The
second street on the left is Brabantstraat, which leads into
rue Gallait and then into Navezstraat. Taking a train to the
Schaarbeek station leaves you much closer to the hotel.
On leaving the station, simply head right until you reach
the hotel.

Cheapest doubles around 1200BF (£20; $35)

George V, 't Kintstraat 23 (tel. 5135093). About 600m from
the Anneessens metro stop. From Bd Lemonnier turn

down rue Soignies and keep on going straight ahead until you reach 't Kintstraat at the end of Washhuisstraat. A 10–15-minute walk from Gare du Midi. Head along Bd de l'Europe, then turn left and follow Bd du Midi. Just beyond the Porte d'Anderlecht turn right along rue de la Senne, then right again at 't Kintstraat.

Yser, Edinburgstraat 13 (tel. 5117459). Closed July–Aug. About 500m from the Porte de Namur metro station. Walk down Chaussée d'Ixelles, turn left along Chaussée de Wavre, then left again.

Sabina, rue du Nord 78 (tel. 2182637). About 200m from the Madou metro station. From Place Madou cross Place Surlet de Chokier heading towards rue du Congrès. Rue du Nord is off to the right.

Aux Arcades, rue des Bouchers 38 (tel. 5112876). Excellent location close to the Grand Place. From rue Marché-aux-Herbes close to the National Tourist Office take Petite rue des Bouchers into rue des Bouchers.

Osborne, 67 rue Bosquet (tel. 5379251). See Bosquet, above, for directions from Gare du Midi. From the Place Louise metro station walk down Av. Louise then turn right along rue Jourdan into rue Bosquet.

Cheapest doubles around 1320BF (£22; $39)

Elysée, rue de la Montagne 4 (tel. 5119682). Good central location. Rue de la Montagne runs uphill from the start of rue Marché-aux-Herbes near the Galeries Royales St Hubert.

Plasky, Plaskylaan 212 (tel. 7337530). Bus 63 from the Madou metro station.

Du Congrès, rue du Congrès 42 (tel. 2171890). About 350m from the Madou metro stop. From Place Madou cross Place Surlet de Chokier and walk down rue du Congrès.

Cheapest doubles around 1380BF (£23; $40)

De France, Jamarlaan 21 (tel. 5227935). About 300m from Gare du Midi. From the station walk down Av. Paul Henri

Spaak to Place Bara. Jamarlaan is off to the right.

Les Bluets, Berckmannstraat 124 (tel. 5343983). Follow the directions for Bosquet, above. Berckmannstraat is right off Jasparlaan coming from Gare du Midi, the second street on the left after rue Bosquet walking from Place Louise.

Pacific, rue Antoine Dansaert 57 (tel. 5118459).

Cheapest doubles around 1480BF (£24.75; $43)

International, rue Royale 344 (tel. 2173344). All rooms have a shower. About 500m from the Botanique metro station; only a little further away from Gare du Nord. From Botanique follow rue Royale past the Church of Jesus and the end of Chaussée de Haecht towards St Mary's Church. From Gare du Nord exit on to Place du Nord or head left around the station from the main exit. Go under the tracks and turn left along Brabantstraat, then right down rue Dupont. At the end of rue Dupont the hotel is a short walk to the right.

Madou, rue du Congrès 45 (tel. 2188375). For directions see the Du Congrès above.

't Zilveren Tasje, rue du Congrès 48 (tel. 2173274). See the Du Congrès above for directions.

Lloyd George, Av. Lloyd George 12 (tel. 6483072).

Cheapest doubles around 1550BF (£26; $45)

Gascogne, Adolphe Maxlaan 137 (tel. 2176962). Closed August. About 600m from Gare du Nord, a few minutes' walk from the Rogier metro station. Exit Gare du Nord on to Place du Nord or walk left round the station from the main exit, then follow rue du Progrès to Place Rogier. Adolphe Maxlaan is on the opposite side of the main road.

Grande-Clôche, Place Rouppe 10–12 (tel. 5126140). A few minutes' walk from the Anneessens metro station; about 750m from Gare du Midi. From Place Anneessens, rue de Tournai leads into Place Rouppe. From Gare du Midi follow Bd de l'Europe into Place de la Constitution. Of the

two main roads on the other side of the street Av. de
Stalingrad on the right runs into Place Rouppe.

IYHF HOSTELS

'Breughel' (Flemish YHA), Heilige Geeststraat 2 (tel.
5110436). Midnight curfew. B&B in dorms around 400BF
(£6.75; $11.50). Singles 650BF (£10.75; $19), doubles 530BF
(£8.75; $15.50) per person, quads 460BF (£7.75; $13.50) per
person. A 5-minute walk from Gare Centrale. Head left
from the station along Keizerinlaan and then Keizerslaan.
Just after the road forks Heilige Geeststraat runs left down
the side of the church.

Centre Jacques Brel (Walloon YHA), rue de la Sablonnière
30 (tel. 2180187). Curfew 1 a.m. B&B in dorms around
400BF (£6.75; $11.50). Singles 630BF (£10.50; $18.50),
doubles 520BF (£8.75; $15) per person, triples and quads
450BF (£7.50; $13) per person. A 10-minute walk from Gare
du Nord; about 400m from the Botanique metro station.
Emerging from the metro station follow rue Royale away
from the Church of Jesus and across the main road, then
take the first street on the left. From Gare du Nord head
left around the station from the main exit (or take the exit
on to Place du Nord) then follow rue du Progrès. At the
major junction by the Rogier metro stop head left until you
reach the crossroads with rue Royale, then turn right and
first left.

'Jean Nihon' (Walloon YHA), rue de l'Eléphant 4 (tel.
2153100). Similar prices to the other Walloon YHA hostel.
Metro: Zwarte Vijvers (slightly closer) or Graaf Van
Vlaanderen. Under 10 minutes' walk from both. From
Graaf Van Vlaanderen follow St Mariastraat across Graaf
Van Vlaanderenstraat into Briefdragerstraat. Turn left
along Schoolstraat, across Gentse Steenweg and on down
Paalstraat. At the fork in the road rue de l'Elephant is to
the right. From Zwarte Vijvers follow Gentse Steenweg
until you see Paalstraat on your right. Going this way you
should pass Ostendstraat on the right a short distance from

the metro station; if not you are going the wrong way.

HOSTELS

Maison Internationale, Chaussée de Wavre 205 (tel. 6488529/
6489787). Curfew 12.30 a.m. Three-day maximum stay.
Very good value. Singles around 400BF (£6.75; $11.50),
doubles around 340BF (£5.75; $10) per person. Price
includes breakfast. In summer, camping in the hostel
garden costs about 260BF (£4.25; $7.50). The hostel is a
5-minute walk from the Quartier Leopold train station;
about 10 minutes' walk from the Luxembourg metro
station. From Quartier Leopold head left along Trierstraat
into Idaliestraat, then turn left down rue Godecharle into
Chaussée de Wavre. From Luxembourg walk down rue du
Trône (the street to the right of rue de Luxembourg), then
go left at the crossroads with Chaussée de Wavre. Bus 38
from Gare du Nord, bus 38 or 60 from Gare Centrale.

CHAB, rue Traversière 8 (tel. 2170158). Curfew 2 a.m. Large
co-ed rooms with mattresses on floor around 330BF (£5.50;
$9.50). Beds in small dorms around 400BF (£6.75; $11.50).
Singles 630BF (£10.50; $18.50), doubles 530BF (£8.75;
$15.50) per person; triples and quads 450BF (£7.50; $13)
per person. Overnight price includes breakfast. Bus 61
from the Gare du Nord to rue Traversière, or a 10-minute
walk. Exit the station on to Place du Nord (or head left from
the main exit), then go under the tracks. Follow the main
road to the right, turn left down Rivierstraat, then
diagonally right at rue Botanique. The latter ends at rue
Royale. Rue Traversière is across the junction. The hostel
is a few minutes' walk from the Botanique metro station,
right off rue Royale on the other side of the Church of
Jesus.

Sleep Well, rue de la Blanchisserie 27 (tel. 2185050). Curfew
1 a.m. Dorms around 350BF (£5.75; $10). Singles 500BF
(£8.75; $14.50), doubles 450BF (£7.50; $13) per person, four-
to six-bed rooms 400BF (£6.75; $11.50) per person. In July
and August only, places are available in very large dorms

for around 280BF (£4.75; $8). Overnight prices include breakfast. Those whose passport includes the number 27 get a discount of a quarter on the overnight price. About 8 minutes' walk from Gare du Nord; a few minutes from Rogier metro station and follow rue du Progrès to the major junction by the Rogier metro stop. Across the junction is Adolphe Maxlaan. Turn left off this street down Mechelenstraat which becomes rue de la Blanchisserie.

Centre International Etudiants Tiers-Monde, rue de Parme 26 (tel. 5379215). A 10-minute walk from Gare du Midi. Follow Bd de l'Europe then turn right along Hallepoortlaan. By the Hallepoort, rue de la Victoire runs away to the right, crossing rue de Parme after Munthofstraat. Slightly closer to the Place Louise metro station. Walk down Av. Louise, turn right along Jourdanstraat, then left at Schotlandstraat which leads into rue de Parme.

Foyer International Protestant 'David Livingstone', Av. Coghen 119 (tel. 3433089).

Entraide Educative et Sociale, Place Loix 20 (tel. 5379642).

CAMPING

Unless you pitch your tent at the Maison Internationale (see the Hostels section above) you are going to have to do a fair bit of commuting to one of the sites in the suburbs.

Beersel, Steenweg op Ukkel 75, Beersel (tel. 3762561). Open all year. Basic, but very cheap. Around 100BF (£1.70; $3) for a solo traveller. From Nord-Bourse tram 55, then bus UH. The most convenient site if you are arriving from Paris, Mons and Charleroi on the E10/A7.

'Paul Rosmant', Warandeberg 52, Wezembeek-Oppem (tel. 7821009). Open Apr.–Sept. Around 85BF (£1.40; $2.50) per tent and per person, plus a municipality tax of 30BF (£0.50; $1). Metro to Kraainem, then change to bus 30 to Place St Pierre. Just off the Brussels ring road. The most convenient site if you are arriving by road from Leuven, Liège or Germany.

'Veldkant', Veldkantstraat, Grimbergen (tel. 2692597). Open
Apr.–Oct. 120BF (£2; $3.50) per tent, 90BF (£1.50; $2.50)
per person. Bus G from Gare du Nord to the end of the
line, then a 10-minute walk. The easiest site to get to if you
are arriving by road from Antwerp.

Ghent (Gent) (tel. code 091)

Tourist Offices
Dienst voor Toerisme, Predikherenlei 2, 9000 Gent. Contact
this office if you want information on the city in advance. On
arrival contact Info-Toerisme in the Stadhuis (Town Hall) (tel.
241555). Open Easter–early Nov. daily, 9.30 a.m.–6.30 p.m.;
at other times of the year the office closes at 4.30 p.m.

Basic Directions
The main train station, Gent–St Pieters, is about 20–25
minutes' walk from the town centre. In front of St Pieters is
Koningin Maria Hendrikaplein, from which Pr. Clemintinalaan
runs off to the right of the station. At the top right hand end
of the square Koningin Elisabethlaan leads into
Kortrijksesteenweg. Turning left at this point and continuing
straight ahead you eventually arrive at the St Niklaaskerk at
the end of Veldstraat. Walking right from the church you arrive
at the Belfry (Belfort). The Stadhuis is on the street running
uphill from the Belfry. Tram 1 (pay the driver) runs from Kon.
Maria Hendrikaplein to the Head Post Office, near the St
Niklaaskerk. Gent–Dampoort station is only ten minutes' walk
from the town centre. From the square in front of the station
pass the end of the dock and take Dampoortstraat or
Hagelandkai (along the water) down to the bridge over the
River Leie. After crossing the Leie go right a little and then
left down Steendam, down the left hand side of St Jacobs and
into Belfortstraat which leads to the Stadhuis. There are
frequent trains between Gent–St Pieters and Gent–Dampoort

(to Kortrijk or Lille/Rijsel). If you want to stock up with food there is a GB supermarket by Dampoort station.

HOTELS

Cheapest singles around 425BF (£7; $12.50), cheapest doubles around 650BF (£10.75; $19), cheapest triples around 950BF (£16; $28)

Le Richelieu, Pr. Clementinalaan 134 (tel. 218644).

Cheapest singles around 540BF (£9; $16), cheapest doubles around 800BF (£13.50; $23), cheapest triples around 950BF (£16; $28) as indicated

La Paix, Pr. Clementinalaan 2 (tel. 222779). Doubles only. Right as you leave the station.
De Ijzer, Vlaanderenstraat 117 (tel. 259873). Singles, doubles and triples. Good location, about 8 minutes' walk from the centre. From the Belfry, walk along to Sint-Baafskathedral, then follow Limburgstraat from the right hand side of the cathedral into Vlaanderenstraat.

Cheapest doubles around 900BF (£15; $26), cheapest triples around 1200BF (£20; $35) as indicated

Buitenbeentje, Charles de Kerchovelaan 191 (tel. 216806). Doubles and triples with showers. The street runs right off Kortrijksesteenweg along the side of the Citadelpark, about 800m from Gent–St Pieters.
Du Progrès, Korenmarkt 10 (tel. 251716). Doubles. Excellent central location. The Korenmarkt starts near the St Niklaaskerk.
De Fonteyne, Goudenleeuwplein 7 (tel. 254871). Singles and doubles. Excellent central location near the Belfry.
Royal, Heernislaan 88 (tel. 258495). Doubles and triples, singles around 800BF (£13.50; $23). From Gent–Dampoort walk past the end of the dock then go left along Kasteellaan, then left as the road forks.

De Palm, G. Callierlaan 93 (tel. 259493). Doubles and triples with showers.

Cheapest doubles 1180BF (£19.75; $35)

La Lanterne, Pr. Clementinalaan 140 (tel. 201318). Singles around 750BF.

Ermitage, Sint-Denijslaan 203 (tel. 224596). Doubles. Turn right on leaving the rear exit of Gent–St Pieters, then a 5-minute walk.

Claridge, Kon. Maria Hendrikaplein 36 (tel. 222587). Doubles with showers.

Cheapest doubles around 1400BF (£23.50; $41), triples around 1850BF (£31; $54) as indicated

Flandria, Barrestraat 3 (tel. 230626/243880). Doubles and triples. Good central location, a few minutes' walk from the Stadhuis. From the Stadhuis, head right along Hoogpoort into Nederpolder, left at Kwaadham, then right.

Adoma, Sint-Denijslaan 203 (tel. 213944). A 5-minute walk from Gent–St Pieters, going left from the rear exit.

Castel, Kon. Maria Hendrikaplein 8 (tel. 202354). Doubles and triples.

The Rambler, Kon. Maria Hendrikaplein 3 (tel. 218877). Doubles, triples around 2100BF (£35.50; $60.50).

Trianon, Sint-Denijslaan 203 (tel. 213944). Doubles with showers. Head right from the rear exit of Gent–St Pieters.

Parkhotel, W. Wilsonplein 1 (tel. 251781). Doubles and triples. A 10-minute walk from the centre. Lies at the end of Vlaanderenstraat (see De Ijzer, above). From St Pieters go right off Nederkouter at Bagattenstraat, left a little, then right along Lammerstraat.

B&B

Around 450BF (£7.50; $13) per person

Peter Klingele, Voorhoutkaai 6. No telephone. Good location on the Leie, near Gent–Dampoort. Follow the directions for M. & L. Laquiere-Seydlitz, below.

Doubles around 1125BF (£18.75; $33) per person

Joost Van Damme-Deltour, Drabstraat 28 (tel. 255568). Good central location. From the St Niklaaskerk walk along the side of the bridge on to the Graslei, turn right along the front of the magnificent guildhouses and walk to the other end of the Graslei. Turn left at this point and follow the road into Drabstraat.

Riet Dhooge, Aannemersstraat 76 (tel. 281939).

Vincent Ronse, Plotersgracht 12 (tel. 256604)

Singles around 620BF (£10.25; $18)

Christin De Muynck, Blekersdijk 46 (tel. 243294). Good location near Gent–Dampoort. Follow Dampoortstraat or Hagelandkaai towards the Leie. At the bridge, turn right down Ham, then left on to Blekersdijk.

Doubles around 1450BF (£24; $42)

May Howard, Leeuwstraat 17 (tel. 251688). Good central location.

Doubles around 1550BF (£26; $45)

M. & I. Laquiere-Seydlitz, Gebroeders Van Eyckstraat 50 (tel. 234530). Well located, a 5-minute walk from the town centre. From Gent–Dampoort walk past the end of the dock and take Schoolkaai (across the inlet of the Leie from Hagelandkaai), left along the waterfront down Voorhuitkaai, then over the bridge and straight on into Gebroeders Van Eyckstraat.

UNIVERSITY ACCOMMODATION

From mid-July to late September single rooms are available in the university's four halls of residence. Prices for 1993 should be around 500BF (£8.25; $14.50), which includes breakfast and the use of showers. The halls are open round the clock. For information and reservations contact K. Van den Broeck, Stalhof 6, 9000 Gent (tel. 220911). The booking office at Stalhof 6 is in the Vermeylen Hall, a 10–15-minute walk from Gent–St Pieters. From the right hand side of Kon. Maria Hendrikaplein follow Kon. Astridlaan to the Citadelpark. Cut diagonally through the park, or follow the road to your right around the park to Overpoortstraat. If you do not want to walk, take bus 9, 70, 71 or 90. Ask if it is possible to have a room in the Vermeylen Hall, or in the Fabiola Hall at Stalhof 4, as the other two halls are far from the centre in the area behind Gent–St Pieters. If you are having trouble getting through to the Vermeylen Hall you can try telephoning the other halls themselves: Fabiola (tel. 226091); Boudewijn, Harelbekestraat 70 (tel. 229721); Astrid, Krijgslaan 250 (tel. 229081).

CAMPING

Blaarmeersen, Zuiderlaan 12 (tel. 215399). Open March–mid-Oct. 130BF (£2.15; $3.75) per tent, 120BF (£2.00; $3.50) per person. From Gent–St Pieters station a 20-minute walk, or bus 51, 52 or 53 to Europaburg, then bus 38.
'Witte Berken', Pontstraat 4, Drongen (tel. 273445/220550). Just outside Ghent. Open mid-May–mid-Sept. 65BF (£1.10; $1.90) per tent and per person. Caravans for hire.

IYHF HOSTELS NEARBY

There are two hostels close to Ghent which may be of interest to railpass holders who are stuck for a bed:

Kampstraat 59 (Recreatiedomein 'De Gavers', Geraardsbergen (tel. 054–416189). Geraardsbergen is roughly 20 miles from Ghent, served by frequent local trains. The hostel is 5 minutes' walk from Schendeleke station.

Passionistenlaan 1A, Kortrijk (tel. 056–201442). Ten minutes from the train station. Kortrijk is about 35 miles from Ghent, with frequent Intercity trains leaving from Gent–St Pieters and Gent–Dampoort.

Liège (tel. code 041)

Tourist Offices

Office de Tourisme de la Ville de Liège, En Féronstrée 92 (tel. 222456). Open Apr.–Oct., Mon.–Fri. 9 a.m.–6 p.m.; Sat. 10 a.m.–4 p.m., Sun. 10 a.m.–4 p.m.; Nov.–Mar., Mon.–Fri. 9 a.m.–5 p.m. City plans, and advice on accommodation possibilities. Close to the Musée d'Art Wallon, along from the Town Hall on Place du Marché.

Office de Tourisme de la Ville de Liège, Gare des Guillemins (tel. 524419). Branch office. Same services as the main office on En Féronstrée.

HOTELS

The city's cheaper hotels are located around Gare des Guillemins. Rue des Guillemins is the street running left from the station down to Place des Guillemins. The red light district is along to the right of Gare des Guillemins, but the area around the station is quite safe to walk around in.

Cheapest singles around 650BF (£10.80; $19), cheapest doubles around 950BF (£15.80; $28)

Le Globe, rue des Guillemins 105 (tel. 527300).
Les Nations, rue des Guillemins 139 (tel. 524434).
Du Midi, place des Guillemins 1 (tel. 522004)

Cheapest singles around 850BF (£14.20; $25), cheapest doubles around 1270BF (£21.20; $37)

Le Berger, rue des Urbanistes 10 (tel. 230080).

Cheapest singles around 950BF (£15.80; $28), cheapest doubles around 1380BF (£23; $40)

Metropole, rue des Guillemins 141 (tel. 524293).

Cheapest doubles around 1650BF (£27.50; $48)

De La Couronne, place des Guillemins 11 (tel. 522168).

IYHF HOSTEL

Rue Blandot 4, Tilff (tel. 882100). This excellent hostel is only 500m from the train station in Tilff, just over 3½ miles from Liège (frequent train services).

FOYER

Foyer International des Etudiants, rue du Vertbois. Three-night minimum stay. 200BF (£3.35; $6) in dorms. The foyer is of poor quality. By the Eglise St-Jacques, off Bd d'Avroy between the Charlemagne statue and the start of Bd de la Sauvenière.

CAMPING

'Camping Club de Sainval', Chemin du Halage, Tilff (tel. 267104). Around 50BF (£0.85; $1.50) per tent and per person. Tilff is just over 3½ miles from Liège (frequent train services).
'Camping du S.I.', rue du Chera, Tilff (tel. 881286/881630). 50BF (£0.85; $1.50) per tent, 40BF (£0.65; $1.20) per person.
'Camping du S.I.', Allée Verte 25, Vise (tel. 793204). Around 30BF (£0.50; $0.80) per tent and per person. Vise is about 15 miles from Liège. On the train line to/from Maastricht (frequent service).

BULGARIA

When travelling in Bulgaria you will find that the reception you will receive from people working in the tourist industry will vary dramatically. In some cases, you will find people who will do their utmost to help you to find suitably priced accommodation, and who will provide you with any other available information to help you enjoy your stay. Sadly, there is currently a dearth in tourist information (particularly town plans showing the places of interest), and in cheap accommodation, so it is often the case that staff in the tourist industry simply cannot help you, no matter how much they might like to. Nowadays, when Tourist Office staff tell you that the supply of cheap accommodation has been exhausted, it is likely that they are telling you the truth. Nevertheless, one of the worst legacies of the former state-controlled tourist industry is the engrained habits and attitudes of some of those who worked in tourism under the old regime (and who were encouraged to wring as much money out of Western tourists as possible). There still remains a hard core of people in the tourist industry who will tell you blatant lies in an attempt to force you to accept expensive accommodation when cheaper lodgings are available.

Unfortunately, it is just not possible to say with any certainty where you might have trouble finding cheap accommodation and where you should not. In many popular destinations (such as Sofia, Plovdiv and Veliko Târnovo) the supply of cheap lodgings just manages to satisfy demand at most times of the year, while in others (such as Varna and the Black Sea resorts) the increase in the number of tourists has swamped the existing accommodation possibilities. While the supply of budget accommodation is rising throughout the country the number of visitors continues to rise also. Assuming ongoing strife in

Yugoslavia continues to make Bulgaria an attractive option for reaching Greece overland, there is likely to be dramatically increased pressure on accommodation possibilities in obvious stopover points such as Sofia, Plovdiv and Veliko Târnovo. At the end of the day, with the accommodation scene in such a state of flux, there is no way of knowing whether you are being told the truth or otherwise when Tourist Office staff tell you there are no cheap beds available.

Difficulties in finding **hotel** accommodation are indicative of those facing Western budget travellers throughout Bulgaria. In the past, Western tourists looking for a hotel room were more or less confined to hotels reserved through Balkantourist or some other official agency. This was part of an orchestrated attempt to keep Western visitors out of the cheaper hotels intended for Bulgarian and East European holidaymakers. The policy was made almost totally effective by the practice of the staff at the cheaper hotels. Only occasionally would they bend the rules and allow someone who had approached the hotel in person to stay the night. Telephoning a hotel was guaranteed to meet with a 'no vacancies' response.

Happily, this situation has changed, and all hotels are eager to accept guests, no matter where they come from. Budget travellers will probably be interested in only the one-and two-star hotel categories (the only difference is that rooms in one-star hotels do not have a private bath). Prices in one-star hotels are usually around £10.25 ($18) for a single, £18 ($32) for a double. Comparable rooms in a two-star hotel cost £13.75 ($24) and £22 ($38) respectively. However, despite the fact that one-star hotels are now open to Western visitors, hotel accommodation is now more difficult to find than it was during the days of state control because of the increased number of visitors. Previously hotels had to be booked in advance during the summer; it is now difficult to find a hotel room on arrival throughout much of the year. One-star hotels in popular towns still tend to be filled with groups of East European holidaymakers, so you still have a better chance of finding a room in a two-star hotel. Because of language difficulties, it is always better to approach hotels in person if you arrive after the Tourist Office has closed, rather than contacting them by telephone. If you are told upfront that there are no rooms available this is likely to be true and not, as is often the case in neighbouring Romania, a ploy to get you to offer a bribe.

Arranging lodgings in the home of a Bulgarian family is both a cheaper and a more interesting option than staying in a hotel. **Private rooms** can be booked through Balkantourist and, in some cases, through other organisations such as ORBITA (the student travel organisation). In Sofia, doubles cost about £4.50–5.75 ($8–10) per person, with the cheaper rooms generally being located out in the suburbs. As the public transport system in Sofia is cheap and reasonably efficient, it is practicable to stay in the suburbs if you cannot find a room in the centre. Outside the capital, doubles in popular destinations like Plovdiv and Veliko Târnovo rarely cost more than £5 ($9) per person. In the countryside, rooms can cost as little as £2.50 ($4.50) per person, though it can be very difficult to find rooms in rural areas. One occasional drawback to booking rooms through an agency in the past has been the existence of a minimum stay requirement: particularly along the Black Sea coast, where a minimum stay of three to five days was required in some towns. In more popular towns, it is not unusual to be approached by touts offering private rooms during the peak season. The rooms on offer are often of lower quality than those offered by accommodation agencies, but they may be your only hope of getting a cheap bed. Touts are well aware of the local lodging situation, so there is not a great deal of room for haggling over their initial asking price, which at the very height of the season can be on a par with rooms booked through a local agency.

The student travel organisation ORBITA controls a network of hotels and **youth hostels**. In the past, ORBITA youth hostels admitted Westerners by prior reservation only. While groups of five or more were sometimes allowed to book hostels on arrival in Sofia, others had to book months in advance. Nowadays, the situation is that while ORBITA still prefers dealing with groups, and while it is still almost impossible to find a space at an ORBITA hostel on arrival, their staff are more likely to admit you to a hostel if there is space available. Realistically, only during university summer vacations, mid-July until mid-September, do independent travellers have a slim chance of finding a place in student accommodation. If you are lucky enough to do so, you can expect to pay around £1.50 ($2.75) for a bed.

The Bulgarian Tourist Union, which is affiliated to the IYHF, also operates a chain of hostels, around 60 of which are listed in the IYHF handbook. Facilities are little more than basic, and the hostels are often located far from the centre of town, but at around £1.50 ($2.75) for a bed the price is fine. Once again, these should be booked well in advance as they are popular with visiting groups. However, as the staff at these hostels were traditionally more accommodating to Western visitors stuck for a bed than their counterparts in hotels, or in the ORBITA hostels, it might be worthwhile making a personal enquiry at any hostel you come across.

Camping is both a cheap way to see the country and an ideal way to meet young East European travellers. Charges are around £1.50 ($2.50) per tent, with a similar fee per occupant. Moreover, taking a tent normally provides insurance against having to pay out for a hotel room if you cannot find a hostel bed or a private room, as virtually all the main tourist destinations have a campsite in or around town (city sites are often located on the outskirts). With the exception of sites along the Black Sea coast which become very crowded in summer, finding a place to pitch your tent is generally straightforward. The Bulgarian National Tourist Office in London/your capital city may be able to provide you with a map of the 120 campsites Western visitors were once restricted to (at the time of writing, the London office was very short of information). This map covers all the places you are likely to visit, and contains details of site facilities and opening periods (normally May–mid-Oct. inclusive). At most of these sites comfortable chalet accommodation is available to let. A chalet sleeping two normally costs in the region of £8–10 ($14–17.50) per night. **Freelance camping** and **sleeping rough** are both illegal and steep fines are usually imposed on those apprehended.

However, in recent years the police have been turning a blind eye to people sleeping rough in some of the Black Sea resorts during the peak season, possibly because they are well aware of the dire shortage of accommodation possibilities in that area.

Hikers and climbers should contact the Bulgarian Tourist Union for permission to use the network of **mountain chalets** (*hizha*) they operate, and to make the necessary reservations. The standard of accommodation in *hizha* varies tremendously, from those with only the bare essentials, to those which seem like hotels.

Tourist Information
As the quality of tourist information available locally to visitors is poor, it is advisable to purchase a good guidebook before setting off on holiday. At the time of writing, this is easier said than done, though hopefully the situation will have improved by 1993. Some of the guidebooks which covered the old Eastern Bloc are good sources of information on the main sights to see, but the information on accommodation in these books is now obsolete.

ADDRESSES

Bulgarian National Tourist Office	18 Princes Street, London, W1R 7RE (tel. 071 499 6988).
Hotels	Balkantourist, Knjaz Dondukov 37, Sofia (tel. 884430).
Private rooms	See Balkantourist above.
Hostels	ORBITA, (Student Travel Office), bul. Alexander Stambolijski 45a, Sofia (tel. 884801).
	ORBITA, bul. Vitosha 4, Sofia (tel. 831659).
	Bulgarian Tourist Union, Zentralrat, bul. Tolbuchin 18, Sofia (tel. 879405).
Mountain huts	Bulgarian Tourist Union. Address above.

Koprivshtitsa

The highly attractive town of Koprivshtitsa is of great
importance in Bulgarian national history. The Koprivshtitsa
train station is about six miles from the town, on the
Sofia–Burgas line. Local buses meet incoming trains to
transport you into the town. Reports differ as to whether the
Balkantourist office (located in the brown house by the river,
to the rear of the cluster of restaurants in the town centre) is
in operation, so collect information on the town before setting
out from Sofia. The Hotel Koprivshtitsa is the best hotel option
in town with singles around £7 ($12) and doubles around £9.75
($17). From the centre, walk to the second stone bridge, cross
over and go up the hill. Private rooms are best fixed up in
advance through Balkantourist in Sofia. Curiously, some maps
show a campsite which has long since ceased to exist (if it ever
did). The closest campsite is about 2½ miles downhill from the
train station in Mirkovo (tel. Mirkovo 484), between Sofia and
Koprivshtitsa. Buses run from the train station to the site,
which is open mid-May–Sept. Bungalows are available for hire
at the site.

Plovdiv (tel. code 032)

Tourist Office
Puldin Tour, bul. Moskva 34 (tel. 553848). Open daily 8.45
a.m.–12.30 p.m. and 1.30–6.30 p.m. The office is close to the
fairgrounds, across the River Marica from the town centre.
From the railway station take bus 1 or 7 to the stop after
crossing the river, or take tram 102 to the ninth stop. The office
is one block along bul. Moskva from the tram stop.

HOTELS

Bulgaria, ul. Patriarch Evtimii (tel. 226064). Two-star hotel.

Singles £14.25 ($25), doubles £23.50 ($35). Follow Vasil
Kolarov from Central Square and then go right.

Leipzig, bul. Ruski 76 (tel. 232250). Two-star hotel. Similar
prices to the Bulgaria. Ruski is the main street which runs
away from the train station. The Leipzig is four blocks
along the street.

Enquire at Puldin Tour about rooms in the centrally located
Republica and any other hotels which may be cheaper than
the two above. In the past, the doors of the city's cheapest
hotels have been closed to Western guests, but the situation
may now have altered.

PRIVATE ROOMS

Available from Puldin Tour. Normally prices are around £4.50
($8) for a double, but prices rise during the Plovdiv Fair (last
two weeks of Sept.) to around £6.75 ($12).

CAMPING

Trakia. Open May–Oct. Twin-bedded bungalows around
£5.75 ($10). Two and a half miles from the centre on the
road to Sofia (an extension of bul. Moskva), by the Gorski
Kat restaurant. Take bus 4 or 18 to the last stop, from which
the site is a 10-minute walk along the main road.

Maritsa. Open May–Oct. Bungalows available. Three miles
further out than the Trakia site.

Sofia (tel. code 02)

Tourist Offices
The main Balkantourist office and the Tourist Information is
operated at Knjaz Dondukov 37 (tel. 884430). From the train
station take tram 1, 7 or 15 along bul. Georgi Dimitrov to Pl.
Sveta Nedelya, the square on the left overlooked by the Balkan

Sheraton hotel. Dondukov leads off to the left at the opposite end of the square. Another Balkantourist office has recently opened at bul. Vitosa 1 (tel. 43331). Vitosa is a continuation of Georgi Dimitrov. Another branch operates in the International Arrivals building at Sofia airport. An accommodation service is available at each of the three offices. In theory, all the offices above are open daily from 7 a.m.–10 p.m., but in practice they do not adhere to these hours. The small Balkantourist booth in the train station is there primarily as an exchange facility but the staff usually speak English if you have an urgent query.

HOTELS

In recent years the amount of hotel accommodation available to Western visitors has been increased as non-Balkantourist hotels which were previously debarred from admitting Westerners now admit anyone. Nevertheless, there are still no real bargains to be found in the centrally located hotels. Singles in the hotels below normally cost around £10–15 ($17.50–26.50), doubles around £20–26 ($35–46). Book hotel rooms through Balkantourist.

Zdravec, Georgi Dimitrov (tel. 833949). Tram 1, 7 or 15 from the train station along Georgi Dimitrov.

Edelvais, Georgi Dimitrov (tel. 835431).

Sredna Gora, Georgi Dimitrov 60 (tel. 835311).

Bulgaria, bul. Ruski 4 (tel. 871977). Where Knjaz Dondukov goes left from Pl. Sveta Nedelya (see Tourist Offices) bul. Ruski heads right.

Serdica, bul. General V. Zaimov 2 (tel. 443411). Bus 13, 213 or 285 from the train station to the junction of Slivnica and Volgograd. Walk down Volgograd (or take trolleybus 1) until you see bul. Gen. V. Zaimov, the second major road on the left.

Pliska, bul. Trakia 87 (tel. 723721). Out from the city centre but easily reached from the train station. Buses 13 and 213 from the station run along Trakia. You will know you are

on Trakia when you see the stadium and the large Park
Na Svobodata on the right.

Slavia, ul. Sofijski Geroi 2 (tel. 525551). Just outside the
centre, easily reached on public transport. Tram 13 from
the train station runs down bul. Hristo Botev before
turning right along General Totleben into 9 Septemvri.
Sofijski is to the left near the start of 9 Septemvri.

Sebastopol, ul. Rakovski 116 (tel. 875941). One of the cheaper
hotels. Prices at the bottom of the ranges quoted above.
Centrally located. To the right of Knjaz Dondukov (see
Tourist Offices) is Ruski which crosses Rakovski.

Hemus, bul. Georgi Trajkov 31 (tel. 661415). Prices at the top
of the ranges quoted but a very clean, pleasant hotel.
Breakfast included. Tram 9 from the train station runs
along Georgi Trajkov.

Preslav, ul. Traiditsa 3 (tel. 876586).

Gorna Banya, Oural 1 (tel. 570086).

Kopitoto (tel. 571256). Far from the centre in the foothills of
Mount Vitosha. From the train station take tram 6, 9 or
13 along Hristo Botev to Pl. Dimitar Blagoev, change to
tram 5 to the terminus, and then again to bus 62.

Iskâr, ul. Iskâr (tel. 835811). B&B in singles £6.25 ($11). Very
cheap, if not especially pleasant. Communal showers and
bathrooms. Walking down Dondukov (see Tourist Offices)
from Pl. Sveta Nedelya, ul. Iskâr is parallel one block to
the left.

PRIVATE ROOMS

Private rooms arranged through an official agency are the best
accommodation option open to travellers in Sofia. Balkantourist
will arrange centrally located doubles for only £4.50–5.75
($8–10), as will the ORBITA youth/student travel office at bul.
Alexander Stambolijski 45A (tel. 801812), but do not delay in
going to the offices as stocks of rooms are not inexhaustible.
Stambolijski runs left off Vitosa, one block beyond Pl. Sveta
Nedelya (see Tourist Offices). The rooms offered by touts at
the train station are frequently of poor quality and/or far from

the centre, and probably only to be considered if you are desperate.

IYHF HOSTELS

Enquire about IYHF hostels at the Tourist Agency 'PIRIN' bul. Alexander Stambolijski 30 (tel. 881079). Turn left off Vitosa close to Pl. Sveta Nedelya (see Tourist Offices).

HOSTELS

ORBITA Student Hostel, Anton Ivanov 76 (tel. 652952). ISIC card required. Tram 9 from the train station to the junction of Georgi Trajkov and Anton Ivanov (also tram 2 from the city centre). Do not expect to find a place here during the peak season. The ORBITA head office is at Stambolijski 45 (see Private Rooms).

CAMPING

The two most convenient sites are both about 6½ miles out from the centre. Both offer bungalows for hire:

Cherniya Kos. (tel. 571129). Open May–Oct. Twin-bedded bungalows £9.25 ($16). Off the road to Pernik, by the foot of Mount Vitosa. From the train station take tram 6, 9 or 13 along Hristo Bonev to Pl. Dimitar Blagoev, then take tram 5 to its terminus, then bus 58 or 59.

Vrana (tel. 781213). Open May–Oct. Off the E80 to Plovdiv. Bus 213 from the train station, then change to bus 5.

There are another two sites about ten miles out from the city centre:

Bankya. Open May–mid Oct. Off the E80 on the way to Yugoslavia.

Lebed. Open May–Oct. Chalets only. £9.25 ($16) for two-bed chalets. Off the road to Samokov.

Varna (tel. code 052)

Tourist Office
Balkantourist, ul. Musala 3. Open Mon.–Fri. 8.30 a.m.–12.30
p.m. and 1.00–6.00 p.m. From the train station walk uphill on
ul. Avram Gachev to Pl. 9 Septemvri, turn right along ul.
Vaptsarov and then go across the little park on the left.

HOTELS

> Musala, ul. Musala (tel. 223925). The cheapest hotel in the
> town. Singles around £8 ($14), doubles around £11.50
> ($20). Beside the Tourist Office.
> Orbita, bul. Vasil Kolarov (tel. 25162). Doubles around £17
> ($30).
> Odessa, bul. Georgi Dimitrov (tel. 25312). Doubles around
> £17 ($30).

PRIVATE ROOMS

Available from Balkantourist. £5.75 ($10). Generally located in
or around the town centre.

CAMPING

> Galata. Open June–Sept., during which time it is frequently
> filled to capacity. There are bungalows, but you will have
> to be very fortunate to get one of them. Bus 17 from bul.
> Botev to Galata.

SLEEPING ROUGH

Given the vastly increased numbers visiting Varna in recent
years there is simply not enough accommodation to go round
during the summer. Perhaps it is in recognition of this fact that
the local police have been tolerant of people sleeping rough,
despite its being illegal. The park by the railway station has

become a popular place for sleeping out. For safety's sake, you can deposit your pack at the left-luggage (*garderob*) opposite the station (open 5.30 a.m.–10.30 p.m.).

Veliko Târnovo (tel. code 062)

Tourist Office
Balkantourist, ul. Vasil Levski 1 (tel. 28165/21814). Useful information service. Just over the street from the theatre, near the junction with ul. Hristo Botev. If for any reason this office is closed in 1993, head for the Hotel Etar which is nearby, just off Hristo Botev.

Arriving by Train
Every train running between Sofia and Varna stops at Gorna Oryahovitsa, eight miles from Veliko Târnovo. There are eight trains a day linking Gorna Oryahovitsa to Veliko Târnovo, but in late morning and early afternoon you can wait a long time for a connection, so it is probably wise to take a bus to the main stop in Gorna Oryahovitsa and then catch one of the half-hourly buses to Veliko Târnovo. The bus station in Veliko Târnovo is just off ul. Hristo Botev, an easy walk from the Tourist Office. The train station is a 20-minute walk away from the centre. Although the station is linked to the town centre by buses 4, 12 and 13, they run so infrequently you are usually best advised to walk.

HOTELS

Etar (tel. 26861). Doubles around £11.50 ($20). Off Hristo Botev.

Yantra, pl. Velchova Zavera. Doubles around £17 ($30). In the old town, off Dimitar Blagoev.

Orbita, Hristo Botev 15. Cheap but frequently filled to capacity, especially during the summer. Ask at the reception at the top of the stairs.

Motel Sveta Gora (tel. 20472). Cheap rooms. See the Sveta Gora campsite for directions.

PRIVATE ROOMS

Available from Balkantourist. The office has a fair supply of rooms in the old town, but these can go quickly at the height of the tourist season.

IYHF HOSTELS

The 'Pirin' travel agency at ul. Dimitar Blagoev 79 (tel. 20373) will make reservations in local hostels for IYHF members. The most convenient is the excellent hostel operating in the Hotel Edelvais at the same address as 'Pirin'.

CAMPING

Sveta Gora. Open May–Oct. Bungalows available. About 1½ miles west of the town, by the Motel Sveta Gora, in the Sveta Gora Park. Ask for directions from the terminus of buses 4, 12 or 13 (infrequent services) which you can catch at the bus or train stations.

Bolyarski Stan. Open May–Oct. Also with bungalows. 2½ miles west of the town. From the theatre on Vasil Levski (see Tourist Offices) take bus 11 to the junction of the main roads to Sofia and Varna.

CROATIA (Hrvatska)

For information on the various accommodation possibilities in Croatia refer to the final chapter on Yugoslavia for the introduction which was included in the 1992 edition of this book.

Due to the war in the former Yugoslavia the information included in the town sections below has not been updated since the 1992 edition. Many of the accommodation possibilities listed may no longer be available – especially in Dubrovnik, where all the city's hotels were damaged to some extent during the fighting and the brief Yugoslav occupation.

Dubrovnik (tel. code 050)

In the peak season (July to September) what hotels are left will
be expensive. Even C-class hotels such as the Stadion and the
Dubravka charge around £14.50 ($27.50; DM42) per person at
this time. Prices at hotels are lower in May and June, but only
if you are travelling in April or October are there more than
a handful of hotels with affordable rooms.

HOTELS

Peak season:
  Gruž, Gruska obala 25 (tel. 24777). Half board £15.25 ($29;
  DM44.25) per person.

May and June:

Expect to pay around £11 ($21; DM32) p.p. for doubles

  Dubravka (tel. 26284).
  Stadion (tel. 23449).

April and October:

Expect to pay around £9.50 ($18; DM27.50) p.p. for doubles

  Neptun (B class) (tel. 23755).
  Sumratin (B), I.L. Ribara 27 (tel. 24722).
  Jadran (B) (tel. 23322/23276).
  Bellevue (B), P. Čingrije 7 (tel. 25077).
  Adriatic (B) (tel. 24144).
  Lapad (B), Lapadska obala 37 (tel. 23473).
  Dubravka and Stadion. Tel. nos as above.
  Gruž. At this time of year half board here costs around £8
  ($15; DM23.25) p.p.

PRIVATE ROOMS

Private rooms can be booked at various offices in town. In July and August prices per person in doubles are: Category I £6.90–9.50 ($13–18; DM20.00–27.50); Category II £5.70–7.60 ($10.75–14.50; DM16.50–22.00); Category III £4.50–5.70 ($8.50–10.75; DM13.00–16.50). At other times prices are: Category I £5.70–7.60 ($10.75–14.50; DM16.50–22.00); Category II £4.50–5.70 ($8.50–10.75; DM13.00–16.50); Category III £3.45–4.50 ($6.50–8.50; DM10–13).

Atlas, Pile 1 (tel. 27333).

Dalmacijaturist, M. Pracata 7 (tel. 29367/24077/24078).

Dubrovnikturist, Put Republike 5 (tel. 32108/29679).

Generalturist, F. Supila 29 (tel. 23554–5–6).

Kvarner-Express, Gručka obala 69 (tel. 22772).

Putnik, F. Supila 7 (tel. 26650/26651/26398).

Razvitakturist, U Pilama 2 (tel. 26677/26111).

Unisturist, Masarykov put 9 (tel. 25594).

Sunturist, F. Supila 8 (tel. 24965/23843).

Turisticki Informativni centar, P. Miličevića 1 (tel. 26354–5/23746).

IYHF HOSTELS

Oktobarske revolucije 17/Vinka Sagrastena 3 (tel. 23241). For information contact FSH-Zagreb, Trg žrtava fašizma 13, Zagreb (tel. 041–415038). Open 15 Apr.–15 Oct. 1 a.m. curfew. Around £4.75 ($9; DM13.75). A 10-minute walk from the bus station.

HOSTELS

International Youth and Student Center Dvorac Rasica, Ivanska 14 (tel. 23841/23241). Bus 2 or 4 from the bus station of ferry terminal, or walk up Od Batale on to Ivanska. Open July–Oct. Advance reservation essential July and Aug. Contact Ferijalni Savez, Mose Pijade 12/1, PO Box 374, 11000 Beograd, or Yugotours-Narom.

CAMPING

Solitudo (tel. 20770). Open 1 Apr.–31 Oct. Roughly 2 miles west of the bus station. Bus 6 from the Old Town, or from near the bus station. £2.10 ($4; DM6) per tent, £3.10 ($6; DM9) p.p.

There is another site in Kupari, about 5 miles out of Dubrovnik, accessible by bus 10 (tel. 486020). Open 15 Apr.–15 Oct. £1.20 ($2.25; DM3.50) per tent, £1.50 ($3; DM4.50) p.p.

SLEEPING ROUGH

There is virtually no chance of you getting away with sleeping on the beach as the police make regular patrols. You can take a chance and bed down in the terraced park overlooking the sea below Marsala Tita, but if you are caught you can expect a steep fine. If you really are stuck, head for the campsites: even if you have to pay the price for one person and a tent, it is far better than being fined.

Split   (tel. code 058)

HOTELS

Hotels in Split are very expensive: for example, the D-class Central (tel. 41132) charges £13.75 ($26; DM39.75) p.p. for doubles with showers during the peak season of June to September. At other times prices fall to around £11 ($21; DM32) p.p. The Slavija (tel. 47053) has doubles which are slightly more expensive, but these rooms lack private showers.

PRIVATE ROOMS

Let by the Tourist Office: OOUR Turist biro, Titova obala 12 (tel. 42142/42544). In July and Aug. prices p.p. in doubles are:

Category I £7.60–9.15 ($14.50–17.25; DM22.00–26.50),
Category II £6.50 ($12.50; DM19), Category III £5.35 ($10.25;
DM15.50). At other times: Category I £6.00–7.25 ($11.50–13.75;
DM17.50–21.00), Category II £5 ($9.50; DM14.50), Category
III £4.25 ($8; DM12).

HOSTELS

Studencki Dom, Maleśina 66 (tel. 551774). B&B in triples £5
($9.50; DM14.50) p.p. Close to Proleterskin Brigada.
Reached by bus 18 from the open-air market.

CAMPING

Trstenik, Put Trstenika (tel. 521971). Open 1 May–1 Oct. Not
the greatest of sites, but preferable to being fined for
sleeping rough.

SLEEPING ROUGH

Probably your best chance of remaining undetected is to bed
down deep in the woods of Marjan Park. The risk is yours.

Zagreb (tel. code 041)

HOTELS

Cheapest doubles around £10.35 ($19.75; DM30) p.p.

Park (tel. 233422).
Jadran (tel. 414600).
Tomislavov Dom (tel. 449821).
Šumski Dvor (tel. 275892/272195).

PRIVATE ROOMS

Expect to pay p.p. in doubles all year round: Category II £4.30 ($8.25; DM12.50), Category III £3.45 ($6.50; DM10)

Generalturist, Zrinjevac 18 (tel. 425566/427723).
Turističko društvo Novi Zagreb, 33 divizije 15 (tel. 529426).

IYHF HOSTEL

Omladinski Hotel, Petrijnska 77 (tel. 434964). Dorms around £4 ($7.50; DM11.50), doubles and triples around £10 ($19; DM29) p.p. Turn right on leaving the station, walk one block and you will see Petrijnska on your left. Fills quickly.

HOSTELS

Studentski Centar, Savska 25 (tel. 274674). Dorms £5.50 ($10.50; DM16) mid-July–Sept. From Trg Republike tram 14 to the junction of Vodnikova and Savska.

CAMPING

Plitvice, Zagreb/Lučko (tel. 522230/529882). £1.70 ($3.30; DM5) per tent, plus £2.25 ($4.25; DM6.50) p.p. Open 1 May–1 Oct. Six miles out on the road to Maribor. Tram 4, 14 or 17 to Savski Most, then bus 112 or 167 to Lucko, followed by a 2-mile walk.

CZECH REPUBLIC AND SLOVAKIA
(České and Slovensko)

Even before the 'Velvet Revolution' of 1989, finding cheap accommodation in Czechoslovakia was not the easiest of tasks. Due to their popularity with East European groups, hostels and the few hotels within the budget travel price range usually had to be booked months in advance. It was not uncommon to see people turned away from the campsites in Prague and Bratislava during July and August. In 1990, the situation worsened dramatically in the main towns when the state railway (CSD) was included in the Inter-Rail scheme for the first time. This had the expected result of drawing unprecedented numbers of young travellers to Czechoslovakia; especially to Prague, and, to a lesser extent, Bratislava and Brno, the west Bohemian spa towns of Mariánské Lázně and Karlovy Vary, and the main town of south Bohemia, České Budějovice. At the same time, there was a considerable growth in both the number of tour groups and of independent travellers. Again, these visitors were heading primarily for the same destinations as Inter-Railers. (Prague was worst affected, seeing a staggering 1000 per cent increase in the number of tourists visiting the city in 1990.) Although there was a sizeable growth in the availability of private rooms and a number of independent hostels were established, this was not enough to stop demand far outstripping supply in the towns mentioned above. Curiously, in some other towns, finding accommodation actually became easier. Without the usual influx of East European tourists (particularly East Germans) who had visited the country several times and so had begun to spread away from the main attractions, some towns initially found themselves short of visitors.

The present position in the Czech Republic and Slovakia is that there is a general shortage of cheap accommodation possibilities in the peak season of July and August (late May to early September in Prague), though a steady improvement seems likely in the next few years. The situation in the major tourist destinations is nowhere near as dire as in 1990–91, though it can still be very difficult to find a cheap bed in the high season. In the smaller towns, the situation is hard to gauge. Happily, more visitors are finding their way out from the usual tourist destinations to the exquisite small towns. However, a growth in accommodation possibilities tends to follow an influx, so if the town has become reasonably well visited, tourists can toil to find accommodation in peak season. On the other hand, there are many smaller towns (particularly in north Bohemia and central and eastern Slovakia) where you will have no trouble at all finding cheap accommodation at any time of year.

Matters would be much improved if easy advance booking of accommodation was possible. The CKM hostels listed in the IYHF handbook can be reserved in advance, though you will have to try to book two to six months before your date of arrival. Čedok (London) recently sent old clients a letter stating that they now booked all grades of hotels and B&B accommodation throughout the country (previously they booked only the more expensive classes of hotels). When asked to elaborate on this, they declined to reply. None the less, you would be advised to contact them on this matter, as otherwise the outlook is bleak given that there is no established procedure for reserving hotels, private rooms, independent hostels or campsites. You can try writing to hotels or independent hostels directly, or to agencies who book hotels, private rooms or hostels, but neither approach guarantees success. None the less, for the little effort and cost involved, it is worth trying to arrange accommodation in the towns listed above prior to your arrival. If you have no reservations, try to avoid arriving in these towns at weekends, as crowds of Austrians and

Germans on weekend breaks only exacerbate the problem of finding suitable accommodation.

Hotels are divided into five categories; A or deluxe/five-star, A*/four-star, B/three-star, B*/two-star, and C/one-star. In Prague, late cancellations and forfeited reservations might offer your best chance of success. These are reallocated from 5 p.m. by Čedok and Pragotur. Čedok says that hotels rated in the C/one-star category 'truly have no frills', but from the budget traveller's point of view they are a real bargain. In most towns, the lower three grades are now within the reach of the budget traveller. Even in some popular tourist destinations there are doubles available for as little as £10 ($17.50). As might be expected, prices are higher in Prague, where it is difficult to find a double room for under £15 ($26). More likely, you will have to pay £20–30 ($35–52) if you want a double room in the capital. Hotel bills often have to be settled in hard currency (Deutschmarks/US dollars are preferred), with travellers' cheques sometimes refused.

Throughout the Czech Republic and Slovakia, it is possible to stay in the homes of local people. Prices for **private rooms** booked through agencies are no longer officially fixed, with the result that they have risen, and rooms are not the bargain they were a couple of years ago. Now you can expect to pay around £10 ($17.50) for a single in Prague, around £6 ($10.50) elsewhere. However, private rooms are the most widely available budget option. With the obvious potential for new agencies in this field there are now alternatives to dealing with Čedok or Pragotur, the only organizations that let private rooms when the industry was state-controlled. Nevertheless, because of the number of rooms they control, Pragotur are still the best to deal with in the capital, with Čedok predominant in the country as a whole (České Budějovice is one notable exception). Some rooms in the cities can be far from the centre, but as public transport systems in the cities are cheap and efficient, distance should not deter you, providing the room on offer is well served by public transport. Whichever agency you deal with, the accessibility of the room should be one of your prime considerations. Unfortunately, beggars cannot be choosers. In a busy office you can expect to be asked to step out of the queue if you refuse a room, as the agencies know there are plenty of people who will be glad to accept it.

The asking price for private rooms offered by individuals will not be too dissimilar to those you will pay at one of the local agencies (although breakfast is usually included in private offers). However, whereas the standard of rooms booked through an agency is reasonably uniform, the quality of privately offered rooms varies dramatically. You might be lucky and get a perfectly acceptable room with a decent location but, especially in Prague and Bratislava, many are situated in the centre of the vast housing schemes on the outskirts of town and can be difficult to reach by public transport. In peak season, your room for manoeuvre as regards price and location can be severely constrained by the sheer numbers of those looking for accommodation. If you are stuck, you can always stay one night, and then get into town early next morning to look for something better. If you do take up a private offer, take care of your valuables.

Hostelling probably offers the best value for money out of all the accommodation possibilites, but finding a hostel bed is not easy. There are roughly 50 hostels listed in the IYHF handbook. These are operated by CKM (the student travel organization). Prices range from £2.50–5.50 ($4.50–9.50)– usually towards the lower end of the scale. The few permanent hostels are a great bargain. Standards are excellent as these are in fact CKM hotels which offer discounts of 70 to 80 per cent to IYHF members and students. However, not only do they have to be booked several months in advance if you plan to arrive during the peak season, but a quick comparison of the hostel list with a guidebook will tell you that apart from Prague and Bratislava, the spa towns of Mariánské Lázně and Karlovy Vary, and Banská Bystrica, the places of major interest lack permanent hostels. Many of the temporary hostels listed in the IYHF handbook (including the four hostels in Brno) are converted student dormitories, which open only during July and August. If you are travelling at that time of year it is always worth contacting the local CKM office, as they control the letting of rooms in student dormitories in many towns not mentioned in the IYHF handbook. Rooms in student dorms generally cost around £2.50–3.50 ($4.50–6).

In recent years, there has been a growth in the number of independent hostels, particularly in Prague and Bratislava. Again, the vast majority of these are in converted student dormitories, operating only in July and August. The established tourist agencies (Čedok, CKM, Pragotur) may not be a fruitful source of information on independent hostels, either because they are genuinely unaware of new hostels, or because they are intent on selling you accommodation they control. Ask other travellers about hostelling possibilities, and keep your eyes open for hostels advertised at bus and train stations.

Most small towns have very basic dormitory hostels known as *turistická ubytovna*, where a bunk bed costs around £1 ($1.75). Facilities seldom extend to anything more than toilets and cold showers. These hostels are meant primarily for workers living away from home, or for groups of workers on holiday, but it is most unlikely you will be turned away if there is room at the hostel. Unfortunately, many such hostels open only when they have a group booking. Nevertheless, it is worth enquiring about *turistická ubytovna* at the local Čedok or CKM offices, as they sometimes offer the only hostel accommodation available in town.

If you are travelling between May and September/mid-October, **camping** is a great way to see the country very cheaply (few sites remain open outside these months). 'Camping Czechoslovakia' (from Čedok) lists around 250 sites, graded A, AB and B, with details of opening times and facilities available, and has a map showing their locations. Prices for a solo traveller are about £1.50–2.50 ($2.50–4.50) per night, but, as Čedok warns, 'don't expect luxury'. Sites are usually clean, but at the B-class sites outside showers are the norm. Very occasionally in peak season, you might have a little trouble finding a space, but even then only at the sites in Prague and Bratislava (and perhaps at weekends in České Budějovice, Tbor, Mariánské Lázně and Karlovy Vary). At the vast majority of the sites listed in 'Camping Czechoslovakia' it is possible to rent two-or four-bed chalets ('*chata*'). The standard of chalets varies from site to site: while some are quite cramped, others are spacious and very comfortable. At some sites you may be required to pay for all the beds in the chalet, even if they are not all occupied. Expect to pay between £2–4 ($3.50–7) per person in a fully occupied chalet.

Most, but not all, of the main places of interest have a convenient campsite listed in 'Camping Czechoslovakia'. However, there are a host of other primitive sites, known in Czech as *tbořiště* or in Slovak as *tborisko*. Facilities at these sites are spartan: you may have to wash in the river nearby, and may prefer to use the woods to the site's toilets. On the plus side, these sites are exceptionally cheap at around £1 ($1.75) per night for a solo traveller. Again, few of these sites remain open outside the months of May to September. In the past, these were aimed at East European holidaymakers, and were not advertised to Westerners. Indeed, the official agencies were loath even to admit their existence. Nowadays, local Čedok offices are more likely to be forthcoming about tbořiště/tborisko in the vicinity, though it is always worth asking locals if Čedok officials say there are none. Alternatively, the book *Ubytovani CSR* lists all the hotels, hostels and campsites in the Czech Republic (in Czech, but easy to follow), while the 1:100,000 tourist map of the country shows the location of all campsites in both the Czech and Slovak Republics.

If you are stuck for a bed, but have an Inter-Rail, Eurail or BIJ ticket, you can always catch a night train (see overnight-train suggestions below). One of the best ways to arrive in Brno reasonably early in the morning is to take an overnight train from Prague to Bratislava, or vice versa, and then catch the early train to Brno. Travelling overnight from Bratislava to Prague can allow you to catch early morning connections to Tabor, Olomouc, Pilsen, Cheb and the spa towns. Even leaving Prague to head out into east and central Slovakia can show you interesting towns such as Bardejor, Presov, Banska Bystrica and Banska Stiavnica.

Tourist Information

At the time of writing, few cities had tourist offices organized along Western lines. In most towns, the information that is available is distributed by accommodation agencies such as Čedok or CKM. In very few towns can you pick up a small plan showing the main sites of interest (even the information distributed in Prague is poor). If you are heading for the Czech Republic or Slovakia, it is best to buy a good guidebook before setting off on holiday. When you arrive, bookshops in the main cities should have English versions of *Czechoslovakia*, published by *Ctibor Rybár*, a useful guide to the country (you can enquire as to whether Čedok in London are still selling copies of this book in 1993). One useful item which you can pick up at some Čedok offices is a list of altered street names. As many of the maps on sale in the country do not yet show current street names, finding your way around can be a confusing matter.

ADDRESSES

Čedok Tours & Holidays	17–18 Old Bond Street, London W1X 4RB (tel. 071 629 6058).
Youth hostels	CKM Club of Young Travellers, Žitná 12, 121 05 Praha 2.
	Travel Section and Secretariat: CKM, Malostranské nbřež 1, 11 00 Praha 1–Mal Strana (tel. 02 538858).

Overnight-train suggestions (check times locally, or with the Thomas Cook timetable):

Praha Hlav. Nad.	23.17	Bratislava	05.35
Praha Hlav. Nad.	00.15	Bratislava	05.16 (continues to Budapest)
Praha Holešovice	22.38	Bratislava	04.55

Early morning connection to Brno:

Bratislava	05.50	Brno	07.20
Bratislava	22.50	Praha Holešovice	05.08
Bratislava	23.50	Praha Hlav. Nad.	05.45
Bratislava	00.35	Praha Hlav. Nad.	06.03

Early morning connections from Prague:

Praha Holešovice	05.57	Brno	09.19		
Praha Hlav. Nad.	06.30	Karlovy Vary	10.07		
Praha Hlav. Nad.	07.49	Tabor	09.45	České Budějovice	11.01
Praha Hlav. Nad.	07.50	Plzen	09.28	Domazlice	10.34
Praha Hlav. Nad.	08.47	Plzen	10.37	Mariánské Lázně	11.58 Cheb 12.32

Praha Holešovice	20.27	Kosice	05.46		
Praha Hlav. Nad.	00.00	Kosice	09.53		
Kosice	20.10	Praha Holešovice	05.32		
Kosice	20.38	Praha Hlav. Nad.	06.31		
Kosice	00.20	Olomouc	06.52	Praha Hlav. Nad.	10.05
Kosice	16.55	Karlovy Vary	07.50	Cheb	09.02
Bratislava	23.00	Kosice	05.25		
Bratislava	00.20	Kosice	07.07		
Kosice	23.10	Bratislava	05.44		
Kosice	23.55	Bratislava	06.27		

Bratislava (tel. code 07)

Tourist Office
BIPS, Laurinská (formerly Leningradská) (tel. 333715/
334325/334370). Open June–Sept., Mon.–Fri. 8 a.m.–6 p.m.,
Sat. 8 a.m.–1 p.m.; Oct.–May, Mon.–Fri. 8 a.m.–4.30 p.m.
General information, plus advice on the hostel situation. Just
off Hviezdoslavovo náměstí.

Accommodation Agencies
Čedok, Jesenkého 1–7 (tel. 499613/52645/52624). Open
Mon.–Fri. 9 a.m.–6 p.m., Sat. 9 a.m.–midday. Tram 13
from the main train station. Also at Štúrova 13 (tel.
52081/52002). Same hours as the office on Jesenkého. A
short walk from Hviezdoslavovo náměstí. Take the street
heading down the side of the Slovak National Theatre to
reach Stúrova.

CKM, Hviezdoslavovo náměstí 16 (tel. 331607). Open Mon.
and Wed. 9 a.m.–6 p.m., Tues., Thurs. and Fri. 9 a.m.–4
p.m., Sat. 9.30 a.m.–12.30 p.m.

Uniatour, Leškova 5 (tel. 43967). First left off Stefnikova, the
main road leading from Bratislava hlavná stanica.

Arriving in Bratislava
Most trains to the Slovak capital arrive at Bratislava hlavná
stanica, about 15 minutes' walk from the Old Town, or a short
trip on trams 1 or 13. Head away from the station past the train
terminal and on to Pražka. Turn left down Pražka and keep
going straight ahead, on down Obrancov Mieru until you arrive
at the Trinity Church. Follow the road round to the left a short
distance, then turn right heading for the old St Michael's Gate
(Michalská brána). Going through the gate follow Michalsk
downhill and continue straight ahead to reach Hviezdoslavovo
náměstí.

Some trains from Slovakia arrive at the Bratislava Nové
Mesto station. Trams 6 and 14 link Nové Mesto to the city
centre. Most buses arrive at the bus station on Bajkalská. Going

right from the bus station for about 100m you reach Vajnorská from which you can take any tram heading down into the city.

HOTELS

For information on hotels and reservations contact Čedok.

Ustav vzdelávania ve stavebnictve, Brodošova 33 (tel. 375212). Doubles with a bath £7 ($12.50), triples £10 ($17.50). From the main train station take tram 44 to the third stop on Bárodošova. Walk back a short distance, then head uphill to the three-storey building with the name of the hotel on top.

Krym (B/two-star), Safarikovo náměstí 7 (tel. 554713). Off Štúrová, close to the Danube.

Palace, Poštová 1 (tel. 333656). Tram 14 from the train station to the fifth stop.

Motel Zlaté Piesky, ul. Vajorská (tel. 65170/66028). On the fringes of the city, by the campsites. See the Camping section for directions.

CKM Juniorhotel Sputnik, ul. Drieňová 14 (tel. 234340). Singles £12 ($21), doubles £20 ($35). From the main train station take tram 8 to the eighth or ninth stop. The hotel is on the opposite side of the small lake visible to your left.

PRIVATE ROOMS

Contact Čedok on Štúrova or Slovakotourist.

HOSTELS

During the summer, Bratislava is well supplied with hostel beds, mostly in converted student dormitories. CKM, BIPS and Uniatour are the organizations to approach for information regarding hostels. The bus station and the main train station are favourite places for hostel operators to pin up advertisements, usually with rates and directions to the hostel.

CKM Juniorhotel Sputnik, ul. Drieňová 14 (tel. 234340/238065). Singles and doubles £4.20 ($7.50) per person for IYHF members and ISIC card holders. Frequently full, so try to reserve ahead. See the entry in the Hotels section above for directions.

CKM Youth Hostel Ružinovsk 1 (tel. 220441 ext. 56) £3.50 ($6) per person for IYHF members in singles, doubles or triples. For non-members singles cost £9 ($16), doubles £13 ($23), and triples £17 ($30). Well advertised at the bus and train stations. From the bus station or hlavn stanica take trolleybus 210 to Račianske myto, followed by bus 54 to the sixth stop.

Studentský domov J. Hronca, Bernolákova 3 (tel. 42612). Open July–Aug. Student dorm converted into a temporary IYHF hostel controlled by CKM. £3.50 ($6) for IYHF members. See the Bernolak YH below for directions

Bernolak Youth Hostel (BIPS), Bernolákova 1 (tel. 58019). Open July–Aug. Doubles £6.25 ($11), triples £8 ($14). Reduced prices for ISIC card holders: £5.75 ($10) and £6.50 ($11.50) respectively. Adverts in the bus and train stations. From hlavná stanica or the bus station take trolleybus 210 to Račianske myto, then follow the posters to the hostel. A 15-minute walk from the centre.

Mladost (BIPS), Asmolovova 53 (tel. 721203). Open July–Aug. £3.75 ($6.50) falling to £2.25 ($4) if you stay more than three nights. From the bus station or main train station take trolleybus 210 to Račianske myto, then bus 39 to the terminus. From the bus stop red footprints signed 'elam' show the way to the hostel.

Mlada Garda, Račianska cesta 103. Operated by Uniatour. Open July–Aug. Around £2 ($3.50) per person. Small reduction for ISIC card holders.

YMCA Interpoint Bratislava, Karpatská 2 (tel. 493267). Open 15 July–15 Aug. £3.50 ($6). From hlavná stanica walk down past the tram terminus on to Malinovského. Turn left and follow Malinovského until you see Karpatská on the left.

CAMPING

Two sites at Zlaté piesky, both with bungalows. Tram 2 from town centre, tram 4 from train station or tram 12 to the Zupka crossroads, then bus 32 to the third stop:

Senecká cesta 10 (tel. 66028/214000). Grade AB site. Open all year round.

Senecká cesta 12 (tel. 65170). Grade A site, open 15 May–15 Sept.

Brno (tel. code 05)

Tourist Information

Čedok, across the street from the main train station, sell maps of the city for around £0.30 ($0.50).

Accommodation Agencies

CKM, Česká 11 (tel. 23641). Open Mon.–Fri. 10 a.m.–noon and 2–5 p.m., Sat. 10 a.m.–noon. A 15-minute walk from the main train station. Cross the road and head down Masarykova into náměstí Svobody. Keep going straight on along the left-hand side of the square into Ceská.

Čedok, Divadeln 3 (tel. 23179). Open Mon.–Fri. 9 a.m.–6 p.m., Sat. 9 a.m.–noon. A 10-minute walk from the main train station. Head right until you come to nám. Cs. Armády. Go along the left-hand side of the square and then down the road leading out of the square. Alternatively, head straight down Masarykova from the station and then turn right and follow Orli to its end.

Arriving in Brno

Most trains arrive at Brno Hlavní nádraží (main train station) on the fringe of the Old Town. Some night trains only stop at Brno Královo Pole on the outskirts of the city. Unless you arrive here on a Sunday morning, you rarely have to wait more than 20 minutes for a connecting train to Hlavní nádraží. The main bus station is located a few blocks behind the main train station.

HOTELS

Information on hotels and reservations available from Čedok on Divadelní, but they invariably try to press you into staying at one of the more expensive hotels.

Společenský dům, Horova 30 (tel. 744185). Cheapest hotel in Brno. Singles around £8 ($14), doubles around £12 ($21). From the main train station take tram 4, 5 or 13 to Husova, then tram 10.

Europa, Jánská 1 (tel. 26611/26621). Singles £8.50 ($15), doubles around £15.50 ($27). Breakfast included. A short walk from the main train station. Head straight down Masarykova and the hotel is at the junction with Jánská, the fourth street on the right.

Astoria, Novabranska 3 (tel. 27526). Singles £12 ($21), doubles £16.50 ($29). Close to the Čedok office on Divadelní. A 10-minute walk from the main train station. Head straight down Masarykova from the station, turn right along Orli, then left after passing the Menin Gate. Tram 2, 11 or 18 from the station to Malinovskeho nám.

If the hotels above are full, the next three hotels as you move up the price scale are the U Jakuba at Jakubské náměstí 6 (tel. 22991), the Avion at Česká 20 (tel. 27606), and the Slovan at Lidická 23 (tel. 745505); useful names to mention if Čedok are trying to be unreasonable.

PRIVATE ROOMS

Contact Čedok on Divadelní. Singles £6.50 ($11.50), doubles £11–13 ($19–23). A three-day minimum stay may still be in force in 1993.

IYHF HOSTELS

Operated by CKM in converted student dorms. All four hostels are open from 1 July–31 Aug. If you arrive in Brno Mon.–Fri. 9 a.m.–5 p.m., you should go to the CKM office before going to the hostels, even if you have a reservation.

Expect to pay around £2.50 ($4.50).

Kolej J E Purkyně, Husova 8.
Brno Studentská Kolej SCSP Brno, Královo Pole, Purkyňova 93.
Kolej VUT, Leninova 8.
Kolej VŠZ, J.A. Komenského, Kohoutova 55.

CAMPING

Both sites are about 10 miles out of town.

Bobrava, Modrice u Brna (tel. 320110). Grade B site. Open 15 Apr.–15 Oct. Tram 2, 14 or 17 to the Modrice terminus, then a 10-minute walk, or a local train to Popovice, 500m from the site.

Obora, Brno-prehrada (tel. 56575). Grade B site. Open 1 Apr.–31 Oct. More difficult to reach by public transport. A CSAD bus runs about every hour. In summer, you can reach the site by taking tram 3, 10, 14, 18, 20 or 21, followed by a boat trip.

České Budějovice (tel. code 038)

Tourist Information
Informačni. In a red trailer on Švermovo náměstí. Open 9–11 a.m. and 2–6 p.m., weekends 9 a.m.–noon and 1–6 p.m. Good source of information on the city in English and German. From Žižkovo náměstí take 5 května and head straight on across the water and Na Sadech into Švermovo nám. From the

bus and train stations head right, turn left up maršále Malinovského just past the train station, then left along Na sadech to Švermovo nám. A more permanent office may be found by 1993. If so the Srba International Travel Agency or CKM should be able to tell you the new location.

Accommodation Agencies

Srba International Travel Agency, 5 května 1 (tel. 25061). Open Mon.–Fri. 2–8 p.m., weekends 9 a.m.–8 p.m. Map of the city £0.35 ($0.60). 5 května runs out of Žižkovo náměstí.

CKM, Osvobození 14 (tel. 36138) Osvobození runs off Žižkovo náměstí.

Čedok, Žižkovo náměstí (tel. 38056). An office much criticized in the past when they have changed money and booked hotels, but made it quite plain they did not want to be bothered by other enquiries.

Basic Directions

The bus and train stations are virtually side by side on Nádraží, a ten-minute walk from the town centre. Just right of the train station exit turn left on to maršále Malinovského. On the left-hand side as you walk up this street is the PRIOR department store with a supermarket. Continuing on down maršále Malinovského you reach the junction with Na sadech, across which you can follow Kanovnická into Žižkovo náměstí, the main square of the town. Turning left along the side of the square brings you to the start of Osvobození. If you continue straight on along the side of the square from Kanovnická, you pass Čedok before arriving at the start of 5 kveětna.

Finding Accommodation

Finding suitable accommodation is not the problem it was a couple of years ago thanks to the increase in the number of rooms available in private homes and small pensions. None the less, it can still be tricky to find a cheap place to stay during July and August, and especially so at weekends, as the town is highly popular with Germans and Austrians taking weekend breaks, as well as Czechs.

HOTELS

Enquiries about hotel accommodation should be made at the Čedok office on Žižkovo náměstí.

   Malše, Nádražní 31 (tel. 27631). Singles around £8.60 ($15), doubles arond £11 ($19). Across the street from the train station.

   Zvon, Žižkovo náměstí 28 (tel. 35361). Singles around £10.50 ($18.50), doubles around £16.50 ($29). Payment in hard currency only.

PENSIONS

In the past few years, the number of pensions has increased in and around the city. If you arrive by road you will see these advertised by the roadside as you enter town. Many of these 'pensions' are really just private rooms, advertised by enterprising owners. Your likeliest source of information on pensions is the Srba International Travel Agency (see above).

PRIVATE ROOMS

Book through the Srba International Travel Agency. Doubles range in price from £8–14 ($14–25). As well as booking rooms locally, the office books similarly priced rooms throughout south Bohemia, a particularly useful service if you are heading for some of the smaller towns in the region.

HOSTELS

During July and August, CKM lets beds in vacant dormitories. Most of the beds are booked well in advance by visiting groups, so you really need to get to the CKM office early to see if there are any spare beds available.

CAMPING

There are two sites right beside each other on the fringes of the town, just off the road to Český Krumlov. Bus 6 from Na sadech stops close to the sites. Otherwise it is a 25-minute walk from the bus and train stations to the campsites. Head left along Nádražní from the train station on to Kasárenská. Turn right, then left along Dvořkova on to Mánesova. Turn right and follow Mánesova across the River Malše and towards the River Vltava. When the road forks near the Vltava head down to the left, and then along the main road. The campsites are signposted on the right.

Dlouhá Louka, Stromovka 8 (tel. 38308). Grade A site. Open May–Sept. Bungalows available.

Stromovka, Litvínovská (tel. 28807). Grade B site. Open Apr.–Oct. Bungalows available.

Karlovy Vary (tel. code 017)

Accommodation Agencies

Čedok operate at various locations in the town. Closest to the bus and train stations is the office at the junction of Dimitrova and Moskevská. In the town centre, there are offices at Karla IV 1 (tel. 26110), and in the Hotel Atlantic at Tržiště 23 (tel. 26705/24378).

'W', nám. Republiky (tel. 27768). Near the bus station (autobusová nádraží).

HOTELS

Čedok recommend reserving hotels three–four months in advance. If you enquire on arrival you can expect to be told that all the hotels are full. Be persistent, and try to get them to give you the names and telephone numbers of hotels that might have space.

Turist, Dimitrovova 18 (tel. 26837). Doubles around £9 ($16). Near the bus station.

Nrodní dům, Masarykova 24 (tel. 23386). Singles £8.75 ($15.50), doubles £12.25 ($21.50). Close to the bus station.

Adria, Koněvova 1 (tel. 23765). Singles £10.50 ($18.50), doubles £15.50 ($27). Payment must be made in hard currency. Along the street from the bus station.

CKM Juniorhotel Alice, ul. Pětiletky 3 (tel. 24848). Singles around £10.50 ($18.50). Set in the woods about 3 miles out of town. A beautiful walk. From the Karlovy Vary horní nídraží train station take bus 11 to the market place, then bus 7. Take bus 7 direct from the bus station.

Jizena, Dimitrovova 7 (tel. 25020). £14.75 ($26) per person. Close to the bus station.

PRIVATE ROOMS

Čedok, Karla IV: doubles around £9 ($16). Office open mid-May–Sept. Mon.–Fri. 9 a.m.–5 p.m., Sat. 9 a.m.–noon; Oct.–mid-May 9 a.m.–4 p.m.

'W': £7–10.50 ($12–19) per person. Office open Mon.–Sat. 10 a.m.–6 p.m.

IYHF HOSTEL

CKM Juniorhotel Alice, ul. Pětiletky 3 (tel. 24848). Around £2.50 ($4.50) per person for IYHF members. See the entry in the Hotels section above for directions.

CAMPING

Březová, Slovenská č. 9 (tel. 25101). Grade A site. Open 1 May–30 Sept. Bungalows available. Close to CKM Juniorhotel Alice. See the entry in the Hotels section above for directions.

Košice (tel. code 095)

Tourist Information
At the time of writing, there were no small maps available locally to help you see around the city. For answers to general enquiries approach Čedok or CKM, where the staff do their best to help. The situation is exactly the same in nearby Prešov and Bardejov, the other two main towns of interest in east Slovakia. Again, the local Čedok offices will do their best to help.

Accommodation Agencies
Čedok (tel. 53121) is located by the Hotel Slovan at Rooseweltova 1, at the foot of námestie Slobody. Open Mon.–Fri. 9 a.m.–5 p.m., Sat. 9 a.m.–noon.

CKM, námestie Slobody 82 (tel. 27858). Open Mon.–Fri. 9 a.m.–4.30 p.m., Sat. 9 a.m.–noon. The office is set back off the square, down an alleyway, but the CKM sign is easily spotted.

Basic Directions
The bus and train stations are located close to each other, about five minutes' walk from námestie Slobody (the main square). Taking the road leading away from the train station you can turn right along the side of the park to reach the Jakabov palác. From there, head straight down Generala Petrova which brings you onto námestie Slobody by the town tower and St Elisabeth's Cathedral. The CKM office is across the square and along to the right. The Hotel Slovan is down to the right, on the same side. Heading for Čedok from the stations, you can save yourself a few minutes' walk by following the road round to the left, then turning right along Rooseweltowa.

Finding Accommodation
Košice is a major international rail crossroads and a town where many travellers have to (or choose to) break their journey. Many of the visitors you see here only stay in town for a few

hours before continuing their journey. In the past, this has ensured that the supply of accommodation has managed to meet demand. Now more people are arriving in Košice and using the main town of east Slovakia as a base from which to visit nearby towns, with the result that finding cheap accommodation is becoming more difficult. This is especially true of late June, just before CKM open up student dormitories as temporary hostels. Hopefully, a supply of private rooms will be available by 1993 to ease the increasing pressure on local hotels.

HOTELS

Rooms in local hotels can be booked through Čedok.

Tatra, Smeralova 1. C-category hotel, the cheapest in Košice. Turn off nám. Slobody by East Slovak Gallery (Východoslovenská galéria).

Europa, Protfašìstických Bojovnkov 1 (tel. 23897). Expect to pay around £12 ($21) for doubles. Close to the Hotel Imperial.

Club, Nerudova (tel. 20214). Similar in price to the Europa.

Centrum. Doubles around £12 ($21). Close to the Čedok office.

Imperial, generala Petrova 16 (tel. 22146). Singles £9 ($16), singles with bath £13 ($23), doubles with bath £19 ($33).

Hutnìk, Tyršovo nábrežie 6 (tel. 37780). Similar rates to the Imperial.

PRIVATE ROOMS

Enquire at Čedok or CKM as to whether they, or any other organization, are booking private rooms in the city.

HOSTELS

CKM control the letting of beds in student dormitories converted into temporary hostels during July and August.

CAMPING

Auto Camping Salas Barca, Alejová (tel. 58309). Open Apr.–Sept. Bungalows available. Three miles from the city, just off the road to Rožňava. From the Slovan hotel take tram 1 or 4, or bus 22 or 52 as far as the flyover. From there the campsite is about 5 minutes' walk along the road to Rožňava.

Olomouc (tel. code 068)

Tourist Information
Despite the obvious tourist potential of the city and the increasing numbers of visitors, there were no small maps showing the city's points of interest available at the time of writing. If copies are still available from bookshops the large *plán města* provides some historical information on the city in Czech, Russian, English, French and German, as well as having a small insert showing the main places of interest. The description of these is in Czech only, but is relatively easy to follow.

Accommodation Agencies
Čedok náměstí Mru 2 (tel. 28831). Helpful staff. German speakers are always available; only rarely is an English speaker not available.
CKM, Denisova 4 (tel. 29009). German- and English-speaking staff.

Basic Directions
The train station (Olomouc hlavní nádraží) is about 1 mile from the centre; the main bus station (autobusové nádraží) slightly further out in the same part of town. From the bus station walk out on to Ostravská and catch tram 4 or 5 heading left along the street. These trams pass the train station, from which you can also take trams 1, 2 and 3 to reach the city centre. Unusually

for Czechoslovakia, you pay the tram driver, so have some small coins ready.

From the train station, the trams run straight down Osvobození. The road then bends left, shortly after which you reach náměstí Republiky with the imposing Jesuit Church. Beyond nám. Republiky you are on Denisova, with the CKM office at the corner of the junction with Ztracená. This street and the next three streets on the left, (Ostružnická, Opletalova and 28 října), all lead up into náměstí Míru. The PRIOR department store on 28 října has a supermarket if you want to buy some groceries.

HOTELS

Enquire about hotel accommodation at Čedok. Unlike some Čedok offices if they tell you the cheap hotels are full they are unlikely to be lying to you in the hope you will accept something more expensive.

Hotelový dům, Volgogradská (tel. 413121). Cheapest hotel in the city, and consequently often full in the summer. Bus 16 runs along the street from its terminus on Kosmonautů near the train station.

Morava, Riegrova 16 (tel. 29671). Prices are a little higher than at the Hotelový dům. Excellent central location. The street runs off náměstí Míru.

PRIVATE ROOMS

Enquire at Čedok and CKM about the availability of private rooms.

HOSTELS

CKM control the letting of beds in student residences converted into temporary hostels in July and August.

CAMPING

Neither of the sites closest to Olomouc are easy to reach unless you have your own transport. Ask Čedok or CKM about precise directions by public transport before setting off to the sites. You can also try asking them about any *tábořiště* which may be more conveniently located.

Dolní Žleb, Šternberk (tel. 2300). Grade A site, open mid-June–mid-Sept. The site is located about 2 miles from the bus and train stations Šternberk, a small town about 10 miles to the north of Olomouc.

Přehrada, Mostkovice (tel. 0508-7279). Grade A site, open mid-May–mid-Sept. The town of Prostějov (12 miles from Olomouc) is on the main road and the railway line between Brno and Olomouc. Přehrada is a good campsite, with a pleasant lakeside setting, but it is 3 3/4 miles away from Prostějov.

Pilsen (Plzeň) (tel. code 019)

Accommodation Agencies

Čedok. On the corner of Sedláčkova and Presková. The latter runs out of one corner of Nám Republiky, the centre of town. Opening hours: Mon.–Fri. 9 a.m.–noon & 1–6 p.m., Sat. 9 a.m.–noon.

CKM, Dominikanská. Just off Nám Republiky.

HOTELS

Enquire at the Čedok office above.

Plzeň, Žižkova 66 (tel. 272656). Doubles £16 ($28). Tram 1 or 4 from the town centre.

PRIVATE ROOMS

Enquire at Čedok or CKM about the availability of private rooms.

HOSTELS

During July and August CKM let beds in converted student dormitories.

CAMPING

Bílá Hora (tel. 35611/62850). Grade A. Open 20 Apr.–15 Sept. Also lets bungalows. In the suburb of Bílá Hora. Bus 20.

Ostende (tel. 520194). In Plzeň-Bolevec. Grade A, open 1 May–15 Sept. Bungalows available.

Prague (Praha) (tel. code 02)

Tourist Information

Pražská Informační služba (PIS), Na Přikopě 20 (tel. 544444). Open June–Sept., Mon.–Fri. 8 a.m.–8.30 p.m., weekends 9 a.m.–3 p.m.; Oct.–May, Mon.–Fri. 8 a.m.–7 p.m., Sat. 8 a.m.–noon. The best source of general information on the city. No accommodation service. Metro: Nměstí Republiky. Na Přikopě runs out of nám. Republiky.

Accommodation Agencies

Pragotur, U Obecnho domu 2 (tel. 2317200/2317281/2317234). Open Mon.–Sat. 9 a.m.– 8 p.m., Sun. 9 a.m.–3 p.m. Metro: Náměstí Republiky. U Obecního domu runs off nám. Republiky.

Čedok, Panská 5 (tel. 225656/227004). Open Apr.–Nov., Mon.–Fri. 9 a.m.–10 p.m., Sat. 8.30 a.m.–6 p.m., Sun. 8.30 a.m.–4.30 p.m.; Dec.–Mar., Mon.–Fri. 9 a.m.–8 p.m., weekends 8.30 a.m.– 2 p.m. Metro: Náměstí Republiky.

Follow Na Přikopě from nám. Republiky, then head left down Panská.

CKM, Žitná 12 (tel. 2296526). Metro: I.P. Pavlova. Walk down Ječná then turn right along either V tůnich or Štěpanská into Žitna.

Top Tour, Rybná 3 (tel. 2296526/2321077/2320860). Open Mon.–Fri. 9 a.m.–8 p.m., weekends 11 a.m.– 7 p.m. Metro: Nám. Republiky. From nám. Republiky walk a short distance down Celetná, turn right on to Králodvorská, then left.

AVE Ltd, Wilsonova 80 (tel. 2362560). AVE have two offices on the upper floor of Praha hlavní nádraží. They also operate an office at Ruzyne Airport (tel. 2362541).

KONVEX, Kamziková 4 (tel. 2366760). Open daily 10 a.m.–7 p.m. Metro: Staroměstská. The metro station is on Kaprova. Ask a local to point you in the direction of Staroměstské náměstí. Keep going more or less straight ahead until you reach the square. The KONVEX office is in a small street off Staroměstské nám., on the same side of the town hall as the astronomical clock.

Hello Ltd, nám. Gorkého-Senovážná 3 (tel. 224283). Open daily 9 a.m.–10 p.m. Metro: Náměstí Republiky. From nám. Republiky walk down Hybernská, then turn right along Dlážděbá into the square.

Finding Accommodation

The growth in the number of private rooms and apartments available has gone some way to alleviating the terrible accommodation shortage in Prague. Nevertheless, there are still only around ten thousand beds in registered accommodation for ten million visitors, the vast majority of whom arrive between June and early September. If you are travelling at that time of year aim to get to Prague early in the morning and start looking for a bed right away. The accommodation situation worsens dramatically at weekends, as the city is exceptionally popular with Germans and Austrians taking a short break, so look to arrive between Monday and Thursday, if at all possible.

Arriving in Prague

Of the city's five main train stations your most likely point of arrival is Praha hlavní nádraží, a short walk from the Václavské náměstí, and within easy walking distance of the old town. Some international trains and overnight internal services drop you at Praha-Holešovice, in the northern suburb of Holešovice. Trains terminating at Praha-Smichov, Masarykovo nádraží (the old Praha-Stred), and Praha-Vysočany are usually local services, or slow trains from the provinces. Connections between Praha hlavní, Praha-Smichov and Praha-Holešovice are easy as all are served by the metro (line C: Hlavní nádraží; line B: Smichovské nádraží; line C: Nádraží Holešovice, respectively). The Masarykovo nádraží is a short walk along Wilsonova from Praha hlavní nádraží and, in the opposite direction, the Florenc metro station (lines B and C). From Praha-Vysočany tram 3 crosses Wilsonova a short distance from the Florenc metro stop. The main bus station, Praha-Florenc, is beside the Florenc metro station. The Masarykovo nádraží and Prah hlvaní nádraží are both within easy walking distance of Praha-Florenc, to the left along Wilsonova. Arriving at Ruzyně airport, your cheapest option is to take bus 119 (three an hour) from opposite the main exit to its terminus at the Dejvická metro station (line A). The CSA bus is dearer, but takes you direct to the CSA office on Revolučni, a short walk from náměstí Republiky.

HOTELS

Čedok deal in B/two-star hotels, but often claim not to in an attempt to persuade you to take a room in a more expensive hotel. Pragotur specialize in C/one-star hotels, and are unlikely to be dishonest about the availability of hotel rooms. Both agencies reallocate late cancellations and forfeited reservations from 5 p.m. onwards.

Hotel prices have fluctuated in the past few years. As a rough guide expect to pay from £11–16 ($19–28) for the cheapest doubles in a C/one-star hotel, and from £15–30 ($26–53) for their equivalent in a B/two-star hotel. Most hotel bills have to be settled in hard currency.

B/two-star hotels

Adria, Václavské nám. 26 (tel. 2352885). Metro: Museum or Můstek. A short walk left along Wilsonova from Praha hlavní nádraží.

Hvězda, Na Rovni 34 (tel. 368037/368965). Tram 18 from the Malostranská metro station to the Heyrovského náměstí terminus, or tram 1 or 18 from the Hradčanská metro station. From the tram terminus follow Polni until it crosses Na Rovni.

Hybernia, Hybernská 24 (tel. 220431). Singles £13.50 ($23.50), doubles £19 ($33). Metro Náměstí Republiky. Walk down Hybernská from nám. Republiky.

Koruna, Opatovická 15 (tel. 293933). Metro: Národni tířda. From Spálená turn down Ostrovní (almost opposite Purkyňova), then head left at Opatovická.

Merkur, Těšnov 9 (tel. 2316951). Metro: Florenc. Těšnov is a continuation of Na Florenci heading down towards the River Vltava, across Wilsonova from the bus station.

Meteor, Hybernská 6 (tel. 2358517). See the Hybernia, above.

Moráň, Na Moráni 15 (tel. 294251). Tram 9 from Hlavní nádraží runs along the street. A short walk from the Karlovo náměstí metro station.

Opera, Těšnov 13 (tel. 2315609/2315735). Singles £12 ($21), doubles £20 ($35). Price includes breakfast. See the Merkur above for directions.

Axa, Na poříčí 40 (tel. 2324467). Metro: Náměstí Republiky. Na poříčí runs out of the square.

Botel Albatross, nábřeží L. Svobody (tel. 2316996). A floating hotel moored on the Vltava by the Švermuv bridge. From the Náměstí Republiky metro station follow Revolučni down to the river.

Kriváň, Nám I.P. Pavlova 5 (tel. 293341) Metro: I.P. Pavlova.

Praga, Plzeňská 29 (tel. 548741). Tram 4 or 9 from Andĕl metro station. A short walk from the Andĕl metro station, left along Nádražní, then left up Plzeňská. Tram 9 runs from the stop to the right of Hlavní nádraží through Václavské náměstí and on up Plzeňská to the Motol terminus.

Savoy, Keplerova 6 (tel. 537458/537459). Singles £7.50 ($13), doubles £15 ($26). Undergoing renovation, so prices may rise sharply. From the Malostranská metro station take tram 22 heading uphill. The tram runs along Keplerova.

Solidarita, Soudružská 2081 (tel. 777145). Metro: Strašnická. Walk along Volšínách about 300m, then turn left. If you see U Vesny on your left you are going the wrong way.

Transit, ul. 25 února 197 (tel. 367108). On the outskirts of the city. From the Dejvická metro station take tram 20 or 26 to the terminus in Liboc, then change to bus 108.

U Blaženky, U Blaženky 1 (tel. 538266). Tram 9 runs from the right of Hlavní nádraží through Václavské náměstí and up Plzeňská. Get off the tram at the junction of Plzeňská and Mozartova, walk down Mozartova and go right at U Blaženky.

Union, Jaromírova 1 (tel. 437858/437859). Metro: Vyšehrad. Follow the main road over the bridge. The hotel is on Jaromírova to the left of the bridge.

Modrá Hvězda, Jandova 3 (tel. 830291). From the Florenc metro station walk right down Wilsonova towards the river. When you see the tram lines crossing Wilsonova follow them to the right and then take tram 3, 8 or 19 to nám. Lidových milicí and the start of Jandova.

C/one-star hotels

Stará Zbrojnice, Všehrdova 16 (tel. 532815). Take tram 9 from the right of Hlavní Nádraží. Shortly after crossing the Vltava you will see Všehrdova on the right, off Vítězná.

Balkán, Svornosti 28 (tel. 540777). From the Anděl metro station on Nádražní walk down either Na belidle or Jindřicha Plachty on to Svornosti.

Libeň, tř. Rudé armády 2 (tel. 828227). Tram 12 from the Malastranská metro station and tram 10 from Vltavská metro station both run along the street (which will almost certainly have been renamed by now). After crossing the river the trams follow Libeňský most. At the point at which they turn left you are on (what was) Rudé Armády. The hotel is near the turn.

Moravan, U Uránie 22 (tel. 802905). Metro: Nádraží Holešovice. From the station head left along Vrbenského which becomes U Uranie.

Národní dům, Bořivojova 53 (tel. 275365). Doubles £11 ($19), triples £13.50 ($24), quads £18 ($32). Also dormitory accommodation, though this is frequently block-booked by visiting groups. From the right-hand side of Hlavní nádraží take tram 9, 10, 13 or 26 heading right towards Žižkov. Get off at Sladkovského nám., cross the square and follow one of the small streets on to Bořivojova. A ten-minute walk if you follow the tramlines.

Ostaš, Orebitská 8 (tel. 272860). Within easy walking distance of Hlavní nádraží. Head right from the exit, then turn right and follow the tramlines. Take Řehořova (on the left after Prběnická) which leads into Orebitská.

Tichý, Seifertova 65 (tel. 273079). A ten-minute walk from Hlavní nádraží, right from the main exit, right again and then follow the tramlines and the main road to the hotel, a few hundred metres past the stadium. Trams 9, 10, 13 and 26 pass the hotel.

PRIVATE ROOMS

With the removal of officially regulated prices, the cost of private rooms has soared so that they no longer offer the good value for money they once did. None the less, they are the most widely available accommodation possibility. Given the obvious potential in this market, new booking agencies are still emerging, so it is always worth asking around amongst other travellers and keeping your eyes open for adverts in the bus and train stations. Whichever office you deal with, try to get a room with a decent location. Ideally, you want a room in the centre, but these are scarce. Realistically, you should expect to be staying a few miles from the centre. Provided you can secure a room with an easy and frequent public transport service to the centre this is no problem, as public transport is cheap and reliable. When paying for a room you will probably be requested to do so in hard currency (Deutschmarks and US dollars are preferred).

Pragotur: control the largest stock of rooms thanks to their pre-eminence when the tourism industry was state-controlled. Singles in the centre cost around £10–11 ($17.50–19.50), outside the centre £9 ($16), doubles in the centre around £11 (19.50), outside the centre £9 ($16). Pragotur guarantee that all rooms located outside the centre are well served by public transport. The three-day minimum stay rule which the organization once enforced was scrapped in 1991.

Čedok: singles from £8–15 ($14–26), doubles from £12–24 ($21–42).

Top Tour: prices for rooms range from £8.50–14.25 ($15–25).

AVE Ltd: around £11.50 ($20) per night.

KONVEX: from £8.50–11.50 ($15–20) per night.

Hello Ltd: from £8.50–11.50 ($15–20) per night.

FURNISHED APARTMENTS

KONVEX offer apartments located in and around the city centre for £14–23 ($25–40) per night.

HOSTELS

There are few year-round hostels in the city. By June, as the numbers of visitors begins to increase steadily, finding a hostel bed becomes extremely difficult. The conversion of vacant student dormitories into temporary hostels in July and August brings a welcome increase in the number of hostel beds available, but since these two months are the most popular time for visitors arriving in Prague you are still going to have to look early in the day if you want a hostel bed. It is possible to approach hostels in person, but it is better to head straight for

CKM as they are well informed as to where beds are available, and will make reservations for you, as well as giving you directions to the hostel by public transport. As a rule, you can expect to pay from £2–4.50 ($3.50–8) for a hostel bed booked through CKM. Although at peak periods you should probably be glad to get any hostel bed at all, it can be worth asking CKM if they have beds in small rooms available, as dormitory beds at some hostels cost as much per person as singles and doubles at others. Top Tour also book beds in dormitory hostels, with prices ranging from £3.50–6.50 ($6–11.50) per person.

These hostels can be booked through CKM:

CKM Juniorhotel Žítna, Žítna 12 (tel. 292984). IYHF hostel. Open year round. Only off-season are you likely to have any chance of getting a bed on arrival. Around £4.50 ($8) for IYHF members. See the CKM entry in the Accommodation Agencies section above for directions.

Admira, Ubytovna TJ, U školsé zahrady. IYHF hostel. Open year round. (Tel. 538858). Trams 10 and 24 from the Vltavsk metro station run along Střelničá. Get off the tram when you reach the junction with Pakoméřická (left) and U měšťanských škol (right). The latter crosses U školsé zahrady.

Internát Konstructiva, Vrbova 1233 (tel. 462641). IYHF hostel. Far from the centre, requiring several changes on public transport. From Hlavní nádraží walk across the grassy area in front of the station and then down Jeruzalémská onto Jindřišská. Head left until you see the stop for tram 3. Take the tram towards its terminus in Braník (also trams 17 and 21 from other parts of the city centre). Passing the islands in the Vltava the tram then runs along Branická towards the Zápotockého bridge. About 400m before the bridge Branická turns left away from the river. Get off the tram at this point, walk a short distance up Branická, and then go right on Ke Krči from which you can catch bus 196 along Vrbova to the hostel.

Hotel Fasádostav, Jemnická 4 (tel. 431244). IYHF hostel.

Metro: Budějovická. From the station take bus 118 heading along Vyskočilova until the street is crossed by Michelská. Walking left up Michelská you will see Jemnická on your left. the hostel is a 10–15-minute walk from the metro stop.

TJ Dukla Karlin, Malého (tel. 222009). Open all year. Around £2 ($3.50) per night, either in bunk beds or cots set up in the gym. If the hostel is full they may let you sleep on the floor. Close to the bus station. Metro: Florenc. From the station go right along Křižíkova. Turn right at the junction with Prvního pluku, followed by a short walk on to Malého.

Zimní Stadion Vokovice, Zalany. £2.50 ($4.50) or £4 ($7) depending on whether you stay in the old or new buildings. Metro to Dejvická, then tram 2, 20 or 26 to Homéřická, the fourth stop.

Akademie Výtanvych Umění (AVU), U Starého Vystaviště 188. £4.50 ($8) per person in doubles with a shower, £4.25 ($7.50) per person in ordinary doubles, £4 ($7) per person in dorms. Tram 12 from the Nádraží Holešovice metro station.

Domov Mládeže, Dykova 20. £3.50 ($6). Two-night maximum stay. From the Náměstí Miru metro station take tram 16 to the second stop.

TJ Slavoj, V náklich (tel. 460070). Four-bed rooms in a boathouse by the Vltava, close to the Braník terminus of trams 3, 17 and 21. £4 ($7) per person. From Hlavní nádraží head straight ahead across the gardens in front of the station and down Jeruzalémská on to Jindřišská. Head left along this street until you reach the stop for tram 3 (take the tram in the direction you were walking).

TJ Doln Mécholupy, Na paloučku 223 (tel. 751262). Open year round. Singles £4 ($7). Seven miles out in the eastern suburbs. From the Želivského metro station take bus 111, 228 or 229 to Dolnomécholupska.

ESTEC Students House, Kolej Strahov, Spartakiádní blok 5 (5th building) (tel. 4637584). Open year round, but the full capacity of 400 beds is only available from July–mid-Sept. At other times only a few beds are available to visitors. Round-the-clock reception. £4.50 ($8) per person in doubles. From the Dejvická metro station take bus 217 to the sixth stop.

Koleje VŠCHT-VOLHA, Kosmonautů 950. £6.30 ($11) per person in doubles with showers. Bus 122, 145 or 154 from the Chodov metro station.

CAMPING

Pragotur distribute the brochure 'Praha Camping' listing all the sites. It is worth picking up a copy in case any of the telephone numbers have changed from those given below. Pragotur may simply say they have none left. If so, ask them to confirm the information given here. They may also tell you all the sites are full. Don't believe them. Call the sites yourself (all the better if you can speak German; if not, English should let you gather basic info).

All sites let bungalows except where indicated otherwise.

Expect to pay around £1.30 ($2.25) per tent and per person; £4.50 ($8) per person in a full bungalow

Sokol Trója, Trojská 171/82, (tel. 842833). Grade A site, open 1 June–31 Aug. Bus 112 from the Nádraží Holešovice metro station passes the site. Take the bus to Na Kazance. If the site is full the house at Trojská 157 (a few minutes' walk away) has a small site to the rear of the house.

Sokol Dolní Počernice, Dolní Počernice Nár. Hrdinů (tel. 718034). Grade A site, open 1 May–30 Sept. Walk right from the exit of Hlavní nádraží to catch tram 9 heading right to its terminus just off Konévova. From the tram terminus take bus 109 to the campsite. Near the Doln Počernice train station.

Caravancamp TJ Vysoké Školy, Plzeňská (tel. 524714). Grade A, open 15 May–15 Sept. Trams 4, 7 and 9 run past the site. Walk right from the exit of Hlavní nádraží to catch tram 9 heading left along the street. From the Anděl metro station walk a short distance left onto Plzeňská to catch tram 4, 7 or 9.

Intercamp Kotva Braník, U ledáren 55 (tel. 466085/461397). Grade A, open 1 Apr.–30 Sept. Close to the Braník terminus of trams 3, 17 and 21. Shortly after passing the Zápotockého bridge (the first after the islands), you can see the campsite down by the river. From Hlavní nádraží head across the gardens in front of the station and down Jeruzalémská onto Jindřišská. Head left along the street to the tram stop and take tram 3 in the direction you were walking.

Motol Sportcamp, V podhájí (tel. 521632/521802). Grade A, open 1 Apr.–31 Oct. Same directions as for the Caravancamp above. Take trams 4, 7 or 9 to their Motol terminus, from which the site is a 5-minute walk uphill, on the left.

Slavoj Suchdol, Za sokolovnou 440, (tel. 342505/342305). Grade B site. No bungalows. Open 1 July–31 Aug. (Details may well have changed after the recent reconstruction.)

Dolní Chabry, Ústeck. Public camping site. No bungalows.

TJ Armita, Nad Iávkou 3 (Džbán swimming pool), Praha 6 (tel. 368551 ext. 33). No bungalows. From Dejvická metro station take tram 20 or 26 heading along Benešova to last stop. From the terminus you follow the path around the left-hand side of the reservoir to reach the site (about 10 minutes' walk).

Chalets only at the following sites:

Na Vlachovce, tř. Rudé armády 217 (note: Red Army Street will probably have been renamed) (tel. 841290). The bungalows are shaped like beer kegs. Follow the directions for the Hotel Liben (see Hotels section, above), but do not get off the tram immediately after turning off Libeňský most. After the tram passes under the flyover look out for the site and the junction with Pod Vlachovkou on the left hand side of the street.

Transit, ul. 25 února 197 (tel. 367108). By the Hotel Transit. See the entry in the Hotels section for directions.

Xaverov, Božanovská, Dolní Počernice (tel. 867348).

Nedvězi, Nedvězi (tel. 750312).

DENMARK (Danmark)

Few countries have responded as imaginatively and constructively to the growth in budget tourism as Denmark. Tourist Offices will take the time to explain the various cheap accommodation possibilities, in stark contrast to the way in which a leaflet is thrown at you in some other countries. Accommodation prices are noticeably lower than in the rest of Scandinavia, increasing the range of your options.

Hotels, however, are still likely to be outside your budget. The cheapest doubles in Copenhagen cost 400Dkr (£36.50; $64); elsewhere around 250–300Dkr (£22.75–27.25; $40–48). Rooms in **private homes** are more affordable, with singles costing around 130–180Dkr (£11.80–16.40; $21–29), doubles 200–290Dkr (£18.20–26.40; $32–46). The addition of an extra bed to a room generally costs around 50–100Dkr (£4.50–9; $8–16). Breakfast is optional: usually 25–35Dkr (2.25–3.25; $4–5.50) for a hearty Danish breakfast. Private rooms are becoming more widely available each year, but they are still in short supply in some areas. For that reason, it is advisable to try and reserve rooms ahead. Where rooms are available Tourist Offices outside Copenhagen will accept requests for reservations made by letter or phone. A fee of around 12Dkr is charged for making a reservation, the same fee paid by personal callers at the office.

Rooms do not have to be booked through the Tourist Office. If you see a house or farmhouse advertising rooms (rooms are invariably advertised in several languages) simply approach the owner. Another option, if there are a few of you, is to rent a **holiday home** for a week. In high season, a simple house sleeping four costs from 1000–2000Dkr (£90–180; $160–320) per week. If this appeals to you, it may be wise to contact the local Tourist Office for advice on booking ahead.

You will seldom be far from one of the hundred or so **IYHF hostels** spread throughout this small country. There is a hostel in all the main towns. In many hostels, you have the chance to stay in small rooms, as well as in dormitories. While you might baulk at the thought of paying £10–14 ($17.50–24.50) in some Norwegian hostels, prices here vary from 69–89Dkr (£6.25–8.10; $11–14) in four-bed rooms, with dormitory accommodation costing around 59Dkr (£5.40; $9.50). Prices are very reasonable considering the standard of Danish hostels. As a result of a drive by the hostel association to attract families, high standards of comfort exist. Outside the large towns and ports, hostels are rarely full but, as they may be a couple of miles out, phoning ahead is advisable in order to let you find out directions, as well as book a bed. Reservations are held until 5 p.m., unless you state that you will arrive later. Receptions close at 9 p.m. and, outside Copenhagen, an 11 p.m. curfew is normal. If advance warning is given, it is possible to arrive later than this but you may be charged 25Dkr (£2.25; $4) for this. Bring your own bed linen as it costs around 30Dkr (£2.75; $5) per night to hire. It is also advisable to have an IYHF card. Otherwise you will have to pay 25Dkr (£2.25; $4) for an overnight card, or 100Dkr (£9.10; $16) for a membership card.

In the main towns, there are often **independent hostels** and local authority run Sleep-Ins. The latter frequently operate only for a period of a few weeks in summer (usually early August), and may be as basic as a mattress on the floor to put your sleeping bag on. Sleep-Ins differ considerably in price, from the 80Dkr (£7.25; $13) for B&B in Copenhagen, to the free Sleep-In in Odense run by DSB, the state railway. In theory, age restrictions and one-night maximum stays exist, but they are seldom stringently enforced. Sleep-Ins apart, **Town Mission Hostels** can often provide the cheapest lodgings in town. Generally clean and well equipped, there is, however, a strict ban on alcohol. The local Tourist Office will inform you on whether a Sleep-In or Town Mission Hostel is in operation.

There is hardly a town of any size that does not have a **campsite**. Graded from one to three stars, the best are the

Denmark   123

three-star sites, at which one person will pay around 45Dkr
(£4.10; $7) per night. All sites are open during the summer
months; a fair number from April to September; and a few all
year round. Unless you have an International Camping Carnet
you will be obliged to buy either a Danish Camping Pass (valid
all year, 28Dkr (£2.20; $4.50), or a one night pass for 7Dkr
(£0.65; $1). Many sites let cabins or static caravans sleeping
up to four people, which cost 1200–3000Dkr (£110–270;
$190–480) per week.

Camping outside official sites is perfectly acceptable,
provided you first obtain the permission of the landowner. Do
not camp on the beaches as this is against the law and
frequently results in an on-the-spot fine. It is also illegal to sleep
rough, so it is asking for trouble to try sleeping in stations,
parks, or on the streets.

Note: All Danish telephone numbers have eight digits. Dial
eight digits at all times.

ADDRESSES

The Danish Tourist Board	169–173 Regent Street, London W1A 2LT (tel. 071 734 2637)
Danish YHA	Landsforeningen Danmarks Vandrerhjem, Vesterbrogade 39, DK–1620 København V (tel. 31–313612).
Camping	Camping Club Denmark, Horsens Turistforening, Søndergade 26, DK–8700 Horsens (tel. 75–623822).
	Official guide 'Camping Denmark' available from Tourist Offices, booksellers, campsites, and by post from Campinggrådet, Olaf Palmesgade 10, DK–2100 København (tel. 31–423222). Not cheap. The National Tourist Office in London (or your capital city) has an abbreviated list, free on request.

124   Cheap Sleep Guide

Holiday homes

Feriehusudlejernes Brancheforening,
Euro Tourist, Vesterbro 89, DK–9100
Aalborg.

Sammenslutningen af Feriehususlejende
Turistforeningen, Odsherreds
Turistbureau, Algade 52, DK–5400
Nykøbing S.

Aalborg

Tourist Office
Turistbureauet, Østerå 8, 9000 Aalborg (tel. 98126022). Open
mid-June–mid-Aug., Mon.–Fri. 9 a.m.–7 p.m., Sat. 9 a.m.–2
p.m., Sun. 10 a.m.–1 p.m.; at other times, Mon.–Fri. 9
a.m.–4.30 p.m., Sat. 9 a.m.–noon.

HOTELS

Turist Hotel, Prinsengade 36 (tel. 98132200). Doubles around
440Dkr (£40; $70).
Aalborg Somandshjem, Østerbro 27 (tel. 98121900/98121986/
98121279). B&B in doubles with a shower around 480Dkr
(£44; $76).

PRIVATE ROOMS

Available from the Tourist Office.

IYHF HOSTEL

Skydebanevej 50 (tel. 98116044). Open mid-May–mid-Aug.
By the marina, to the west of the town. Bus 2, 12 or 14
from the town centre to the terminus.

CAMPING

Strandparkens, Skydebanevej 20 (tel. 98116044). A few
minutes' walk from the IYHF hostel. See above for
directions.

Århus

Tourist Office
Århus Turistbureauet, Rådhuset, 8000 Århus (tel. 86121600).

Open 14 June–11 Aug., daily 9 a.m.–8 p.m.; 12 Aug.–15 Sept., daily 9 a.m.–7 p.m.; 16 Sept.–31 Dec., Mon.–Fri. 9.30 a.m.–4.30 p.m., Sat. 10 a.m.–1 p.m.; 1 Jan–23 June, Mon.–Fri. 9 a.m.–4.30 p.m., Sat. 9 a.m.–noon. A short walk from the train station. Head left from Banegårdspladsen then right along Park Alle.

HOTELS

Windsor, Skolebakken 17 (tel. 86122300). Doubles from 310Dkr (£28; $49) with breakfast.
Park, Sønder Allé 3 (tel. 86123231). Doubles from 340Dkr (£31; $54).

PRIVATE ROOMS

Available from the Tourist Office. Around 110Dkr (£10; $17.50) per person.

IYHF HOSTEL

Pavillonen, Marienlunsvej 10, Risskov (tel. 86167298). Open year round. 1½ miles from the town centre, in the Risskov forest, about 500m from the beach. Bus 1 or 6. The hostel is signposted from the Marienlund terminus.

SLEEP-IN

Frederiksallé 20. Open 1 July–1 Sept. Check with the Tourist Office to see if this is in operation in 1993.
City Sleep-In, Kulturgyngen, Mejlgade 53 (tel. 86192255). 90Dkr (£9.50; $16.00), extra for single and double rooms.

CAMPING

Blommehaven, Ørneredevej 35, Højbjerg (tel. 86270207). Open mid-Apr.–mid-Sept. In the Marselisborg forest, close to the Århus bay beach. In summer take bus 19 straight

to the site, otherwise take bus 6 to Horhavevej.
Århus Nord, Randersvej 400, Lisbjerg (tel. 86231133). Open
year round. Chalets available. Buses 117 and 118 run
straight to the site.

Bornholm

Ferries to the island arrive at Rønne. The accommodation
possibilities listed below form a rough circular tour of the
island, with all but those between Dueodde and Rønne being
along the coast. Distances are so small as to make this an easy
walking tour.

Rø nne

Tourist Office
Beside the Bornholmstreffiken terminal (tel. 56950810). The
office distributes information covering the whole island and
will help you plan a route around the island. Rooms in private
homes can be booked through this office at the normal rates.

IYHF HOSTEL

Galløken, Sdr Alle 22 (tel. 53951340). Open 4 Apr.–31 Oct.

CAMPING

Galløken, Strandvejen 4 (tel. 53952320). Open
mid-May–Aug.
Nordskovens, Antoinettevej 2 (tel. 53952281). Open
June–mid-Sept.
Sandegårds, Haslevej 146 (tel. 53952990). Tents for hire.

Hasle

HOTELS

Pension Svalhøj, Simblegårdsvej 28 (tel. 53964018). Open 15 May–15 Sept. B&B in singles and doubles for around 140Dkr (£12.75; $22) per person.

Vendelbogå, Grønnegade 3 (tel. 53964140). Open year round. Doubles with a shower from 330Dkr (£30; $53).

IYHF HOSTEL

Fælledvej 28 (tel. 53964175). Open Easter and 1 May–15 Sept.

CAMPING

'Friheden', Fælledvej 30 (tel. 53964202). Tents for hire. Not a year round site.

Although the towns of Sandvig, Allinge, Sandkås and Tejn are listed separately there is very little distance between them. Sandvig and Allinge are actually joined to each other; Sandkås is about a mile from Allinge; with Tejn roughly another mile down the coast.

Sandvig

HOTELS

Pension Holiday, Strandvejen 82 (tel. 53980216). Open 1 May–1 Oct. B&B in doubles for around 340Dkr (£31; $54), in doubles with a shower around 370Dkr (£34; $59), in singles around 185Dkr (£17; $30).

Gretha's Pension, Nygade 7 (tel. 53981010). Open mid-

Apr.–mid-Oct. Singles around 185Dkr (£17; $30), doubles
with shower around 370Dkr (£34; $59).
Pension Lindesdal, Hammersøvej 1 (tel. 53981750). Open
mid-May–mid-Oct. Doubles around 330Dkr (£30; $53).

IYHF HOSTEL

Hammershusvej 94 (tel. 53980362). Open Easter–31 Oct.

CAMPING

Lyngholt, Borrelyngvej 43 (tel. 53980574). Hires out tents.
Open all year.
Sandvig, v/Ostersobadet (tel. 53980447).

Allinge

HOTELS

Sandboggard, Landemærket 3 (tel. 53980303). Open 1 May–1
Oct. Doubles around 320Dkr (£29; $51).
Havsten, Strandvejen 45 (tel. 53981884). Open 25 June–25
Aug. Singles around 190Dkr (£17.50; $30), doubles around
380Dkr (£35; $60).
Lis, Hammershusvej 74 (tel. 53981172). Open 1 May–1 Oct.
Singles around 180Dkr (£16.50; $29), doubles with showers
around 360Dkr (£33; $57).
Pension Olsker, Rønnevej 62 (tel. 53980957). Open year
round. Doubles from 330Dkr (£30; $53).
Pension Kilden, Brinkevej 7 (tel 53980909). Open mid
May–mid Oct. Doubles with and without showers around
270Dkr (£24.50; $43).

Sandkås

HOTELS

Expect to pay around 300Dkr (£27.50; $48) for B&B in doubles

Store Lærkegard, Lærkegardsvej 5 (tel. 53980053). Open 1
Feb.–21 Oct.
Det Hvide Hus Tejnvej 52 (tel. 53980582). Open 15 Apr.–25
Oct.

CAMPING

Sandkås, Poppelvej 2 (tel. 53980441).

Tejn

CAMPING

Tejn, Kåsevej 5 (tel. 53984171).

Gudhjem

HOTELS

Feriegården, Brøddegade 14 (tel. 53985066). Open year
round. Singles from 110Dkr (£10; $17.50), singles with
bath/shower from 140Dkr (£12.75; $22), doubles from
200Dkr (£18; $32), doubles with bath/shower from 230Dkr
(£21; $37).
Pension Havglimt, Gartnervænget 3 (tel. 53985415). Open
1 May–1 Oct. Doubles from 280Dkr (£25.50; $45).

IYHF HOSTEL

Sct Jorgens Gård (tel. 53985035). Open Easter–1 Nov.

CAMPING

Bådsted, Sdr. Strandvej 91 (tel. 53984230).
Sannes, Melstedvej 39 (tel. 53985211).
'Sletten', Melsted Langgade 45 (tel. 53985256).

Melsted

CAMPING

Strandlunden, Melstedvej 33–35 (tel. 53985245).

Svaneke

IYHF HOSTEL

Reberbanevej 5 (tel. 53996242). Open 1 Apr.–1 Nov.

CAMPING

Møllebakkens, Møllebakken 8 (tel. 53996462).
Hullehavn, Reberbanevej (tel. 53996363).

Nekso

CAMPING

Nexø, Stenbrudsvej 26 (tel. 53992721).

Dueodde

IYHF HOSTEL

Skrokkegårdsvej 17 (tel. 53988119). Open 1 May–1 Oct.

CAMPING

At the Youth Hostel. See above.
  Dueodde, Duegårdsvej 2 (tel. 53988149).
  Bornholms Familie Camping, Krogegårdsvej 2 (tel. 53988150).

Åkirkeby

CAMPING

Aakirkeby, Haregade 23 (tel. 53975551). Tents for hire.

Copenhagen (København)

Tourist Offices
Danmarks Turistråd, Hans Christian Andersen Boulevard 22, 1553 København V (tel. 33111325). Open June–mid-Sept., daily 9 a.m.–6 p.m.; mid-Sept.–Apr., Mon.–Fri. 9 a.m.–5 p.m., Sat. 9 a.m.–2 p.m.; Sun. 9 a.m.–1 p.m. The office hands out a reasonable free map of the city and the informative *Copenhagen This Week*, as well as being an excellent source of information on the city and the country as a whole. On the other side of the Tivoli amusement park from the main train station. Go left along the side of the park from the station, then right along Besterbrogade into Rådhuspladsen from which Hans Christian Andersen Boulevard runs right past the Town Hall.

USE-IT, Rådhuspladsen 13 (tel. 33156528). Open 15 June–15 Sept., daily 9 a.m.–7 p.m.; at other times, Mon.–Fri. 10 a.m.–4 p.m. An office oriented towards the budget traveller. Free help with finding accommodation. Their free map is superior to that of the Tourist Office. The organization also publishes useful guides to seeing the city on foot, by bike, or by bus, as well as an entertainment guide.

Public Transport
Copenhagen has an integrated network of buses and electric trains (S-tog) with prices calculated on a zonal system. Railpasses are valid on the S-tog network. The Copenhagen Card (available from the Tourist Office) covers the whole metropolitan network. The three-day card costs around 230Dkr (£21; $36). As well as usage of public transport, the card allows free entry to almost all the museums in the region. For 90Dkr (£8.25; $14.50) you can buy the Rabatkort, a multi-ride ticket containing ten stamps. By cancelling one stamp you can use the network as much as you like within one zone for an hour (two stamps 1½ hours, three stamps 2 hours). Several people can use the same Rabatkort; simply cancel the appropriate number of stamps for each person. The Grundbillet – around 10Dkr (£0.90; $1.50) – allows you to make as many changes as you want over two zones for up to one hour. Important bus terminals include Rådhuspladsen (see Tourist Offices) and Kongens Nytorv. Buses 1, 6, 28, 29 and 41 run between the two squares. To reach the other two main termini buses 14, 16, 50 and 75E link Rådhuspladsen to Norreport (S-tog station), while bus 10 runs between Kongens Nytorv and Toftegardsplads.

Finding Accommodation
During the summer, hostel beds can disappear at an alarming rate, so try to reserve ahead. If you arrive without reservations USE-IT (see Tourist Offices) are your best bet for finding a hostel bed. Otherwise, unless you have a tent, you will either have to sleep rough, or pay for a hotel room, neither of which is a good option.

HOTELS

Søfolkenes Mindehotel, Peder Skramsgade 19 (tel. 33134882). B&B in singles around 235Dkr (£21.50; $37), in doubles around 420Dkr (£38; $67). Bus 28 or 41 from Vesterbrogade or Rådhuspladsen passes the end of the street by the Inderhavnen.

Skt. Jørgen, Julius Thomsengade 22 (tel. 31371511). B&B in doubles from 440Dkr (£40; $70).

Jørgensen, Rømersgade 11 (tel. 33138186). Doubles from around 440Dkr (£40; $70). See the entry in the Hostels section below for directions.

Amager, Amagerbrogade 29 (tel. 31549005/31545009). B&B in doubles starts around 460Dkr (£42; $73). Bus 30, 33 or 34 along Amager Boulevard to Amagerbrogade from Rådhuspladsen.

Cab Inn, Danasvej 32–34 (tel. 31210400). Doubles with a shower around 520Dkr (£47; $83). With breakfast. Bus 29 from Vesterbrogade runs along the street. To walk follow Vester Farimagsgade away from Vesterbrogade by the train station. Turn left along Kampmannsgade and over the Skt Jøgens Sø into Dansavej.

Ibsens, Vendersgade 23 (tel. 33131913). Doubles around 490Dkr (£44; $78) per person with breakfast. S-tog to Nørreport, then walk down the street to the hotel.

Missionshotellet Hebron, Helgolandsgade 4 (tel. 31316906). B&B in doubles around 530Dkr (£48; $84). From Banegardspladsen in front of Central Station turn left down Reventlowsgade then right along Istedgade into Helgolandsgade.

Turisthotellet, Reverdilsgade 5 (tel. 31229839). B&B in doubles from 500Dkr (£46; $80). From Banegardspladsen in front of Central Station turn left down Reventlowsgade then right at Reverdilsgade. A few minutes' walk.

PRIVATE ROOMS

Værelseanvining, Central Train Station. Rooms found for a

15Dkr (£1.40; $2.50) commission. Prices start around 130Dkr (£11.75; $21). Personal callers only.

H.A.Y.4U, Kronprinsengade 10 (tel. 33330805). Room prices start around 130Dkr (£11.75; $21) no commission. From the Nørreport S-top station follow Frederiksborggade, cross Kultorvet, and then walk along Købmagergade until you see Kronprinsengade on the left.

USE IT (see Tourist Offices). No commission, and often capable of undercutting the prices of rooms from the two agencies above.

Skandinavisk Logi/Morgenmad (S.L.M.), St Kongensgade 94 (tel. 33919115).

IYHF HOSTELS

Expect to pay around 68Dkr (£6.25; $11).

Bellahøj, Herbergsvejen 8 (tel. 31289715). Three miles from the town centre. From the station, or from Rådhusplein take bus 2 or nightbus 902. Get off at Fuglsang Allé.

Amager, Sjællandsbroen 55 (tel. 32522908). Mon.–Fri. bus 46 from Central Station. Weekends bus 37 from Holmens Bro. S-train B, C, H, or L to Valby station (S-trains free with railpasses) to join bus 37 saves a bit of time and money.

Lyngby Vandrerhjem, Rådvad 1 (tel. 42803074/42803032). Far out, and not easy to get to. Fine if you are stuck for a first night. S-train A, B or L to Lyngby. From there, bus 182 or 183 to Lundtoftvej and Hjortekærsvej. The two-mile walk to Rådvaad is marked. Bus 187 provides a direct link between Central Station and the hostel, but only runs four times a day. The only IYHF hostel with a curfew, 11 p.m.

HOSTELS

City Public Hostel, Absalonsgade 8 (tel. 31312070). Open 5 May–31 Aug. No curfew and round-the-clock reception. More expensive than the IYHF hostels but central location.

90Dkr (£8.25; $14.50), or 105Dkr (£9.50; $17) if you want the breakfast, where you can eat as much as you like. In the Vesterbro Ungdomsgård. From the train station walk left along Vesterbrogade to Vesterbros Torv. Absalonsgade is off Svendsgade on the left of the square.

KFUM/KFUK (YMCA/YWCA) Interpoint, Store Kannikestræde 19 (tel. 31113031). Open 1 July–22 Aug. Check in from 8 a.m.–noon, or between 2.30 p.m. and the 12.20 a.m. curfew. 60Dkr (£5.50; $9.50). Excellent central location. The street runs from Frue Plads (site of Our Lady's Cathedral). From Rådhuspladsen walk away from the Town Hall down Vester Voldgade, right along Vestergade, then left up Nørregade to Frue Plads. Walking down Nørregade from the Nørreport S-tog station is about half the distance.

KFUK (YWCA) Interpoint, Valdermarsgade 15 (tel. 31311574). Open 15 July–15 Aug. Same entry requirements as the KFUK hostel. Similar hours and prices. Outside the centre.

Hotel Jørgensen, Rømersgade 11 (tel. 33138186). From June–Aug. the hotel operates a mixed dorm in its basement. 70Dkr (£6.50; $14.50), 90Dkr (£8.25; $14.50) with breakfast. From the Nørreport S-tog station Vendersgade and Frederiksborggade lead into Rømersgade.

SLEEP-IN

Per Hendriks Lings Allé 6 (tel. 31265059). Open 19 June–27 Aug. Mixed dorms or mattresses on the floor. 80Dkr (£7.25; $13) with continental breakfast. Usually will find space for last-minute arrivals. Bus 1 from Rådhuspladsen or nightbus 953 to Per Hendriks Allé. Alternatively bus 6 or 14 from Rådhuspladsen, or nightbus 914 to Vedidrætsparken.

CAMPING

There are a total of seven sites around Copenhagen. Expect

to pay around 40Dkr (£3.75; $6.50) per person, tent included, at the sites below.

Strandmøllen, Strandmøllenweg 2 (tel. 42803883). Open mid-May to Sept. Nine miles out, but only 20 minutes on S-train C dir. Klampenborg.

Absalon, Kordalsvej 132 (tel. 31410600). Open year round. 5½ miles out of town. S-train B or L to Brondbyøster, then a 3/4 mile walk. Ask locals for directions.

Bellahøj, Hvidkildevej (tel. 31101150). Same buses as for the Bellahøj IYHF hostel, but get off at the stop after Hulgårdsvej.

Esbjerg

Tourist Office
Turistbureauet, Skolegade 33, 6700 Esbjerg (tel. 75125599). Open Mon.–Fri. 9 a.m.–5 p.m., Sat. 9 a.m.–noon. The office is on the corner of the main square.

Arriving in Esbjerg
Arriving by ferry from Harwich, Newcastle or Tórshavn, the town centre is a well-signposted 20-minute walk from the ferry terminal. Trains to Copenhagen depart from the train station by the ferry terminal. The main train station is located near the town centre, at the opposite end of Skolegade from the main square.

HOTELS

Tarp Kro, Tarpbyvej 50 (tel. 75167011). Doubles around 300Dkr (£27; $48)

Ølufvad Kro, Ølufvadhovedvej 85 (tel. 75169006. Doubles around 320Dkr (£29; $51) with breakfast.

Sømandshjemmet, Auktionsgade 3 (tel. 75120688). Doubles around 330Dkr (£30; $53). At the harbour.

PRIVATE ROOMS

Available from the Tourist Office.

IYHF HOSTEL

Gammel Vardevej 80 (tel. 7512458). About 1 3/4 miles from
the centre. Bus 1, 9, 11, 12 or 31 from Skolegade.

CAMPING

Strandskovens, Gl. Vardevej 76 (tel. 75125816). See the IYHF
hostel above for directions.

Frederikshavn

Tourist Office
Brotorvet 1 (tel. 98423266). Open mid-June–mid-Aug.,
Mon.–Sat. 8.30 a.m.–8.30 p.m., Sun. 11 a.m.–2 p.m.; mid-
Apr.–mid-June, Mon.–Fri. 9 a.m.–5 p.m., Sat. 11 a.m.–2 p.m.;
Oct.–Mar., Mon.–Fri. 9 a.m.–4 p.m. By the Stena Line ferry
terminal at the corner of Havnepladsen and Rådhus Allé,
a 5-minute walk from the train station.

HOTELS

Discountlogi Teglgaarden, Teglsgaardvej 3 (tel. 98420444).
Open all year. Singles from 190Dkr (£17.50; $30), doubles
from 300Dkr (£27; $48).

IYHF HOSTEL

'Fladstrand', Buhlsvej 6 (tel. 98421475).

CAMPING

Nordstrand, Apholmenvej 40 (tel. 98422982/98429350). Open Apr.–Sept.

Legoland

Situated in Billund, the mini-town made out of Lego is one of the main tourist attractions in Denmark. Legoland is open from May until mid-September, with a number of indoor exhibitions from Easter to mid-December. Hotels in Billund are expensive, so either camp at the local site, or visit Legoland on a daytrip from Vejle or Varde.

Billund

DCU-Camping Billund, Nordmarksvej 2 (tel. 75331521). Open 24 June–16 Sept. Very close to Legoland.

Vejle

Bus 912 to Billund. Most days an hourly service operates.

HOTELS

Grejsdalens Hotel and Kro, Grejsdalsvej 384 (tel. 75853004). Singles from 250Dkr (£22.75; $40), doubles from 400Dkr (£36.50; $64).

Park Hotel, Orla Lehmannsgade (tel. 75822466). Cheapest doubles around 460Dkr (£42; $73) including breakfast.

IYHF HOSTEL

Vejle Vandrerhjem, Gl. Landevej 80 (tel. 75825188).

SLEEP-IN

In the Sports Hall, Vestre Engvej. Details from the Tourist Office (tel. 75821955).

CAMPING

Nørremarksvej 18 (tel. 75823335).

Varde

HOTELS

Hojskolehjemmet, Storegade 56 (tel. 75220140). Doubles around 380Dkr (£35; $61) including breakfast.

IYHF HOSTEL

Ungdomsgården, Pramstedvej 10 (tel. 75221091). Open 15 May–1 Oct.

Odense

Tourist Office

Odense Tourist Information, Town Hall, 5000 Odense C (tel. 66127520). Open mid-June–Aug., Mon.–Sat. 9 a.m.–7 p.m., Sun. 11 a.m.–7 p.m.; Sept.–mid-June, Mon.–Fri. 9 a.m.–5 p.m., Sat. 10 a.m.–1 p.m. About 10 minutes' walk from the train station. Head right along Ostre Stationsvej then left at Jernbanegade, or walk through the park in front of the station on to Jernbanegade. At the end of Jernbanegade, turn left along Vestergade to the Town Hall.

HOTELS

Ansgarhus Motel, Kirkegårds Alle 17–19 (tel. 66128800). Open Jan.–Sept. Doubles without breakfast around 330Dkr (£30; $53).

B&B in doubles around 370–410Dkr (£33–37; $58–65)

Kahema, Dronningensgade 5 (tel. 66122821).
Staldgården, Rugårdsvej 8 (tel. 66178888).
Ydes, Hans Tausengade 11 (tel. 66121131).

B&B in doubles around 430Dkr (£39; $69)

Fangel Kro, Fangelvej 55 (tel. 65961011). Not central, but the bus stops about 100m from the hotel.

PRIVATE ROOMS

Available from the Tourist Office. Around 110Dkr (£10; $17.50) per person.

IYHF HOSTEL

Kragsbjergvej 121 (tel. 65130425). 70Dkr (£6.50; $11). Bus 62 or 63 from the train station. A 20-minute walk from the town centre.

HOSTELS

KFUM/KFUK (YMCA/YWCA) Interpoint, Rodegårdsvej 91 (tel. 66142314). Open 15 July–15 Aug. 60Dkr (£5.50; $9.50). Detailed map at station.

SLEEP-IN

Run by the State Railway DSB. Enquire by phone whether it

is in operation either at the train station, or at the Tourist
Office (tel. 66127520).

CAMPING

Odense, Odensevej 102 (tel. 66114702). Open Easter–mid-
Oct. Around 35Dkr (£3.25; $5.50) per person, tent
included. Bungalows available. Bus 13. The site is within
easy walking distance of the Fruens Bøge train station on
the line to Svendborg. Walk down Stationsvej, then right
along Odensevej.

'Blommenslyst', Middelfartvej 494 (tel. 65967641). Open
May–mid-Sept. Farther out than the site above, to the west
of town.

FINLAND (Suomi/Finland)

In common with the other Scandinavian countries, simply feeding yourself in Finland costs a fair amount of money, making it all the more vital to keep the price of your accommodation down. Unless you are desperate you will want to avoid staying in **hotels**, as even the cheapest hotels charge around 140FIM (£16.70; $29) for singles, 200FIM (£23.80; $42) for doubles. In the main tourist destinations, you can expect to pay closer to 300FIM (£36; $63) for the cheapest doubles in town. At least the invariably excellent standards and large breakfasts provide some consolation if you are forced to take a hotel room.

B&B accommodation is a cheaper option than hotels, with overnight prices generally in the 75–150FIM (£8.90–17.80; $15.50–31) range. A substantial breakfast and use of a sauna are usually included in the overnight price. Unfortunately B&B accommodation is nowhere near as widespread as hotel accommodation, and is available mainly in the north of the country, particularly on farms.

Hostelling is an excellent way to see Finland, especially if you are travelling outside the peak season of mid-July to mid-August. There are roughly 160 **IYHF hostels** scattered around the country, with at least one operating in all the main tourist destinations during the summer. Finnish hostels are classified from one up to four stars. Prices in two-star hostels range from 35–55FIM (£4.20–6.50; $7.50–16.50), depending on whether you stay in a dorm or a small room. Most common in the larger towns are three-star hostels which charge 35–80FIM (£4.20–6.50; $7.50–16.50) per night in two- to eight-bed rooms. Prices in the four-star hostels (known as Finnhostels) start at 57FIM (£6.80; $12), rising to 160FIM (£19; $33.50). The largest rooms in four-star hostels are quads.

Only in the most expensive hostels are IYHF cards obligatory, but at others you can expect to be charged a supplement of 10FIM (£1.20; $2) if you are without a card. Bearing in mind that hiring bed linen can cost a similar amount (only included in the overnight price at four-star hostels), it is better to come well prepared and save your money. Only from June to August, and particularly from mid-July to mid-August, will you experience any difficulty in getting a hostel bed. At this time, hostels in the large cities and in areas popular with hikers are often full, making it imperative to reserve ahead, by letter or by telephone. Reservations are held until 6 p.m., unless you make it clear that you will be arriving later. In contrast to other Scandinavian countries, Finland has seen little growth in the number of **independent hostels**. Converted student dorms, known as 'Summerhotels', are generally clean and modern. Accommodation is in singles or doubles: around 160FIM (£19; $33.50) is the normal price for singles: 100–125FIM (£11.90–14.90; $21–26) per person the usual price for doubles.

There are over 350 well-equipped official **campsites**, graded from one to three stars, covering all the main tourist areas. Prices vary from 30–80FIM (£3.60–9.50; $6–17) upwards, according to the classification of the site. If you are not in possession of an International Camping Carnet, you will have to buy a Finnish camping pass at the first site you visit. Few sites remain open all year round. Most open for the period May/June to August/September only. Many of the sites in and around the larger towns are very big, with a tent capacity of 2000. During July and August, these sites become very busy at weekends. Some sites let cottages (usually without bedding) for two to five people – well worth enquiring about if there are several people prepared to share. Cottages are available for anything between 150–300FIM (£17.90–35.80; $31–62) per day. In July and August, it is advisable to try and reserve cottages in advance.

It is possible to **sleep rough** in Finland and stay within the law. More advisably, you can take advantage of an old law which allows you to camp anywhere as long as you have the landowner's permission. It is normal practice to camp out of sight of private homes. Despite a growing tendency (officially encouraged) to camp only on established sites, you will have no trouble with the authorities, provided you leave no litter, and don't do anything which might start a forest fire.

ADDRESSES

Finnish Tourist Board   66–68 Haymarket, London SW1Y 4RF
(tel. 071 839 4048). Lists of hotels,
hostels and campsites.

Finnish YHA   Suomen Retkeilymajajärjestö-SRM ry,
Yrjönkatu 38 B 15, 00100 Helsinki
(tel. 90–6940377).

Helsinki (Helsinki/Helsingfors)
(tel. code 90)

Tourist Offices

Kaupungin Matkailutoimisto, Pohjoisesplanadi 19, 00100 Helsinki (tel. 1693757). Open mid-May–mid-Aug., Mon.–Fri. 8.30 a.m.–6 p.m., Sat. 8.30 a.m.–1 p.m.; otherwise, Mon. 8.30 a.m.–4.30 p.m., Tues.–Fri. 8.30 a.m.–4 p.m. Free telephone to call local hotels and hostels. A 10-minute walk from the train station, left down Mannerhaeimintie, then left again along Pohjoisesplanadi.

Hotellikeskus, Asema-aukio 3 (tel. 171133). Open in summer, Mon.–Fri. 9 a.m.–9 p.m., Sat. 9 a.m.–7 p.m., Sun. 10 a.m.–6 p.m.; at other times, Mon.–Fri. 9 a.m.–6 p.m. Dispenses city maps and hotel/hostel lists but, first and foremost, the office is an accommodation service: 10FIM (£1.20; $2.10) commission for a hotel room, half that fee for a hostel bed. A few minutes' walk from the train station in the direction of the post office.

HOTELS

The least expensive hotels charge 260–300FIM (£31–36; $55–63) for their cheapest doubles.

Kongressikoti, Snellmanink 15 A (tel. 174839).

Clairet, Itäinen Teatterikuja 3 (tel. 669707). Near the train station.

Erottajanpuista, Uudenmaankatu 9–11 (tel. 642169).

Lönnrot, Lönnrotinkatu 16 (tel. 6932590).

Pilvilinna-Irmala-Terminus, Vilhonkatu 6B (tel. 630260/607072). Near the train station.

Mekka, Vuorikatu 8B (tel. 630265).

Tarmo, Siltasaarenk 11 B 40 (tel. 7014735).

Regina, Puistokatu 9 A 2 (tel. 656937).

Omapohja, Itäinen Teatterikuja 3 (tel. 666211). Near the train station.

Hotel Finn, Kalevankatu 3B (tel. 640904).

IYHF HOSTELS

Stadionin maja, Pohj Stadiontie 3 B (tel. 496071). Curfew 2 a.m. Three-star hostel. Prices for IYHF members start at 40FIM (£4.75; $8.50) in small dorms, rising to 60FIM (£7.25; $12.50) per person in doubles. Tram 3T or 7A to the Olympic Stadium, or a 25-minute walk. From the train station turn right down Mannerheimintie. At the junction with Helsingkatu and Runeberginkatu you will see the stadium complex.

Satakuntatalo, Lapinrinne 1A (tel. 695851). Student accommodation converted into a temporary four-star hostel. Open 28 May–3 Sept. Around 220FIM (£26; $46) for singles, 160FIM (£19; $33.50) per person in doubles. Ask about student discounts (20–50 per cent). A 10-minute walk from the train station. Tram 4 stops nearby.

Eurohostel, Linnankatu 9 (tel. 664452). Recently opened four-star hostel. Doubles around 130–150FIM (£15.50–18; $27–31) per person. Close to the harbour, a 20-minute walk from the train station. Tram 4 stops nearby.

Finnhostel Academica, Hietaniemenkatu 14 (tel. 4020206/4020575). Student accommodation converted into a temporary hostel. Open 1 June–1 Sept. Singles from 200–250FIM (£23.75–29.75; $42–52), doubles from 130–155FIM (£15.50–18.50; $27–32) per person. Ask about student reductions. Bus 18 or tram 3T run to the hostel. A 10-minute walk from the train station. Cross Mannerheimintie near the post office, follow Salamonkatu past the bus station, and then turn right at Runeberginkatu. After crossing Pohjoinen Rautaiekatu, you will see Hietaniemenkatu running off to the left.

Vantaan retkeilyhotelli, Tikkurilan Urheilupuisto, 01300 Vantaa (tel. 8393310). Four-star hostel. Ten miles from the city centre; just over half a mile from the Tikkurila train station.

HOSTELS

Kallionnretkeilymaja, Porthaninkatu 2 (tel. 70992590). Mid-May–Aug. 2 a.m. curfew. 55FIM (£6.50; $11.50; DM16). Only 30 beds. Run by the city's youth organization. Fifteen-minute walk from the train station along Unionkatu, or the metro to Hakaniemi.

YWCA Interpoint. In both 1991 and 1992, the hostel was located at Raumantie 5 (tel. 557849), accessible by bus 18. Hopefully, the hostel will again be at this location in 1993, but if not, for information on the current location contact the Tourist Office, or Minna Muukonen (tel. 448066). The hostel is usually open from 1 July–15 Aug., to both men and women. 12.30 a.m. curfew. 1993 price should be around 50FIM (£6; $10.50). The staff may let you sleep on the floor when all the city's hostels are full.

YMCA Interpoint (tel. 557849). Take bus 18.

CAMPING

Rastila (tel. 316551). Open mid-May–mid-Sept. Prices at this municipal site start at 27FIM (£3.25; $5.50) p.p. (tent included). Also lets cabins. 4½ miles from the city centre. Metro to Itäkeskus, then bus 90, 90A or 96.

Rovaniemi (tel. code (9)60)

Tourist Office

Aallonkatu 1 (tel. 16270). Open June–Aug., Mon.–Fri. 8 a.m.–7 p.m.; weekends, 10 a.m.–7 p.m.; rest of the year, Mon.–Fri. 8 a.m.–4 p.m. A short walk from the bus and train stations. Turn left from the bus station, right from the train station, on to Rantakatu, which leads into Hallituskatu. Turn left along Valtakatu, and continue until you see the Tourist Office.

HOTELS

Cheapest doubles 300FIM (£36; $63)

Matkakoti Matka-Kalle, Asemieskatu 1 (tel. 20130).
Outa, Ukkoherrantie 16 (tel. 312474).
Rovaniemi Summerhotel, Kairatie 75 (tel. 392651).

IYHF HOSTEL

Retkeilymaja Tervashonka, Hallituskatu 16 (tel. 14644).
Three-star hostel. For directions, see Tourist Office, above.

CAMPING

Ounaskoski (tel. 345404). Open 1 June–31 Aug. Just over the
river from the centre of town.
Napapiirin Saari-Tuvat (tel. 60045). Site opens in May.

Savonlinna (tel. code (9)57)

Tourist Office
Savonlinna Tourist Service, Puistokatu 1, 57100 Savonlinna
(tel. 5713492). Open June–Aug., daily 8 a.m.–10 p.m., at other
times, Mon.–Fri. 9 a.m.–4 p.m. Accommodation-finding
service (invaluable in July when the town is packed) and free
baggage-storage.

Arriving in Savonlinna by Train
The most convenient stop for the town centre and the Tourist
Office is Savonlinna-Kauppatori, one stop before the main
station if you are arriving from Helsinki.

HOTELS

Hospits, Linnankatu 20 (tel. 22443). Cheapest doubles
around 280FIM (£33.50; $59).

IYHF HOSTELS

Retkeilymaja Malakias, Pihlajavedenkuja 6 (tel. 23283). Open 29 June–9 Aug. Just over 10 minutes' walk from the train station.

Retkeilymaja Vuorilinna, Kasinosaari (tel. 5750495/5750494). Open 1–28 June and 9–31 Aug.

CAMPING

Vuohimäki (tel. 537353). Open 1 June–19 Aug. 4½ miles from the centre. Bus 3 runs twice hourly.

Korkeamäen Majatalo, Ruokolahti, Kerimäki (tel. 312186 and, in summer, tel. 4827).

Turku (Turku/Åbo) T(tel. code (9)21)

Tourist Offices

The City Tourist Office operates at several locations in the city. The main office is at Käsityöläiskatu 3, 20100 Turku (tel. 336366), about 50m from the train station. Open June–Aug., Mon.–Fri. 8 a.m.–4 p.m.; at other times, Mon.–Fri. 8.30 a.m.–4 p.m. During the peak season, June–Aug., there is an accommodation-finding service in the train station, open Mon.–Fri. 9.30 a.m.–7.30 p.m., weekends 9.30 a.m.–2.30 p.m. Another branch is at the ferry terminal (Silja Line counter), open daily 7.30 a.m.–noon and 6–9.30 p.m.

Arriving in Turku/Åbo

If you arrive at the train station you are only a short walk from the centre of the town. The ferry terminal is about two miles from the city centre, but bus 1 runs frequently from the harbour to the Market Place in the town centre.

HOTELS

Cheapest doubles 300FIM (£36; $63)

Matkakievari, Läntinen Pitkäkatu 8 (tel. 503506). Left from the square in front of the train station.

Aura, Humalistonkatu 13 (tel. 311973). The street leads away from the front of the train station.

Turisti-Aula, Käsityöläiskatu 11 (tel. 651111). The street leads away from the front of the train station.

St Birgittas Convent Guesthouse, Ursininkatu 15a (tel. 501910). Follow Käsityöläiskatu from the train station, right on Puutarhakatu, then left.

Ikituuri Summer Hotel, Pispalantie 7 (tel. 376111). Converted student accommodation. Open 1 June–31 Aug.

Asuntohotelli Astro, Humalistonkatu 18 (tel. 511800). See Aura, above.

IYHF HOSTELS

Turun kaupungin retkeilymaja, Linnankatu 39 (tel. 316578). Four-star hostel. From the ferry terminal a 20-minute walk along Linnankatu or bus 1. A 15-minute walk from the train station. Down Käsityöläiskatu, right at Puutarhakatu, left at Koulukatu, then right on Linnankatu.

Finnhostel Kòren, Hämeenkatu 22 (tel. 320421). Student accommodation serving as a temporary four-star hostel. Open 1 June–31 Aug.

CAMPING

Ruissalo (tel. 589249). Open 1 June–2 Sept. About 6½ miles out of town. Bus 8 runs twice hourly from the Market Square.

Baltic States

If you're travelling on to Latvia, it's useful to know about a
new tourist agency in Tallinn, specializing in budget
accommodation. The Baltic Accommodation and Travel Service
runs a Youth Hostel in the centre of Riga and a B&B service
with more than 50 Estonian families in Tallinn, Parnu, Tartu
and Kuressnare. By summer 1993, this family B&B network
should have also expanded to Latvia and Lithuania and they
will have an office in the Youth Hostel in Riga. Current prices
are $9 per night for the hostel in Riga; $10 first night, $5
subsequent nights for the family B&B accommodation in
Estonia.

In Tallinn, contact: SAKALA 11c, EE0001, Tallinn, Estonia
(tel. 70142-681-893). Open 1 May–15 Sept. In Riga, contact:
GRECINIEKU IELA 28 (tel. 70132-224-296). Open 1 May–30
Sept. Only 500m from the station.

FRANCE

As a rule, budget travellers should have little difficulty in finding a cheap place to stay in France. There is probably a wider range of good options here than anywhere else in Europe. Even in Paris there are plenty of cheap places to stay. For most of the year, you should be able to find a cheap bed on arrival anywhere outside the capital, unless there is a special event on in the town (such as the Festival d'Avignon). However, it is best to try and reserve hotels ahead in July and August when the French themselves are on holiday. In Paris, hotel reservations are a good idea at any time of year, but especially from Easter to late September when the city is buzzing with visitors. Youth hostels in Paris should be reserved in advance (around 3–4 months ahead if you are planning a visit in summer), while the two youth hostel associations advise advance reservations of hostels in popular tourist destinations between May and September.

Although the French have no national reservations centre on the Dutch model, they have made great strides in facilitating the easy booking of accommodation. While French hoteliers will invariably accept a request for a reservation over the phone you may be able to save yourself the trouble of phoning around to book in advance by using the 'Accueil de France' or 'Loisirs Accueil' services. Around fifty French cities' Tourist Offices are part of the 'Accueil de France' scheme, which allows you to book hotel accommodation in any other town which is also part of the system. (Details on whether a city included in this guide is a participant is given in the Tourist Office sections. As the number of cities taking part is increasing, this information may change, so it is always worth asking locally.) Reservations can be made for the same day or for up to eight days in advance; a small charge is made for this service to cover the cost of the phone call or telex. The 'Accueil de France' service is particularly useful if you are heading for Paris. Because looking for accommodation in Paris on your own can be frustrating, it makes sense to use one of the accommodation services in the capital to find you a bed, but it is even smarter to arrive with your accommodation already booked and bypass the very long queues which are common at these offices during the main tourist season. A variation on 'Accueil de France' are the 'Loisirs Accueil' services which have been established by many of the French départements (regional authorities). These offices reserve not just some hotels in the area but also campsites, more often than not free of charge. A list of such offices is available from the French Government Tourist Office; simply send a stamped self-addressed envelope with your request.

The French Ministry of Tourism categories for **hotels** range from one star up to four stars, and then the deluxe 'four stars L', according to the facilities available and the level of comfort. The actual grading and inspection of hotels is carried out on a regular basis by the prefecture of the département (only a relatively small number of hotels remain unclassified). Standards of comfort and cleanliness in French hotels should give you little to worry about but, as is the case everywhere, there is always the occasional hotel which lets standards slip between inspections. Given that the authorities are committed to maintaining a consistently high standard of accommodation do not hesitate to contact them (c/o the local Tourist Office) if you have any grounds for complaint.

In contrast to other countries, two people can easily stay every night in a hotel without worrying unduly about their budgets as hotel prices are very low (Parisian hotels are ridiculously cheap when compared to their counterparts in London). French custom is to set a price for a room, which means that the charge is the same whether it is occupied by one or two people. In practice, some hoteliers will let rooms to solo travellers at a reduced rate (typically 70–75 per cent of the cost of the room), but often only outside the peak season when trade is beginning to tail off. A third bed normally adds about 30 per cent to the cost of a room.

One-star hotels will be of primary interest to budget travellers, though it is worth noting that many unclassified hotels, particularly in rural areas, offer perfectly adequate standards of accommodation. One-star hotels seldom offer more than the basic comforts, but they represent good value for what you pay. The cheaper two-star establishments are also within the range of the budget traveller. Despite the fact that these are described by the Ministry of Tourism as merely 'comfortable', you will probably find them a bit luxurious when compared to similarly priced accommodation in other west European countries. The cheapest one-star hotels charge around 100–110FF (£10.50–11.50; $18.50–20), except in Paris where you will do well to find a room for under 140FF (£14.50; $26). Prices for two-star hotels start at around 140–150FF (£14.50–15.50; $26–27.50) outside Paris, around 170–180FF (£17.75–18.75; $31–33) in the capital.

Although hotel rooms are cheap and good value for money, on the whole hotel breakfasts are not. You can expect to pay 15–25FF (£1.60–2.60; $2.75–4.50) for a basic continental breakfast; very poor value for money when you consider what that amount might buy at the supermarket or baker's, or even in a local café. Legally, hoteliers have no right to insist that you take breakfast (or any other meal), but in practice there are always a few who will try to force your hand in popular towns at the height of the season. While you have the right to refuse breakfast, they have the right to refuse your custom. Another cost over and above what you pay for a room may be a charge for taking a shower or a bath. You will normally be asked to pay from 10–25FF (£1–2.60; $1.75–4.50) to use the bath or shower when these are not included in the overnight price.

Throughout the provincial towns there are over 5000 family-run hotels and inns belonging to an organization known as 'Logis de France', easily identifiable by their distinctive green-and-yellow emblem. These establishments have generally taken advantage of government grants and now provide guaranteed standards of service, mainly in one- or two-star accommodation, though a number of unclassified 'auberges' are also included in the association. A complete guide to these hotels and inns can be purchased from the Logis Department of the French Government Tourist Office. A considerably abridged list of these accommodations is available from 'Gîtes de France'.

Bed and Breakfast accommodation is found mainly in the countryside, though there are some B&B possibilities in a few of the larger cities. Rural chambres d'hôtes (B&B in private homes) are generally similar in price to cheap hotels, but probably offer even better value for money. Another alternative to hotel accommodation open to the budget traveller is to rent self-catering accommodation. Again, this is an option far more prevalent in rural France, most conspicuously in the form of **'Gîtes de France'**: self-catering accommodation let by an association of French families. Sleeping between four and six people, they can usually be rented for 900–1500FF (£95–155; $165–275) per week. The gîtes are normally located in and around small villages, and may be village houses, rural or farm cottages, or flats in private homes. Over 2,500 gîtes can be booked through the offices of 'Gîtes de France Ltd' in London. For an annual membership fee of £3 you receive an illustrated guide to all the properties, free use of the reservation service, and discounts on 21 ferry routes across the Channel if you are travelling by car or motorbike.

There are two **youth hostel** associations in France; the IYHF-affiliated Fédération Unie des Auberges de la Jeunesse (FUAJ), and the Ligue Française pour les Auberges de la Jeunesse (LFAJ). Relations between the two are strained, to say the least. The IYHF handbook lists the FUAJ hostels, but only a few of the LFAJ establishments. It is worthwhile finding out about the LFAJ hostels, as they fill in many of the gaps in the FUAJ network, so that there are not many places of major interest that lack a hostel (contact the associations' head offices for up-to-date hostel lists).

Most hostels stay open all year round, except perhaps for a few weeks in winter. Hostelling can certainly be a cheap way to see the country, at virtually any time of year, provided you take the trouble to reserve well ahead for hostels in the more popular tourist towns. The drawbacks are the poor quality of some of the hostels, and the curfews. Even the top-rated hostels vary enormously in quality. While some are well maintained and efficiently run, at the other extreme are those in dilapidated buildings, where the warden only appears at certain times and is not on the premises at night. In the very worst of this latter type, you may well have reason to worry about your personal safety. Curfews are normally 11 p.m. at the latest, except in a very small number of hostels.

Generally, hostel prices vary according to the grade of establishment. Prices can be as low as 30FF (£3.10; $5.50), but are normally around 40–50FF (£4.20–5.20; $7.50–9). However, in popular tourist destinations such as Paris, Strasbourg, Avignon and Bayeux even low-grade hostels may charge well above the normal hostel price. In these towns, expect to pay around 75–85FF (£7.80–8.80; $13.50–15.50) in the hostels of either association. The IYHF card permits entry to both FUAJ and LFAJ hostels. Technically, the IYHF card is obligatory at FUAJ hostels, but non-members are normally allowed to stay on the payment of a 10–20FF (£1.05–2.10; $1.75–3.50) supplement per night, or are restricted to a one-night stay.

In some of the larger towns, a further possibility available to IYHF members and students are the 'Foyers des Jeunes Travailleurs/Travailleuses'. These are residential hostels, whose main function is to provide cheap living accommodation for young workers and students. As such, they tend to offer a higher standard of accommodation than hostels (mainly singles and doubles). Prices are usually on a par with local hostels, but you are getting better value for money. It is worth enquiring about 'foyers' at any time of year, but your chances of finding a place are obviously better during the student vacations.

Gîtes d'étapes (not to be confused with Gîtes de France) are widespread in rural areas, particularly those popular with hikers and cyclists. They provide basic, cheap accommodation; normally bunk-beds in dorms, and simple cooking and washing facilities. The LFAJ maintains 11 gîtes d'étapes in the Aveyron-Le Lot region, and another 27 in Corsica (details are included in the LFAJ hostel list). These are ideal for cycling or walking tours in two of the most beautiful areas of the country. Overnight fees range from about 25–45FF (£2.60–4.75; $4.50–8.50). If you are heading into the mountains, there is a plentiful supply of mountain huts, the majority of which are operated by the Club Alpin Français (CAF). Huts are open to non-members, but members of the CAF and its associated clubs receive a reduction on the usual overnight charge of 50FF (£5.25; $9).

Camping is very popular in France. Practically every town of any size has a campsite. There are over 7000 in all, rated from one to four stars. The overnight fee varies from 5–20FF (£0.50–2.00; $0.90–3.60) per person, depending on the classification of the site. Usually, the cheapest you will find is a site run by the local authority (*camping municipal*). Charges are normally under 10FF (£1; $1.80) per night. Outside the main season there may not even be an attendant to collect the fees, so you can camp for free. At other times, these sites are clean and well maintained, and lack only the shopping and leisure facilities of higher-graded sites.

With a few exceptions, camping is a cheap, convenient and pleasant way to see France. There is no centrally located site in Lyon, so you will have to travel to one of the sites on the outskirts. The only site in Nice is pitifully small, and far from the centre. Along the Mediterranean, many sites become ridiculously overcrowded during the summer months; so much so that 11 regional information posts, 21 telephone information centres, and 59 local reception centres have been established to deal with the problem. The addresses and telephone numbers of these centres are listed in the brochure *Mémento du Campeur Averti*, available from Tourist Offices. Try to reserve coastal sites in advance.

In rural areas, many farms are part of a scheme which allows you to camp on the farm (*camping à la ferme*). These are listed in 'Accueil à la Campagne', a useful publication for anyone wanting to explore rural France. Facilities are very basic, yet prices are similar to those of other campsites. Many farmers will allow you to camp on their land free of charge, provided you ask their permission first. If you pitch your tent without their consent, expect a hostile confrontation.

Sleeping rough is legal, and the weather will seldom cause you any problems, except in the north outside the summer months. However, sleeping rough is not advisable, especially in the cities, or along the beaches of the Mediterranean. Petty criminals realized the easy pickings to be had from those sleeping in and around stations a long time ago (Paris and Marseilles are particularly unsafe). The beaches are 'worked' by French and North African gangs who steal for a living. If you are stuck for a place to stay, some stations have emergency lodgings. Ask for the 'Accueil en Gare'. Failing this, you would be better to take an overnight train. If you are going to sleep rough, leave your pack at the station, and try to bed down beside other travellers. If you are attacked, hand over your money. Thieves have been known to become violent if their victims try to resist. If you have been sensible and taken out travel insurance you will incur only a small loss, which is preferable to risking serious injury.

Note: All French telephone numbers have eight digits and, with the exception of the capital, there are no dialling codes. Dial the eight digits for each number below at all times and when dialling Paris from outside the city, add 1 before the eight digits given.

ADDRESSES

French Government Tourist Office	178 Piccadilly, London W1V 0AL (tel. 071 499 6911; 24-hours, recorded message). If purchasing any guides send cheques only, made payable to 'Maison de la France'.
Hotels	The Logis de France guide is available from the 'Logis Department' of the French Government Tourist Office from March onwards. The 1992 price was £6.50, plus £1 for postage and packing.

Gîtes de France	Gîtes de France Ltd, 178 Piccadilly, London W1V 9DB (tel. 071 493 3480).
Youth hostels	Fédération Unie des Auberges de la Jeunesse, 27 rue Pajol, 75018 Paris (tel. (1) 46 07 00 01).
	Ligue Français pour les Auberges de la Jeunesse, 38 bd Raspail, 75007 Paris (tel. (1) 45 48 69 84).
Camping	'The Camping Traveller to France 1990/9' is available from the French Government Tourist Office. £1, including postage and packing.
Rural Accommodation	The book *French Country Welcome*, available from bookshops, lists selections of chambres d'hôtes, gîtes, farms which are part of camping à la ferme, and mountain huts.

Aix-en-Provence

Tourist Office
Office du Tourisme, 2 Place Général de Gaulle, 13100 Aix-en-Provence (tel. 42 26 02 93). 'Accueil de France' service unavailable. A few minutes' walk from the train station. See Basic Directions, below.

Basic Directions
Going left from the train station you find yourself on av. Victor Hugo which leads to Place du Général de Gaulle. Right off av. Victor Hugo near the train station is bd du Roi René, part of a series of roads running around the Old Town back to av. Victor Hugo at Place du Général de Gaulle. From Place du Général de Gaulle, cours Mirabeau heads right to Place Forbin. The small road left of cours Mirabeau leads to Place des Augustins from which you can follow rue Espariat, left at rue Bedarrides, and then on down Maréchal Foch into Place Richelme where you'll find the Town Hall. Bd de la République is diagonally left across Place du Général de Gaulle from av. Victor Hugo. At Place Niollon, cours Sextus heads off to the right of bd de la République.

HOTELS

Cheapest rooms around 120FF (£12.50; $22)

Vendôme, 10 cours des Minimes (tel. 42 64 45 01).

Cheapest rooms around 140–160FF (£14.50–16.75; $25–29)

Bellegarde, 2 Place Bellegarde (tel. 42 23 43 37). From Place Richelme head right along rue Paul Bert, left at the junction of rue Pierre et Marie Curie and rue Mathéron, then right along rue du Puits Neuf to Place Bellegarde.

Paul, 10 av. Pasteur (tel. 42 23 23 89). From the foot of Place Richelme near the Town Hall, rue Gaston de Saporta leads into av. Pasteur.

Cheapest rooms around 190–210FF (£19.75–22; $35–38)

Vigouroux, 27 rue Cardinale (tel. 42 38 19 53). Right off av. Victor Hugo.

Le Moulin, 1 av. Robert Schumann (tel. 42 59 41 68).

Des Arts (Sully), 69 bd Carnot (tel. 42 38 11 77).

Concorde, 68 bd du Roi René (tel. 42 26 03 95).

De France, 63 rue Espariat (tel. 42 27 90 15).

Du Globe, 74 cours Sextius (tel. 42 26 03 58).

Splendid, 69 cours Mirabeau (tel. 42 38 19 53).

Casino, 38 rue Victor-Leydet (tel. 42 26 06 88). The street runs between Pl. des Augustins and Pl. Niollon.

YOUTH HOSTEL

3 av. Marcel Pagnol (FUAJ), Quartier Jas de Bouffan (tel. 42 20 15 99). IYHF cards obligatory. Sold at the hostel for 100FF (£10.50; $17). First night B&B 75FF (£7.75; $14), then 65FF (£6.75; $12) per night. 1½ miles from the station. Bus 8 or 12 dir. Jas de Bouffan to the Etienne d'Orves Vasarely stop. Watch for the Vasarely building.

FOYERS

Club des Jeunes Travailleurs, Les Milles, av. Albert Einstein (Zone Industrielle) (tel. 42 24 41 38). Four miles from the centre.

St Eloi, 9 av. Jules Isaac (tel. 42 23 44 99).

Foyer Hotel Sonacotra, 16 av. du petit Bartélémy (tel. 42 64 20 87). (Men only.)

Foyer pour les Filles, 15 rue du Bon Pasteur (tel. 42 23 33 98 (females only). At Pl. Niollon go into the Old Town from the main roads. At the junction of rue Victor-Leydet and rue Lisse des Cordeliers follow the latter, on down rue de la Treille to the corner of rue des Bons Enfants.

Sed Abeilles, av. Maréchal Leclerc (tel. 42 59 25 75). (Men and women aged 16–25 only).

CAMPING

Airotel Chantecler, Val St-André (tel. 42 26 12 98).
Arc en Ciel, Pont des Trois Sautets (tel. 42 26 14 28). Off
Route Nationale 7.

Avignon

Tourist Offices
Office de Tourisme, 41 cours Jean-Jaurès, 8400 Avignon (tel.
90 82 65 11). Head office. Open Mon.–Fri. 9 a.m.–6 p.m., Sat.
9 a.m.–noon and 2–6 p.m., except during the Festival when
the office is open from 9 a.m.–7 p.m. daily. 'Accueil de France'
service available.

Office de Tourisme, du Pont d'Avignon 'Le Châtelet'. Branch
office. Open Apr.–Sept., daily 9 a.m.–6.30 p.m.; Oct.–Mar.,
open 9 a.m.–1 p.m. and 2–5 p.m. daily, except Mon. when
the office is closed.

Hotel Reservations and 'Accueil de France' service. In the
train station (tel. 90 82 05 81).

Finding Accommodation
Accommodation in all price categories becomes difficult to find
during the Festival d'Avignon (early July to late August) so
reserve in advance if possible at this time.

Basic Directions
The train station is just outside the old city walls by the Porte
de la République, a 5-minute walk from the Tourist Office and
a 15-minute walk from Place de l'Horloge in the town centre.
After going through the Porte de la République, cours Jean-
Jaurès and then rue de la République lead into Place de
l'Horloge. Rue Joseph Vernet runs left off cours Jean-Jaurès.
Near the end of rue Joseph Vernet going left down rue
Baroncelli leads you into Place Crillon and to the Porte de
l'Oulle. Beyond the Porte de l'Oulle, the Pont Deladier crosses

the River Rhône. the area known as the Ile de la Barthelasse is to the right on the opposite side of the river.

HOTELS

Cheapest rooms around 120FF (£12.50; $22)

Du Parc, 18 rue Agricol-Perdiguier (tel. 90 82 71 55). Right off cours Jean-Jaurès.

Cheapest rooms around 130FF (£13.50; $24)

Le Splendid, 17 rue Agricol-Perdiguier (tel. 90 86 14 46). Right off cours Jean-Jaurès.

Cheapest rooms around 150FF (£15.50; $27.50)

Monclar, 13 avenue Monclar (tel. 90 86 20 14). Head right on leaving the station. The street is on your right before you reach the Gare Routière.

Cheapest rooms around 160FF (£16.75; $29)

Des Arts, 9 rue de l'Aigarden (tel. 90 86 63 87). Centrally located.

Cheapest rooms around 170FF (£17.75; $31)

Saint-Roch, 9 impasse Mérindol (tel. 90 82 18 63). Close to the train station, just outside the city walls.
Provençal, 13 rue Joseph Vernet (tel. 90 85 25 24). Left off cours Jean-Jaurès.

Cheapest rooms around 180FF (£18.75; $33)

D'Angleterre, 29 bd. Raspail (tel. 90 86 34 31). Left off cours Jean-Jaurès.
De la Bourse, 6 rue Portail Boquier (tel. 90 82 34 43). Turn left off cours Jean-Jaurès immediately after passing the Chambre de Commerce to reach rue Portail Boquier.

Le Magnan, 63 rue Portail Magnanen (tel. 90 86 36 51). Head right from the train station and follow the city walls past the Port St-Michel to the Porte Magnanen, then turn left through the walls on to rue Portail Magnanen.

Medieval, 15 rue Petite Saunerie (tel. 90 86 11 06). Centrally located.

Mignon, 12 rue Joseph Vernet (tel. 90 82 17 30). Left off cours Jean-Jaurès.

Cheapest rooms around 200FF (£20.75; $36.50)

De Garlande, 20 rue Galante (tel. 90 85 08 85). Centrally located.

De Mons, 5 rue de Mons (tel. 90 82 57 16). Centrally located.

Cheapest rooms around 220FF (£23; $40)

Regina, 6 rue de la République (tel. 90 86 49 45).

GUESTHOUSE

Ferme Etienne Jamet, Ile de la Barthelasse (tel. 90 86 16 74).

B&B

Mme Salaun, 34 rue de la Masse (tel. 90 86 19 05).
Les Logis St-Eloi, 14 Pl. de l'Oratoire (tel. 90 25 40 36).

HOSTELS/FOYERS

The Squash Club, 32 bd Limbert (tel. 90 85 27 78). Bed 50FF (£5.25; $9).

Foyer Hameau de Champfleury, 33 av. Eisenhower (tel. 90 85 35 02). Open 15 June–15 Sept. B&B from 120–150FF (£12.50–15.50; $22–27.50).

Residence Pierre Louis Loisil, av. Pierre Sémard (tel. 90 25 07 92). Bed 57FF (£6; $10.50).

Foyer Bagatelle, Ile de la Barthelasse (tel. 90 86 30 39). Bed 52FF (£5.50; $9.50).

Foyer International de Pont d'Avignon (YMCA), 7 bis, bd
de la Justice (tel. 90 25 46 20). B&B 85FF (£8.75; $15.50).
La Bastide de Bonpas, route de Cavaillon, Montfavet (tel. 90
23 04 57). Bed 77FF (£8; $14).

CAMPING

There are four sites grouped closely together on the Ile de la
Barthelasse, just across the river. Within walking distance of
the station, or take the infrequent bus 10 from the Post Office
(to the left after passing through the Porte de la République).
Bagatelle (tel. 90 86 30 39). Open all year.
Camping Municipal Pont St-Benézet (tel. 90 82 63 50). Open
1 Mar.–31 Oct.
Camping Parc des Libertés (tel. 90 85 17 73). Open for a few
weeks around Easter, then from 15 June–15 Sept.
Les Deux Rhônes, Chemin de Bellegarde (tel. 90 85 49 70).
Open all year round.

Bordeaux

Tourist Offices
Office de Tourisme Bordeaux Centre, 12 cours du XXX Juillet,
33080 Bordeaux cedex (tel. 56 44 28 41). Open June–Aug.,
Mon.–Fri. 9 a.m.–7 p.m., Sat. closes at 6 p.m., Sun. closes
at 2 p.m.; at other times, Mon.–Fri. 9 a.m.–12.15 p.m. and
1.45–6.30 p.m., Sat. closes at 6 p.m. 'Accueil de France' service
available. Next to the Opera.
Office de Tourisme Bordeaux Gare St-Jean (tel. 56 91 64 70).
Office de Tourisme Bordeaux Aéroport (tel. 56 34 39 39).

Basic Directions
Bordeaux St-Jean is about three miles from the town centre.
CGFTE buses link the station to various points in the city
centre. Maps of the network are available from the Tourist
Office. If you want to walk, the simplest route (not the shortest,

but the safest) is to follow cours de la Marne from the station to Place de la Victoire. Then you can walk right along rue Sainte-Catherine into the heart of the city, across cours Victor Hugo, cours d'Alsace et Lorraine and rue de la Porte Dijeaux/rue St-Rémi, then on to the Opéra and the beginning of cours du XXX Juillet. Going along cours du XXX Juillet you reach the Girondins monument on Esplanade des Quinconces.

HOTELS

Centrally located hotels (one-star unless shown otherwise). Expect to pay around 140–160FF (£14.60–16.70; $25–29)

De la Boëtie, 4 rue de la Boëtie (tel. 56 91 76 68). Go left from the Porte Dijeaux at the end of rue de la Porte Dijeaux.

D'Amboise, 22 rue de la Vieille Tour (tel. 56 81 62 67). Unclassified hotel, slightly cheaper than the other hotels listed.

Abadie, 127 rue Dubordieu (tel. 56 91 60 85).

De Biarritz, 21 rue de Loup (tel. 56 44 38 51).

Le Blayais, 17 rue Mautrec (tel. 56 48 17 87). Near Notre-Dame. From the Opéra, take Allées de Tourny, then left.

Le Bourgogne, 16 cours Victor Hugo (tel. 56 92 82 27). Near the Porte des Salinières, down towards the River Garonne.

Dauphin, 82 rue du Palais-Gallien (tel. 56 52 24 62). From the Opéra follow Allées de Tourny into Place Tourny, then take rue Hugerie.

De Dax, 7 rue Mautrec (tel. 56 48 28 42). See the Le Blayais, above.

De Famille, 76 cours Georges-Clemenceau (tel. 56 52 11 28). From the Opéra follow Allées de Tourny, then go left from Place Tourny.

Du Parc, 10 rue de la Verrerie (tel. 56 52 78 20). By the Jardin Public, on the fringe of the town centre. From the Girondins monument follow cours de Maréchal Foch, turn right at cours de Verdun, right again at cours Xavier Arnozan, then left.

Du Parlement de Bretagne, 38 rue des Piliers-de-Tutelle (tel. 56 44 58 18). The street runs between cours du Chapeau Rouge (by the Opéra) and rue du Cancera (off rue Sainte-Catherine).

Saint-François, 22 rue de Mirail (tel. 56 91 56 41). Rue du Mirail faces the beautiful Grosse Cloche, on cours Victor Hugo heading down towards the river.

Saint-Rémi, 34 rue Saint-Rémi (tel. 56 48 55 48).

Lafaurie, 35 rue Lafaurie-de-Monbadon (tel. 56 48 16 33). The street crosses rue Hugerie (see the Dauphin, above).

Unotel, 37 cours du Maréchal-Juin (tel. 56 90 10 00). More expensive at 200FF (£20.80; $36.50), but the hotel has a very large capacity if you find you are having difficulty finding a room elsewhere. Follow cours d'Alsace et Lorraine away from the river past the Cathédrale St-André and along rue des F. Bonie.

One-star hotels near Gare St-Jean. Expect to pay around 140–160FF (£14.60–16.70; $25–29) for rooms without a shower/bath

Noël, 8 rue St-Vincent-de-Paul (tel. 56 91 62 48). The street runs diagonally right away from the station, between the arrival and departure halls.

San Michel, 32 rue Charles-Domercq (tel. 56 91 96 40). The street running along the front of the station.

Du Lion d'Or, 38 pl. André-Meunier (tel. 59 91 71 62). Follow rue St-Vincent-de-Paul (see the Noël, above) on to cours de la Marne, then head left until you see the square on your right.

Hôtel-Bar-Club Les 2 Mondes, 10 rue St-Vincent-de-Paul (tel. 56 91 63 03). See the Noël, above.

HOSTELS

22 cours Barbey (FUAJ) (tel. 56 91 59 51). Turn right on leaving the station, left up cours de la Marne, then fourth on the left. 11 p.m. curfew.

Maison des Etudiants, 50 rue Ligier (tel. 56 96 48 30). Oct–June women only, open to men July–Sept. Half-hour walk from the station. Up cours de la Marne, straight across Pl. de la Victoire to cours Aristide-Briand which runs into cours de la Libération. Rue Ligier is on the right. Alternatively, bus 7 or 8 from the station to the Bourse du Travail stop on cours de la Libération. Keep on going the same way, then right on rue Ligier.

CAMPING

No really convenient site.

Lorréjean. From the bus station on Quai Richelieu by the river take bus B to the end of the line (30-minute trip), then a couple of minutes' walk.

Les Gravières, Pont-de-la-Maye, Villeneuve d'Ornon (tel. 56 87 00 36). Open all year round.

Chamonix

Tourist Offices
Office de Tourisme, Place du Triangle de l'Amitié, 74402 Chamonix-Mont-Blanc (tel. 50 53 00 24). Open daily July–Aug., 8.30 a.m.–7.30 p.m.; Sept.–June, 8.30 a.m.–12.30 p.m. and 2–7 p.m. Reserves rooms free of charge (tel. 50 53 23 33) or write in advance. 'Accueil de France' service not available. About 500m from the train station. Down Avenue Michel Croz, then round to the left of the Town Hall.

Accommodation in Chamonix
As it can be very difficult to find accommodation on arrival, try to reserve ahead. If you have not done so you may have to stay outside Chamonix in one of the towns nearby. Those with a railpass will have no problem getting to accommodation outside Chamonix as most of the towns along the valley are

served by SNCF (this includes all those mentioned below, unless stated otherwise).

HOTELS

Prices quoted for the hotels below are for the room only. Breakfast adds another 25FF (£2.60; $4.50) p.p. on average to these prices.

Cheapest rooms around 120FF (£12.50; $22)

Valaisanne, 454 av. Ravanel le Rouge (tel. 50 53 17 98).

Cheapest rooms around 130FF (£13.50; $24)

Carrier (tel. 50 54 02 16). In Argentière

Cheapest rooms around 160FF (£16.75; $29)

Aiguille Verte, 683 rue Joseph Vallot (tel. 50 53 01 73). Stade, rue Whymper (tel. 50 53 05 44).

Cheapest rooms around 170FF (£17.75; $31)

Marti (tel 50 54 11 01). In Argentière.

Cheapest rooms around 180FF (£18.75; $33)

Prairie (tel. 50 53 19 96). In Les Praz. No SNCF station in Les Praz, but the Les Bois station is a 10–15-minute walk away.

Cheapest rooms around 200FF (£20.75; $37)

Dahu (tel. 50 54 01 55). In Argentière.
Bon Coin (tel. 50 53 15 67).

Prices quoted for the hotels below are for half-board based on two people sharing a room.

Cheapest price around 170FF (£17.75; $31)

Chaumière (tel. 50 53 13 25).
Chardonnet (tel. 50 54 02 80). In Argentière.
Gorges de la Diosaz (tel. 50 47 20 97). In Servoz.

Cheapest price around 180FF (£18.75; $33)

Mont-Blanc (tel. 50 54 60 02). In Vallorcine.
Cimes Blanches (tel. 50 47 20 05). In Servoz.

Cheapest price around 190FF (£19.75; $35)

Arve (tel. 50 53 02 31).
Boule de Neige (tel. 50 53 04 48).

YOUTH HOSTEL

103 Montée J. Balmat (FUAJ), Les Pélerins (tel. 50 53 14 52).
A 30-minute walk from Chamonix. Nearest train station
Les Pélerins. The hostel is about half a mile uphill from
the station. Alternatively, take the bus dir. Les Houches
from Pl. de l'Eglise in Chamonix to the school (école) in
Les Pélerins.

DORMITORY ACCOMMODATION

Cheap accommodation is provided in several refuges, gîte
d'étapes and chalets in and around Chamonix.

Ski Station, 6 route des Moussoux (tel. 50 53 20 25). Bed only
around 50FF (£5.25; $9). Up the hill from the Tourist Office.
Le Chamoniard Volant, 45 route de la Frasse (tel. 50 53 14
09). Beds around 65FF (£6.75; $12), breakfast around 25FF
(£2.60; $4.50), half-board starts around 150FF (£15.75;
$27.50).
Le Belvedère, 501 route du Plagnolet, Argentière (tel. 50 54
02 59). Beds around 45–60FF (£4.75–6.25; $8–11), breakfast
around 22FF (£2.25; $4), half-board around 120–130FF
(£12.50–13.50; $22–24).

CAMPING

Three sites are located about 10–15 minutes' walk from the centre of town, just off the road to Les Pélerins. A full list of the 18 sites in the area is available from the Tourist Office.

Les Arolles, 281 Chemin du Cry-Chamonix (tel. 50 53 14 30). Open 25 June–30 Sept. 100 places.

L'Ile des Barrats (tel. 50 53 51 41). Open 1 June–30 Sept. 150 places.

Les Tissourds (tel. 50 55 94 97). Open 1 July–31 Aug. 20 places. Cold water only.

Les Moliasses (tel. 50 53 18 61). Open 1 June–15 Sept. A 15-minute walk from the town centre.

Dieppe

Tourist Office
Office de Tourisme-Syndicat d'Initiative de Dieppe, Boulevard Général-de-Gaulle, B.P. 152, 76204 Dieppe cedex (tel. 35 84 11 77/35 84 83 97). 'Accueil de France' service not available. To get there, see Basic Directions below.

Basic Directions
Trains from Paris connecting with ferry services run to Dieppe-Maritime station, next to the ferry terminal. Other trains stop at Dieppe station, about 10–15 minutes' walk from the ferry terminal. From Dieppe station go straight ahead on to bd G. Clemenceau. On the right is the fishing port. Going along the side of the water you pass bd Général-de-Gaulle on the left (the Tourist Office is on the second block), then rue d'Ecosse. Continuing, you reach the Avant-Port and the ferry terminal.

HOTELS

Cheapest rooms around 110FF (£11.50; $20)

La Pêcherie, 3 rue Mortier-d'Or (tel. 35 82 04 62). Near the fishing port. Take the second left off Quai Duquesne after rue d'Ecosse.

Du Havre, 13 rue Thiers (tel. 35 84 15 02). Left off bd G.-Clemenceau.

Cheapest rooms around 120FF (£12.50; $22)

Beauséjour, 2 and 4 Place Louis-Vitet (tel. 35 84 13 90). Near the fishing harbour. Take the first right off Quai Duquesne after rue d'Ecosse.

De la Jetée, 5 rue de l'Asile-Thomas (tel. 35 84 89 98). In the area between the Quai Henri IV and Quai du Hable and the beach, around the Avant-Port from the ferry terminal.

Cheapest rooms around 150FF (£15.50; $27.50)

Au Grand Duquesne, 15 Place Saint-Jacques (tel. 35 84 21 51). Great location near St James' Church in the heart of the Old Town. Take the third right off rue d'Ecosse.

Les Arcades, 1 and 3 avenue de la Bourse (tel. 35 84 14 12). Near the ferry terminal.

Windsor, 18 bd de Verdun (tel. 35 84 15 23). Cheapest of the hotels on the seafront. A 15-minute walk from the station. Straight on from Quai Duquesne, second left after Grande Rue.

Cheapest rooms around 170FF (£17.75; $31)

Tourist Hotel, 16 rue de la Halle-au-Blé (tel. 35 06 10 10). Straight on from Quai Duquesne, then left after Grande Rue.

L'Ancrage, 9 arcades de la Poisonnerie (tel. 35 84 21 45). Near the ferry terminal.

Pontoise, 10 rue Thiers (tel. 35 84 14 57). Left off bd G.-Clemenceau.

YOUTH HOSTEL

48 rue Louis Fromager (FUAJ), Quartier Janval, Chemin des

Vertus (tel. 35 84 85 73). Forty minutes' walk from the station. Bus 2 dir. Val Druel to Château Michel.

CAMPING

No really convenient site.

Camping du Pré St-Nicolas (tel. 35 84 11 39). Two-star site. Open all year. Located near the golf course, just off the road to Pourville. A 25-minute walk from the station. Left along bd G.-Clemenceau, right at bd Maréchal Joffre, left rue Cl. Groulard, left rue du Faubourg de la Barre, then right at the fork in the road and straight on.

Camping Vitamin, Dieppe–Les Vertus (tel. 35821111). Three-star site. Open 1 Apr.–31 Oct.

Dijon

Tourist Office

Office de Tourisme-Syndicat d'Initiative de Dijon, Pavillon du Tourisme, Place Darcy, 21000 Dijon (tel. 80 43 42 12). Open daily, July–Aug. 9 a.m.–9 p.m.; mid-Apr.–June and Sept.–mid-Oct., 9 a.m.–noon and 2–9 p.m.; at other times of year, 9 a.m.–noon and 2–7 p.m. If you arrive without reservations, the staff will find hotel rooms for you. 'Accueil de France' service available. When the office is closed an information board in front of the office gives round-the-clock information on the availability of hotel rooms in the city. A 5-minute walk from the train station. See Basic Directions below.

Basic Directions

As you leave the train station rue Guillaume Tell runs away to the left, rue du Dr Albert Rémy to the right. Directly in front of you av. Maréchal Foch leads off towards Place Darcy and the Tourist Office. Rue des Perrières and bd Sevigné, the streets immediately to the left and right respectively of av. Maréchal

Foch, both lead into Place Darcy as well. From Place Darcy, bd de Brosses takes you to Place St-Bernard, from which you can carry straight on down bd de la Tremouille into Place de la République. Taking rue de la Liberté from Place Darcy, you arrive at Place de la Libération, formerly known as Place Royale. If, however, you turn left off rue de la Liberté at Place François Rudé, you can then follow rue des Forges with its beautiful sixteenth- and seventeenth-century houses, past the Church of Our Lady (Eglise Notre-Dame) with its unique row of gargoyles, into Place des Ducs. Walking from the train station to Place de la République, Place des Ducs or Place de la Libération takes about 15 minutes.

HOTELS

Cheapest rooms around 100FF (£10.50; $18.50)

Du Théâtre, 3 rue des Bons Enfants (tel. 80 67 15 41). The street is off Place de la Libération.

Cheapest rooms around 130FF (£13.50; $24)

L'Etendard, 4 rue des Perrières (tel. 80 41 51 32).
Monge, 20 rue Monge (tel. 80 30 55 41). From the end of rue du Dr Rémy left on rue Mariotte and straight on to Place St-Bénigne. Right into rue de la Prévote, left, then a quick right down rue Condorcet and first left into rue Monge.

Cheapest rooms around 150FF (£15.50; $27.50)

Du Sauvage, 20 rue Monge (tel. 80 30 55 41). See Hôtel Monge, above.
Saint-Bernard, 7 bis, rue Courtepée (tel. 80 30 74 67). From Place St-Bernard go left down rue Bernard (virtually at a right angle to bd des Brosses) into Place Depuis, right along rue Devosge, then left at rue Courtepée.
Des Rosiers, 22 bis, rue de Montchapet (tel. 80 55 33 11). A 15-minute walk from the train station, 10–15 minutes' walk from the Church of Our Lady. Right off rue Guillaume Tell

at rue Pierre Palliot and straight on, across the main road to Troyes into Place Auguste Dubois. From here, go right along rue Jacques Cellerier, then right at rue de Montchapet.

KCNIL, 11–13 avenue Junot (tel. 80 65 30 29). A 15–20-minute walk from the town centre, in the opposite direction to the train station. From Place des Ducs go left up rue Verrerie, quick right on to rue Jeannin, straight on, then across rue Diderot/rue Berlier and down rue Paul Carnet into Place du 30 Octobre. Directly opposite rue Carnet is bd de Strasbourg, from which av. Junot is the second left.

Du Stade, 3 bd de Strasbourg (tel. 80 65 35 32). See Hôtel KCNIL, above.

De la Gare, 16 rue Mariotte (tel. 80 30 46 61). Left at the end of rue du Dr Rémy.

Lamartine, 12 rue Jules Mercier (tel. 80 30 37 47). Right off rue de la Liberté near Place de la Libération.

Cheapest rooms around 170FF (£17.75; $31)

De la Poste, 5 rue du Château (tel. 80 30 51 64). Left off rue de la Liberté, a short distance from Place Darcy.

Thurot, 4 and 6 Passage Thurot (tel. 80 43 57 46). Rue Thurot is left off rue Guillaume Tell. Impasse Thurot is on the right-hand side.

Le Jacquemart, 32 rue Verrerie (tel. 80 73 36 76). Right off bd de la Trémouille near Place de la République.

Cheapest rooms around 200FF (£20.75; $36.50)

Montchapet, 26 rue Jacques Cellerier (tel. 80 55 33 11). A 10-minute walk from the historic centre, slightly closer to the train station. See Hôtel des Rosiers, above.

La Résidence, 17 bis, rue Chancelier de l'Hôpital (tel. 80 66 18 87). A 5-minute walk from Place de la Libération. Straight on into Place du Théâtre, then along rue Vaillant to Place St-Michel. Right down rue Buffon, then left to the hotel.

Des Ducs, 5 rue Lammonnoye (tel. 80 67 31 31). From Place des Ducs, rue Longpierre runs across rue Lammonnoye.

Du Nord, Place Darcy (tel. 80 30 58 58).

Du Palais, 23 rue du Palais (tel. 80 67 16 26). Off Place de la Libération.

Du Globe, 67 rue Jeannin (tel. 80 66 13 86). From Place des Ducs go left up rue Verrerie, then a quick right.

Continental, 7/9 rue du Dr Rémy (tel. 80 43 34 67). Rooms are only slightly more expensive than the prices quoted above.

HOSTELS

1 bd Champollion (tel. 80 71 32 12). Take bus 5 from Place Grangier to the last stop, Epirey. Place Grangier is near Place Darcy. From the latter, rue de la Poste runs into Place Grangier. From rue de la Liberté take rue du Château. Bus 4 runs to Place Grangier from the train station.

FOYERS

Foyer International des Etudiants, 1 av. Maréchal Leclerc (tel. 80 71 51 01). Offers singles for about the same as you would pay for a dorm bed at the hostel, but is only open May–June. Bus 4 dir. Grézille to Parc des Sports.

UNIVERSITY ACCOMMODATION

Singles in university dorms are let by CROUS, 3 rue Docteur Maret (tel. 80 50 16 03). Again, prices are similar to those of dorm beds at the hostel. The office is open Mon.–Fri. 9–11.30 a.m. and 2–4.30 p.m. During the university vacation (July–Sept.) you can try the dormitories on your own if the CROUS office is closed. The Résidence Universitaire Mansard is on bd Mansard (tel. 80 66 18 22), while the Résidence Universitaire Montmuzzard is on bd Gabriel (tel. 80 39 68 01). Bus 9 serves both dormitories.

CAMPING

Camping du Lac, bd Kir (tel. 80 74 53 19). Open 1 Apr.–15
Sept. 3FF (£0.30; $0.50) per tent, 7FF (£0.75; $1.25) per
person. About 10 minutes' walk from the train station away
from the town centre. At the end of rue du Dr Rémy turn
right through the underpass, then follow av. Albert 1er
to the right of the exit.

Lille

Tourist Office
Office de Tourisme de Lille, Palais Rihour, Place Rihour, B.P.
205, 59002 Lille cedex (tel. 20 30 81 00). Open Mon. 2–6 p.m.,
Tues.–Sat. 10 a.m.–6 p.m. A well-stocked office with plenty
of information on the city and the Pas de Calais. Rooms found
in local hotels. 'Accueil de France' service available.

Basic Directions
The train station is about 10 minutes' walk from the Tourist
Office in the heart of the old city. From Place de la Gare follow
rue Faidherbe towards Place du Théâtre. At Place du Théâtre,
turn left down the side of the square and follow rue des
Manneliers, then go straight ahead at the junction with Place
De Gaulle (right) and rue Neuve (left) into Place Rihour.
From the left-hand side of Place de la Gare, rue de Tournai
runs back along the side of the train station. A short distance
along rue de Tournai, rue du Molinel runs off to the right,
passing the end of rue Sainte-Anne (right) before being crossed
by rue de Paris. Rue du Molinel ends at Place Richebe, just
off bd de la Liberté, across which is Place de la République.
Heading right along bd de la Liberté, the street is crossed by
rue Nationale (a point more easily reached from the train
station by walking to Place De Gaulle, where rue Nationale
begins). Turning left down Nationale from here you quickly
arrive at Place de Strasbourg, and ultimately at Place Maréchal-

Leclerc. If instead of turning down rue Nationale you continue along bd de la Liberté, you arrive at Place Daubenton, from which bd Vauban runs left down to Place Maréchal-Leclerc.

HOTELS

Cheapest rooms around 90FF (£9.50; $16.50)

Des Voyageurs, 10 Place de la Gare (tel. 20 06 43 14).
Paris Nord, 14 rue du Molinel (tel. 20 06 27 54).

Cheapest rooms around 100FF (£10.50; $18.50)

Constantin, 5 rue des Fossés (tel. 20 54 32 26). Just off Place Rihour. The street runs between rue de la Vieille Comédie and rue de l'Hôpital-Militaire.
Coq Hardi, 34 Place de la Gare (tel. 20 06 05 89).
Floréal, 21 rue Sainte-Anne (tel. 20 06 36 21).
De Londres, 16 Place de la Gare (tel. 20 06 12 67).
De Namur, 10 rue du Molinel (tel. 20 06 34 88).

Cheapest rooms around 110FF (£11.50; $20)

Chopin, 4 rue de Tournai (tel. 20 06 35 80).
Faidherbe, 42 Place de la Gare (tel. 20 06 27 93).
De la Tradition, 73–75 rue Masséna (tel. 20 57 14 52). Rue Masséna crosses rue Nationale at Place de Strasbourg.

Cheapest rooms around 120FF (£12.50; $22)

Du Globe, 1 bd Vauban (tel. 20 57 29 58)
Du Moulin d'Or, 15 rue du Molinel (tel. 20 06 12 67).
Liberty, 16 rue Baptiste-Monnoyer (tel. 20 57 31 16). At the junction with 169 bd de la Liberté.
Saint-Nicholas, 11 bis, rue Nicolas-Leblanc (tel. 20 57 73 26). The street runs off Place de la République.

Cheapest rooms around 130FF (£13.50; $24)

Central Hôtel, 91 rue Boucher-de-Perthes (tel. 20 54 64 63).

The street crosses rue Nationale just beyond Place de Strasbourg.

De France, 10 rue de Béthune (tel. 20 57 14 78). From rue du Molinel turn right along rue des Tanneurs, then left at rue de Béthune. From Place Rihour take rue de la Vieille Comédie, then turn right up rue de Béthune.

Cheapest rooms around 140FF (£14.50; $25.50)

Minerva, 28 rue Anatole-France (tel. 20 55 25 11). From rue Faidherbe turn right down rue des Comines, left along rue Quenette, then left again on to rue Anatole-France.

Cheapest rooms around 150FF (£15.50; $27.50)

Brueghel, 35 Parvis St-Maurice (tel. 20 06 06 69). Between rue Sainte-Anne and rue de Paris.

Saint-Maurice, 8 Parvis St-Maurice (tel. 20 06 27 40). Between rue Sainte-Anne and rue de Paris.

Cheapest rooms around 160FF (£16.75; $29)

Monte Carlo, 17 place des Reigneaux (tel. 20 06 06 93). Just off Place de la Gare, to the right of rue Faidherbe.

Cheapest rooms around 170FF (£17.75; $31)

Continental, 11 Place de la Gare (tel. 20 06 22 24).

Cheapest rooms around 190FF (£19.75; $34.50)

Grand Hôtel de l'Univers et des Reigneaux, 19 Place des Reigneaux (tel. 20 06 99 69). Just off Place de la Gare, to the right of rue Faidherbe.

Cheapest rooms around 200FF (£20.75; $36.50)

De la Paix, 46 bis, rue de Paris (tel. 20 54 63 93).

HOSTEL

1 av. Julien-Destrée (FUAJ) (tel. 20 52 98 94). Around 45FF (£4.75; $8.50). Opposite the Foire Commercial (Métro station: Foire Commercial), a 10-minute walk from the train station. Follow rue de Tournai, head left on rue Javary, then right on to av. Julien-Destrée.

CAMPING

There are a number of campsites in the surrounding area. Information is available from the Tourist Office, or from the Camping Club de Lille, 13 rue Baggio (tel. 20 53 77 40).

If you are heading into Belgium there are two sites which may be of particular interest:

Sportstadion, Westerlaan 2, Waregem (tel. 056 606289). Around 65BF (£1.10; $2) per tent, 55BF (£0.90; $1.50) per person. Waregem is about 30 miles from Lille, on the Lille-Kortrijk-Gent-Antwerpen train line just beyond Kortrijk, and just off the A14-E3.

Camping Communal de l'Orient, Vieux Chemin de Mons, Tournai (tel. 069 222635). Open all year round. Around 70BF (£1.20; $2) per tent, 60BF (£1; $1.75) per person. Tournai is about 20 miles from Lille, just over the Belgian border. There are good road and rail links between Lille and Tournai, and onwards from Tournai to Brussels or Mons.

Lyon

Tourist Offices
Office de Tourisme/Bureau des Congrès de Lyon/ Communauté, Place Bellecour, B.P. 2254, 69214 Lyon cedex 02 (tel. 78 42 25 75). The Tourist Board operates several Tourist Information offices throughout the city.

Pavillon du Tourisme, Place Bellecour. Open mid-June–mid-

Sept., Mon.–Fri. 9 a.m.–7 p.m., Sat. 9 a.m.–6 p.m., Sun. 10 a.m.–6 p.m.; at other times of year, the office closes one hour earlier each day. 'Accueil de France' service available. Métro: Bellecour, or 10 minutes' walk along rue Victor Hugo from Lyon-Perrache train station.

Bureau d'Information Perrache. In the Carte Perrache, in front of Lyon-Perrache. Open Mon.–Sat. 9 a.m.–12.30 p.m. and 2–6 p.m.

Fourvière. Open, in peak season, daily from 9 a.m.–1 p.m. and 2–6.30 p.m.

Agence de Villeurbaine, 3 av. Aristide Briand (tel. 78 68 13 20) Open Mon.–Fri. 9 a.m.–6 p.m., Sat. 9 a.m.–5 p.m.

Finding Accommodation
Finding suitable accommodation in Lyon should be relatively easy. Many of the cheapest hotels are in the area around Lyon-Perrache train station. In contrast, the hotels around the Part-Dieu train station are relatively expensive. If you arrive at Part-Dieu, there are frequent connections to Lyon-Perrache by main line train, while the two stations are also linked by the city's Métro. If for any reason you cannot find a bed, head for the 'Accueil en Gare', located in the covered walkway linking Lyon-Perrache train station to the Centre Perrache.

HOTELS

Cheapest rooms around 110FF (£11.50; $20)

Vichy, 60 bis, rue de la Charité (tel. 78 37 42 58). Perrache district.

Cheapest rooms around 120FF (£12.50; $22)

Vaubecour, 28 rue Vaubecour (tel. 78 37 44 91). Perrache.
Croix-Pâquet, 11 Place Croix-Pâquet (tel. 78 28 51 49). Terreaux district.
Des Facultés, 104 rue Sébastien-Gryphe (tel. 78 72 22 65). Préfecture-Guillotière.

Nicolaï, 8 rue Nicolaï (tel. 78 72 48 43). Préfecture-Guillotière.

Cheapest rooms around 130FF (£13.50; $24)

Célestins, 4 rue des Archers (tel. 78 37 63 32). Bellecour.

Cheapest rooms around 140FF (£14.50; $25.50)

Simplon, 11 rue Duhamel (tel. 78 37 41 00). Perrache.
D'Ainay, 14 rue des Remparts d'Ainay (tel. 78 42 43 42).
   Perrache.
Alexandra, 49 rue Victor-Hugo (tel. 78 37 75 79). Perrache.
Chez-Soi, 4 Place Carnot (tel. 78 37 18 30). Perrache.
Saint-Étienne, 39 rue Victor-Hugo (entrance on rue Jarente)
   (tel. 78 37 01 92). Perrache.
Du Tourisme, 44 bis, quai Jar (tel. 78 83 73 48). Vaise.
Saint-Michel, 64 rue Saint-Michel (tel. 78 72 48 84).
   Préfecture-Guillotière.

Cheapest rooms around 150FF (£15.50; $27.50)

Victoria, 3 rue Delandine (tel. 78 37 57 61). Perrache.
De Genève, 10 quai Perrache (tel. 78 37 11 59). Perrache.
Saint-Pothin, 110 rue Vendôme (tel. 78 52 09 31). Brotteaux.

Cheapest rooms around 160FF (£16.75; $29)

Le Terme, 7 rue Sainte-Cathérine (tel. 78 28 30 45). Terreaux.
Valmy, 15 rue des Tanneurs (tel. 78 83 55 59). Vaie.
Celtic, 5 Place Saint-Paul (tel. 78 28 01 12). Vieux Lyon.

Cheapest rooms around 170FF (£17.75; $31)

La Loire, 19 cours de Verdun (tel. 78 37 44 29). Perrache.
   Closed 1–15 Aug.
Touring, 37 cours de Verdun (tel. 78 37 39 03). Perrache.
Morand, 99 rue de Créqui (tel. 78 52 29 96). Brotteaux.

Cheapest rooms around 180FF (£18.75; $33)

Dauphiné, 3 rue Duhamel (tel. 78 37 24 19). Perrache.

Mont-Blanc, 26 cours de Verdun (tel. 78 37 35 36). Perrache.
Montesquieu, 36 rue Montesquieu (tel. 78 72 47 47).
Préfecture-Guillotière.

Cheapest rooms around 200FF (£20.75; $36.50)

La Marne, 78 rue de la Charité (tel. 78 37 07 46). Perrache.
Closes for three weeks in August.
Normandie, 3 rue de Bélier (tel. 78 37 31 36). Perrache.
Foch, 59 av. Maréchal-Foch (tel. 78 89 14 01). Brotteaux.
De Saxe, 127 rue Vendôme (tel. 78 24 53 89). Brotteaux.
Closes for two weeks in August.

Cheapest rooms around 210FF (£22; $38.50)

Dubost, 19 Place Carnot (tel. 78 42 00 46). Perrache.
Moderne, 15 rue Dubois (tel. 78 42 21 83).
Cordeliers-République.
Iris, 36 rue de l'Arbre-Sec (tel. 78 39 93 80). Terreaux.
Le Salon Doré, 55 cours Richard-Vittan (tel. 78 54 33 41).
Hôpitaux-Monplaisir-Montchat. Closed in August.

B&B

Association Bed & Breakfast, 4 rue Joliot-Curie (tel. 78 36 37
19). The office in Vieux-Lyon is open Mon.–Sat. 2–6 p.m.
Singles from 90–200FF (£9.50–20.75; $16.50–36.50),
doubles from 75–130FF (£7.75–13.50; $13.50–24) per
person.

HOSTELS

Lyon-Venissieux (FUAJ), 51 rue Roger Salengro (tel. 78 76
39 23). 50FF (£5.25; $9) for IYHF members, 20FF (£2.10;
$3.50) supplement for non-members. Two and a half miles
from the centre. From Perrache, before 9 p.m., take the
métro to Bellecour then bus 35 to av. Georges Levy. After
9 p.m., take bus 53 from Perrache to Avenue Viviani/bd
des Etats-Unis. From Part-Dieu, leave the station by the

Vivier Merle exit and take bus 36 dir. Minguette to av. Viviani/bd Joliot Curie.

Résidence Benjamin Delessert, 145 avenue Jean Jaurès (tel. 78 61 41 41). Open July–Aug. Singles 80FF (£8.50; $14.50), doubles 125FF (£13; $23). Métro: Macé, then a 10-minute walk.

CAMPING

All the sites are about six miles out of the city.

Dardilly, Camping International 'Porte de Lyon' (tel. 78 35 64 55). Four-star site. 50FF (£5.25; $9) per tent, 18FF (£1.90; $3.50) p.p. Open 1 Mar.–31 Oct. Bus 19 from the Town Hall (métro: Hôtel de Ville) dir. Ecully-Dardilly to the Parc d'Affaires stop.

'Les Barolles', Saint Denis Laval (tel. 78 56 05 56). One-star site to the south-west of the city. Open 1 Mar.–31 Dec.

There are another three sites at the Parc de Loisirs de Miribil-Jonage, north-east of the city.

Marseilles (Marseille)

Tourist Offices
Office Municipal de Tourisme de Marseille, 4 La Canabière, 13001 Marseille (tel. 91 54 91 11). July–Sept., open daily 8 a.m.–8 p.m.; Oct.–June, 9 a.m.–7.30 p.m., Sun. 10 a.m.–5.30 p.m. Free accommodation service and a good range of information on the city. 'Accueil de France' service not available. From Gare St-Charles (the main train station) go down the steps into bd d'Athènes. Go straight ahead along bd d'Athènes and then rue Dugommier into La Canabière, then head left to the Tourist Office. Another branch operates in Marseille St-Charles (tel. 91 50 59 18). Open, in summer, daily 8 a.m.–8 p.m.; in winter, Mon.–Fri. 9 a.m.–noon and 2–6.30 p.m.

HOTELS

Cheapest rooms in the one-star hotels below cost 110–160FF (£11.50–16.75; $20–29). Most of the hotels are within easy walking distance of the train station.

Salvator, 6 bd Louis Salvator (tel. 91 48 78 25). Métro: Estrangin or N.D. du Mont.

Nady, 157 cours Lieutaud (tel. 91 48 70 21). Métro: Castellane.

Caravelle, 5 rue Guy-Moquet (tel. 91 48 44 99). Métro: Noailles.

Lutia, 31 av. du Prado (tel. 91 79 22 63). Métro: Perier or Castellane.

Gambetta, 49 Allée Léon Gambetta (tel. 91 62 07 88). Métro: Réformés or Noailles.

Moderne, 11 bd de la Libération (tel. 91 62 28 66). Métro: Réformés.

Pavillon, 27 rue Pavillon (tel. 91 33 76 90). Métro: Vieux-Port.

Provenal, 32 rue Paradis (tel. 91 33 11 15). Métro: Vieux-Port.

Quillici, 13 Place des Marseillaises (tel. 91 90 14 48). By the main train station. Métro: St-Charles.

Sphinx, 16 rue Sénac (tel. 91 48 70 59). Métro: Réformés or Noailles.

Athènée, 63 rue de la Palud (tel. 91 54 36 74). Métro: Estrangin or N.D. du Mont.

Bearn, 63 rue Sylvabelle (tel. 91 37 75 83). Métro: Estrangin.

Edmond Rostand, 31 rue Dragon (tel. 91 37 74 95). Métro: Estrangin.

Impéria, 36 bd Louis Salvator (tel. 91 48 67 01). Métro: Estrangin or N.D. du Mont.

Montgrand, 50 rue Montgrand (tel. 91 33 33 81). Métro: Pierre Puget.

Guillemain, 357 av. du Prado (tel. 91 77 88 53). Métro: RD–PT du Prado.

Azur, 24 cours Franklin Roosevelt (tel. 91 42 74 38). Métro: Réformés.

Beaulieu Glaris, 1 Place Marseillaises (tel. 91 90 70 59). By the main train station. Métro: St-Charles.

De Bourgogne, 31 allées Léon Gambetta (tel. 91 62 19 49). Métro: Réformés or Noailles.

De la Bourse, 4 rue Paradis (tel. 91 33 74 75). Métro: Vieux-Port.

Little Palace, 39 bd d'Athènes (tel. 91 90 12 93). Go down the steps from Gare St-Charles. Métro: St-Charles.

Sevigné, 28 rue Bretueil (tel. 91 81 29 20). Métro: Vieux-Port.

Monthyon, 60 rue Montgrand (tel. 91 33 85 55). Métro: Pierre Puget.

Hotel Grill Balladins, 35 bd Rabatau (tel. 91 25 75 75). Métro: RT–PT du Prado.

Fortia, 32 rue Fortia (tel. 91 33 33 75).

The cheapest rooms at the two-star hotels below cost around 150–200FF (£15.50–20.75; $27.50–36.50). Most are within easy walking distance of Marseille St-Charles.

Bellevue, 34 quai du Port (tel. 91 91 11 64). By the old port. Métro: Vieux-Port.

Estérel, 124 rue Paradis (tel. 91 37 13 90). Métro: Estrangin or Castellane.

La Préfecture, 9 bd Louis Salvator (tel. 91 54 31 60). Métro: Estrangin or N.D. du Mont.

Sainte-Anne, 23 rue Bretueil (tel. 91 33 13 21). Métro: Vieux-Port.

Du Velay, 18 rue Berlioz (tel. 91 48 31 37). Métro: Castellane.

Du Pharo, 71 bd Charles Livon (tel. 91 31 08 71).

Peron, 119 corniche Kennedy (tel. 91 31 01 41).

YOUTH HOSTELS

Both the hostels are about four miles out from the city centre.

Marseille-Bois Luzy (FUAJ), Château de Bois Luzy, Allée des Primivères (tel. 91 49 06 18). The smaller of the two hostels, with 90 beds in summer. Also has space for tents. Bus 8 from Bourse, near La Canabière.

Marseille-Bonneveine (FUAJ), 47 av. Joseph Vidal (Impasse de Bonfils), Bonneveine (tel. 91 73 21 81). 185 beds. From

St-Charles train station take the métro to RD–PT du Prado, then bus 44 dir. Roy d'Espagne to Pl. Bonnefons.

CAMPING

Camping de Bonneveine, 187 av. Clot-Bey (tel. 91 73 26 99). About four miles from the city centre. Métro and bus as for the Bonneveine hostel (see above). Ask the driver for the stop near the campsite.

Nice

Tourist Offices
Nice Office de Tourisme, Acropolis, 1 Esplanade Kennedy, 06508 Nice cedex. Write to this office if you want information on the city in advance. On arrival, head for one of the information offices the Tourist Board operates in the city.

Bureau d'Accueil Gare SNCF, avenue Thiers (tel. 93 87 07 07). Open June–Sept., Mon.–Sat. 8.45 a.m.–6.30 p.m., Sun. 8.45 a.m.–12.15 p.m. and 2–5.45 p.m.; Oct.–May, Mon.–Sat. 8.45 a.m.–12.30 p.m. and 2–6 p.m. Free plan of the city. Reserves local hotels for a 10FF (£1.10; $1.75) fee, but not before 10 a.m. 'Accueil de France' service available. The office is next to the train station.

Bureau d'Accueil, 5 avenue Gustav-V (tel. 93876060). This branch office near Place Masséna keeps the same hours as the office by the train station.

Bureau d'Accueil Nice-Ferber (tel. 93833264). Close to the airport.

Finding Accommodation
Beds are difficult to find in Nice at any time in summer, but especially so during the Jazz Parade in July. If you arrive early in the morning at this time, try phoning a few hotels or searching for a room in the area around the train station. If you are not having any success, try to get to the Tourist Office

for about 9.30 a.m. and start queueing so you get the best
rooms they have to offer.

HOTELS

All the hotels listed below are close to the station or the town
centre. Prices quoted are for two people sharing a room. Some
hotels offer reductions of up to 30 per cent for single occupancy;
others offer no reduction at all.

Cheapest rooms around 110FF (£11.50; $20)

Miron, 4 rue Miron (tel. 93 62 16 60).
Le Commodore, 10 rue Barbéris (tel. 93 89 08 44).
Mignon, 26 rue de la Buffa (tel. 93 88 07 43).
Pastoral, 27 rue Assalit (tel. 93 85 17 22).

Cheapest rooms around 120FF (£12.50; $22)

Astrid, 26 rue Pertinax (tel. 93 62 14 64).
De France, 24 bd Raimbaldi (tel. 93 85 18 04/93 62 11 44).
Little Masséna, 22 rue Masséna (tel. 93 87 72 34).
Lyonnais, 20 rue de Russie (tel. 93 88 70 74).
Saint-François, 3 rue Saint-François (tel. 93 85 88 69/93 13 40
    18
Wilson, 39 rue Hôtel-des-Postes (tel. 93 85 47 79).
Chauvain, 8 rue Chauvain (tel. 93 85 34 01).
Corédia, 19 rue Alsace-Lorraine (tel. 93 88 25 15).

Cheapest rooms around 130FF (£13.50; $24)

La Belle Meunière, 21 av. Durante (tel. 93 88 66 15).
De Calais, 2 rue Chauvain (tel. 93 62 22 44).
Darcy, 28 rue d'Angleterre (tel. 93 88 67 06).
Family, 34 bd Gambetta (tel. 93 88 58 92).
Idéal Bristol, 22 rue Paganini (tel. 93 88 60 72).
Interlaken, 26 av. Durante (tel. 93 88 30 15).
Les Mimosas, 26 rue de la Buffa (tel. 93 88 05 59).
Au Picardy, 10 bd Jean-Jaurès (tel. 93 85 75 51).

Rialto, 55 rue de la Buffa (tel. 93 88 15 04).

Cheapest rooms around 140FF (£14.50; $25.50)

Central, 10 rue de la Suisse (tel. 93 88 85 08).
Novelty, 26 rue d'Angleterre (tel. 93 87 51 73).
Petit Louvre, 10 rue Emma Tiranty (tel. 93 80 15 54).
H0tel du Forez, 27 rue Gloffnedo (tel. 93 85 36 75).
Les Orangers, 10 bis, av. Durante (tel. 93 87 51 41).
Astoria, 6 bd François Grosso (tel. 93 44 74 10).

Cheapest rooms around 150FF (£15.50; $27.50)

Du Centre, 2 rue de Suisse (tel. 93 88 83 85).
Carlone, 2 bd François Grosso (tel. 93 44 71 61).
Les Cigales, 16 rue Dalpozzo (tel. 93 88 33 75).
Notre-Dame, 22 rue de Russie (tel. 93 88 70 44).

Cheapest rooms around 160FF (£16.75; $29)

Canada, 8 rue Halévy (tel. 93 87 98 94).
Carnot, 8 bd Carnot (tel. 93 89 56 54).
Maru, 11 rue Alexandre Mari (tel. 93 80 06 83).
D'Orsay, 18–20 rue Alsace-Lorraine (tel. 93 88 45 02).
Regency, 2 rue Saint-Siagre (tel. 93 62 17 44).
Soleda, 16 av. St-Jean-Baptiste (tel. 93 85 39 05).

Cheapest rooms around 170FF (£17.75; $31)

Crillon, 44 rue Pastorelli (tel. 93 85 43 59).
Imperial, 8 bd Carabacel (tel. 93 62 21 40).
Des Nations, 25 av. Durante (tel. 93 88 30 58).
Le Congrès, 11 rue du Congrès (tel. 93 87 35 62).
Les Mouettes, 11 rue du Congrès (tel. 93 88 17 76).

Cheapest rooms around 180FF (£18.75; $33)

De Berne, 1 av. Thiers (tel. 93 88 25 08).
Châteauneuf, 3 rue Châteauneuf (tel. 93 96 82 74/93 96 28 33).
Excelsior, 19 av. Durante (tel. 93 88 18 05).

Ostende, 3 rue Alsace-Lorraine (tel. 93 88 72 48).

Cheapest rooms around 190FF (£19.75; $34.50)

Camélias, 3 rue Spitalieri (tel. 93 62 15 54).
Clair Hôtel, 23 bd Carnot/Impasse Terra Amata (tel. 93 89
    69 89).
Flor-Amy, 13 rue d'Italie (tel. 93 88 56 92).
D'Italie, 9 rue Paul Déroulède (tel. 93 88 35 90).
De la Mer, 4 Place Masséna (tel. 93 92 09 10/93 80 87 96).
Paradis, 1 rue Paradis (tel. 93 87 71 23).
Lorrain, 6 rue Gubernatis (tel. 93 85 42 90).
Rex, 3 rue Masséna (tel. 93 87 87 38).

Cheapest rooms around 200FF (£20.75; $36.50)

Des Anges, 1 Place Masséna (tel. 93 82 12 28).
Cresp, 8 rue St-François-de-Paule (tel. 93 85 91 76).

Cheapest rooms around 215FF (£22.50; $39)

Armenonville, 20 av. des Fleurs (tel. 93 96 86 00).
Avenue, 47 bis, av. Jean Médecin (tel. 93 88 48 73).
Carlyna, 8 rue Sacha-Guitry (formerly rue St-Michel) (tel. 93
    80 77 21).
Colmar, 19 rue Assalit (tel. 93 62 14 02).
Cronstadt, 3 rue Cronstadt (tel. 93 82 00 30).
Des Flandres, 6 rue de Belgique (tel. 93 88 78 94).
La Malouine, 62 bd Carnot (tel. 93 89 56 80/93 26 08 46).
De Savoie, 39 rue d'Angleterre (tel. 93 88 35 73).

UNIVERSITY ACCOMMODATION

Rooms in vacant student dormitories can often be let during
the summer. Details are available from CROUS, 18 av. des
Fleurs (tel. 93 96 73 73). At any time of year, women can try
calling Cité Universitaire, Residence 'Les Collinettes', 3 av.
Robert Schumann (tel. 93 97 06 64/93 89 23 64), where singles
cost around 100FF (£10.50; $18.50).

HOSTELS/FOYERS

Route Forestière du Mont Alban (FUAJ) (tel. 93 89 23 64). Midnight curfew. B&B around 70FF (£7.25; $13). On top of a hill, about three miles from the train station. Bus 5 from the train station to Place Masséna, then bus 14 to Alban Fort. Both buses cost 8FF (£0.85; $1.50). Services run until 7.30 p.m.

Let's Go Meublés, 3rd floor, 22 rue Pertinax (tel. 93 80 98 00). Near the train station. No curfew. 51FF (£5.20; $9.75) including showers and blankets.

Meublé Abadie, 2nd floor, 22 rue Pertinax (tel. 93 85 81 21). Midnight curfew.

Espace Magnan, 31 rue Louis de Coppet (tel. 93 86 28 75). Open June–Sept. 55FF (£5.75; $10). Close to the beach and the Promenade des Anglais. From the train station, take bus 23 and ask the driver where to get off.

Bale des Anges, 55 Chemin de St-Antoine (tel. 93 86 76 74).

Relais International de la Jeunesse 'Clairvallon', 26 av. Scudéri (tel. 93 81 27 63). Midnight curfew. B&B 70FF (£7.25; $13). Set in an old house in Cimiez, about six miles out of Nice. Easily reached by bus 15 from Place Masséna.

Jean Médecin, 25 Ancien Chemin de Lanterne (tel. 93 83 34 61).

Forum Nice-Nord, 10 bd Comte de Falicon (tel. 93 84 24 37).

Montebello, 96 av. Valrose (tel. 93 84 19 81).

Saint-Antoine, 69 Chemin de St-Antoine (tel. 93 86 37 19).

De la Plaine (tel. 93 29 90 04) and Des Bluets (tel. 93 29 90 05). Both at 273 Route de Grenoble. Open to men aged 18 and over only.

'Les Sagnes', 59 bis, Route de Grenoble (tel. 93 83 76 28). Open to men aged 18 and over only.

Riquier, 248 bd du Mont-Boron (tel. 93 55 44 28). Men aged 18 and over only.

Sonacotra, Quartier du Château, St-André de Nice (tel. 93 54 85 70).

HOSTELS NEARBY

Plateau St-Michel, Menton (FUAJ) (tel. 93 93 59 31 4). A short trip away by train.

CAMPING

No really convenient site in Nice. Camping Terry, 768 Route de Grenoble St-Isidore (tel. 93 08 11 58) has only 30 places. The site is four miles north of the airport, far from any bus route. There is a good choice of sites in Villeneuve-Loubet, only five miles along the coast on the railway line to Cannes. The Tourist Information Centre at Nice station can give you a map of these sites, some of which are listed below. Open all year unless otherwise stated.

L'Orée de Vaugrenier, bd des Groules (tel. 93 33 57 30). Open 15 Mar.–31 Oct.

La Vieille Ferme, bd des Groules (tel. 93 33 41 44). Two sites: four star and one star.

De l'Hippodrome, 2 av. des Rives (tel. 93 20 02 00).

L'Ensoleillado, 49 av. de l'Eglise Christophe (tel. 93 20 90 04). Open 15 Feb.–15 Oct.

Neptune, av. des Baumettes (tel. 93 73 93 81). Open 15 Mar.–15 Oct.

La Tour de la Madone, Route de Grasse (tel. 93 20 96 11). Open 15 Mar.–31 Oct.

Paris

Unless you have booked accommodation in advance the first thing you should do on arrival is head for a room-finding service. Making use of these room-finding services will probably save you time, frustration and money; except perhaps in winter, when the number of visitors has fallen off. The best rooms go early in the day, so the quicker you get there the better. If you arrive by train, there is at least one room-finding organization at all the stations, with the exception of St-Lazare (which is unfortunate if you are arriving on the boat-train from Dieppe, or from anywhere in Normandy).

The Office du Tourisme et des Congrès de Paris operates seven offices in the city during the peak season. A fee of 15FF (£1.60; $3) per person is charged for finding a room in a one-star hotel (if this seems high to you, consider the fact that the same service in London costs over three times as much), while for beds in hostels/foyers the fee is 5FF (£0.50; $1) per person.

Bureau d'Accueil Central, 127 av. des Champs-Élysées 75008 Paris (tel. (1) 47 23 61 72). The head office. Open daily 9 a.m.–8 p.m. The 'Accueil de France' service is available at this office. Métro: Charles de Gaulle-Etoile.

Bureau Gare du Nord, 18 rue de Dunkerque (tel. (1) 45 26 94 82). Open, in peak season, Mon.–Sat. 8 a.m.–9 p.m., Sun. 1–8 p.m.; at other times, Mon.–Sat. 8 a.m.–8 p.m. Métro: Gare du Nord.

Bureau Gare de l'Est (tel. (1) 46 07 17 73). In the station arrivals hall. Open, in peak season, Mon.–Sat. 8 a.m.–9 p.m.; at other times, Mon.–Sat. 8 a.m.–8 p.m. Métro: Gare de l'Est.

Bureau Gare de Lyon (tel. (1) 43 43 33 24). By the exit from the main lines. Same hours as Gare de l'Est. Métro: Gare de Lyon.

Bureau Gare d'Austerlitz (tel. (1) 45 84 91 70). In the main line arrivals hall. Open, in peak season, Mon.–Sat. 8 a.m.–9 p.m.; at other times, Mon.–Sat. 8 a.m.–3 p.m. Métro: Gare d'Austerlitz.

Bureau Gare Montparnasse, 15 bd de Vaugirard (tel. (1) 43 22 19 19). Same hours as Gare de l'Est. Métro: Montparnasse-Bienvenue.

Bureau Tour Eiffel, Champ de Mars (tel. (1) 45 51 22 15). Open May–Sept., daily 11 a.m.–6 p.m. Métro: Champ de Mars Tour Eiffel.

Accueil des Jeunes en France (AJF) is a tourist agency especially for young travellers. AJF is run on a non-profit-making basis, which helps keep charges low. The commission for finding a room in a hotel or hostel/foyer is 10FF (£1.10; $1.80) per person, except for beds in AJF hostels/foyers, which are located free of charge. Payment on booking with AJF is the norm. AJF operate four offices in the city, all of which will help with general tourist information as well as booking beds.

Beaubourg, 119 rue Saint-Martin (tel. (1) 42 77 87 80). The head office of AJF, opposite the Pompidou Centre. Open all year round, Mon.–Sat. 9.30 a.m.–7 p.m. The office also runs a poste restante service. Métro: Rambuteau or Les Halles; RER: Châtelet–Les Halles

Gare du Nord (tel. (1) 42 85 86 19). Inside the new suburban station. Open June–Oct., daily 8 a.m.–10 p.m. Métro: Gare du Nord.

Hôtel de Ville, 16 rue du Pont Louis-Philippe (tel. (1) 42 78 04 82). Open all year round, Mon.–Fri. 9.30 a.m.–6.30 p.m. Métro: Hôtel de Ville or Pont Marie. From Hôtel de Ville, walk a short distance along the street and turn right. From Pont Marie, face the Seine and then follow the river along to your left.

Quartier Latin, 139 bd Saint-Michel (tel. (1) 43 54 95 86). Open Mar.–Oct., Mon.–Fri. 9.30 a.m.–6.30 p.m. RER: Port Royal. Walk down bd Saint-Michel from the RER station.

Arriving by Bus or Plane

The Gare Routière International at 8 Place Stalingrad is the terminus for most international services arriving in Paris. Access to the city centre is easy from the Stalingrad métro station. Most international flights touch down at the Roissy–Charles de Gaulle airport. A free bus connects the airport to the Roissy train station, from which RER lines B and D run to Gare du Nord and Châtelet–Les Halles. Catch the bus from Aérogare 1 arrival gate 28, Aérogare 2A gate 5, Aérogare 2B gate 6 or Aérogare 2D gate 6. From Orly airport, a free bus service operates between Orly Sud gate H or Orly Ouest gate F and the Orly train station from which the RER runs into the city.

Trouble Spots

The areas around Pigalle and Montmartre (the Moulin Rouge and Sacré Coeur are the main attractions) are a favourite haunt of petty thieves and pickpockets during the day, so take care of your valuables. Some of the cheaper hotels in these districts (9ème and 18ème *arrondissements*) are used by prostitutes. In the evening, young women walking in these parts without a male companion are likely to be harassed, almost certain to be verbally abused. These areas can be dangerous for anyone after dark, but particularly if you are alone and noticeably foreign. Day and night you should avoid the Pigalle, Anvers and Barbes-Rocheouard métro stations.

HOTELS

The number after the street name (e.g. 7e) refers to the arrondissement (district) of the city. Hotels in the 10e arrondissement are always within easy walking distance of Gare du Nord and Gare de l'Est (the two stations are virtually side by side).

Cheapest rooms around 110FF (£11.50; $20)

Brabant, 18 rue des Petits Hôtels, 10e (tel. (1) 47 70 12 32). Métro: Poissonière. The street runs between rue Lafayette (at Place Liszt) and bd de Magenta.

Cheapest rooms around 120FF (£12.50; $22)

Cambrai, 129 bis, bd de Magenta, 10e (tel. (1) 47 78 32 13). Métro: Gare de l'Est. From the station head right along rue de 8 mai 1945 on to bd de Magenta. From Gare du Nord follow bd de Denain away from the station, then head left down bd de Magenta.

Grand Hôtel d'Amiens, 88 rue de Faubourg Poissonière, 10e (tel. (1) 48 78 71 18). The street runs between the Poissonière and Bonne Nouvelle métro stations.

Cheapest rooms around 130FF (£13.50; $24)

De Lille, 2 rue Montholon, 9e (tel. (1) 47 70 38 76). Off rue

Lafayette between the Poissonière and Cadet métro stations.

De l'Industrie, 2 rue Gustave Goublier, 10e (tel. (1) 42 08 51 79). Off bd de Strasbourg between the Château d'Eau and Strasbourg-St-Denis métro stations. You can walk straight down bd de Strasbourg from Gare de l'Est.

Lafayette, 198 rue Lafayette, 10e (tel. (1) 40 35 76 07). Métro: Gare du Nord or Louis-Blanc. From Gare du Nord, walk left along place Roubaix, then turn left up rue Lafayette. Louis-Blanc is on rue Lafayette.

Sans-Souci, 113 bd de Ménilmontant, 11e (tel. (1) 43 57 00 58). Between the Ménilmontant (closest) and Père-Lachaise métro stations.

Cheapest rooms around 140FF (£14.60; $25.50)

Pacific, 70 rue du Château d'Eau, 10e (tel. (1) 47 70 07 91). Along rue du Château d'Eau from the Château d'Eau métro station. From the Jacques Bonsergent métro station, walk down rue de Lancry from bd de Magenta on to rue du Château d'Eau. From the République métro station, walk up bd de Magenta, then head left along rue du Château d'Eau.

Lux Hotel Picpus, 74 bd de Picpus, 12e (tel. (1) 43 43 08 46). Between the Picpus and Bel Air métro stations.

Printania, 91 av. du Dr Arnold Netter, 12e (tel. (1) 43 07 651 3). Off cours de Vincennes between the Porte de Vincennes (closest) and Nation métro stations.

Wattignies, 6 rue de Wattignies, 12e (tel. (1) 46 28 43 78). Métro: Dugommier. From bd de Reuilly turn down rue de Charenton, then left at rue de Wattignies.

Sthrau, 1 rue Sthrau, 13e (tel. (1) 45 83 20 35). At the corner with 74 rue Tolbiac. Walk along rue Tolbiac from the Tolbiac métro station.

Résidence Chalgrin, 10 rue Chalgrin, 16e (tel. (1) 45 00 19 91). Métro: Argentine. From av. de la Grande Armée, rue d'Argentine leads into rue Chalgrin.

Cheapest rooms around 150FF (£15.60; $27.50)

Des Alliés, 20 rue Berthollet, 5e (tel. (1) 43 31 47 52). Métro:
Gobelins. From av. des Gobelins turn left along bd du Port
Royal, then right at rue Berthollet.

Du Marché, 6 rue Faubourg St-Martin, 10e (tel. (1) 42 06 44
53). Métro: Strasbourg–St-Denis. The street runs parallel
to bd de Strasbourg, one block away.

Métropole Lafayette, 204 rue Lafayette, 10e (tel. (1) 46 07 72
69). See Hôtel Lafayette, above, for directions.

Arian-Hôtel, 102 av. de Choisy, 13e (tel. (1) 45 87 34 58).
Métro: Tolbiac or Place d'Italie. Rue Tolbiac crosses av. de
Choisy one block from the métro station. From Place
d'Italie, walk along av. de Choisy.

Cheapest rooms around 160FF (£16.70; $29)

Grand Hôtel des Arts-et-Métiers, 4 rue Borda, 3e (tel. (1) 48
87 73 89). Off rue Turbigo at the junction with rue Volta,
a short walk from the Arts-et-Métiers métro station.

Herse d'Or, 20 rue Saint-Antoine, 4e (tel. (1) 48 87 83 89).
Between the Bastille and St-Paul métro stations.

Port-Royal, 8 bd du Port Royal, 5e (tel. (1) 43 31 70 06). Métro:
Gobelins. Bd du Port Royal runs from the end of av. des
Gobelins.

Des Carmes, 5 rue des Carmes, 5e (tel. (1) 43 29 78 40). Métro:
Maubert-Mutualité. The street runs off Place Maubert.

Palais Bourbon, 49 rue de Bourgogne, 7e (tel. (1) 47 05 52
33). Métro: Varenne. From bd des Invalides both rue de
Varenne and rue de Grenelle lead into rue de Bourgogne.

Du Centre, 24 bis, rue Cler, 7e (tel. (1) 47 05 52 33). Métro:
Ecole Militaire. Rue Cler is left off av. de la Motte Piquet,
one block from the junction of the latter with av. Bosquet.

Blanche, 69 rue Blanche, 9e (tel. (1) 48 74 16 94). Between
the Blanche and Trinité métro stations.

Athèna, 16 rue Papillon, 9e (tel. (1) 47 70 56 43). The street
is off rue Lafayette between the Cadet (closest) and
Poissonière métro stations.

D'Alsace, 85 bd de Strasbourg, 10e (tel. (1) 40 37 75 41).
Between the Gare de l'Est and Château d'Eau métro
stations.

De Chabrol, 46 rue de Chabrol, 10e (tel. (1) 47 70 10 77).
Métro: Poissonière or Gare de l'Est. From Gare de l'Est,
head right along rue du 8 mai 1945.

Des Familles, 216 Faubourg Saint-Denis, 10e (tel. (1) 46 07
76 56). Métro: Gare du Nord or Chapelle. From Gare du
Nord, Faubourg Saint-Denis runs up the left-hand side of
the station as you leave by the main exit.

Grand Hôtel des Voyageurs, 9 rue du 8 may 1945, 10e (tel.
(1) 40 34 54 34). Métro: Gare de l'Est. The hotel is on the
street in front of the station.

De l'Europe, 74 rue Sedaine, 11e (tel. (1) 47 00 54 38). Métro:
Bréguet-Sabin. Rue Sedaine is off bd Richard Lenoir, close
to the métro station.

Baudin, 113 av. Ledru-Rollin, 11e (tel. (1) 47 00 18 91). Métro:
Ledru-Rollin.

Luna Park, 1 rue Jacquard, 11e (tel. (1) 48 05 65 50). Left off
rue Oberkampf, a short walk from the Parmentier métro
station (follow descending street numbers along rue
Oberkampf).

De l'Aveyron, 5 rue d'Austerlitz, 11e (tel. (1) 43 07 86 86).
Métro: Gare de Lyon (closest) or Bastille. Rue d'Austerlitz
is off rue de Lyon, between the two métro stations.

De Marseille, 21 rue d'Austerlitz, 11e (tel. (1) 43 43 54 22).
See Hôtel De l'Aveyron for directions.

Royal, 65 bd Saint-Michel, 13e (1) 45 35 02 48). Between the
Luxembourg and Port Royal RER stations.

Des Arts, 8 rue Coypel, 13e (tel. (1) 47 07 76 62). Métro: Place
d'Italie. The street runs between av. des Gobelins and bd
de l'Hôpital.

Des Beaux Arts, 2 rue Toussaint-Féron, 13e (tel. (1) 47 07 52
93). Métro: Tolbiac. The street runs off av. d'Italie one block
from the junction of rue Tolbiac and av. d'Italie.

Lebrun, 33 rue Lebrun, 13e (tel. (1) 47 07 97 02). Métro:
Gobelins. Rue Lebrun runs between av. des Gobelins and
bd St-Marcel.

De la Place des Alpes, 2 Place des Alpes, 13e (tel. (1) 43 29 78 40). Place des Alpes is on bd St-Vincent, between the Place d'Italie (closest) and Nationale métro stations.

Floridor, 28 Pl. Denfert Rochereau, 14e (tel. (1) 43 21 35 53). Métro: Denfert Rochereau.

Télémaque, 64 rue Daguerre/19 rue Roger, 14e (tel. (1) 43 20 72 92). Métro: Denfert Rochereau. Follow rue Froidevaux from Pl. Denfert Rochereau, then turn left.

Du Mont Blanc, 11 bd Victor, 15e (tel. (1) 48 28 16 79). Métro: Porte de Versailles.

Villa d'Auteil, 28 rue Poussain, 16e (tel. (1) 42 88 30 37). Métro: Porte d'Auteil or Michel Ange Auteil. From Porte d'Auteil rue Poussain runs parallel to the left of rue d'Auteil. From Michel Ange Auteil, rue Girodet and rue Bonizetti both run from Pl. J. Lorrain into rue Poussain.

Polonia, 3 rue de Chaumont, 19e (tel. (1) 42 49 87 15). Off av. Secrétan between the Jaurès and Bolivar métro stations.

Cheapest rooms around 170FF (£17.70; $31)

Henri IV, 25 Pl. Dauphine, 1e (tel. (1) 43 54 44 53). Métro: Pont-Neuf or Cité. From Pont Neuf, cross the bridge, go straight ahead, then turn left along rue H. Robert into the square. Place Dauphine is on the opposite side of the Conciergerie and the Palais de Justice from the Cité station.

Sainte Marie, 6 rue de la Ville Neuve, 2e (tel. (1) 42 33 21 61). Off bd de Bonne Nouvelle between the Bonne Nouvelle (closest) or Strasbourg–St-Denis métro stations.

De Bretagne, 87 rue des Archives, 3e (tel. (1) 48 87 83 14). Métro Rambuteau or Hôtel de Ville. From Rambuteau, follow rue Rambuteau into rue des Archives. From Hôtel de Ville, turn along rue des Archives from rue de Rivoli.

Sainte-Elisabeth, 10 rue Sainte-Elisabeth, 3e (tel. (1) 42 72 01 66). Off rue de Turbigo between the Arts et Métiers and Temple métro stations.

Andrea, 3 rue Saint-Bon, 4e (tel. (1) 42 78 43 93). Métro: Hôtel de Ville. Rue Saint-Bon is off rue de Rivoli as you head in the direction of bd de Sebastopol and the Palais de Louvre.

Maxime, 28 rue Censier, 5e (tel. (1) 43 31 16 15). Métro: Censier-Daubenton.

Marignan, 13 rue du Sommerard, 5e (tel. (1) 43 25 31 03). Métro: Maubert-Mutualité. At Pl. Maubert turn off bd St-Germain down rue des Carmes, then head right at rue du Sommerard.

Delhy's, 22 rue de l'Hirondelle, 6e (tel. (1) 43 26 58 25). Métro: St-Michel. The street runs off Pl. St-Michel one block from the Seine.

Peiffer, 6 rue de l'Arcade, 8e (tel. (1) 42 66 03 07). Off bd. Haussmann between the St-Augustin and Havre-Caumartin métro stations. From the Madelaine métro station, walk down the right-hand side of the church and then take one of the small streets into rue de l'Arcade.

Milan, 17 rue de St-Quentin, 10e (tel. (1) 40 37 88 50). Métro: Gare du Nord. Off Pl. de Roubaix, left of the train station exit.

Parmentier, 91 rue Oberkampf, 11e (tel. (1) 43 57 02 09). A short walk along rue Oberkampf from the Parmentier métro station.

Grand Hôtel Chaligny, 5 rue Chaligny, 12e (tel. (1) 43 43 87 04). Rue Chaligny crosses bd Diderot a short distance from the Reuilly-Diderot métro station.

Nievre, 18 rue d'Austerlitz, 12e (tel. (1) 43 43 87 04). See Hôtel De l'Aveyron, above, for directions.

De Bourgogne, 15 rue Godefroy, 13e (tel. (1) 45 35 37 92). Métro: Place d'Italie. Rue Godefroy runs off the square.

Paris Didot, 20 rue Ledion, 14e (tel. (1) 45 42 33 29). Métro: Plaisance. Walk along rue d'Alésia, turn right at rue Didot, then left at rue Ledion.

Ribera, 66 rue Lafontaine, 16e (tel. (1) 42 88 29 60). Métro: Jasmin. From av. Mozart follow rue Ribera into rue Lafontaine.

Ermitage, 42 bis, rue de l'Ermitage, 10e (tel. (1) 46 36 23 44). Métro: Jourdain (slightly closer) or Pyrénées. From Jourdain, walk down rue de Jourdain, then left along rue

des Pyrénées until the street is crossed by rue de
l'Ermitage. From the Pyrénées métro station, head straight
down rue des Pyrénées.

Cheapest rooms around 180FF (£18.75; $33)

De Rouen, 42 rue Croix-des-Petits-Champs, 1er (tel. (1) 42
61 38 21). Métro: Palais Royal Musée de Louvre. Turn left
off rue St-Honoré.

Studia, 51 bd Saint-Germain, 5e (tel. (1) 43 26 81 00). Between
the Odéon and Maubert-Mutualité métro stations.

Gay-Lussac, 29 rue Gay-Lussac, 5e (tel. (1) 43 54 23 96). The
street runs off bd St-Michel by the Luxembourg RER
station.

Grand Hôtel Léveque, 29 rue Cler, 7e (tel. (1) 47 05 49 15).
See Hôtel du Centre above for directions.

De France, 57 rue des Petites Ecuries, 10e (tel. (1) 47 70 15
83). Métro: Château D'Eau. The street runs off bd de
Strasbourg by the métro station.

De France, 159 av. Ledru-Rollin, 11e (tel. (1) 43 79 53 22).
Between the Voltaire and Ledru-Rollin métro stations.

Sport, 258 av. Daumesnil, 12e (tel. (1) 43 43 61 36). Métro:
Michel Bizot.

Terminus et des Sports, 96 cours de Vincennes, 12e (tel. (1)
43 43 97 93). Métro: Porte de Vincennes.

Home Fleuri, 75 rue Daguerre, 14e (tel. (1) 43 20 02 37).
Métro: Denfert-Rochereau. From Pl. Denfert-Rochereau
follow av. du Général Leclerc until you see rue Daguerre
on the right.

Royal Lecourbe, 286 rue Lecourbe, 15e (tel. (1) 45 58 06 05).
Métro: Boucicaut. Walk down av. Felix Faure, then turn
left down rue Duranton into rue Lecourbe.

Camélia, 24 bd Pasteur, 15e (tel. (1) 47 83 76 35). Métro:
Pasteur.

Atlas, 12 rue de l'Atlas, 19e (tel. (1) 42 08 50 12). Métro:
Belleville. The street runs right off bd de la Villette.

Mary's, 118 rue Orfila, 20e (tel. (1) 43 61 51 68). The street
runs off Pl. P. Signac by the Pelleport métro station. Rue

Orfila crosses rue des Pyrénées close to the Gambetta métro station.

Cheapest rooms around 190FF (£19.80; $35)

De Nice, 42 bis, rue de Rivoli, 4e (tel. (1) 42 78 55 29). Between the St-Paul and Hôtel de Ville métro stations on rue de Rivoli.

Des Academies, 15 rue de la Grande Chaumière, 6e (tel. (1) 43 26 66 44). Off bd de Raspail by the Vavin métro station.

Eiffel Rive Gauche, 6 rue du Gros Caillou, 7e (tel. (1) 45 51 24 56). From the Ecole Militaire métro station head along av. Bosquet, turn left at rue de Grenelle, then left at rue du Gros Caillou.

Paris Opéra, 76 rue de Provence, 9e (tel. (1) 48 74 12 15). Métro: Chaussée d'Antin or Trinité. From either station, follow rue de la Chaussée until it is crossed by rue de Provence.

Aviator, 20 rue Louis Blanc, 10e (tel. (1) 46 07 79 24). Métro: Louis-Blanc or Colonel-Fabien. The street runs out of place du Colonel-Fabien.

Kuntz, 2 rue des Deux Gares, 10e (tel. (1) 40 35 77 26). Métro: Gare du Nord or Gare de l'Est. From Gare du Nord follow rue du Faubourg St-Denis out of Pl. Roubaix away from the train station, then go left. From Gare de l'Est, follow rue d'Alsace up the side of the station (on the right as you leave the train station), then turn left.

Véronèse, 5 rue Véronèse, 13e (tel. (1) 47 07 20 90). Off av. des Gobelins between the Place d'Italie and Gobelins métro stations.

Novex, 8 rue Caillaux, 13e (tel. (1) 47 07 42 58). Off av. d'Italie close to the Maison Blanche métro station.

Victoria, 47 rue Bobillot, 13e (tel. (1) 45 80 59 88). Métro: Place d'Italie or Tolbiac. Walk down the street from Place d'Italie. From Tolbiac follow the ascending street numbers on rue Tolbiac until it reaches rue Bobillot.

Petit-Palace, 131 av. du Maine, 14e (tel. (1) 43 22 02 25). Métro: Montparnasse-Bienvenue.

Amiral, 90 rue de l'Amiral Roussin, 15e (tel. (1) 48 28 53 89).
Métro: Vaugirard. From Pl. A. Cherioux follow rue Blomet,
then turn left down rue de l'Amiral Roussin.

Mondial, 136 bd de Grenelle, 15e (tel. (1) 45 79 08 09). Métro:
La Motte Picquet-Grenelle.

Niel, 11 rue Saussier-Leroy, 17e (tel. (1) 42 27 99 29). From
the Ternes métro station walk along av. des Ternes, turn
right at rue Poncelet, then left at rue Saussier-Leroy.

Santana, 109 rue Legendre, 17e (tel. (1) 46 27 60 40). From
the La Fourche métro station follow av. de Clichy into rue
Legendre.

Cheapest rooms around 200FF (£20.80; $36.50)

Richelieu-Mazarin, 51 rue de Richelieu, 1cr (tel. (1) 42 97 46
20). Métro: Bourse, 4 Septembre or Richelieu-Drouot. The
street crosses rue de 4 septembre between the Bourse and
4 Septembre métro stations.

Nevers Luxembourg, 3 rue de l'Abbé-de-l'Epée, 5e (tel. (1)
43 26 81 83). The street is off bd St-Michel between the
Luxembourg and Port Royal RER stations.

Grand Hôtel Moderne, 33 rue des Ecoles, 5e (tel. (1) 43 54
37 78). Métro: Maubert-Mutualité.

De Chevreuse, 3 rue de Chevreuse, 6e (tel. (1) 43 20 93 16).
Off bd du Montparnasse close to the Vavin métro station
(follow ascending street numbers on bd du Montparnasse).

De Belgique, 10 rue de Bruxelles, 9e (tel. (1) 43 20 93 16).
Métro: Blanche or Place de Clichy. Rue de Bruxelles runs
out of Pl. Blanche, and off rue de Clichy, a short walk from
Pl. de Clichy.

Grand Hôtel du Prince Eugene, 12 rue du Château d'Eau,
10e (tel. (1) 42 39 89 13). See Hôtel Pacific. Jacques
Bonsergent and République are closer than Château d'Eau.

Modern'Hôtel, 89 bis cours de Vincennes, 12e (tel. (1) 43 43
11 24). Métro: Porte de Vincennes.

Du Midi, 4 av. René-Coty, 14e (tel. (1) 43 27 23 25). Métro:
Denfert-Rochereau. The street runs out of Pl.
Denfert-Rochereau.

Du Parc, 6 rue Jolivet, 14e (tel. (1) 43 20 95 54). Métro: Edgar-Quinet. The street runs right off rue de la Gaité.

De Blois, 5 rue des Plantes, 14e (tel. (1) 45 40 99 48). Métro: Alésia. Walk up av. du Maine, then head left along rue de la Sablière into rue des Plantes.

Eden, 7 rue J.B. Dumay, 20e (tel. (1) 43 61 51 68). Off rue de Belleville between the Jourdain (closest) and Pyrénées métro stations.

Cheapest rooms around 210FF (£22; $38.50)

De la Vallée, 84–86 rue Saint-Denis, 1er (tel. (1) 42 36 46 99). The street crosses rue Etienne Marcel close to the Etienne Marcel métro station.

Tiquetonne, 6 rue Tiquetonne, 2e (tel. (1) 42 36 94 58). Métro: Etienne Marcel. From the métro station follow rue de Turbigo. Rue Tiquetonne is one block away from rue de Turbigo down both rue St-Denis and rue Française.

Sansonnet, 48 rue de la Verrerie, 4e (tel. (1) 48 87 96 14). Métro: Hôtel de Ville. Rue de Renard, rue du Temple and rue des Archives all cross rue de la Verrerie one block from rue de Rivoli.

Flatters, 3 rue Flatters, 5e (tel. (1) 43 31 74 21). Métro: Les Gobelins. At the end of av. des Gobelins turn left down bd du Port Royal, then right at rue Flatters.

Alsace Lorraine, 14 rue des Cannettes, 6e (tel. (1) 43 25 10 14). Métro: St-Sulpice. Walk along rue du Vieux Colombier into Pl. St-Sulpice, then turn left.

Résidence Bosquet, 19 rue Champ de Mars, 7e (tel. (1) 47 05 25 45). Métro: Ecole Militaire. The street crosses av. Bosquet.

Montyon, 15 rue Montyon, 9e (tel. (1) 47 70 92 70). Métro: Rue Montmartre. Rue Montyon runs right off rue du Faubourg Montmartre.

De Hollande, 4 rue Cadet, 9e (tel. (1) 47 70 50 79). Métro: Cadet is closest, but it is an easy walk from the Le Peletier or Poissonière métro stations to the junction of rue Lafayette and rue Cadet.

Austin's, 26 rue d'Amsterdam, 9e (tel. (1) 48 74 48 71). Métro: St-Lazare. The street runs down the side of the train station, on the left as you leave by the main exit.

De Bruxelles, 85 rue de Clichy, 9e (tel. (1) 48 74 48 71). Métro: Place de Clichy or Liège. Rue de Clichy runs out of Pl. de Clichy. From Liège, rue de Liège leads into rue de Clichy after one block.

Pierre-Dupont, 1 rue Pierre-Dupont, 10e (tel. (1) 46 07 93 66). Off rue du Faubourg St-Martin between the Louis-Blanc and Château-Landon métro stations.

Grand Hôtel Voltaire, 150 bd Voltaire, 11e (tel. (1) 43 79 07 12). Between the Charonne (closest) and Voltaire métro stations.

Pax, 12 rue de Charonne, 11e (tel. (1) 47 00 40 98). Métro: Ledru-Rollin. From the métro station, follow rue du Faubourg St-Antoine towards Pl. de la Bastille, then turn right at rue de Charonne.

Du Midi, 31 rue Traversière, 12e (tel. (1) 43 07 88 68). Métro: Ledru-Rollin. The street runs left off av. Ledru-Rollin a short distance from the métro station as you head in the direction of av. Daumesnil.

Mistral, 3 rue Chaligny, 12e (tel. (1) 46 28 10 20). Métro: Reuilly-Diderot or Faidherbe Chaligny. From Reuilly-Diderot follow bd. Diderot in the direction of Gare de Lyon until the street is crossed by rue Chaligny.

Celtik, 15 rue d'Odessa, 14e (tel. (1) 43 20 93 53). Métro: Montparnasse-Bienvenüe or Edgar-Quinet. Rue d'Odessa runs between bd Edgar Quinet and rue du Départ in front of Gare Montparnasse.

Le Royal, 49 rue Raymond Losserand, 14e (tel. (1) 43 22 14 04). Métro: Pernety on rue Raymond Losserand.

De Sèvres, 92 bd Garibaldi, 15e (tel. (1) 47 83 22 79). Métro: Sèvres-Lecourbe.

Cheapest rooms around 220FF (£23; $40)

Picard, 26 rue de Picardie, 3e (tel. (1) 48 87 53 82). From the Temple métro station walk along rue du Temple, turn left at rue Dupetit-Thouars, then left at the end of the street.

Muguet, 11 rue Chevert, 7e (tel. (1) 47 05 05 93). Métro: Ecole Militaire. From Pl. de Ecole Militaire, walk along av. de Tourville until you see rue Chevert on your left.

Grand Hôtel Lafayette-Buffault, 6 rue Buffault, 9e (tel. (1) 47 70 70 96). The street crosses rue Lafayette a short walk from the Le Peletier métro station. An easy walk down rue Lafayette from the Cadet métro station. From the Notre Dame de Lorette métro station, follow rue Châteaudun in the direction of Cadet métro station. Rue Buffault crosses rue Châteaudun just beyond Pl. Kossuth.

Rex, 4 bis, Cité Rougemont, 9e (tel. (1) 48 24 60 70). Métro: Rue Montmartre or Bonne-Nouvelle. Turn off bd Poissonière down rue Rougemont, then turn left at the top of the street along rue Bergère to reach Cité Rougemont.

Apollo, 11 rue de Dunkerque, 10e (tel. (1) 48 78 04 98). Métro: Gare du Nord. Head right from the main exit of the station.

Du Nord, 47 rue Albert Thomas, 10e (tel. (1) 42 01 66 00).

B&B

Pension les Marroniers, 78 rue d'Assas, 6e (tel. (1) 43 26 37 71; for reservations (1) 43 26 37 71). Bed, breakfast and evening meal. Singles and doubles from around 160FF (£16.70; $29) per person, slightly cheaper per person in triples. RER: Port Royal. Rue d'Assas begins near the RER station, between bd St-Michel and rue Notre-Dame-des-Champs.

Bed & Breakfast 1, 73 rue Notre-Dame-des-Champs, 6e (tel. (1) 43 25 43 97). This organization has singles starting around 230FF (£24; $42), doubles around 270FF (£28; $49). Métro: Notre-Dame-des-Champs.

UNIVERSITY ACCOMMODATION

Cité Universitaire de Paris, 15 bd Jourdan, 14e (tel. (1) 45 89 35 79). In summer, there is a 7-to 10-night minimum stay. Singles 100–130FF (£10.40–13.50; $18.50–24), doubles around 95FF (£10; $17.50) per person. Full payment in advance is usually required. For further details and reservations contact: M. le Délégue, Général de Cité Universitaire de Paris, 19 bd Jourdan, 75690 Paris cedex 14. RER: Cité Universitaire. The closest métro stop is Porte d'Orléans Général-Leclerc, a 10-minute walk away along bd Jourdan.

HOSTELS/FOYERS

AJF operate five Hôtels de Jeunes in the city, four of which are open all year round. Accommodation is usually in two- or four-bed rooms with B&B costing around 95FF (£10; $17.50). No reservations are accepted, so arrive early at an AJF office, or at one of the Foyers.

Le Fauconnier, 11 rue de Fauconnier, 4e (tel. (1) 42 74 23 45). The largest of the five foyers. Métro: Pont Marie or St-Paul. From Pont Marie follow the Seine downstream about 100m, then turn left up rue de Fauconnier. From St-Paul turn left down rue Prévôt from rue Franois Miron, then left along rue Charlemagne until you see rue du Fauconnier on the right.

Le Fourcy, 6 rue de Fourcy, 4e (tel. (1) 42 74 23 45). Off rue de Rivoli and rue François Miron, a short walk from the St-Paul métro station.

Maubisson, 12 rue des Barres, 4e (tel. (1) 42 72 72 09). The smallest of the five foyers. Right off rue de l'Hôtel de Ville, a short walk from the Pont Marie métro station.

Résidence Bastille, 151 av. Lédru Rollin, 11e (tel. (1) 43 79 53 86). Some singles available. Between the Voltaire (closest) and Ledru-Rollin métro stations.

Residence Luxembourg, 270 rue St-Jacques, 5e (tel. (1) 43 25 06 20). Open July–Sept. RER: Luxembourg. Rue St-Jacques runs parallel to bd St-Michel, one block away. Follow Souflot from near the RER station.

Centre International de Paris (BVJ) run four foyers. Accommodation is mainly in multi-bedded rooms, though there are a few singles. B&B costs around 100FF (£10.40; $18.50). No reservations are accepted, so arrive early, preferably before 9 a.m. Three-night maximum stay.

Paris Quartier Latin, 44 rue des Bernardins, 5e (tel. (1) 43 29 34 80). Métro: Maubert-Mutualité. Rue des Bernardins crosses bd St-Germain about 150m from Pl. Maubert.

Paris Louvre, 20 rue Jean-Jacques Rousseau, 1er (tel. (1) 42 36 88 18). From the Louvre Rivoli métro station head up rue du Louvre from rue de Rivoli, turn left along rue St-Honoré, then right. From the Palais Royal Musée du Louvre métro station, walk along rue St-Honoré until you see rue Jean-Jacques Rousseau on the left.

Paris Les Halles, 5 rue du Pélican, 1er (tel. (1) 40 26 92 45). From the Louvre Rivoli métro station, follow the directions for the foyer above until you see rue du Pélican, going left off rue Jean-Jacques-Rousseau. From the Palais Royal/Musée du Louvre métro station, follow rue St-Honoré, turn left up rue Croix-des-Petits-Champs, then right.

Paris Opéra, 11 rue Thérèse (tel. (1) 42 60 77 23). Off av. de l'Opéra near the Pyramides métro station. An easy walk from the Opéra or Palais Royal/Musée de Louvre métro stations at either end of av. de l'Opéra.

Centre International de Séjour de Paris (CISP) run two foyers. 140FF (£14.60; $25.50) for singles, 110FF (£11.50; $20) in two- to five-bedded rooms, 93FF (£9.70; $17) in 12-bedded dorms. Reception open 6.30 a.m.–1.30 a.m. The foyers are frequently full by noon.

CISP Ravel, 6 av. Maurice Ravel, 12e (tel. (1) 43 43 19 01). Métro: Porte de Vincennes.

CISP Kellerman, 17 bd Kellerman, 13e (tel. (1) 45 80 70 76). Bd Kellerman runs off av. d'Italie by the Porte d'Italie métro station.

Association des Etudiants Protestants de Paris (AEPP), 46 rue de Vaugirard (tel. (1) 46 33 23 30/43 54 31 49). Ages 18–25 only. Singles 92FF (£9.60; $17), doubles 83FF (£8.60; $15) per person, dorms 70FF (£7.30; $13). From Pl. Edmond Rostand (by the Luxembourg RER station) follow rue des

Médicis into rue de Vaugirard. From the Odéon métro station, follow rue l'Odéon from bd St-Germain to Pl. de l'Odéon, then walk down the side of the theatre on to rue de Vaugirard.

'Jules Ferry' (FUAJ), 8 bd Jules Ferry (tel. (1) 43 57 55 60). 2 a.m. curfew. Reception open 8 a.m.–9 p.m. Four-night maximum stay. 95FF (£10; $17.50) for B&B in two- to six-bed rooms. Advance reservation advisable at all times, but particularly from Easter to September (use the IYHF advance booking vouchers). Otherwise get to the hostel early. The 'Jules Ferry' hostel handles reservations for the temporary FUAJ hostel set up in the university during the summer vacation (July–mid-Sept.). Bd Jules Ferry crosses rue du Faubourg du Temple, a short distance along the latter from Pl. de la République and the République métro station.

'Le D'Artagnan' (FUAJ), 80 rue Vitruve (tel. (1) 43 61 08 75). No curfew. Round-the-clock reception. 103FF (£10.75; $19) for B&B in three- to eight-bed rooms. Will not accept reservations for individuals. Rue Vitruve is off bd Davout between the Porte de Bagnolet (closest) and Porte de Montreuil métro stations.

Relais Européen de la Jeunesse (FUAJ), 52 av. Robert Schumann, Athis Mons (tel. 64 84 81 39). No curfew. Round-the-clock reception. 95–105FF (£10–10.90; $17.50–19). 500m from the RER station in Athis Mons (line C).

3 rue Marcel Duhamel (FUAJ), Arpajon (tel. 64 90 28 55). Around 50FF (£5.20; $9). 400m from the RER station in Arpajon (line C4 dir. Dourdan from Paris Austerlitz). Camping spaces available.

LFAJ hostels. The booking office for the six LFAJ hostels in the city is opposite the Pompidou Centre at 119 rue St-Martin (tel. (1) 42 72 72 09). Métro: Rambuteau or Les Halles. RER: Châtelet-les-Halles. LFAJ also let space in houseboats (*peniches*) along the Seine.

C.A.I. (LFAJ), 25 rue de 8 mai 1945, Acheres (tel. 39 11 14 97). Around 50FF (£5.20; $9). From Paris St-Lazare take the

RER dir. Cergy-St Christophe to Acheres. The hostel is about 700m from the station.

Y&H Hostel, 80 rue Mouffetard, 5e (tel. (1) 45 35 09 53). 1 a.m. curfew. 87FF (£9; $16). Weekly rate 540FF (£56; $98). Reserve in advance with the first night's payment, or get to the hostel early. Métro: Place Monge. From Pl. Monge follow rue Ortocan until it is crossed by rue Mouffetard.

3 Ducks Hostel, 6 Pl. E. Pernet, 15e (tel. (1) 48 42 04 05). 1 a.m. curfew. 83FF (£8.65; $15). Reservations accepted with one night's payment. By the Jean Baptiste de Grenelle church. Métro: Felix Fauré or Commerce. From Commerce, follow the ascending street numbers on rue du Commerce.

Maison des Clubs UNESCO, 43 rue de Glacière, 13e (tel. (1) 43 36 00 63). Three-night maximum stay. Singles 135–150FF (£14.10–15.60; $24.50–27.50), two- to four-bed rooms 120FF (£12.50; $22) per person. No reservations accepted for individuals. Rue de Glacière crosses bd Auguste Blanqui by the Glacière métro station.

Aloha Hostel, 42 rue Borromée, 15e (tel (1) 42 73 03 03). Curfew 1 a.m. 83FF (£8.65; $15) per person in singles, doubles, quads and six-bed rooms. Reservations accepted with the first night's payment. Métro: Volontaires. Turn down rue Borromée at 243 rue Vaugirard.

Foyer Franco-Libannais, 15 rue d'Ulm, 5e (tel. (1) 43 29 47 60). No curfew. Singles 110FF (£11.50; $20), singles with shower 120FF (£12.50; $22), doubles 90FF (£9.40; $16.50), doubles with shower 110FF (£11.50; $20) per person, triples with shower 90FF (£9.40; $16.50) per person. From the Cardinal Lemoine métro station, follow rue du Cardinal Lemoine past the end of rue Clovis, turn right down rue Thouin, then right again along rue de l'Estropade until it is crossed by rue d'Ulm. From the Luxembourg RER station, head down rue Gay-Lussac from bd St-Michel, turn left at rue Collard, right again at rue St-Jacques, then almost immediately left along rue Pierre et Marie Curie, which is crossed by rue d'Ulm.

Maison International des Jeunes, 4 rue Titon, 11e (tel. (1) 43 71 99 21). Three-night maximum stay. Ages 18–30, but this rule is not rigorously enforced. 100FF (£10.40; $18.50). Written requests for reservations accepted. Métro: Faidherbe-Chaligny.

Foyer International des Etudiantes, 93 bd St-Michel, 6e (tel. (1) 43 54 49 63). July–Sept., open to both sexes; Oct.–June, women only. Singles 155FF (£16.20; $28.50), doubles 105FF (£11; $19) per person. Best reserved in writing two months in advance. A short walk along bd St-Michel from the Luxembourg RER station.

CAMPING

Camping du Bois de Boulogne, allée du Bord de l'Eau (tel. (1) 45 24 30 00). Solo travellers pay around 60FF (£6.25; $11). In summer, the site fills fast and becomes very crowded. Métro: Port Maillot. Then bus 244, followed by a short walk.

Rheims (Reims)

Tourist Offices
Office de Tourisme de Reims, Square du Trésor, 2 rue Guillaume de Machault, B.P. 2533, 51071 Reims cedex (tel. 26 47 25 69). Open Easter–30 Sept., daily 9 a.m.–7.30 p.m., except Sun. and holidays 9.30 a.m.–6.30 p.m.; 1 Oct–Easter, the office closes one hour earlier than the times above. 'Accueil de France' service available. By the cathedral, a 15-minute walk from the train station (see Basic Directions below).

Basic Directions
On leaving the train station, bd Joffre runs left to Pl. de la République. Crossing the square in front of the station, bd Foch heads left, parallel to bd Joffre, to the Porte de Mars, while bd Général Leclerc runs right to the canal. At the junction of these two boulevards, rue Noël leads off diagonally left. To the right of rue Noël, Pl. Drouet d'Erlon heads towards St

James's Church (St-Jacques), beyond which is rue Vesle. Left
of rue Noël, rue Thiers leads towards the Town Hall on Pl.
de l'Hôtel de Ville. Taking the third right off rue Thiers, you
can follow cours J-B-Langlet to the Cathedral and the Tourist
Office. From the station to the cathedral is about a 15-minute
walk.

HOTELS

Cheapest rooms around 90FF (£9.50; $16.50)

Au Bon Accueil, 31 rue de Thillois (tel. 26 88 55 74). Right
off Pl. Drouet d'Erlon near St James's Church.
Linguet, 14 rue Linguet (tel. 26 47 31 89). Near the Town Hall
and Pl. de la République.

Cheapest rooms around 110FF (£11.50; $20)

Cecyl, 24 rue Buirette (tel. 26 47 57 47). Right off Pl. Drouet
d'Erlon.
Thillois, 17 rue de Thillois (tel. 26 40 65 65). See Au Bon
Accueil, above.
Le Parisien, 3 rue Périn (tel. 26 47 32 89). In the area
immediately to the left of, and behind, the train station.
Saint-André, 46 av. Jean Jaurès (tel. 26 47 24 16). From the
Town Hall follow rue Jean-Jacques Rousseau on to bd
Lundy, right to Pl. Aristide Briand, then left, or go right
round bd Lundy from Pl. de la République.

Cheapest rooms around 120FF (£12.50; $22)

Les Arcades, 16 passage Subé (tel. 26 47 42 39). Near the train
station.
Central, 16 rue des Telliers (tel. 26 47 30 08). Follow rue Noël
into rue des Telliers.
Monopole, 28 Pl. Drouet d'Erlon (tel. 26 47 10 33).

Cheapest rooms around 130FF (£13.50; $24)

D'Anvers, 2 Pl. de la République (tel. 26 40 28 35).

Alsace, 6 rue du Général Sarrail (tel. 26 47 44 08). The street runs between Pl. de la République and Pl. de Hôtel de Ville.

Porte-Paris, 39 rue du Colonel Fabien (tel. 26 08 73 50). Cross the canal by Pont de Vesle (left from the end of bd du Général Leclerc) into rue du Colonel Fabien.

Saint-Maurice, 90 rue Gambetta (tel. 26 85 09 10). From cours J-B-Langlet, right on rue Carnot/rue de Vesle, then left along rue Chanzy which leads into rue Gambetta. About 20 minutes' walk from the station.

Cheapest rooms around 140FF (£14.50; $25.50)

Ardenn'Hôtel, 6 rue Caqué (tel. 26 47 42 38). In the area bounded by bd du Général Leclerc, rue Jeanne-d'Arc, the canal and rue de Vesle.

Azur, 9 rue des Ecrevées (tel. 26 47 43 39). Near the Town Hall.

Les Consuls, 7 rue de Général Sarrail (tel. 26 88 46 10). See Hôtel d'Alsace, above.

Cheapest rooms around 160FF (£16.75; $29)

Le Baron, 85 rue de Vesle (tel. 26 47 46 24).

Cheapest rooms around 170FF (£17.75; $31)

Victoria, 35 Pl. Drouet d'Erlon (tel. 26 47 21 79).

Saint-Nicaise, 6 Pl. Saint-Nicaise (tel. (26 85 01 26). Far from the station, a 20–25-minute walk from the catheral. Head left at the cathedral on rue R.-de Courcy, then right along cours A.-France. Continuing straight on you reach Pl. Saint-Nicaise.

Cheapest rooms around 180FF (£18.75; $33.50)

Touring, 17 ter, bd du Général Leclerc (tel. 26 47 38 15).

Cheapest rooms around 220FF (£23; $40)

Gambetta, 13 rue Gambetta (tel. 26 47 41 64). About 15

minutes' walk from the train station. See Hôtel Saint-Maurice, above.

Grand Hôtel Continental, 93 Pl. Drouet d'Erlon (tel. 26403935).

UNIVERSITY ACCOMMODATION

Available July and August.

Contact CROUS, 34 bd Henri Vasnier (tel. 26 85 50 16). Rooms are quite far from the centre.

HOSTELS

Centre International de Séjour et de Rencontres (FUAJ), 1 Chaussée Bocquaine (tel. 26 40 52 60). A 15-minute walk from the station. Cross the canal by Pont de Vesle (left from the end of bd du Général Leclerc), down rue du Colonel Fabien, then left.

A.L.E.J.T., 66 rue de Courcelles (tel. 26474652). Open all year. A 5–10-minute walk from the train station. Right from the exit along bd Louis Röderer, then left on to rue de Courcelles.

Méridienne, 36 rue de la Cerisaie (tel. 26 85 65 17). Open all year except August. Around 100FF (£10.50; $18.50) per person in doubles.

CAMPING

Airotel de Campagne, avenue Hoche (Route de Châlons) (tel. 26 85 41 22). Open 23 Mar.–30 Sept.

Rouen

Tourist Offices

Office de Tourisme, 25 Pl. de la Cathédrale, B.P. 666, 76008 Rouen cedex (tel. 35 71 41 77). Open May–Sept., Mon.–Sat.

9 a.m.–7 p.m., Sun. and holidays 9.30 a.m.–12.30 p.m. and 2.30–6 p.m.; at other times, Mon.–Sat. 9 a.m.–12.30 p.m. and 2–6.30 p.m. Finds rooms in local hotels for 12FF (£1.25; $2.25). 'Accueil de France' service available. To get there, see Basic Directions below.

Basic Directions

The historical centre of the city is small. From the train station to the Pont Jeanne-d'Arc over the River Seine is about a 10-minute walk. From Pl. Bernard-Tissot in front of the train station rue Jeanne-d'Arc runs straight to the Pont Jeanne-d'Arc. Just under half way down, rue Jeanne-d'Arc is crossed by rue Thiers. By going left, you would reach the Church of St-Ouen. On down rue Jeanne-d'Arc, you pass Pl. Maréchal Foch with the Court on the left, then about two thirds of the way to the Seine, the street is crossed by rue du Gros-Horloge. To the right is the Old Market, on the left the road leads to the Tourist Office and the cathedral. Crossing over the river by the Pont Jeanne-d'Arc av. J-Cartier leads into av. de Bretagne. Bus 12 from the station runs down rue Jeanne-d'Arc, over the Seine and then down av. de Bretagne.

HOTELS

Cheapest rooms around 65FF (£6.75; $12)

Normandy, 47 rue du Renard (tel. 35 71 13 69). From rue Jeanne-d'Arc go right down bd de la Marne into Pl. Cauchoise, then across the square into rue Renard.

Cheapest rooms around 75FF (£7.75; $14)

Saint-Ouen, 43 rue des Faulx (tel. 35 71 46 44). From rue Thiers head to the right around the Church of St-Ouen into rue des Faulx.

Cheapest rooms around 90FF (£9.50; $16.50)

Du Palais, 12 rue du Tambour (tel. 35 71 41 40). Runs off Pl.

Maréchal Foch and rue aux Juifs to rue du Gros-Horloge.

Du Square, 9 rue du Moulinet (tel. 35 71 56 07). Off rue Jeanne-d'Arc by rue Blanchard, a short distance after bd de la Marne.

Napoléon, 58 rue Beauvoisine (tel. 35 71 43 59). Left from Pl. Tissot along rue de la Rochefoucault, right down Champ des Oiseaux, over bd de la Marne, and on down rue Bouvrreuil, then left along rue du Cordier which leads into Beauvoisine.

De Lille, 79 rue Lafayette (tel. 35 72 89 91). From av. de Bretagne head left along rue A. Glatigny, across Pl. des Emmurées and rue St-Sever to take rue de Lessard into rue Lafayette.

Du Sphynx, 130 rue Beauvoisine (tel. 35 71 35 86). See Napoléon, above.

Le Vieux-Logis, 5 rue de Joyeuse (tel. 35 71 55 30). Left from Pl. Tissot along rue de la Rochefoucault, right then left up bd de l'Yser to Pl. Beauvoisine. Right down Louis-Ricard, from which rue de Joyeuse runs off to the left.

Normandy, 32 rue du Cordier (tel. 35 71 46 15). Immediately after crossing bd de l'Yser, go left along rue Donjon to its end, then across the square into rue du Cordier.

Cheapest rooms around 100FF (£10.50; $18.50)

Rochefoucault, 1 rue de la Rochefoucault (tel. 35 71 86 58). By the station, left off Pl. Bernard-Tissot.

Cheapest rooms around 110FF (£11.50; $20)

Des Arcades, 52 rue des Carmes (tel. 35 70 10 30). Right off rue Thiers heading towards St. Ouen.

De la Gare, 3 bis rue Maladrerie (tel. 35 71 57 90). To the right off Pl. Tissot.

Beauséjour, 9 rue Pouchet (tel. 35 71 93 47). Rue Pouchet runs out of Pl. Tissot to the right of rue Jeanne-d'Arc.

Cheapest rooms around 120FF (£12.50; $22)

Boieldieu, 14 Pl. du Gaillardbois (tel. 35 70 50 75). From the cathedral, take rue Grand Pont towards the Seine, then left along rue de la Savonnerie into the square.

Regina, 2 av. de Bretagne (tel. 35 73 02 74).

De la Tour de Beurre, 20 quai Pierre-Corneille (tel. 35 71 95 17). Overlooking the Seine. From the foot of rue Jeanne-d'Arc go left.

Cheapest rooms around 130FF (£13.50; $24)

Du Havre, 27 rue Verte (tel. 35 71 46 43). Rue Verte runs down the side of the train station (right from the exit) across Pl. Bernard-Tissot and into rue Jeanne-d'Arc.

De Nice, 73 rue Lafayette (tel. 35 72 21 72). See Hôtel de Lille, above.

Des Familles, 4 rue Pouchet (tel. 35 71 69 61). See Hôtel Beauséjour above.

De Chapeau Rouge, 129 rue Lafayette (tel. 35 72 32 72). See Hôtel de Lille, above.

Vieille-Tour, 47 Pl. de la Haute-Vieille-Tour (tel. 35 70 03 27). To the left of Pl. du Gaillardbois. See Hôtel Boieldieu, above.

Solferino, 51 rue Thiers (tel. 35 71 10 07). Right off rue Jeanne-d'Arc.

De Lisieux, 4 rue de la Savonnerie (tel. 35 71 87 73). See Hôtel Boieldieu above.

De l'Europe, 87 rue aux Ours (tel. 35 70 83 30). Crosses rue Jeanne-d'Arc one street on from rue du Gros-Horloge.

Cheapest rooms around 140FF (£14.50; $25.50)

La Cache-Ribaud, 10 rue du Tambour (tel. 35 71 04 82). See Hôtel du Palais, above.

D'Albion, 52 rue des Augustins (tel. 35 70 05 15). From the St-Ouen church, rue de la République runs down to the Seine. Rue des Augustins is on the left near the river.

De la Préfecture, 35 av. Champlain (tel. 35 72 93 89). Immediately after crossing the Pont Jeanne-d'Arc, turn left along quai Jean-Moulin, then right.

Cheapest rooms around 160FF (£16.75; $29)

De Normandie, 19 rue du Bec (tel. 35 71 55 77). Near the Court. Left off Jeanne-d'Arc along rue aux Juifs at Pl. Maréchal Foch, then right.

De la Terrasse, 26 rue de Campully (tel. 35 71 95 23). From Pl. Tissot head right on rue de la Maladrerie, then first left.

Du Gaillardbois, 12 Pl. du Gaillardbois (tel. 35 70 34 28). See Hôtel Boieldieu, above.

Morand, 1 rue Morand (tel. 35 71 46 07). Left off rue Jeanne-d'Arc, about 250m from the station.

Cheapest rooms around 170FF (£17.75; $31)

De Paris, 12 rue de Champmeslé (tel. 35 70 09 26). Right off rue du Gros-Horloge heading towards the cathedral.

Foch, 6 rue Saint-Etienne-des-Tonneliers (tel. 35 88 11 44). Right off rue Jeanne-d'Arc near the river along rue Général Leclerc, right down rue J-le-Lieur, then left.

De la Cathédrale, 12 rue Saint-Romain (tel. 35 71 57 95). The street runs along the left-hand side of the cathedral.

De Bordeaux, 9 Pl. de la République (tel. 35 71 93 58). See Hôtel d'Albion, above. At the end of rue de la République by the Seine.

Du Gros-Horloge, 91 rue du Gros-Horloge (tel. 35 70 41 41). Left off rue Jeanne-d'Arc.

Cardinal, 1 Pl. de la Cathédrale (tel. 35 70 24 42).

IYHF HOSTEL

Centre de Séjour, 17 rue Diderot (tel. 35 72 06 45). 57FF (£6; $10.50) in mixed dorms. Off av. de Bretagne. A 20-minute walk from the train station, or bus 12 to the end of rue Diderot.

UNIVERSITY ACCOMMODATION

CROUS, 3 rue d'Herbouville (tel. 35 71 46 15). This office lets singles to those with a student ID card for 50FF (£5.25;

$9) from June–Sept. The university is in Mont-St-Aignan, far from the town centre but easily reached by bus 10.

CAMPING

Neither of the two sites are centrally located. Camping Municipal, rue Jules-Ferry (tel. 35 74 07 59) is in Déville-lès-Rouen, off the main road (Route National 27) to Dieppe. Camping 'L'Aubette', 23 rue Vert-Buisson (tel. 35 08 47 69) is in Saint-Leger-du-Bourg-Denis, in the direction of Beauvais.

St Malo

Tourist Offices
Office de Tourisme, Port des Yachts, 35400 Saint-Malo (tel. 99 56 64 48). Open July–Aug., Mon.–Sat. 8.30 a.m.–8 p.m., Sun. 10 a.m.–6.30 p.m.; at other times, Mon.–Sat. 9 a.m.–noon and 2–6 p.m. 'Accueil de France' service not available. To get there see Basic Directions below.

Basic Directions
From Pl. de l'Hermine (the square by the train station), bd des Talards runs off towards the St-Servan district of town. By going right off bd des Talards down av. Franklin-Roosevelt you can follow the quayside to the ferry terminal. Bd de la République is on the opposite side of Pl. de l'Hermine from bd des Talards. Between these two roads av. Louis-Martin takes you down past the Tourist Office (a 10-minute walk) to the nearby Porte St-Vincent, the entry to the Old Town. From bd de la République, red buses 2 and 3, and the purple bus 4 maintain a frequent service to the Porte St-Vincent until 7.30 p.m. To reach the Tourist Office from the ferry terminal, it is a 10-minute walk along the quayside, left over the water by the swimming pool, then follow Chaussée des Corsaires on to av. Louis-Martin, then left.

HOTELS

Rooms can be very difficult to find in July and August, so reserve ahead if possible. If you want to stay in the Old Town, book as far in advance as you can.

Cheapest rooms around 110FF (£11.50; $20)

Faisan Doré, 1 rue de l'Orme (tel. 99 40 91 70). In the Old Town, between the Halle-aux-Blés and the Marché-des-Légumes.

La Petite Vitesse, 42 bd de la République (tel. 99 56 31 76). A short walk from the station.

L'Avenir, 31 bd de la Tour d'Auvergne (tel. 99 56 13 33). Close to the train station. Right off bd de la République.

Cheapest rooms around 130FF (£13.50; $24)

Le Vauban, 7 bd de la République (tel. 99 56 09 39). A few minutes' walk from the train station.

Suffren, 4 bd des Talards (tel. 99 56 31 71). Around 100m from the station.

Hostellerie du Malouin, 6 rue Hélène Boucher (tel. 99 56 31 08). A 10-minute walk from the station. Right off bd de la République down rue Jean-Jaurés. Straight on until you see rue Boucher on the right.

Le Tivoli, 61 Chaussée du Sillon (tel. 99 56 11 98). Near the main beach (Grande Plage). Follow bd de la République to Pl. Duguesclin, from which rue Roger Vercel heads down to the beach. A 10-minute walk from the station.

De la Mer, 3 rue Dauphine (tel. 99 81 61 05). In St-Servan, a 15–20-minute walk from the station. Head for the ferry terminal (see Basic Directions). From the Quai de Trichet, head left into rue Georges-Clemenceau, cross over and take one of the streets on the other side into rue Dauphine.

Vieille Ville, 40 av. Aristide-Briand (tel. 99 56 12 25). A 10–15-minute walk from the station. From bd de la République, turn right on rue Jean-Jaurès, which leads into av. Aristide-Briand.

Les Chiens du Guet, 4 Pl. du Guet (tel. 99 40 46 77). In the Old Town, beside the Porte St-Pierre.

Le Neptune, 21 rue de l'Industrie (tel. 99 56 82 15). A 10-minute walk from the station and from the Old Town. Left off rue Roger Vercel (see Le Tivoli, above).

Cheapest rooms around 150FF (£15.50; $27.50)

Cap à l'Ouest, 2 rue St-Benoît (tel. 99 40 87 03). In the Old Town off rue Maclaw, near the Sous-Préfecture.

Brasserie Armoricaine, 6 rue de Boyer (tel. 99 40 89 13). In the Old Town, near the post office (P.T.T.) between Place-aux-Herbes and the Porte des Bes.

La Rotonde, 1 bd Châteaubriand (tel. 99 40 89 13). For directions, see main FUAJ hostel, below. At the end of av. Louis-Pasteur the road forks. Bd Châteaubriand is to the left of av. du Rév.-Père-Umbricht.

Auberge de l'Hermine, 4 Place de l'Hermine (tel. 99 56 31 32). A few steps away from the train station.

Pomme d'Argent, 24 bd des Talards (tel. 99 56 12 39). A short walk from the station.

Cheapest rooms around 160–180FF (£16.75–18.75; $29–33)

Auberge au Gai Bec, 4 rue des Lauriers/9 rue Thévenard (tel. 99 40 82 16). In the Old Town. Rue des Lauriers runs off the Place-aux-Herbes.

Armeric, 5 bd de la Tour d'Auvergne (tel. 99 40 52 00). A 5-minute walk from the station, right off bd de la République.

Châteaubriand, 8 bd Hébert (tel. 99 56 01 19). Directions: main FUAJ hostel below. To the left, off av. Louis-Pasteur.

Les Voyageurs, 2 bd des Talards (tel. 99 56 30 35). By the train station.

Du Commerce, 11 rue St-Thomas (tel. 99 40 85 56). In the Old Town, off Pl. Châteaubriand, to the right of Porte St-Vincent.

Paris, 3 rue Alphonse Thébault (tel. 99 56 31 44). Off Pl. de l'Hermine, about 100m from the train station.

Victoria, 4 rue des Orbettes (tel. 99 56 34 01). In the Old Town. Follow the walls left from Porte St-Vincent, then right off rue Jacques-Cartier. The hotel offers a chance to play French billiards.

Cheapest rooms around 200FF (£20.75; $36.50)

L'Arrivée, 52 bd de la République (tel. 99 56 30 78). A 5-minute walk from the station.

Le Bristol-Union, 4 Pl. de la Poissonerie (tel. 99 40 83 36). In the Old Town. Diagonally left from Porte St-Vincent and down rue Ste-Marguerite.

Croiseur, 2 Pl. de la Poissonerie (tel. 99 40 80 40). Directions: see Bristol-Union, above.

Le Louvre, 2 rue des Marins (tel. 99 40 86 62). In the Old Town. Directions: see Bristol-Union above, then rue des Merciers, across Grande Rue into rue des Marins.

YOUTH HOSTELS

37 Avenue du Révérend-Père-Umbricht (FUAJ) (tel. 99 40 29 80). 65FF (£6.75; $12). Fills quickly in summer. Red bus 2 to rue Coutoisville, then a short walk along av. du R-P-Umbricht, or a 20-minute walk from the train station. From bd de la République, right along av. Ernest-Renan to the end, left av. de Moka, right av. Louis-Pasteur and straight on.

Avenue de Moka (FUAJ) (tel. 99 56 31 55). The annex of the main FUAJ above. Roughly half the price, and roughly half the distance from the train station. Directions above.

L'Hermitage (IFAJ), 13 rue des Ecoles (tel. 99 56 22 00). In Paramé, a 15-minute walk from the main FUAJ hostel. Continuing more or less straight on you will arrive at Pl. du Prieuré. Out the other side on rue des Six-Frères-Ruellan, rue Legavre at the bend, then right to rue des Ecoles.

CAMPING

La Cité d'Aleth, Cité d'Aleth (tel. 99 81 60 91). The Cité d'Aleth adjoins the St-Servan district of town. This municipal site overlooks the Old Town and, less enchantingly, the ferry terminal.

Les Nielles, av. John Kennedy (tel. 99 40 26 35). This municipal site is located near one of the beaches (Plage du Minihic), beyond the Paramé district.

Le Nicet, av. de la Varde (tel. 99 40 26 32). This municipal site is far from the centre in the Rotheneuf district, near the coast at the Pointe du Nicet.

Les Ilôts, av. de la Guimorais (tel. 99 56 98 72). Also in Rotheneuf, this municipal site is well inland from the coast, but close to the coastal route to Mont-St-Michel.

De la Fontaine, rue de la Fontaine-aux-Pélerins (tel. 99 81 62 62). Open 15 June–15 Sept. Well out from the centre, on the main route to Mont-St-Michel.

Strasbourg

Tourist Offices

Office du Tourisme de Strasbourg et de sa Région, Palais des Congrès, av. Schutzenberger, 67082 Strasbourg cedex. Head office of the Tourist Board. Contact this office if you want information in advance. On arrival, head for one of the information bureaux the Tourist Board operates in the city.

Accueil Gutenberg, Chambre de Commerce, 10 pl. Gutenberg (tel. 88 32 57 07). Open daily June–Sept., 8 a.m.–7 p.m.; Easter–May and Oct., 9 a.m.–6 p.m.; at other times, Mon.–Sat. 9 a.m.–12.30 p.m. and 1.45–6 p.m. 'Accueil de France' service. In the town centre, a short walk from the cathedral (see Basic Directions below).

Accueil Gare, Pl. de la Gare (tel. 88 32 51 49). In front of the train station. Open June–Sept., 8 a.m.–7 p.m. daily; Easter–May and Oct., daily 9 a.m.–12.30 p.m. and 1.45–6 p.m.

Accueil Pont de l'Europe (tel. 88 61 39 23). Same hours as Accueil Gare.

Basic Directions

From Pl. de la Gare in front of the train station, bd de Metz runs right into Pl. Ste-Aurélie and bd de Nancy, which leads in turn to Pl. de la Porte and bd de Lyon. Diagonally left across Pl. de la Gare from the station is rue Kuhn, to the right of which (almost opposite the station exit) is rue du Maire Kuss. Following this street and then crossing the Pont du Maire Kuss you arrive at the church near the intersection of rue du Vieux-Marché-aux-Vins (to the left) and Grande Rue (right of the church). Grande Rue leads into rue Gutenberg, which ends at Pl. Gutenberg with the statue of the famous printer. From the train station to Pl. Gutenberg is about 15 minutes' walk. Going right from Pl. Gutenberg, you can follow rue du Vieux-Marché-aux-Poissons down to the l'Ill, across which is Pl. du Corbeau.

HOTELS

Cheapest rooms around 110FF (£11.50; $20)

Michelet, 48 rue du Vieux-Marché-aux-Poissons (tel. 88 32 47 38). One-star hotel.

La Cruche d'Or, 6 rue des Tonneliers (tel. 88 32 11 23). One-star hotel. Closed 1–15 Aug. In the area between Grande Rue and the l'Ill.

Henriette, 69 rue Leclerc (tel. 88 78 03 84) One-star hotel in the suburb of Wolfisheim.

Cheapest rooms around 120FF (£12.50; $22)

Du Jura, 5 rue du Marché (tel. 88 32 12 72). One-star hotel. Left off rue du Vieux-Marché-aux-Vins.

Astoria, 7a rue de Rosheim (tel. 88 32 17 22). Two-star hotel. Left off bd de Nancy near Pl. Ste-Aurélie.

Schutzenbock, 81 av. Jean Jaurès (tel. 88 34 04 19). One-star hotel. Closed 1–25 Aug. A 20-minute walk from the centre. Off Pl. l'Etoile near the city council offices.

Au Cygne, 38 rue de la 1ère Division Blindée (tel. 88 64 04
79). One-star hotel in the suburb of Eschau.

Cheapest rooms around 130FF (£13.50; $24)

Weber, 22 bd de Nancy (tel. 88 32 36 47). One-star hotel.
Patricia, 1a rue des Puits (tel. 88 32 14 60). One-star hotel.
In the area between Grande Rue and the I'Ill.

Cheapest rooms around 170FF (£17.75; $31)

Gutenberg, 31 rue des Serruriers (tel. 88 32 17 15). Two-star
hotel. From Grande Rue turn right down rue des
Cordonniers then left at rue des Serruriers.
De l'Ill, 8 rue des Bateliers (tel. 88 36 20 01). Two-star hotel.
From Pl. du Corbeau head left along quai des Bateliers,
then right at rue des Bateliers. A 5–10-minute walk from
the town centre.
Du Rhin, 7–8 Pl. de la Gare (tel. 88 32 35 00). Two-star hotel.
De Bruxelles, 13 rue Kuhn (tel. 88 32 36 47). Two-star hotel.

Cheapest rooms around 190–220FF (£19.75–23; $34.50–40)

Auberge du Grand Duc, 33 route de l'Hôpital (tel. 88 34 31
76). One-star hotel. About 20 minutes' walk from the city
centre, near the city council offices.
Du Couvent du Franciscain, 18 rue Faubourg de Pierre (tel.
88 32 93 93). Two-star hotel. From the train station walk
left along bd du Président Wilson, then right along bd du
Président Poincaré to Pl. du Faubourg de Pierre and the
start of rue du Faubourg de Pierre.
Eden, 16 rue d'Obernai (tel. 88 32 41 99). Two-star hotel. Left
off bd de Lyon.
Pax, 24/26 rue du Faubourg National (tel. 88 32 14 54). Two-
star hotel. Petite rue de la Course (diagonally right across
Pl. de la Gare from the train station exit) leads into rue du
Faubourg National. Alternatively you can walk right from
the station along bd de Metz and then turn left.

YOUTH HOSTELS

'René Cassin' (FUAJ), 9 rue de l'Auberge de Jeunesse (tel. 88 30 26 46). 1 a.m. curfew. 65FF (£6.75; $12) for B&B. Also has space for 60 tents. Bus 3, 13, or 23 from Marché Ste-Marguérite (follow Petite rue de la Course and then rue St-Michel from Pl. de la Gare), or a 20-minute walk from the train station. Right off bd de Lyon down rue de la Broque. Straight on under the motorway, then along the cycle path through the park to the bridge. Up and over the bridge to the hostel.

Centre International de Rencontres du Parc du Rhin (FUAJ), rue des Cavaliers (tel. 88 60 10 20). Bus 1, 11 or 21 from Strasbourg train station to Pont-du-Rhin. The nearest train station is Kehl/Rhein, half a mile away in Germany.

Amitel Galaxie (LFAJ), 8 rue de Soleure (tel. 88 25 58 91). One and a half miles from the train station. Ten minutes' walk from the town centre. Bus 10 to Pl. du Maréchal de Lattre de Tassigny, then walk up rue de Soleure, or bus 1, 11 or 21 to Pl. Corbeau, then walk down rue d'Austerlitz into rue de la Brigade Alsace-Lorraine before turning left at rue de Soleure..

CIARUS, 7 rue Finkmatt (tel. 88 32 12 12). 75FF (£7.75; $14). A 10–15-minute walk from the train station. Do not cross the Pont du Maire Kuss, but turn left along the water. Keep going until you see rue Finkmatt on the left at the end of Quai Finkmatt.

Altrheinweg 11, Kehl/Rhein (tel. 19 49 78 51/19 49 23 30). DM17 (£6; $10.50). Although the pleasant town of Kehl/Rhein is in Germany it is virtually a suburb of Strasbourg. Trains run more or less hourly from Strasbourg and there is a frequent bus service.

FOYERS

Du Jeune Travailleur, rue du Maçon (tel. 88 39 69 01).
Du Jeune Ouvrier Chrétien, 6 rue de Bitche (tel. 88 35 12 75).
De l'Ingenieur, 54 bd d'Anvers (tel. 88 61 59 89).

De l'Etudiant Catholique, 17 Pl. St-Etienne (tel. 88 35 36 20).
De la Jeune Fille, 8 rue de Soleure (tel. 88 36 15 28). Women
only.

CAMPING

7 rue l'Auberge de Jeunesse (tel. 88 30 26 46). Next to the
'René Cassin' hostel. For directions see above. Camping
is also available at the hostel itself.

Toulouse (Toulouse/Tolosa)

Tourist Offices
Office de Tourisme Syndicat d'Initiative de Toulouse, Donjon
du Capitole, place du Capitole, 31000 Toulouse (tel. 61 23 32
00). Open daily May–Sept., 9 a.m.–7 p.m.; Oct.–Apr.,
Mon.–Sat. 9 a.m.–6 p.m. A branch office operates in the train
station.

Basic Directions
Trains arrive at Toulouse Matabiau, about one mile from the
city centre. Almost directly across the canal from the station
is rue de Bayard, which leads down to bd de Strasbourg.
Slightly to the right across bd de Strasbourg is rue de Remusat,
which takes you right into Pl. du Capitole, site of the Tourist
Office. Alternatively you can head left from Gare Matabiau,
and then turn right on to Allée Jean-Jaurès. This street passes
the junction of bd de Strasbourg (right) and bd Lazare-Carnot
(left) before reaching Pl. Wilson, with the statue of the Occitan
poet Pierre Goudoli. From Pl. Wilson, rue Lafayette crosses
rue d'Alsace-Lorraine before reaching Pl. du Capitole.

HOTELS

Cheapest rooms around 80FF (£8.25; $14.50)

Beauséjour, 4 rue Caffarelli (tel. 61 62 77 59). Right off Allée Jean-Jaurès.

Cheapest rooms around 100FF (£10.50; $18.50)

Antoine, 21 rue Arnaud Vidal (tel. 61 62 70 27). Left off Allée Jean-Jaurès.

Des Arts, 1 bis, rue Cantegril (tel. 61 23 36 21). Off rue des Arts. From Pl. Wilson follow rue St-Antoine-du-T. into Pl. St-Georges, across which is rue des Arts.

Astrid, 12 rue Denfert Rochereau (tel. 61 23 36 21). Between rue de Bayard and Allée Jean-Jaurès, rue Bertrand-de-Born runs parallel to these two streets into Pl. du Belfort, across which is rue Denfert Rochereau.

Splendid, 13 rue Caffarelli (tel. 61 62 43 02). See Beauséjour, above.

Donjon, 12 rue du Poids de l'Huile (tel. 61 21 86 44). The street runs between Pl. du Capitole and rue d'Alsace-Lorraine. Head left from rue Lafayette as you walk from Pl. Wilson.

Excelsior, 82 rue Riquet (tel. 61 62 71 25). Left off Allée Jean-Jaurès, close to the canal.

Cheapest rooms around 110FF (£11.50; $20)

Anatole France, 46 Pl. Anatole France (tel. 61 23 19 96).

Héliot, 3 rue Héliot (tel. 61 62 47 66). From rue de Bayard turn left down rue Maynard into Pl. de Belfort. Rue Héliot is directly across the square.

Le Lutetia, 33 rue Maynard (tel. 61 62 51 57). Left off rue de Bayard.

Bourse, 11 rue Clémence Isaure (tel. 61 21 55 86). Follow rue Gambetta from Pl. du Capitole, turn left along rue Ste-Ursule. Rue Clémence Isaure is off to the right near the junction with rue de Cujas.

Nouvel Hôtel, 13 rue du Taur (tel. 61 21 13 93). The street runs from Pl. du Capitole.

Cheapest rooms around 120FF (£12.50; $22)

Olivier, 75 av. Honoré-Serres (tel. 61 21 39 94). From rue de Bayard head right along bd de Strasbourg on to bd d'Arcole, then right down av. Honoré-Serres.

Palais, 4 Allée Paul Feuga (tel. 61 52 96 23). Between the Palais de Justice and the Point St-Michel. From Pl. Wilson walk down rue Lapeyrousse on to rue d'Alsace-Lorraine, turn left, and go straight ahead until you eventually reach Grande rue de Nazareth. Turn right, then left at the end of the street to reach Allée Paul Feuga.

Brasserie Pierre, 48 rue de Périole (tel. 61 48 58 75). In the area to the rear of Gare Matabiau. Head left from the station along the canal, turn left down the main road, and watch for rue Périole on the left-hand side, off Allée Georges-Pompidou.

Unic, 26 Allée Jean-Jaurès (tel. 61 62 38 19).

Au Père Leon, 2 Pl. Esquirol (tel. 61 21 70 39). From Pl. Wilson walk down rue Lapeyrousse on to rue d'Alsace-Lorraine. Turn left, and then right down rue de Metz to reach Pl. Esquirol.

François 1er, 4 rue d'Austerlitz (tel. 61 21 54 52). Off Pl. Wilson.

Grand Balcon, 8 rue Romiguières (tel. 61 21 48 08). Off Pl. du Capitole.

Cheapest rooms around 130FF (£13.50; $24)

Real, 30 Allée Jean-Jaurès (tel. 61 62 94 34).
Le Toulouse, 63 rue de Bayard (tel. 61 62 41 03).

Cheapest rooms around 140FF (£14.50; $25.50)

Chaumond, 19 rue Lafayette (tel. 61 21 86 42).

Cheapest rooms around 160FF (£16.75; $29)

Croix Baragnon, 17 rue Croix Baragnon (tel. 61 52 60 10). From Pl. Wilson follow rue St-Antoine-de-T. into Pl. St-

Georges, then take rue des Arts, which is crossed by rue
Croix Baragnon.
Guillaume Tell, 42 bd Lazare-Carnot (tel. 61 62 44 02).
Riquet, 92 rue Riquet (tel. 61 62 55 96). See Hôtel des Arts,
above.
Saint-Severin, 69 rue de Bayard (tel. 61 62 71 39).

Cheapest rooms around 170FF (£17.75; $31)

Jacobins, 52 rue Pargaminières (tel. 61 21 86 42). From Pl.
du Capitole follow rue Romiguières into rue Pargaminières.
Grand Hôtel d'Orléans, 72 rue Bayard (tel. 61 62 98 47).
Trianon, 7 rue Lafaille (tel. 61 62 74 74).

Cheapest rooms around 180FF (£18.75; $33)

Cosmos, 20 rue Caffarelli (tel. 61 62 57 21). See Hôtel
Beauséjour.
Junior, 62 rue du Taur (tel. 61 21 69 67).

Cheapest rooms around 190FF (£19.75; $34.50)

Le Bristol, 75 rue de Bayard (tel. 61 62 90 76).

Cheapest rooms around 200FF (£20.75; $36.50)

Clocher de Rodez, 14–15 pl. Jeanne d'Arc (tel. 61 62 42 92).
From rue de Bayard turn right along rue des Moutons into
the square.
Lafayette, 5 rue Caffarelli (tel. 61 62 75 73). See Hôtel
Beauséjour.
Metropole, 18 rue d'Austerlitz (tel. 61 21 68 51). See Hôtel
François.
L'Ours Blanc, 2 rue Victor Hugo (tel. 61 21 62 40). Off bd
de Strasbourg, left from the end of rue de Bayard.

HOSTELS

Villa des Rosiers, 125 av. Jean-Rieux (FUAJ) (Tel. 61 80 49
93). Curfew 11 p.m. Around 45FF (£4.75; $8.50). Bus 14

from the train station, then bus 22 to the hostel, or a 25-minute walk. Head left from the train station along the canal, then head left up av. Jean-Rieux at the fifth roadbridge.

UCJG (YMCA) San Francisco, 92 Route d'Espagne (tel. 61 40 29 28). Around 56FF (£5.80; $10.50). Bus 12 to Barrier de Muret.

CAMPING

Camping Municipal du Pont de Rupé, avenue des Etats-Unis, Chemin du Pont de Rupé (tel. 61 70 07 35). On the northern fringe of the city. Take bus P from the train station.

GERMANY (Deutschland)

The money already ploughed into tourism in the east of the country has, even at this early stage, ensured that the old DDR has a tourist infrastructure much more akin to the western European norm than any of the other former Eastern bloc countries. There is no discernible difference in the amount or quality of tourist information on offer between the east and the west of the country. However, there are great differences in the standard of accommodation: Germany will still be two separate countries for several years to come, though the difference is only really apparent if you are looking for a room of your own. In that case your most likely options are cheap hotels, pensionen, gasthäuse and private rooms. It is the relative abundance of these different forms of accommodation that is as good a guide as any to whether you are in the east or west of the country.

Cheap hotels, **pensionen** and **gasthäuse** are widely available in the west. Prices in the main tourist destinations generally start around DM32,50–35,00 (£11.40–12.25; $20–21.50) per person in singles and doubles, elsewhere around DM27,50 (£9.60; $17). The west also boasts a good supply of **farmhouse accommodation** (available mainly in summer) and **private rooms** (found mainly in the smaller towns). Prices for farmhouse accommodation and private rooms start around DM25–30 (£8.75–10.50; $15.50–18.50) per person. The standards of comfort and cleanliness in all the forms of accommodation mentioned above are invariably high, so you are virtually assured excellent value for money, particularly if you make comparisons with similarly priced accommodation in Italy or the UK. In the east of the country, cheap hotels, pensionen and gasthäuse are few and far between when compared to the west. Here it is **private rooms** which are the mainstay of the accommodation scene. They are by far the most widely available cheap accommodation possibility, no matter where you travel in the east. The increase in the number of private rooms available to let since the practice was legalized in the DDR in 1990 has averted a potentially serious accommodation shortage in the east. Now there is an ample supply of rooms, even in particularly popular destinations such as Dresden, Weimar, Potsdam and Eisenach. On average, prices are in the DM20–30 (£7–10.50; $12.50–18.50) per person range, in singles or doubles. While the standards of comfort in private rooms in the east may not yet match their western counterparts, rooms are normally scrupulously clean so that, on the whole, reasonable value for money is guaranteed. Tourist Office accommodation services throughout Germany are usually more than willing to help you find a room in any of the types of accommodation listed above. In smaller towns, it is feasible to look for rooms on your own. Simply make enquiries at hotels, or wherever you see a *'gasthof'* or *'zimmer frei'* sign. With the possible exception of staunchly Roman Catholic rural Bavaria, unmarried couples are unlikely to face any difficulties when requesting to share a room.

At a first glance, the impressive network of nearly 700 **IYHF hostels** created in 1991 by the fusion of West Germany's Deutsches Jugendherbergswerk (DJH) and the Jugend-herbergsverband der DDR would suggest that the budget traveller need look no further for a cheap bed. It is certainly possible to see the country cheaply if you hostel, as there is one in almost every town you are likely to visit, even during a four-month trip. As in other countries, hostelling is a good way to meet other travellers. One thing that should not deter you from hostelling in Germany is the image of German hostels as highly institutional and impersonal establishments, run by dour and officious staff. This is no more true than in most countries. Generally, the staff are approachable and happy to provide you with any information to help you enjoy your stay in town. However, there are some real drawbacks to hostelling as a means of visiting Germany. German hostels are open to IYHF members only. In Bavaria, there is a maximum age

restriction of 26; elsewhere hostels are open to people of all
ages. Curfews, which are rigorously enforced, are normally
10 p.m., except in the larger cities where hostels may stay open
until midnight or 1 a.m. Whether you are in a small town or
a large city, the curfew coincides with the time that the local
nightlife starts to get going.

The Association recommends that hostels should be reserved
in advance at all times, but particularly between 15 June and
15 September (good advice, but not always possible to adhere
to). Unless your reservation is for a longer period, you will be
limited to a three-night stay, except where there is plenty of
space at a hostel. If you have a reservation be sure to arrive
before 6 p.m. unless you have notified the hostel that you will
arrive later, otherwise your reservation will not be held, and
your bed may be given to someone else. If you turn up without
a reservation, priority is given to visitors aged up to 27 until
6 p.m. where beds are available. In theory, this means anyone
older is not assigned a bed until after 6 p.m. in case younger
guests arrive. In practice, this rule is often ignored. The
association handbook states that no beds are let after 10 p.m.,
even in the city hostels which are open late. Again this is a
rule that many wardens choose to ignore, so if you are stuck
there is nothing to be lost by approaching city hostels after
10 p.m.

There are six types of hostel and prices vary according to the
standard of comfort, facilities available, location, and the time
of the curfew. Prices at the different types of hostel also vary
according to the age of the user, with those aged 25 and over
paying a surcharge of around DM5 (£1.75; $3) at all hostels.
The main price divide amongst the various grades of hostel
is between **Jugendherbergen** (youth hostels) and
Jugendgasthäuse (youth guest houses). Juniors (age 24 and
under) pay between DM12,50–20,00 (£4.40–7.00; $7.50–12.50)
for B&B in dormitories at a Jugendherbergen. Unless you have
your own sheet sleeping bag, you will also have to pay for sheet
hire: the charge varies between the 15 regional associations,
but you can expect to pay at least DM5 (£1.75; $3) for the
duration of your stay. In a Jugendgasthäuse, prices for juniors

range from DM21–37 (£7.35–13.00; $13–23), with DM26–32 (£9.10–11.20; $16–20) being normal. Accommodation is mainly in two- or four-bed rooms, with breakfast and the hire of bed linen included in the overnight price.

Jugendgasthäuse are more expensive partly because they have been modernized in an effort to attract groups. This means that individual travellers are obliged to pay extra for leisure and recreation facilities that will rarely be available for their use. Groups can be a great source of annoyance to individual travellers. Hostels are frequently full of school and youth groups. This is especially true of hostels in the cities, along the Rhine and in the Black Forest, and in the more picturesque small towns; in short, all the places you are most likely to visit. The worst times are weekdays during the summer months, and weekends throughout the rest of the year. Space for individual travellers in hostels is often at a premium, and even by 9.30 a.m. you may be turned away. Even if you do squeeze into a hostel packed with groups it may not be too pleasant. As groups bring in a lot of money, wardens tend to turn a blind eye to poorly controlled or noisy groups, no matter what the rules say. While the various problems discussed above are by no means peculiar to Germany (English hostels can be just as bad), the sheer number of groups you encounter here causes greater irritation than in most other countries. Possibly the best advice is neither to avoid the hostels, nor to try and stay in them all of the time.

As well as the IYHF hostels, the western part of Germany has a network of hostels run by the 'Naturfreundehaus' organization (Friends of Nature Hostels). Most are located in the countryside just outside the towns. Accommodation is in singles, doubles, or small dorms, and prices are on a par with those of Jugendgasthäuse. Again, you may have problems finding a bed because of groups: not of schoolchildren this time, but of middle-aged guests, with whom the hostels are very popular.

Camping is an excellent way to see Germany cheaply, and without worrying about the likelihood of finding a cheap bed. The chances of you being turned away from a site because it is full are virtually nil (Munich's campsites manage to cope with the huge influx at the time of the Oktoberfest). At present, the sites in the east of the country are very quiet, since the numbers of campers coming from the west has failed to compensate for the loss of East European holidaymakers (primarily from the DDR and Czechoslovakia). In the west of Germany there are over 2,000 sites, covering all the main places of interest, and most towns and villages with even a minimal tourist trade. The two main operators are local authorities and the Deutscher Camping Club (DCC). Municipal sites are usually cheaper than those run by the DCC, but the standards of amenities and cleanliness are normally very high, irrespective of who operates the site. Some DCC sites are quite exceptional. Charges are around DM3–6 (£1.05–2.10; $1.80–3.60) for a tent, DM4,50–7,00 (£1.60–2.50; $3.00–4.50) per person, which, considering the standards of the sites, represents excellent value for money. Camping in the old DDR was a nightmare for Western visitors, as only a handful of the hundreds of sites were open to them, which often meant that long and tortuous journeys had to be made from the main tourist attractions to the 'nearest' site. With the removal of bureaucratic restrictions, camping immediately became a convenient way to see the east of Germany. Sites tend to be similarly priced to those in the west, or slightly cheaper. While levels of cleanliness are now on a par with sites in the west, the standards of facilities are generally lower. The one drawback to camping in the east is that you may still have to make a short journey of about five miles from one of the main towns to a smaller town nearby to find the closest campsite. This is rarely the case in the west, with sites usually being within the limits of the main towns (Heidelberg is one notable exception). In any large city where there is a choice of sites with similar prices, railpass holders may save on transportation costs if there is a site located near a local train station or an S-Bahn stop (railpasses are often valid on city S-Bahn systems). Even if they are not primarily interested in camping, anyone travelling extensively in Germany would be well advised to take a tent, as this will stand you in good stead if you happen to arrive in town during one of the many trade fairs or local festivals that take place in German cities throughout the year. At these times all the cheaper beds fill rapidly, so unless you can camp you will most likely have to either pay for an expensive hotel room, sleep rough, or leave town.

In an effort to safeguard the environment **camping outside official sites** has been made illegal, but it is still possible to sleep rough, providing you obtain the permission of the landowner and/or the police. There is little point trying to sleep out in parks or town centres. Apart from this being dangerous in some cities, the police will send you on your way if they find you. Police attitudes to **sleeping in stations** vary from place to place. In some of the smaller towns and cities they will wake you to check if you have a valid rail ticket, and if you have they will then let you lie until around 6 a.m., but when they come back at that time be prepared to move sharpish. If you do not have a ticket you will be ejected from the station, and arrested if you return later. In Munich, tolerance is shown (especially during the Oktoberfest) but do not expect a peaceful night before you are asked to move on in the morning. The stations of the northern ports and the central cities around Frankfurt are rough, and potentially dangerous at night. It is also unwise to try sleeping in the stations of the large towns in the east of the country. Although the media tends to overstate the level of neo-fascist activity in the former DDR, it is not unusual to see small groups of young neo-fascists in and around train stations late at night.

Railpass holders can always take a **night train** if they are stuck for somewhere to sleep. Trains leave the main stations for a multitude of destinations, internal and international. In the central area around Mainz-Heidelberg-Mannheim-Würzburg-Nuremberg there are trains leaving at all hours through the night. Alternatively, there is the 'Bahnhofs-mission', a church-run organization which operates in the stations of all reasonably sized towns in the west of the country (shelters will no doubt be opened in the east as well). They are meant for travellers who have no place to stay, or who are leaving early in the morning. If you approach the

Bahnhofsmission during the day it is likely that you will be told to return before 8 p.m. This highly restrictive curfew helps prevent abuses of the system by those who are simply looking to fix themselves up with a cheap bed. You cannot stay more than one night in the shelter. B&B and use of the showers usually costs DM10–15 (£3.50–5.25; $6.00–9.50).

Note: There is no unified telephone system in Germany, so codes quoted for eastern cities may be useless if phoning from the west of the country (and vice versa). As the telephone system in the east is overhauled codes quoted may also become obsolete, even for phone calls within the east of the country. Check which code you should be using when you telephone across the old border. Most telephone boxes have a panel showing main city codes; if not, enquire at a post office or contact directory enquiries.

ADDRESSES

German National Tourist Office	Nightingale House, 65 Curzon Street, London W1 7PE (tel. 071-495 3990).
German YHA	Deutsches Jugendherbergswerk (DJH), Hauptverband, Bismarckstrasse 8, Postfach 1455, 4930 Detmold (tel. 05231–74010).
Friends of Nature Hostels	NaturfreundeJugend, Grossglockner Strasse 28, 7000 Stuttgart 60 (tel. 0711 481076).
Camping	Deutscher Camping-Club (DCC), Mandlestrasse 28, 8000 München 23 (tel. 089–334021).
	The DCC sell the official, comprehensive guide to Germany's campsites. Expect to pay around DM25 (£8.75; $15.50) for the guide.
	A considerably abridged list is available from the German National Tourist Office.

Berlin

Tourist Offices

Verkehrsamt Berlin, Europa Center, Budapesterstrasse 45 (tel. 2626031). (Charlottenburg.) Open daily 8 a.m.–10.30 p.m. Basic plan of the city. Rooms found in local hotels for a fee of DM3 (£1.05; $1.80). From the Zoologischer Garten train station (main line, S-bahn and U-bahn) head along Budapesterstrasse past the ruins of the Kaiser-Wilhelm-Gedächtniskirche. The Europa Center is on the right after about 500m. There are Verkehrsamt Berlin branch offices at the Zoologischer Garten station (tel. 3139063/3139064) and at Tegel Airport (tel. 41013145), both open 8 a.m.–8 p.m. daily.

Informationszentrum Berlin, Hardenbergstrasse 20, 3rd floor. Open Mon.–Fri. 8 a.m.–7 p.m., Sat. 8 a.m.–4 p.m. Close to Zoologischer Garten station. Well worth visiting to pick up **Berlin for Young People**, a highly useful guide to the sights and entertainment which includes a detailed pull-out plan of the central area (both east and west).

Informationszentrum am Fernsehturm, Panaramastrasse 1 (tel. 2124675/2124512). (Mitte.) This office should provide the same services as the Verkehrsamt Berlin offices, but (on past performance) do not head here first. At the foot of the radio tower on Alexanderplatz (S-bahn and U-bahn: Alexanderplatz).

HOTELS

Cheapest doubles around DM56 (£19.60; $34.50)

Gasthaus Waldowstrasse, Waldowstrasse 47 (tel. 52774) (Hellersdorf). Singles around DM30 (£10.50; $18.50). Breakfast not included.

Pension 'Monika', Schrägerweg 26 (tel. 9494502) (Weissensee). Without breakfast.

Haus Schliebner Pension, Dannenwalderweg 95 (tel. 4167997) (Reinickendorf). Without breakfast.

Cheapest doubles around DM65 (£22.75; $40)

Pension Zum Alten Fischerdorf, Dorfstrasse 14 (tel. 6489320)
(Köpenick).
Gästehaus Karlshorst, Aristotelessteig 6 (tel. 5042568)
(Lichtenberg).
Privatzimmer Wolfram, Steinkirchenerstrasse 6 (tel. 4151362)
(Reinickendorf). Without breakfast.
Pension 22, Schambachweg 22 (tel. 3655230) (Spandau).
Breakfast not included.
Pension Elton, Pariserstrasse 9 (tel. 8836155/8836156)
(Wilmersdorf).

Cheapest doubles around DM70 (£24.50; $43.50)

Hotel-Pension Trautenau, Trautenaustrasse 14 (tel. 8613514)
(Wilmersdorf).

Cheapest doubles around DM75 (£26.25; $46.50)

Hotelpension Neues Tor, Invalidenstrasse 102 (tel. 2823859)
(Mitte). Without breakfast.
Hotel Hamburger Hof, Kinkelstrasse 6 (tel. 3334602)
(Spandau).
Wilhelmshöhe, Brandensteinweg 6 (tel. 3619094/3625711)
(Spandau).
Hotel-Pension Haus Konstanz, Konstanzerstrasse 30 (tel.
860268) (Wilmersdorf).
Hotel-Pension München, Güntzelstrasse 62 (tel. 854226)
(Wilmersdorf).

Cheapest doubles around DM80 (£28; $50)

Hotel Pension Majesty, Mommsenstrasse 55 (tel. 3232061)
(Charlottenburg).
Wirtshaus zum Finkenhanel, Steinkirchenerstrasse 17 (tel.
415953) (Reinickendorf).

Cheapest doubles around DM85 (£29.75; $53)

City-Pension Alexandra, Wielandstrasse 32 (tel. 8812107) (Charlottenburg).

Centrum Pension Berlin, Kantstrasse 31 (tel. 316153) (Charlottenburg). Without breakfast.

Motel Grünau, Libboldallee 17 (tel. 6814198) (Köpenick).

Hotel Reichspost, Urbanstrasse 84 (tel. 6911035) (Kreuzberg).

Pension Helga, Formerweg 19 (tel. 6621010) (Neukölln). Breakfast not included.

Hotel Benn, Ritterstrasse 1a (tel. 3331061) (Spandau). Without breakfast.

Gästehaus Ingeborg, Ruthnerweg 15 (tel. 8177632) (Steglitz).

Pension Am Elsterplatz, Plönerstrasse 25 (tel. 862880) (Wilmersdorf). Without breakfast.

Haus Tannenhöhe, Ulrichstrasse 31 (tel. 8051531) (Zehlendorf).

Cheapest doubles around DM90 (£31.50; $56)

Hotel Charlottenburger Hof, Stuttgarterplatz 14 (tel. 3244819) (Charlottenburg). Without breakfast.

Hotel Pension Metropol, Fasenenstrasse 71 (tel. 8817579) (Charlottenburg). Without breakfast.

Hotel Transit, Hagelbergerstrasse 53–54 (tel. 7855051) (Kreuzberg).

Pension Schultze, Friedrichrodaerstrasse 13 (tel. 779970) (Steglitz). Breakfast not included.

Pension 'Dorf-Aue', Alt-Lichtenrade 128 (tel. 7444581) (Tempelhof).

Hotel-Pension Pariser Eck, Pariserstrasse 19 (tel. 8812145) (Wilmersdorf). Breakfast not included.

Cheapest doubles around DM95 (£33.25; $59)

Hotelpension Cortina, Kantstrasse 140 (tel. 3139059/317396) (Charlottenburg).

Hotel Crystal, Kantstrasse 144 (tel. 3129047/3129048/3129049) (Charlottenburg).

Pension Oliva, Schlüterstrasse 36 (tel. 8815895) (Charlottenburg). Without breakfast.

Pension Silvia, Knesebeckstrasse 29 (tel. 8812129) (Charlottenburg). Breakfast not included.

Pension Viola Nova, Kantstrasse 146 (tel. 316457) (Charlottenburg). Breakfast not included.

Pension Cäcilie, Motzstrasse 52 (tel. 2116514) (Schöneberg). Breakfast not included.

Haus zur Linde am See, Alt-Gatow 1–3 (tel. 3626094) (Spandau). Without breakfast.

Hotel-Pension Margret, Breitestrasse 36 (tel. 3333088) (Spandau).

Pension Dalg, Woltmannweg 46 (tel. 7734908) and Ritterstrasse 6B (tel. 7124076) (Steglitz). Without breakfast.

Hotel Pichlers Viktoriagarten, Leonorenstrasse 18–22 (tel. 7716088) (Steglitz).

Pension Finck, Güntzelstrasse 54 (tel. 8612940/8618158) (Wilmersdorf).

Hotel-Pension Insel Rügen, Pariserstrasse 39/40 (tel. 8818204) (Wilmersdorf).

Hotel-Pension Uhlietz, Lietzenburgerstrasse 77 (tel. 8836177) (Wilmersdorf).

Haus La Garde, Bergengruenstrasse 16 (tel. 8013009) (Zehlendorf). Without breakfast.

Cheapest doubles around DM100 (£35; $62)

Hotelpension 'a b c', Grolmanstrasse 32/33 (tel. 8811496) (Charlottenburg).

Hotel Am Park-Pension, Sophie-Charlotten-Strasse 57/58 (tel. 3213485) (Charlottenburg).

Hotel-Pension Charlottenburg, Grolmanstrasse 32/33 (tel. 8815254) (Charlottenburg).

Hotel-Pension Leibniz, Leibnizstrasse 59 (tel. 3238495) (Charlottenburg).

Hotel-Pension Curtis, Pariserstrasse 39/40 (tel. 8812757/ 8834931) (Wilmersdorf).

Pension am Rüdesheimer Platz, Rüdesheimerplatz 7 (tel. 8217732) (Wilmersdorf).

Hotel-Pension Kleist, Darmstadterstrasse 7 (tel. 8814701) (Wilmersdorf).

Hotelpension Wien, Brandenburgischestrasse 37 (tel. 8918486) (Wilmersdorf).

PRIVATE ROOMS & APARTMENTS

Verkehrsamt Berlin, Europa Center, Budapesterstrasse 45 (tel. 2626031) (Charlottenburg). Around DM35 (£12.25; $21.50) per person, with breakfast for private rooms. Two-night minimum stay. For opening hours and directions, see the Tourist Office section above.

Europäisches Reisebüro (Haus des Reisens), Alexanderplatz 5 (tel. 2154415) (Mitte). Rooms DM18–30 (£6.30–10.50; $11.00–18.50) per person. Office open Mon.–Fri. 10.00 a.m.–6 p.m., Sat. 10 a.m.–5 p.m. S-bahn and U-bahn: Alexanderplatz.

Zeitraum, Horstweg 7 (tel. 3256181) (Charlottenburg). From DM27,50 (£9.60; $17) per person in rooms and apartments. Office open Mon.–Fri. 9.00 a.m.–1 p.m. and 3–8 p.m., Sat. noon–4 p.m.

Berlin City-Apartments, Rheinstrasse 159 (tel. 9753122) (Lichtenberg). From DM60 (£21; $37) for doubles. Apartments available.

Berlin City-Apartments, Landsbergerallee 203 (tel. 978080) (Hohenschönhausen). From DM70 (£24.50; $43.50) for doubles. Apartments available.

Mitwohnzentrale, Kurfürstendamm 227/228, 2nd floor (tel. 883051) (Charlottenburg). Prices for apartments start around DM35 (£12.25; $21.50) per person for one night, falling with the length of your stay. Open Mon.–Fri. 10.00 a.m.–7 p.m., weekends 11 a.m.–4 p.m.

Wohnagentur Q-3-A, Prenzlauer Allee 17 (tel. 4371515). Lets apartments in the east of the city, frequently at lower rates than the Mitwohnzentrale above. Open Mon.–Fri. 10.00 a.m.–7 p.m., Sat. 11 a.m.–4 p.m.

IYHF HOSTELS

Advance reservation is advisable, particularly if you are travelling in summer, or will be arriving in Berlin at the weekend. Requests for reservations should be sent to the head office of the regional hostel association in Tempelhof: DJH Landesverband Berlin-Brandenburg, Tempelhofer Ufer 32, 1000 Berlin 61 (tel. 2623024). The hostels are open to IYHF members only. Cards can be purchased from the regional head office for around DM30 (£10.50; $18.50). Office open 10.00 a.m.–3 p.m. Mon., Wed. and Fri., and from 2–5.30 p.m. Tues. and Thurs.

'Ernst Reuter', Hermsdorfer Damm 48–50 (tel. 4041610) (Hermsdorf). Midnight curfew. Juniors DM21,50 (£7.35; $13.50) for B&B. U-bahn: Tegel (line 6), then bus 125 dir. Frohnau to the fourth stop.

Jugendgasthaus Berlin, Kluckstrasse 3 (tel. 2611097) (Tiergarten). Midnight curfew. Juniors DM27 (£9.50; $16.50) for B&B. Bus 129 from Kurfürstendamm towards Oranienplatz or Hermannplatz.

Jugendgasthaus Wannsee, Badeweg 1 (tel. 8032034) (Wannsee). Midnight curfew. Juniors DM27 (£9.50; $16.50) for B&B. S-bahn: Nikolassee (line 3) then a 10-minute walk towards the beach. The hostel is at the junction of Badeweg and Kronprinzessinnenweg.

HOSTELS/DORMITORY ACCOMMODATION

Jugendgasthaus am Zoo, Hardenbergerstrasse 9a (tel. 3129410) (Charlottenburg). Singles DM44 (£15.40; $27.50); doubles DM77,50 (£27.20; $48). DM29 (£10.20; $18) per person in quads. Without breakfast. U-Bahn: Ernst-Reuter-Platz.

Studenthotel, Meiningerstrasse 10 (tel. 7846720) (Schöneberg). B&B in doubles DM35 (£12.25; $21.50) per person, in quads DM32 (£11.20; $20) per person. U-Bahn: Rathaus Schöneberg, or Bus 146 from Zoologischer Garten train station to the same stop.

Jugendhotel Am Tierpark, Franz-Mett-Strasse 7 (5100114) (Lichtenberg). Doubles, triples and quads. DM29–32 (£10.15–11.20; $18–20) per person, breakfast included. Huge capacity, 150m from the Tierpark U-Bahn stop.

Studentenwohnheim Hubertusallee, Hubertusallee 61, at the junction with Delbrückstrasse (tel. 8919718) (Wilmersdorf). Students with ID pay DM44 (£15.40; $27.50) for singles, DM66 (£23.20; $40.50) for doubles, and DM78 (£27.40; $48) for triples. The prices for non-students are DM83 (£29; $51) for singles, DM100 (£35; $62) for doubles, and DM110 (£38.50; $68) for triples. Breakfast included. Bus 110 or 129.

Jugendgasthaus Central, Nikolsburgerstrasse 2–4 (tel. 870188) (Wilmersdorf). 1 a.m. curfew. Two-to eight-bed rooms. DM33 (£11.60; $20.50) for B&B, DM38 (£13.30; $23.50) for full board. U-Bahn: Güntzelstrasse.

Jugendgasthaus Feurigstrasse, Feurigstrasse 63 (tel. 7815211/7815212) (Schöneberg). DM33 (£11.60; $20.50) for B&B. U-Bahn: Kleistpark.

Jugendhotel International, Bernburgerstrasse 27/28 (tel. 2623081/2623082) (Kreuzberg). DM40 (£14; $25) for B&B in three-to seven-bed rooms, DM44 (£15.40; $27) per person in doubles, DM50 (£17.50; $31) for singles.

INTERNATIONAL YOUTH CAMP

Internationales Jugendcamp, Ziekowstrasse 161 (tel. 4338640) (Reinickendorf-Hermsdorf). A similar idea to 'The Tent' in Munich; a large covered area, with mattresses and sheets provided. Open 21 June–31 Aug. Age limit 26. DM9 (£3.20; $5.50) per night. Bus 122 from the Tegel U-bahn station.

CAMPING

The campsites below are all open year round. DM8 (£2.80; $5) per person is the standard charge at all four sites. Advance reservations can be made by contacting the Deutscher Camping Club e.V. at Geisbergstrasse 11, 1000 Berlin 30 (tel. 246071) (Schöneberg).

Kladow, Krampnitzerweg 111/117 (tel. 3652797) (Spandau).
From the Rathaus Spandau U-bahn station take bus 135
to its terminus, then continue along Krampnitzerweg about
500m.

Haselhorst, Pulvermühlenweg (tel. 3345955). From the
Haselhorst U-bahn station follow Daumster into
Pulvermühlenweg.

Dreilinden, Kremnitz Ufer (Albrechts-Teerofen) (tel. 8051201)
(Wannsee). Bus 118 from the Oskar-Helene Heim U-bahn
station, then a 20-minute walk along Kremnitz Ufer to
Albrechts-Teerofen.

International Campsite Krossinsee, Wernsdorferstrasse (tel.
6858687) (Schmöckwitz). A 1½ mile walk from the terminus
of tram 86, across the bridge, then down the third turning
on the right.

SLEEPING ROUGH

The Grunewald is the most obvious, but there are lots of places
at the end of the S-Bahn lines, or along the shores of the
Krossinsee.

If you are stuck for a bed, but do not want to sleep out, go
to the Bahnhofsmission in Zoologischer Garten station, where
you will be given a bed for DM15 (£5.25; $9.50). One night
only.

Bremen (tel. code 0421)

Tourist Offices

Verkehrsverein der Freien Hansestadt Bremen,
Hillmannplatz 6, 2800 Bremen 1 (tel. 30800). Open
Mon.–Thurs. 9 a.m.–4 p.m., Fri. 9 a.m.–2 p.m. Contact
this office only for information on hotels and for
reservations.

Tourist-Information am Hauptbahnhof. Open Mon.–Thurs.
8 a.m.–8 p.m., Fri. 8 a.m.–10 p.m., Sat. 8 a.m.–6 p.m.,

Sun. 9.30 a.m.–3.30 p.m. Information on the city and on accommodation. Outside the main train station (Bremen Hbf).

Tourist-Information Bremen-Nord, Alte Hafenstrasse 30 (tel. 663120). Open Mon. 2–6 p.m., Tues.–Fri. 10 a.m.–6 p.m., Sat. 10 a.m.–2 p.m. Information on the city and on accommodation.

HOTELS

Few of the city's cheaper hotels are located close to the centre, or to the train station.

Cheapest doubles around DM70 (£24.50; $43.50)

Pension Haus Hohenlohe, Hohenlohestrasse 5 (tel. 342395/342364). A 5-minute walk from Bremen Hbf. Head left from the exit, turn left under the lines, right at the fork in the road, and then right along Hohenlohestrasse off Hermann-Böse-Strasse.

Sillingers Hotel, Osterholzer Heerstrasse 152 (tel. 405600).

Cheapest doubles around DM75 (£26.25; $46.50)

Grollander Krug, Oldenburgerstrasse 11 (tel. 510755).

Gästehäus Walter, Buntentorsteinweg 86 (tel. 558027/554773) Off Friedrich-Ebert-Strasse, across the Kleine Weser.

Lütkemeyer, Rockwinkeler Landstrasse 83 (tel. 259461).

Hans Neustadt, Graudenzerstrasse 33 (tel. 551749). In the Sudervorstadt district.

Enzensperger, Brautstrasse 9 (tel. 503224). Reasonable location. Just across the Weser, between the Bürgermeister-Smidt-Brücke and the Wilhelm-Kaiser-Brücke.

Regenbogen Apartments, Hastedter Osterdeich 206 (tel. 442769).

Cheapest doubles around DM80 (£28; $50)

Pension Kosch, Cellerstrasse 4 (tel. 447101). Close to the
Weserstadion (home of Werder Bremen).

Pension Galerie, Thedinghauserstrasse 46 (tel. 530753). In
the area off Friedrich-Ebert-Strasse.

Pension Haus Bremen, Verdenerstrasse 47 (tel.
4987777/4987778). In the area close to the Weserstadion.

Cheapest doubles around DM85 (£29.75; $53)

Hotel-Pension Weidmann, Am Schwarzen Meer 35 (tel.
4940557). In the area close to the Weserstadion.

Krone, Hastedter Osterdeich 209b (tel. 443151).

Heinisch, Wachmannstrasse 26 (tel. 342925). By the
Burgerpark, a 10-minute walk from Bremen Hbf. From the
train station, head left and then turn left under the lines.
At the fork in the road, head right along Hermann-Böse-
Strasse. Wachmannstrasse is directly across the junction
with Hollerallee when you reach the park.

Cheapest doubles around DM90 (£31.50; $56)

Weltvreden, Am Dobben 62 (78015/704091). Reasonable
location, just outside the historic centre.

Zum Werdersee, Holzdamm 104 (tel. 83504/83505). Just off
the Werderseebrücke.

IYHF HOSTELS

Jugendgasthaus Bremen, Kalkstrasse 6 (tel. 171369). 1 a.m.
curfew. DM25–28 (£8.75–9.75; $15.50–17.00). Fine location
by the Weser, a short walk from the city centre. From the
train station walk down Bahnhofstrasse, cross the water,
and turn right along Am Wall past the windmill. Turn left
off Am Wall down Bürgermeister-Smidt-Strasse, then go
right when you reach the river.

Jugendherberge Bumenthal, Bürgermeister-Dehnkamp-

Strasse 22 (tel. 601005). DM18–21 (£6.30–7.40; $11–13). Far from the centre.

HOSTELS

Seemansheim Bremen, Jippen 1 (tel. 18361). Singles DM22–34 (£7.70–12.00; $13.50–21.00), doubles DM17–20 (£6–7; $10.50–12.50) per person in quads. In the same part of town as the DJH Jugendgasthaus, only slightly further out from the centre

IYHF HOSTELS NEARBY

Jugendherberge Worpswede, Hammeweg, 2, Worpswede (tel. 04792–1360). Around DM20 (£7; $12.50). Worpswede is about ten miles from Bremen. No train service, but regular buses.

CAMPING

Campingplatz Freie Hansestadt Bremen, Am Stadtwaldsee 1 (tel. 212002). Close to the university. Buses 23 and 28 pass close to the site.

Cologne (Köln) (tel. code 0221)

Tourist Office
Verkehrsamt der Stadt Köln, Unter Fettenhennen 19, 5000 Köln (tel. 2213345). Open May–Oct., daily from 8 a.m.–10.30 p.m. except Sun. and public holidays 9 a.m.–10.30 p.m.; Nov.–Apr., open daily from 8 a.m.–9 p.m. except Sun. and public holidays 9.30 a.m.–7 p.m. The office accepts requests to book hotel accommodation in advance by letter, but not by telephone. Room-finding service for those who arrive without prior reservation. DM4 (£1.40; $2.50) commission.

Basic Directions
Leaving Köln Hbf by the main exit on to Bahnhofvorplatz the
vast bulk of the cathedral is to your left. Going right along the
front of the train station as far as you can, and then following
the street which runs away to your left, you arrive at the
junction with Marzellanstrasse. Going right along
Marzellanstrasse to the end of the street you can turn right
under the train lines, or turn left into Ursulaplatz. Across
Bahnhofvorplatz from the train station, almost opposite the
main entrance to the cathedral is the Tourist Office on Unter
Fettenhennen. Running away from the cathedral near the
Tourist Office is Hohe Strasse. To the left of Hohe Strasse is
the old market (Alter Markt) and the Town Hall, beyond which
is the Rhine. The Hohenzollern-brücke crosses the Rhine by
the cathedral. The next bridge downstream is the Deutzer
Brücke. Along the Rhine between the two are the Frankenwerft
and the Rheingarten. Continuing on down Hohe Strasse the
street is crossed by I.d. Höhle and Gürzenichstrasse. Turning
right along either of these streets and continuing straight on
you reach the Neumarkt. Further on down Hohe Strasse the
street is crossed by Cäcilienstrasse. Heading right,
Cäcilienstrasse leads into the Neumarkt, going left on to the
Deutzer Brücke. Beyond Cäcilienstrasse. Hohe Strasse becomes
Hohe Pforte, which in turn becomes Severinstrasse, a long
street which runs all the way to the Severinstor (one of the
old city gates) on Chlodwigplatz. From Köln Hbf to the end
of Hohe Pforte is just over 10 minutes' walk, to the Severinstor
about 20 minutes' walk.

Buses 32 and 33 from Köln Hbf wind their way through the
area around the Town Hall before running the whole length
of Severinstrasse and on beyond the Severinstor. Leaving Köln
Hbf by the rear exit, you emerge on to Breslauer Platz. Going
left from the square, you pass the end of Domstrasse. A short
distance down Domstrasse you pass the ends of
Brandenburgerstrasse and then Jakordenstrasse. Following
Domstrasse to its end, you can turn left on to Ebertplatz.

HOTELS

Cheapest doubles around DM65 (£22.75; $40)

Pension Kirchner, Richard-Wagner-Strasse 18 (tel. 252977).
A 20-minute walk from Köln Hbf. From the Neumarkt,
follow Hahnenstrasse, then go left at Pilgrimstrasse, which
leads into Richard-Wagner-Strasse. Pilgrimstrasse begins
by the U-bahn station at Rudolfplatz, between the
Habsburgerring and the Hohenzollernring.

Henn, Norbertstrasse 6 (tel. 134445). Head right from the
Tourist Office to the end of Unter Fettenhennen. Turn left
and go straight on, along Komödienstrasse and on down
Zeughausstrasse and Friesenstrasse until you see
Norbertstrasse on the right.

Hubertushof, Mühlenbach 30 (tel. 217386). A 10-minute walk
from Köln Hbf, left off Hohe Pforte.

Alter Römer, Am Bollwerk 23 (tel. 212385/216290). One street
back from the Frankenwerft, between Bischofsgarten-
strasse and Grosse Neugasse.

Schützenhof, Mengenicherstrasse 12 (tel. 5902739). Far from
the centre in the suburb of Pesch. Take a train to Köln
Westbahnhof then take tram 3 to the terminus on
Venloerstrasse. Continue on down Venloerstrasse then go
right at the fork in the road along Grevenbroicherstrasse
and Nüssenbergerstrasse.

Haus Schallenberg, Bergisch-Gladbacherstrasse 616 (tel.
633091/633092). Far from the centre but easy to reach. From
Evertplatz take tram 16 to the junction of Isenburgstrasse
with Maria-Himmelfahrt, then walk up the latter on to
Bergisch-Gladbacherstrasse. The hotel is nearby.

Cheapest doubles around DM70 (£24.50; $43.50)

An der Oper, Auf der Ruhr 3 (tel. 245065). Just over 5
minutes' walk from Köln Hbf. Turn right off Hohe Strasse
along Minoritenstrasse and continue straight on until Auf
der Ruhr crosses Breite Strasse.

Rossner, Jakordenstrasse 19 (tel. 122703).

Göbbels, Stammstrasse 2a (tel. 523414). Take a local train to
the Köln Ehrenfeld station. Stammstrasse begins by the
station.

Cheapest doubles around DM75 (£26.25; $46.50)

Flintsch, Moselstrasse 16–20 (tel. 232142). Take a local train
to Köln Südbahnhof. Moselstrasse is the street running
along the front of the station.

Am Blomekörvge, Josephstrasse 15 (tel. 323660).
Josephstrasse runs left off Severinstrasse about half-way
down the street.

Brandenburger Hof, Brandenburger Strasse 2–4 (tel. 122889).

Schmitze-Lang, Severinstrasse 62 (tel. 318129).

Pension Jansen, Richard-Wagner-Strasse 18 (tel. 251875). See
Pension Kirchner above for directions.

Cheapest doubles around DM80 (£28; $50)

Rhein-Hotel St Martin, Frankenwerft 31–33 (tel.
234031/234032/234033).

Thielen & Tourist, Brandenburger Strasse 1–7 (tel. 123333).

Dom-Pension, Domstrasse 28 (tel. 123742).

Am Rathaus, Bürgerstrasse 6 (tel. 216293). By the Town Hall,
about 8 minutes' walk from Köln Hbf. Turn left off Hohe
Strasse at Grosse Budengasse, go straight on, then right
at Bürgerstrasse.

Berg, Brandenburger Strasse 6 (tel. 121124).

Autohof SVG, Kreuznacherstrasse 1 (tel. 380535). Well out
from the centre in the suburb of Raderberg. From Köln Hbf,
take bus 33 to the junction of the Brühlerstrasse with
Raderthaler Gürtel and Raderberger Gürtel. Walk up
Raderbergerstrasse and take the first left.

Im Kupferkessel, Probsteigasse 6 (tel. 135338). From
Bahnhofvorplatz, head away from the station down
Ketzerstrasse and then An den Dominikan. Keep on going
straight ahead until you see Probsteigasse on the right off
Christophstrasse.

Cheapest doubles around DM85 (£29.75; $53)

Wever, Jahnstrasse 22 (tel. 233282). A 15–20-minute walk from the Köln Hbf. From the Neumarkt take Hahnenstrasse, turn left down Mauritiussteinweg and go around the church to the start of Jahnstrasse. You can take the U-bahn to the Neumarkt from Köln Hbf. From Ottoplatz in front of the Köln Deutz train station, trams 1 and 2 run along Jahnstrasse.

Heinzelmännchen, Hohe Pforte 5–7 (tel. 211217).

Drei Könige, Marzellenstrasse 58–60 (tel. 132088/132089).

Haus Trost, Thebäerstrasse 17 (tel. 516647/513232). Take a local train to Köln Ehrenfeld then follow Stammstrasse from the station and turn right along Simrockstrasse into Thebäerstrasse. A 5–10-minute walk from Köln Ehrenfeld.

Tagungs und Gästehaus St Georg, Rolandstrasse 61 (tel. 383046/383047). Bus 32 or 33 from Köln Hbf or a 25-minute walk. Rolandstrasse is to the right off Bonnerstrasse just beyond the Severinstor.

Lindenhof, Lintgasse 7 (tel. 231242). From Hohe Strasse turn left down Grosse Budengasse and continue on along Kleine Budengasse and Mühlengasse. Turn right down Unter Käster and then right again. Bus 32 and 33 from Köln Hbf pass the end of the street, but it takes just over 5 minutes to walk.

Graf Adolph, Adolphstrasse 12 (tel. 316611). From Ottoplatz by the Köln Deutz train station, take Neuhöfferstrasse and continue straight ahead until you reach Adolphstrasse.

Weisser Schwan, Thieboldsgasse 133/135 (tel. 217697). The street runs off the Neumarkt. A 15–20-minute walk from Köln Hbf, but an easy walk from the U-bahn station on the Neumarkt.

Zum Boor, Bonnerstrasse 217 (tel. 383998). Bus 32 from Köln Hbf runs along Bonnerstrasse.

City-Hotel, Ursulagartenstrasse 26 (tel. 133646). In a quiet street by St Ursula's Church, just under 10 minutes' walk from Köln Hbf. Follow Marzellanstrasse to its end and turn

left into Ursulaplatz from which Ursulagartenstrasse is off
to the right.

IYHF HOSTELS

Siegestrasse 5a (tel. 814711). Curfew 12.30 a.m. DM22 (£7.70;
$13.50). Fills quickly. Reception opens 12.30 p.m. 150m from
Köln-Deutz station. Well signposted. Frequent connections
from the main train station by local train or S-Bahn (free with
railpasses). Twenty minutes from town centre across the
Deutzer Brücke, 15 minutes from Köln Hbf across the
Hohenzollernbrücke.

Jugendegasthaus Köln-Riehl, An der Schanze 14 (tel. 767081).
Phoning ahead will enable to find out whether rooms are
available, but no reservations are accepted. Reception opens
at 11 a.m. Rooms go fast, so get there as soon as possible.
DM29 (£10.15; $18). Two miles from the main train station.
From Breslauer Platz, walk right down to the river, turn left,
on under the Zoobrücke, along Niederlander Ufer into An
der Schanze. From Köln Hbf take U-bahn lines 5, 16 or 18
to Boltensternstrasse.

CAMPING

All the sites are quite a distance from the centre. If you take
tram 16 to Marienburg there are two sites on the opposite side
of the Rhine, about 15 minutes' walk over the Rodenkirchener
Brücke in Köln-Poll.

Campingplatz der Stadt Köln, Weidenweg (tel. 831966).
Open 1 May–10 Oct. Intended mainly for families, but you
will not be turned away.

Alfred-Schütte-Allee (tel. 835989). Open 1 July–15 Sept. Site
for young people.

Campingplatz Berger, Uferstrasse 53a is in Köln-
Rodenkirchen (tel. 392421). Open all year round.

Campingplatz Waldbad, Peter-Baum-Weg is in Köln-
Dünnwald (tel. 603315). Open all year round.

IYHF HOSTELS NEARBY

'Jugendhof', Macherscheiderstrasse 113, Neuss-Uedesheim (tel. 02101–39273). There are frequent connections between Cologne and Neuss by train and S-Bahn.

Dresden (tel. code 051)

Tourist Offices

Dresden Werbung und Tourismus GmbH, Goetheallee 18, 0-8053 Dresden (tel. 35621). Contact this office in advance for information on the city and help in planning your visit. On arrival in Dresden, you can obtain information and book accommodation at either of the two offices the Dresden Tourist Board operate in the city.

Dresden Information, Pragerstrasse 10, 0-8010 Dresden (tel. 4955025). Open Apr.–Sept., Mon.–Sat. 9 a.m.–8 p.m., Sun. 9 a.m.–1 p.m.; Oct.–Mar., Mon.–Fri. 9 a.m.–8 p.m., Sat. 9 a.m.–2 p.m., Sun. 9 a.m.–1 p.m. A 5-minute walk from Dresden Hbf. You cannot miss the tall Hotel Newa on Pragerstrasse on leaving the Dresden Hbf.

Dresden Information (Branch Office), Neustadter Markt (tel. 53539). Open Mon.–Fri. 9 a.m.–6 p.m., weekends 9 a.m.–4 p.m. A 5–10-minute walk from Bahnhof Dresden-Neustadt. From the square in front of the statin, head left along Antonstrasse into Platz der Einheit from which Strasse der Befreiung runs to the Neustadter Markt with the famous Goldener Reiter statue. The Tourist Office is in the underpass leading to the Augustusbrücke.

Arriving in Dresden by Train

Trains not terminating in Dresden frequently stop at Bahnhof Dresden-Neustadt only. However, there are regular connnecting trains between the two stations. It is unlikely that you will have to wait more than 15 minutes for a connection. Dresden

Hbf and Dresden Neustadt are also linked by a frequent tram service (lines 3 and 11).

Public Transport

The Dresdner Verkehrsbetriebe AG operate an integrated transport system consisting mainly of the suburban railway (SV-bahn), trams and buses. Their head office is near the Dresden-Neustadt station at Antonstrasse 2a (tel. 52001). There is an information booth in front of Dresden Hbf. Dresden Transport sell a particularly cheap day-ticket for visitors (DM2 (£0.70; $1.25) in 1992). As well as the trams, buses and SV-bahn, the ticket covers the Elbe ferry (on the route to the Pillnitz Palace) and the funicular railway.

Trouble Spots

Unlike in most German cities, the 1FC Dynamo Dresden football stadium is close to the main train station, so opposition fans walk to the ground, inevitably accompanied by groups of local fans taunting their rivals, and the police, complete with dogs, and riot police waiting in the wings. While the police in eastern Germany have learned from their western counterparts how to deal with the novel and hence very dangerous problem of football hooliganism which emerged in the wake of reunification, the spectacle can be unnerving for anyone unaccustomed to such a scene. There is virtually no chance of you being set upon, but, as with all such situations, there is no knowing what damage the throwing of even one missile can do. The best advice is to avoid the area between Dresden Hbf and the Altmarkt and Pirnaischer Platz before and after matches (usually Saturday afternoons, occasionally Wednesday evenings; match posters are displayed by Dresden Information).

Accommodation In and Around Dresden

Dresden is highly popular, so accommodation is best reserved in advance. The cheapest hotels and pensions are all located outside central Dresden, as are the majority of the private rooms on offer, which means you are going to have to use the public transport system to get to them. Several of the accommodation options listed below are in Radebeul which is, effectively, a suburb of Dresden. Those with a railpass can travel free to Radebeul by taking one of the frequent local trains.

HOTELS

Cheapest doubles around DM45 (£15.75; $28) for B&B

Pension Dorn, Am Wehr 7, 0-8017 Dresden (no telephone).
Pension Zimmel, Marienstrasse 9, Radebeul (tel. 78432).

Cheapest doubles around DM50 (£17.50; $31) for B&B

Fremdenheim Lössnitzer Hof, Meissnerstrasse 202, Radebeul (tel. 75353).

Cheapest doubles around DM55 (£19.25; $34) without breakfast

Pension Magvas, Gondelweg 3 (tel. 2236084).
Pension Im Grünen an der Elbe, Pillnitzer Landstrasse 174 (tel. 376517). From Dresden Hbf take tram 10 to Altenbergerplatz, then change to bus 85, which runs along Pillnitzer Landstrasse.

Cheapest doubles around DM70 (£24.50; $43.50)

Touristenhotel Haus der Kultur und Bildung, Maternistrasse 17 (tel. 4845266). Breakfast included.
Pension Haus Hohenblick, Höhenweg 28, Pappritz (tel. 36363). All rooms have shower and WC. Breakfast not included.

Cheapest doubles around DM75 (£26.25; $46.50) for B&B

Frendemheim Bellmann, Kretschmerstrasse 16 (tel. 38150).

Cheapest doubles around DM85 (£29.75; $53) for B&B

Pension Renate Deckwer, Rädestrasse 26 (tel. 4327192). All
rooms have a shower and WC.
Pension Eichlepp, Dr-Rudolph-Friedrichs-Strasse 15,
Radebeul (tel. 78742/728742). All rooms have shower and
WC.
Hotel Glasewald's Ruh, Berggasse 27 (tel. 75552/75322).
Pension Peter Ogon, Burgwartstrasse 10 (tel. 4326209).

PRIVATE ROOMS

Available from the Tourist Office. Singles DM20–30
(£7.00–10.50; $12.50–18.50), doubles and larger rooms
DM30–80 (£10.50–28.00; $18.50–50.00).

IYHF HOSTELS

Hübnerstrasse 11 (tel. 470667). DM14,50 (£5.25; $9) for
juniors, DM17,50 (£6.25; $11) for seniors. Tram 3 from
Dresden Hbf to the Südvorstadt terminus, or a 10-minute
walk from the station. Out of the exit to the right of the
main exit, head right along Juri-Gagarin-Strasse, then right
again at Reichenbach, then straight on, along
Altenzellerstrasse to Hübnerstrasse.
Oberloschwitz, Sierksstrasse 33 (tel. 36672). DM13,50 (£4.75;
$8.50) for juniors, DM16,50 (£5.75; $10) for seniors. Tram
5 to Nürnburger Platz, then bus 61 or 93 to the second stop
over the River Elbe, followed by a short walk.
Weintraubstrasse 12, Radebeul (tel. 74786) DM14 (£5; $8.50)
for juniors; DM17 (£6; $10.50) for seniors.

IYHF HOSTELS NEARBY

Weintraubenstrasse 12, Radebeul (tel. 74786). Juniors pay
DM14 (£5; $9), seniors DM17 (£6; $10.50). On the edge of
the city. Short train trip to Radebeul, then a 10-minute walk
to the hostel.

Pirna-Copitz, Birkwitzer Strasse 51, Pirna (tel. 04–2388).
Juniors (£5; $9), seniors DM17 (£6; $10.50). About 15
minutes' walk from the train station, bus L dir. Sportplatz.
Pirna is about 10 miles from Dresden.

CAMPING

Mockritz, Boderitzerstrasse 8 (tel. 478226). Open all year.
Bungalows for hire, sleeping up to four people. DM15–20
(£5.25–7.00; $9.50–12.50) p.p.

Wostra, Triesdestrasse (tel. 2231903). Open Apr.–Oct. Tents
for hire.

Reichenberg, Am Bad Sonnenland (tel. 75070). Open
Easter–Oct. Four-bed bungalows available for DM50
(£17.50; $31) per night.

Mittelteichbad Moritzburg, Dresdner Strasse 115,
Reichenberg (tel. Moritzburg 442). Open Apr.–Oct. Ten
miles north-west of Dresden. The site offers a view over
the lake to Moritzburg, the magnificent baroque hunting
lodge of the Electors of Saxony. Take the Moritzburg bus
from the bus station (100m to the right of the main exit
of Dresden Hbf).

Eisenach (tel. code 0623)

Tourist Office
Fremdenverkehrsamt Eisenach-Information, Bahnhofstrasse
3–5, 0-5900 Eisenach (tel. 76162/2284 for general information;
tel. 4895 for enquiries regarding accommodation). Open Mon.
10 a.m.–6 p.m., Tues.–Fri. 9 a.m.–6 p.m., Sat. 9 a.m.–3 p.m.
After the office closes, the accommodation line is open for
several hours. The accommodation service covers hotels,
private rooms and apartments. A few minutes' walk along
Bahnhofstrasse from the bus and train stations.

Finding Accommodation

Just outside Eisenach is the Wartburg, the most visited tourist attraction in the former DDR, and even more popular nowadays (the town offers numerous other attractions, plus easy access to the Thuringian countryside). Although large numbers of coach tourists come to Eisenach, most stay somewhere else, which means that at most times of year finding a bed is easier than you might imagine. Nevertheless, finding a room can be difficult if you arrive at the weekend during the summer, as the town is very popular with people taking weekend breaks.

HOTEL

Burghof, Karlsplatz 24/26 (tel. 3387). The cheapest hotel in the town. B&B starts around DM38 (£13.50; $23.50) per person. From the Tourist Office continue along Bahnhofstrasse through the old town gate into Karlsplatz.

PENSIONS

Anita Meister, Querstrasse 11a. No telephone. B&B DM28 (£9.75; $17) per person. From Bahnhofstrasse go through the old town gate into Karlsplatz. Both Alexanderstrasse and Karlstrasse on the opposite side of the square across Querstrasse.

Palmental Haus II (tel. 72045). Bed only from DM28 (£9.75; $17) per person.

Haus Schönblick, Fritz-Koch-Strasse 12 (tel. 2722). B&B from DM32,50 (£11.50; $20) per person.

PRIVATE ROOMS

Book through the Tourist Office. B&B from DM25 (£8.75; $15.50) per person.

APARTMENTS

Available from the Tourist Office. Well worth enquiring about if there are three or four of you. Stays of one night are possible, though your chances of finding a vacant apartment for a short stay are much slimmer if you are travelling in summer.

IYHF HOSTELS

Despite the fact that Eisenach has two hostels you cannot guarantee finding a bed in either of them off-season as they are frequently filled to capacity with visiting school and youth groups. Try to reserve ahead.

Mariental 24 (tel. 3613). DM13,50 (£4.75; $8.50) for those aged under 27, DM16,50 (£5.75; $10) otherwise. About 25 minutes' walk from the bus and train stations. From Bahnhofstrasse, turn left along Wartburg-Allee. Shortly after passing the Automobil-Pavilon, the street bends right to the junction of Marienstrasse (right) and Mariental (left).

Bornstrasse 7 (tel. 2012) Similar in price to the hostel on Mariental. A 15–20-minute walk from the bus and train stations. From Bahnhofstrasse head left along Wartburg-Allee, then turn left down Johann-Sebastian-Bach-Strasse. At the fork in the road go left, then right down Bornstrasse.

CAMPING

Enquire at the Tourist Office as to the whereabouts of the most convenient campsites.

Frankfurt-am-Main (tel. code 069)

Tourist Offices

Verkehrsamt Stadt Frankfurt-am-Main, Kaiserstrasse 52, 6000 Frankfurt 1 (tel. 21236869). Write to this office for information or to book accommodation in advance.

Telephone enquiries are only accepted during the Trade Fair.

Tourist Information Hauptbahnhof (tel. 21238849/21238851). Open Apr.–Oct., Mon.–Sat. 8 a.m.–10 p.m., Sun. and public holidays, 9.30 a.m.–8 p.m.; rest of the year, the office closes at 9 p.m. Mon.–Fri. Only handles personal enquiries for accommodation or information. DM3 (£1.05; $1.80) commission for finding a room. Opposite track 23 in Frankfurt Hbf.

Tourist Information Römer, Römerberg 27 (tel. 21238708/ 21238809). Open Mon.–Fri. 9 a.m.–7 p.m., weekends and public holidays 9.30 a.m.–6 p.m. Personal enquiries regarding information or accommodation only. DM3 (£1.05; $1.80) commission for finding a room. Römerberg is the heart of the beautiful Old Town, a short walk from the Römer stop on U-bahn line 4. The closest S-bahn station (all lines) is Hauptwache (see Basic Directions below).

DER Deutsches Reisebüro GmbH, Flughafen Frankfurt/Main (tel. 693071). Open daily 8 a.m.–9 p.m. One of two offices at the airport which will book rooms for you. Located in the middle of Arrival Hall B.

Flughafen Frankfurt/Main AG-Reisebüro (tel. 69066211). Open daily 8 a.m.–9 p.m. Arrivals Level B of the airport.

City Transport
The city transport system includes trams, buses and S-and U-bahn networks. Railpass holders can use the S-bahn free of charge. There is a frequent S-bahn service between the airport and the city centre and Frankfurt Hbf.

Trouble Spots
Kaiserstrasse (see Basic Directions below) is the main thoroughfare leading from Frankfurt Hbf to the city centre. The Red Light district is in the area to the left of Kaiserstrasse. Kaiserstrasse itself is safe, as is the Red Light district until the small hours of the morning. Even then it is not really violent, but it is the place you are most likely to find trouble in the city

centre. The crowds drawn to the famous flea market (Flohmarkt), over the River Main from the Flosserbrücke, create opportunities for pickpockets. Use some common sense and you will have no problems.

Basic Directions
In front of Frankfurt Hbf is the busy Am Hauptbahnhof. To the right, this street runs into Baselerstrasse, to the left, into Düsseldorferstrasse which takes you to Platz der Republik. Of the streets opposite the station Kaiserstrasse (take the underpass from Frankfurt Hbf) offers the simplest route if you are walking to the town centre. Follow Kaiserstrasse into the Rossmarkt and on to the Hauptwache. The main shopping street Zeil begins at Hauptwache. From Zeil, you can reach the Römerberg, the heart of the beautiful Old Town, by turning right down Liebfrauenstrasse, past the church and on down Neue Krame into the Römerberg. The walk from Frankfurt Hbf to the Hauptwache takes about 15 minutes, another few minutes takes you to the Römerberg.

HOTELS

Cheapest doubles around DM65 (£22.75; $40)

Goldener Stern, Karlsruherstrasse 8 (tel. 233309). A 5-minute walk from the Hbf. Mannheimerstrasse runs along the side of the station, right from the main exit. Karlsruherstrasse is off Mannheimerstrasse

Am Schloss, Bolongarostrasse 168 (tel. 301849). Well out from the centre in the area between the Nied and Höchst S-Bahn stations.

Cheapest doubles around DM75 (£26.25; $46.50)

Atlas, Zimmerweg 1 (tel. 723946). Just over 5 minutes' walk from Frankfurt Hbf. From Platz der Republik head right along Mainzer Landstrasse, then left at Zimmerweg. The S-Bahn station Taunusanlage (all lines) is closer. Walk a short distance along Mainzer Landstrasse, then right.

Bruns, Mendelssohnstrasse 42 (tel. 748896). A 15-minute walk from Frankfurt Hbf. From Platz der Republik follow Friedrich-Ebert-Anlage, then go right along Wilhelm-Hauff-Strasse, which leads into Mendelssohnstrasse. Tram 19 heading left from Frankfurt Hbf passes the hotel. From U6: Westend, the hotel is only a short walk, left off Bockenheimer Landstrasse.

Cheapest doubles around DM85 (£29.75; $53)

Backer, Mendelssohnstrasse 92 (tel. 747992). Just over 15 minutes' walk from the Hbf. Easily accessible by tram or U-bahn. See Hotel Bruns, above.

Wall, Stuttgarterstrasse 92 (tel. 253545). Just over 5 minutes' walk from the Hbf, off Mannheimerstrasse one street after Karlsruherstrasse. See Hotel Goldner Stern, above.

Am Anlagenring, Eschenheimer Anlage 23 (tel. 590768). S-bahn (all lines): Konstablerwache, then bus 36 along Eschenheimer Anlage, or a ten-minute walk. From Zeil, go right at Grosse Friedbergerstrasse, then straight on down Alte Gasse and Petersstrasse into Eschenheimer Anlage. U1 U2 U3: Eschenheimer Tor is closer. Go up Eschenheimer Landstrasse, then right along Eschenheimer Anlage.

IYHF HOSTEL

'Haus der Jugend', Deutscherrnufer 12 (tel. 619058). Midnight curfew. DM20 (£7; $12.50). During the morning and evening rush hours, take bus 46 from Frankfurt Hbf to the Frankensteinerplatz stop, only 50m from the hostel. After 7.30 p.m., take tram 16 to Textorstrasse, again leaving you a short walk. The closest S-bahn station is about 8 minutes' walk away. From Lokalbahnhof (all lines) take Dammstrasse off Mühlbruchstrasse, then straight on into Dreieichstrasse. Go right, down to the riverside, then follow the Main to the right.

IYHF HOSTELS NEARBY

Beckerstrasse 47, Aschaffenburg (tel. 06021–92763). Trains hourly (at least), 45-minute journey.

Schützengraben 5, Gelnhausen (tel. 06051–4424). Hourly trains, 40-minute trip.

Blücherstrasse 66, Wiesbaden (tel. 0611–48657/449081). Forty-five minutes by S–14 or regular train, every 20–30 minutes.

CAMPING

Heddernheim, An der Sandelmühle 35 (tel. 570332). U2: Sandelmühle is a short walk from the site by the River Nidda. S6: Escherheim is about 5 minutes' walk away. Cross the Nidda by the Maybachbrücke. The site is along the river to your right.

Niederrad, Niederräder Ufer 2 (tel. 673846). Tram 15 runs past the Hbf to the site by the River Main. A 15–20-minute walk from the Hbf. Follow Baselerstrasse into Baseler Platz, then cross the Main by the Friedensbrücke. Then turn right and walk along the side of the Main to the site, just beyond the next bridge (Main-Neckar-Brücke).

Freiburg-im-Breisgau (tel. code 0761)

Tourist Office
Freiburg-Information, Rotteckring 14, Postfach 1549, 7800 Freiburg-im-Breisgau (tel. 36890-90). Open May–Oct., Mon.–Wed. and Sat. 9 a.m.–6 p.m., Thurs.–Fri. open until 9 p.m., Sun. and public holidays 10 a.m.–noon; Nov.–Apr., Mon.–Fri. 9 a.m.–6 p.m., Sat. 9 a.m.–3 p.m. If you have not reserved accommodation in advance the staff will find hotel rooms and private rooms (*privatzimmer*) for a DM3 (£1.05; $1.80) commission. Private rooms are normally only available for stays of three days and longer. To get there, see Basic Directions below.

Basic Directions

The bus and train stations are both on Bismarckallee. Heading left along Bismarckallee, you will see Friedrichstrasse on the right, part of the ring road round the Old Town. Going right, Bismarckallee runs into Schnewlinstrasse, which leads to the River Dreisam, across which are the St Georgen and Merzhausen suburbs. From the front of the station, Eisenbahnstrasse heads off in the direction of the town centre. After a few minutes' walk you reach Rotteckring. The Tourist Office is across Rotteckring, on the left. Continuing straight on you pass Rathausplatz, then Kaiser-Joseph-Strasse, at which point Rathausgasse becomes Schusterstrasse. Turning right along Herrengasse, then following Oberlinden you arrive at the Schwaentor on Schlossbergring. The walk from the station to the Schwabentor takes about 15–20 minutes.

Public Transport

Depending on where you are staying, you may want to purchase a 24-, 48-or 72-hour ticket for the city's public transport system. These tickets are very reasonably priced (the 24-hour ticket costs only slightly more than the cost of two single journeys.) You can buy any of these tickets from the Tourist Office. If your accommodation is within walking distance of the centre there is no point buying such a ticket as all the sights are contained within the historic centre of Freiburg. Anyone staying outside the centre who has a German railpass should check before buying tickets of any kind to see if a Deutsche Bundesbahn bus stops nearby.

HOTELS

Cheapest doubles around DM65 (£22.75; $40) B&B

  Hirschen-Dionysos, Hirschstrasse 2 (tel. 29353). A 20-minute walk from the centre, in the Guntersal area of town, two miles from the main train station. Nearest train station is Freiburg-Wiehre, a 15-minute walk away.

Gästehaus Löwen, Dürleberg 9 (tel. 07655-1260). In Opfingen, 6½ miles from the centre.

Gästehaus Zur Sonne, Hochdorferstrasse 1 (tel. 07665-1288). In Hochdorf, 6½ miles from the town centre.

Gästehaus Schauinsland, Grostalstrasse 133 (tel. 69483). Rooms with showers. About 6½ miles from Freiburg Hbf in Kappel.

Cheapest doubles around DM70 (£24.50; $43.50) B&B

Schemmer, Eschholzstrasse 63 (tel. 272424). Only 400m from Freiburg Hbf. From Bismarckallee, follow Wannerstrasse past the bus station and the church into Eschholzstrasse, then left.

Gästehaus Zur Tanne, Altgasse 2 (tel. 07664-1810). In Opfingen, about 6 miles from the centre.

Cheapest doubles around DM75 (£26.25; $46.50) with breakfast (unless shown otherwise)

Adler, Im Schulerdobel 1 (tel. 65413). In Kappel, 5 miles from the train station.

Am Stadtgarden, Bernhardtstrasse 5 (on the corner of Karlstrasse) (tel. 28290/28202). Overnight price does not include breakfast. Good location, on the fringe of the Old Town. A 10–15-minute walk from the bus and train stations. From Friedrichstrasse, follow the ring road until you see Karlstrasse, heading left from Leopoldring.

Gästehaus Hirschen, Breisgauerstrasse 47 (tel. 82118). Two miles from the station in the opposite direction from the centre.

Löwen, Breisgauerstrasse 62 (tel. 84661). Near Gästehaus Hirschen above.

Cheapest doubles around DM80 (£28; $50) B&B

Stadt Wien, Habsburgerstrasse 48 (tel. 36560/39898). A 10–15-minute walk from the train station. Down

Friedrichstrasse and Friedrichring, then left. A 5–10-minute walk from the town centre.

Cheapest doubles around DM85 (£29.75; $53) B&B

Alleehaus, Marienstrasse 7 (tel. 34892/33652). Excellent location, right on the edge of the Old Town, a 10–15-minute walk from the bus and train stations. Go right along Rotteckring, across Bertoldstrasse and along Werderring. Turn left at the Kempartstrasse and head straight on, across Kaiser-Joseph-Strasse, through the Holzmarkt and on down Wallstrasse, then right at Marienstrasse.

Gästehaus Goldene Sternen, Emmendingerstrasse 1 (tel. 278373). A 10-minute walk from Freiburg Hbf. Go left, then left off Stefan-Meier-Strasse at Lortzingstrasse. A 15-minute walk from the town centre.

Sonne, Baslerstrasse 58 (tel. 403048). About 15 minutes' walk from the stations, and from the centre. Cross the River Dreisam, down Heinrich-von-Stephan-Strasse, then left.

Gästehaus St Ottilien, Kartäuserstrasse 135 (tel. 63230). On the Schlossberg, 4 miles from the station, 2 miles from the centre, uphill from the IYHF hostel.

PRIVATE ROOMS

Private rooms are best reserved in advance. However, although private rooms arranged through the Tourist Office are normally only available to those staying at least three days, if you are stuck for a bed it is doubtful if any owner with a room available will quibble about letting you stay one night if you ring up in the evening.

Cheapest rooms around DM17 (£6; $10.50) per person

Sumser, Neuhäuserstrasse 2 (tel. 63623). No singles available. About 4½ miles from the stations.

Cheapest rooms around DM22 (£7.75; $13.50) p.p.

Faubert, Häherweg 25 (tel. 131651). Singles and doubles,
with shower and WC. About 2 miles from the stations, in
the opposite direction from the town centre.

Höll, Haierweg 30 (tel. 445343). Singles not available. About
1 mile from the stations, slightly further from the centre.

Burger, Waldallee 14 (tel. 84357). Singles and doubles. Non-
smokers only. About 2 miles from the stations, in the
opposite direction from the town centre.

Cheapest rooms around DM24 (£8.50; $15) p.p.

Brodmann, Langackern 21 (tel. 29397). Singles about 20 per
cent more expensive. About 15–20 minutes' walk from the
centre. Two miles from Freiburg Hbf. Closest train station
is Freiburg-Wiehre.

Heise, Kleintalstrasse 58 (tel. 62927). No singles. Non-
smokers only. About 4½ miles from the stations.

Kern, Im Bohrer 46 (tel. 29474). Doubles only. About 15–20
minutes' walk from the centre. Two miles from Freiburg
Hbf. Closest train station is Freiburg-Wiehre.

Tritschler, Ziegelhofstrasse 40 (tel. 86077). Singles only.
About 2 miles from the stations in the opposite direction
from the centre of town.

Cheapest rooms around DM27 (£9.50; $16.50) p.p.

Ehret, Mozartstrasse 48 (tel. 33387). One single only. Non-
smokers only. A 15–20-minute walk from the stations.
Follow the ring road from Friedrichstrasse, then go left after
Stadtstrasse, along the side of the park where Leopoldring
joins Schlossbergring. A 10-minute walk from the centre.

Busse, Waldseestrasse 77 (tel. 72938). Singles and doubles.
Singles are slightly more expensive. Non-smokers only.
Near the Mösle-Park camping site. Tram 1 dir: Litterweiler
from Freiburg Hbf to Stadthalle or the terminus.

Idhe, Marchstrasse 5 (tel. 273421). No singles. Non-smokers
only. A 10-minute walk from the stations.

IYHF HOSTEL

Kartäuserstrasse 151 (tel. 67656). Curfew 11.30 p.m. DM19 (£6.75; $12). Far from the centre. Tram 1 dir. Littenweiler from the station to Römerhof. Along Fritz-Geiges-Strasse, over the water, then right.

UNIVERSITY ACCOMMODATION

Enquiries about the availability of rooms during the university vacation to Studentenhaus 'Alte Universität', Wohnraumabteilung, Bertoldstrasse 12, 7800 Freiburg (tel. 2101272).

CAMPING

Hirzberg, Kartäuserstrasse 99 (tel. 35054). Open 1 Apr.–15 Oct. DM3 (£1.05; $1.75) per tent, DM6 (£2.10; $3.50) per person. Tram 1 dir. Littenweiler to Messeplatz from Freiburg Hbf. A 20-minute walk from the nearest train station, Freiburg-Wiehre on the Höllentalbahn. Go right from the station along Turkenlouisstrasse, left up Hildastrasse, then right along Kartäuserstrasse. A 10–15-minute walk from the town centre. Go right from the Schwabentor, then left along Kartäuserstrasse.

Mösle-Park (tel. 72938). Open 20 Mar.–31 Oct. DM3,50–5,00 (£1.20–1.75; $2–3) per tent, DM6,50 (£2.20; $4) per person. Near the FFC stadium. Tram 1 dir. Littenweiler from Freiburg Hbf to the Stadthalle. A 15–20-minute walk from the nearest train station, Freiburg-Wiehre. Right from the station to the end of Turkenlouisstrasse, left up Dreikönigstrasse, right along Talstrasse, then right down Schützenallee, from which you can see the stadium complex. A 20-minute walk from the town centre.

St Georg, Basler Landstrasse 62 (tel. 43183). Open all year. DM4–5 (£1.40–1.75; $2.50–3.00) per tent, DM6,50 (£2.20; $4) per person. A 25-minute walk from the centre, and from Freiburg Hbf. Cross the Dreisam, on down Heinrich-von-

Stephan-Strasse, then right. Closest station is Freiburg St
Georgen, about 5–10 minutes' walk from the site.

There are another two sites in Freiburg-Hochdorf, about four
miles out from the centre, but these sites cater more for
those with caravans/caravanettes. Although prices per
person are similar to those at the sites above, prices for
tents are much higher at around DM7,50–8,50
(£2.60–£3.00; $4.50–5.00).

Tunisee (tel. 07665–2249/1249). Open 1 Apr.–31 Oct. The
cheaper of these two sites.

Breisgau (tel. 07665–2346). Open all year.

IYHF HOSTELS NEARBY

Rheinuferstrasse 12, Breisach-am-Rhein (tel. 07667–7665).
DM16 (£5.50; $10). Breisach is a beautiful small town about
12½ miles from Freiburg. Trains and/or German railway
buses hourly. (German railpasses are valid on these DB
buses.)

Hamburg (tel. code 040)

Tourist Offices

Tourist Information im Bieberhaus, Hachmannplatz (tel.
30051-245). The main office. Open Mon.–Fri. 9 a.m.–6
p.m., Sat. 9 a.m.–3 p.m. Go out the main Kirchenallee exit
of Hamburg Hbf. You cannot miss the tall Bieberhaus at
the left hand end of Kirchenallee.

Tourist Information im Hauptbahnhof (tel. 30051-230). By the
main exit on to Kirchenallee. Open daily 7 a.m.–11 p.m.

Tourist Information am Hafen, St Pauli Landungsbrücken
(tel. 30051-200). Between landing stages 4 and 5 of the port.
Open daily Mar.–Oct., 9 a.m.–6 p.m., at other times, 10
a.m.–5 p.m.

Tourist Information im Flughafen (tel. 30051-240). In the
airport at Terminal 3 (Arrivals). Open daily 8 a.m.–11 p.m.

Tourismus-Zentrale Hamburg GmbH, Postfach 10 22 49, 2000 Hamburg (tel. 30051-0). Contact this office to reserve hotel accommodation in advance.

City Transport
Railpasses are valid on the city's S-bahn network (in second class only, unless you have a first-class Eurail pass), but not the U-bahn. All the main tourist attractions are close to an S-bahn station. Those without railpasses have the option of several passes covering the whole Hamburger Verkehrs-verbund (HVV) network of S- and U-bahn, buses and port ferries. Day tickets and 3-day tickets are available from automatic ticket machines, or from bus drivers (day tickets cannot be used before 9 a.m. Mon.–Fri.). If you want more information on these tickets contact HVV on tel. 322911, or ask at the Tourist Office. The Tourist Office will also have up-to-date information on the Hamburg CARD (1992 price DM9,50 £3.25; $6). As well as allowing you to use the public transport system, the Hamburg CARD also gains you free entry to eleven museums.

Basic Directions (around Hamburg Hbf)
The area around Hamburg Hbf contains some of the city's least expensive hotels. Leaving the train station by the main exit on to Kirchenallee and heading left you arrive at the main Tourist Office in the multi-storey Bieberhaus. At this point, Kirchenallee runs into St Georg-Strasse, while Lange Reihe runs away to your right. Turning around so that Lange Reihe is on your left, then walking along Kirchenallee, you come to Ellmenreichstrasse on the left. This street leads into Hansaplatz, as does the next street on the left, Bremer Reihe. Continuing along Kirchenallee, you reach Steintorplatz, from which three streets run off to the left: sharp left is Steintorweg, leading into Bremer Reihe, then Steindamm, then, almost at a right angle to Kirchenallee is Adenauerallee. While there are relatively inexpensive hotels in all of these streets, Bremer Reihe and Steindamm offer the most possibilities. Unfortunately, the cheapest hotels in these streets are often

used by prostitutes, which, even though the hotels are invariably safe for you and your belongings, hardly makes for a peaceful night.

HOTELS

Cheapest doubles around DM70 (£24.50; $43.50)

Inter-Rast, Reeperbahn 154–166 (tel. 311591). S-bahn: Reeperbahn. In the Red Light district. Street noise is a problem, unless you are a sound sleeper.

Cheapest doubles around DM75 (£26.25; $46.50)

Kochler, Bremer Reihe (tel. 249511). S-bahn/U-bahn: Hauptbahnhof.
Schanzenstern, Bartelsstrasse 13 (tel. 4398441). S-bahn: Sternschanze. Bartelsstrasse runs between Schanzenstrasse and Susannenstrasse.

Cheapest doubles around DM80 (£28; $50)

Auto-Hotel 'Am Hafen', Spieldudenplatz 11 (tel. 316631). S-bahn: Reeperbahn. Walk up the Reeperbahn, right at Davidstrasse, then left.
Benecke, Lange Reihe 54–56 (tel. 245860). S-bahn/U-bahn: Hauptbahnhof.
Wernecke, Hartungstrasse 7a (tel. 455357). U-bahn: Hallerstrasse, then a few minutes' walk down Rothenbaumchaussee, passing Hermann-Behn-Weg to Hartungstrasse on the right. A 10-minute walk from mainline S-bahn station Dammtor. Follow Rothenbaumchaussee from Theodor-Heuss-Platz to Hartungstrasse on the left.

Cheapest doubles around DM85 (£29.75; $53) S-bahn/U-bahn stop Hauptbahnhof, unless otherwise indicated

Village, Steindamm 4 (tel. 246137).
Polo, Adenauerallee 7 (tel. 2803556).
Sarah Petersen, Lange Reihe 50 (tel. 249826).

Hager, Hansaplatz 7 (tel. 243404).

Kieler Hof, Bremer Reihe 15 (tel. 243024).

Remstal, Steintorweg 2 (tel. 244560).

Pfeifer, Hallerstrasse 2 (tel. 447830). U-bahn: Hallerstrasse.

Ingeborg, Hartungstrasse 7a (tel. 455357). See Hotel
Wernecke above.

Garni Schaub, Martinistrasse 12 (tel. 4603430). U-bahn:
Eppendorfer Baum. Follow Eppendorfer Baum across
Hegestrasse into Curschmannstrasse, which is crossed by
Martinistrasse.

**Cheapest doubles around DM90 (£31.50; $56). Unless shown
otherwise, S-bahn/U-bahn stop: Hauptbahnhof**

Zentrum, Bremer Reihe (tel. 2802528).

Meyn, Hansaplatz 2 (tel. 245309).

Köhler, St Georgstrasse 6 (tel. 249065).

Annenhof, Lange Reihe 23 (tel. 243426).

Graf Moltke, Steindamm 1 (tel. 2801154).

Krone, Schäferkampsallee 61 (tel. 445886). U-bahn: Schlump
or Christus-Kirche.

Bergunde, Eppendorfer Baum 5 (tel. 482214). U-bahn:
Eppendorfer Baum.

IYHF HOSTELS

'Auf dem Stintfang', Alfred-Wegener-Weg 5 (tel. 313488).
Curfew 1 a.m. From the Hauptbahnhof, take S1, S2, S3
(S-Bahn free with railpasses) or the U3 to Landungsbrücke.
The hostel is on top of the hill.

Jugendgasthaus 'Horner-Rennbahn', Rennbahnstrasse 100
(tel. 6511671). Open Mar.–Dec. Curfew 1 a.m. Quite far
out. U3 to Horner-Rennbahn, then a 10-minute walk.
Alternatively take the Wandsbek bus from the centre.

HOSTELS

Zeltdorf Hamburg, Sylvesterallee 3 (tel. 8319939). DM17,50
(£6.25; $11). Open May–Sept.

Kolpinghaus St Georg, Schmilinskystrasse 78 (tel. 246609). Reception open round the clock. Singles DM41 (£14.50; $25.50), doubles DM65–80 (£22.75–28.00; $40–50), triples DM100 (£35; $62). A 10-minute walk from Hamburg Hbf. S-bahn/U-bahn Hauptbahnhof. Take the exit on to Kirchenallee, go left, then right down Lange Reihe, which is crossed by Schmilinskystrasse.

Jugendhotel MUI, Budapester Strasse 45 (tel. 431169). Singles around DM48 (£17; $29.50), doubles from DM65 (£22.75; $40), larger rooms around DM28 (£9.75; $17). U-bahn: St Pauli, then walk along Budapesterstrasse.

Sternschanze, Schanzenstrasse 101 (tel. 433389). S-bahn: Sternschanze. Singles DM45 (£15.75; $28), doubles DM75 (£26.25; $46.50).

Zeltdorf Hamburg, Sylvesterallee 3 (tel. 8319939) DM17,50 (£6.25; $11). Open May–Sept.

IYHF HOSTELS NEARBY

Soltauerstrasse 133, Luneberg (tel. 04131–41864). The beautiful town of Luneberg is about 30 miles from Hamburg. Frequent trains. About 45 minutes from Hamburg Hbf.

Konrad-Adenauer-Ring 2, Bad Oldesloe (tel. 04531–504294). Trains at least twice hourly, 25–45-minute trip depending on classification of train.

CAMPING

Buchholz, Kielerstrasse 374 (tel. 5404532). Near the Hamburger SV football stadium. S3 dir. Pinneberg, or S21 dir. Elbgaustrasse to the Stellingren (Volksparkstadion) stop. If HSV are playing at home it is best to avoid travelling to the campsite when there will be football fans about (Sat. noon–2.30 p.m. and around 5 p.m., Wed. 5–7 p.m. and around 9.30 p.m.). The best of the city's campsites. Phone ahead to see if they have space. If not, there are several other sites on Kielerstrasse.

Ramcke, Kielerstrasse 620 (tel. 5705121).
Anders, Kielerstrasse 650 (tel. 5704498).
City Camping Park, Kronsaalweg, 86/Kielerstrasse (tel. 5404994).

Hannover (tel. code 0511)

Tourist Offices
Verkehrsbüro Hannover, Ernst-August-Platz 8 (tel. 1683903). Opposite Hannover Hbf. Open Mon.–Thur. 8.30 a.m.–6 p.m., Fri. 8.30 a.m.–3 p.m.
Amt für Fremdenverkehrsund Kongresswesen, Friedrichswall 5, Postfach 404, 3000 Hannover. Write to this office if you want to reserve accommodation in advance. For private rooms write to: Incoming and Congress Service Hannover, at this address at least three weeks before your arrival.

Trade Fairs in Hannover
Unlike in most other German cities, there are no hotel rooms available in the DM30–40 (£10.50–14.00; $18.50–25.00) per person range, as accommodation prices are inflated by the large number of trade fairs the city plays host to. If possible, try not to arrive during a fair, as finding a bed of any sort becomes very difficult. Dates of the fairs are available from the Hannover Tourist Promotion Board in the UK, Nyumbani, Lynwick Street, Rudgwick, Sussex RH12 3DJ (tel. 040382-2837), from the German National Tourist Office in London, from the Hannover Trade Fair Organization in Croydon (tel. 081 688 9541), or from Tourist Offices in Germany.

HOTELS

Cheapest doubles around DM85 (£29.75; $53)

Flora, Heinrichstrasse 36 (tel. 342334). Triples are available at around the same price p.p. as doubles. Only 800m from Hannover Hbf. From the rear exit walk right until you see Volgersweg heading left off Augustenstrasse. Heinrichstrasse runs parallel to the right of Volgersweg on the other side of Berliner Allee.

Hotel Haus Tanneneck, Brehmstrasse 80 (tel. 818650). About 2 miles from the train station. Bus 39 from Hannover Hbf runs along Brehmstrasse. Closest train station is Hannover-Bismarckstrasse.

Cheapest doubles around DM90 (£31.50; $56)

Hotel Eden, Waldhausenstrasse 30 (tel. 830430). A short walk from U-bahn Döhrener Turm.

Cheapest doubles around DM100 (£35; $62)

Hospiz am Bahnhof, Joachimstrasse 2 (tel. 324297). A few minutes' walk from the train station, to the left of Ernst-August-Platz.

Hotel Eilenriede, Guerickstrasse 32 (tel. 5476652). About 3 miles from Hannover Hbf. Follow Klingerstrasse from Klingerstrasse U-bahn stop. Guerickstrasse is to the left.

Hotel Gildehof, Joachimstrasse 6 (tel. 363680/363691/36392). Triples are available for around the same price p.p. as doubles.

PRIVATE ROOMS

Bed and breakfast accommodation is available with local families during the Hannover Fair. Singles cost around DM55 (£19.25; $34), doubles around DM85 (£29.75; $53). Book in advance (see above), or make enquiries on arrival at the Tourist Office, or at the airport (Arrival Level A, Gates 1–6).

IYHF HOSTEL

Ferdinand-Wilhelm-Fricke-Weg 1 (tel. 322941/1317674).

DM16 (£5.75; $10). A more expensive Jugendgasthaus
operates at the same location. Near the football stadium
(Niedersachsen-Stadion, home of Hannover 96), a
20-minute walk from Hannover Hbf. From Ernst-August-
Platz follow Bahnhofstrasse then Karmarschstrasse into
Frederikenplatz. Take Lavesallee, left on Waterloostrasse,
to the right around the stadium, then left along the
waterside to the site. The closest train station is Hannover-
Linden, if you have a railpass. A short distance down
Göttingerstrasse, then right. Follow Lodemannweg over
the water, then head right to the site. The Fischerhof U-
bahn stop (lines 3 and 7 dir: Mühlenberg) is only slightly
closer than Hannover-Linden. Turn right off Ricklinger
Hauptweg on to Lodemannweg.

HOSTELS

Naturfreundhaus in der Eilenriede, Hermann-Bahlsen-Allee
8 (tel. 691493). Listed in the IYHF handbook, but a
Naturfreundhaus establishment, with discounts for
Naturfreundhaus members. Normal prices similar to those
of a Jugendgasthaus. Stadtbahn U3 dir. Lahe or U7 dir.
Fasanenkrug to Spannhagengarten, or a 30-minute walk
from the station.

IYHF HOSTELS NEARBY

If the hostels in Hannover are full and you cannot afford a hotel
or private room, there are IYHF hostels in three towns near
Hannover, all of which are well worth visiting in their own
right.

Weghausstrasse 2, Celle (tel. 05141–53208). At least two
trains each hour, 20 minutes by express train, 30–45
minutes by local train.

Fischbeckerstrasse 33, Hameln (of Pied Piper fame) (tel.
05151–3425). Hourly trains, 45-minute trip.

Schirrmannweg 4, Hildesheim (tel. 05121–42717). Trains at
least once an hour, 25-minute trip by local train.

CAMPING

Birkensee, Hannover-Laatzen (tel. 529962). Laatzen is a 10-minute journey from Hannover Hbf. Frequent local trains.

Heidelberg (tel. code 06221)

Tourist Offices

Verkehrsverein Heidelberg, Postfach 10 58 60, 6900 Heidelberg (tel. 10821). Room reservations and information in advance.

Tourist-Information am Hauptbahnhof (tel. 21341). On the square outside the main train station. General information and a room-finding service. DM2 (£0.70; $1.25) commission. Open Mar.–Oct., Mon.–Sat. 9 a.m.–7 p.m. (Fri. open until 9 p.m.), Sun. 10 a.m.–6 p.m.; at other times, Mon.–Sat. 9 a.m.–7 p.m.; Sun. 10 a.m.–3 p.m. When closed, details of hotels with rooms available at closing time are posted outside.

Tourist-Information am Schloss, Neue Schlosstrasse 54. Open 10 a.m.–5 p.m. At the top of the Bergbahn funicular railway, a short walk from the castle.

Tourist-Information Neckarmünzplatz. Open 9 a.m.–6.30 p.m. (closed in winter). Follow the River Neckar upstream from the Karl-Theodor-Brücke (Alter Brücke) along Am Hackteufel to the coach park.

Basic Directions

The main train station (Heidelberg Hbf) is about 20 minutes' walk from the town centre. From the station, Mittermaier-strasse leads down to the River Neckar and the Ernst-Walz-Brücke, across which is the Neuenheim district of the city. The tree-lined Kurfürsten-Anlage leads away from the station in the direction of the town centre. Bahnhofstrasse runs parallel to the right of Kurfürsten-Anlage. Kurfürsten-Anlage leads into

Friedrich-Ebert-Anlage, which runs along the fringe of the Old Town to the Schlossberg. At the junction of Kurfürsten-Anlage and Friedrich-Ebert-Anlage, turning left takes you into Bismarckplatz, a major hub of public transport. To the right of Bismarckplatz is Hauptstrasse, initially a busy shopping street but then running right through the Old Town to the Karlstor, an old city gate which marks one of the boundaries of the Old Town. On the way to the Karlstor, Hauptstrasse passes Universitätsplatz before reaching the Marktplatz with the Town Hall and the Church of the Holy Ghost. Buses 10 and 11 link Heidelberg Hbf with Universitätsplatz. Bus 33 runs from the station to the Kornmarkt, just beyond Marktplatz, while bus 11 continues from Universitätsplatz to the Bergbahn stop, close to the Kornmarkt at the foot of the funicular railway leading up to the castle and the Königsstühl. Railpass holders can save money by taking a train from Heidelberg Hbf to Heidelberg-Karlstor, about 8 minutes' walk from the Marktplatz.

Public Transport
Single journeys on the city's trams and buses cost around DM2 (£0.70; $1.25). A 36-hour pass is available which pays for itself after four trips. Up-to-date prices, tickets, and general information are available from the HSB Verkaufs-Stelle, across from the side entrance to Heidelberg Hbf.

Finding Accommodation
Finding suitable accommodation can be difficult in Heidelberg because the city is popular with older, more affluent tourists, guaranteeing the hotels a steady trade and pushing hotel prices above the norm for Germany. As the city also receives large numbers of young visitors, you cannot always count on getting a bed in the IYHF hostel, even with its large capacity (451 beds). Even camping is not without its problems: the two sites are about 5 miles out of town, and although there is a train station nearby, the service is so infrequent that you will almost certainly have to travel by bus, adding to the cost of an overnight stay at either of the sites.

HOTELS

Cheapest doubles around DM45 (£15.75; $28)

Jeske, Mittelbadgasse 2 (tel. 23733). Two- to five-bed rooms. All the same price p.p. Right in the centre of the Old Town. Understandably popular, so try to reserve ahead. Mittelbadgasse runs off the Marktplatz.

Cheapest doubles around DM55 (£19.25; $34)

Waldhorn, Peter-Wenzel-Weg 11 (tel. 800294). Beautifully located, high in the hills above the suburb of Ziegelhausen. Fine if you have your own transport.

Cheapest doubles around DM70 (£24.50; $43.50)

Alter Kohlhof, Kohlhof 5 (tel. 21915). Near the Königsstuhl, in the hills above the castle.

Cheapest doubles around DM75 (£26.25; $46.50)

Goldenes Lamm, Pfarrgasse 3 (tel. 480834).

Cheapest doubles around DM80 (£28; $50)

Elite, Bunsenstrasse 15 (tel. 25734). Turn right off Bahnhofstrasse down Landhausstrasse, then left along Bunsenstrasse.

Endrich, Friedhofweg 28 (tel. 801086). In the suburb of Ziegelhausen.

Haus Sedlmayer, Gerhart-Hauptmann-Strasse 5 (tel. 412872/ 402372). In Neuenheim. A 15-minute walk from Heidelberg Hbf. Cross the Neckar by the Ernst-Walz-Brücke, go straight ahead on Berlinerstrasse, then right at Gerhart-Hauptmann-Strasse.

Cheapest doubles around DM85 (£29.75; $53)

Auerstein, Dossenheimer Landstrasse 82 (tel. 480798).
Brandstätter, Friedrich-Ebert-Anlage 60 (tel. 23944).

Burgfreiheit, Am Schlosseingang (tel. 22768). By the entrance
to the castle.

Goldene Rose Kirchheim, Hegenichstrasse 10 (tel. 782058).

Kohler, Goethestrasse 2 (tel. 24360/166088). Right off
Bahnhofstrasse shortly after Landhausstrasse.

Cheapest doubles around DM90 (£31.50; $56)

Zum Pfalzgrafen, Kettengasse 21 (tel. 20489). Centrally
located. Kettengasse runs off the Marktplatz.

PRIVATE ROOMS

The staff in the second-hand clothes shop **Flic-Flac** at
Unterestrasse 12 can help young travellers find lodgings with
local people. Unterestrasse runs between the Heumarkt and
the Fischmarkt. The Heumarkt is on the other side of
Hauptstrasse from Universitätsplatz. The Fischmarkt is on the
side of the Holy Ghost Church as you enter Marktplatz from
Hauptstrasse or the Kornmarkt.

IYHF HOSTEL

Tiergartenstrasse 5 (tel. 412066). DM18 (£6.30; $11). Two and
a half miles from Heidelberg Hbf. Bus 33 from the station,
or Bismarckplatz. After 8 p.m., tram 1 to Chirurgische
Klinik, then bus 330 to the first stop after the zoo.

DORMS

Hotel Jeske (see above) charges around DM22,50 (£7.90, $14)
per person in two- to five-bed rooms.

IYHF HOSTELS NEARBY

'Lindenhof', Rheinpromenade 21, Mannheim (tel.
0621–822718). DM15 (£5.25; $9.50). In many ways the best
hostel option for anyone with a railpass. Set on the banks

of the Rhine, the Mannheim hostel is both cheaper and more pleasant to stay in than the Heidelberg hostel. Midnight curfew. Ten–fifteen minutes' walk from Mannheim Hbf (main station). Train journey from Heidelberg around 12–20 minutes.

As well as the hostel in Mannheim, railpass holders stuck for a bed have the option of staying in the IYHF hostels in Worms or Speyer, two towns well worth a visit in their own right. There are frequent trains between Mannheim and Worms. Local trains take about 20 minutes. Journey time from Heidelberg to Speyer is about 1 hour. You may have to change at Mannheim, Ludwigshafen or Speyer. Deutsche Bundesbahn bus 7007 provides a direct connection between the two towns (1 hour trip, railpasses valid). The bus leaves from Stance 2 at Heidelberg Hbf.

Dechaneigasse 1, Worms (tel. 06241-27580). The hostel is about 15 minutes' walk from Worms Hbf, looking out on to the cathedral (Dom). Walk right from the cathedral along Bahnhofstrasse, left up Kriemhildenstrasse and then right along Lutherring to the cathedral.

Geibstrasse 5, Speyer (tel. 06232-75380). Two miles from Speyer Hbf. Bus 2 (phone the hostel or the Tourist Office in Speyer tel. 06232-14395, to check this).

CAMPING

Haide (tel. 06223–2111). Located between Ziegelhausen and Kleingemünd. Bus 35 to the Orthopedic Clinic in Schlierbach-Ziegelhausen, about 5 miles out of town. The site is across the Neckar. Popular with groups on camping holidays.

Neckartal (tel. 06221–802506). Same bus as above, but get off at the Im Grund stop. The site is near the clinic. More basic than the site across the river, but perfectly adequate. Tends to be free of groups. Passports held at reception, which means you cannot leave before the office opens at 8 a.m.

CAMPING NEARBY

'Strandbad', Karin Ebner, Mannheim-Neckarau (tel. 0621–856240). Probably the best site if you have a railpass. The site is close to Mannheim-Neckarau station. Frequent trains from Mannheim Hbf. Last train around 11.45 p.m. except Sat. and Sun. night. Also local buses. About 2 miles from Mannheim Hbf, so you will pay less travelling by bus to this site than those above. If you stay late in Heidelberg there are trains to Mannheim Hbf at 11.49 p.m., 1.20 a.m. and various trains between 2–3 a.m. (check times locally).

Kiel (tel. code 0431)

Tourist Office
Tourist Information Kiel e.V., Sophienblatt 30, 2300 Kiel 1 (tel. 67910). A few minutes' walk from the train station.

HOTELS

Cheapest doubles around DM45 (£15.75; $28)

Pension Schnoor, Hof Wulfsdorf 5 (tel. 04348-1479, 8266). Six miles out of town in Probsteierhagen.

Cheapest doubles around DM50 (£17.50; $31)

Hotel Neu-Schönberg, Strandstrasse 207 (tel. 04344-883). In Schönberg, 9½ miles from the centre.

Cheapest doubles around DM55–65 (£19.25–22.75; $34–40)

Pension-Gasthof Margarethenhöh, Kirschberg 17 (tel. 202725). In Kiel-Dietrichsdorf, 3 3/4 miles from the centre.
Gästehaus Landwehr, Am Plotzenbrook 3 (tel. 04346-289). Singles are similarly priced. In Landwehr, 3 3/4 miles from the town centre.

Gästehaus Meyer, Rosenkranzer Weg 15 (tel. 04346-6596). In Schinkel, 3 3/4 miles from centre.

Gaststätte-Pension Villa Fernsicht, Fernsichtweg (tel. 04307-222). In Raisdorf, 4½ miles from the centre.

Cheapest doubles around DM68–75 (£23.75–26.25; $42.50–46.50

Motel Karlstal, Karlstal 18–20 (tel. 731690). In Kiel-Gaarden, about 1½ miles from the centre.

Pension Waldeck, Trondelweg 11 (tel. 722311, 727605). In Kiel-Ellerbek, 3 miles from the centre.

Privat Pension Karin Krauthammer, Grabastrasse 73 (tel. 722810). In Kiel-Ellerbek, 2½ miles from the centre.

Hotel Dietrichsdorfer Hof, Heikendorfer Weg 54 (tel. 26108). In Kiel-Dietrichsdorf. 3½ miles from the centre.

Hotel Zur Kreuzung, An der B4 (tel. 04322-4586). In Bordesholm, about 2 miles from the centre.

Cheapest doubles around DM78–85 (£27.25–29.75; $49–53)

Hotel Runge, Elisabethstr. 16 (tel. 731992). In Kiel-Gaarden. 1½ miles from the centre.

Touristhotel Schweriner Hof, Königsweg 13 (tel. 61416/62678). About 250m from the train station.

Reimers Gaststätte, Dorfstrasse 2 (tel. 783108). In Kiel-Elmschenhagen, 3½ miles from the centre.

Pension Petra, Gravensteiner Strasse 4 (tel. 362100). In Kiel-Holtenau, 3 3/4 miles from the centre.

IYHF HOSTEL

Johannesstrasse 1 (tel. 731488). In Kiel-Gaarden, about 1½ miles from the centre. Bus 4, 24, 34 or 64 to Karlstal, then walk up Schulstrasse into Johannesstrasse and go left.

IYHF HOSTEL NEARBY

'Haus der Jugend', Franz-Rohwer-Strasse 10, Neumünster (tel. 04321–403416). Hourly trains, 20-minute journey.

CAMPING

Campingplatz Falckenstein, Palisadenweg 171 (tel. 392078). DM5 (£1.75; $3) for a small tent; same fee per person. In Kiel-Friedrichsort, 12 kms from the town centre.

Leipzig (tel. code 041)

Tourist Offices

Rat der Stadt Leipzig, Fremdenverkehrsamt und Kongressamt, Hainstrasse 16–18, 0-7010 Leipzig. The office offers a full information and accommodation service if you contact them in advance. The Tourist Board operate several offices in the city and at the airport.

Touristen-Information/Zimmernachweis LEIPZIG-INFORMATION, Sachsenplatz 1 (tel. 799340/7959315). General information and a room-finding service for those arriving without prior reservations. Tourist Information open Mon.–Fri. 9 a.m.–7 p.m., Sat. 9 a.m.–2 p.m. Accommodation Service open Mon.–Fri. 9 a.m.–9 p.m., Sat. 10 a.m.–7 p.m., Sun. 5–9 p.m. A 5-minute walk from Leipzig Hbf. Head straight on from the station across Platz der Republik and Richard-Wagner-Strasse until you reach Brühl. Head right, then left at Katharinenstrasse to Sachsenplatz.

LEIPZIG-INFORMATION, Hauptbahnhof (tel. 275318). Open Mon.–Fri. 9 a.m.–6 p.m. In the Westhalle of Leipzig Hbf.

Flughafen Leipzig-Halle. Open Mon.–Fri. 7 a.m.–9 p.m., weekends 7 a.m.–6 p.m.

Trouble Spots

In 1990–91, newspapers reported that the city was suffering

from certain troubles, mainly as a result of low morale in an under-staffed and under-funded police force which had lead to a breakdown in order in some areas. This problem has long since been resolved, so visitors can enjoy this refreshingly vibrant city with no fears.

Public Transport
The city's transport system includes buses, trams and two S-bahn lines. Railpass holders can use the S-bahn free of charge.

HOTELS

Cheapest doubles around DM90 (£31.50; $56)

Hotel Bürgerhof, Grosse Fleischergasse 4 (tel. 209496). Second left off Brühl, after Katharinenstrasse (see Tourist Offices above).

Cheapest doubles around DM95 (£33.25; $59)

Hotel Am Auewald, Paul-Michael-Strasse 12–14 (tel. 4511003/4511025).

PRIVATE ROOMS

Available from LEIPZIG-INFORMATION in Leipzig Hbf or on Sachsenplatz

IYHF HOSTELS

Käthe-Kollwitz-Strasse 62–66 (tel. 475888/470530). Tram 2 from the front of Leipzig Hbf, or tram 1 from the stop to the far right of the main exit, or a 10–15-minute walk. Head left along Tröndlin-Ring, left at the first main junction down Goerdeleiring, then right at the fork in the road along Käthe-Kollwitz-Strasse.

Am Auensee, Gustav-Esche-Strasse 4 (tel. 57189). Five miles from the town centre, but easily reached by tram 11 or 28 from Leipzig Hbf. The hostel is about 10 minutes' walk

from the Wahren station, down Linkelstrasse into Strasse
der Jungen Pioniere.
Hauptstrasse 23, Grossdeuben (tel. 396651). S-bahn to
Gaschwitz, then a 10–15-minute walk towards
Grossdeuben. Bus 1 dir: Zwenkau to the first stop in
Grossdeuben leaves you with an 8-minute walk.

IYHF HOSTELS NEARBY

'Halle', August-Bebel-Strasse 48a, Halle (tel. 041–24716 from
Leipzig, normal code for Halle is 046). Halle is a historically
interesting city about 22 miles from Leipzig. The two cities
are linked by frequent express trains.

CAMPING

Am Auensee, Gustav-Esche-Strasse 5 (tel. 52648). Same
directions as the IYHF hostel of the same name. Pleasant
site near the lake. DM4 (£1.40; $2.50) per person, DM3
(£1.05; $2) per tent. Also lets bungalows and *Finnhütten*.
Twin-bedded bungalows DM30 (£10.50; $18.50) per night,
triple-bedded bungalows DM45 (£15.75; $28) per night,
four-bed bungalows DM40 (£14; $25) per night. A twin-
bedded *Finnhütte* costs DM20 (£7; $12.50) per night.

Lübeck (tel. code 0451)

Tourist Offices
Amt für Lübeck-Werbung und Tourismus, Postfach 2132,
2400 Lübeck. Contact this office if you want information
on the city in advance. The organization operates two
information points in the city.
Touristbüro am Markt (tel. 1228106). Open Mon.–Fri. 9.30
a.m.–6 p.m., weekends 10 a.m.–2 p.m. Wide range of
information on the city.
Touristbüro Beckergrube, Beckergrube 95 (tel. 1228109).

Open Mon.–Fri. 8 a.m.–4 p.m. Beckergrube runs between An der Untertrave and Breite Strasse. The office is near the junction with An der Untertrave.

Lübecker Verkehrsverein e.V., Postfach 1205, Breite Strasse 75 (tel. 72339/72300). Write to this office to reserve accommodation in advance. On arrival you can use their accommodation service. DM3 (£1.05; $2.50) commission. Breite Strasse runs from the Markt.

Informationsschalter im Hauptbahnhof (tel. 72300). Operated by the Lübecker Verkehrsverein. Same commission for finding accommodation. Relatively poor information service.

Basic Directions

From the train station you can follow Beim Retteich or Konrad-Adenauer-Strasse down to the Puppenbrücke. After crossing the bridge the road forks, but either way will take you to the Holstentor, the old gate which is the symbol of the city. Crossing the Holstenbrücke, you arrive at the start of Holstenstrasse. To your left, at this point, is An der Untertrave, to your right, An der Obertrave. Going up Holstenstrasse, you arrive at the Kohlmarkt, from which you can turn left into the Markt. From Lübeck Hbf to the Markt is about 12 minutes' walk. At the end of the Kohlmarkt is Wahmstrasse, from which Königstrasse and then Grosse Burgstrasse lead left to the Burgtor.

HOTELS

Cheapest doubles around DM60 (£21; $37) B&B

Frau Scharnweber, Moislinger Allee (tel. 891042)

Cheapest doubles around DM70 (£24.50; $43.50) B&B

Pension am Park, Hüxtertorallee 57 (tel. 797598). Just outside the Old Town. From Wahmstrasse follow Kranenstrasse into Huxtertorallee, then go right.

Cheapest doubles around DM75 (£26.25; $46.50)

Hotel Marienburg, Katharinenstrasse 41 (tel. 42512). B&B.
Left from the station, left at Fackenburger Allee across the
railway line, first right, then first right again, then left along
Katharinenstrasse.

Hotel Stadtpark, Roeckstrasse 9 (tel. 34555). B&B.

Hotel Schönwald, Chasotstrasse 25 (tel. 64169/64162). English
spoken.

Cheapest doubles around DM80 (£28; $50) B&B

Bahnhofs-Hotel, Am Bahnhof 21 (tel. 83883). Buffet breakfast.
By Lübeck Hbf.

Pension Köglin, Kottwitzstrasse 39 (tel. 622432/823733).

Cheapest doubles around DM90 (£31.50; $56) B&B

Hotel Hanseatic, Hansestrasse 19 (tel. 83328/83330). Buffet
breakfast. The street runs off Beim Retteich.

Hotel Petersen, Hansestrasse 11a (tel. 84519). The street runs
off Beim Retteich.

PRIVATE ROOMS

Famile Schräger, Ginsterweg 5 (tel. 891407). B&B in singles
and doubles DM32,50 (£11.50; $20) per person.

Frau Reimer, Vermehrenring 11e (tel. 65596). B&B DM37,50
(£13.25; $23) per person.

Frau Zingel, Vermehrenring 119 (tel. 625029. Room for up
to three persons. B&B DM37,50 (£13.25; $23) per person.

APARTMENTS

Herr Nickel, Engelsgrube 61 (tel. 593139/705120). DM42,50
(£15; $26) per person per day for two sharing. DM35
(£12.25; $21.50) per person per day for three sharing. In
the historic centre of the city between An der Untertrave
and Breite Strasse.

Familie Nickel, Kahlorststrasse 1a (tel. 593139). Sleeps 2–4. DM60–85 (£21.00–29.75; $37–53) per day.

Ferienwohnung Kottwitzstrasse 42 (tel. 64289) DM90–100 (£31.50–35; $56–62) per day. Sleeps up to three persons.

Pension 'Santa Monika', Monika Schlei, Kronsdorfer Allee 101a (tel. 581328). DM32,50 (£16.75; $20) p.p. per day for two sharing.

Historisches Altstadt-Ferienhaus, Hartengrube 44 (Heynathsgang). DM47,50 (£16.75; $29.50) p.p. per day for two sharing: DM38 (£13.25; $23.50) p.p. per day for three sharing: DM33 (£11.50; $20.50) p.p. per day for four sharing. In the Old Town. Contact Antje Pröpper, Engelsgrube 85 (tel. 74629/3909181).

E. Lorenz, Steinstrasse 2 (tel. 791708). In the Old Town. Similar prices to the Historisches Altstadt-Ferienhaus, above.

IYHF HOSTEL

Folke-Bernadotte-Heim, Am Gertrudenkirchhof 4 (tel. 33433). Curfew 11.30 p.m. DM16 (£5.50; $10). Outside the historic centre, about 5 minutes' walk from the Burgtor. A 25–30-minute walk from Lübeck Hbf. From the station take bus 1 or 3 to Am Burgfeld.

Lübeck Jugendgasthaus, Mengstrasse 33 (tel. 70399). In the Old Town. Turn right off An der Untertrave.

HOSTELS

Sleep-In (YMCA), Gross Petersgrube 11 (tel. 78982). Open to men and women. Midnight curfew. DM14 (£5; $9). Located in one of the most beautiful streets in the town. Turn left off An der Obertrave.

Rucksackhotel, Kanalstrasse 70 (tel. 706892). DM70 (£24.50; $43.50) for doubles, DM90 (£31.50; $56) for triples, DM20–23 (£7–8; $12.50–14.00) per person in larger rooms. About 20 minutes' walk from Lübeck Hbf. From Königstrasse, turn right up Glockengiesserstrasse and walk

the whole length of the street to Kanalstrasse. The hostel
is at the junction of the two streets.

CAMPING

Steinrader Damm 12, Lübeck-Schönböcken (tel.
893090/892287). DM8 (£2.80; $5) per tent, DM6 (£2.10; $4)
p.p. Open 1 Apr.–31 Oct. From the centre of town only
a 10-minute trip on bus 7 or 8 dir. Dornbreite. Both stop
near the entrance to the site.

Meissen (tel. code 053)

Tourist Office
Fremdenverkehrsamt der Stadt Meissen, Meissen-Information,
An der Frauenkirche 3, 0-8250 Meissen (tel. 4470). Open
Mon.–Fri. 9 a.m.–6 p.m. and, during the main tourist season,
Sat. 10.30 a.m.–2.30 p.m. From the Meissen Hbf, head left until
you reach the Elbe. Cross the bridge and go straight ahead,
or down Elbstrasse until you reach the Marktplatz. The
Frauenkirche and the Tourist Office are on the left of the
Marktplatz.

HOTELS

Pension Jägerhof, Heinrich-Heine-Strasse 47 (tel. 7515). B&B
in doubles DM70 (£24.50; $43.50).
Hotel Goldener Löwe, Heinrichsplatz 6 (tel. 3304). B&B from
DM75 (£26.25; $46.50). Heinrichsplatz is halfway along
Elbstrasse as you walk to the Tourist Office.

PRIVATE ROOMS

Rooms must be booked through the Fremdenverkehrsamt
Meissen Information. Prices for B&B are normally in the range
DM20–35 (£7.00–12.25; $12.50–21.50) per person.

Cheapest price around DM17.50 (£6.25; $11) p.p.

Ilse Stelzner, Weinberggasse 8b. Doubles/triples only. Price does not include breakfast.

Cheapest price around DM20–23 (£7–8; $12.50–14.00) p.p.

Andrea Berger, Tonberg 18. Price for doubles. Singles are about 50 per cent more expensive.

Herbert Börsdorf, Dresdnerstrasse 101 (tel. 4158). Doubles/triples only.

Edelgard Bursche, Trinitaskirchweg 20 (tel. 2945). Singles only.

Ingrid Kanis, Am Hohen Gericht 12 (tel. 3777). No singles or doubles. Larger rooms only.

Pia Hampf, Tonberg 10. Doubles only.

Helmut Queisser, Oberspaarerstrasse 55. Doubles only.

Frank Lützner, Niederspaarerstrasse 17. Doubles only.

Jutta Weder, Stadtparkhohe 11d (tel. 4006). Singles and doubles.

Cheapest price around DM25 (£8.75; $15.50) p.p.

Sabine Göckert, Bohnitzscherstrasse 12. Doubles/triples. Price does not include breakfast.

Elisabeth Kursawe, Grossenhainerstrasse 136. Doubles only.

Ingeborg Müller, Gelegegasse 9b. Doubles only.

Ingeborg Münch, Grüner Weg 8. Doubles/triples.

Claus Reichenbach, Rauhentalstrasse 67. No singles. Doubles and larger rooms. Price does not include breakfast.

Cheapest price around DM28–30 (£9.75–10.50; $17–18.50) p.p.

Steffen Zimmermann, Stadtblick 27 (tel. 3641). Singles only.

Werner Bartscht, Gelegegasse 6b (tel. 7519). Doubles/triples.

Hans Fölck, Heinrich-Heine-Strasse 54. Doubles/triples.

Helga Nickel, Grossenhainerstrasse 95 (tel. 3365). Doubles only.

Helmut Porsche, Korbitzerstrasse 18b. No singles. Doubles and larger rooms.

APARTMENTS

Also available through the Fremdenverkehrsamt Meissen Information. DM50–80 (£17.50–28.00; $31–50) per night.

IYHF HOSTEL

Wilsdrufferstrasse 58 (tel. 3065). Around DM14 (£5; $9).

CAMPING

Campingplatz Scharfenberg (tel. 2680). By the River Elbe, in the direction of Dresden. For further information contact Dietmar Sieber, Siebeneichen 6b, 0-8250 Meissen.

Munich (München) (tel. code 089)

Tourist Office
Fremdenverkehrsamt der Landeshauptstadt München, 8000 München (tel. 23911). Hotels can be reserved in advance by writing to this office. The Fremdenverkehrsamt operate three branches in the city which will book rooms for you on arrival. A fee of DM5 (£1.75; $3) is payable for this service.

München Hauptbahnhof (tel. 2391256/2391257). Open daily 8 a.m.–10 p.m. Opposite track 11 in the main train station, by the Bayerstrasse exit. Queues can be lengthy in summer, expect to wait 15–30 minutes. If all you want is a simple city map with the main tourist attractions, these are normally available from the self-service brochure stand.

Ruffinihaus, Rindermarkt/Pettenbeckstrasse. Open Mon.–Fri. 9.30 a.m.–1 p.m. and 2–6 p.m. except public holidays. S1-7/U3, U6: Marienplatz. Follow Rindermarkt down the side of St Peter's Church from Marienplatz. At the fork in the road, go either way (going left, Pettenbeckstrasse is first right, and vice versa). Queues at this office are usually considerably shorter than at the train station.

Flughafen Riem (tel. 907256). In the arrivals hall of the airport. Open daily 8.30 a.m.–10 p.m., except Sun. and public holidays 1–9 p.m.

Public Transport

All integrated tram, bus, S-and U-bahn systems are operated by the Münchner Verkehrs- und Tarifsverband (MVV). Prices are based on a zonal system. Various types of tickets are available to visitors. Simplest of all are single journey tickets, priced according to the zone of your destination. Strip-tickets (ten strips) work out cheaper per journey than single tickets. The number of strips you cancel in the automatic machines depends on how many zones you are travelling. If your journey is of four stops or less (two stops on the S- and U-bahn) cheaper short-distance single and strip-tickets are available. MVV day tickets are valid on the whole network. Cancel the ticket when you first use it. If there is a group of you a special day ticket for groups is available which offers a saving on the cost of buying individual day tickets. Unlike the day ticket, you cannot use these tickets before 9 a.m. Mon.–Fri. A similar restriction applies to the monthly Green Card. Single tickets and strip-tickets are available from automatic vending machines, and from tram/bus drivers (tickets bought from drivers must be cancelled on board the bus/tram). Strip-tickets are also available at all MVV sales points. Daily tickets are available at MVV sales points, Tourist Offices, in many hotels, and at the Obermanzing and Thalkirchen campsites. Monthly tickets are available from MVV sales outlets. Automatic machines for cancelling tickets are located at the entrance to the S-and U-bahn, and on the platforms of trams and buses. Railpass holders can travel free on the S-bahn only. Assuming you have a railcard and find accommodation in the centre, or close to an S-bahn station, then it is worth noting that most of the main attractions are near S-bahn stations or within easy walking distance of the centre (exceptions are the Olympic stadium complex and the nearby BMW museum, and the Nymphenburg Palace).

Accommodation in Munich

Munich is one of the most popular destinations in Europe, so advance reservation of accommodation is advisable at any time of year, as far in advance as possible. To reserve hotel accommodation write directly to the hotel, or to the Tourist Office (you can give the names of a few hotels in order of preference). The city is exceptionally busy between June and August, then, in September, just when it is becoming easier to find accommodation elsewhere, Munich receives a huge influx of visitors for the start of the Oktoberfest. If you are arriving without reservations at this time it is highly unlikely you will find a hostel bed, or even a room in one of the cheaper hotels listed below. Railpass holders totally stuck for a bed should refer to the Sleeping Rough section below for details of a useful train service.

HOTELS

Note: Roman numerals in an address refer to the floor of the building.

Singles around DM38 (£13.25; $23.50) doubles around DM55 (£19.25; $34)

Maisinger, Pippingerstrasse 105 (tel. 8112920). S2: Obermenzing, then bus 75 along Verdistrasse and into Pippingerstrasse, or a 10-minute walk along the same route.

Cheapest doubles around DM60 (£21; $37)

Eberl, Josef-Frankl-Strasse 56 (tel. 3132638).

Cheapest doubles around DM65 (£22.75; $40)

Gästehaus Obermenzing, Verdistrasse 80 (tel. 8112763). S2: Obermenzing, then a 300m walk along Verdistrasse.
Schiller, Schillerstrasse 11 (tel. 592435). About 300m from Munich Hbf. Leaving the station by the main exit,

Schillerstrasse begins almost opposite the right hand end of Bahnhofplatz, across Bayerstrasse.

Cheapest doubles around DM70 (£24.50; $43.50)

Am Kaiserplatz, Kaiserplatz 12 (tel. 349190). U3, U6: Münchener Freiheit, then a few minutes' walk along Herzogstrasse, first left, then right along Kaiserstrasse.

Fleischmann, Bischof-Adalbert-Strasse 10 (tel. 3595379/3508126) U2, U3: Petuelring. From Petuelring, a short walk down Riesenfeldstrasse, right after Keferloherstrasse, then left.

Theresia, Luisenstrasse 51 (tel. 521250/5233081/5233082). U2: Theresienstrasse. Follow Theresienstrasse two blocks in the direction of the Alte Pinakothek, then right on Luisenstrasse (about 300m in all).

Würmtalhof, Eversbuschstrasse 91 (tel. 8122185). S2: Allach, then a 250m walk along Versaliusstrasse into Eversbuschstrasse. The hotel is near the junction.

Cheapest doubles around DM75 (£26.25; $46.50)

Augsburg, Schillerstrasse 18 (tel. 597673). See Hotel Schiller, above. About 300m from Munich Hbf.

Beck, Thierschstrasse 36 (tel. 225768). Tram 20 heading right from the front of the Munich Hbf runs along the street. S1–S7: Isartor, then a 5-minute walk along Thierschstrasse from Isartorplatz.

Diana, Altheimer Eck 15/3 (tel. 2603107). Excellent central location, 5–10 minutes' walk from Munich Hbf. Through the underground shopping centre to Karlsplatz (S1–S7/U4, U5: Karlsplatz /Stachus is the nearest stop to the hotel), along Neuhauserstrasse, right at Eisenmannstrasse, then left along Altheimer Eck.

Härtl, Verdistrasse 135 (tel. 8111632). S2: Obermenzing, then a 5-minute walk along Verdistrasse or bus 73 or 75.

Isabella, Isabellastrasse 35 (tel. 2713503). U2: Hohenzollern-platz, a 400m walk along Kurfürstenstrasse, then right down Isabellastrasse.

Scheel, Isabellastr. 31/II (tel. 2713611). See Hotel Isabella, above.

Zöllner, Sonnenstrasse 10/IV and V (tel. 554035). A 5–10-minute walk from Munich Hbf, left along Bayerstrasse from Bahnhofplatz, then right down Sonnenstrasse, or take tram 20, 25 or 27 heading right from Bahnhofplatz.

Sollner Hof, Herterichstrasse 63–65 (tel. 792090/794045).

Josefine, Nordenstrasse 13 (tel. 2710043). U2, U3: Scheidplatz, then tram 13 to Nordendstrasse, or U3, U6: Giselastrasse, then a 500m walk along Leopoldstrasse in the direction of the university (Universität) right along Georgenstrasse, left at Nordendstrasse.

Cheapest doubles around DM80 (£28; $50)

Am Knie, Strindbergstrasse 33 (tel. 886450). Tram 19 from Munich Hbf heading towards Pasinger Marienplatz. Get off by the junction of Landsbergerstrasse and G.-Habel-Strasse. Walk down the latter, then left.

Doria, Hohenstaufenstrasse 12/IV (tel. 333872). U3, U6: Giselastrasse, then a 5-minute walk. Down Leopoldstrasse toward the university (Universität), right along Georgenstrasse, right again at Friedrichstrasse, then left.

Frankfurter Ring, Riesenfeldstrasse 79a (tel. 3511309). Good value, as rooms have a shower/bath. U3, U6: Münchener Freiheit, then bus 43 or 143 to the junction of Frankfurter Ring and Riesenfeldstrasse (the hotel is near the junction), or U2, U3: Petuelring, then a 600m walk along Riesenfeldstrasse from Petuelring.

Herzog-Heinrich, Herzog-Heinrich-Strasse 3 (tel. 532575/5380750). A 10-minute walk from Munich Hbf. Exit on to Bayerstrasse, right, left down Paul-Heyse-Strasse and across Georg-Hirth-Platz into Herzog-Heinrich-Strasse. Exit left from the station on to Arnulfstrasse and you can take bus 58 to Georg-Hirth-Platz.

Hungaria, Briennerstrasse 42/II (tel. 521558). A 10-minute walk from Munich Hbf. Exit left on to Arnulfstrasse, cross over and take Dachauerstrasse, second right, across

Karlstrasse, on down Augustenstrasse into Brienner-strasse. The hotel is located roughly 250m from both. U1: Stiglmaierplatz and U2: Königsplatz.

Lutz, Hofenfelsstrasse 57 (tel. 152970).

Marie-Luise, Landwehrstrasse 37/IV (tel. 554230). A 5-minute walk from Munich Hbf, right when Landwehrstrasse crosses Schillerstrasse (see Hotel Schiller above).

Maximilian, Reitmorstrasse 12 (tel. 222433) U4, U5: Lehel, or tram 20 heading right from Munich Hbf to the second stop after Maximilian II monument. Walk along Thiersch-strasse away from the monument, right down Robert-Koch-Strasse, then left.

Olympia, Maxhofstrasse 23 (tel. 754063/754064).

Strigl, Elisabethstrasse 11/II (tel. 2713444/2716250). U2: Hohenzollernplatz, then a few minutes' walk down Tengstrasse and left along Elisabethstrasse.

Westfalia, Mozartstrasse 23 (tel. 530377–78). A 15-minute walk from Munich Hbf. Right when Mozartstrasse crosses Herzog-Heinrich-Strasse (see Hotel Herzog-Heinrich, above). U3, U6: Goetheplatz, then a 300m walk along Mozartstrasse.

Wilhelmy, Amalienstrasse 71 (tel. 283971). U3, U6: Universität, then about an 800m walk. From Ludwig-strasse, both Schellingstrasse and Adalbertstrasse lead into Amalienstrasse (go right and left respectively to the hotel).

Cheapest doubles around DM85 (£29.75; $53)

Clara, Wilhelmstrasse 25 (tel. 348374). U3, U6: Münchener Freiheit, then a few minutes' walk along Herzogstrasse from Leopoldstrasse, then left at Wilhelmstrasse.

Erbprinz, Sonnenstrasse 2 (tel. 594521/594522) A 5–10-minute walk from Munich Hbf (see Hotel Zöllner, above).

Erika, Landwehrstrasse 8 (tel. 554327). A 5-minute walk from Munich Hbf, left where Landwehrstrasse crosses Schillerstrasse (see Schiller, above).

Frank, Schellingstrasse 24 (tel. 281451). See Hotel Wilhelmy, above. A 5-minute walk from the U-bahn station.

Frauenhofer, Frauenhoferstrasse 10 (tel. 2607238). U1, U2:
Frauenhofer, then a 150m walk. Tram 25 or 27 heading
right from Munich Hbf to Müllerstrasse also leaves 150m
walk down Frauenhoferstrasse.

Haydn, Haydnstrasse 9 (tel. 531119). A 10–15-minute walk
from Munich Hbf, left off Herzog-Heinrich-Strasse at
Kaiser-Ludwig-Platz (see Hotel Herzog-Heinrich, above).
U3, U6: Goetheplatz, then a few minutes' walk along
Mozartstrasse, then right.

Lugano, Schillerstrasse 32 (tel. 591005). A 5-minute walk from
Munich Hbf, see Hotel Schiller, above.

Locarno, Bahnhofplatz 5 (tel. 555164). On the left as you leave
Munich Hbf by the main exit.

Münch, Heimdallstrasse 2b (tel. 605222).

Süzer, Mittererstrasse 1/III (tel. 533521/536642). A few
minutes' walk from Munich Hbf. Exit on to Bayerstrasse,
right, then left down Mittererstrasse.

Utzelmann, Pettenkoferstrasse 6 (tel. 594889). A 10-minute
walk from Munich Hbf, left off Schillerstrasse (see Hotel
Schiller, above). U1, U2: Sendlinger Tor, or tram 20, 25
or 27 heading right from Munich Hbf to the Sendlinger Tor,
followed by a short walk. From Sonnenstrasse take
Nussbaumstrasse, then right.

Cheapest doubles around DM90 (£31.50; $56)

Alba, Mühlbaurstrasse 2 (tel. 472458). U4: Prinzregentenplatz. The hotel is right at the start of Mühlbaurstrasse as
it leaves Prinzregentenplatz.

Am Nordbad, Schleissheimerstrasse 91 (tel. 180857). U2:
Hohenzollernplatz, then a short walk along Hohenzollern-
strasse, then left on Schleissheimerstrasse.

Armin, Augustenstrasse 5 (tel. 593197). About 800m from
Munich Hbf (see Hotel Hungaria, above). U1: Stiglmaierplatz, then a few minutes' walk down Dachauerstrasse,
left at Karlstrasse, then left again.

Beim Haus der Kunst, Bruderstrasse 4/I (tel. 222127). Tram
20 heading right from Munich Hbf to the junction of

Wagmüllerstrasse and Prinzregentenstrasse. Go left along
the latter, then left at Bruderstrasse.

Brunner, Untere Mühlstrasse 13 (tel. 8131528). Rooms have
shower/bath. S2: Allach, then a few minutes' walk along
Vesaliusstrasse, then left.

Flora, Karlstrasse 49 (tel. 597067). Just over 5 minutes' walk
from Munich Hbf, left off Dachauerstrasse (see Hotel
Hungaria, above).

Hedwig, Hedwigstrasse 7/III (tel. 1293302) U1: Rotkreuzplatz, then a short walk along Nymphenburgerstrasse, left
on the second street after crossing the main road
(Landshuter Allee).

Kronprinz, Zweigstrasse 10 (tel. 593606). A 5-minute walk
from Munich Hbf. On leaving the station turn right, then
left along Bayerstrasse, right at Zweigstrasse.

Lex, Briennerstrasse 48 (tel. 522091). See Hotel Hungaria,
above, then left off Augustenstrasse.

Lindner, Dultstrasse 1 (tel. 263413). Good location near the
Asamkirche, a short walk from the town centre. S1–S7/U3,
U6: Marienplatz, then a 400m walk. Follow Rindermarkt
down past St Peter's Church. Dultstrasse runs between
Oberanger and Sendlingerstrasse (turn right and left
respectively).

Lucia, Linprunstrasse 12 (tel. 5234016). A 15-minute walk
from Munich Hbf. Right along Dachauerstrasse into
Stiglmaierplatz, (U1: Stiglmaierplatz) left along Brienner-
strasse, right Sandstrasse, then left.

München, Valpichlerstrasse 49 (tel. 564045) U4, U5: Laimer
Platz is about 200m away. Follow Fürstenriederstrasse from
the station, then left.

Schubert, Schubertstrasse 1/I (tel. 535087). A 10–15-minute
walk from Munich Hbf, right off Herzog-Heinrich-Strasse
at Kaiser-Ludwig-Platz. About 500m from U3, U6: Goetheplatz. Schubertstrasse is to the right off Mozartstrasse.

IYHF HOSTELS

The IYHF hostels in Munich are part of the Bavarian section

of the Deutsches Jugendherbergswerk, which admits only those aged 27 or under to hostels under its control. Because of the popularity of the hostels in Munich there is virtually no chance of this rule being ignored, as can be the case in some cities in the region.

DJH Jugendgasthaus München, Miesingerstrasse 4 (tel. 7236550/7236560). 1 a.m. curfew. Singles DM32 (£11.25; $20), doubles DM28 (£9.75; $17) p.p., larger rooms around DM24 (£8.50; $15) p.p. Prices include breakfast. S7, S27: Mittersendling, then a short walk along Leipartstrasse and straight on to the hostel, or S7: Harras, then bus 66 to the hostel.

DJH München, Wendl-Dietrich-Strasse 20 (tel. 131156). 1 a.m. curfew. B&B in dorms around DM20 (£7; $12.50) p.p. U1: Rotkreuzplatz, then a short walk along Wendl-Dietrich-Strasse. The entrance is on Winthirplatz, second on the right.

DJH Burg Schwaneck, Burgweg 4–6, Pullach (tel. 7930643/4). 1 a.m. curfew. B&B in dorms from DM14–16 (£5.00–5.75; $8.50–10.00) p.p. About 7½ miles from the city centre, but the trip on the S7 to Pullach from the main train station or city centre only takes about 25 minutes. From the S-bahn station the hostel is a well signposted 10-minute walk.

HOSTELS

CVJM, Jugendgasthaus, Landwehrstrasse 13 (tel. 555941). YMCA hostel, but open to girls as well. 12.30 a.m. curfew. Singles DM42–57 (£14.75–20.00; $26–35), doubles DM36–45 (£12.75–15.75; $22–28), per person, larger rooms DM33–41 (£11.50–14.50; $20–25) p.p. Overnight price includes breakfast. Prices fall after two nights. A 5–10-minute walk from Munich Hbf. Leaving by the main exit, go right, across Bayerstrasse and down Schillerstrasse, then left along Landwehrstrasse.

Haus International, Jugendhotel, Elisabethstrasse 87 (tel. 12006). All rooms have showers and WC. Singles DM49–72 (£17.25–25.25; $30–44), doubles DM46–61 (£16.00–21.50;

$28–38) p.p., larger rooms DM37–42 (£13.00–14.75;
$23–26) p.p. U2: Hohenzollernplatz, then a 5-minute walk
along Hohenzollernplatz and left down Schleissheimerstrasse into Elisabethstrasse

Jugendhotel Marienberge, Goethestrasse 9 (tel. 555891).
Women only. Age limit 25. Midnight curfew. Singles DM32
(£11.25; $19.50), doubles and larger rooms DM27 (£9.50;
$16.50) p.p. Overnight price includes breakfast. A five-
minute walk from Munich Hbf. Leave by the Bayerstrasse
exit, turn right, then left on to Goethestrasse.

Kolpinghaus St Theresia, Hanebergstrasse 8 (tel. 126050).
Singles DM46 (£16; $28), doubles DM39 (£13.75; $24) p.p.,
larger rooms DM30 (£10.50; $18.50) p.p. From Munich Hbf,
take tram 20, 25 or 27 heading left from the station to the
stop after Dachauerstrasse crosses Landshuter Allee. Walk
back, then right down Landshuter Allee, then right again
at Hanebergstrasse (a 5-minute walk).

IYHF HOSTELS NEARBY

Beim Pfaffenkeller 3, Augsburg (tel. 0821–33909). DM18
(£6.25; $11) for B&B in dorms. Trains run to Augsburg
every 20–30 minutes from Munich, a 30–40-minute trip.
To get to the hostel from Augsburg Hbf, take tram 2 to
Stadtwerke. As Augsburg is a popular destination itself
(and rightly so), the hostel is often full in summer so phone
before making the trip out to Augsburg.

'THE TENT'

Jugendlage Kapuzinerhölzl, Franz-Schrank-Strasse 8 (tel.
1414300). Actually two circus tents, with mattresses and
blankets provided. Open 5 p.m.–9 a.m., late June–early
September. DM7 (£2.50; $4.50). Three-night maximum
stay. Maximum age 24, not rigorously enforced. Leave your
pack at the station. U1 to Rotkreuzplatz, then tram 12 dir.
Amalienburgstrasse to the Botanischer Garten stop on

Miesingerstrasse. Along Franz-Schrank-Strasse and left at the top on to In den Kirschen. 'The Tent' is on the right.

CAMPING

Munich-Thalkirchen, Zentralländstrasse 49 (tel. 7231707). Cheap, municipal site. Open 15 Mar.–31 Oct. Crowded, especially during the Oktoberfest. From the train station, S1–S7 to Marienplatz, then U3 dir. Forstenrieder Allee to Thalkirchen (Tierplatz), followed by bus 57 to Thalkirchen (last stop).

Munich-Obermenzing, Lochhausenerstrasse 59 (tel. 8112235). S2: Obermenzing, then bus 75 to the junction of Pippingerstrasse and Lochhausenerstrasse, followed by a 5-minute walk along the latter. Open 15 Mar.–31 Oct.

SLEEPING ROUGH

The police tolerate people sleeping in the main train station during the Oktoberfest, though make sure you move quickly when they wake you in the morning (usually around 6 a.m.). For obvious reasons, you cannot expect a peaceful night's sleep. A useful train for railpass holders stuck for a bed is the D14164, which leaves Munich Hbf at 0123 and runs as a local service to Stuttgart, arriving at 0512. At 0538, the D2111 Norddeich-Munich train arrives in Stuttgart, departing at 0553 and arriving in Munich at 0845. Leave your pack at Munich Hbf.

Nuremberg (Nürnberg)   (tel. code 0911)

Tourist Offices
Nuremburg's Tourist Information (tel. 23360) has two branches: one in Nürnberg Hbf, open Mon.–Sat. 9 a.m.–8 p.m., the other in the Rathaus (Town Hall) off Hauptmarkt, open Mon.–Sat. 9 a.m.–1 p.m. and 2–6 p.m. To reserve hotels

in advance, write to: Congress- und Tourismus-Zentrale
Nürnberg, Frauentorgraben 3, 8500 Nürnberg 70.

Basic Directions
The historic core of Nuremberg is quite small, so in 20 minutes
you can walk from the train station to the castle on the opposite
side of the Old Town. From the station, take the underpass
to Königstor, then walk down Königstrasse to reach St
Lawrence's Church on Lorenzplatz. Go downhill over the
River Pegnitz by the Museumsbrücke and into Hauptmarkt.
Head diagonally left across the square, turn right into
Rathausplatz, from which Burgstrasse leads uphill to the castle.
Near the Church of St Lawrence (just over one third of the way)
is the Lorenzkirche U-bahn stop, linked to Nürnberg Hbf by
U-bahn lines 1 and 2. Directions in the various sections below
are often given from points on this route.

HOTELS

**Cheapest singles around DM30 (£10.50; $18.50) cheapest
doubles around DM50 (£17.50; $31)**

Alt-Nürnberg, Breite Gasse 40 (tel. 224129). Left off Königstrasse, a short distance before the Lorenzkirche.

Cheapest doubles around DM60 (£21; $37)

Zum Schwänlein, Hintere Sterngasse 11 (tel. 225162). First
left off Königstrasse from the Königstor.

Cramer-Klett, Pillenreutherstrasse 162 (tel. 44921). Singles
DM30 (£10.50; $18.50). U-bahn lines 1 and 11 to
Frankenstrasse take you virtually to the door.

Eberlein, Jägerstrasse 11 (tel. 632821). Out of the centre, but
a 15-minute walk from Nürnberg-Eibach train station (head
for Weissenburgerstrasse). U-bahn line 2 to Röthenbach
is slightly closer.

Cheapest doubles around DM68 (£24; $42)

Melanchthon, Melanchthonplatz 1 (tel. 412626). A 20-minute walk from Nürnberg Hbf. Left from the exit, left through the Celtis underpass, across Celtisplatz and down Pillenreutherstrasse, then right along Breitscheidstrasse and Wiesenstrasse. U-bahn line 1 or 11 to Aufsessplatz will save you half the walk.

Süd, Ingolstädterstrasse 51 (tel. 445139). U-bahn line 1 or 11 to Frankenstrasse. Head right from the junction with Pillenreutherstrasse, then right again a few blocks on.

Vater Jahn, Jahnstrasse 13 (tel. 444507). A 15-minute walk from Nürnberg Hbf. From Celtisplatz (see Melanchthon above) go right along Celtisstrasse and Tunnelstrasse, then left.

Fischer, Brunnengasse 11 (tel. 226189). Left off Königstrasse, just before the Lorenzkirche.

Cheapest doubles around DM70–75 (£24.50–26.25; $43.50–46.50)

Brendel, Blumenstrasse 1 (tel. 225618). Follow Königstor-Marientorgraben from the Königstor, then right.

Keim, Peuntgasse 10 (tel. 225940). A short walk down Königstrasse from the Königstor, then right.

Christl, Laufamholzstrasse 216c (tel. 501249). Well out from the centre, but a 10–15-minute walk from the Nürnberg-Laufamholz S-bahn stop.

Jugend- und Economy-Hotel, Gostenhofer Hauptstrasse 47–49 (tel. 289581). Large capacity.

Cheapest doubles around DM80 (£28; $50)

Hannweber, Peter-Henlein-Strasse 1–14 (tel. 413770). Close to the Melanchthon (directions above). The street crosses Pillenreutherstrasse one block before Breitscheidstrasse.

Keiml, Luitpoldstrasse 7 (tel. 226240/208775). To the left off Königstrasse, a short walk from the Königstor.

Altstadt, Hintere Ledergasse 2 (tel. 226102). Walking from

Lorenzplatz towards the River Pegnitz, go left on Kaiserstrasse which leads into Hintere Ledergasse.

Cheapest doubles around DM85 (£29.75; $53)

Haus Vosteen, Lindenstrasse 12 (tel. 533325). A 20-minute walk from Nürnberg Hbf. From the Königstor, take Königstor-Marientorgraben, then follow the old walls to Maxtorgraben. Go right into Veilodterstrasse, then left.

Schweizer-Hof, Karl-Bröger-Strasse 38 (tel. 443860). From Pillenreutherstrasse (see Melanchthon above) go right along Bogenstrasse into Karl-Bröger-Strasse. A 10-minute walk from the train station. U-bahn line 1 or 11 to Aufsessplatz leaves a short walk.

Peter Henlein, Peter-Henlein-Strasse 15 (tel. 412912). Over the street from the Hannweber (directions above).

Royal, Theodorstrasse 9 (tel. 533209). A 15-minute walk from the Nürnberg Hbf. Follow Gleissbühlstrasse into Laufertorgraben, right at Kesslerstrasse, then sharp right.

Berndt, Wölckernstrasse 80 (tel. 448066). A 10-minute walk from Nürnberg Hbf. Take the Allersberger underpass to the right of the station and follow Allersbergerstrasse into Wölckernstrasse.

Aquamarin, Lorenzstrasse 11 (497705). Right from Lorenzplatz.

Blaue Traube, Johannesgasse 22 (tel. 221666). A short walk from the Königstor, right on Theatergasse, then right.

Pfälzer Hof, Am Gräslein 10 (tel. 221411). A short walk from the Königstor along Königstrasse, left at Hallplatz across the Kornmarkt, then left after Kartäusergasse.

Albrect Dürer Klause, Bergstrasse 25 (tel. 204592). From Burgstrasse go left along Obere Krämersgasse into Bergstrasse.

Goldener Adler, Klaragasse 21 (tel. 208500/221360). The entrance is on Klaragasse, left off Königstrasse a short distance from the Königstor.

Sonne, Königstrasse 45 (tel. 227166). A short walk from the Königstor. The entrance is on Theatergasse.

More double rooms in the DM50–60 (£17.50–21.00; $31–37) range are available in nearby Fürth and Erlangen, both about 15–30 minutes' journey by frequent local trains. In both Fürth and Erlangen there is a branch of the Tourist Office near the train station (tel. 776682/772670 for the office in Fürth; tel. 09131-25074 for the office in Erlangen).

IYHF HOSTEL

Jugendgasthaus 'Kaiserstallung', Burg 2 (tel. 241352). DM25 (£8.75; $15.50). Age limit 27. 1 a.m. curfew. Formerly the castle stables. A 20-minute walk from Nürnberg Hbf (see Basic Directions), or take tram 9 dir. Thon to Krelingstrasse. The castle is on the left. Walk through the grounds to the hostel.

HOSTELS

Jugend-Hotel Nürnberg, Buchenbühl, Rathsbergerstrasse 300 (tel. 529092). Small dorms cost DM22–27 (£7.75–9.50; $13.50–16.50) depending on whether the dorm has its own shower and toilet. Breakfast included. Thirty minutes' walk from the centre. Tram 3 to the terminus, then bus 41 to Felsenkeller.

Jugend- und Economy-Hotel, Gostenhofer Hauptstrasse 47–49 (tel. 289581). Doubles start around DM70 (£24.50; $43.50).

IYHF HOSTEL NEARBY

'Frankenhof', Südlicher Stadtmauerstrasse 35, Amt für Freizeit, Erlangen (tel. 09131–862555/862274). DM16 (£5.50; $10). Frequent local trains make the 30-minute trip to Erlangen. From the station go straight ahead on to Hauptstrasse, turn right, then left along Friedrichstrasse. The hostel is in the sport and leisure area to the right of Friedrichstrasse.

CAMPING

Campingplatz am Stadion, Haus-Kalb-Strasse 56 (tel.
811122). Open May–Sept. Those with a railpass can take
atrain to Nürnberg-Dutzendteich. The site is behind the
football stadium (IFC Nürnberg, one of Germany's all-time
greats). The U-Bahn stop Messenzentrum is slightly closer.
Naturfreunde Erlangen, Wöhrmühle 6, Erlangen (tel.
09131–28499). Year round site. Near the station in
Erlangen, a 30-minute trip by frequent local trains from
Nürnberg. From the rear of the station, go right until you
see the road heading left under the A73 road. The site is
on the other side of the A73.

Potsdam (tel. code see below)

Tourist Office
POTSDAM-INFORMATION, Touristenzentrale Am Altem
Markt, Friedrich-Ebert-Strasse 5, 0-1561 Potsdam (tel. 23385).
Open daily from 9 a.m.–8 p.m., except Sat., Sun. and public
holidays when the office closes at 6 p.m. From Potsdam
Stadtbahnhof, cross the Havel by the Lange Brücke and go
right at the fork in the end of the road, down Friedrich-Ebert-
Strasse to the Tourist Office.

Telephoning Potsdam and Towns Nearby
Codes vary according to where you are calling from:
Potsdam:from west Berlin 03733
  from east Berlin 023
  from the former West Germany 003733
Werder:from west Berlin 0373352
  from the former West Germany 00373352
Caputh:from west Berlin 03733594
  from the former West Germany 003733594

Arriving in Potsdam by Train
In contrast to most German cities, do not get off at the Hauptbahnhof as it is far from the centre. Potsdam-Stadt is closest to the Tourist Office and the town centre. Potsdam Charlottenhof (previously known as Potsdam West) is the closest station to the Sanssouci Palace and the New Palace.

HOTELS

There is a shortage of hotels offering doubles in the DM60–80 (£21–28; $37–50) range in Potsdam, though there are rooms available around these prices in neighbouring towns.

B&B in doubles around DM60 (£21; $37)

Havelblick, Dorfstrasse 17, Töplitz (tel. 214). Singles from DM30 (£10.50; $18.50).

B&B in doubles around DM80 (£28; $50)

Gindowsee, Puschkinstrasse 21, Werder (tel. Werder 2342).
Melodie, Am Markt, Werder (tel. Werder 2508/2591).
Babelsberg, Stahnsdorferstrasse 68, Potsdam (tel. 78889). The closest train station is S-bahn: Griebnitzsee, about 750m away. Walk from the station to Stahnsdorferstrasse, then go right along the street.

PRIVATE ROOMS AND APARTMENTS

The Tourist Office book rooms and apartments in Potsdam and within a 12½ mile radius of the town. If no rooms are available in town, railpass holders should ask for a room in a town on the railway. Prices range from DM20–35 (£7.00–12.25; $12.50–21.50) per person per night, depending on the quality of the accommodation. Bookings can be made at any time the Tourist Office is open.

IYHF HOSTELS

'Am Neuen Garten', Eisenhartstrasse 5 (tel. 22515). Bus F from the Hauptbahnhof to Am Neuen Garten, or tram 1, 4 or 6 Platz der Einheit, or tram 2 or 5 to Johannes-Dieckmann-Strasse. From Potsdam Stadt station, follow the directions for the Tourist Office but continue right through the town centre on Friedrich-Ebert-Strasse until you see Johannes-Dieckmann-Strasse. Heading right takes you to Am Neuen Garten. This hostel was closed in 1992. Check the IYHF handbook or with the local Tourist Office to see if it has re-opened.

IYHF HOSTELS NEARBY

'Werder', Am Schwielowsee 110, Werder (tel. Werder 2850). Previously a Youth Tourist Hotel operated by the East German hostel association (more expensive than a normal Youth Hostel). Enquire about current prices at POTSDAM-INFORMATION.

CAMPING

Potsdam-Stadt, Potsdam Gaisberg, Geltow (tel. Werder 2412). Open 1 Apr.–15 Oct. DM5 (£1.75; $3) per person, DM6 (£2.10; $4) per tent. By the Templiner See.

Werder-Riegelspitze, Werder (tel. Werder 2397/2331). Open 15 Apr.–15 Oct. Beside the Glindower See. Bus D-631 runs to the site from Potsdam Hbf.

Caputh-Himmelreich, Caputh (tel. Werder 475). Open May–Oct.

Caputh Flottstelle, Caputh (tel. Caputh 497).

Stuttgart (tel. code 0711)

Tourist Offices

'I-Punkt', Königstrasse 1a. Open May–Oct., Mon.–Sat. 8.30 a.m.–10 p.m., Sun. 11 a.m.–6 p.m.; at other times, 1–6 p.m.

Das Verkehrsamt der Landeshauptstadt Stuttgart, Lautenschlagerstrasse 3, Postfach 10 50 44, 7000 Stuttgart 10 (tel. 2228-0). Advance reservation of hotel rooms can be made free of charge through this office.

City Transport

Railpasses are valid on the S-bahn, but not on the U-bahn.

HOTELS

Cheapest doubles around DM68 (£24; $42)

Schilling, Kernerstrasse 63 (tel. 240860). U-bahn lines 15 and 16 to Eugensplatz, then a short walk along Kernerstrasse. About 10 minutes' walk from the main train station. Follow directions for the IYHF hostel below. On the fringe of the town centre.

Cheapest doubles around DM75 (£26.25; $46.50)

Solitude, Hohewartstrasse 10 (tel. 854919). In the Feuerbach district. U-bahn lines 6 and 16 to Feuerbach Krankenhaus. With the hospital on your right, follow Stuttgarterstrasse until you see Hohewartstrasse on your right.

Eisenmann, Osterbronnerstrasse 5 (tel. 742779). In Rohr. S-bahn 1 and 2 to Rohr. Osterbronnerstrasse crosses the S-bahn line near the station.

Cheapest doubles around DM78 (£27.50; $48)

Eckel, Vorsteigstrasse 10 (tel. 290995). About 20 minutes' walk from the centre, further from Stuttgart Hbf. Bus 40 (heading right from in front of the train station) to Hölderlinplatz.

Schwarzwaldheim, Fritz-Elsas-Strasse 20 (tel. 296988). Central location. S-bahn lines 1–6 to Stadtmitte. The street runs off Rotebühlplatz. A 10-minute walk from the train station down Lautenschlägerstrasse and Theodor-Heuss-Strasse to Rotebühlplatz.

Adler, Filderbahnstrasse 25 (tel. 711304). In Möhringen. U-bahn lines 5 and 6 to Möhringen Bahnhof. From Filder-bahnplatz, a short walk down Filderbahnstrasse.

Traube, Kornwestheimerstrasse 11 (tel. 802696). In Stamm-heim. U-bahn line 15 to Korntalerstrasse.

Cheapest doubles around DM85 (£29.75; $53)

Silberwald, Kirchheimerstrasse 58–60 (tel. 474503). In Sillenbuch. U-bahn lines 15 and 16 to Eduard-Steinle-Strasse. At the end of Eduard-Steinle-Strasse, on the main road passing through Sillenbuch.

Lamm, Karl-Schurz-Strasse 7 (tel. 267328). U-bahn line 14 to Mineralbäder. Karl-Schurz-Strasse runs out of Am Schwanenplatz.

Museum-Stube, Hospitalstrasse 9 (tel. 296810). Central location. S-bahn lines 1–6 to Stadtmitte. From Theodor-Heuss-Strasse, take Langestrasse one block into Hospital-strasse. Just over 5 minutes' walk from Stuttgart Hbf, along Lautenschlägerstrasse, then right on Willi-Bleicher-Strasse into Hospitalstrasse.

Cheapest doubles around DM90 (£31.50; $56)

Haus Berg, Karl-Schurz-Strasse 16 (tel. 261875). See Lamm, above.

Krämer's Bürgerstuben, Gablenberger Hauptstrasse 4 (tel. 465481). In Gablenberg. Bus 40 or 42 (heading left from the front of Stuttgart Hbf) to Wagenburg/Ostendstrasse.

Schnaich, Paulinenstrasse 16 (tel. 602679). Just outside the centre. U-bahn line 14 to Österreichischer Platz, then a short walk along Paulinenstrasse.

Stoll, Brunnenstrasse 27 (tel. 562331). In Bad Cannstatt. S-bahn lines 1–3 to Bad Cannstatt. A 5–10-minute walk from the station. Left along Bahnhofstrasse, across Wilhelms-platz and down Wilhelmstrasse into Brunnenstrasse.

Arche, Bärenstrasse 2 (tel. 245759). Central location near the Marktplatz. U-bahn lines 5, 6, 15 and 16 to Charlottenplatz. Follow Holzstrasse, right Dorotheenstrasse, left Münz-strasse, then first right into Bärenstrasse. A 10-minute walk from Stuttgart Hbf. Through the Klett-Passage, down Königstrasse, left along Schulstrasse into Marktplatz, then along Bärenstrasse.

IYHF HOSTEL

Haussmannstrasse 27 (tel. 241583) DM18 (£6.25; $11). The entrance is on the corner of Werastrasse and Kernerstrasse. U-bahn lines 15 and 16 to Eugensplatz then a short walk along Kernerstrasse, or a 10-minute walk from Stuttgart Hbf. Leave the station by the ZOB exit (right, facing the tracks), under the tunnel then right. At the monument, go into Schillerstrasse, across Neckarstrasse at the crossing, up the path to the right of the police station, past the school, then up the steps to the corner of Werastrasse and Kernerstrasse.

IYHF HOSTELS NEARBY

There are hostels in two towns nearby which are well worth a visit. Esslingen-am-Neckar has retained much of its historic core, while Ludwigsburg has a superb palace. Esslingen is easily reached by frequent local trains, or by S-bahn line 1 dir. Plochingen (15–30-minute journey). There are regular local trains to Ludwigsburg (10–15-minute journey). Unfortunately, both hostels are located far from the respective stations. For details on which buses to take contact the hostels or the local Tourist Information Offices: for Ludwigsburg (tel. 07141-910252); in Esslingen the office is a 10-minute walk from the train station on the Marktplatz (along Bahnhofstrasse, over the Neckar and straight on).

Neuffenstrasse 65, Esslingen (tel. 0711-3512441/3512645).

Gemsenbergstrasse 31, Ludwigsburg (tel. 07141-51564).

CAMPING

By the Neckar on the Cannstätter Wasen (tel. 556696/561503). Not central, but easily reached from the centre or the train station. The site is only a few minutes' walk from U-bahn stop Hedelfingen (lines 9 and 13). S-bahn station Bad Cannstatt (lines 1–3) is a 10-minute walk away. Head right from the station, then right down Daimlerstrasse to the Cannstätter Wasen. The site is within walking distance of the fabulous Daimler-Benz Museum and off the football stadium (Neckarstadion, home of VfB and Stuttgarter Kickers).

Trier (tel. code 0651)

Tourist Office
Verkehrsamt der Stadt Trier, Simeonstift an der Porta Nigra, Postfach 3830, 5500 Trier (tel. 48071). Open Apr.–mid-Nov., Mon.–Sat. 9 a.m.–6.45 p.m., Sun. 9 a.m.–3.30 p.m.; mid-Nov.–Dec., Mon.–Fri. 9 a.m.–6 p.m.; weekends, 9 a.m.–1 p.m.; Jan.–Feb., Mon.–Fri. 9 a.m.–5 p.m., Sat. 9 a.m.–1 p.m.; Mar., Mon.–Fri. 9 a.m.–6 p.m., Sat. 9 a.m.–1 p.m. Contact the office in writing to reserve hotels in advance.

Basic Directions
The main train station (Trier Hbf) is about 10–15 minutes' walk from the Hauptmarkt in the heart of the Old Town. From the station, Bahnhofstrasse takes you to the tree-lined main avenue Theodor-Heuss-Allee. Follow this street until you see the imposing bulk of the Roman Porta Nigra, at which point you should turn left (use the underpass). Walking past the Porta

Nigra you are on Simeonstrasse. The Tourist Office is located over to the right. Simeonstrasse leads straight down into the Hauptmarkt, which is dominated by the spire of St Gandolph's Church. To the right of the spire is the start of Fleischstrasse, to the left, Brotstrasse. Following Brotstrasse and going straight ahead, Neustrasse leads into Saarstrasse. Left off Saarstrasse is Leoplatz, just off which is Trier Süd (the southern railway station). Continuing along Saarstrasse and then Matthiasstrasse you reach the Basilica of St Matthew, with the remains of the only apostle buried on German soil. The Basilica is about 30 minutes' walk from the Hauptmarkt. From Matthiasstrasse, at this point, the road right takes you on to the Konrad-Adenauer-Brücke over the Mosel.

HOTELS

All the hotels and pensions listed at DM60 or less are out in the suburbs of the city.

Cheapest doubles around DM45 (£15.75; $28)

Weinhaus E. Thiel, Ruwererstrasse 10 (tel. 52233).
Pension Anna Rudolf, Peter-Klöckner-Strasse 28 (tel. 69449).
  In Trier-Quint.

Cheapest doubles around DM50 (£17.50; $31)

Maximin, Ruwererstrasse 12 (tel. 52577).

Cheapest doubles around DM55 (£19.25; $34)

Haus Magda, Biewererstrasse 203 (tel. 66372).

Cheapest doubles around DM60 (£21; $37)

Gästehaus Filscher Häuschen, Filscher Häuschen 1 (tel. 10600).
Pension Ursula Monzel, Fröbelstrasse 9 (tel. 86376).
Pension Fritz Metzen, Wolkerstrasse 2 (tel. 37575).

Pension Waltraud Heinz, Marianholzstrasse 26 (tel. 57231). In Trier-Ruwer.

Cheapest doubles around DM65 (£22.75; $40)

Saarbrücker Hof, Saarstrasse 45 (tel. 75161). An easy walk from Trier Süd.

Zur Glocke, Glockenstrasse 12 (tel. 73109). Great location. Off Simeonstrasse.

Zur Römerbrücke, Karl-Marx-Strasse (tel. 73467). Follow Fleischstrasse into Brückenstrasse, past Marx's birthplace, and on into Karl-Marx-Strasse.

Cheapest doubles around DM75 (£26.25; $46.50)

Klosterklause, Balthasar-Neumann-Strasse 1 (tel. 25613). From Theodor-Heuss-Allee, turn right down Gobenstrasse, then right again at Thebäerstrasse. Follow the street towards the St Paulin church until you see Balthasar-Neumann-Strasse on the left.

In der Olk, In der Olk 33 (tel. 41227). Near the junction of the Hauptmarkt and Fleischstrasse, turn down Dietrichstrasse, head left along Zuckerbergstrasse (opposite Walramsneustrasse), right at Salvianstrasse, then left at In der Olk.

Haus Marianne, Eurenerstrasse 190a (tel. 800103). All rooms have bath/shower and WC. On the other side of the Mosel from the centre, close to the Konrad-Adenauer-Brücke. The closest train station is Trier West.

Cheapest doubles around DM80 (£28; $50)

Grund, Paulinstrasse 7 (tel. 25939). Right off Theodor-Heuss-Allee at the Porta Nigra.

Kurfürst Balduin, Theodor-Heuss-Allee 22 (tel. 25610).

Weinhaus Haag, Stockplatz 1 (tel. 72366). Well located. From Simeonstrasse a short walk down Stockstrasse takes you into Stockplatz.

Cheapest doubles around DM85 (£29.75; $53)

Monopol, Bahnhofsplatz 7 (tel. 74755/74754). Right in front of Trier Hbf.

Neutor, Neusstrasse 50 (tel. 48626). Trier Süd is the closest train station.

Aulmann, Fleischstrasse 47–48 (tel. 40033/73530). Excellent location.

IYHF HOSTEL

Jugendherberge Trier, Maarstrasse 156 (tel. 29292). Midnight curfew. Juniors DM18 (£6.25; $11), seniors DM24 (£8.50; $14.75). Pleasant setting by the Mosel, within easy walking distance of the centre. About 20 minutes' walk from Trier Hbf. Follow Theodor-Heuss-Allee to the Porta Nigra, turn right up Paulinstrasse, then left down Maarstrasse. Bus 2 dir: Trierweilerweg, or bus 8 dir: Pfalzel/Ehrang/Quint stop at Georg-Schmidt-Platz, about 500m from the hostel. Take the footpath and follow the river downstream.

HOSTEL

Jugendgästehaus Kolpinghaus, Dietrichstrasse 42 (tel. 75131). DM21–24 (£7.50–8.50; $13–15). Well located. Near the junction of the Hauptmarkt and Fleischstrasse head along Dietrichstrasse.

CAMPING

Campingpark Trier-City, Luxemburgerstrasse 81 (tel. 86921). Cheap municipal site. Across the Mosel from the city centre, close to the Konrad-Adenauer-Brücke. Trier West is the closest train station.

Weimar (tel. code 0621)

Tourist Office
WEIMAR-Information, Marktstrasse 4, 0-5300 Weimar (tel. 65384). From the train station head downhill on Carl-August-Allee, straight on until you reach Goetheplatz (a 15-minute walk), or take bus 1. From the far end of Goetheplatz, head left along Geleitstrasse, turn right at Windischenstrasse, then left.

HOTELS

Cheapest doubles around DM80 (£28; $50)

Hotel Kaiserin Augusta, Carl-August-Allee 17 (tel. 2162). Singles start at DM45 (£15.75; $28). Just over 100m downhill from the train station.

Guest House of the Hotel Belvedere, Ernst-Busse-Strasse 9 (tel. 61566).

Cheapest doubles around DM90 (£31.50; $56)

Hotel Thüringen, Brennerstrasse 2 (tel. 3675). Brennerstrasse runs downhill from the left-hand side of the square in front of the train station.

Hotel-Pension Liszt, Lisztstrasse 3 (tel. 61911). Close to the centre. From Goetheplatz (see Tourist Office above), take Heinrich-Heine-Strasse at the bottom right of the square, left on Sophienstiftsplatz, right on Philipp-Müller-Strasse, right again into Steubenstrasse, then left.

PRIVATE ROOMS

From the Tourist Office. Mar.–Oct., Mon.–Fri. 10 a.m.–7 p.m., Sat. 9 a.m.–4 p.m.; Nov.–Feb., 9 a.m.–1 p.m. only. Prices range from DM20–30 (£7–10.50; $12.50–18.50) per person without breakfast.

IYHF HOSTELS

'Germania', Carl-August-Allee 13 (tel. 2076). Bed only DM4
(£1.40; $2.50). A 100m walk downhill from the train station.
'Am Poseckschen Garten', Humboldtstrasse 17 (tel.
4021/64021). Bed only DM4 (£1.40; $2.50). Just outside the
centre. From Goetheplatz (see Tourist Office above), take
Wielandstrasse at the bottom left of the square, straight
on through Theaterplatz, right along Schützengasse, left
at Steubenstrasse, then a quick right into Humboldtstrasse.
Am Wilden Graben, Zum Wilden Graben 12 (tel. 3471). B&B,
DM18 (£6.25; $11). A 15-minute walk from the town centre.
From Schützengasse (see the hostel above), head left into
Wielandplatz, right down Amalienstrasse, then along the
sides of the cemeteries until you see Zum Wilden Graben
on the right.

CAMPING

Although there are no campsites in Weimar itself, it is easy
to get to sites in the vicinity by public transport. The closest
site is in Öttern, 6 miles from Weimar and accessible by bus.
Fifteen miles out of town is the site at Lake Hohenfelden, which
can be reached by bus or local trains (a 40-minute trip).

Würzburg (tel. code 0931)

Tourist Offices
Frendemverkehrsamt Würzburg, Am Congress Centrum, 8700
Würzburg (tel. 37371/37436). Handles the advance reservation
of rooms (written enquiries preferred). The office confirms the
reservation once it has been made.

Tourist Information, Pavillon am Hauptbahnhof. Open
Mon.–Sat. 8 a.m.–8 p.m. Room reservation on arrival. DM3
(£1.05; $2) commission. By the train and bus stations.

Tourist Information, Haus Zum Falken, Markt. Open

Mon.–Fri. 9 a.m.–6 p.m., Sat. 9 a.m.–2 p.m. Room reservation on arrival. DM3 (£1.05; $2) commission.

Basic Directions

Leaving Würzburg Hbf walk round the right-hand side of the square, past the Tourist Office and cross the busy Röntgenring to the start of the Kaiserstrasse. Walk down Kaiserstrasse and you arrive at the junction with Theaterstrasse (virtually straight ahead) and Juliuspromenade (on the right). Follow Juliuspromenade a short distance and then turn left along Schönbornstrasse, passing the Markt and the new cathedral to reach the Cathedral. By turning right down Domstrasse at this point and going straight on, you arrive at the Alte Mainbrücke spanning the River Main. The walk from the train station to the river takes about 15–20 minutes.

HOTELS

Cheapest doubles around DM60 (£21; $37)

Gästehof Schlier and Pension Schlier are both in Bergtheim, about 10 miles out of Würzburg. Local trains to Schweinfurt stop in the town. There are trains every 90 minutes through the day. The last train leaves just before 9 p.m. and does not run on Saturdays, but there are later buses.

Gasthof Schlier, Bergtheim (tel. 09367-501)
Pension Schlier, Bergtheim,(tel. 09367-448)

Cheapest doubles around DM65 (£22.75; $40)

Hotel Groene, Scheffelstrasse 2 (tel. 74449). About 1 1/3 miles from the town centre.
Hotel Fischzucht, Julius-Echter-Strasse 15 (tel. 64095). Two and a half miles from the centre.

Cheapest doubles around DM75 (£26.25; $46.50)

Gasthof Wörther Hof, Frankfurterstrasse 9 (tel. 42051).

Cheapest doubles around DM80 (£28; $50)

Pension Spehnkuch, Röntgenring 7 (tel. 54752).

Gasthof Jägerruh, Grombühlstrasse 55 (tel. 281412/21892). Two miles from the centre.

Gasthof Zur Klinge, Rathausplatz (tel. 42051). Two and a half miles from the town centre in the suburb of Heidingsfeld. Tram 3 from Würzburg Hbf.

Pension Siegel, Reisgrubengasse 7 (tel. 54156/17456). Excellent central location.

Cheapest doubles around DM85 (£29.75; $53)

Hotel Zum Winzermännle, Domstrasse 32 (tel. 54156/17456). Excellent central location.

Gasthof Hemmerlein, Balthasar-Neumann-Promenade 5 (tel. 51300). Good location on the street running past the Residenz (Palace of the Prince-Bishops). Follow Theaterstrasse to its end, then go left.

Hotel Dortmunder Hof, Innerer Graben 22 (tel. 56163). Central location. First right off Schönbornstrasse.

Cheapest doubles around DM90 (£31.50; $56)

Hotel Schönleber, Theaterstrasse 5 (tel. 12068/12069).

Hotel Russ, Wohlfahrtsgasse 1 (tel. 50016). Good central location. Left off Domstrasse near the Rathaus along Augustenstrasse then left again.

Hotel Stift Haug, Textorstrasse 16–18 (tel. 53393). From the square in front of the station take Bahnhofstrasse (left of Kaiserstrasse) into Textorstrasse.

Hotel Meesenburg, Pleichertorstrasse 8 (tel. 53304). Head right along Röntgenring until you see Pleichertorstrasse on your left at the crossroads.

APARTMENTS

Elisabeth and Victor Zander, Rübezahlweg 51 (tel. 62939). Four-bed apartment with TV, shower and kitchen facilities.

DM75 (£26.25; $46.50) daily based on two sharing. DM10 (£3.50; $6) for each extra person. The apartment is in the suburb of Heidingsfeld, easily reached by tram 3 from Würzburg Hbf.

IYHF HOSTEL

DJH-Jugendgästehaus, Burkarderstrasse 44 (tel. 42590). B&B DM23 (£8; $14). A 20–25-minute walk from Würzburg Hbf (left after crossing the Alte Mainbrücke, then straight on), or tram 3 dir: Heidingsfeld from the station.

STUDENT ACCOMMODATION

Haus International, Friedenstrasse 2 (tel. 8005140/8005615). Sept.–Oct. only. DM50 (£17.50; $31) for singles, DM80 (£28; 50) for doubles. All rooms with shower and WC. Behind the Residenz, about 15 minutes' walk from Würzburg Hbf. Down Theaterstrasse, straight along Rennweg past the palace, right at the crossroads then follow Friedrich-Ebert-Ring until you see Friedenstrasse on the left.

CAMPING

Kanu-Club, Mergentheimerstrasse 13b (tel. 72536). Tram 3 dir: Heidingsfeld from Würzburg Hbf to Judenbühlweg, then a short walk following the signs for the canoe club. Check in at the restaurant.

Kalte Quelle, Winterhäuserstrasse 160 (tel. 65598).

GREECE (Hellas)

Although accommodation prices have risen relatively sharply over the past few years, by European standards accommodation in Greece is still a bargain. At most times of the year, there is an ample supply of cheap beds and, except in the peak months of July and August, you are unlikely to encounter any trouble in finding a place to stay, even if you arrive late in the day. However, finding a cheap bed in Athens during the peak season becomes a bit of a problem (especially if you start looking after midday), while the supply of reasonably priced accommodation on most of the islands fails miserably to satisfy the huge demand.

Hotels are graded into six categories; deluxe, and then downwards from A to E. D-and E-class hotels are well within the range of the budget traveller, with singles in the 1500–3300dr (£4.50–10.00; $8.00–17.50) range, and doubles from 1700–4000dr (£5.20–12.20; $9–21) (prices are for rooms without a shower/bath). Prices in C-class hotels generally start around 3250dr (£9.80; $17.50) for singles and 5400dr (£16.40; $28.50) for doubles, though some C-class hotels offer much cheaper rooms. Beds in triples or quads invariably work out much cheaper per person than those in singles or doubles. During the peak season, hotels may levy a 10 per cent surcharge if you stay for less than three nights. Off-season, hotels cut their rates by up to 40 per cent. At this time of year, hoteliers are often prepared to negotiate about room prices, as they know you can easily take your custom elsewhere.

Pensions are cheaper than hotels. Though you may not notice much of a difference between the prices of pensions and those of cheap hotels in Athens, the difference is readily apparent elsewhere: even in such popular destinations as Rhodes where pensions are often cheaper than private rooms, but especially so in rural areas, where prices can be as low as 600dr (£1.80; $3.20) per person.

Private rooms (*dhomatia*) are normally a fair amount cheaper than hotels. These are also officially classified, from A down to C. C-class rooms start around 1300dr (£4; $7) for singles, 1900dr (£5.75; $10) for doubles and 2500dr (£7.60; $13.50) for triples. Comparable A-class rooms start around 2000dr (£6; $10.50), 2300dr (£7; $12) and 3200dr (£9.70; $17) respectively. Private rooms are most common on the islands and in the coastal resorts. In most towns with a considerable supply of rooms, they can be booked through the local Tourist Office or Tourist Police. In some places, these offices operate an annoying policy of only booking rooms when the local hotels are filled to capacity. It is possible to look for rooms on your own: they are frequently advertised in several languages in an effort to attract tourists' attention (typically Greek, German, English, French and Italian). If you spot such a sign, you can try to fix yourself up with a room on the spot. At the height of the tourist season, travellers arriving by bus or ferry in popular destinations are almost certain to encounter locals touting rooms in their homes at train and bus stations, or ferry terminals. Given the severe accommodation shortage on most of the islands, it makes sense to accept any offer where the price and the location are reasonable. Few private rooms remain open during the period from November to April. This is the direct result of an official policy intended to maintain a steady trade for the hotels. Few owners flout this system, and there is little point searching for those who do. For obvious reasons, miscreants cannot advertise their rooms openly, but they will tout them when they have vacancies. For any small group looking to stay put for a week or so, renting a house or a flat can be an excellent option, particularly on the islands. Unfortunately, you will have to make enquiries locally on arrival to see what possibilities exist.

The **youth hostel** network is not extensive, numbering around 30 hostels in total. Generally, they are a bit ramshackle, but the atmosphere is usually quite relaxed. Only rarely are IYHF membership cards asked for. Even then you can buy a

card at the hostel, or will be allowed to stay on the payment
of a small surcharge. The overnight fee ranges from 700–1200dr
(£2.10–3.60; $4.00–6.50). Between June and September,
curfews are usually 1 a.m.; at other times of the year, midnight.
However, there are some hostels which close as early as 10
p.m. With the warden's agreement, you can stay longer than
the normal three-day maximum. In Athens, there are a number
of **student houses**. These are non-official hostels which offer
cheap dormitory accommodation. As international trains
approach Athens, young people from various student houses
often board the train to hand out leaflets advertising their
establishment. The leaflets are always flattering, of course, but
some of these places are fine. Others, however, are of very
poor quality. By and large, the cheapest of these hostels are
also the least secure for your belongings. The average price
for dorms is 1300dr (£4; $7).

Student houses frequently offer sleeping accommodation on
their roof, as do some hotels and IYHF hostels. In the
countryside, and on the islands, the best bet for **renting roof
space** are the local 'tavernas'. To find out about availability you
will have to ask in person, question the hostel touts, or rely
on word of mouth. The Tourist Office are unlikely to be very
expansive regarding the availability of roof space, as the
practice was made illegal in 1987, ostensibly because the
government was concerned about hoteliers overcharging. At
present, the law is flouted on a wide scale, and renting a spot
on a roof to throw down a mat and a sleeping bag remains
a cheap and pleasant way to spend the summer nights. In
Athens, you can expect to pay about 750dr (£2.30; $4), but
elsewhere you will rarely pay as much as this – around 600dr
(£1.80; $3.20) being more normal.

There are around 90 official **campsites**, of which 13 are run
by the Greek National Tourist Organization (EOT); the rest are
privately operated. The EOT sites are usually large, regimented
establishments. The standard of the private sites varies widely.
While some are very pleasant, others, especially those on the
islands, are often little more than fenced off patches of land
(or sand). Typical prices are around 450dr (£1.40; $2.50) for a

small tent, 650dr (£2; $3.50) per occupant. While private sites may be prepared to drop their prices a little, there is no chance of this at state-run sites. If you are travelling between late June and early September, it is advisable to pack a tent as it guarantees you a cheap night's sleep. Travelling without a tent in the peak season, you are going to have to be incredibly fortunate to find a cheap bed every night of your trip.

Freelance camping and **sleeping rough** were made illegal as long ago as 1977, although many travellers are completely unaware of this. In part this is because many people still camp and sleep rough without encountering any difficulties with the authorities. Certainly, the law is not always stringently enforced. In the rural parts of the mainland there is virtually no chance of you having any problems, provided you ask permission before you pitch a tent, and do not litter the area. Even on the islands, the police are tolerant of transgressions of the law, within certain limits. You will usually be all right if you show some discretion in your choice of site. This is important because in July and August your chances of finding a room or hostel bed are slim, so at some point you are likely to have to camp or sleep rough. *Avoid the main tourist beaches as the local police patrol them regularly*. Raids are also likely if the police hear that large numbers are beginning to congregate in one spot. The police are increasingly prone to using force to clear people away.

In most of the mountainous regions of the country the Hellenic Alpine Club (HAC) maintains **refuge huts** for the use of climbers and hikers. Some of these are unmanned, so you have to visit the local HAC office in advance to pick up a set of keys. Unless you are a member of the HAC, or one of its foreign associates, you will have to pay a surcharge on the normal overnight fee.

ADDRESSES

EOT   National Tourist Organization of
                                                   Greece, 4 Conduit Street, London
                                                   W1R 0DJ (tel. 071 734 5997).

Hotels	Advance reservations. Greek Chamber of Hotels, 6 Aristidou Street, Athens (tel. 01–3236962).
Greek YHA	Greek Youth Hostel Association, 4 Dragatsaniou Street, Athens 105–59 (tel. 01–3234107/3237590).
Camping	List of sites and facilities from the EOT National Tourist Organization of Greece.
Mountain Refuges	Hellenic Alpine Club (HAC), 7 Karageorgi Street, Athens (tel. 01–3234555).

Athens (Athina) (tel. code 01)

Tourist Offices
Greek National Tourist Organization (EOT), Amerikis 2 (tel. 3223111). EOT head office. Contact this office for information on the city or the country before you set off on holiday. On arrival, you can obtain information at any of the information counters they operate in the city, but most will not give help with finding accommodation.

Karageorgi Servias 2 (tel. 3222545). The office is located in the National Bank on Sindagma Square. Open Mon.–Fri. 8 a.m.–8 p.m., Sat. 9 a.m.–2 p.m.

Ermou 1 (tel. 3252267/3252268). In the General Bank of Greece on Sindagma Square. Open Mon.–Fri. 8 a.m.–8 p.m., Sat. 8 a.m.–2 p.m.

Airport (tel. 9612722). Round-the-clock service in the East Air Terminal.

Pireaus, Zea Marina (tel. 4135716). Information and help with accommodation is available.

Hellenic Chamber of Hotels. Room-finding service. A–C-class hotels only. In the National Bank on Sindagma Square. Open Mon.–Fri. 8 a.m.–2 p.m., Sat. 9 a.m.–2 p.m.

Finding Accommodation in Athens
Unless you arrive late in the day during July or August you should find a reasonably cheap place to stay quite easily. Expect to pay 2200–3300dr (£6.70–10.00; $11.50–17.50) in singles, 3000–5000dr (£9–15; $16–27) in doubles, around 1300dr (£4; $7) in dorms, and 750dr (£2.30; $4) for roof space in a pension or student hostel.

PENSIONS/STUDENT HOSTELS

In the area stretching from the train station towards the Areos Park and Omonia Square. The road going right from the station is Theodorou Diligiani, which bends left at its junction with Mezonos (left) before running into Karaiskaki Square. Agiou

Konstandinour links Karaiskaki Square to Omonia Square. The main road leading away from the train station is Filadelfias, which subsequently becomes Ioulianou, ending near the Areos Park. A short distance along this road, Liossion crosses Filadelfias. Going right down Liossion brings you to Anexartissias Square at the heart of the Vathi district, a short walk from Omonia Square. Continuing straight along Ioulianou, the street is crossed by a number of important roads: Aharnon, Aristotelous, Tritis Septemvriou (going right the street runs into Omonia Square) and 28 Oktovriou, also known as Patission. Patission starts just off Omonia Square and runs up past the Areos Park.

Olympos (tel. 5223433). Right opposite the train station.

Diethnes, Peoniou 52 (tel. 8832878). Walk left from the station, then turn right on to Peoniou.

Aphrodite, Einardou 12 (tel. 8832878). Walk left from the station, past the end of Peonious, then turn right up Karditsas on to Liossion. Cross the street, head left, and then almost immediately right at Einardou.

Athens Connection, Ioulianou 20 (tel. 8213940). Doubles 3900dr (£11.80; $20.50), doubles with bath 4800dr (£14.50; $25.50). Dorms 1300–1500dr (£4–4.50; $7–8). Free baggage storage. Beds go swiftly.

San Remo, Nissirou 8 (tel. 5222404). Left off Theodorou Diligiani, just before Mezonos.

Santa Mavra, Mezonos 74 (tel. 5223138/5225149).

Athens Inn, Viktoros Ougo 13 (tel. 5246906). Singles 2400dr (£7.30; $13), doubles 3400dr (£10.30; $18), doubles with bath 3900 (£11.80; $20.50), triples with bath 5400dr (£16.40; $28.50). Dorms 1300–1700dr (£4.00–5.20; $7–9). Free baggage storage. Viktoros Ougo crosses Theodorou Diligiani a short distance from Karaisaki Square.

Argo, Viktoros Ougo 25 (tel. 5225939). Singles 1800dr (£5.50; $9.50), doubles 3400dr (£10.30; $18), triples 3600dr (£11; $19), quads 4800dr (£14.50; $25.50). Free luggage storage.

Rio, Odisseos 13 (tel. 5227075). Singles 3000dr (£9; $16), doubles 3600dr (£11; $19), triples 4700dr (£14.20; $23), quads 5800dr (£17.50; $31). Free baggage storage. Right off Theodorou Diligiani, virtually at Karaiskaki Square.

Annabel, Koumoundourou 28 (tel. 5245834). Doubles 3900dr (£11.80; $20.50), triples 5000dr (£15.20; $26.50), six-bed rooms 7900dr (£24; $42). Dorms 1000dr (£3; $5.50). Roof space 750dr (£2.30; $4). Free baggage storage. From Theodorou Diligiani go left along Viktoros Ougo after crossing Marni.

Appia, Menandrou 21 (tel. 5241209). Singles 1800dr (£5.50; $9.50), singles with bath 2600dr (£7.90; $14), doubles 2800dr (£8.50; $15), doubles with bath 3900 (£11.80; $20.50), triples 3400dr (£10.30; $18), triples with bath 4200dr (£12.70; $22.50). Free luggage storage. Left off Agiou Konstandinou.

Lydia, Liossion 121 (tel. 8219980).

Joy's, Feron 38 (tel. 8231012). A few blocks beyond Liossion turn left off Ioulianou up Mihail Voda, then turn right along Feron. The pension is at the junction with Aharnon.

Feron, Feron 43 (tel. 8232083). See Joy's, above.

Pergamos, Aharnon 104 (tel. 5231991).

Elli, Heiden 29 (tel. 8815876). Left up Aharnon, then right.

Angela, Stournara 38 (tel. 5233262/5233263/5234263). Off Aharnon and Marni, one block from Anexartissias Square.

Sun Light, Filis 68 (tel. 8811956). Filis crosses Ioulianou one block after Aharnon.

Athens House, Aristotelous 4 (tel. 5240539). Single 2400dr (£7.30; $13), doubles 3600dr (£11; $19), triples 4800dr (£14.50; $25.50), quad 6000dr (£18.20; $32). Aristotelous crosses Ioulianou a couple of blocks after Aharnon.

Iokastis' House, Aristotelous 65 (tel. 8226647). At the junction with Ioulianou.

Hellas, Tritis Septemvriou 5 (tel. 5224550/52285447). Singles 1900dr (£5.75; $10), doubles 3100dr (£9.40; $16.50), triples 3300dr (£10; $17.50).

Zorbas, Giifordou 10 (tel. 8232543). Turn left up Tritis Septemvriou from Ioulianou, then head right.

Patissia, Patission 221 (tel. 8627511/8657512).

Athens City, Patission 232 (tel. 8629115/8629116).

Diana, Patission 70 (tel. 8223179).

Milton,m Kotsika 4 (tel. 8216806). From Ioulianou turn left up Patission, then right along Kotsika.

Accommodation around Sindagma Square is slightly more expensive than on average, but is conveniently located near the centre and the places of interest. As you look across Sindagma with the Parliament to your rear, Ermou is the road leading out of the centre of the square. Kar. Servias (which becomes Perikleous) runs from the far right-hand corner, Mitropoleos from the far left. Filelinon runs from the left-hand side of the square.

Festos, Filelinon 18 (tel. 3232455). 2 a.m. curfew. Singles 2200dr (£6.70; $11.50), doubles 3400dr (£10.30; $18), triples 4700dr (£14.20; $25), quads 5800dr (£17.60; $31). Dorms 1100dr (£3.30; $6.50). Roof space 750dr (£2.30; $4). Free baggage storage.

George's, Nikis 46 (tel. 3226474). Doubles 3000dr (£9; $16), triples 4000dr (£12.20; $21). Small dorms 1200dr (£3.60; $6.50). Nikis crosses Ermou and Mitropoleos one block from Sindagma.

Peter's, Nikis 32 (tel. 3222697). See George's, above.

Myrto, Nikis 40 (tel. 3227237/3234560). See George's, above.

Christ, Apolonos 11 (tel. 3220177/3234581). From Mitropoleos turn left down Nikis, then turn right along Apolonos.

Aphrodite, Apolonos 21 (tel. 3234357/3226047). See Christ, above.

Amazon, Pentelis 7 & Mitropoleos (tel. 3234002/3234004). Pentelis is off Mitropoleos, three blocks from Sindagma.

John's Place, Patroou 5 (tel. 3229719). Off Mitropoleos, four blocks from Sindagma.

Theseus, Thissios 10 (tel. 3245960). Curfew 1 a.m. Doubles 2400dr (£7.30; $13), triples 3600dr (£11; $19). Small dorms 1200dr (£3.60; $6.50). Right off Perikleous.

Hermion, Ermou 66 (tel. 3212753). Singles 2700dr (£8.20; $14.50), doubles from 3800–4300dr (£11.50–13.00; $20–23), triples from 4700–5000 (£14.20–15.20; $25.00–26.50). In an alleyway off Ermou.

Ideal, Eolou (tel. 3213195/3220542). Singles 2500dr (£7.60; $13.50), doubles 3900dr (£11.80; $20.50), triples 5000dr (£15.20; $26.50), quads 6400dr (£18.20; $32). Eolou crosses Ermou about ½ mile from Sindagma, beyond the Kapnikarea church.

Pella Inn, Ermou 104 (tel. 3250598). Singles 2600dr (£7.90; $14), doubles 3400dr (£10.30; $18), triples 4800dr (£14.50; $25.50), quads 5800dr (£17.60; $31). Free baggage storage. The entrance is on Karaisaki. A 10-minute walk from Sindagma, close to the Monastariki underground station.

Kolonaki district. Close to the National Garden, at the opposite end of Sindagma Square from Ermou and Mitropoleos.

Athenian Inn, Haritos 22 (tel. 723097/7239552). From Sindagma walk past the left-hand side of the parliament. At the Benaki Museum turn left away from the National Garden up Koumbari into Filikis Eterias Square. Cross the square and head right along Patriarhi Iokm, turn left up Irodotou, then right into Haritos.

The Plaka, beneath the Acropolis, is both centrally located, and a cheap area to stay in:

Dioscouri, Pitakou 6 (tel. 3248165).

Student Inn, Kidathineon 16 (tel. 3244808). 1.30 a.m. curfew. Singles 1800dr (£5.50; $9.50), doubles 3100dr (£9.40; $16.50), triples 4300dr (£13; $23), quads 5800dr (£17.60; $31). small dorms 1200dr (£3.60; $6.50). Luggage storage. Turn right off Filelinon as you walk from Sindagma Square (see below).

Kouros, Kodrou 11 (tel. 3227431). Walking from Sindagma Square along Mitropoleos (see below), turn left down Voulis and continue straight on across Nikodimou into Kodrou.

Acropolis House, Kodrou 6–8 (tel. 3222344/3226241). Singles 5100dr (£15.40; $27) for one night, 7200dr (£21.80; $38) for two nights. Doubles 4900dr (£14.80; $26) for one night 5500dr (£16.70; $29) for two nights. Adding an extra bed to a room increases the original price by 20 per cent. Luggage storage. See Kouros, above.

Adonis, Kodrou 3 & Voulis (tel. 3249737/3249741). See Kouros.

Veikou district. On the other side of the Acropolis from the Plaka. Linked to Sindagma Square by trolleybuses 1 and 5.

Art Gallery, Erehthiou 5 (tel. 9238376/9231933). Singles 4200dr (£12.70; $22.50), doubles 5400dr (£16.40; $28.50), triples 6400dr (£19.40; $34), quads 7600dr (£23; $40). Luggage storage.

Greca, Singrou 48 (tel. 9215262). Singles 3100dr (£9.40; $16.50), singles with bath 4200dr (£12.70; $22.50), doubles 5500dr (£16.70; $29), doubles with bath 6200dr (£18.80; $33), triples 5500dr (£16.70; $29), triples with bath 7200 (£21.80; $38).

Koukaki district. A little further out than Veikou. Also accessible by trolleybuses 1 and 5 from Sindagma Square.

Marble House, An. Zini 35 (tel. 9234058). Singles 2800dr (£8.50; $15), singles with bath 3400dr (£10.30; $18), doubles 4600dr (£14; $24.50), doubles with bath 5100dr (£15.50; $27), triples 5400dr (£16.40; $28.50), triples with bath 6000dr (£18.20; $32). Free luggage storage. Get off the trolleybus at the Zini stop.

Arditos district. Near the Panathenian Stadium:

Joseph House, Markou Moussouro 13 (tel. 9231204). Singles with bath 3000dr (£9; $16), doubles 4000dr (£12.20; $21.50), triples 5000dr (£15.20; $26.50). Dorms 1300dr (£4; $7). Roof space 650dr (£2; $3.50).

Pangrati district. Out beyond Arditos:

Youth Hostel No. 5, Damareos 75 (tel. 7519530). Take trolleybus 2, 11 or 12 to Pangratiou Square, then walk down Frinis until it is crossed by Damareos.

IYHF HOSTEL

Kypselis 57 (tel. 8225860). Kipseli district. Trolleybus 2, 4 or 9 from Sindagma to Zakinthou.

YMCA HOSTEL

XAN, Omirou 28 (tel. 3624291). From Sindagma Square (standing with your back to the parliament), take Stadiou, the main road heading right. Walk past the junction with Amerikis and the GNTO head office, then take the next right.

YWCA HOSTEL

XEN, Amerikis 11 (tel. 3626180). For directions, see the YMCA hostel above.

CAMPING

190 Athinon Avenue, Peresteri (tel. 5814114). Bus 822 or 823 from Eleftherias Square. (Underground: Thission.)

Voula, 2 Alkyonidon (tel. 8952712). Bus 118, 122 or 153 from Vass. Olgas Avenue.

Dafni Camping. Eight miles out in Dafni (tel. 5811562/5811563). Bus 853 or 870.

SLEEPING OUT

Definitely not to be advised. It is illegal and the police make regular checks on the city's parks, especially those located close to the train station. The police, however, are likely to be the least of your worries given the considerable numbers of travellers who are robbed or assaulted while sleeping rough.

Corfu Town (Kerkira) (tel. code 0661)

Tourist Offices

EOT and the local Tourist Police both have offices in the palace. Follow the street along the waterfront from the new port. The EOT office distributes a list of local hotels and has information on the availability of private rooms. Another office operates in the Governor's House between Dessila and Mantzarou. For information, tel. 30298/30360.

Finding Accommodation

At most times of year you should find yourself an E-class hotel without too much trouble, either from the list given out by the EOT office or simply by looking round on your own (the streets between the Igoumentsa Dock and N. Theotki are your best bet, especially if it is singles you are after). In summer, you are more likely to have to ask the Tourist Office about a private room, but it is worth noting that many of the tourist agencies lining Arseniou (between the Old Port and the Old Fortress) and Stratigou (beside the New Port) book rooms in pensions, frequently without commission. To avoid any frustration looking for a room in peak season simply accept any reasonable offer made by the hoteliers and room owners who meet the ferries arriving from Italy or Patras. However, as the island is quite large, be sure to find out the location of the room on offer, otherwise you could end up far from the town.

HOTELS

Europa (tel. 39304). Not far from the new port ferry terminal. Doubles 3400dr (£10.30; $18).

Cyprus, 13 Agion Pateron (tel. 30032). Close to the National Bank on Voulgareos. Doubles 3800dr (£11.50; $20), triples 5000dr (£15.20; $26.50).

Elpis, 4,5H Parados N. Theotki (tel. 30289). In an alley across from 128 N. Theotki, near the Old Port. Singles 1500dr (£4.50; $8); doubles 2400dr (£7.30; $13); triples 3000dr (£9; $16).

Konstantinoupoli, 11 Zavitsanou (tel. 39826). At the end of N. Theotki. Doubles 3200dr (£9.70; $17); triples 4000dr (£12; $21).

Crete, 43 N. Theotki (tel. 38691). Doubles 3300dr (£10; $17.50).

Spilia, 2 Solomou (tel. 25648). Doubles 2750dr (£8.30; $14.50). Close to the KTEL bus station.

C-class hotels. Expect to pay from 3250dr (£9.80; $17.50) in singles, and from 5400dr (£16.40; $28.50) in doubles

Atlantis (Neo Lamani) (tel. 35560–62).
Bretannia (tel. 30724).
Hermes (tel. 39321).
Dalia (tel. 32341).
Calypso (tel. 30723).
Splendid (tel. 30034).
Ionion (tel. 39915).

IYHF HOSTEL

Kontokali Beach (tel. 91202). Three miles north of town, a 20-minute trip on bus 7 from Platia San Rocco, every 30 minutes.

CAMPING

Kontokali Beach International (tel. 91170). Same bus as the hostel.

Crete (Kriti) – Agios Nikalaos

(tel. code 0841)

Tourist Office
Akti I. Koundourou 20 (tel. 22357). By the bridge near the port. Room-finding service.

Finding Accommodation
The best places to look for rooms are the streets up the hill from the IYHF hostel, or the side streets leading off the roads heading out of town. However, in summer when it is exceptionally difficult to find rooms, you will probably save yourself a lot of effort by heading straight to the Tourist Office.

HOTELS

Pension Katerina, 33 Koraka Street (tel. 22766). Doubles 2200dr (£6.70; $11.50), triples 2750dr (£8.30; $14.50). Six blocks from the IYHF hostel.

Christodoulakis Pension, 7 Stratigou Koraka Street (tel. 22525). Doubles 3100dr (£9.40; $16.50), triples 3300dr (£10; $17.50). Kitchen facilities available. Next to the IYHF hostel.

Argiro Pension, 1 Solonos Street (tel. 28707). Doubles 2200dr (£6.70; $11.50), doubles with bath 2750dr (£8.30; $14.50), triples 3000dr (£9; $16), triples with bath 3300dr (£10; $17.50). From the Tourist Office head up 25th Martirou, turn left along Manousogianaki, then right at Solonos.

The Green House, 15 Modatsou Street (tel. 22025). Doubles 2100dr (£6.40; $11). From the Tourist Office follow Koudourou to the left, go left again at Iroon Polytechniou, then right at Modatsou.

Pension Perla, 4 Salaminos (tel. 23379). Singles 2400dr (£7.30; $13), doubles 2750dr (£8.30; $14.50), doubles with bath 3300 (£10; $17.50), triples 3000dr (£9; $16).

C-class hotels. Expect to pay from 3250dr (£9.80; $17.50) in singles, and from 5400dr (£16.40; $27) in doubles

Atlantis (tel. 28964). Situated close to the bus station.
New York, 21 Kondoyanni St (tel. 28557). Close to the bus station.
Lato, 12 Iossif Kountourioutou St (tel. 23319).
Acropole (tel. 22998).
Argyro (tel. 28707).
Istron (tel. 23763).
Pergola (tel. 28152).
Perla (tel. 23379).
Acratos (tel. 22721).
Alcestis (tel. 22454).
Alfa (tel. 23701).
Almyros Beach (tel. 22865).
Apollon (tel. 23023).

Arion (tel. 23778).
Astoria (tel. 25148).
Caravel (tel. 28937).
Castello Maris (tel. 24759).
Creta (tel. 22518).
Cronos (tel. 28761).
Crystal (tel. 24407).
Delta (tel. 28991).
Dias (tel. 28263).
Doxa (tel. 24214).
Du Lac (tel. 22711).
Elena (tel. 28189).
Kamara (tel. 23717).
Kera (tel. 28711).
Knossos (tel. 24871).
Kouros (tel. 23264).
Lito (tel. 23067).
Myrsini (tel. 28590).
Nikos (tel. 24464).
Panorama (tel. 28890).
Pangalos (tel. 22936).
Possidonas (tel. 24086).
Sgouros (tel. 28931).
Zephyros (tel. 23631).

IYHF HOSTEL

3 Odos Stratigou Koraka (tel. 22823). Walk up the concrete
steps from the bridge at the harbour.

CAMPING

Although some people camp on the beach in front of the bus
station, this is not to be recommended. It is better to head out
of town to some of the beaches along the coast. The cove at
Kalo Horio, about 8 miles out, is one of the best places to pitch
a tent.

Crete (Kriti) – Hania (Xania)

(tel. code 0821)

Tourist Office
EOT, 'Pantheo' building (4th floor), 40 Kriari (tel. 26426). Head office. Well organized, and extremely helpful. A branch office operates in the old mosque at the east end of the harbour (tel. 43300). Open Mon.–Sat. 8.30 a.m.–2 p.m. and 3–8 p.m., Sun. 9 a.m.–3 p.m.

Finding Accommodation
Finding a reasonably priced room is considerably easier in Hania than in the other main towns on the island. Even in high season, you should not have to contemplate staying in one of the local C-class hotels. There are concentrations of cheap pensions around the harbour, and slightly further afield, around the cathedral, and in the slightly dilapidated Spiantza district. Outside the peak season, you will rarely have to stray far from the harbour to find suitable accommodation.

HOTELS

Hotel Piraeus, 10 Zambeliou (tel. 54154). Singles 1350dr (£4; $7), doubles 2200dr (£6.70; $11.50), triples 3000dr (£9; $16). At the junction of Halidon and Zambeliou.

Meltemi Pension, 2 Angelou Street (tel. 40192). Singles 1700dr (£5.20; $9), doubles and triples 2200–2800dr (£6.70–8.50; $11.50–15.00). By the Naval Museum, at the western end of the harbour.

Pension Teris, 47 Zambeliou (tel. 53120). Doubles 1700dr (£5.20; $9). Off Halidon.

Hotel Viennos, 27 Skalidi Street (tel. 22470). Singles 1200dr (£3.60; $6.50), doubles 1900dr (£5.75; $10). Dormitory 700dr (£2.10; $4). Beyond 1866 Platia as you walk from the harbour.

Hotel Fidias, 6 Sarpaki Street (tel. 52494). Singles 1700dr (£5.20; $9), doubles 2000dr (£6; $10.50). 200dr (£0.60; $1), extra for singles and doubles with baths. Small dorms 900dr (£2.70; $5). Turn right off Halidon at the cathedral, along Athinagora which subsequently becomes Sarpaki.

Pension Kasteli, 39 Kanevaro Street (tel. 57057). Singles 1700dr (£5.20; $9), singles with bath 2000dr (£6; $10.50), doubles 2800dr (£8.50; $15), doubles with bath 3300dr (£10; $17.50). The owner also lets apartments with kitchen facilities in a house nearby. Kanevaro runs from the eastern end of the harbour.

Pension Efi, 15 Sorvolou Street (tel. 23986). Singles 1450dr (£4.40; $7.50), doubles 2000dr (£6; $10.50), triples 2800dr (£8.50; $15). Signposted from the market.

Hotel Manos, 17 Zambeliou (tel. 52152). Singles 1650dr (£5; $9), doubles 2200dr (£6.70; $11.50). Although the entrance is on Zambeliou, the hotel overlooks the shore from above the Dionisos Taverna.

Rooms for Rent No.47, 47 Kandanolou (tel. 53243). Singles 1450dr (£4.40; $7.50), doubles 2200dr (£6.70; $11.50). On Kastelli Hill. Follow Kanevaro from the eastern end of the harbour, then turn off to the left.

Antonis Rooms, 8 Kountoriotou Street (tel. 20019). Doubles 1700dr (£5.20; $9), triples 2200dr (£6.70; $11.50). Overlooking the western end of the harbour.

C-class hotels. Expect to pay from 3250dr (£9.80; $17.50) for singles, and from 5400dr (£16.40; $27) for doubles

Afroditi (tel. 57603).
Manos (tel. 29493).
Mary Poppins (tel. 26357).
Theofilos (tel. 53294).
Amphitriti (tel. 53294).
Astor (tel. 55557).
Candia (tel. 26660).
Canea (tel. 24673).
Dictynna (tel. 21101).
Hellinis (tel. 28070).
Irene (tel. 54203).

Kriti (tel. 21881).
Kydonia (tel. 57561).
Lato (tel. 56944).
Lucia (tel. 91821).
Omalos (tel. 57171).
Plaza (tel. 22540).
Zepos (tel. 44921).

IYHF HOSTEL

33 Drakonianou Street (tel. 53565). Open Mar.–Nov. No
curfew. Well out from the centre on the outskirts of Hania.
Bus 4, 11, 12 or 13 from the junction of Apokoronou and
Yianari.

CAMPING

Hania (tel. 51090). 330dr (£1; $1.75) for a small tent, 450dr
(£1.40; $2.50) per person. Close to the beach. One and a
half miles west of Hania, reached by taking the Kalamaki
bus from 1866 Platia.
Agia Marina (tel. 68555/68556/68596). 350dr (£1; $1.75) per
tent, 650dr (£2; $3.50) per person. In the village of Agia
Marina, 6 miles west of Hania. Close to the beach. The
Kastelli bus serves Agia Marina.

Crete (Kriti) – Heraklion (Iraklio)

(tel. code 081)

Tourist Offices
EOT, 1 Xanthoudidou Street (tel. 228203/228225). Open
Mon.–Fri. 7.30 a.m.–2.30 p.m. Plans of the town, lists of local
hotels. Just off Platia Eleftherias, across from the Archaeological
Museum. A branch office operates at the airport (tel. 225636),
open 9 a.m.–9 p.m. daily. The Tourist Police office is on
Dhikeosinis, on the way from Platia Eleftherias to the market.

Finding Accommodation

Rooms become very difficult to find in the peak season. The majority of the cheaper rooms are located in the area between Platia Venizelou and the shore, especially Handakos Street and the streets on either side. On leaving the port head right, then go right again when you reach the town walls and follow the water for about half a mile, until you see Handakos on the left after the Xenia Hotel.

HOTELS

Hotel Rea, 1 Kalimeraki Street (tel. 223638). Doubles 2750dr (£8.30; $14.50), triples 3650dr (£11; $19), quads 4400dr (£13.30; $23.50). Off Handakos, close to the Historical Museum, a couple of blocks from the shore.

Rent-a-Room Vergina, 32 Hortatson (tel. 242739). Doubles 2750dr (£8.30; $14.50), triples 3600dr (£11; $19). Dorms 750dr (£2.30; $4). Between the OTE office (telephone company) and the Morosini Fountain.

Kretan Sun, 10 1866 Street (tel. 243794). Singles 1650dr (£5; $9), doubles 2450dr (£7.40; $13), triples 2900dr (£8.80; $15.50). Above the market.

Hotel Ideon Andron, 1 Perdikari Street (tel. 283624). Singles 1650dr (£5; $9), doubles 2200dr (£6.70; $11.50), triples 2750dr (£8.30; $14.50). From Platia Venizelou walk along Dedalou Street, then turn left and follow Perdikari to its end.

Rent Rooms Mary, Handakos 67 (tel. 281135).

C-class hotels. Expect to pay from 3250dr (£9.80; $17.50) for singles, and from 5400dr (£16.40; $27) for doubles

Apollon (tel. 250025).
Asterion (tel. 227913).
Athinaikon (tel. 229312).
Atlas (tel. 288989).
Blue Sky (tel. 254612).
Castello (tel. 251234).

Daedalos (tel. 224391).
Domenico (tel. 228703).
El Greco (tel. 281071).
Evans (tel. 223928).
Gorgona (tel. 821180).
Gortis (tel. 255820).
Gloria (tel. 288223).
Grabelles (tel. 241205).
Heracleion (tel. 281881).
Irene (tel. 226561).
Knossos (tel. 283247).
Kronos (tel. 282240).
Lato (tel. 225001).
Marin (tel. 220737).
Metropole (tel. 244280).
Mirabello (tel. 285052).
Olympic (tel. 288861).
Santa Elena (tel. 251770).
Selena (tel. 226377).
Sofia (tel. 224971).

IYHF HOSTEL

5 Vironos Street (tel. 286281). Open year all round. 11.30 p.m.
curfew. Luggage storage. Vironos is off 25th Augustou.

HOSTEL

Yours Hostel, 24 Handakos (tel. 280858).

CAMPING

Camping Iraklio (tel. 250986). Four and a half miles away on
Amoudhari beach, reached by bus 6 (thrice-hourly service
until 10 p.m.).

Crete (Kriti) – Rethimno (tel. code 0831)

Tourist Office
E. Venizelos Ave. (tel. 29148/24143). Open Mon.–Fri. 9
a.m.–3.30 p.m. Local maps and bus and ferry schedules. By
the waterfront.

Finding Accommodation
Rooms in the cheaper D- and E-class hotels become very hard
to find during the summer season, so start looking for a room
as early as possible. The majority of the cheaper rooms are
located in the streets to your left as you make your way down
from the bus station to the shore.

HOTELS

Vrisinas, 10 Hereti Street (tel. 26092). Doubles 2300dr (£7;
$12). Off Arkadiou Street, a short walk from the bus
station.

Olga's Pension, 57 Souliou (tel. 29851). Singles 2000dr (£6;
$10.50), doubles 2900dr (£8.75; $15.50), triples 3300dr (£10;
$17.50), quads 4000dr (£12; $21). Roof space 600dr (£1.90;
$3.20). Souliou is off Ethnikis Antistaseos.

Hotel Paradisos, 35 Igoum Gavril Street (tel. 22419). Singles
2200dr (£6.70; $11.50), doubles 3300dr (£10; $17.50), triples
4200dr (£12.70; $22.50). From the bus station head for the
Venizelou monument, then go left along Kountouroitou,
which runs into Igoum Gavril.

Hotel Zania, 3 Pavlou Vlastou Street (tel. 28169). Doubles
3300dr (£10; $17.50), triples 4400dr (£13.30; $23.50). Off
Arkadiou.

Hotel Achillo, 151 Arkadiou (tel. 22581). Singles 2000dr (£6;
$10.50), doubles 2750dr (£8.30; $14.50), triples 3300dr (£10;
$17.50), 5-bedded room 4400dr (£13.30; $23.50).

Hotel Acropol, 2 Makariou Street (tel. 21305). Singles 2000dr
(£6; $10.50), singles with bath 2750dr (£8.30; $14.50),
doubles 2750dr (£8.30; $14.50), doubles with bath 3300dr

(£10; $17.50), triples 3300dr (£10; $17.50). Off Iroon Square, close to the shore.

Rent Rooms. To the rear of the Taverna Helona, at the junction of Eleftheriou Venizelou and Petichaki. Doubles 2700dr (£8.20; $14.50).

Barbara Dokimaki, 14 Plastira Street (tel. 22319). Doubles 3400dr (£10.30; $18), five-bed room 6300dr (£19; $33.50). All rooms have a private bath. Roof space 650dr (£2; $3.50).

Pension Anna, Katehaki (tel. 25586). Close to the fortress.

C-class hotels. Expect to pay from 3250dr (£9.80; $17.50) in singles, and from 5400dr (£16.40; $27) in doubles

Lefteris (tel. 23803).
Astali (tel. 24721).
Green (tel. 22225).
Ionia (tel. 22902).
Kyma Beach (tel. 21503).
Park (tel. 29958).

IYHF HOSTEL

45 Topazi Street (tel. 22848). No curfew.

CAMPING

There are two sites located close to each other on the beach at Myssiria Rethimno, 2 miles from town at the start of the old Iraklion road (buses from Iraklion pass the sites). Buses run frequently from Rethimno bus station to the sites.

Camping Elizabeth (tel. 28694). 450dr (£1.40; $2.50) per tent, 650dr (£2; $3.50) per person. Grassed areas for pitching tents.

Arkadia Camping (tel. 23361/28825/24693/29927). 450dr (£1.40; $2.50) per tent, 650dr (£2; $3.50) per person. Tents are pitched on gravel, not grass.

Ios – Ios Town (Hora) (tel. code 0286)

Tourist Office

The Tourist Office (tel. 91028) is by the bus stop in Ios Town. Open daily 9 a.m.–3 p.m. and 4.30–10.30 p.m. Local information and ferry schedules. Ios Town is easily reached from the ferry port in Yialos by bus, or by a 20-minute walk up the hill.

Finding Accommodation

Accommodation on Ios is noticeably cheaper than on most of the Cyclades, with the exception of the ferry port of Yialos. Elsewhere you can expect to pay around 1900dr (£5.75; $10) for singles, 2000–2450dr (£6.00–7.50; $10.50–13.00) for doubles and 3000–3300dr (£9–10; $16.00–17.50) for triples in a local pension. That said, singles are in short supply at any time of year, while rooms of any type become difficult to find during the peak season of July and August.

HOTELS

Draco Pension. Immediately to the right of the bus stop.
Francesco's (tel. 91223). Doubles from 2200–2800dr (£6.70–8.50; $11.50–15.00). Up the hill from the bank.
The Wind (tel. 91139). Doubles from 2100–2900dr (£6.40–8.80; $11.00–15.50). Below the George Irene Hotel.
Marko's Pension (tel. 91060). Doubles around 3500dr (£10.60; $18.50). Just to the left of The Wind.
Petradi's (tel. 91510). Doubles 3300dr (£10; $17.50), triples 5000dr (£15.20; $26.50). On the main road between the beach and the Old Town.

C-class hotels in the Old Town. Expect to pay from 3250dr (£9.80; $17.50) in singles, and from 5400dr (£16.40; $27) in doubles

Corali (tel. 91272).
Filippou (tel. 91290).

Flisvos (tel. 91315).
Fragakis (tel. 91231).
Homer's Inn (tel. 91365).
Armadoros (tel. 91201).

CAMPING

Camping Ios (tel. 91329). About 700dr (£2.10; $4) per person.
In Yials, close to the ferry terminal.

There are two sites in Milopotamos, about 1¼ miles away. Both
charge much the same price as Camping Ios, but are much
more pleasant:
Stars (tel. 91302, or 01–4821083) (Athens number of the
company who run the site).
Souli (tel. 91554 or 01–8940657).

SLEEPING ROUGH

Sleeping on the beach is no longer to be recommended, despite
its past popularity. Not only is there a considerable risk of theft
but police patrols are becoming increasingly regular, as is their
readiness to clear the beach forcibly. Although it is still illegal,
you should have little trouble with the authorities if you stick
to quieter beaches such as Koumbara or Manganari.

Kos – Kos Town (tel. code 0242)

Tourist Office
Municipal Tourist Information, 7 Akti Kountouritou (tel.
28724/24460). Open daily 7.30 a.m.–9.30 p.m. from 15 Apr.–31
Oct; Mon.–Fri. 7.30 a.m.–3 p.m. at other times. Information
on accommodation, local maps and transport schedules. On
the shore, at the junction of Akti Kountouritou with Vas.
Pavlou.
Tourist Police (tel. 28227). Next door to the Tourist Office.

Finding Accommodation

Looking towards town from the harbour, the majority of the cheaper establishments are located over to your right. In July and August, you will struggle to find a bed in a pension or private room if you look on your own, unless you begin your search early in the day. At this time of year, it is better to accept any reasonable offer you receive from locals touting at the ferry port.

HOTELS

Pension Alexis, 9 Irodotou (tel. 28798). Doubles 3300dr (£10; $17.50), triples 4400dr (£13.30; $23.50). The owners will often accommodate those stuck for a room in beds on the patio for 550dr (£1.70; $3). Off Megalos Alexandrou Street.

Xenon Australia, 39 Averof (tel. 23650). Doubles 3300dr (£10; $17.50), triples 3900dr (£11.80; $21). In summer, reservations four weeks in advance are virtually essential. Close to the town's northern beach.

Pension Popi, 37 Averof (tel. 23475). Doubles Doubles 3300dr (£10; $17.50), triples 3900dr (£11.80; $21). Next door to the Xenon Australia.

Hotel Dodecanissos, 2 Alex. Ipsilantou (tel. 28460/22860). Singles 2000–2700dr (£6.00–8.20; $10.50–14.50), doubles 3300dr (£10; $17.50), doubles with bath 4400 (£13.30; $23.50), triples 5300dr (£16; $28). From the Tourist Office head away from the shore, then take the first right.

Hotel Hara, Halkonos (tel. 22500). Doubles with baths 3900dr (£11.80; $21). Close to Arseniou Street, one street back from the town's eastern shore.

CAMPING

Kos Camping (tel. 23910/23275). Open Apr.–Oct. 300dr (£0.90; $1.50) per tent, 550dr (£1.70; $3) per person. In the village of Psaldi, 1½ miles from Kos.

Mykonos – Mykonos Town (Hora)

(tel. code 0289)

Tourist Office
Tourist Information (tel. 23990) is beside the Town Hall, at the other end of the waterfront from the ferry port and the Olympic Airways office. Open daily 9 a.m.–9 p.m. Free local accommodation service and information on ferry schedules. The Tourist Police office (tel. 22716/22482) (open round the clock) can also help with accommodation. Follow the signs marked 'Bus to Plati Yialos' as far as Platia Dim. Koutsi, at which point you turn left.

Finding Accommodation
In the high season (May to Oct.) cheap rooms can be very difficult to find, especially if you do not start looking until after midday. At this time of year, unless you are prepared to camp, or to sleep rough, it makes sense to accept any offer from the touts at the port that seems reasonable, bearing in mind the inflated price of accommodation on the island. In peak season, doubles in local pensions are rarely available for under 3000dr (£9; $16).

HOTELS

Hotel Phillipi, 32 Kalogera Street (tel. 22294). Open 15 June–15 Sept. only. Singles 2850–3300dr (£8.60–10.00; $15.00–17.50), doubles 4400–5400dr (£13.30–16.40; $23.50–29.00), triples 6000–7000dr (£18–21; $32–27).

Hotel Maria, 18 Kalogera Street (tel. 24213). Doubles with bath 5500–6500dr (£16.70–19.70; $29–35).

Rooms Chez Maria, 30 Kalogera Street (tel. 22480). Open Apr.–Oct. Doubles 4400dr (£13.30; $23.50), doubles with baths 5500dr (£16.70; $29), triples 7500dr (£22.70; $40).

Apollon Hotel, Mavroyenous (tel. 23271/22223). Open Apr.–Oct. Singles from 4400dr (£13.30; $23.50), doubles from 5000dr (£15.20; $26.50), doubles with baths from

7500dr (£22.70; $40), triples 7500dr (£22.70; $40). By the harbour.

13 Mitropoleos Street. This old white house offers doubles for 2400dr (£7.30; $13); triples for 3100dr (£9.50; $16.50).

Mina Hotel (tel. 23024). Doubles with bath 6400dr (£19.40; $34). Breakfast included. By the beach.

Panorama Hotel (tel. 22337). Singles 3300dr (£10; $17.50), doubles 4400dr (£13.30; $23.50). By the beach.

Angela's Rooms, Taxi Square (tel. 22967). Roof space 800dr (£2.40; $4.50).

Delfines, Mavroyenous (tel. 22292).

Karbonaki, 21 Panahrandou (tel. 23127).

Karbonis, Andronikou Matoyianni (tel. 22475).

C-class hotels. Expect to pay from 3250dr (£9.80; $17.50) in singles, and from 5400dr (£16.40; $27) in doubles. In the peak season, prices are likely to be raised by 20 per cent.

Adonis (tel. 22434).
Marianna (tel. 22072).
Pelekan (tel. 23454).
Vencia (tel. 23665).
Aeolos (tel. 23535).
Marios (tel. 22704).
Zannis (tel. 22481).
Mykonos Beach (tel. 22572).
Bellou (tel. 22589).
Matogianni (tel. 22217).
Thomas (tel. 23148).
Zorzis (tel. 22167).
Manto (tel. 22330).
Mykonos (tel. 22434).
To Horio (tel. 23148).
Korfos (tel. 22850).

CAMPING

Paradise Beach (tel. 22129/22852/22937). 250dr (£0.75; $1.30) per tent, 450dr (£1.40; $2.50) per person. A van meets all incoming ferries, offering free transport to the site.

FREELANCE CAMPING AND SLEEPING ROUGH

Despite being illegal both are widely practised on the Paradise, Super Paradise and Elia beaches. All three beaches are periodically cleared by the police.

Naxos – Naxos Town (Hora)

(tel. code 0285)

Tourist Office
The Tourist Office (tel. 24525/24358) is on the waterfront. Open daily 8 a.m.–12.30 a.m. from 15 Mar.–31 Oct; at other times, open daily 8 a.m.–9.30 p.m. Free local accommodation service, bus and ferry timetables and luggage storage.

Finding Accommodation
Finding cheap accommodation in Naxos is not as easy as it used to be. As the island has become more popular with package-tour operators, so there has been a fall in the number of cheap rooms available as prices have been forced up. However, unless you arrive during July or August, you should still be able to find a double for 2000–3000dr (£6–9; $10.50–16.00), even less if you are travelling in the winter, when rates can be cut by anything up to 50 per cent. The best area to search for accommodation is up the hill from the OTE office (the telephone company) where there is a substantial concentration of pensions and cheap hotels. In summer, incoming ferries are met by locals touting rooms: typical prices are 2000dr (6; $10.50), for singles, 3100dr (£9.50; $16.50) for doubles, and 3500dr (£10.60; $18.50) for triples. As a rule, rooms offered at the port are more expensive than many of the rooms on offer in the town, but it can save you a lot of effort and frustration to fix up a room at the port.

HOTELS

Hotel Okeanis (tel. 22436). Directly opposite the docks. Doubles around 2400dr (£7.30; $13).

Hotel Pantheon, Old Market Street (tel. 22379). Doubles 2000dr (£6; $10.50), doubles with shower 3000dr (£9; $16).

Hotel Dionyssos, Amfitritis (tel. 22331). Singles 1300dr (£4; $7); doubles 1800dr (£5.50; $9.50); triples 2200dr (£6.70; $11.50), basement dorms 600dr (£1.80; $3.20). Roof space 450dr (£1.40; $2.50). Close to the Venetian Kastro in the Old Market quarter, straight up the hill from the docks. Painted red hands mark the way to the pension, while arrows point the way to the Annixis next door.

Eleni (tel. 24042). Doubles 2200dr (£6.70; $11.50), triples 2750dr (£8.30; $14.50). Turn left before the post office, and then watch for the white house with the brown balcony on your left.

Anna Legaki's (tel. 22837). Singles 1200dr (£3.60; $6.50), doubles 2750dr (£8.30; $14.50), triples 3000 (£9; $16). Roof space 550dr (£1.70; $3). Over the road from the Eleni, above.

Hotel Annixis, 330 Amfitritis (tel. 22112). Next to the Dionyssos. See above for directions.

Hotel Proto, 13 Protopapaki (tel. 22394)

C-class hotels in the Old Town. Expect to pay from 3250dr (£9.80; $17.50) in singles, and from 5400dr (£16.40; $27) in doubles.

Aegeon (tel. 22852).
Aeolis (tel. 22321).
Hermes (tel. 22220).
Panorama (tel. 22330).
Sergis (tel. 23195).
Apollon (tel. 22468).
Grotta (tel. 22215).
Koronis (tel. 22626).
Renetta (tel. 22952).
Sfinx (tel. 23811).

CAMPING

Naxos (tel. 41291/23500). 250dr (£0.75; $1.30) per tent, 450dr
(£1.40; $2.50) per person. Located by the Agios Giorgios
beach.

Paros – Parikia   (tel. code 0284)

Tourist Office
In the old windmill by the port (tel. 22079). Open 8 a.m.–10
p.m. daily. Local maps and transport schedules, but no
accommodation service.

Finding Accommodation
Paros is not only one of the most popular of the Cyclades in
its own right, bit it is also an island many people pass through
due to its importance as a ferry hub. Consequently, finding
hotels in the peak season can be a frustrating experience (many
are block-booked by tour operators). At this time of year, locals
touting private rooms await the arrival of every ferry. Provided
the price is not extravagant you should take the first offer you
receive. Outside the peak season you should have no trouble
finding a double for 2200–2800dr (£6.70–8.50; $11.50–15.00)
in a local pension.

HOTELS

Hotel Dina (tel. 21325). Open May–Oct. Doubles 3300dr (£10;
$17.50), doubles with showers 4400dr (£13.50; $23.50).
Advanced reservation advised, preferably in writing. Just
off the main street, at the foot of Market Square, past the
National Bank.

Rooms Mimikos (tel. 21437). Singles 1900dr (£5.75; $10),
doubles 2500dr (£7.60; $13.50), triples 3200dr (£9.70; $17).
Close to the National Bank, just off Agorakitau
(signposted).

Hotel Kontes (tel. 21246). Singles 2800dr (£8.50; $15), doubles 3500dr (£10.60; $18.50), triples 4400dr (£13.30; $23.50). All rooms have private baths. Behind the Tourist Office.

Hotel Kypreou (tel. 21383/22448). Doubles with bath 3900dr (£11.80; $21), triples with bath 6000dr (£18.20; $32). Not far from the Tourist Office, by the Olympic Airways office.

Hotel Parko (tel. 22213). Doubles 3900dr (£11.80; $21); doubles with bath 6000dr (£18.20; $32), triples 7700dr (£23.50; $41). Along the street from the Olympic Airways office.

C-class hotels. Expect to pay from 3250dr (£9.80; $17.50) in singles, and from 5400dr (£16.40; $27) in doubles.

Alkyon (tel. 21506).
Argo (tel. 21367).
Asterias (tel. 21797).
Cyclades (tel. 22048).
Galinos (tel. 21480).
Georgy (tel. 21667).
Grivas (tel. 22086).
Hermes (tel. 21217).
Louisa (tel. 21480).
Nicolas (tel. 22259).
Oassis (tel. 21227).
Paros (tel. 21319).
Paros Bay (tel. 21140).
Stella (tel. 21502).
Vaïa (tel. 21575/21576).
Zannet (tel. 22063).

CAMPING

Koula (tel. 22081/22082/84400). 250dr (£0.75; $1.30) per tent, 550dr (£1.70; $3) per person. At the northern end of the town's beach, only a quarter of a mile from the centre.

Parasporas (tel. 21394/21944). 250dr (£0.75; $1.30) per tent, 550dr (£1.70; $3) per person. One and a half miles out of town, but less crowded than the site above. Buses run from the port.

Krios (tel. 21705). 250dr (£0.75; $1.30) per tent, 550dr (£1.70; $3) per person. On Krios Beach across the harbour. A small boat makes the trip to Krios Beach from the port.

Rhodes (Rodhos) – Rhodes Town

(tel. code 0241)

Tourist Offices

City of Rhodes Tourist Office, Rimini Square (tel. 35945). Open Mon.–Sat. 8 a.m.–8 p.m., Sun. 9 a.m.–noon. Accommodations service. Free town plan and bus and ferry information.

EOT, 5 Archbishop Makariou/Papagou Street (tel. 23255/23655). Open Mon.–Fri. 7.30 a.m.–3 p.m. Closed outside the main season.

Finding Accommodation

You should not have much trouble finding suitably priced accommodation in Rhodes Town. There are plenty of cheap pensions, virtually all of which are conveniently situated within the Old Town, in the area roughly bounded by Sokratous on the north, Perikléos on the east, Omrou on the south, and Ippodhamou on the west. Rhodes Town also has a good supply of private rooms, with prices averaging 650–850dr (£2.00–2.60; $3.50–4.50) per person – about the same as you might pay in some of the cheaper pensions. In the winter, many pension owners close their doors; those that remain open will often drop their rates if you haggle.

HOTELS

Steve Kefalas's Pension, 60 Omrou Street (tel. 24357). Beds in dorms 1000dr (£3; $5.50), cots on the roof, 600dr (£1.80;

$3.20). From the beginning of Sokratous go left on to Ag. Fanourious, then turn right into Omrou.

Billy's Pension, 32 Perikléos Street (tel. 35691). Doubles 1650dr (£5; $9), dorm beds 650dr (£2; $3.50).

Dionisos Pension, 75 Platonos Street (tel. 22035). 900dr (£2.70; $5) per person in doubles and triples, 700dr (£2.10; $4) for longer stays. Roof space 450dr (£1.40; $2.50). Down the alley between 73 and 75 Sokratous Street.

Pension Massari, 42 Irodotou Street (tel. 22469). Singles 1750dr (£5.30; $9.50), doubles 3000dr (£9; $16), triples 3600dr (£11; $19), quads 4400dr (£13.30; $23.50). All rooms with private baths. The pension is signposted on Omrou.

Minos Pension, 5 Omrou (tel. 31813). Doubles 2650dr (£8; $14).

Artemis Pissa, 12 Dimosthenes Street (tel. 34235). 700dr (£2.10; $4) per person in beds in small rooms, in the hallway or in the garden.

Hotel Faliron, Faliriki (tel. 85483).

Santorini (Thera) – Fira (tel. code 0286)

Tourist Office
The Tourist Police office (tel. 22649) is close to the main square on 25th Martiou, the road leading to Oia.

Finding Accommodation
Considering its size, Fira has a large number of pensions and cheap hotels, but in summer (particularly the peak months of July and August), these are frequently filled by midday. At this time of year you will hardly find a double in Fira for under 3300–3800dr (£10.00–11.50; $17.50–20.00). Keeping these prices in mind you might be well advised to take up the first reasonable offer you receive from the locals with rooms to let, who are on hand every time a boat docks in the harbour. If you are having no luck finding a room in Fira, there are good supplies of pensions and private rooms in many of the small

towns nearby, such as Karteradhos (only 20 minutes' walk away), Messaria, Pirgos and Emborio. A double in a pension in one of these towns should cost around 2500dr (£7.50; $13.50), the usual rate for Fira's cheaper pensions outside the main season (peak season rates are quoted below).

HOTELS/PENSIONS

Villa Litsa, 25th Martiou (tel. 22267) Doubles 3800dr (£11.50; $20), triples 4400dr (£13.30; $23.50).

Delfini (tel. 71272). Doubles 3300dr (£10; $17.50). Near the IYHF hostel.

Hotel Tataki (tel. 22389). Singles with bath 4900dr (£15; $26), doubles with bath 6400dr (£19.40; $34).

C-class hotels. Expect to pay from 3250dr (£9.80; $17.50) in singles, and from 5400dr (£16.40; $27) in doubles

Antonia (tel. 22879).
Kavalari (tel. 22455).
Roussos (tel. 22752).
Theoxenia (tel. 22455).
Kallisti Thira (tel. 22317).
Panorama (tel. 22481).
Pelikan (tel. 23113).

IYHF HOSTEL

Kontohori Youth Hostel, Agios Eleftherios (tel. 22722/22577). Dorm beds and roof space. About 400m north of the town, uphill from 25th Martiou (signposted).

HOSTEL

Kamares Hostel (tel. 23142). Dorm beds and roof space at the same prices as the IYHF hostel. Also uphill from 25th Martiou (follow the yellow signs).

CAMPING

Perissa (tel. 81343). 400dr (£1.20; $2) per tent, 600dr (£1.80; $3.20) per person. On the beach.

Sifnos – Kamares and Appollonia

(tel. code 0284)

Tourist Office
By the waterfront in Kamares (tel. 31977). Open 1–11 p.m. daily.

Finding Accommodation
In peak season, the island as a whole is short on cheap accommodation, but this is particularly true of the port Kamares, and even more so of nearby Appollonia, the island's main town. The Tourist Office books private rooms (doubles around 2500dr (£7.60; $13.50), but their supply is quickly exhausted in July and August). Similarly priced doubles are available at some of Appollonia's tavernas, but again these fill up quickly. In the peak season, it is a good idea to accept any reasonable offer of a private room you may receive at the port.

HOTELS

Pension Appollonia (tel. 31490) Singles 2300dr (£7; $12), doubles 3200dr (£9.70; $17), triples 3800dr (£11.50; $20). In Appollonia, along the road leading from the main square towards Platis Gialos (buses from Kamares stop in the square).
Katsoulakis Travel Agency. Near the quayside in Kamares. Rooms are available above the office.

C-class hotels. Expect to pay from 3250dr (£9.80; $17.50) in singles, and from 5400dr (£16.40; $27) in doubles

Hotel Anthoussa (tel. 31431). Singles 3600dr (£11; $19), doubles 5000dr (£15.20; $26.50). Over a pastry shop, opposite the bus stop located just off Appollonia's main square.

Hotel Sofia (tel. 31238). Good value for money. Singles 2800dr (£8.50; $15), doubles 3500dr (£10.60; $18.50), triples 4400dr (£13.30; $23.50). All rooms have private baths. Just off Appollonia's main square.

Hotel Sifnos (tel. 31624). In Appollonia.

Hotel Stavros (tel. 31641). A short distance from the church in Kamares.

CAMPING

In Kamares, over the road from the beach. 400dr (£1.20; $2) per person, tent included.

FREELANCE CAMPING AND SLEEPING ROUGH

The beach at Faros is one of the most popular. Faros is 4½ miles from Kamares on the opposite side of the island.

Skiathos – Skiathos Town

(tel. code 0424)

Tourist Office
Tourist Police, Papadiamandi Street (tel. 21111). Just past the Post Office. Virtually any small kiosk will sell you a plan covering the town on one side, the island on the reverse, for 200dr (£0.60; $1).

Finding Accommodation
In July and August, finding rooms in pensions or cheap hotels

becomes very difficult, with singles being particularly scarce. At this time of year, your most likely options are private rooms; either those advertised in the town or those offered by locals greeting the ferries.

PRIVATE ROOMS

Orania Thamianidou (tel. 22435). Singles 2200dr (£6.70; $11.50), doubles 2400dr (£7.30; $13). From the post office turn right off Papadiamandi down Evangelistria. Take the second left off Evangelistria, then turn right at the Taverna Ilias.

Maria Papagiorgiou (tel. 21574). Singles 1200dr (£3.60; $6.50), doubles 2200dr (£6.70; $11.50). From Platiou 25 Martiou go left at the Taverna Alexandros sign, and watch for the house with the bright green gates (just off Grigoriou).

Hadula Tsourou, 17 Mitrop. Ananiou (tel. 22364). Doubles 2200dr (£6.70; $11.50), triples 2800dr (£8.50; $15). Right from Papadiamandi opposite the Dionyssos restaurant.

HOTELS

Hotel Kastro (tel. 22623). Singles 1700dr (£5.20; $9), doubles 3300dr (£10; $17.50). In an alley off Evangelistria, close to the Taverna Stavros.

Australia House (tel. 22488). Doubles 3100dr (£9.40; $16.50), triples 3900dr (£11.80; $21). Off Evangelistria (signposted).

CAMPING

Kolios (tel. 49249). 350dr (£1; $1.75) per tent, 550dr (£1.70; $3) per person. The Koukounaries bus passes the site.

Aselinos (tel. 49312). 350dr (£1; $1.75) per tent, 550dr (£1.70; $3) per person. The better of the two sites, close to a pleasant beach but further from town and a 20-minute walk from the closest bus stop. Ask the driver of the Koukounaries bus for the stop.

Thessolonika (Thessoloniki)

(tel. code 031)

Tourist Office
EOT, Aristotelous Square 8 (tel. 222935/271888). Hotel lists, town plans and transport schedules. Very helpful office. Bus 3 from the train station.
Tourist Police (tel. 517000). At the New Railway Station.

Finding Accommodation
With the exception of the festival season (Sept. to Oct.) finding a bed in an E- or D-class hotel, or in one of the city's hostels should be relatively simple.

HOTELS

D- and E-class hotels. Expect to pay from 1400dr (£4.25; $7.50) in singles, and from 2000dr (£6; $10.50) in doubles

Argo, Egnatia 11 (tel. 519770). Doubles 2100dr (£6.40; $11).
Atlantis, Egnatia 14 (tel. 540131). Singles 2000dr (£6; $10.50), doubles 2200dr (£6.70; $11.50).
Augoustos, Elénis Svorono 4 (tel. 522550). Singles 1750dr (£5.30; $9.50), doubles 2650dr (£8; $14).
Ilios, Egnatia 27 (tel. 512620).
Atlas, Egnatia 40 (tel. 537046).
Alexandria, Egnatia 18 (tel. 536185).
Lido, Egnatia 60 (tel. 223805).
Tourist, Mitropleos 21 (tel. 270501).
Nea Orestias, Selefkidon 20 (tel. 519411). Singles 1600dr (£4.80; $8.50), doubles 2450dr (£7.50; $13).
Kastoria, Egnatia 24 (tel. 536280). Singles 2400dr (£7.25; $13), doubles 3000dr (£9; $16).

C-class hotels. Expect to pay from 3250dr (£9.80; $17.50) in singles, and from 5400dr (£16.40; $27) in doubles

ABC, Angelaki 41 (tel. 265421).

Continental, Komninon 5 (tel. 277553).
Grande Bretagne, Egnatia 46 (tel. 530735).
Delta, Egnatia 13 (tel. 516321).
Mandrino, Antigonidon 2 & Egnatia (tel. 526321).
Thessalonikon, Egnatia 60 (tel. 223805).
Vergina, Monastiriou 19 (tel. 527400).
Rex, Monastiriou 39 (tel. 517051).
Park, Ionos Dragoumi 81 (tel. 524121).
Pella, Ionos Dragoumi 61 (tel. 524221/4) (five lines).

IYHF HOSTEL

Alex. Svolou 44 (tel. 225946). 11 p.m. curfew. Tram 8, 10,
11 or 31 from Egnatia to the Arch of Galerius. Walk towards
the water for a few blocks, then turn left along Alex. Svolou
(also known as Pringipos Nikolaou).

YWCA HOSTEL

XEN, Agias Sofia 11 (tel. 276144). Women only. Dormitory
accommodation similar in price to the IYHF hostel. 1250dr
(£3.80; $6.50) per person in doubles.

YMCA HOSTEL

XAN, Hanth Square (tel. 27400). Men only. Ring ahead to
check the hostel is open.

CAMPING

There are no really convenient sites. There are sites on the
beaches of Perea and Agia Trias, but both are about 13 miles
away. The various sites charge around 800dr (£2.40; $4.50) per
tent, 600dr (£1.80; $3) per person. Bus 69 from Platia
Eleftherias, or bus 72. In summer, the sites can also be reached
by taking a boat from the White Tower.

HUNGARY (Magyarorszag)

In the wake of Hungary's democratization, a country where cheap accommodation had previously been easy to find suddenly became a nightmare for budget travellers. This was solely due to the unprecedented volume of tourists swamping the supply of accommodation, rather than due to price increases. Thankfully, the accommodation situation has improved considerably since the particularly bleak year of 1990, to the extent that outside the capital you are more or less assured a cheap bed if you arrive when the accommodation agencies are open. Even in Budapest, you will get a bed, though you may have to pay £10–12 ($17.50–21.00) if you want a room to yourself.

Neither the local offices of the national tourist agency IBUSZ, nor the regional or local tourist agencies, will attempt to pressure you into staying in expensive hotels (uniquely for the Soviet Bloc, this was the case even before 1989). On the contrary, they will generally do their best to arrange the type of accommodation you want, or at the very least direct you to organizations who will help you out. IBUSZ can be an expecially useful organization for travellers as their nationwide presence allows them to operate an advance reservation system so that you can book hotels or private rooms ahead for a fee of around £1.50 ($2.50). This service is well worth using if you are heading for Budapest in peak season, when queues at accommodation agencies can be horrendous, or if you know you will arrive at a future destination in late evening or on a Saturday afternoon or a Sunday (many accommodation agencies outside Budapest are closed at these times).

Hotels (*szálló* or *szállóda*) are rated from one up to five stars. There is a shortage of singles throughout the country in all the various grades of hotels. Unless you are looking for a private bathroom, rooms in one-star hotels are normally perfectly acceptable, assuming you can find them: in recent years the number of one-and two-star hotels has dwindled considerably. Outside of Budapest and the Lake Balaton area, where prices are normally about 30 per cent higher, the remaining one-star hotels charge on average around £10–12 ($17.50–21.00) for doubles. Three-star hotels are much more common, but with prices for doubles with a shower starting at around £35 ($61), these are unlikely to be of interest to budget travellers, unless you are travelling in the winter months when rates can be cut to around £20 ($35) for doubles with showers. The Hungarian National Tourist Office or local offices will provide details on any three-star hotels offering substantially reduced rates.

Rooms in a **pension** (*penzio* or *panzio*) or **inn** (*fogado*) are normally slightly cheaper than at a one-star hotel, with singles (more widely available than in hotels) costing around £5–7 ($9.00–12.50), doubles £8–10 ($14.00–17.50). Breakfast is included in the overnight price at all hotels, pensions and inns. This may be only an uninspiring continental breakfast, but on other occasions you may be treated to a substantial buffet of cold meats. In the countryside it is possible to stay in **farm cottages** and **B&Bs**. Details of these establishments are contained in the brochure 'Holidays in the Countryside' available from IBUSZ, although in the vast majority of cases it is the regional tourist agencies rather than IBUSZ with whom you must make reservations.

Whereas, in 1990, the increase in the number of rooms available in private homes acted as a palliative to the general accommodation shortage, now as more and more Hungarians see the possibility of earning some extra money by letting rooms in their homes, the number of **private rooms** (*fizetovendégszolglat* or *Fiz* for short) available manages to more or less satisfy demand. The vast majority of private rooms are controlled by the old state tourist organizations IBUSZ or EXPRESS (the student travel organization), or by more specialized local agencies such as Szegedtourist or Egertourist (in the towns of those names), or Balatontourist (around Lake Balaton). Some new agencies have been established, and, with such a potentially lucrative market to be tapped, further growth cannot be ruled out. However, in the more popular towns, long queues can act as a deterrent to finding out what various agencies are charging. As a rough guide, IBUSZ offers the best service in Budapest as they control the major share of the market and have a good supply of very cheap rooms. If you arrive in Budapest from another Hungarian town, it is well worth getting the local IBUSZ to reserve one of the cheaper rooms for you. Outside the capital, IBUSZ generally cannot compete with more local agencies in terms of price, or the numbers of rooms they control. However, if you are arriving late at your next destination it is probably worth paying a little extra to reserve a room through IBUSZ.

You should have little cause for complaint about the standard of rooms booked through an agency, but try to make sure the location is acceptable. It might be hoping for a bit much to get a centrally located room in one of the cities, but make a point of asking for one that is well served by public transport. There is a shortage of singles (especially in Budapest), so solo travellers might want to find someone to share with. If you do not want to share, the option of taking a cheap or moderately priced double for yourself is usually available until reasonably late in the day. Only in Budapest are you likely to have to pay out for one of the more expensive doubles, as these tend to be the only rooms remaining after 5 p.m. in peak season. Expect to pay from £4.50–7.00 ($8.00–12.50) for singles, £6–12.00 ($10.50–21.00) for doubles. A surcharge may be added to the price of the room if you stay less than four days (common in Budapest); for example, another 30 per cent for one-night stays. It is standard practice to pay the agency rather than the householder.

In peak season, it is still quite common to be approached by locals offering rooms; most likely in and around the train stations and outside IBUSZ offices. Outside Budapest these rooms are likely to be fine, but you should be wary of offers made in Budapest. The rooms on offer in the capital are generally of an inferior standard to rooms booked through an agency and are likely to be poorly located as well, although the asking price will be similar. However, solo travellers arriving late in the afternoon might want to consider such offers for the first night. If you do accept a private offer, keep an eye on your valuables or, better still, leave them at the station. In the smaller towns, it is feasible to look for rooms on your own. Watch out for houses displaying a 'szobe kiado' or 'Zimmer frei' sign, then simply approach the owner to view the rooms on offer.

EXPRESS operates a chain of 30 **youth hostels** and **youth hotels**, a number of which are listed in the IYHF handbook. They also control the letting of some of the non-EXPRESS hostels listed in the IYHF handbook, and many of the temporary hostels set up in college dormitories during the summer vacation (late June to the end of August). You can expect to pay around £3.50–4.00 ($6–7) for a bed in a dormitory, and up to £6.50 ($11.50) per person in doubles or quads in one of the EXPRESS youth hostels. Whereas previously any individual occupying a small room on their own had to pay for all the bed space, this rule no longer seems to be enforced. Couples wishing to share a double will encounter no difficulties. There are no curfews in EXPRESS accommodation, but you are expected to remain quiet after midnight. In the past, EXPRESS have published a comprehensive list of Hungarian hostels each July. Now, with more companies running hostels, it may be that EXPRESS will produce only a list of their own establishments for 1993 (ask at local EXPRESS offices). The emergence of new companies operating hostels has, not surprisingly, been greatest in Budapest, where several organizations have signed contracts allowing them to operate hostels in a number of student dormitories during the summer vacation for the next three to five years.

In 1990, the prospect of IYHF hostels being touted in Budapest's train stations around 4 p.m. in August would have seemed unthinkable, but this does now occur. Nevertheless, it is advisable to try and reserve hostels in advance, as it is not unusual for EXPRESS accommodation to be filled to capacity by school groups and youth organizations. The IYHF handbook advises the use of Advance Booking Vouchers which should effect a reservation, and to put a deposit against it. Unfortunately, this is not certain to succeed, as EXPRESS make a habit of sending vouchers back and explaining that their value was less than that of the accommodation requested, so you may have no choice but to try and book at an EXPRESS office on arrival in Hungary. Dealing with the companies who have recently begun to operate hostels in the capital is a more straightforward proposition, as they say they will accept requests for reservations made in writing.

As well as youth hostels, there are also a number of local hostels, which are known by different names according to their location. In provincial towns, enquiries should be made regarding the availability of beds in *'turistaszalle'* but, in highland areas, they are referred to as *'turistahaz'*. Local and regional accommodation agencies are generally the best source of information on these hostels. Standards vary much more than the simple A or B grading implies. While some are spartan, others can be very comfortable. As a rule, however, the overnight price of £1.75-10.00 ($3.00–17.50) tends to match the level of comfort provided.

In 1990, increasing numbers of illegal hostels opened in Budapest. The locations of these hostels were passed amongst travellers by word of mouth, or by owners approaching travellers, as they could not be advertised publicly. While some of these hostels were reasonable, the vast majority were being run by unscrupulous persons taking advantage of the desperate accommodation shortage by squeezing as many people as possible into small rooms. Thankfully, the improvement in the accommodation situation has eradicated all but a few of these hostels.

Camping is highly popular with Hungarians, and the Magyar Camping and Caravanning Club (MCCC) is very active. Both the MCCC and an organization called Tourinform produce excellent, easy-to-follow lists of the sites, complete with opening times, facilities available, and a map showing their locations. The recently revised, comprehensive guide *Camping Hungary* is generally available from IBUSZ, or from local tourist agencies. There are about 140 sites in total, the heaviest concentration of which are along the shores of Lake Balaton, though there are sites in all the places you are likely to visit. The season runs from May to October inclusive, but many sites only open for the peak months of July and August. Outside July and August, there is usually no need to make reservations, or to check about the availability of space before heading out to the site, and even at peak times this should only be necessary in Budapest and the Lake Balaton area. Sites are graded from one up to three stars. The three-star sites usually have a supermarket and leisure facilities, whereas the one-star sites seldom offer more than the basic necessities. A solo traveller can expect to pay £2.50–3.50 ($4.50–6.00) for an overnight stay at a two- or three-star site, though discounts are available to members of the International Camping and Caravanning Club (FICC). Either side of the high season, most sites reduce their prices by 25–30 per cent. At the larger sites it is possible to rent bungalows (*fahz*). To hire a typical bungalow sleeping two generally costs around £10 ($17.50), four-person bungalows around £16 ($28). You pay for the bungalow, so there is no discount for unoccupied bed space. Details of sites letting bungalows are contained in the various camping lists mentioned above. Freelance camping is illegal but is practised by many young people (Hungarians especially); most likely because offenders are rarely heavily punished. Favourite locations are the forests of the Danube Bend, and the highland regions of the country where rain shelters (*esöhz*) are common.

As is the case with most of the recently democratized countries, the quality of **tourist information** available locally is poor, even in the capital, so it is advisable to buy a good guidebook before setting off on holiday. Given the relative ease with which Hungary could be visited in the past, there was always a market for guidebooks on the country, so in contrast with other former Soviet Bloc countries there is a wide range of good quality guides to Hungary on offer.

ADDRESSES

Hungarian National
Tourist Office

Danube Travel Agency, 6 Conduit
Street, London W1R 9TG
(tel. 071 4930263).

Youth hostels and
youth hotels

Magyar Ifjsgi Hzak
-EXPRESS, Szabadsg tér 16, 1395
Budapest V (tel. 1129887/1530660).

Camping

Magyar Camping & Caravanning Club
(MCCC), Üllı útja 6, 1085 Budapest
(tel. 336536).

Tourinform, Sütő u.2, 1052
Budapest (tel. 1179800)

Lists of sites are available from the
Hungarian National Tourist Office.

Budapest (tel. code 01)

Tourist Office

Tourinform, Sütö u.2 (tel. 1179800). Open daily 8 a.m.–8 p.m. Not only a good source of general information on the city, but the multilingual staff do their best to answer more unusual enquiries. The staff can advise you on accommodation possibilities, but the office does not make bookings. About 50m from the Tanács körút exit of the Deák tér metro station.

Accommodation Agencies

IBUSZ book the more expensive hotels in Budapest which are of little interest to the budget traveller, but the agency also has the best supply of private rooms. The head office is at Tanács körút 3c (tel. 1186866), a short walk from the Tanács körút exit of the Deák tér metro station. Open Mon.–Fri. 8.30 a.m.–5 p.m., Sat. 8 a.m.–1 p.m. There are branch offices in the three main train stations, open daily 8 a.m.–8 p.m.; at Felszabadulás tér 5 (tel. 186866), open Mon.–Fri. 8 a.m.–7.45 p.m.; and at Petöfi tér 3 (tel. 1185707) open round the clock. The latter two offices are best approached from the Ferenciek tér metro station. From the station, walk down Kossucht Lajos u. to Felszabaduls tér. Continuing on you reach the Elisabeth Bridge. Petöfi tér is to the right along the riverside.

Budapest Tourist book private rooms, and two- and four-bed bungalows at the city's campsites. Roosevelt tér 5–6 (tel. 1186600). Open Mon.–Sat. 8 a.m.–8 p.m., Sun. 9 a.m.–3 p.m. About ten minutes' walk from the Deák tér metro station. From the Tenács körút exit, head left along Bajcsy-Zsilinszky út, then left down Jósef Attila u. into Roosevelt tér.

EXPRESS book beds in hostels and converted student dorms. The EXPRESS head office is at Semmelweis utca 4 (tel. 117860). From the Deák tér metro station, exit on to Tenács körút, walk along the street then turn right down Gerlóczy u., and then first left. An EXPRESS branch office operates at the Keleti train station (tel. 142772). Open daily 8 a.m.–9 p.m. As well as hostel beds, this office books private rooms.

Coopturist books private rooms. Their office is at Bajcsy-Zsilinszky út 17 (tel. 1310992). From the Deák tér metro station, exit on to Tenács körút, and then head left along Bajcsy-Zsilinszky út.

HungaroHotels at Petöfi utca 16 (tel. 1183393), Pannonia Service at Kigyó utca 4/6 (tel. 1183910), and Danubius Travel at Martinelli tér 8 (tel. 173652) all make hotel bookings.

HOTELS

The prices of hotels and pensions have risen sharply over the last few years, with the result that few remain within the budget category. The exception is if you are travelling in winter when hotels often drop their rates substantially. Enquire about current prices at IBUSZ on Petöfi tér or at HungaroHotels, Pannonia Service or Danubius Travel.

Cheapest doubles generally around £10–15 ($17.50–26.50)

Citadella, Gellérthegy (tel. 1665794). Doubles £11 ($19.50), quads £15 (26.50). Recommended. Advance reservation advised. From the Deák tér or Kalvin tér metro stations take tram 49 to Móricz Zsigmond körtér, then change to bus 27 which runs up to the Citadel.

Hala dás Motel, Udülo sor 7 102 (tel. 1891114). Doubles £7 ($12.50). By the Danube, across from Szentendre Island. From the Ujpest-Városkapu metro station take bus 104 or 104A along Váci út. Rev u. runs right off Váci út down to Udulo sor.

Hotel Kandó, Bécsi út 104–108 (tel. 1682032). Doubles £9 ($16), triples £11 ($19.50), quads £12.50 ($22). Bus 60 from the Batthyáni tér metro station runs along the street.

Strand penzió, Pusztakúti út 3 (tel. 1671999). Doubles £10 ($17.50). Next to the Arpád baths. A short walk from the Csillaghegy HÉV. Catch the HÉV at the Batthyáni tér metro station.

Trio penzió, Ördögorom u. 10 (tel. 865742). Open 15 May–15 Oct. No singles. From Marcius 15 tér near the Ferenciek tér metro station take bus 8 to its terminus in the Buda hills. The pension is a 10-minute walk from the bus stop.

Saturnus, Pillangó u. 10 (tel. 421789). Reasonably located in the east of Pest, a short walk from the Pillangó u. metro station.

Ifjúság, Zivitar u. 1–3 (tel. 353331/154260). Well located. From Moskva tér metro station bus 84 runs along Rómer Flóris u., passing the end of Zivitar u. Bus 191 from the Nyugati train station runs down Margit u. before turning into Apostol u., Zivitar u. is a short walk from the junction of these two streets.

Épitök, Nagy Lajos Király útja 15–17 (tel. 1840677). From the Örs vezér tér metro station, bus 32 and tram 62 run along Nagy Lajos Király útja.

Duna-Party penzió, Kossuth Lajos üdülöpart 43–44 (tel. 687029). From the Batthyány tér metro station, take the HÉV to Rómaifürdo. Cross the road, and continue in the direction the train was going, then turn right down Emod u. At the end of this street, turn left, then right down Kalászi u. to the river, then left.

Unikum penzió, Bod Péter u. 13 (tel. 1891114). From Marcius 15 tér near the Ferenciek tér metro station, take bus 8 across the river to Zolyomi út. Keeping the hill (Sas-Hegy) on your right, walk along Zolyomi út until you see Bod Péter on the right.

PRIVATE ROOMS

IBUSZ have the best supply of rooms, and the largest stock of well-located rooms. Prices start around £5 ($9), for singles, £8 ($14) for doubles. During the summer, you will have to get to one of their offices early to be sure of getting one of the cheaper rooms. Otherwise you may find that only the more expensive doubles are left – around £12 ($21). If the offices at the train stations have allocated their whole stock, or if you arrive before they open, or after closing time, head for the IBUSZ office on Petofi tér. On the whole, the rooms on offer at Coopturist, Budapest Tourist, and the EXPRESS office at the

Keleti train station are slightly more expensive than those controlled by IBUSZ. The touting of rooms in the train stations (particularly outside the IBUSZ offices) is still common in summer. As a rule, these will be of lower quality than the rooms you can book through an agency, and possibly poorly located as well. If you can agree on a suitable price the main thing to find out is how easy it is to get to the room.

HOSTELS

The grave shortage of beds in the city in 1990 led to the establishment of many disreputable (and illegal) 'hostels'. In effect, these amounted to nothing more than unscrupulous house owners taking advantage of the situation by packing as many people as possible into small rooms. In the past couple of years, the situation has improved dramatically. In 1992, there were twelve well-run IYHF hostels operating in the city during the peak summer period (mostly in converted student dormitories). It is now common to see young students in the train stations touting spaces in IYHF hostels at around 5 p.m. in the summer, a sight which would have seemed unthinkable only a few years ago. Another bonus is that whereas in the past the locations of the IYHF hostels changed almost annually it seems that the majority of these hostels will be using the same premises for the next few years at least. Independent hostels still come and go from year to year. Any that you see advertised have official approval. There are still a few rogue hostels about, but the choice is now sufficiently wide that you should be able to avoid them.

IYHF HOSTELS

EXPRESS advise the advance reservation of IYHF hostels they control by sending Advance Booking Vouchers to the Budapest Central Office, Semmelweis utca 4, Budapest V, or to their office at Szabadság tér 16, Budapest V. From the list below you should try to book the Hotel Lido, Diak Hotel and Csillebérci Gyermek-és Ifjúsági Központ through the Central Office, and

376 Cheap Sleep Guide

the Asmara YH through the Szabadság tér office. The word 'try' is appropriate, as, in the past, dealing with EXPRESS has often been something of a fiasco (see the introduction above). A variety of companies now control the other hostels. Write to the relevant office requesting a reservation. For the Landler, Rózsa and Vásárhelyi hostels contact the UNIVERSUM Company for Tourism Ltd., Pusztaszeri út 24, 1025 Budapest II. For the Sote Balassa Kollégium and the Donà and Felvinci hostels contact 'Panda', Bajcsy-Zsilinszky út 17, Budapest IV. For Student Hostel 'KEK' and the Schönherz and Bárczy hostels contact City Center Hostels, Irinyi József u. 42, 1117 Budapest XI.

At the hostels below dormitory accommodation is usually around £3.50 ($6). Some of the hostels offer singles at around the same price. The most you are likely to pay for a single (where available) in any of these hostels is £7 ($12).

Diàk Hotel, Dózsa György t 152 (tel. 1408585). Open all year round. Singles £3 ($5.50), doubles £4 ($7). From the Dózsa Györgyút metro station, walk one block down Dózsa György út. The hotel entrance is on Angyyalföldi út, left off Dózsa György út.

Csillebérci Gyermek-és Ifjásági Központ, Konkoly Thege Miklós u. 21 (tel. 1565772). Open all year round. High in the Buda hills. Dificult to reach by public transport.

Asmara Youth Hostel, Bajcsy-Zsilininszky út 51 (tel. 1317777). Open all year. Far from the centre, near the airport, but easy to reach. From the Határ út metro station bus 50 runs along Üllo út, passing Bajcsy-Zsilininszky út on the left.

Hotel Lidó, Nánási út. 67 (tel. 1886865/805576). Open all year round. A 10-minute walk from the Római-Fürdo HÉV stop (take the HÉV from Batthyány tér metro station). Cross the main road and continue in the direction the train was going. Turn right down Emod út, which leads into Nánási út.

Landler, Bartók Béla út 17 (tel. 1851444). Open 1 July–1 Sept.

Two-, three-, and four-bed rooms. £3.50 ($6). Free luggage storage. Well located. Tram 49 from the Deák tér or Kalvin tér metro stations runs along the street.

Vásárhelyi, Kruspér u. 2–4 (tel. 1853794). Open 1 July–1 Sept. Two- and four-bed rooms. £4.25 ($7.50) per person. Free luggage storage. Good location, close to the Landler hostel. Taking the same tram, walk down Bertalan Lajos u. from Bartók Béla út, turn right along Budafoki út, then take the first left. From the Batthyány tér metro station bus 86 runs along Budafoki út passing the end of Kruspér u.

Rózsa, Bercsenényi u. 28–30 (tel. 1666677). Open 1 July–1 Sept. Two- and three-bed rooms. £4 ($7) per person. Free luggage store. Also close to the Landler hostel. Take tram 49, get off at Móricz Zsigmond körtér and walk down Karinthy Frigyes út, which is crossed by Bercsenényi u.

Hostel Donáti, Donáti u. 46 (tel. 1690788). Open 22 June–24 Aug. Dorms £3.50 ($6). Free baggage storage. Great location. From the Batthyány tér metro station follow Batthyány u. until you see Donáti u. on your left. Keep your eyes open for the painted footprints showing the way to the hostel.

Hostel Felvinci, Felvinci u. 8 (tel. 1168932). Open 16 June–22 Aug. Dorms £3.50 ($6). Free baggage storage. Good location. From the Moskva tér metro station, walk uphill a little then turn right down Ezredes u. to cross Fillér u. and Alvinci út. Take the first street on the left after passing Marczibányi tér.

Sote Balassa Kollégium, Tömö u 39/43 (tel. 1330135). Open 5 July–23 Aug. From the Kliniták metro station on Ülloi út Szigony u. runs across Tömö u.

Hostel Schönherz, Irinyi József u. 42 (tel. 1665021). Open 1 July–31 Aug. Tram 6 from the Nyugati train station or from the Blaha Lujza tér or Ferenc körút metro station runs along the street. From the Ferenc körút station it is an easy walk down the street of that name, over the Danube by the Petöfi bridge, and straight on to the hostel.

Hostel Bárczy, Damjanich u. 41–43 (tel. 213526). Open 1 July–25 Aug. Within easy walking distance of the Keleti station (mainline trains and metro). The main street leading away from Keleti is Rákcózi út. Take Rottenbiller út to the right of Rákcózi út and keep going until you see Damjanich u. on the right.

Student Hostel 'KEK', Szüret u. 2–18 (tel. 1852369). Open 1 July–25 Aug. From the Deák tér or Kalvin tér metro stations take tram 49 to Móricz Zsigmond körtér. Here you can change to bus 27 which runs along Szüret u. but it is an easy walk down Villányi út until you see Szüret u. on the right.

OTHER HOSTEL ACCOMMODATION

The Citadella Hotel (see Hotels section for details) offers beds in a dormitory for just over £1 ($1.75).

CAMPING

Budapest Tourist book two- and four-bed bungalows at the city's campsites. A two-bed bungalow costs around £10 ($17.50), a four-bed bungalow around £14 ($24.50). Budapest Tourist is the best organization to approach with any enquiries regarding camping. Solo travellers can now expect to pay £2.00–3.50 ($3.50–6.00) to camp. By the time you add on the cost of leaving your pack at the station, camping becomes a poor option in comparison to a hostel bed.

Hárs-hegyi, Hárshegyi ut 5–7 (tel. 1151482/1761921). Open mid-May–mid-Oct. Bungalows available. Bus 22 from the Moskva tér metro station stops about 100m from the site.

Római, Szentendrei út 189 (tel. 1686260). Open all year round. Bungalows available. From Batthyány tér take the HÉV to Rómaifürdo. The site is just over the road from the HÉV station.

Zugligeti 'NICHE', Zugligeti út 101. Open mid-Mar.–mid-Oct. Bungalows available. From the Moskva tér metro station take bus 158.

Tündérhegyi 'Feeberg', Szilágyi t 8. Open year round.

Bungalows available. Close to the Istenhegy stop on the cog railway. To reach the foot of the cog railway, walk uphill from the Moskva tér metro station.

Rosengarten, Pilisi út 7. Open mid-June–mid-Sept. Bungalows available. From the Örs vezér tere metro station take bus 45 along Kerepesi ut. Pilisi út is right off Kerepesi út.

Metró-Tenis, Csömöri út 158 (tel. 1638505). Open June–Oct. In the Pest suburb of Rákosszentmihály. Bus 31 from the Örs vezér tere metro station runs along Csömöri út.

Római Mini Camping, Rozgonyi Piroska u. 19. Open May–Oct. See the Római site above for directions. Rozgonyi Piroska u. is virtually straight across from the HÉV station.

FREE CAMPSITE

In the Budapest X district, close to the Jászberényi út bridge. From the Örs vezér tere metro station, take bus 61 to the Jászberényi út bridge. Do not leave anything at the site during the day. Before making your way out, check with Tourinform or Budapest Tourist as to whether the site is operating in 1993.

Eger (tel. code 36)

Tourist Information
The accommodation agencies below hand out a small photocopied map of the town which will be quite sufficient if you have a good guide book to help you locate the sights. If you want a more detailed plan there is one with a street index which costs around £0.20 ($0.35). Copies should still be available from Egertourist. If not, ask them which bookstore is likely to have a copy.

Accommodation Agencies

Egertourist, Bajcsy-Zsilinszky u (tel. 11724). Open Mon.– Sat. 8 a.m.–6 p.m. Well-informed staff speaking excellent English and German.

IBUSZ, Bajcsy-tömb belsö (tel. 11451). Located in a passage behind the Egertourist office. Open Mon.–Fri. 8 a.m.–noon. IBUSZ book private rooms and hotels.

EXPRESS, Széchenyi István u. 28 (tel. 10727/11865). Open Mon.–Fri. 8 a.m.–4 p.m.

Cooptourist, Dobó tér 3 (tel. 11998). Open Mon.–Fri. 9 a.m.– 4.30 p.m., Sat. 9 a.m.–noon.

HOTELS

The Tourist at Mekcsey utca 2 (tel. 10014) is good value with doubles around £7 ($12.50). The hotel is just along from the castle. There are cheap pensions at Kapasi u. 35a and at Deák Ferenc utca 11. Enquire at Egertourist about rooms in these. More expensive is the Hotel Minaret, Harangöntő utca 5 (tel. 362020), across the street from the minaret. Doubles around £21 ($37).

PRIVATE ROOMS

Egertourist: singles from £4 ($7); doubles from £8 ($14).
Cooptourist: doubles from £6 ($10.50).
IBUSZ: doubles from £8 ($14).

HOSTELS

The hostel at Dobó tér 6 charges around £2 ($3.50) for a bed and is open all year round. Enquire about the availability of beds in this hostel at Egertourist or EXPRESS. EXPRESS book beds in converted student dormitories during the summer. Dormitory accommodation generally costs about £2.50–4.00 ($4.50–7.00). It is possible to approach the dormitories direct, but as these are usually far from the

town centre it is advisable to make a reservation at the
EXPRESS office.

Középiskolai Kollégium, Dobó tér 25. Excellent central
location.

Berzeviczy Kollégium, Leányka u.2.

Kun Kollégium, Leányka u.6.

Mezögazdasági Kollégium, Mátyás Király u. 132–134.

Mátyás Hotel, Mátyás Király u. 140.

Sas Hotel, Sas u. 92. Four-bedded rooms £7 ($12.50) per
person.

CAMPING

Egercamping, Rákóczi út 79 (tel. 10558). Open mid-
May–mid-Oct. Bungalows available. Book in advance at
Egertourist, or at the site. A 10-minute walk from the town
centre. Bus 5, 10, 11 or 12.

Tulipán. In the Szépasszony Valley.

Esztergom (tel. code 27)

Accommodation Agencies

IBUSZ, Lörinc u. 1 (formerly Martirok u.) (tel. 12552). Open
Mon.–Fri. 8 a.m.– 11.50 a.m. and 12.30–4 p.m., Sat. 8–11
a.m. IBUSZ book hotels and private rooms.

Komtourist, Lörinc u 6 (tel. 12082). Open Mon.–Fri. 9 a.m.–5
p.m., Sat. 9 a.m.–noon.

EXPRESS, Szechenyi tér 7 (tel. 13133/13712).

HOTELS

Fürdö, Bajcsy-Zsilinszky utca 14 (tel. 11688). Doubles from
£10 ($17.50).

Volán, József Attila tér 2 (tel. 11257/12714). Doubles from £140
($25).

PRIVATE ROOMS

Komtourist: doubles from £10 ($17.50).

IBUSZ: doubles start at £12 (£21). Although Komtourist offer cheaper rooms the IBUSZ staff speak much better English should you have any special requirements.

EXPRESS: similar rates to IBUSZ, but a much smaller supply of rooms than either IBUSZ or Komtourist.

HOSTELS

The Tourist Hostel at Dobó u. 8 (near Béke tér) (tel. 12714) is very cheap, as is the turistaszallo at Dolozi Mihály út 8 (close to the cathedral). You can enquire about beds in these hostels or in other turistaszalle at Komtourist. For information on temporary summer hostels, contact Komtourist or EXPRESS.

CAMPING

Vadvirág, Bánomi-dûlo (tel. 12234). Open 15 Apr.–15 Oct. Bungalows available. Two miles from the train station. A 10-minute bus trip. From the station or the town centre take the Visegrad bus (departs the station at 55 minutes past the hour). A few minutes' walk from the stop nearest the site.

Gran Tours, és üdültolep, Primás-sziget, Nagyduna-sétány. Open 1 May–30 Sept. Bungalows available. 1¼ miles from the train station. Ten minutes' walk from the nearest bus stop.

Pécs (tel. code 72)

Accommodation Agencies

IBUSZ, Széchenyi tér 8 (tel. 12176). Open Mon.–Thurs. 8 a.m.–5 p.m., Fri. 8 a.m.–2 p.m., Sat. 8 a.m.–noon.

Mecsek Tourist, Széchenyi tér 9 (tel. 13300).
EXPRESS, Bajcsy-Zsilinszky u. 6. Close to the bus station.
Open Mon.–Thurs. 8 a.m.–4 p.m., Fri. 8.15 a.m.–2 p.m.
MAV Travel Agency. In the train station.

HOTELS

The one-star hotel by the campsite offers singles for £10 ($17.50), doubles for £13 ($23). See Camping section, below, for directions.

PRIVATE ROOMS

Mecsek Tourist: singles from £3.50 ($6), doubles from £5.50 ($9.50).
IBUSZ: singles from £4–5 ($7–9), doubles from £5.00–6.75 ($9–12).
MAV Travel Agency: limited supply of rooms.

HOSTELS

EXPRESS operate a hostel at Universitas u. During the summer, you can also ask EXPRESS, IBUSZ or Mecsek Tourist about beds in converted student dormitories. The dormitories are located on Jakabhegyi ut. From the train station take bus 30 to the terminus, then follow the sign for the Hotel Nyar.

CAMPING

Mandulás (tel. 15981). Open mid-Apr.–mid-Oct. Around £3.50 ($6) for a solo traveller. Three-bed bungalows are available for £10 ($17.50). To reserve on the day call the campsite, to book ahead contact Mecsek Tourist. Located close to the zoo, in the woods under the television tower. Bus 34 runs infrequently to the site. Bus 35 stops at the zoo, five minutes' walk away. Bus 44 runs past the site. Get off the bus at Demokrácia út.

Siófok (tel. code 84)

Tourist Information
Siótour, Szabadság tér 6 (tel. 10800). Off Fo utca. Open
Mon.–Sat. 8a.m.–8p.m., Sun. 9a.m.–1p.m. and 2–6p.m.
  IBUSZ, Fo utca 174 (tel. 11066). Head left from the bus or
train station to reach Fo utca.

HOTELS

In the short period from the opening of the hostel until mid-
May and from late Sept. until the hotel closes, doubles in
two-and three-star hotels may be available for under £20
($35). On arrival, you can enquire at IBUSZ about vacancies
at the three-star Hungária, Balaton, Europa or Lidó, or at the
two-star Napfény, Vènus or Szantòd Touring. For advance
enquiries contact Danube Travel in London, or their
equivalent (usually IBUSZ) in your capital city.

PRIVATE ROOMS

Some rooms can be a considerable distance from the beach.
Try to coax the agencies into giving you a room near the lake.

Siótour: doubles from £8 ($14).
IBUSZ: doubles from £9 ($16).
Doubles at around £10 ($17.50) are available in a number of
the elegant houses which line Balthyány Lajos u. Excellent
value, and close to the beach. Look for the 'Zimmer frei'
or 'szobe kiado' signs and then approach the owner to
book a room.

HOSTELS

Altálános School, Fo tér. Open 1 July–20 Aug.

CAMPING

Kék Balaton (tel. 10851). Open 15 June–31 Aug. One of several sites near Aranypart (the so-called 'Golden Beach'). Close to Siófok, but sandwiched between the train lines and the road.

Aranypart Nyaralótelep (tel. 11801). Open 1 May–30 Sept. Bungalows available.

Ifjúság, Pusztatorony tér (tel. 11471). Open 15 May–25 Sept. With bungalows. Close to the lakeside, as is Gamasza campsite, open July and Aug.

Fűfza, Szolo-hegy, Fo u. 7/a. Open July and Aug. Bungalows available.

Strand, Szent László u. 183, Fürdőtelep (tel. 11804). Open 15 May–15 Sept. By the lake.

Bus 2 runs from Siófok train station 21/2 miles away. Nearest train station is 100m from the site.

Mini Camping, Szent László út 74. Open 1 May–15 Sept.

TOT, Viola u. 19–21, Fürdőtelep. Open 1 June–31 Aug. 500m from the nearest train station.

Sopron (tel. code 99)

Accommodation Agencies

IBUSZ, Várkerület 41 (tel. 12455). Open Mon.–Fri. 8 a.m.–4 p.m., Sat. 8 a.m.–noon.

Ciklámen Tourist, Ogabona tér 8 (tel. 12040). In summer, open Mon.–Sat. 8 a.m.–8 p.m., Sun. 8 a.m.–1 p.m.; in winter, Mon.–Thurs. 7.30 a.m.–4 p.m., Fri. 7.30 a.m.–7.30 p.m., Sat. 8 a.m.–8 p.m., Sun. 8 a.m.–1 p.m.

Basic Directions

From the train station on Gysev pu, take bus 1, 2 or 12 to Várkerület, or walk straight down Mátyás Király utca for ten minutes. IBUSZ is about 600m along Várkerület. Following the main road another 500m as it loops around the Old Town, you will see the Ciklámen Tourist office on the right at the junction with Lackner Kristof utca. The bus station is a short walk along Lackner Kristof utca.

HOTELS

Lokomotiv, Várkerület. 90 (tel. 11111). Doubles from £4.50–8.00 ($8–14). The hotel also lets furnished apartments.

Pannonia, Várkerület 75 (tel. 12180). Doubles from £17.50 ($31).

PENSIONS

Kállai, Ferencz J. utca 66.

PRIVATE ROOMS

IBUSZ: singles and doubles are both around £6 ($10.50). Ciklámen Tourist: Singles around £4 ($7), doubles around £7 ($12.50).

HOSTELS

The Brennbergi Gyermek és Ifjúsági Tábor on Brennbergi út (tel. 13116) is affiliated to the IYHF. For information on this and any other hostels operating in Sopron in 1993 contact Ciklámen Tourist.

CAMPING

Lövér, Koszegi út (tel. 11715). Around £3.50 ($6) for a solo traveller. Two- and four-bed bungalows available: £6.50 ($11.50) and £9 ($16) respectively. Bus 12 runs hourly from Várkerület until 9.50 p.m. The site is about 25 minutes' walk from the train station. Walk one block down Mátyás Király utca, turn right and keep going until you reach Koszegi út. Turn right and keep going straight ahead

(Kőszegi út bends away to the left at one point, but by
going straight on down Harkai út you rejoin Kőszegi út)
until you see the site on the right.

Szentendre (tel. code 26)

Accommodation Agencies

IBUSZ, Bogdányi u. 11 (tel. 2610333). Open Mon.–Fri. 10
a.m.–4 p.m.

   Dunatour, Bogdányi u. 1 (tel. 2611311). Open June–Aug.,
Mon.–Fri. 8a.m.–4p.m., Sat. 7a.m.–7p.m., Sun.
10a.m.–4p.m.

HOTELS

**Expect to pay £7 ($12.50) for singles, and £10 ($17.50) for
doubles**

   Party, Ady utca (tel. 12491).
   Danubius, Ady utca (tel. 12511).

PENSIONS

**Doubles are around £8–9 ($14–16); similar in price to a
private room**

   Coca Cola, Dunakanyar körút 50 (tel. 10410).
   Hubertus, Tyukosdűlo 10 (tel. 10616).

PRIVATE ROOMS

   IBUSZ: doubles start around £8.50 ($15).
   Dunatours: similar prices to IBUSZ. Dunatours can often find
     you a room when IBUSZ have filled the rooms they
     control.
   Dunatours, Bajcsy Zsilinszky ut 17, Budapest (tel. 1314533).

The Budapest office can book rooms in advance. Open Mon.–Fri. 8 a.m.–4 p.m., Sat. 9 a.m.–1 p.m. From the Deák tér metro station, exit on to Tanacs körut and head left along Bajcsy Zsilinszky ut.

HOSTELS

ET Hostel 'Duna-Parti Diaakhotel', Szentendre Somogyi Basco Part 12. Open mid-July to mid-Aug. About £1.50 ($2.50). Ask Dunatours about the availability of space at this hostel (or at any others).

CAMPING

Pap-sziget (tel. 10697). On Pap Island. Open 1 May–30 Sept. Bungalows available. About half a mile from the town centre. There is also a smaller site on Szentendrei Island. This site lacks many of the facilities of the three-star Pap-sziget campground, but is much less crowded. Take the ferry from the northern landing stage.

REPUBLIC OF IRELAND
(Eire)

Budget travellers should have few problems finding reasonably priced accommodation in the Irish Republic. **Bed & Breakfast** accommodation is the most widely available option throughout the country as hotels are expensive. Prices for B&B start around IR£11–12 (£10.30–11.20; $18.00–19.50) per person in doubles, but in the most popular tourist towns you can expect to pay IR£13–14 (£12.20–13.10; $21.50–23.00) per person. A supplement is charged for the single occupancy of a double room; usually around IR£2–3 (£1.80–2.80; $3.50–5.00), but occasionally as high as IR£8 (£7.50; $13). In the countryside, B&B is often available at farmhouses. Again, prices start around IR£11–12 (£10.30–11.20; $18.00–19.50). Many farmhouses offering B&B are members of the Irish Farm Holidays Association.

Hostelling is probably the best way to see the Irish Republic. There are around 50 **IYHF hostels** throughout the country, operated by the Irish YHA, An Óige. Many of these are set out in the country, ideally spaced for a day's walking or cycling, though most (but not all) of the main towns have a hostel. Impeccable levels of cleanliness are virtually guaranteed at An Óige hostels. Prices are normally IR£4–5 (£3.75–4.75; $6.50–8.00) for dormitory accommodation between October and May, rising to IR£5.00–6.50 (£4.75–6.00; $8.00–10.50) in the peak season of June to September. A few hostels are more expensive. Peak season prices for the hostels in Dublin and Galway are IR£9–10 (£8.40–9.30; $14.50–16.50), with the price of the main Dublin hostel falling to IR£7.70 (£7.20; $12.50) off season (the Galway hostel and the other Dublin hostels operate in summer only). There are no daytime lockouts, and the midnight curfew at all hostels is late by IYHF standards.

Booking other hostels ahead is easy as wardens will do this for you free of charge. Although you are expected to do any domestic duties required by the warden, An Óige hostels are more friendly and easygoing than is the norm. Indeed, the high esteem in which An Óige hostels are held by hostellers is reflected by their consistently high rating in surveys of European IYHF members.

Few countries have seen such a growth in **independent hostels** as the Irish Republic. Around 50 of these hostels have joined together to form the Independent Hostel Owners (IHO) association, while another 21 are united under the name Irish Budget Hostels. Both organizations issue lists of their establishments. Like the An Óige hostels, a number of these independent hostels (currently around 40, but likely to increase) have been officially approved by the Irish Tourist Board. Such hostels are referred to as 'holiday hostels' (all the Irish Budget Hostels are officially approved). Independent hostels frequently fill in the gaps in the An Óige network, as well as offering an alternative to An Óige hostels in some towns. Unlike An Óige hostels where IYHF membership is obligatory, these hostels have no such requirements, and they are almost always free of curfews. Most independent hostels cost around IR£6.00–7.50 (£5.60–7.00; $10.00–12.50) for dormitory accommodation, although several in Dublin charge IR£8–10 (£7.50–9.30; $13.00–16.50). A feature of some independent hostels is the availability of more expensive singles and doubles, as well as dormitory accommodation.

Unless you are planning on getting right out into the countryside, carrying a tent may not be particularly worthwhile, other than as insurance in case you cannot find suitably priced accommodation. Some of the official **sites** serving the main towns are located well outside town. With prices generally in the range of IR£2–5 (£1.85–4.65; $3.50–8.00), a solo traveller can spend almost as much as the cost of a hostel bed once the cost of getting to the site is taken into account. Where there is no convenient site, one possibility can be camping in the grounds of an independent hostel. For around IR£2.50 (£2.35; $4) you can camp outside some of the independent hostels, and make use of their facilities. In rural areas, farmers seldom object to you pitching a tent on their land if you ask their permission. It is also quite legal to **sleep rough**, though this leaves you open to a soaking at any time of year.

ADDRESSES

Irish Tourist Board	150 New Bond Street, London W1Y 0AQ (tel. 071 493 3201). The office sells a guide to all the registered B&Bs, officially approved hostels and official campsites (1992 price £4).
B&B	Town and Country Homes Association, 'Killeadan', Bundoran Road, Ballyshannon, Co. Donegal (tel. 072---51653/51377).
	The Secretary, Irish Farm Holidays Association, Desert House, Clonakilty, Co. Cork (tel. 023–33331).
Youth Hostels	An Óige, 39 Mountjoy Square, Dublin 1 (tel. 01–363111).
	Paddy and Josephine Moloney, Irish Budget Hostels, Doolin Village, Co. Clare (tel. 065–74006).
	Independent Hostel Owners (IHO), Dooey Hostel, Glencolumcille,Co. Donegal (tel. 073–30130).
Camping	Irish Caravan Council, 2 Offington Court, Sutton, Dublin 13 (tel. 01–323776).

Cork (Corcaigh) (tel. code 021)

Tourist Office

Tourist House, Grand Parade (tel. 273251). Open July–Aug., Mon.–Sat. 9 a.m.–7 p.m.; June, closes at 6 p.m.; Sept.–May, Mon.–Fri. 9.15 a.m.–5.30 p.m., Sat. 9.15 a.m.–1 p.m. Just over 10 minutes' walk from the train station. Walk left along Lower Glanmire Road, turn left at the end of the street and cross the River Lee, walk right along the riverside then left at the next bridge down St Patrick's Street into Grand Parade.

B&Bs

Expect to pay around IR£13 (£12; $21.50) p.p. in doubles, and around IR£15 (£14; $24.50) for a single

Mrs Lelia Holmes, 'Olivet', Bishopstown Road, Bishopstown (tel. 543105). City centre 1½ miles away. Bus 8.

Mrs Kay O'Donavan, 38 Westgate Road, Dunderg, Bishopstown (tel. 543078). City centre 1½ miles away. Bus 5 or 8.

Mrs Greta Murphy, 'San Antonio', 46 Maryville, Ballintemple, Blackrock (tel. 291489). City centre 1 mile away. Bus 2.

Mrs Mary O'Leary, 50 Maryville, Ballintemple, Blackrock (tel. 292219). City centre 1 mile away. Bus 2.

Mrs Nancy Kenefick, 3 Carrig-Fern, College Road, Wilton/University (tel. 543423). Bus 5.

Mrs Rita O'Herlihy, 55 Wilton Gardens, Wilton/University (tel. 541705). 1¼ miles from the centre. Bus 5 or 8.

Mrs Margaret Reddy, St Anthony's, Victoria Cross, Wilton/University (tel. 541345). City centre 1¼ miles away. Bus 8 stops outside the house.

Mrs Catherine Whelan, 'Rose Villa', 1 Donscourt, Bishopstown Road, Wilton/University (tel. 545731). City centre 1½ miles away. Bus 8.

Mrs H. O'Driscoll, Hawthorn, Dublin Pike (tel. 302899). A 20-minute walk from the centre.

Mrs E. Burke, Kent House, 47 Lower Glanmire Road (tel. 504260). A 10-minute walk from the centre. Close to the train station.

Mrs Ann Fanning, The Haven, 5 Cahergal Gardens, Ballyhooly (tel. 505329). A 10-minute walk from the town centre.

Mrs B. Higgins, 7 Ferncliff Villas, Bellevue Park, St Lukes (tel. 508963). A 10-minute walk from the centre. Rooms are cheaper than on average.

Mrs E. Murray, Oakland, 51 Lower Glanmire Road (tel. 500578). A 10-minute walk from the centre of Cork. Close to the train station.

Mrs M. Sheridan, Tara House, 52 Lower Glanmire Road (tel. 500294). A 10-minute walk from the town centre. Close to the train station.

Mrs M. Smythe, Ashford House, Donovans Road (tel. 276324). Doubles are slightly cheaper than average, but at times of special events, e.g. the Jazz Festival, and at holidays, they become more expensive than average. A 10-minute walk from the centre of Cork.

Mrs Nuala Kennedy, San Antone, 10 Park View, Victoria Road (tel. 963513). Less than quarter of a mile from the centre.

Mrs E. O'Sullivan, Coolfadda House, Douglas Road (tel. 363489). Just over half a mile from the town centre.

IYHF HOSTEL

1–2 Redclyffe, Western Road (tel. 543289). Curfew 11.55 p.m. June–Sept., IR£6.50 (£6; $11); Oct.–May, IR£5 (£4.75; $8). Prices fall slightly for the rest of the year. Bus 5 or 8.

HOLIDAY HOSTELS

Kinlay House, Bob & Joan Walk, Shandon (tel. 508966). Irish Budget Hostel. No curfew. Round-the-clock reception. B&B around IR£8 (£7.50; $13). In an alley beside St Anne's Church in Shandon. From the train station, walk left along

Lower Glanmire Road, turn left down to the river and the bridge (the bus station is across this bridge). Do not cross the river but turn right and follow the River Lee to the second bridge, then turn right again up Watercourse Road to St Anne's Church.

ISAACS, 48 MacCurtin Street (tel. 500011). Irish Budget Hostel. Twenty-four hour reception. Six-bed rooms around IR£6 (£5.50; $10). A few more expensive small rooms are available. Near the bus and train stations. From the train station head left along Lower Glanmire Road to the junction with MacCurtin Street. From the bus station cross the River Lee and head straight on to the same junction.

Sheila's Hostel, Belgrove Place, Wellington Road (tel. 505562). No curfew. Reception open 8 a.m.–10 p.m. Around IR£5 (£5.50; $10). Near the bus and train stations by the junction of York Street and Wellington Street.

HOSTELS

Cork City Hostel, 100 Lower Glanmire Road (tel. 509089). No curfew. Around IR£6 (£5.50; $10). Along the road from the train station. From the bus station cross the River Lee and go straight ahead, then right along Lower Glanmire Road.

Campus House, 3 Woodland View (tel. 343531). Around IR£6 (£5.50; $10). Close to the IYHF hostel, one mile from the centre on Western Road. Bus 5 and 8.

YMCA Interpoint, 11–12 Marlboro Street (tel. 270187). Located in the city centre. Find Patrick's St, left at Porter's Shop, YMCA 100 yards.

CAMPING

Cork City Caravan and Camping Park (tel. 961866). Three-star site. Open Easter–30 Sept., and during the Jazz Festival. Bus 14 stops at the gate. Small tent IR£1 (£0.90; $1.50), large tent IR£4 (£3.75; $6.50), IR£1 (£0.90; $1.50) per adult.

Bienvenue Caravan and Camping Site (tel. 312171). One-star

site. Open Easter–31 Oct. On the main road to Kinsale
(R600). Free pick-up from the bus station or the Tourist
Office. IR£3.50 (£3.50; $6) for all tents, IR£0.75 (£0.60; $1)
per adult.

Dublin (Baile Átha Cliath/Dublin)

(tel. code 01)

Tourist Offices
Tourist Information, 14 Upper O'Connell Street (tel. 747733).
Open July–Aug., Mon.–Sat. 8.30 a.m.–8 p.m., Sun. 10.30
a.m.–3 p.m.; June, Mon.–Sat. 8.30 a.m.–6 p.m.; otherwise,
Mon.–Fri. 9 a.m.–5 p.m. Books rooms locally for IR£1 (£0.90;
$1.50).

Tourist Information, Dublin Airport (tel. 376387). Open 8
a.m.–10.30 p.m., June–Sept.; 8 a.m.–8 p.m., in May; 8
a.m.–6.30 p.m., Sept.–Dec.; and 8 a.m.–6 p.m., Jan.–Apr.

Tourist Information, North Wall Ferryport (B&I Terminal),
Alexander Road. Open late June–early Sept. only.

Finding Accommodation
On the whole, you should have little trouble finding a bed in
a hostel or in one of the cheaper B&Bs. The one time of year
when it can become tricky to find cheap accommodation are
the days leading up to and after one of Ireland's home games
in the Five Nations rugby championship, when hordes of
visiting rugby fans descend on the city. However, it is doubtful
if you will be in Dublin at that time as the games are played
in the winter months.

Public Transport
Although most of the cheaper B&Bs are outside the city centre,
you will have no trouble getting to them as the city has an
efficient bus service while the DART commuter train can be
useful, depending on where you are staying (same price as

buses to similar destinations). Information on the city's bus network is available from the office at 59 Upper O'Connell Street (tel. 366111 during office hours, tel. 734222 thereafter). Most city buses depart from the streets off Upper O'Connell Street (see Tourist Office for directions), especially the Eden Quay, Abbey Street and Talbot Street. B&B proprietors will invariably be able to tell you which bus to get to their establishment, where to catch the bus and where to get off.

Trouble Spots

The area around the Connolly train station is one of the more depressed parts of the city. Most of the hostels are in this part of town. Although the district is in no way dangerous it is advisable not to leave rucksacks and valuables lying in the hostels. Either make use of hostel storage facilities (where available) or leave your pack at the station.

B&Bs

All prices quoted below are per person and based on two people sharing a room without a bath/shower. A supplement is added for single occupancy, usually around IR£4–5 (£3.75–4.75; $6.50–8.00). During public holidays and special events some owners increase their prices, usually by IR£1.50–2.50 (£1.40–2.30; $2.50–4.00) per person.

Around IR£11 (£10.30; $18)

Mrs E. Trehy, 110 Ringsend Park, Sandymount (tel. 689447). Single supplement IR£2.50 (£2.30; $4).

Around IR£12 (£11.20; $19.50)

Mrs M. Birmingham, 8 Dromard Terrace, Sandymount (tel. 683861). Single supplement IR£1.50 (£1.40; $2.50).
Mrs R. Casey, Villa Jude, 2 Church Avenue, Sandymount (tel. 684982). Single supplement IR£2 (£1.80; $3).
Mrs S. Doyle, 35 Seafort Avenue, Sandymount (tel. 689850). Single supplement IR£2.50 (£2.30; $4).

Mrs Ryan, 10 Distillery Road, Clontarf (tel. 374147).

Around IR£13 (£12.25; $21.50)

Mrs D. Abbot-Murphy, 14 Sandymount Castle Park, Sandymount (tel. 2698413). Off the Guildford Road.

Around IR£14 (£13; $23)

Mrs E. Byrne-Poole, Sea-Front, 278 Clontarf Road, Clontarf (tel. 336118). Bus 30.

Mrs C. Canavan, 81 Kincora Road, Clontarf (tel. 331007). Bus 30.

Mrs M. Dunwoody, Eldar, 19 Copeland Avenue, Clontarf (tel. 339091).

Mrs K. Greville, Mona, 148 Clonliffe Road, Clontarf (tel. 376723).

Mrs B. Creagh, St Aidan's, 150 Clonliffe Road, Clontarf (tel. 376750).

Mrs Margo Harahan, Jaymara, 67 Hampton Court/Vernon Avenue, Clontarf (tel. 336992).

Mrs Mary Hosford, 1 Park View, Kincroa Court, Clontarf (tel. 334851).

Mrs Moira Kavanagh, Springvale, 69 Kincora Drive, Clontarf (tel. 333413). Off Kincora Grove. Bus 28, 29A, 31, 32 or 44A.

Mrs R. McDonagh, Rionore, 17 Mount Prospect Avenue, Clontarf (tel. 332351).

Mrs J. Murnane, 56 Castle Avenue, Clontarf (tel. 336402).

Mrs A. O'Donavan, 132 Seafield Road East, Clontarf (tel. 333707).

Mrs E. O'Mahony, 222 Clonliffe Road (tel. 375295).

Mrs C. Drain, Bayview, 265 Clontarf Road, Clontarf (tel. 339870). Bus 30.

Mrs Oonagh Egan, Currow, 144 Kincora Road, Clontarf (tel. 339990). Bus 30.

Mrs Erna Doherty, 16 Beechlawn Avenue, Woodville Estate, Artane (tel. 474361). Bus 27A or 27B.

Mrs M. O'Reilly, Rathleek, 13 Brookwood Road, Artane (tel. 310555).

Mrs Rita Kenny, Seaview, 166 Bettyglen, Raheny (tel. 315335). Bus 31, 31A, 32, 32B or the DART.

Mrs M. Moran, 90 Foxfield Road, Raheny (tel. 313119).

Mrs N. Patton, Rathmullan, 110 Bettyglen, Raheny (tel. 318463).

Mrs Mai Bird, St Dunstans, 25A Oakley Road, Ranelagh (tel. 972286). Just under one mile from the centre. Bus 11, 11A, 11B or 13.

Mrs A. Boyle, St Judes, 6 Fortfield Terrace, Upper Rathmines (tel. 972517).

Mrs M. MacMahon, 64 Sandford Road, Ranelagh (tel. 970654).

Mrs E. O'Brien, 24 Ormond Road, Rathmines (tel. 977801).

Mrs Roma Gibbons, Joyville, 24 St Alphonsus Road, Drumcondra (tel. 303221). One mile from the city centre. Bus 3, 11, 11A, 16, 16A, or 41A.

Mrs M. Smyth, 21 Sandymount Road, Sandymount (tel. 683602).

IYHF HOSTELS

Dublin International Youth Hostel, 61 Mountjoy Street (tel. 301776/301396). Relatively flexible midnight curfew. June–Sept., IR£10 (£9.35; $16.50); Oct.–May, IR£7.50 (£7; $12.50). Best reserved in advance during July and Aug. Free luggage lockers. Near the city centre. Follow O'Connell Street away from the quayside up past the Tourist Office and straight on across Dorset Street into Blessington Street, from which Mountjoy Street runs off to the left. From the airport take bus 41A to Dorset Street. A free bus meets incoming ferries.

Scoil Lorcáin, Monkstown (tel. 2804252). Open July–Aug., IR£6.50 (£6; $10.50). Five and a half miles from the centre.

69/70 Harcourt Street (tel. 782632). Open 24 June–31 Aug., IR£10 (£9.35; $16.50). Just off St Stephen's Green, a 15-minute walk from the Connolly Station across the Liffey. Buses 11, 13 and 46A run to St Stephen's Green.

HOLIDAY HOSTELS

The Dublin Tourist Hostel (ISAACS), 2–5 Frenchman's Lane
(tel. 363877/749321). Phone the latter number for
information or to make a reservation. Irish Budget Hostel.
No curfew. 24-hour reception. Basic dorms IR£5.50 (£5; $9),
6-and 8-bed dorms IR£6 (£5.50; $10), singles IR£13 (£12;
$21.50), doubles IR£17 (£16; $28). Free baggage storage,
lockers available. Close to the Connolly Station, off Lower
Gardiner Street. Walking along Talbot Street from the
station turn left down Lower Gardiner Street.

Kinlay House, 2–12 Lord Edward Street (tel. 6796644). Irish
Budget Hostel. Dorms from IR£8.00 (£7.50; $13), doubles
from IR£14 (£13; $23) per person. Price includes breakfast.
Lockers available. Centrally located near Christ Church
Cathedral. From O'Connell Street walk down to the River
Liffey, cross the river and follow the quayside along to the
left. At the third bridge turn left off the Merchants' Quay
down to the cathedral.

Avalon House, 55 Aungier Street (tel. 750001). No curfew.
Dorms IR£7.50 (£7; $12.50), quads IR£12 (£11.25; $19.50)
per person, doubles IR£13.50 (£12.50; $22) per person,
singles IR£18.50 (£17.25; $30). Breakfast included. 250m
from St Stephen's Green, a 15-minute walk from the
Connolly Station across the Liffey. Buses 16, 16A and 19
stop at the door, buses 11, 13 and 46A run to St Stephen's
Green. Follow York Street from the west side of the square.

YWCA, Radcliffe Hall, St John's Road, Sandymount (tel.
2694521). Open June–Sept. 11 p.m. curfew. IR£9 (£8.40;
$15) for dorms, IR£13–14 (£12.20–13.00; $21–23) per
person in small rooms. 700m from the Sydney Parade
DART station. Bus 3 runs along the street.

HOSTELS

M.E.C., 43 North Great George Street (tel. 726301). Round
the clock reception. Dorms IR£7.50 (£7; $12.50), doubles
IR£10 (£9.35; $16.50) per person, singles IR£14 (£13; $23)

with breakfast. Reduced weekly rates available. Off Parnell Street. Follow O'Connell Street away from the quayside into Parnell Street.
Young Traveller, St Mary's Place (tel. 305000). 24-hour reception. B&B IR£9.50 (£9; $15.50). Close to the Connolly Station, off Talbot Street.
Goin' My Way/Cardijn House, 15 Talbot Street (tel. 788484/741720). Midnight curfew. Off-B IR£6 (£5.50; $10). Baggage room with a safe. No lockers. Over Tiffany's shoe shop, close to the Connolly train station.
YMCA Interpoint, Amgier St (tel. 782607/780594).

CAMPING

Shankhill Caravan & Camping Park (tel. 820011). Open all year round. IR£5 (£4.75; $8) per tent, IR£0.50 (£0.45; $0.80) per person in peak season (27 June to 28 Aug.). The price for tents falls slightly at other times of the year. The closest site to Dublin, 10 miles south of the city on the N11 to Wexford. Bus 45, 45A, 84, or the DART to Shankill.
North Beach Caravan and Camping Park, Rush (tel. 437131/437602). Open all year round. IR£3.50 (£3.25; $6) per person, tent included. Seventeen miles north of the city.

Galway City (Gaillimh/Galway City)

(tel. code 091)

Tourist Office
Tourist Information, Victoria Place, off Eyre Square (tel. 63081). Open July–Aug., daily 9 a.m.–7 p.m., Sept.–June, Mon.–Sat. 9 a.m.–6 p.m. Accommodation service. IR£1 (£0.90; $1.50) commission. One block from the bus and train stations.

Finding Accommodation
Throughout most of the year finding suitable accommodation in Galway is straightforward, but this is not the case in late

July and August. The International Busking Festival on the last weekend in July draws many visitors to the city, as does the Westend Traditional Festival on the last weekend in August. Sandwiched between these two events is the Galway Races (first week in August), which attracts even more visitors. Unless you have a tent, reservations are essential if you are arriving during this period.

B&Bs

All prices quoted below are per person based on two people sharing a room without a bath/shower. A supplement is added for single occupancy, usually around IR£2–3 (£1.85–2.75; $3.25–5.00). During public holidays and special events some owners increase their prices, usually by IR£2–3 (£1.85–2.75; $3.25–5.00) per person. All the B&Bs listed below are within the central area of the city or within 10–15 minutes' walking distance. There are plenty of similarly priced B&Bs further out.

Around IR£12 (£11.20; $19.50)

Mrs T. Collins, 31 Grattan Court, Lower Salthill (tel. 63667).

Mrs S. Davy, Ross House, 14 Whitestrand Avenue (tel. 67431).

Mrs D. Glynn, Montmartre, 41 Whitestrand Park (tel. 64927).

Mrs P. Heffernan, Merrion House, 28 Lower Salthill (tel. 25964).

Mrs A. Larkin, Rosglen, 11 Whitestrand Park, Lower Salthill (tel. 64300).

Mrs B. Lyons, Mount Perpetua, 28 Whitestrand Park, Lower Salthill (tel. 65563).

Mrs C. Ruane, 25 Grattan Court, Fr. Griffin Road (tel. 66513).

Around IR£13 (£12.25; $21.50)

Mrs Mary Corless, 22 Newcastle Road (tel. 22415).

Mrs Colette O'Donnell, Seabreeze, 13 Whitestrand Avenue (tel. 61530).

Mrs K. Stephens, Inishmore House, 109 Fr. Griffin Road, Lower Salthill (tel. 62639).

Mrs Eileen Storan, Dunree, 57 Lower Salthill (tel. 23196).

Mrs M. Tarpey, The Dormers, Whitestrand Road, Lower Salthill (tel. 65034).

Mrs A. Cox, Thirroul, 26 Upper Newcastle (tel. 21551).

Mrs C. Carey, The Greenways, 9 Glenard Crescent (tel. 22308).

Mrs S. Comer, Towerhill, 33 Glenard Crescent (tel. 22150).

Mrs K. McGloin, 13 Glenard Crescent (tel. 21437).

Mrs S. D. Moloney, Ermland, 16 Glenard Crescent (tel. 23781).

Mrs M. O'Gorman, Setanta, 2 D'Alton Place (tel. 23538). Off Dr Mannix Road.

Mrs Joan Wright, Padua, 27 Oaklands (tel. 23520).

John & Theresa Geraghty, Cill Dara, 23 Rockhill Avenue (tel. 22367). Off Dalysfort Road.

IYHF HOSTEL

St Mary's College, St Mary's Road (tel. 27411). Open 26 June–28 Aug. B&B IR£8.50 (£8; $14). In the Salthill area of the city, one mile from the train station.

HOLIDAY HOSTELS

Arch View Hostel, 11 Upper Dominick Street (tel. 66661). Irish Budget Hostel. IR£6.00–7.50 (£5.50–7.00; $10.00–12.50). Prices fall slightly Oct.–May. Right in the centre of town.

The Stella Maris Holiday Hostel, 151 Upper Salthill (tel. 21950/26974). No curfew. IR£7–8 (£6.50–7.50; $11.50–13.00). Price falls slightly Oct.–June.

Grand Holiday Hostel, 244 Upper Salthill (tel. 21150). No curfew. IR£6–7 (£5.50–6.50; $10.00–11.50). Bus 1.

Woodquay Hostel, 23–24 Woodquay (tel. 62618). IR£7–8 (£6.50–7.50; $11.50–13.00).

HOSTELS

Corrib Villa, 4 Waterside (tel. 62892). No curfew. IR£5.50 (£5; $9). Centrally located. Follow Eglinton Street past the court to Waterside.

Owens, Upper Dominick Street (tel. 66211). No phone reservations, but phoning ahead will let you know if there is space. No curfew. IR£6 (£5.50; $10). In the centre of town.

Eyre Hostel, 35 Eyre Street. No telephone. Central location.

Galway Tourist Hostel, Gentian Hill, Knocknacarra, Salthill (tel. 25176).

CAMPING

The Ballyloughane Caravan Park on the Dublin Road has space for tents. Open Apr.–Sept. Hunter's Silver Strand, 4 miles west of the city along the coast is the best of a number of sites in Salthill. Open Apr.–Sept. No one will object to you pitching a tent on the grassy area by the Spanish Arch.

Limerick City (Luimneach/ Limerick City) (tel. code 061)

Tourist Offices
Tourist Information, the Granary, St Michael Street (tel. 317522). Open June–Aug., Mon.–Sat. 9 a.m.–7.30 p.m., Sun. 10 a.m.–3 p.m.; Sept. and May, Mon.–Sat. 9 a.m.–6 p.m.; Sun. 11 a.m.–3 p.m., Oct.–Apr., Mon.–Sat. 9 a.m.–6 p.m.

B&Bs

The Ennis Road, running from the River Shannon in the direction of the airport, and the streets leading off it, are the best places to look for Bed & Breakfast accommodation in

Limerick. Buses 2, 3, 10 and 59 all run along parts of the Ennis Road.

Expect to pay around IR£13 (£12; $21.50) p.p. in doubles, IR£15 (£14; $24.50) if you want a single

Mrs Noreen Marsh, 'Shannon Grove House', Athlunkard, Killaloe Road (tel. 345756/343838). Only slightly more expensive than the prices quoted above. All rooms have private shower/bath and toilet. Just over half a mile from the city centre.

Mrs Bernadette Clancy, St Rita's, Ennis Road (tel. 55809). Five minutes' walk to the centre. Buses stop outside the house.

Clifden House, Ennis Road (tel. 51166). A 10-minute walk from the centre. Doubles slightly cheaper than average.

Mrs M. White, Derryleigh, 40 Merval Drive, Clareview (tel. 53717). Doubles slightly cheaper than average. A 10-minute walk from the town centre.

Mrs Dolores Benson, Arkview, 6 Janemount Park, Corbally (tel. 346986). All rooms cheaper than average.

Mrs B. Feeney, Dellastrada House, 136 Upper Mayorstone Park (off the Ennis Road) (tel. 52300). Cheap rooms. Singles cost less than usual price for doubles. A 10-minute walk from the town centre.

Mrs J. Kennedy, Cragville, Castleview Gardens, Clancy Strand (tel. 55216). Cheap doubles.

Mrs S. Roche, St Martin's, 4 Clanmorris Gardens (off the Ennis Road) (tel. 55013). Cheap rooms. Singles less than usual price for doubles.

Mrs M. Volke, Coolgreen, Ennis Road (tel. 54375). A 15-minute walk from the town centre.

John and Betty O'Shea, 'Lisheen', Connagh East (just off Ennis Road) (tel. 55393). Two miles from the city centre.

Mrs Mary Power, Curraghgower House, Ennis Road (tel. 54716). Singles are more expensive than average. Just over half a mile from the city centre. Buses 2, 3, 59 and 10 stop 100m away.

Mrs Carole O'Toole, Gleneagles, 12 Vereker Gardens, Ennis Road (tel. 55521). Singles are more expensive than normal. Within easy walking distance of the town centre.
John O'Toole, Ennis House, 2 Inagh Drive, Ennis Road (tel. 326257). Just over half a mile from the city centre. Bus stops 20m away. All rooms have shower/bath and toilet. Doubles are only slightly more expensive than the price quoted above; singles actually cheaper than normal.

IYHF HOSTEL

1 Pery Square (tel. 312107). June–Sept. IR£6.50 (£6; $11); Oct.–May IR£5 (£4.75; $8). Midnight curfew. Close to the bus and train stations.

ITALY (Italia)

Anyone who thinks of Italy as a place where accommodation prices are low is likely to be disappointed. Compared to Greece, Portugal and Spain, accommodation is no bargain and, in some ways, this is also true when comparisons are made with northern Europe. In the major Italian cities, hostels are around the same price as those in the Netherlands and Denmark, but rarely approach the standard of hostels in those countries. Similarly, cheap Italian hotels cost roughly the same as their German counterparts, but the latter offer much higher standards of comfort and cleanliness.

In the main places of interest, accommodation options for solo travellers can be restricted to hostelling or camping, unless they can find someone to share a room with, or can afford to pay upwards of 20,000–30,000L (£9.30–14.00; $16.50–24.50) for one of the limited supply of singles. For two or more people travelling together, hostelling or staying in cheap hotels are the best, easily available options. Rooms in private homes (*camere libere*) can be much cheaper than hotels, but are not easy to find. Ask the Tourist Office for details of their availability.

Hotels are rated from one up to five stars. Charges, which are fixed by the Provincial Tourist Board, should be clearly displayed in the room. It should also be stated whether overnight price is inclusive of breakfast, showers and IVA (VAT), as these are often charged separately. If there is no notice in the room, ask the management for written confirmation of the relevant details. At the lower end of the hotel market IVA is charged at 10 per cent. Showers normally cost 1500–3000L (£0.70–1.40; $1.25–2.50). Breakfast can add anything from 3000–10,000L (£1.40–4.60; $2.50–8.00) to the overnight price per person, but, legally, breakfast is optional for those staying only a few days. Hoteliers can insist, however, that you take half-board if you stay for a lengthy period.

In most of the main towns you should consider yourself fortunate if you find a double in the region of 35,000L (£16.30; $28.50). It is more likely that you will have to pay around 45,000–50,000L (£21–23; $37–41). For triples, you will rarely pay more than another third on top of the price of doubles. Florence, Milan, Bologna and Venice are the places most likely to cause you problems in your search for one of the cheaper rooms, due to a combination of higher than average prices and demand exceeding supply. If you are beginning to despair in Venice, consider staying in nearby Mestre, or Padua (regular trains leave right up to midnight; 10- and 30-minute trips respectively). In the off-season, hotels often reduce their prices. If they have not already done so, you can expect some success if you try to bargain them down.

The **Italian YHA** operates about 50 hostels, split into three grades. Even the top-rated hostels can vary dramatically in quality. Prices start at around 12,000L (£5.60; $10), but normally you will pay around 14,000–16,000L (£6.50–7.50; $11.50–13.00). In some of the main cities, such as Rome, Venice, Florence, Milan and Naples, prices range from 18,000–20,000L (£8.40–9.30; $14.50–16.50). At hostels charging 15,000L (£7; $12.50) and over, breakfast is included in the price. Non-members are usually admitted on the payment of a small surcharge of 2000L (£0.90; $1.60) per night. In Venice, non-members are only admitted if they buy a membership card, costing 15,000L (£7; $12.50). In summer, hostel curfews are normally 11.30 p.m. Hostels are seldom conveniently located in the centre of town and many of the smaller towns of particular interest have no hostel.

In the cities, there are also a number of independent hostels and some run by local authorities. Prices and curfews are similar to those of IYHF hostels. In most of the larger cities, women have the option of staying in one of the dormitories run by the various religious orders. These establishments, known as 'Protezione della Giovane', offer high standards of accommodation and security to female travellers. Prices are normally around 18,000L (£8.40; $14.50) in singles, 12,500L

(£5.80; $10) per person in doubles, but can reach 28,000L (£13; $23) per person in some institutions in Venice. Curfews are usually between 10.00 and 11.30 p.m. During university vacations, it is possible to stay in vacant **student accommodation**. Applications should be made to the local 'Casa dello Studente'. Ask the local Tourist Office for the location and the telephone number.

There are over 2000 registered **campsites**. Strictly speaking, you are not supposed to camp outside these sites, but the authorities are unlikely to trouble you if you are camping on privately owned land with the permission of the owner. Unless you are planning to do a considerable amount of touring outside the main cities there is not much to commend taking a tent, other than as an insurance should all else fail. Sites serving the cities are usually large, crowded, noisy and located far from the centre; by and large, they are more suited to those travelling by car than those relying on public transport. Camping is also quite expensive. Normally, charges are around 3500L (£1.60; $3) per tent, and 5500L (£2.50; $4.50) per occupant, but can rise well above this at city sites. It is not unusual to be charged 6500L (£3; $5.50) per tent and per person. Some of the sites near Venice charge a ridiculous 15,000L (£7; $12.50) per tent, 6000L (£2.80; $5) per person, and above, in peak season. Security is also a problem, so you can add the cost of storing your pack at the station (1500L (£0.70; $1.25) per day, or each time you want access to it within that period, to the cost of camping and of public transport.

Sleeping in train stations has recently been made illegal, and the police are not too well disposed to those sleeping rough elsewhere. If you are **sleeping rough**, however, the police are likely to be the least of your problems. Places which seem well suited to sleeping out also tend to be the places where naïve and foolish travellers are stripped of their cash and belongings (and, where the thieves have a sense of humour, their clothes too). The Borghese Gardens in Rome is one prime example. Naples is especially dangerous, but you should avoid sleeping rough in Italy as a whole.

Anyone who would like to spend some time in the

countryside might consider **renting a cottage or a farmhouse**. These can be rented for as little as 4000–10,000L (£1.85–4.65; $3.50–8.00) per person per night, which represents excellent value for money. Hikers and climbers should contact the Italian Alpine Club for details of the 465 refuge huts in the Italian Alps. The overnight fee is normally around 7000L (£3.25; $6), but this rises by 20 per cent in winter.

ADDRESSES

Italian State Tourist Office	1 Princes Street, London W1R 8AY (tel. 071 408 1254).
Italian YHA	Associazione Italiana Alberghi per la Gioventù, Via Cavour 44 (terzo piano), 00184 Roma (tel. 06-4746755/4871152).
Student accommodation	'Guide for Foreign Students' booklet is available through the Ministry of Education, Viale Trastevere, Roma.
Camping	Federcampeggio, Casella Postale 23, 50041 Calenzalo (Firenze) supplies lists and maps, as does the Italian State Tourist Office.If you want to buy a guide while in Italy, the 'Euro Camping' guide is easy to pick up and one of the best available, for around 10,000L (£4.75; $8.50).
Farmhouses and cottages	Agriturist, Corso V Emanuele 101, Roma (tel. 06-6512342).
Mountain Refuges	Club Alpino Italiano (Rifugi Alpini), Via Ugo Foscolo 3, Milano (tel. 02-72022555).

Assisi (tel. code 075)

Tourist Office
Azienda di Promozione Turistica, Piazza del Commune (tel. 812534). Opposite the Roman Temple of Minerva. Open 9 a.m.–1 p.m. and 3.30–6.30 p.m.

Arriving by Train
Trains stop in Assisi-Santa Maria degli Angeli, three miles from the Old Town. A regular bus service operates between the station and the Old Town.

Finding Accommodation
Despite the fact that relatively few of those who visit Assisi actually stay there (most pass through on coach trips) it can be difficult to find a cheap place to stay the night. The Tourist Office will book hotel rooms for you, either in the Old Town or in Assisi-Santa Maria degli Angeli. Unfortunately, hotel prices have been rising sharply over the past few years with the result that there are now relatively few hotels in the budget category. If you want to stay in the Old Town but cannot afford a hotel room, the Tourist Office has lists of local families and religious institutions which accept paying guests.

HOTELS

Cheapest doubles around 33,000L (£15.25; $27)

Donnini, Via Los Angeles 47, Santa Maria degli Angeli (tel. 8040260). One-star hotel. Singles start around 22,000L (£10.25; $18), singles with bath/shower around 33,000L (£15.25; $27), doubles with bath/shower around 44,000L (£20.50; $36).

Cheapest doubles around 37,000–39,000L (£17.25–18.50; $30–32)

Ancajani, Via Ancajani 16 (tel. 812472). One-star hotel.

Dal Moro, Via G. Becchetti 12, Santa Maria degli Angeli (tel. 8041666). One-star hotel.

Porziuncola, Piazza Garibaldi 10, Santa Maria degli Angeli (tel. 8041020). Two-star hotel. The hotel has the best location possible in Santa Maria degli Angeli, on the square facing the Basilica of St Mary amongst the Angels.

Anfiteatro Romano, Via Anfiteatro (tel. 813025). One-star hotel.

Italia, Vicolo della Fortezza (tel. 812625). One-star hotel.

Marconi, Piazza Dante Alighieri 3 (tel. 8040277). One-star hotel.

Cheapest doubles around 42,000L (£19.50; $34)

La Rocca, Via Porta Perlici 27 (tel. 812284). One-star hotel.

Cheapest doubles around 45,000L (£21; $37)

Lieto Soggiorno, Via A. Fortini (tel. 816191). Two-star hotel.

Moderno, Via G. Carducci 37, Santa Maria degli Angeli (tel. 8040410). Two-star hotel.

Cheapest doubles around 50,000L (£23.50; $41).

Belvedere, Via Borgo Aretino 13 (tel. 812460). Two-star hotel.

Porziuncola, Via Micarelli, Santa Maria degli Angeli (tel. 8041020). One-star hotel. An annex of the two-star hotel listed above. The price here is for doubles with a bath/shower, which is a good deal lower than at the two-star hotel. The annex has no basic doubles.

Cheapest doubles around 53,000L (£24.50; $43).

Rina, Piazzia S. Pietro 20 (tel. 812817). Two-star hotel.

Cheapest doubles around 55,000L (£25.50; $45).

Sole, Corso Mazzini 35 (tel. 812373). Two-star hotel.

Villa Cherubino, Via Patrone d'Italia 39, Santa Maria degli

Angeli (tel. 8040226). One-star hotel. Doubles with shower/bath only.
Europa, Via Metastasio 2 (tel. 812412). Two-star hotel.

Cheapest doubles around 57,000L (£26.50; $46).

Los Angeles, Via Los Angeles, Santa Maria degli Angeli (tel. 8041339). One-star hotel. An annex of the two-star hotel of that name. Price quoted is for doubles in the annex with shower/bath.

HOSTEL

In the small village of Fontemaggio, just over a mile outside the old town (tel. 813636). Around 17,000L (£8; $14).

CAMPING

Also in Fontemaggio. Same telephone number as the hostel.

Bari (tel. code 080)

Tourist Office
Piazza Aldo Moro. Beside the train station. Open Mon.–Fri. 8.30 a.m.–1 p.m., Sat. 8.30–11 a.m.

The City
Bari has much more to offer than just ferries to Greece. The second city of southern Italy has enough of interest to justify a visit in its own right, though neither the city nor the Italian Tourist Board strongly promote Bari as a tourist destination (in stark contrast to some other towns and countries who will try to entice tourists anywhere). Although some travellers without railpasses have always found their way to Bari (ferries to Greece cost around the same as those from Brindisi for those not holding railpasses) it is safe to say that the growth in budget

travellers visiting the city in recent years has been overwhelmingly due to the highly innovative 'Stop-over in Bari' programme, an excellent accommodation scheme for the under-30s described in more detail below.

Stop-over in Bari
Between mid-June and mid-Sept, the Stop-over in Bari organization operate a site where you can **camp** or **sleep out** for free for one night at Pineta San Francesco (tel. 441186, 24 hours). The site is on the fringe of the city, but is easily reached by bus 5 from the train station, or by bus 1 from Corso Cavour. Toilet and washing facilities are available on site, as is free luggage storage. Stop-over in Bari also offer two-night stays in **private flats** for 26,000L (£12; $21), great value if you want to spend a couple of days looking around Bari. Any of the four Stop-over offices will give you details of the other offers open to under-30s for one day, such as free bus travel, free bike hire. Stop-over offices:

OTE, Via Dante 111 (tel. 5214538).

Piazza Aldo Moro. By the main train station.

At the Maritime Station, c/o the Adriatica Office.

Registration desk at Pineta San Francesco.

HOTELS

Singles with bath/shower around 10,000L (£4.75; $10).

Milanese, Via Piccini 216 (tel. 5210131).

Doubles around 13,500 (£6.25; $11).

Smeralda, Via Capruzzi 234 (tel. 364400). No singles.

Cheapest doubles around 19,000L (£8.75; $15.50).

Residenza Universitaria, Via de Rossi 23 (tel. 235226). Singles around 11,000L (£5; $9).

414 Cheap Sleep Guide

Cheapest doubles around 27,000L (£12.50; $22).

Maria, Via Crisanzio 26 (tel. 232592). Singles around 17,250L (£8; $14).

Loizzo, Via Crisanzio 46 (tel. 5211284). Singles around 13,600L (£6.25; $11).

Cheapest doubles around 30,000L (£14; $24.50).

Fiorini, Via Imbriani 69 (tel. 540185). Singles around 15,600L (£7.25; $13).

Modernissimo, Corso Vittorio Emanuele 30 (tel. 210203). Singles around 13,600L (£6.25; $11).

Casa della Studentessa, Via Carruba 58 (tel. 512415). Two-star. Open to women only. Singles around 15600L (£7.25; $13), with bath/shower 17,800L (£8.25; $14.50).

Patricia, Via Fiume 5 (tel. 235702). Singles around 16,250L (£7.50; $13.50).

Serena, Via Imbriani 69 (tel. 540283). Singles around 20,000L (£9.25; $16.50).

Cheapest doubles around 32,500L (£15; $26.50).

Romeo, Via Crisanzio 12 (tel. 5216380). Two-star hotel. Singles around 23,000L.

Darinka, Via Calefati 15a (tel. 235049). No singles.

Cheapest doubles around 35,500L (£16.50; $29).

Giulia, Via Crisanzio 12 (tel. 5216630). Two-star hotel. Cheapest singles around 20,000L (£10.75; $19).

Cheapest doubles around 38,000 (£17.75; $31).

Bristol, Via Cadefati 15a (tel. 5211503). Singles start at around 22,500L (£10.50; $18.50).

Cheapest doubles around 40,000L (£18.50; $32.50).

La Medusa, Piazza L. di Savoia 22 (tel. 543294). Two-star hotel. No singles.

PRIVATE ROOMS

The Tourist Office has a list of private rooms available in the
city.

IYHF HOSTEL

'Del Levante', Via Nicola Massaro 33 (tel. 320282). In Bari-
Palese, about four miles from the town centre.

CAMPING

San Giorgio (tel. 491175). Open all year round. By the SS16,
about four miles south of the centre. From the Teatro
Petruzzeli take bus 12.

Bologna (tel. code 051)

Tourist Offices
Ente Provinciale per il Turismo (EPT), Via Marconi 45. The
administrative office. Contact for information in advance.
  EPT, Piazza della Medaglia d'Oro (tel. 246541). Outside the
train station. Open Mon.–Sat. 9 a.m.–7 p.m., Sun. 9 a.m.–1
p.m. The staff will find you a room or phone any suggestions
you have. After closing time a list of hotels with vacancies is
displayed.
  EPT, Piazza del Nettuno 1c (tel. 239660). The main
information office, located in the Palazzo Communale. Same
hours and services as the office at the train station, but this
office has a greater range of information.

Basic Directions
After leaving the train station, cross Piazza della Medaglia
d'Oro and go left along the busy Viale Pietro Pietramellara until
you see the square on the right-hand side with the Porta
Galliera. Via Galliera and Via dell'Indipendenza run from this

square. After about 300m both streets meet Via dei Mille. Going right along Via dei Mille, and then turning left at Via Montebello, you arrive at the start of Via del Porto. Continuing straight on down Via dell'Indipendenza you reach the end of the street opposite Piazza del Nettuno. At this point, Via Ugo Bassi heads right. Going to the left you can join Via Rizzoli, which leads to the two towers ('Due Torri') on Piazza di Porta Ravegna which are the symbol of the city. Crossing the street from the end of Via dell'Indipendenza you can walk through Piazza del Nettuno into the larger Piazza Maggiore, the main square in the city.

HOTELS

Hotel prices in Bologna are comparatively high. Although there are a few inexpensive hotels, it is usually difficult to find one with rooms available. Room prices in Bologna's one-star hotels are more or less standard, at around 32,500L (£15; $26.50) for a single, 45,000L (£21; $37) for a double, and 66,000L (£31; $54) for a double with bath/shower. A few one-star hotels offer less expensive rooms, but they are seldom more than 10 per cent cheaper. Surprisingly, some of the cheapest rooms are found in two- and three-star hotels, but these are in short supply, and similar rooms are usually twice the price.

Cheapest doubles around 28,000L (£13; $23).

Gianna, Via Belle Arti 8 (tel. 270653). Doubles without bath/shower only at this one-star hotel. Some rooms are slightly more expensive. From Via dell'Indipendenza go left along Via A. Righi, then straight on down Via delle Moline into Via Belle Arti.

Minerva, Via De Monari 3 (tel. 239652). Doubles without bath/shower only at this one-star hotel. Most rooms are priced at the standard rate. Left off Via Galliera after Via Volturno.

Cheapest doubles around 31,000–34,000L (£14.50–15.75; $25–28).

Nuovo, Via del Porto 6 (tel. 247926). This two-star hotel also has singles available at 21,000L (£9.75; $17). Most are twice that price.

Touring, Via Mattuiani 1/2 (tel. 584305). This two-star hotel offers some cheap rooms of all types. Singles 20,000L (£9.25; $16.50), singles with bath/shower 32,000L (£15; $26.50), doubles 31,000L (£14.50; $25), and doubles with bath/shower 43,000L (£20; $35).

Due Torri, Via degli Usberti 4 (tel. 269826/239944). Two-star hotel with some singles at 22,500L (£10.50; $18.50). Go right at the end of Via Galliera along Via Parigi and watch out for Via degli Usberti on the left.

Ideale, Via Sirani 5 (tel. 358270). One-star hotel. Standard price for most doubles. Singles with bath/shower are relatively cheap at 34,000–39,500L (£15.75–18.50; $27.50–22.00).

Cheapest doubles around 37,000–39,000L (£17.25–18.50; $30–32).

Orologio, Via IV Novembre 10 (tel. 231253). This well-located three-star hotel has a few very cheap rooms. Singles 21,500L (£10; $17.50), doubles 37,000L (£17.25; $30). Also doubles with bath/shower at the normal price for a double in a one-star hotel. Right at Via Ugo Bassi, then left up Via della Zecca, straight on down the side of Piazza Roosevelt, and then right into Via IV Novembre.

Accademia, Via Belle Arti 6 (tel. 232318). This two-star hotel offers a few cheap rooms of all types. Singles 22,500L (£10.50; $18.50), singles with bath/shower 34,000L (£15.76; $27.50), doubles 39,500L (£18.50; $32), doubles with bath/shower 45,000L (£21; $37). See Hotel Gianna, above, for directions.

Atlantic, Via Galliera 46 (tel. 248488). A few cheap rooms of all types in this two-star hotel. Singles 28,500L (£13.25; $23), singles with bath/shower 34,000L (£15.75; $27.50), doubles 39,500L (£18.50; $32), doubles with bath/shower 50,000L (£23; $41).

Cheapest doubles around 45,000L (£21; $37).

Tuscalano, Via Tuscalano 29 (tel. 324024). Two-star hotel. Only a few rooms at this price.

Apollo, Via Drapperie 5 (tel. 223955). Some singles at 27,500L and some doubles at the prices quoted above. Otherwise rooms at this one-star hotel are the standard price. Right off Via Rizzoli at Via Calzolerie, and straight on into Via Drapperie.

Tre Poeti, Via Caldarese 7 (tel. 228605). One-star hotel. A few doubles at the price quoted above. Others are about 20 per cent dearer. Some singles around 28,500L (£13.25; $23). Some doubles with bath/shower are about 10 per cent cheaper than normal for a double in a one-star hotel. The hotel is only a few minutes' walk from the 'Due Torri'. Via Calderese runs between Via S. Vitale and Via Strada Maggiore.

Cheapest doubles around 49,000L (£22.75; $40).

Perla, Via San Vitale 77/2 (tel. 224579). A few singles at this one-star hotel cost about 27,500L (£12.75; $22.50). Otherwise singles and doubles are the same price as at most one-star hotels. Via S. Vitale begins at the 'Due Torri'.

Cheapest doubles around 54,000L (£25; $44) in the one-star hotels below. Singles are the normal price for one-star hotels.

Farini, Via Farini 13 (tel. 271969). Doubles with bath/shower are also about ten per cent cheaper than normal. From Piazza Maggiore, follow Via dell'Archiginassio down the side of the Church of San Petronio and go straight on to Via Farini.

Ferraresi, Via Livraghi 1 (tel. 221802). Right at Via Ugo Bassi, then left after Via della Zecca.

Garisenda, Via Rizzoli 9, Galleria del Leone 1 (tel. 272902).

Cheapest doubles around 58,000L (£27; $47) A few doubles with bath/shower are available at this price in the two-and three-star hotels listed below.

City, Via Magenta 10 (tel. 372676). Three-star hotel.

Dei Commercianti, Via de'Pignattari 11 (tel. 233052). Three-star hotel.

Maggiore, Via Emilia Ponente 62/3 (tel. 381634). Three-star hotel.

Paradise, Via Cattani 7 (tel. 231792). Three-star hotel. Turn left off Via dell'Indipendenza, then right at Via Cattani.

San Felice, Via Riva de Reno 2 (tel. 557457). Three-star hotel. Right off Via Galleria.

San Giorgio, Via delle Moline 17 (tel. 248659). Three-star hotel. See Hotel Gianna, above, for directions.

Saragozza, Via Senzanome 10 (tel. 330258). Three-star hotel. About 10 minutes' walk from the centre, 20 minutes' walk from the train station. Walking from the station, turn right off Via Galliera at Via Riva de Reno, left at Via N. Sauro, across Via Ugo Bassi and on down Via Cesare Battisti, left at Via Barberia, right at Via del Riccio, first right along Via Lo Stradellaccio, right at Via del Fossato, left at Vicolo della Neve, then left.

Holiday, Via Bertiera 13 (tel. 263649/276952). Two-star hotel.

Borsa, Via Goito 4 (tel. 222978). One-star hotel. Left off Via dell'Indipendenza.

Marconi, Via Marconi 22 (tel. 262832). One-star hotel. Left off Via del Porto.

Pedrini, Strada Maggiore 79 (tel. 346912). One-star hotel. The street begins at the 'Due Torri'.

Roveri, Via Mattei 72 (tel. 532118). One-star hotel.

San Mamolo, Via Falcone 8 (tel. 583056). One-star hotel.

San Vitale, Via San Vitale 94 (tel. 225966). One-star hotel. See Hotel Perla, above, for directions.

Villa Azurra, Via Felsina 49 (tel. 535460). One-star hotel.

IYHF HOSTEL

'San Sisto', Via Viadagola 2 (tel. 501810) and Via Viadagola

14 (tel. 519202). 18,000L (£8.40; $14.50). About 4 miles from the main train station. From Via Irnerio (near the main station, off Via dell'Indipendenza) take bus 93 heading east. Mon–Sat. Last bus 8.15 p.m. Sundays and during 1–24 August bus 301.

CITY HOSTEL

Ask at the Tourist Office if the 'Dormitorio Comunale' is in operation.

CAMPING

No convenient site. Piccolo Paradiso is in Marzabotto, some distance away (tel. 842680). Open Mar.–Dec. Ask the Tourist Office how to get to the site.

Brindisi (tel. code 0831)

Tourist Office
Ente Provincial per il Turismo (EPT), Viale Regina Margherita 5 (tel. 21944). Open Mon.–Sat. 8.30 a.m.–12.30 p.m. and 4.30–7.30 p.m. Very helpful office.

Arriving in Brindisi
The train station is on Piazza Crispi, about 20 minutes' walk from the ferry terminal at the Stazione Marittima down Corso Garibaldi to its end, then along Via del Mare. There are plenty of buses which make the journey along the length of Corso Garibaldi (around 700L (£0.35; $0.60) for the trip).

Finding Accommodation
Finding a place to stay in Brindisi is seldom a problem as most of the people who arrive in town depart on one of the overnight ferries.

HOTELS

Cheapest singles around 8500L (£4; $7), doubles around 14000L (£6.50; $11.50).

Doria, Via Fulvia 38 (tel. 26453). The cheapest in town, but best avoided by women travelling alone. Well out from the centre. Follow Via Appia into Via Arione, from which Via Fulvia is the second street on the right.

Cheapest doubles around 34,000–36,000L (£15.75–16.75; $28–29.50).

Villa Blanca, Via Armengol 23 (tel. 25438). Singles around 22,500L (£10.50; $18.50). Doubles with a shower/bath are only slightly more expensive than basic doubles.
Venezia, Via Pisanelli 6 (tel. 25411). Singles around 20,000L (£9.25; $16.50).

Cheapest doubles around 40,000L (£18.50; $32.50).

Europa, Piazza Cairoli 5 (tel. 528546/528547). Singles around 26,000L (£12; $21).
Altair, Via Tunisi 2 (tel. 24911). Singles around 22,500L (£10.50; $18.50).

HOSTELS

Via Brandi 2 (tel. 413100). About 1½ miles from the centre, but easily reached by bus 3, 4 or 5 from the train station. Call ahead to make sure that the hostel is open before making the trip.

CAMPING

Materdomin. Three miles from town on the road to Punta Penne. During the summer, the site can be easily reached by taking a local bus heading for the coast.

Florence (Firenze) (tel. code 055)

Tourist Offices

Azienda Autonoma di Turismo, Via Tornabuoni 15, 50123 Firenze (tel. 217459/216544). Open Mon.–Sat. Contact this office if you want information in advance, or on arrival. Free map of the city, efficient and knowledgeable staff. No accommodation service.

Ente Provinciale per il Turismo (EPT), Via Manzoni 16 (tel. 2478141). Open Mon.–Sat. 8.30 a.m.–1.30 p.m. Free map and information on the city. No accommodation service, but you should address any complaints regarding hotels to this office.

Informazione Turistiche. In a booth outside Firenze Santa Maria Novella train station (take the exit by track 16). Open daily 8 a.m.–9 p.m. Free map of the city.

Informazione Turistiche Alberghiere. Beside track 16 in the train station. Open daily, mid-Apr.–mid-Nov., 8 a.m.–9.30 p.m.; at other times, 9 a.m.–8.45 p.m. Room-finding service. Commission around 2000L (£0.90; $1.50) per person. State clearly the price range you are interested in, as otherwise they will offer you expensive rooms.

Basic Directions

The vast majority of the accommodation suggestions below are within reasonable walking distance of the Santa Maria Novella train station. The cathedral is 10–15 minutes' walk away from the station. Piazza della Stazione is the square in front of the train station. Via Nazionale leads out of the left-hand side of the square. Within a short distance, Via Nazionale passes one end of Via Fiume and crosses Via Faenza, two streets with a good supply of relatively inexpensive hotels. A few blocks further on Via Faenza crosses Via Guelfa. There are also a number of cheap hotels in the streets running off Via Guelfa, parallel to the right of Via Nazionale. At the bottom left of Piazza della Stazione is Piazza della Unità Italiana, from which Via de' Panzani runs to Via de' Cerretani, crossing Via del Giglio on the way. Going along Via de' Cerretani you arrive at Piazza S. Giovanni with the baptistry, beyond which is the cathedral. If from Piazza della Unità Italiana you head round the Santa Maria Novella church you arrive at Piazza Santa Maria Novella. Down the left-hand side of the square Via de' Banchi runs straight into Via de' Cerretani. Following Via d. Belledonne and then going left, you arrive at Via de' Tornabuoni. Three streets converge at the foot of Piazza Santa Maria Novella: Via del Sole (also leading towards Via de' Tornabuoni), Via de' Fossi (heading down towards the River Arno) and Via della Scala. The latter can also be reached by taking Via S. Caterina di Siena from the right hand side of Piazza della Stazione. Crossing Via della Scala, you can take a series of small streets right down to the Arno, crossing Via Palazzuolo, Borgo Ognissanti and Via Montebello on the way.

Street Numbers
The city's streets are not numbered in the conventional manner. Instead, there are two sets of numbers: red indicating business premises and blue or black denoting residential properties. Most hotels have blue or black numbers. In local publications, an *r* is added to the street number of commercial buildings.

HOTELS

Room prices in Florence's one-star hotels are more or less standard. With a few exceptions, you can expect to pay around 29,500 (£13.75; $24) for a single; 37,500L (£17.50; $31) for a single with bath/shower; 43,000L (£20; $35) for a double; and 54,000L (£25; $44) for a double with bath/shower. Hotels 1–8 in the list below offer slightly cheaper rooms, generally around 26,000 (£12; $21) for a single; 33,000L (£15.50; $27) for a single with bath/shower; 39,000L (£18; $32) for a double; and 48,000–51,000L (£22.25–23.75; $39.00–41.50) for a double with shower/bath. All other hotels charge the standard rate.

1. Rina, Via Dante Alighieri 12 (tel. 213209). A few really cheap rooms. Single around 13,500L (£6.25; $11), double

around 26,000L (£12; $21). Others as described above.
No rooms with shower/bath. Near the Badia. Follow Via
della Studio from the cathedral and go straight on into
Via Dante Alighieri.

2. Ausonia e Rimini, Via Nazionale 24 (tel. 496547).
3. Colorado, Via Cavour 66 (tel. 217310). No doubles with bath/shower.
4. La Mia Casa, Piazza Santa Maria Novella 23 (tel. 213061). No singles with bath/shower.
5. Montreal, Via della Scala 43 (tel. 262331).
6. Marilena Tourist House, Via Fiume 20 (tel. 261705). No doubles with bath/shower.
7. Sampaoli, Via San Gallo 14 (tel. 284834). The street runs off Via Guelfa, three blocks to the right of Via Nazionale.
8. San Marco, Via Cavour 50 (tel. 284235). Some singles at 22,000L (£10.25; $18), some doubles with bath/shower at 44,000L (£20.50; $36).
9. ABC, Borgo Ognissanti 67 (tel. 218882).
10. Adria, Via Montebello 49 (tel. 212029).
11. Adua, Via Fiume 20 (tel. 287506).
12. Aldini, Via Calzaiuoli 13 (tel. 214752).
13. Anna, Via Faenza 56 (tel. 298322).
14. Apollo, Via Faenza 77 (tel. 284119).
15. Armonia, Via Faenza 56 (tel. 211146).
16. Azzi, Via Faenza 56 (tel. 213806).
17. Bavaria, Borgo degli Albizi 26 (tel. 2340313). From the cathedral, head down Via del Proconsolo, then left.
18. Brunori, Via del Proconsolo 5 (tel. 263648). See 17.
19. Burchianti, Via del Giglio 6 (tel. 212796).
20. Canada, Borgo San Lorenzo 14 (tel. 210074). Left from the end of Via de' Cerretani, by the baptistry.
21. Casci, Via Cavour 13 (tel. 211686). Via Cavour crosses Via Guelfa, four blocks to the right of Via Nazionale.
22. Cely, Piazza Santa Maria Novella 24 (tel. 218755).
23. Cestelli, Borgo SS Apostoli 25 (tel. 214213). From the Piazza Santa Maria Novella, take Via delle Belledonne (just to the right of Via de' Banchi). At the end of the street head left until you reach Via de'Tornabuoni. Turn

right down this street and continue on, passing Via Porta Rossa on the left as you enter Piazza S. Trinità. Borgo SS Apostoli is then the second street on the left. Walking from the train station to Piazza S. Trinità takes just over 15 minutes.

24. Colomba, Via Cavour 21 (tel. 263139). See 21.
25. Colore, Via Calzaiuoli 13 (tel. 210301).
26. D'Errico, Via Faenza 69 (tel. 214059).
27. Davanzati, Via Porta Rossa 15 (tel. 283414).
28. Diana's Guest House, Via Panzani 10 (tel. 216730).
29. Elite, Via della Scala 12 (215395).
30. Enza, Via S. Zanobi 45 (tel. 490990). The street runs off Via Guelfa, one block to the right of Via Nazionale.
31. Erina, Via Fiume 17 (tel. 284343).
32. Esplanade, Via Tornabuoni 13 (tel. 287078).
33. Etrusca, Via Nazionale 35 (tel. 213100).
34. Fani, Via Guelfa 28 (tel. 283731).
35. Ferdy, Via S. Gallo 39 (tel. 475302). See 7.
36. Fiorentina, Via dei Fossi 12 (tel. 219530). The street runs from the far end of Piazza Santa Maria Novella.
37. Fiorita, Via Fiume 20 (tel. 283693).
38. Genzianella, Via Cavour 112 (tel. 573909). See 21.
39. Giacobazzi, Piazza Santa Maria Novella 24 (tel. 294679).
40. Giappone, Via dei Banchi 1 (tel. 210090).
41. Gigliola, Via della Scala 40 (tel. 287981).
42. Giovanna, Via Faenza 69 (tel. 261353).
43. Guelfa, Via Guelfa 28 (tel. 215882).
44. House for Tourists-Aglietti, Via Cavour 29 (tel. 287824). See 21.
45. Il Bargellino, Via Guelfa 87 (tel. 262658).
46. Iris, Piazza Santa Maria Novella 22 (tel. 296735).
47. Joly, Via Fiume 8 (tel. 292079).
48. Kursaal, Via Nazionale 24 (tel. 496324).
49. La Romagnola, Via della Scala 40 (tel. 211597).
50. La Scala, Via della Scala 21 (tel. 212629).
51. Le Vigne, Piazza Santa Maria Novella 24 (tel. 294449).
52. Lombardi, Via Fiume 8 (tel. 283151).
53. Lucia, Via Borgo Ognissanti 8 (tel. 215391).

54. Magliani, Via Santa Reperata 1 (tel. 287378). The street runs off Via Guelfa two blocks to the right of Via Nazionale.
55. Marcella, Via Faenza 58 (tel. 213232).
56. Margaret, Via della Scala 25 (tel. 210138).
57. Mariella, Via Fiume 11 (tel. 212302).
58. Marini, Via Faenza 56 (tel. 284824).
59. Merlini, Via Faenza 56 (212848).
60. Mia Cara, Via Faenza 58 (tel. 216053).
61. Monica, Via Faenza 66 (tel. 283804).
62. Nazionale, Via Nazionale 22 (tel. 262203).
63. Nella, Via Faenza 69 (tel. 284256).
64. Palazzuolo, Via Palazzuolo 71 (tel. 214611/244883).
65. Pina, Via Faenza 69 (tel. 212231).
66. Orchidea, Borgo degli Albizi 11 (tel. 2480346). See 17.
67. Polo Nord, Via Panzani 7 (tel. 287952).
68. Righi, Via San Zanobi 89 (tel. 486350). See 30.
69. Rudy, Via S. Gallo 51 (tel. 475519). See 7.
70. San Giovanni, Via Cerretani 2 (tel. 213580).
71. Scoti, Via Tornabuoni 7 (tel. 292128). See 23.
72. Serena Tourist House, Via Fiume 20 (tel. 213643).
73. Sofia, Via Cavour 21 (tel. 283930).
74. Sole, Via del Sole 8 (tel. 296094). The street runs left from the far end of Piazza Santa Maria Novella.
75. Tamerici, Via Fiume 5 (tel. 214156).
76. Tina, Via S. Gallo 31 (tel. 483519/483593). See 7.
77. Tony's Inn, Via Faenza 77 (tel. 217975).
78. Toscana, Via del Sole 8 (tel. 213156). See 74.
79. Universo, Piazza Santa Maria Novella 20 (tel. 211484).
80. Varsavia, Via Panzani 5 (tel. 215615).
81. Bandini, Piazza Santo Spirito 9 (tel. 215308). Fine location on the square in front of the Church of the Holy Spirit, on the opposite side of the Arno from the station. A 20-minute walk from the station. Follow Via de' Fossi down to the Arno, cross the river and head up Via dei Serragli from the Ponte Alla Carraia. Via San Agostino on the left leads into Piazza San Spirito. If you don't want to walk, take bus 36 or 37 from Piazza Santa Maria

Novella to the first stop after crossing the Arno. Around Santo Spirito is the best area for good value meals.

IYHF HOSTEL

Viale Augusto Righi 2–4 (tel. 601451). Members only. Reservations by letter only. 20,000L (£9.30; $16.50) per night. About 3½ miles from the town centre. Bus 17B from the station.

HOSTELS

Ostello Santa Monaca, Via Santa Monaca 6 (tel. 268338). Midnight curfew. Around 17,000L (£8; $14), sheets 3000L (£1.40; $2.50). No reservations, so arrive anytime after 9.30 a.m. to sign the list and put some form of ID in the box. Go back to check in between 4.00–4.30 p.m. No toilet facilities for female guests. Bus 36 or 37 from Piazza Santa Maria Novella to the first stop over the river, or 20 minutes on foot. Via Santa Monaca is right off Via dei Serragli, opposite Via S. Agostino. See 81 for directions to walk to the hostel.

Pensionato Pio X, Via de' Serragli 106 (tel. 225044). Midnight curfew. Two-day minimum stay. No reservations accepted, so get there early. 16,500L (£7.75; $13.50). Bus 36 or 37 from Piazza Santa Maria Novella to the second stop after crossing the Arno, or just over 20 minutes' walk. See 81 for directions.

Istituto Gould, Via de' Serragli 49 (tel. 212576). No curfew. No arrivals or departures on Sundays. Singles 29,500–33,000L (£13.75–15.50; $24–27), doubles 48,000–53,000L (£22.25–24.75; $39–43), triples 60,000–80,000L (£28–37; $49–65), quads 76000L (£35; $62). Bus 36 or 37 from Piazza Santa Maria Novella to the first stop after crossing the river, or a 20-minute walk (see 81 for directions).

Suore Oblate dell'Assunzione, Via Borgo Pinti 15 (tel. 2480582). Open mid-June–July and Sept. Midnight curfew.

Singles and doubles around 25,000L (£11.75; $20.50) per
person. From the Duomo, follow Via dell'Oriuolo to the
start of Via Borgo Pinti.
Suore Oblate dello Spirito Santo, Via Nazionale 8 (tel.
298202). Open mid-June–Oct. Midnight curfew. Singles,
doubles and triples from around 25,000L (£11.75; $20.50)
per person with breakfast.

CAMPING

Parco Communale. Viale Michelangelo 80 (tel. 6811977).
Open April to October. 6500L (£3; $5.50) per tent, 6000L
(£2.75; $5) per person. Frequently crowded. Tend to say
they are full if you phone during the peak season, but
usually find space if you turn up. Bus 13 from the station.
Villa di Camerata, Viale Augusto Righi 2–4 (next to the youth
hostel) (tel. 610300). Open Apr.–Oct. 6000L (£2.75; $5) per
tent, 5000L (£2.25; $4) per person. Bus 17b from the station.

'AREA DE SOSTA'

A covered area where you can put down a mat and a sleeping
bag. Run by the city authorities at Via Rocca Tedalda in Villa
Favard, about 4 miles from the town centre. Washing and toilet
facilities are available at the site. No charge. Maximum stay
one week. Open from 7 p.m.–10 a.m. (tel. 690022). Bus 14a,
14b or 14c from the station. Leave your pack at the station.

Genoa (Genova)   (tel. code 010)

Tourist Offices
The head office is at Via Roma 11 (tel. 581407). Open
Mon.–Thurs. 8 a.m.–2 p.m. and 4–6 p.m., Fri.–Sat. 8 a.m.–1
p.m. There are branch offices at the two main train stations,
both open daily 8 a.m.–8 p.m.; Porta Principe (tel. 262623) and
Brignole (tel. 562056). Another branch office operates at the
airport.

Around the Porta Principe Train Station

Genova Porta Principe occupies one side of Piazza Acquaverde. At the right-hand end of the square, Via Andrea Doria runs back along the side of the train station. From the far right-hand end of Piazza Acquaverde, Salita S. Giovanni leads out of the square into Via Pre'. On the opposite side of the square from the station, past the Columbus monument, is Via Balbi. Taking this street and continuing more or less straight ahead through Piazza dell'Annunziata and along Via Bensa, Largo Zecca and Galleria G. Garibaldi you arrive at Piazza Portello, from which Galleria M. Bixio leads past Piazzale Mazzini into Piazza Corvetto. Via Roma runs from Piazza Corvetto down towards Piazza de Ferrari.

Around the Brignole Train Station

In front of Genova Brignole is Piazza Verdi. Going right from the station exit brings you to Via de Amicis. From the end of this street, Via Serra runs into Piazza Corvetto. Also on the right of Piazza Verdi, Via Fiume runs away from the station to Via Cadorna, across which is the large Piazza della Victoria. Going right at this point, Via Cadorna leads into Via XX Settembre which ends at Piazza de Ferrari. Via S. Vicenzo runs between Via Fiume and Via XX Settembre. Heading left from Piazza Verdi along Via Tolemaide you pass the end of Corso Torino on the right.

Trouble Spots

Genoa's Old Town is dangerous at night (roughly the area bounded by the waterfront, Piazza Carignano, Piazza Dante, Piazza de Ferrari and Piazza Caricamento). For the most part, there is nothing to worry about during the day, though you may not want to venture into the labyrinthine area between Piazza Cavour and the Porta Siberia o del Molo. In a totally different area of the city, above Galleria G. Garibaldi, is the Belvedere Montaldo from which there is a panoramic view over the city and the port (a view tourist brochures advise you not to miss). The simplest way to the Belvedere Montaldo is to take either of the two narrow sets of steps heading left from Galleria

G. Garibaldi (Salita Superiore della Rondinella or Salita Alla Spianata Castelletto) but the profusion of empty syringes is testimony to what goes on here. The best way to walk up to the viewpoint is to follow Via Cafarco from Piazza Fortello, then go left at the top along Corso Paganini.

HOTELS

Cheapest doubles around 16,000L (£7.50; $13).

    Capri, Via Cairoli 4/3 (tel. 208922). To the right by the junction of Via Bensa and Largo Zecca.

    Parigi, Via Pre' 72/1 (tel. 252172).

Cheapest doubles around 17,000–19,000L (£8–9; $14–16).

    Arcobaleno, Corso Torino 17/7 (tel. 595477). Rooms have a shower/bath.

Cheapest doubles around 22,500–25,500L (£10.50–12.00; $18.50–21.00).

    Gina, Via Goito 20 (tel. 891512). Near Piazza Corvetto. From Piazzale Mazzini take Via Bacigalupo to Piazza Marsala and the start of Via Goito.

    Mirella, Via Groppalo 4/4 (tel. 893722). Walk along Via de Amicis, go right at the first junction, over the railway line and up Via Groppalo.

    Rinascente, Via Pre' 59 (tel. 261113).

    Valle, Via Groppalo 4/11 (tel. 882257). See Hotel Mirella for directions.

Cheapest doubles around 27,000–29,500L (£12.50–13.75; $22–24).

    Alicia, Via Balbi 15/5 (tel. 280166).

    Armonia, Via Pre' 46/r (tel. 207660).

    Balbi, Via Balbi 21/3 (tel. 280912).

    Delfino, Via Pre' 19/h (tel. 200673).

Mediterranee, Via Cairoli 14/4 (tel. 206531). See Hotel Capri
for directions.
Rampone, Via Balbi 15/11 (tel. 280101).
Romano, Via Andrea Doria 4/4 (tel. 261070).
San Marco, Via Andrea Doria 4/a (tel. 261517).

Cheapest doubles around 31,000–33,000L (£14.50–15.50; $25–27)

Astro, Via XX Settembre 3/21 (tel. 581533/587286).
Bruxelles Margherita, Via XX Settembre 19/7 (tel. 589191).
Riva, Via Balbi 29/6 (tel. 265415).
Roma, Via S. Vicenzo 26/10 (tel. 586689).
Soana, Via XX Settembre 23/8a (tel. 562814).
Soana (dipendenza), Via XX Settembre 23/7a (tel. 561486).

Cheapest doubles around 34,000–36,000L (£15.75–16.75; $27.50–29.50)

Acquaverde, Via Balbi 29/8 (tel. 265427).
Barone, Via XX Settembre 2/23 (tel. 587578).
Fieramare, Corso Torino 17/5 (tel. 540450).
Ginevra, Via Balbi 15/7 & 15/9 (tel. 280109).
Nido, Via Fiume 4/6 (tel. 542116).
Piemontese, Via Andrea Doria 6/n (tel. 261812).
Rita, Via Groppola 8/c (tel. 870207). See 5 for directions.

Cheapest doubles around 37,500L (£17.50; $31)

Olympia, Via XX Settembre 21/8 (tel. 592538).

Cheapest doubles around 44,000L (£20.50; $36)

Carola, Via Groppalo 4/12 (tel. 891340). See Hotel Mirella for
directions.

Cheapest doubles around 47,000L (£22; $38)

Meuble Suisse, Via XX Settembre 21/6 (tel. 541176). Rooms
with shower/bath.

IYHF HOSTEL

Cristoforo Colombo, Via Costanzi (tel. 586407). Around 20,000L (£9.25; $16.50). Opened last year.

HOSTELS/DORMITORIES

Casa della Giovane, Piazza Santa Sabina 4 (tel. 206632). Women only. B&B 12,000–16,500L (£5.50–7.75; $10.00–13.50).

CAMPING

Villa Doria, Via Vespucci (tel. 680613). Open year round. Far from the centre in the Genova-Pegli district. Ask the Tourist Office for directions to the site from the centre, or from the train station in Genova-Pegli.

Milan (Milano) (tel. code 02)

Tourist Offices
Ente Provinciale per il Turismo (EPT), Via Marconi 1, 20123 Milano. The administrative office of the regional tourist board. Contact this office if you want information in advance. A Tourist Information office operates at the same address (tel. 809662). Open Mon.–Fri. 9.45 a.m.–12.30 p.m. and 1.30–5 p.m., Sat. 9 a.m.–12.30 p.m. and 1.30–5 p.m. The office is near the cathedral (metro: Duomo). This office has a more efficient and wide-ranging room-finding service than the other office, located in Milano Centrale train station (tel. 6690532/6690432). Open 9 a.m.–12.30 p.m. and 2.15–6 p.m. Hotel Reservation Milano is at Via Palestro 24, 20121 Milano (tel. 76006095).

Around Milano Centrale Train Station
In front of the station is Piazza Duca d'Aosta, to the right running alongside of the station is Piazza IV Novembre, to the

left also running alongside the station is Piazza L. di Savoia. Along the side of the station, Via Tonale leads out off Piazza IV Novembre. Diagonally right from the main exit of Milano Centrale is the start of Via Galvani. Via Copernico runs right off Via Galvani after one block. The main road leading away from Piazza Duca d'Aosta in the direction of the city centre is Via Pisani. At the start of Via Pisani, Via Vitruvio runs left out of Piazza Duca d'Aosta to Corso Buenos Aires at Piazza Lima (metro MM1: Lima), across which is Via Plinio. Walking down Via Pisani, you pass the ends of Via S. Gregorio and then Viale Tunisia on the left-hand side. The next street on the left after Viale Tunisia leads into Via Castaldi. Continuing on to the end of Via Pisani you arrive in Piazza Repubblica. Heading left at this point brings you into Via V. Veneto, which ends at the Porta Venezia (metro MM1: Porta Venezia). Via Lazzaretto runs parallel to the left of Via Piani between Via Vitruvio and Piazza Repubblica. One block to the left of Via Lazzaretto is Via Settela. Diagonally left from the main exit of Milano Centrale, Via A. Doria runs away at an angle through Piazza Caiazzo (metro MM2: Caiazzo) into Piazzale Loreto (metro MM1 and MM2: Loreto). Via Settembrini runs from Via Vitruvio (opposite Via Lazzaretto) across Piazza Caiazzo to Viale Brianza. Viale Monza and Via Porpora both run out of Piazzale Loreto as do Corso Buenos Aires and Viale Abruzzi. Via Iulli is to the left off Via Porpora. Walking down Viale Abruzzi you can turn left at Via G. Pecchio, on along Via della Vallaze and then right into Via F. Lippi.

It can be easier to reach some hotels in Via Porpora or Via F. Lippi from Milano Lambrate (local train or metro MM2: Lambrate FS). From the station, walk right on to Piazza Gobetti, the start of Via Porpora and Via Vallaze.

HOTELS

Singles around 16,000L (£7.50; $13) doubles around 25,000L (£11.50; $20.50)

Firenze Mare, Via Porpora 143 (tel. 2846223).
Vitruvio, Via B. Marcello 65 (tel. 2711807).

Singles around 18,000L (£8.50; $14.50) doubles around 28,000L (£13; $23)

Ballarin, Via Soncino 3 (tel. 800822). Within easy walking distance of Piazza del Duomo (metro MM1: Duomo). Follow Via Torino into Largo Carrobbio then left).
Cecconi, Via Settembrini 54 (tel. 224514).

Doubles around 30,000L (£14; $24.50)

Comercio, Via Mercato 1 (tel. 8048003). Price quoted is for doubles with bath/shower. Singles with bath/shower 21,000L (£9.75; $17). Close to the city centre. Metro M2: Lanza is a few minutes' walk from the hotel.
Andrea Doria, Via Andrea Doria 16 (tel. 6692372). Singles 17,000L (£8; $14).

Doubles around 32,000L (£15; $26), singles around 21,000L (£9.75; 17)

Mongelli, Via Iulli 20 (tel. 2361265).

Doubles around 34,000L (£15.75; $28), singles around 22,500L (£10.50; 18.50)

Isolabella, Viale Montegrappa 6a (tel. 6599865). From Stazione Porta Garibaldi (train station and metro M2), a short walk down Corso del Como towards the Porta Garibaldi and then left near the gate. From metro M2: Moscova walk towards the gate.
ABC, Via Molino delle Armi 12 (tel. 867501). Near the San Lorenzo Maggiore church, off Corso Italia.

Doubles around 38,000L (£17.75; $31)

Arlecchino, Via Paganini 7 (tel. 278174). Singles 26,000L (£12; $21).
Golden Gate, Corso di Porta Vittoria 58 (tel. 5458096). Singles 25,000L (£11.50; $20.50). Metro M1: Palestro. From Piazza S. Babila follow Via Durini into Via Verziere, go left and cross the road into Corso di Porta Vittoria.

Helen, Via Paganini 8 (tel. 2042001). Singles 27,000L (£12.50; $22).

Internazionale, Via Dante 15 (tel. 873697). Singles 26,000L (£12; $21). Excellent location, a few minutes' walk from Piazza del Duomo. Metro MM1: Cairoli. The street runs out of Piazza Cairoli.

Ischia, Via F. Lippi 43 (tel. 2666235). Singles 22,000L (£10.25; $18).

Merano, Via Lazzaretto 10 (tel. 279378).

Mercurio, Via Ascanio Sforza 73 (tel. 8466774). Singles 24,500L (£11.50; $20). From Porta Genova (mainline and metro M2 station) walk to the harbour (*Darsena*), right along the waterfront into Piazza XXIV Maggio, then right down Via Ascanio Sforza.

Paganini, Via Paganini 6 (tel. 278443). No singles.

Rovello, Via Rovello 18a (tel. 873956). Singles 25,500L (£12; $21). Excellent location, a few minutes' walk from Piazza del Duomo. Metro M1: Cordusio. The street runs out of Piazza Cordusio.

Argentario, Corso di Porta Vittoria 58 (tel. 5458172). Singles 27,000L (£12.50; $22). See Hotel Golden Gate for directions.

Doubles around 41,000L (£19; $33.50)

Bussentina, Via Settala 3 (tel. 288517). Singles 27,000L (£12.50; $22).

Canna, Viale Tunisia 6 (tel. 224133). Singles 26,000L (£12; $21).

Dante, Via Dante 14 (tel. 866471). Singles 27,000L (£12.50; $22). Well located, a short walk from Piazza del Duomo. See Hotel Internazionale for directions.

Nicosia, Corso Vercelli 1 (tel. 4814411). Singles 27,000L (£12.50; $22).

Trentina, Via F. Lippi 50 (tel. 2361208). No singles.

Ullrich, Corso Italia 6 (tel. 873177). About 8 minutes' walk from Piazza del Duomo.

Eva, Via Lazzaretto 17 (tel. 6592898).

Iride, Via Porpora 170 (tel. 2666695).

Magic, Via Copernico 8 (tel. 683382).

Oriente, Via Porpora 52 (tel. 2361298).

Sorriso, Corso di Porta Vittoria 51 (tel. 55192226). See Hotel
Golden Gate for directions.

Ugoletti, Via Settala 56 (tel. 222366).

Doubles around 45,000L (£21; $37)

Adri, Via Iulli 18 (tel. 235692).

Arthur, Via Lazzaretto 14 (tel. 2046294).

Brera, Via Pontaccio 9 (tel. 873509). Close to the city centre.
Metro M2: Lanza is a very short walk from the hotel.

Charly, Via Settala 78 (tel. 278190).

Cremona, Via Porpora 168 (tel. 235312).

Giglio, Via P. Castaldi 26 (tel. 29406995).

Italia, Via Vitruvio 44 (tel. 6693826).

Kennedy, Viale Tunisia 6 (tel. 29400934).

Marte, Via Ascanio Sforza 81 (tel. 8433136). See Hotel
Mercurio for directions.

Metro, Viale Monza 120 (tel. 2856918).

Nazionale, Via Vitruvio 46 (tel. 6693059).

Paola, Via Porpora 16 (tel. 29400965).

Salerno, Via Vitruvio 18 (tel. 2046870).

Veneta, Via Iulli 22 (tel. 2361271).

Doubles around 48,000L (£22.50; $39); expect to pay at least 30,000L (£14; $24.50) in singles

Aurora, Corso Buenos Aires 18 (tel. 278960).

Ca'Grande, Via Porpora 87 (tel. 2850295).

Casa Mia, Via Vittorio Veneto 30 (tel. 6575249). An easy walk
from Stazione Centrale. Closest metro is M1: Porta
Venezia.

Eden, Via Tonale 2 (tel. 66980609).

Jolanda, Corso Magenta 78 (tel. 463317). From metro M1 M2:
Cadorna, follow Via Carducci out of Piazza Cadorna then
right at Corso Magenta.

Manzoni, Via Senato 45 (tel. 791002). Good location off
Piazza Cavour, within easy walking distance of Piazza del
Duomo.

Paradiso, Via B. Marcello 85 (tel. 279448).
San Tomaso, Viale Tunisia 6 (tel. 209747).

Doubles around 51,000L (£24; $42)

Giulio Cesare, Via Rovello 10 (tel. 876250). Excellent location,
close to Piazza del Duomo. See Hotel Rovello for
directions.
Kent, Via Corridoni 2a (tel. 55187635). Within easy walking
distance of the centre. Metro M1: Palestro. From Piazza
S. Babila follow Via Durini, go left as you enter the square
and head down to Via Visconte di Modrone. Via Corridoni
begins on the opposite side of the street.
Mondial, Via Vitruvio 24 (tel. 202695).
Principe, Corso Buenos Aires 75 (tel. 6694377).
Siena, Via P. Castaldi 17 (tel. 206108). Price quoted is for a
room with bath/shower.

IYHF HOSTEL

Ostello Piero Rotta, Via Martino Bassi 2/Viale Salmoiraghi
2 (tel. 367095). Curfew 11.30 p.m. 22,000L (£10.25; $18).
Members only, but IYHF cards are sold at the hostel.
16,000L (£7.50; $13). (Not far from the San Siro/Giuseppe
Meazza stadium. Football every Sunday. Milan or
Internazionale.) From Central Station metro line 2 to
Cadorna, then line 1 heading for S. Leonardo to QT8/San
Siro. Line 1 splits, so make sure you don't get on a train
to Inganni.

DORMITORIES

Casa Famiglia ACISJF, Corso Garibaldi 121a–123 (tel.
6595206). Women under 30 only. Around 23,000L (£10.75;
$19) per night. Very safe, but a 10.30 p.m. curfew. A
5–10-minute walk from Milano Porta Garibaldi train
station. Take a train from Milano Centrale, walk down
Corso Como which leads into Corso Garibaldi. Metro
MM2: Moscova is much closer.

CAMPING

The three closest sites are all a considerable distance away:

Il Barregino, Via Corbettina, Bareggio (tel. 9014417). Open
all year.

Autodromo, Parco di Monza, Monza (tel. 387771). Open
Apr.–Sept. Close to the famous Formula One circuit.
Accessible by bus from Milano Centrale train station.

Agip Metanopoli, Via Emilia, San Donato Milanese (tel.
5272159). Open all year.

Ask at the Tourist Office for directions to the sites.

Naples (Napoli) (tel. code 081)

Tourist Offices

Ente Provinciale per il Turismo (EPT), Via Partenope 10a (tel.
7644871). The main EPT office on the bay near Villa
Communale. Open Mon.–Sat. 8.30 a.m.–2 p.m., Sun. 8.30
a.m.–noon. Free city maps and information on accommodation
possibilities.

EPT, Stazione Napoli Centrale (tel. 268779). Open Mon.–Sat.
8.30 a.m.–8 p.m., Sun. 8.30 a.m.–2 p.m. The office will phone
hotels to see if they have vacancies. Free city map.

EPT, Piazza Gesù Nuovo (tel. 5523328). Open Mon.–Sat. 9
a.m.–7 p.m., Sun. 9 a.m.–2 p.m. The best of the EPT offices
for information on the city and surrounding area.

Azienda di Turismo, Piazza Reale (tel. 418744). Open
Mon.–Sat. 8.30 a.m.–2.30 p.m. The best of all the offices for
information on the city.

There are two other information offices which open on an
irregular basis, one in the Napoli Mergellina train station and
the other at the Capodochino Airport.

Around Napoli Centrale Train Station

In front of the train station is Piazza Garibaldi. Immediately to the right of the station Corso Novara runs off the square. Parallel to Corso Novara, one street back from Piazza Garibaldi, Via Aquila runs away from the side of Stazione Napoli Centrale. Continuing along the right-hand side of Piazza Garibaldi from Corso Novara, you pass the ends of Via Bologna, Via Torino and Via Milano before arriving at Corso Giuseppe Garibaldi, which runs across the far end of Piazza Garibaldi. Turning right up Corso Garibaldi, you arrive at Piazza Principe Umberto. The small Vico Ferrovia runs between Via Milano and Piazza Principe Umberto. Walking along Corso Novara from Piazza Garibaldi after one block you arrive at the junction with Via Firenze (heading left to Piazza Principe Umberto) and Corso Meridionale (going right). One block further on down Corso Novara, Via Palermo leads off to the left, ending at Via Milano, while Via Genova goes off to the right. After another block Via Venezia runs left from Corso Novara, running parallel to Via Firenze and Via Palermo, and crossing Via Bologna, Via Torino and Via Milano. Via Giuseppe Pica runs parallel to the left-hand side of Piazza Garibaldi, one block back from the square. Corso Umberto I runs from the far left-hand corner of Piazza Garibaldi as you look out from Napoli Centrale station.

Finding Accommodation
Hotel prices in Naples are lower than in the other major cities, and you should seldom struggle to get a room in a cheap one-star hotel. Unfortunately, on the whole, the standard of accommodation in Neapolitan one-star hotels does not compare favourably with their more northern counterparts, especially as regards cleanliness and security for your belongings. You might want to leave your pack at the station. There are a few two-star hotels which are reasonably cheap, and which are safer for your belongings. Do not allow hotel owners to cheat you (reputedly, this is second nature to many of them). The price for rooms must be clearly displayed on the door of the room.

Finding a hotel with a decent location can be difficult. Many of the hotels listed below are in the area around the Napoli

Centrale train station. Although this part of town is hardly choice, it is intimidating rather than dangerous (unless you are stupid enough to wander through it with your pack at night). The area around the Mergellina train and metro station is one of the best, but unfortunately hotel options here are limited. The IYHF hostel is in this part of town. Even those who are usually none too keen on hostels might want to consider staying here. The hostel is one of the best in Italy, and you will have no problems with personal security (although you are probably still best to leave your pack at the train station).

Trouble Spots

As is the case with many cities, Naples suffers from a reputation gained in the past. Many travellers bypass the city or visit it with trepidation, yet walk around more dangerous places with no qualms at all. That is not to say that Naples is safe to wander about in, but it has long surrendered its title as the mugging capital of Europe. Provided you make your way to the sights by the main thoroughfares (use public transport to get to the port) and take obvious precautions with cameras and other valuables, you should not encounter any trouble. Petty thieves in Naples are no different from anywhere else; opportunists ready to take advantage of tourists' stupidity. Two areas which are dangerous at night are the university quarter (around Via Roma and Piazza Dante) and the Santa Lucia district (down towards the bay). Sadly some of the best hotels in the city are in those areas.

HOTELS

Cheapest doubles around 21,000L (£9.75; $17)

Tirreno, Via Giuseppe Pica 20 (tel. 281750). No singles.
Annadea, Via Milano 77 (tel. 5543311). Singles around 13,500L (£6.25; $11).
Fiore, Via Milano 109 (tel. 5538798). No singles. Doubles with shower/bath only slightly more expensive.

Manzoni, Vico Ferrovia 6 (tel. 5542960). Singles from 13,500L (£6.25; $11).

Sorrento, Via Milano 77 (tel. 282948). Singles around 13,500L (£6.25; $11).

Cheapest doubles around 24,000L (£11.25; $19.50)

Corso, Corso Umberto I 377 (tel. 283201). Singles around 14,750L (£7; $12).

Vittorio Veneto, Via Milano 96 (tel. 201539). Singles around 14,750L (£7; $12).

Cheapest doubles around 27,500–30,000L (£12.75–14.00; $22.50–24.50)

Bella Napoli, Via Carraciolo 10 (tel. 680234). Two-star hotel. Singles start around 14,250L (£6.75; $11.50). Via Carraciolo lines the waterfront near the Mergellina train station, so just walk down to the sea from the station.

Potenza, P. Garbaldi 120 (tel. 286330). Singles around 17,000L (£8; $14).

Teresita, Via Santa Lucia 90 (tel. 412105). Singles around 17,500L (£8.25; $14.50). A very safe and pleasant hotel, but in unsafe surroundings at night.

Zara, Via Firenze 81 (tel. 287125). Singles around 17,000L (£8; $14).

Cheapest doubles around 31,000–34,000L (£14.50–15.75; $25–28)

Al Trentino, Corso Umberto I 31 (tel. 5540397). No singles. Doubles with shower/bath are only slightly more expensive. A particularly good hotel.

Aurora, Piazza Garibaldi 60 (tel. 201920). Singles around 20,500L (£9.50; $17).

Crispi, Via Francesco Giordani 2 (tel. 664804). Singles around 17,000L (£8; $14). From the Mergellina train station, walk away from the sea, turn right along Via A. d'Isernia, then left on to Via Giordani. From Piazza Garibaldi you can take bus 4 to Via M. Schipa which is crossed by Via Giordani.

Cheapest doubles around 35,000–37,000L (£16.25–17.25; $28.50–30)

Casanova, Via Venezia 2 (tel. 268287). Singles around 17,000L (£8; $14).

Ginevra, Via Genova 116 (tel. 283210). Singles around 21,000L (£9.75; $17).

Imperia, Piazza Miraglia 386 (tel. 459347). Singles around 21,000L (£9.75; $17). Another very good hotel, but the area is unsafe at night. Take bus 185, CD or CS from Piazza Garibaldi to Piazza Dante in the heart of the university quarter.

Cheapest doubles around 38,000–41,000L (£17.75–19.00; $31.00–33.50)

Muller, Piazza Mergellina 7 (tel. 669056). A good two-star hotel near the Mergellina train station. Singles around 27000L (£12.50; $22).

Giglio, Via Firenze 16 (tel. 287500).

Sayonara, Piazza Garibaldi 59 (tel. 220313). Singles start around 24,500L (£11.50; $20).

Cheapest doubles around 43,000–45,500L (£20–21; $35–37)

Ausonia, Via Carraciolo 11 (tel. 682278). Two-star hotel on the waterfront near the Mergellina train station. Walk down to the sea from the station.

Speranza, Via Palermo 31 (tel. 269286) Two-star hotel.

Primus, Via Torino 26 (tel. 5547354).

Viola, Via Palermo 23 (tel. 269368).

Cheapest doubles around 47,500L (£22; $39)

Garden, Corso Garibaldi 92 (tel. 5336069). Singles start around 25,000L (£11.75; $20.50).

Cheapest doubles around 54,000L (£25; $44)

Cesare Augusto, Viale Augusto 42 (tel. 615981). Two-star

hotel near the Campi Flegrei train station. Walk round the right-hand side of the square on leaving the station until you see Viale Augusto on the right.

IYHF HOSTEL

'Mergellina', Salita della Grotta a Piedigrotta 23 (tel. 7612346). A fine hostel in a good location. 11.30 p.m. curfew. Three-day maximum stay in July and August. 18,000L (£8.50; $14.50). Only 300m from the Mergellina train station. Turn right, then right again from the station. From Napoli Centrale take a local train or the metro to Mergellina, or bus 152 from Piazza Garibaldi.

CAMPING

Camping Vulcano Solfatara, Via Solfatara 161, Pozzuoli (tel. 8673413). On the edge of a volcano crater. Open Apr.–Oct. Bus 152 from Piazza Garibaldi runs right to the site. Alternatively, you can take the metro or a local train (free with railpasses) to Pozzuoli. The site is a half-mile walk from the station in Pozzuoli, mostly uphill. When this site is closed ask the Tourist Office for details of the sites in Pompeii or Sorrento.

Padua (Padova) (tel. code 049)

Tourist Office
Azienda di Promozione Turismo di Padova, Riviera dei Mugnai 8, 35137 Padova. Write to this office if you want information on the city in advance. On arrival, head for one of the two APT information offices in the city. One is at the train station (tel. 8752077), open Mon.–Sat. 8 a.m.–6 p.m., Sun. 8 a.m.–noon; the other in the Museo Civico Eremitani on Piazza Eremitani (tel. 8751153), open daily 9 a.m.–6 p.m.

Basic Directions

Padua's train station on P. Stazione is just outside the sixteenth-century walls which run right round the historical centre of the city. Two main roads lead away from the train station out of P. Stazione: Viale Codalunga (on the right) and Corso del Popolo. The latter becomes Corso Garibaldi, which runs into Piazza Garibaldi, passing Piazza Eremitani on the way. From Piazza Garibaldi, you can walk straight ahead down Via Cavour, Via VII Febbraio, Via Roma and Via Umberto I to reach the area known as Prato delle Valle. From the train station to Prato delle Valle is a 15–20-minute walk.

Finding Accommodation

Except in the period June to early September, when many tourists unable to find suitable accommodation in Venice make their way to Padua (shamefully many never even bother to visit the wonderful attractions of Padua itself), you should have little trouble finding a reasonably priced bed in the city.

HOTELS

Prices for rooms without showers are more or less standard in the city's one- and two-star hotels. In one-star, hotels you can expect to pay around 25,000 (£11.75; $20.50) for a single, 34,000L (£15.75; $28) for a double. Rates in a two-star hotel are around 29,000–37,000L (£13.50–17.25; $23.50–30.00) and 47,000L (£22; $38) respectively. At the few one-star hotels offering singles with showers, prices range from 28,750–37,000L (£13.50–17.25; $23.50–30.00). Doubles with showers are more common, and usually cost in the region of 54,000L (£25; $44).

One-star hotels. Normal price for doubles; singles slightly cheaper at around 23,500L (£11; $19)

Basilea, Via Michele Sanmicheli 54 (tel. 44642). Doubles with showers around 46,000L (£21.50; $37.50). From Prato delle Valle, head down the left-hand side of the Basilica S.

Giustina and follow Via Cavazzana on to Via Micheli
Sanmicheli. The hotel is to your right.

Piccola Vienna, Via Beato Pellegrino 133 (tel.
8716331/8720020). From P. Stazione take Viale Codalunga
and head straight on until you see Via Beato Pellegrino on
your right.

Junior, Via L. Faggin 2 (tel. 611756). In the area between Via
T. Aspetti and Via A. Da Bassano. The former runs out
of P. Stazione, heading into the part of town to the rear
of the train station.

One-star hotels. Normal prices for singles and doubles

Al Camin, Via Felice Cavallotti 44 (tel. 687835). At the
opposite end of the old town from the train station. From
Prato delle Valle head down Corso Vittorio Emanuele. Go
straight ahead across Piazzale S. Croce into Via Felice
Cavallotti.

Al Pozzetto, Via N. Sauro 16 (tel. 664741). Great location,
just off Piazza dei Signori. From Piazza Garibaldi head
along Via S. Lucia and watch out for Via N. Sauro on the
left.

Al Santo, Via del Santo 147 (tel. 8752131). Singles with
showers are relatively cheap. Normal price for doubles
with showers. Central location. From Piazza Eremitani
follow Via degli Zabarelli into Via del Santo.

All'Ancora, Via del Santo 125 (tel. 651693). See the Al Santo
above.

All'Arca, Via del Santo 24 (tel. 656287). At the end of Via
del Santo. See the Al Santo above.

Arcella, Via Jacopo D'Avanzo 7 (tel. 605581). Singles with
showers are relatively cheap, doubles with showers slightly
above normal prices. From P. Stazione take Via T. Aspetti
heading into the area behind the train station. Via Jacopo
D'Avanzo is off to the right.

Bellevue, Via Luca Belludi (tel. 8755547). No basic doubles.
Doubles with showers at the normal price. Singles with
showers are available at the top of the price range quoted

above. The street runs between Prato delle Valle and Piazza del Santo.

Da Marco, Via Sorio 73 (tel. 8717296). Doubles with showers at the usual prices. Outside the city walls on the way to the airport.

Dante, Via San Paolo 5 (tel. 8760408). From Piazza Garibaldi follow Via S. Fermo into Via S. Pietro, then turn left.

Eden, Via Cesare Battisti 255 (tel. 650484). Doubles with showers available at the usual price. From Piazza Eremitani follow Via degli Zabarella, then turn left.

Giotto, Via Catania 1 (tel. 8711003). Outside the old town.

La Perla, Via Cesarotti 67 (tel. 8758939). From Piazza degli Eremitani follow Via degli Zabarella and then Via del Santo into Piazza del Santo, from which Via Cesarotti runs off to the left.

Pace, Via Papafava 3 (tel. 8751566). From Via Roma take the right turning after Solferino and look for Via Papafava running left off Via Marsala.

Pavia, Via Papafava 11 (tel. 661558). See the Pace above.

Riviera, Via Rodena 12 (tel. 665413). Doubles with showers available at the usual price. From Piazza Eremitani follow Via degli Zabarella and then Via del Santo. Via Rudena runs left off Via del Santo.

Venezia, Via Venezia 30 (tel. 8070499). Doubles with showers at the normal price. Head left from the station exit on to Via Nicol Tommasseo, which leads into Via Venezia.

Verdi, Via Dondi dell'Orologio 7 (tel. 663450). Good location, close to Piazza del Signori.

Two-star hotel. Singles around 26,500L ($12.25; $21.50), doubles around 40,000L (£18.50; $32.50)

Casa del Pellegrino, Via Cesarotti 21 (tel. 8752100). See the La Perla, above.

Two-star hotels. Singles around 31,000L (£14.50; $25), doubles around 47,000L (£21.75; $38.50)

Vienna, Via Beata Pellegrino 106 (tel. 8720020). See the

Piccola Vienna above.

Alla Fiera, Via Ugo Bassi 20 (tel. 8755094). From the train station head left on to Via Nicol Tommasseo. Continue straight ahead until you see Via Ugo Bassi on the right.

Buenos Aires, Via Luca Belludi 37 (tel. 651844). See the Bellevue, above.

Two-star hotels. Singles from 33,000L (£15.50; $27), doubles around 47,000L (£22; $38)

Maritan, Via Gattemalata 8 (tel. 850177). Just outside the city walls, close to the Ospedale Busonera.

Two-star hotels. Singles from 37,000L (£17.25; $30), doubles around 47,000L (£22; $38)

Sant'Antonio, Via S. Fermo 118 (tel. 8751393). The street runs off Piazza Garibaldi.

Svevo, Piazzale Pontecorvo 33a (tel. 650985). By the Parco Treves. From Piazza Eremitani, take Via degli Zabarella and keep going straight ahead until you see Via S. Francesco on your left. This street leads into Piazzale Pontecorvo.

Gattemalata, Via Gattemalata 78 (tel. 8071121). Just outside the city walls, close to the Ospedale Busonera.

HOSTEL

Centro Ospitalità Città di Padova, Via A. Aleardi 30 (tel. 8752219). Curfew 11 p.m. B&B around 15,500L (£7.25; $12.50). Bus 3, 8 or 18 from the train station.

IYHF HOSTELS NEARBY

'Rocca degli Alberi', Castello degli Alberi (Porta Legnago), Montagnana (tel. 429–81076/81320). Open Apr.–mid-Oct. B&B around 13,500L (£6.25; $11). Montagnana is about 25 miles from Padua, accessible by local train and bus. The hostel is 500m from the train station.

CAMPING

Strada Romana Aponense 104, Montegrotto Terme (tel.
793400). Open Mar.–Dec. The closest site to Padua. Bus
M runs to Montegrotto Terme, just over 10 miles away.

Pisa (tel. code 050)

Tourist Offices

Ente Provinciale per il Turismo (EPT), Lungarno Mediceo 42,
56100 Pisa (tel. 20351/20352). The administrative office of EPT
in Pisa. Contact this office if you require information in
advance.

EPT, Piazza del Duomo. Open July–Aug., Mon.–Sat. 8
a.m.–8 p.m.; at other times, 8.30 a.m.–12.30 p.m. and
2.30–6.30 p.m. The staff will help you find accommodation.
Bus 1 from the station, or a 15–20-minute walk. From the
station go straight ahead until you arrive in Piazza Vittorio
Emanuele II. Head left into Piazza S. Antonio, past the church
and then take Via Francesco Crispi down to the River Arno.
On the other side of the river, Via Roma leads you right into
Piazza del Duomo with the baptistry, the cathedral and the
Leaning Tower. Go right to the Tourist Office. Alternatively,
you can take Corso Italia from Vittorio Emanuele II right down
to the river. Cross the Arno and continue virtually straight
ahead (passing the EPT head office in the Casino dei Nobili
on the quayside) until you reach the Roman Baths. Turn left
along to the Leaning Tower. Taking the second route lets you
see more of the places of interest on the way.

HOTELS

In any of Pisa's one-star hotels you can expect to pay around
24,500–28,500L (£11.50–13.25; $20–23) for a single, 3900L (£18;
$32) for a double, though some hotels do have a limited number
of rooms available at lower prices. It is rare to find singles or

doubles with a bath/shower in a one-star hotel. Some two-star hotels have rooms which are the same price (or cheaper) than their equivalents in one-star hotels, but again these are limited in number. Normal prices in two-star hotels are 34,000L (£15.75; $28) for singles, 46,000L (£21.50; $37.50) for singles with bath/shower, 51,000L (£23.75; $41.50) for doubles, and 61,500–66,500L (£28.50–31.00; $50–54) for doubles with bath/shower.

Clio, Via San Lorenzo 3 (tel. 28446). One-star hotel. Doubles with a shower/bath around 43,000L (£20; $35).

Di Stefano, Via Sant'Apollonia 35 (tel. 26359). One-star hotel.

Galileo, Via Santa Maria 12 (tel. 40621). A few singles slightly cheaper than the norm for one-star hotels. See directions for the Tourist Office.

Giardino, Via C. Cammeo (tel. 562101). One-star hotel. Some singles slightly cheaper than normal, as well as a few doubles for 34,000L (£15.75; $28). Doubles with bath/shower are available at 43,000–51,000L (£20.00–23.75; $35–41.50).

Graziella, Via La Nunziatina 24 (tel. 42152). One-star hotel with a few singles slightly cheaper than normal and some doubles for 34,000L (£15.75; $28). From Piazza Vittorio Emanuele II (see Tourist Offices) take the street to the left of Corso Italia, and go straight down until you see Via La Nunziatina on the right of Via Mazzini.

Gronchi, Piazza Arcivescovado 1 (tel. 561823). One-star hotel with a few singles slightly cheaper than normal and some doubles around 34,000L (£15.75; $28). A short walk from Piazza del Duomo.

Helvetia, Via Don G. Boschi 31 (tel. 41232). One-star hotel with some singles available for around 17,000L (£8; $14) and some doubles at around 29,000L (£13.50; $23.50). Also has doubles with shower/bath for 40,000–47,000L (£18.50–22.00; $32–39). A short walk from Piazza del Duomo.

Maggiore, Via Colombo 49–51 (tel. 501459). One-star hotel. Singles with bath/shower available for around

28,000–34,000L (£13–15.75; $23–28), doubles with bath/shower around 47,000L (£22; $38)

Milano, Via Mascagni 14 (tel. 23162). One-star hotel.

Rinascente, Via del Castelletto 28 (tel. 502436). Doubles only in this one-star hotel, but some are as cheap as 21,000L (£9.75; $17)

San Rocco, Via Contessa Matilde 110 (tel. 42380). One-star hotel with some singles and doubles slightly cheaper than average. Via Contessa Matilde is the street at the back of the wall behind the Cathedral and the Leaning Tower. Go through the wall near the Leaning Tower.

Serena, Via D. Cavalca 45 (tel. 24491). Singles start around 14,500L (£6.75; $12), doubles around 22,500L (£10.50; $18.50) in this one-star hotel.

Amalfitana, Via Roma 44 (tel. 47830). Two-star hotel. Singles and doubles start at one-star hotel prices. See Tourist Office for directions.

Campaldimo, Via Tagliamento 24 (tel. 562363). Doubles with shower/bath only at this two-star hotel. Prices start at about 36,000L (£16.75; $29.50).

Cecile, Via Roma 54 (tel. 29328). Prices in this two-star hotel start around 20,500L (£9.50; $17) for singles, 28,500L (£13.25; $23) for singles with bath/shower, 34,000L (£15.75; $28) for doubles and 45,000L (£21; $37) for doubles with bath/shower. See Tourist Office for directions.

Roseta, Via P. Mascagni 24 (tel. 42596). Two-star hotel with a few doubles around the price normally paid in one-star hotels.

DORMITORIES

Casa della Giovane, Via Corridoni 31 (tel. 22732). Women only. Around 18,000L (£8.40; $15) per night, including breakfast. Reception open until midnight. A short distance from the station. Turn right on leaving the station.

CAMPING

Torre Pendente, Viale delle Cascine 86 (tel. 560665). Open
mid-Mar. to Oct. About 5 minutes' walk from the Leaning
Tower, past the cathedral and baptistry, out through the
old walls, turn right, then left.

Rome (Roma) (tel. code 06)

Tourist Offices
Ente Provinciale per il Turismo (EPT), Via Parigi 5 (tel. 4883748).
EPT Head Office, open Mon.–Sat. 8.15 a.m.–7 p.m. Much
shorter queues than at the EPT branch office in the Roma
Termini train station. Only 500m from Termini. On leaving the
station, head for the far left-hand corner of the square in front
of you (Piazza dei Cinquecento), go up Viale L. Einaudi,
around Piazza della Repubblica to the right, then along Via G.
Romita to the start of Via Parigi on the right.

EPT, Stazione Termini (tel. 4871270/4824078). Platform 3.
Open daily 9 a.m.–1 p.m. and 3–8 p.m. Very long queues are
the norm in summer. The office claims to have no information
on campsites.

EPT, Aeroporto Intercontinentale 'Leonardo da Vinci' (tel.
6000255). In the arrivals hall of the airport.

EPT, Autostrada del Sole A1 (Salaria services).

EPT, Autostrada del Sole A2 (Frascati services).

Ente Nazionale per il Turismo (ENIT), Via Marghera 2/6 (tel.
4971282). Open Mon.–Tues. and Thurs.–Fri. 9 a.m.–1 p.m.,
Wed. 4 –5 p.m. Information on the rest of the country only.
To get there, see **Around Roma Termini** below.

CTS (Student Travel Centre), Via Nazionale 66 (tel. 479931).
Open Mon.–Fri. 9 a.m.–1 p.m. and 4–7 p.m., Sat. 9 a.m.–1
p.m. As well as the usual travel services the office will help
find you accommodation. To get there, see **Around Roma
Termini** below.

Finding Accommodation

Rome has a vast stock of hotel rooms, so even in July and August when hordes of visitors flock into the city, there are still enough beds to go round. Nevertheless, finding one can still be frustrating. The area around the Termini station has the largest concentration of rooms and is the cheapest area of the city to stay in. Understandably, this is the area most popular with budget travellers. The sheer number of rooms in the area means you can make personal enquiries at a lot of hotels without having to walk very far, but consider leaving your pack at the station as many establishments are on the upper floors. Prices are generally higher in the city centre, and over the River Tiber around the Vatican City. Few owners will show you their cheapest rooms if they have others available. Cheaper rooms are usually only offered if you are on the point of leaving. The price set by the Tourist Authority for a room should be displayed in the room. Make sure what you are being asked to pay tallies with the price shown. It is not really wise to try and haggle an owner down from the official price in summer, as they can send you packing, safe in the knowledge that someone else will be along shortly. Although both the EPT offices in the city centre find rooms, they are not interested in finding rooms at the prices you will want to pay. Usually, however, they can be persuaded to phone any suggestions you give them, but do not expect them to consider such requests during July and August. At these times, the Student Travel Office (CTS) is likely to be more help. Railpass holders stuck for a bed should refer to the **Sleeping Rough** section below.

Trouble Spots

There is no area of the city you are likely to visit that is really violent, although the area around Termini station can get rough late at night. Unless you are stupid enough to sleep rough, there is little chance of you being robbed at knifepoint, but there is a high incidence of non-violent petty theft, particularly amongst crowds where wallets can be taken or rucksacks cut open. Obviously, the metro and buses offer a perfect setting for the sneak thief, so pay particular attention to your

belongings as you travel about (keep your rucksack in front
of you; hold small daysacks to your chest).

Around Roma Termini

Emerging from Roma Termini you face Piazza dei Cinquecento.
Turning left you can see Via Cavour running away from the
station and the square towards the Forum. Walking the whole
length of Via Cavour to the Forum takes about 12 minutes. On
the way, about 750m from Termini, you pass the Via Cavour
metro station. At the station, Via Giovanni Giolitti runs left
from the start of Via Cavour down the side of the station. Two
blocks down the side of the station you can turn right along
Via Gioberti. One block further on Via Cavour is crossed by
Via Giovanni Amendola. Following this road left leads you into
Via Filippo Turati. Another block along, Via Cavour is crossed
by Via Principe Amadeo. Again going left you can follow this
street as far as Via Lamarmora. Walk right a short distance
along Via Lamormora and you see the start of Via Principe
Eugenio. Going right from Via Cavour down either Via G.
Amendola or Via Principe Amadeo you cross Via Massimo
d'Azeglio before both streets end at Via del Viminale. Via
d'Azeglio runs out of the left-hand side of Piazza dei
Cinquecento, one street up from Via Cavour, while Via del
Viminale is an extension of Largo di Villa Peretti, one street
up from Via d'Azeglio. Viale L. Einaudi runs diagonally left
from the far left hand corner of Piazza dei Cinquecento to
Piazza della Repubblica. Going right around the Piazza you
can take Via Orlando into Via XX Settembre, going left you
can follow Via Nazionale to Trajan's Forum and the Vittorio
Emanuele II monument (an 8-minute walk away). From the
right-hand side of Piazza dei Cinquecento Via Marsala runs
down the side of the station. Walking right from the station
exit, you arrive at the point where Via Vicenza runs away from
the square. One block down Via Marsala, Via Marghera runs
off parallel to Via Vicenza, another block down Via Marsala
and Via Milazzo runs off parallel to Via Marghera and Via
Vicenza. Going up the right-hand side of Piazza dei
Cinquecento, Via Marsala becomes Largo Montemartini, and

then Via Volturno. From Largo Montemartini, Via Solferino
runs out of Piazza dei Cinquecento parallel to Via Vicenza. Via
Solferino runs into Piazza Indipendenza, on the other side of
which is Via San Martino della Battaglia. Via Gaeta, the small
Via Calatafimi, and then Via Montebello all run right off Via
Volturno as you head away from the station. Walking along
Via Solferino, Via Magenta runs from the Piazza Indipendenza
to Via Milazzo. Further along Piazza Indipendenza, Via dei
Mille and then Via Varese run to Via Milazzo and on to Via
Castro Pretorio. Opposite Via Varese, Via Castelfidardo runs
left from Piazza Indipendenza, crossing Via Gaeta and Via
Montebello before reacing Via XX Settembre. One block from
Piazza Indipendenza, Via San Martino della Battaglia is crossed
by Via Palestro, which runs between Via Castro Pretorio and
Via XX Settembre.

HOTELS

Cheapest doubles around 11,500L (£5.50; $9.50)

Ines, Via del Viminale 58 (tel. 4755972).

Cheapest doubles around 21,000L (£9.75; $17)

Margherina, Via Marghera 13 (tel. 491625).
Sibilla, Via Marghera 29 (tel. 4952336).

Cheapest doubles around 22,500L (£10.50; $18.50)

Termini, Via G. Amendola 77 (tel. 463667).
Valparaiso, Viale G. Cesare 47 (tel. 381076). Near the Vatican
  City. Metro stations Lepanto and Ottaviano are on the
  Viale Giulio Cesare.

Cheapest doubles around 24,500L (£11.50; $20)

Adas, Via Cavour 233 (tel. 4741432). Via Cavour runs left
  from Piazza dei Cinquecento to the Forum. Walking the
  whole length of Via Cavour from Termini station takes

about 20 minutes. Metro station Cavour is about 750m from Termini.

Di Rienzo, Via Principe Amedeo 79a (tel. 736956). Most rooms are more expensive.

Martini, Via Nazionale 18 (tel. 460994). Via Nazionale runs left from Piazza della Repubblica to Trajan's Forum and the Vittorio Emanuele II monument. Walking the whole length of the street takes about 8 minutes.

Paho Pehi, Via Vicenza 42 (tel. 491997).

Cheapest doubles around 27,000L (£12.50; $22)

Andreina, Via G. Amendola 77 (tel. 4818657).

Irpinia, Via Principe Amedeo 76 (tel. 4818016).

Lachea, Via San Martino della Battaglia 11 (tel. 4957256).

Rita, Via Volturno 42 (tel. 4040639).

Schiavo, Viale G. Cesare 47 (tel. 380021).

Urbis Romae, Piazza S. Pantaleo 3 (tel. 6540377). Piazza S. Pantaleo is on Corso Vittorio Emanuele II, near Piazza Navona in the heart of the city.

Wetzler, Piazza della Repubblica 47 (tel. 4827994).

Cheapest doubles around 31,000L (£14.50; $25)

Acropol, Via Principe Amedeo 76 (tel. 483726).

Aquila, Via Milazzo 8 (tel. 491837).

Katty, Via Palestro 35 (tel. 4751385).

Malian, Via Principe Amedeo 76 (tel. 481356).

Marciano, Via Cavour 136 (tel. 4753761).

Marini, Via Palestro 35 (tel. 4040058).

Moscatello, Via Principe Eugenio 51 (tel. 733675).

Orlanda, Via Principe Amedeo 76 (tel. 460637).

Cheapest doubles around 34,000L (£15.75; $28)

Bergamo, Via Gioberti 30 (tel. 7316308).

Cathrine, Via Volturno 27 (tel. 483634).

Cervia, Via Palestro 55 (tel. 491057).

Cipriani, Via Massimo d'Azeglio 24 (tel. 462713).

Cottorillo, Via Principe Amedeo 79a (tel. 7316064).

Fiorella, Via del Babuino 196 (tel. 3610597). Near the Spanish Steps. Via del Babuino runs between Piazza di Spagna and Piazza del Popolo. The two squares are only about 500m apart. Metro: Spagna or Flaminio.

Giulia, Via Calatafimi 19 (tel. 4817582).

Montestella, Via Palestro 88 (tel. 491269).

Noemi, Via Principe Amedeo 67 (tel. 485645).

Ortensia, Via Magenta 53/2–4 (tel. 495300).

Otello, Via Marghera 13 (tel. 490383).

Ottaviano, Via Ottaviano 6 (tel. 383956). A short walk from St Peter's Square. Metro: Ottaviano.

Restivo, Via Palestro 55 (tel. 492172).

Sardegna, Via Principe Amedeo 9 (tel. 4819887).

Silvia, Via Principe Amedeo 67 (tel. 4745518).

Stefanella, Via Magenta 39 (tel. 4451646).

Tony, Via Principe Amedeo 79d (tel. 736994).

Cheapest doubles around 37,000L (£17.25; $30)

Blanda, Via Castelfidardo 31 (tel. 4941378).

Chic, Via Cavour 266 (tel. 4758614).

Cressy, Via Volturno 27 (tel. 486956).

Giugiu', Via del Viminale 8 (tel. 4827734).

Leale, Via Milazzo 4 (tel. 4455661).

Mari II, Via Calatafimi 38 (tel. 4740371).

Marzia, Via Magenta 13 (tel. 4041551).

Perugia, Via del Colosseo 7 (tel. 6797200/6784635). Near the Colosseum. Off Via Cavour at Largo C. Ricci near the Forum. Metro: Colosseo or Cavour.

Cheapest doubles around 41,000L (£19; $33.50)

A. Marina, Via Gioberti 30 (tel. 737766).

Ascot, Via Montebello 22 (tel. 4741675).

Aurora, Via Magenta 39 (tel. 4957613).

Bruna, Via Maghera 13 (tel. 4959370).

Capri, Via Magenta 13 (tel. 491367).

Dell'Urbe, Via dei Mille 27a (tel. 4455767).

Galli, Via Milazzo 20 (tel. 4456859).
Giulia, Via Calatafimi 19 (tel. 4817582).
Jonella, Via della Croce 41 (tel. 6797966). Near the Spanish
   Steps. Via della Croce runs off Piazza di Spagna. Metro:
   Spagna.
Lucy, Via Magenta 13 (tel. 4451740).
Mari, Via Palestro 55 (tel. 492137/4462137).
Milani, Via dei Mille 7b (tel. 491313).
Milo, Via Principe Amedeo 76 (tel. 4745360).
Petrucci, Via Palestro 87 (tel. 491803).
Sud America, Via Cavour 116 (tel. 4745521).
Tortoriello, Via Principe Amedeo 76 (tel. 4743575).

Cheapest doubles around 44,000L (£20.50; $36)

Arrivederci, Piazza della Repubblica 47 (tel. 460334).
Baltic, Via XX Settembre 89 (tel. 485509).
Bianca, Via Volturno 48 (tel. 4040672).
Castelfidardo, Via Castelfidardo 31 (tel. 4742894).
Cherie, Via Cavour 238 (tel. 4741789).
Corallo, Via Palestro 44 (tel. 4456340).
Danubio, Via Palestro 34 (tel. 4041305).
Dolomiti, Via San Martino della Battaglia 11 (tel. 491058).
Eliana, Via Gioberti 30 (tel. 737764).
Ethel, Via Palestro 34 (tel. 4958134).
Eureka, Piazza della Repubblica 47 (tel. 4755806).
Everest, Via Cavour 47 (tel. 461629).
Fenecia, Via Milazzo 20 (tel. 490342).
Giorgina, Via Principe Amedeo (tel. 4817118).
Guidi, Via G. Amendola 95 (tel. 4756290/4826290).
Ida, Via Germanico 198 (tel. 386717). Near the Vatican City.
   Metro: Ottaviano, then follow Via Ottaviano to the start
   of Via Germanico.
Josè, Via Palestro 55 (tel. 490895).
Licia, Via Principe Amedeo 76 (tel. 4755293).
Lucia, Via G. Amendola 77 (tel. 4744722).
Palestro, Via Palestro 88 (tel. 4953218).
Pezzotti, Via Principe Amedeo 79a (tel. 734633).

Primerose, Via Montebello 104 (tel. 4041327).
Rosanna, Via XX Settembre 4 (tel. 483902).
Sallecchia, Via Principe Amedeo 85a (tel. 7310389).
Tokyo, Via Marsala 64 (tel. 4450365).
Vita, Via Magenta 38 (tel. 44653742).

Cheapest doubles around 47,000L (£22; $38)

Bolognese, Via Palestro 15 (tel. 490045).
Cosimo, Via Gaeta 71 (tel. 483027).
Esedra, Piazza della Repubblica 47 (tel. 463912).
Germano, Via Calatafimi 14a (tel. 486919).
La Fontanella, Via Palestro 87 (tel. 4455770).
Liz, Via Marsala 98 (tel. 491413).
Onella, Via Principe Amedeo 47 (tel. 465257).
Orbis, Via Principe Amedeo 62 (tel. 4745428).
Sant'Andrea, Via XX Settembre 89 (tel. 4814775).
Selene, Via del Viminale 8 (tel. 474478).
Taormina, Via Principe Eugenio 51 (tel. 7311378).
Tre Stelle, Via San Martino della Battaglia 11 (tel. 493095).
Ventura, Via Palestro 88 (tel. 4451951).

Cheapest doubles around 51,000L (£23.75; $42)

There are plenty of hotels around Termini Station with rooms
at these prices. Most of the hotels listed below have better
locations.

Amalia, Via Germanico 66 (tel. 314519/351968). See Hotel Ida.
Argentina, Via Cavour 41 (tel. 463263).
Ferraro, Via Cavour 266 (tel. 4743755).
Giuggioli, Via Germanico 198 (tel. 314938). See Hotel Ida.
Lady, Via Germanico 198 (tel. 314938). See Hotel Ida.
Nautilus, Via Germanico 198 (tel. 315549). See Hotel Ida.
Navona, Via dei Sediari 8 (tel. 6543802). Right in the centre
   of the city. Via dei Sediari runs out of Piazza Navona.
Piemonte, Via Vicenza 34 (tel. 4452240).
Primavera, Piazza San Pantaleo 3 (tel. 6543109). See Hotel
   Urbis Romae.

Cheapest doubles around 56,500L (£26.50; $46)

Davos, Via degli Scipioni 239 (tel. 389012). The street runs parallel to Via G. Cesare, one block closer to the Vatican City. Metro: Ottaviano or Lepanto.

Panda, Via della Croce 35 (tel. 6780179). See Hotel Jonella.

Suez, Via Filippo Turati 62 int. 6 (tel. 737353). All rooms have shower/bath.

IYHF HOSTELS

'Foro Italico-A.F. Pessina', Viale delle Olimpiadi 61 (tel. 3964709). 11 p.m. curfew. About 20,000L (£9.25; $16.50) for B&B. Well out from the centre, by the Olympic stadium (football every Sunday during the season, Roma or Lazio; occasional top-class athletics meetings). Metro A to Ottaviano, then bus 32.

The Italian YHA also let rooms in three university halls from about 20 July to 20 Sept. The price for B&B at these three residences is similar to that of the IYHF hostel. Enquiries for all three residences tel. 3242571 or 324573, or ask at EPT. Advance reservation: AIG, Via Carlo Poma 2, 00195 Roma.

Via Cesare de Lollis 20. About a mile from Roma Termini. Bus 492 from the station.

Viale del Ministerio degli Affari Esteri 6. Near the IYHF hostel. The hostel is the check-in point for this residence.

Via Domenico de Dominicis 13. Just over 2 miles from Roma Termini. Metro A to Colli Albani, then bus 409.

HOSTELS

YWCA, Via Cesare Balbo 4 (tel. 460460). Midnight curfew. Women only. Safe, if not cheap. Singles around 40,000L (£18.50; $33), doubles around 62,000L (£29; $51), triples around 75,000L (£35; $61). Near Roma Termini. Follow Via D'Azeglio from Piazza d. Cinquecento, go right at Via Torino, then left along Via Cesare Balbo.

Locando del Conservatorio, Via del Conservatorio 62 (tel.

659612). Singles around the price you will pay for dorms at the IYHF hostel, doubles slightly cheaper. Central location. Understandably popular, so write in advance.

Centro dei Giovani, Via degli Apuli 40 (tel. 4953151). Near the station. Fills fast.

CAMPING

No central site.

Flaminio, Via Flaminia Nuova (tel. 3332604). Open Mar.–Oct. Quite expensive. One of the closest to the centre (5 miles out). Metro A to Flaminio, then bus 202, 203, 204 or 205.

Roma, Via Aurelia 831 (tel. 6623018). Open all year. Bus 38 from Termini station to Piazza Fiume, then bus 490 to the last stop. Change to bus 246.

Nomentano, Via Nomentana (corner of Via della Cesarina) (tel. 6100296). Open Mar.–Oct. Bus 36 from Termini to Piazza Sempione, then bus 336 to Via Nomentana.

Salaria, Via Salaria 2141 (tel. 8887642). Open June to Oct. About 10 miles from the centre.

Capitol, Via Castelfusano 195, Ostia Antica (tel. 5662720). Open all year. Two miles from the ruins. Metro to Piramide, train to Lido Centro then bus 5 to the campsite. The train from Piramide to Ostia Antica leaves you a 2-mile walk to the site.

SLEEPING ROUGH

Lunacy. Even putting all your valuables in the left luggage and sleeping in the station is not advisable. Far better to sleep out at one of the campsites after leaving your pack and valuables at the station (Nomentano and Flaminio are the closest). Railpass holders can check in their luggage and valuables and then take the 0010 from Roma Termini to Ancona. The train arrives in Ancona at 0435. Ten minutes later you can catch a train back to Rome (arrives 0845). If you want to be absolutely sure of catching the return train get off in Falconara, the station before Ancona (arrives 0427, departs 0454).

Siena (tel. code 0577)

Tourist Office
The city Tourist Office was for many years located on the main square at Piazza del Campo 55 (tel. 280551). In 1992, the office was relocated to Via di Città 43, just off Piazza del Campo (open Mon.–Fri. 9 a.m.–12.30 p.m. and 3.30 –7.00 p.m.). If the Tourist Office is not operating in Via di Città in 1993, try the old location. Hotel accommodation can be booked at the Cooperative booth near the church of San Domenico on Viale Curtatone (tel. 288084). Open Mon.–Sat. 9 a.m.–8 p.m.

Finding Accommodation
With the exception of the days around the Palio (2nd July and 16th August), finding suitable accommodation has been relatively straightforward in the past. Although the city has few one-star hotels, private rooms are available and the city did have one of the best IYHF hostels in Italy, with a capacity of 110 beds. This hostel was closed in 1992. Unless it (or another hostel) opens in 1993 the competition for cheap rooms in Siena is likely to be fierce.

Basic Directions
The train station is about 1½ miles from the city centre. Incoming trains are met by a bus which drops passengers at Piazza Matteotti, a short walk from Piazza del Campo. From the square, head down Via dei Termini and turn left down any of the small streets on to Banchi di Sopra. Turn right and follow Banchi di Sopra to Piazza del Campo (head right from the end of the street to reach Via di Città). Intercity buses stop on Viale Curtatone, close to the church of San Domenico; again a short walk from Piazza del Campo. From the church, follow Via d. Paradiso, head right along Via della Sapienza, then right again at Costa S. Antonio. Going straight ahead, Via d. Galluzza and then Via d. Beccheria bring you on to Via di Citta, just off Piazza del Campo.

HOTELS

Singles around 25,500L (£12; $21), doubles from around 39,500–43,500L (£18.25–20.25; $32–36)

Bernini, Via della Sapienza 15 (tel. 289047).
Garibaldi, Via G. Dupré 18 (tel. 284204). Off Piazza del Campo to the right of the Palazzo Pubblico.

Singles around 25,500L (£12; $21), doubles around 43,500L (£20.25; $36)

Nuove Donzelle, Via delle Donzelle 3 (tel. 288088). Just off Piazza del Campo.
Tre Donzelle, Via delle Donzelle 5 (tel. 280358). Just off Piazza del Campo.
Cannon d'Oro, Via Montanini 28 (tel. 443211). Two-star hotel. No basic singles. Singles with showers start around 28,500L (£13.25; $23). Only a few doubles at the price quoted above. Others are much more expensive.

Singles around 23,000L (£10.75; $19), doubles from 46,000L (£21.50; $38)

Lea, Viale XXIV Maggio 10 (tel. 283207). Two-star hotel. Only a few rooms at these prices.

Singles from 23,000L (£10.75; $19), doubles from 49,000L (£23; $40)

Moderno, Via Peruzzi 19 (tel. 288453). Just outside the old city walls. From Piazza del Campo, take Banchi di Sopra and head straight on, turn right along Via di Vallerozzi, then right after passing through the town gate.

PRIVATE ROOMS

Book through the Tourist Office. Around 43,000L (£20; $35) for a double.

IYHF HOSTEL

'Guidoriccio', Via Fiorentina (Lo Stellino) (tel. 52212). A 20-minute walk from the city centre. Bus 10 or 15 from Piazza Matteotti. Arriving by bus from Florence you can ask the driver to let you off at Lo Stellino. The 1991 price was 11,000L (£5.25; $9). This hostel was closed in 1992. Check with the Tourist Office or the IYHF handbook to see if it has re-opened in 1993.

HOSTELS

Conservatori Feminili Riuniti, Via del Refugio (tel. 280376). Open to women only. Around 16,000L (£7.50; $13).

CAMPING

Campeggio Siena Colleverde, Strada di Scacciapensieri 37 (tel. 280044). Open 21 Mar.–20 Oct. About 1½ miles from the city centre. Until 10 p.m. you can take bus 10 from Piazza Matteotti to the site.

Turin (Torino) (tel. code 011)

Tourist Offices
Ente Provinciale per il Turismo (EPT), Via Roma 222 (tel. 535181/535901). The main EPT office on Piazza San Carlo. Open Mon.–Fri. 9 a.m.–5 p.m., Sat. 9 a.m.–noon. An EPT branch office operates in the main hall of the Porta Nuova train station, same hours as the main office.

Basic Directions
Torino Porta Nuova (the main train station) is located on the Corso Emanuele II. Just under 15 minutes' walk away is Corso Regina Margherita. The remarkably compact historic centre of Turin is located between these two main thoroughfares. Across

Corso Vittorio Emanuele II from Porta Nuova is Piazza Carlo
Felice, from which Via Roma runs into the impressive Piazza
San Carlo. Crossing the square, Via Roma leads into a second
important square: Piazza Castello with the Palazzo Madama.
Via Garibaldi leads out of the left-hand side of Piazza Castello
in the direction of Piazza d. Statuto by the Porta Susa train
station. From the right-hand side of the Piazza Castello, Via
Giuseppe Verdi runs into Corso San Maurizio, close to the
River Po, while Via Po leads into Piazza Vittorio Veneto, across
which is the Ponte Vittorio Emanuele I.

Trouble Spots
To the right of the main exit of Torino Porta Nuova Via Nizza
runs off Corso Vittorio Emanuele II down the side of the train
station. The area bounded by Via Nizza, Corso Vittorio
Emanuele II and the Parco Valentino contains many of the
cheapest hotels in the city. Women travelling without a male
companion, and certainly those travelling alone, would be
better to look for accommodation elsewhere in the city.
Although the area is not dangerous to walk about in, it is
slightly run down and on the sleazy side, and unaccompanied
women are likely to face harassment. The area on the opposite
side of Corso Vittorio Emanuele is fine, with hotels convenient
to both the train station and the city centre.

HOTELS

Cheapest doubles around 30,500L (£14.25; $25)

  Nettuno, Via Po 4 (tel. 8397291).

Cheapest doubles around 34,000L (£15.75; $28)

  Nelly, Via Palmieri 23 (tel. 740647). A 15-minute walk from
    Porta Nuova. Head left until you see the street heading
    right off Corso Vittorio Emanuele II.
  Palmieri, Via Palmieri 23 (tel. 740538). See Hotel Nelly.
  Passatempo, Corso Francia 318 (tel. 740538). Out from the

city centre. Corso Francia runs out of Piazza d. Statuto.
Studium, Via Carlo Alberto 47 (tel. 8395681). Head right from
the exit of Porta Nuova until you see the street running
left off Corso Vittorio Emanuele II.

Cheapest doubles around 38,500L (£18; $31.50)

Real Piemonte, Piazza Lagrange 1 (tel. 535447). Follow Via
Lagrange, parallel to the right of Piazza Carlo Felice.

Cheapest doubles around 40,500L (£18.75; $33)

Canaletto, Via Accademia Albertina 5 (tel. 832434). Head
right from the exit of Porta Nuova until you see the street
heading left off Corso Vittorio Emanuele II.
Domus, Via Giulia di Barolo 5 (tel. 830229). The street runs
out of Piazza Vittorio Veneto.
Serenella, Via Torino 4 (tel. 837031). By the River Po, well
out from the centre.
Aspromonte, Via Maria Vittoria 21 (tel. 8396818). Right off
Piazza San Carlo at the far end of the square as you walk
from Porta Nuova.
Fata Morgana, Via Maria Vittoria 21 (tel. 8396818). See Hotel
Aspromonte.
Soggiorno Flora, Via Nizza 3 (tel. 6698691). Right from the
exit of Porta Nuova, then right again down the side of the
station.

Cheapest doubles around 43,000L (£20; $35)

Kariba, Via San Francesco d'Assisi 4 (tel. 542281). Head left
from the exit of Porta Nuova until you see the street
running right off Corso Vittorio Emanuele II.
Massena, Via Massena 51 (tel. 588375). Head left from the
exit of Porta Nuova until you see the street running left
off Corso Vittorio Emanuele II.
San Carlo, Piazza San Carlo 197 (tel. 553522).
San Maurizio, Corso San Maurizio 31 (tel. 882434). The street
runs between the Po and Corso Regina Margherita.

Edelweiss, Via Madama Cristina 34 (tel. 6507208). Head right from the exit of Porta Nuova until you see the street running right off Corso Vittorio Emanuele II.

Lagrange, Piazza Lagrange 1 (tel. 538861). See Real Piedmont.

Via B. Galliari 9 (tel. 657257). Head right from the exit of Porta Nuova, turn right down the side of the station along Via Nizza then left at Via B. Galliari.

Cheapest doubles around 45,000L (£21; $37)

Ariston, Via Assieta 3 (tel. 543995). Go left from the exit of Porta Nuova, left down the side of the station on Via Sacchi, then right at Via Assieta.

Aurora, Via Carlo Alberto 47 (tel. 8397011). See Hotel Studium.

Casa Mariana, Via Principe D'Acaja 8 (tel. 761729). A 15-minute walk from Porta Nuova. Head left from the exit until you see the street running right off Corso Vittorio Emanuele II.

Castagnole, Via Berthollet 3 (tel. 6698678). Go right from the exit of Porta Nuova, right down the side of the station on Via Nizza, then left along Via Berthollet.

Florida, Piazza di Statuto 9 (tel. 518916).

Graziella, Via Mazzini 22 (tel. 877810). From Corso Vittorio Emanuele II take Via Lagrange, the street parallel to the right of Piazza Carlo Felice. Via Mazzini is on the right as you walk down Via Lagrange.

La Consalata, Via Nizza 21 (tel. 669879). Go right from the exit of Porta Nuova, then right down the side of the station.

La Primula, Piazza Carignano 8 (tel. 535102).

Marina, Via B. Galliari 12 (tel. 6699121). See Via B. Galliari 9.

Nuovo, Via B. Galliari 12 (tel. 689839). See Via B. Galliari 9.

Porta Nuova, Corso Vittorio Emanuele II 65 (tel. 543009).

Principe Tomasso, Via Principe Tomasso 8 (tel. 6698612). Head right from the exit of Porta Nuova, turn right down the side of the train station on Via Nizza and head straight on until you see Via Principe Tomasso on the left.

Romagnola, Via Carlo Alberto 47 (tel. 8395765). See Hotel
Studium.

Cheapest doubles around 47,500L (£22; $39)

Antico Distretto, Corso Valdocco 10 (tel. 5213713). Walking
down Via Garibaldi from Piazza Castello the street is on
the right just before you arrive at Piazza d. Statuto.
Doria, Via Accademia Albertina 42 (tel. 540222) See Hotel
Caneletto.

IYHF HOSTEL

'Torino', Via Alby 1 (tel. 6602929/683738). Around 17,500L
(£8.25; $14.50). Bus 52 from Corso Vittorio Emanuele II,
or a 20-minute walk from Porta Nuova. Head right from
the station, cross the Po by Ponte Umberto I, and head
straight on. At the fork in the road, go right on to Corso
Giovanni Lanza. Cross the road and follow Viale Enrico
Thovez, from which the hostel is off to the right.

CAMPING

Riviera sul Po, Corso Moncalieri 422 (tel. 6611485). Open year
round. Bus 67 from Corso Vittorio Emanuele II.

Venice (Venezia) (tel. code 041)

Tourist Offices
The APT Head Office at Ascensione 71f near Piazza San Marco
(tel 5226365) does not find rooms, which means anyone
wanting information only should go to this office to avoid the
queues at other APT offices. Open Mon.–Sat. 8.30 a.m.–7 p.m.
The APT office in Venezia Santa Lucia train station (tel. 715016)
finds rooms and gives out information. Open 8 a.m.–8 p.m.
daily. Exceptionally long queues in summer. From May to

September, the AVA Hotel Information at the bus station on Piazzale Roma offers advice on accommodation and books hotel rooms (tel. 5227402). Open Mon.–Sat. 9.30 a.m.–7.30 p.m., Sun. 1.30–5.00 p.m. The Centro Turistico Studentesco (CTS) at Dorsoduro 3252 on the Fondamenta Tagliapietra will help find rooms (tel. 705660). Open Mon.–Fri. 7 a.m.–12.30 p.m. and 3.30–6.30 p.m., Sat. 9 a.m.–12.30 p.m. Queues are shorter than at the train station.

Finding Accommodation

If you arrive in Venice during the summer it is safe to say you will never have seen a city so packed with tourists. This is especially true of August, when the Italians themselves are on holiday. Many visitors only stay in the city a few hours, but sufficient numbers stay overnight to make finding a room difficult. Ideally, you should reserve hotels in writing well in advance (Italian or English) stating clearly the type of room you want. Inform the hotelier at what time you expect to arrive, but if you get to Venice early go to the hotel as soon as you arrive just to make sure the room has been held. You can try phoning ahead, but even if you can communicate with an owner, they are generally loath to reserve one of their cheaper rooms. They will probably try to get you to accept a room with a private shower/bath, and breakfast, which can easily add 10,000–16,000L (£4.50–7.50; $8–13) per person to what you would pay for a basic double. If you arrive in Venice early in the morning, start queueing at one of the offices before opening time, as it could make the difference between getting one of the cheaper rooms or not. As reasonably inexpensive singles are few and far between, solo travellers might also find someone in the queue to team up with and get a double.

The Tourist Office hands out *Dormire Giovane*, a publication listing all the youth accommodations and their respective prices. If you want to stay in the IYHF hostel, reservations are recommended at all times. In the summer, you have to spend about three hours in a queue to have a hope of getting in without a reservation. Reservations for the city-run hostels are best made in writing one month in advance. Girls can stay at one of the dorms run by the religious orders. Curfews can be restrictive, but they are safe, and are more likely to have rooms than cheap hotels. Prices vary: some cost the same as hostels, others as much as hotels.

If you are having trouble finding suitably priced accommodation, consider staying in nearby Venezia-Mestre, where hotel prices are slightly lower, or in Padua. Both are linked to Venice by frequent trains, right up to midnight (Mestre is a 10-minute trip, Padua is only 30 minutes away).

Public Transport
Although the city has a few buses the routes are severely restricted. Boats are the main way to get about the city. An efficient *vaporino* service operates between 5 a.m. and midnight. All the stops are shown on most maps of the city, including the ones distributed by the Tourist Office. The *vaporetti* come in two forms: the slower boats known as *accelerati*, and faster boats for which a higher fare is charged. Passes are available for 24 hours and for three days, paying for themselves after six and ten trips respectively. Depending on how long you are staying, a Carta Venezia might be a good purchase. This pass gives the holder a 60 per cent discount on fares for a period of up to three years. You can get this pass (passport photo required) at the ACTV office by the S. Angelo stop.

Addresses
Streets and buildings in Venice are not numbered in the normal manner. Instead, districts are numbered at once, so that the number a house bears is its district number rather than a street number. There are six districts in the city: Cannaregio, San Polo, Santa Croce, Dorsoduro, San Marco and Castello.

HOTELS

Most of the city's one-star hotels charge around 50,000L (£23.25; $41) in doubles, though some do have a number of rooms which are cheaper than this. It is rare to find a single for under 27,000L (£12.50; $22). Normally, prices for singles in one-star hotels start at around 33,000–37,000L (£15.25–17.25; $27–30). A few two-star hotels offer some comparatively cheap rooms, but these are in short supply. Prices are slightly cheaper in Venezia-Mestre, where singles in one-star hotels generally start around 32,000L (£14.75; $26), doubles about 47,000L (£21.75; $38).

Cheapest doubles around 34,000L (£15.75; $28).

Alle Guglie, Rio Terra San Leonardo, Cannaregio 1523 (tel. 717351). Doubles only 34,000–39,500L (£15.75–18.50; $28–32). Head left from the station along Lista da Spagna, cross the Ponte d. Guglie. The hotel is not far from the bridge on Rio Terra San Leonardo.

Caneva, Ramo della Favia, Castello 5515/5518 (tel. 5228118). Some singles around 22,500L (£10.50; $18.50). Otherwise normal one-star prices for singles and doubles.

San Salvador, Calle Galiazza, San Marco 5264 (tel. 5289147). Singles 21,500–30,000L (£10–14; $17.50–24.50), some singles with shower/bath 27,000L (£12.50; $22), and some doubles with shower bath about 45,000L (£21; $37).

Alla Fava, Campo della Fava, Castello 5525 (tel. 5229224). This two-star hotel has some singles at 22,500L (£10.50; $18.50), and some doubles with bath/shower for around 51,000L (£23.75; $42).

Atlantico, Castello 4416 (tel. 709244). This two-star hotel has a number of singles for 22,500L (£10.50; $18.50) and some doubles with shower bath for 47,500L (£22; $38.50).

Diana, Calle Specchieri, San Marco 449 (tel. 5206911). Two-star hotel with a few rooms at the same prices as the Atlantico, above. A short walk from St Mark's Square. Calle Specchieri runs from S. Zulian towards San Marco.

Serenissima, Calle Goldoni, San Marco 4486 (tel. 700011). Two-star hotel with some singles for 23,500L (£11; $19) some doubles with bath/shower for 51,000L (£23.75; $42).

Tivoli, Dorsoduro 3838 (tel. 5237752). Two-star hotel with some singles at 22,500L (£10.50; $18.50) and some doubles with shower/bath for 56,500 (£26.25; $46). In the off-season prices are reduced by a fifth.

Trovatore, Calle delle Rasse, Castello 4534 (tel. 5224611). Two-star hotel with some rooms at the same prices as the Atlantico above. Excellent location, a few minutes' walk from St Mark's Square. Left from the waterfront at the second street after passing the Bridge of Sighs ('Ponte dei Sospiri').

Firenze, San Marco 1490 (tel. 5222858). Two-star hotel with some rooms similarly priced to the Atlantico above.

Walter, Fondamenta Tolentini, Santa Croce 240 (tel. 5286204). Two-star hotel with some rooms similarly priced to the Atlantico above.

Canal, Santa Croce 553 (tel. 5235480). Two-star hotel with some very cheap rooms. Singles from 22,500L (£10.50; $18.50), doubles from 34,000L (£15.75; $28), doubles with shower/bath from 47,000L (£22; $38.50). Other rooms of the same time in the hotel are about twice the price.

Sturion, Calle del Sturion, San Polo 679 (tel. 5236243). Some singles around 25,000L (£11.75; $20.50). Other singles and doubles at the usual price for one-star hotels. Excellent location overlooking the Grand Canal. From the Rialto Bridge follow Riva del Vin along the Grand Canal then take the fourth street on the right.

Alla Torre, Via Calle del Sale 52/54, Mestre (tel. 984646). Doubles only.

Col di Lana, Via Fagarese 19, Mestre (tel. 926879). Some singles at 20,500L (£11.75; $20.50), some doubles with bath/shower for 45,000L (£21; $37).

Primavera, Via Orlanda 5 (tel. 5310550). Also some singles at 22,500L (£10.50; $18.50), some doubles with shower/bath at 45,000L (£21; $37).

Doubles around 36,500L (£17; $30)

Casa Linger, Castello 3451 (tel. 5285920). Singles around 28,000L (£13; $23).

Cavallino, Via S. Dona 39, Mestre (tel. 611191). Doubles only.

Trento, Via Fagare 2, Mestre (tel. 926090). Singles 30,000L
(£14; $24.50).

Cheapest doubles around 36,500L (£17; $30), others at the normal price for one-star hotels

Bernardi Semenzato, SS Apostoli, Cannaregio 4363/4366 (tel.
5227257). Also some singles around 25,000L (£11.75;
$20.50). English speaking owner. Just off Strada Nuova,
near the Church of the Holy Apostles. Walk left from the
station along Lista de Spagna and keep going straight on
until you reach Strada Nuova, or take a boat to the stop
by the Ca d'Oro.

Da Bepi, Fondamenta Minotto, Santa Croce 160 (tel.
5226735). Cross the bridge near the station, turn left and
follow the Grand Canal to the Rio dei Tolentini. Do not
cross the water, but turn left and keep going, past the S.
Nicola da Tolentino church, then left onto Fondamenta
Minotto.

Eden, Cannaregio 2357 (tel. 720228).

Cheapest doubles around 39,000L (£18; $32)

Antiche Figure, S. Simeon Piccolo, Santa Croce 686a (tel.
718290). Singles 29,500L (£13.75; $24). The hotel is near S.
Simeon Piccolo, the church directly across the Grand Canal
from the train station.

Basilea (dipendenza), Rio Manin, Santa Croce 804 (tel.
718667). Other singles and doubles at the usual price for
one-star hotels. Close to the station. Cross the Grand Canal
and head up Calle Lunga, left across the Rio Marin, then
right along Fondamenta Rio Marin.

Da Pino, Crossera S. Pantalon, Dorsoduro 3941 (tel. 5223646).
Other doubles at the normal price for one-star hotels. Near
the S. Pantaleone Church, a short walk from Campo S.
Rocco across the Rio della Frescada.

Dalla Mora, Salizzada San Pantalon, Santa Croce 42a (tel.
5235703). Other doubles are slightly cheaper than average

for one-star hotels. In the off-season prices are reduced by a fifth.

Fiorita, Campiello Nuovo, San Marco 3457a (tel. 5234754). Other doubles are at the normal price for one-star hotels.

Marin, Ramo del Traghetto, Santa Croce 670b (tel. 718022). Also some singles around 26,000L (£12; $21), some doubles with shower/bath for 51,000L (£23.75; $42). Other singles and doubles at usual one-star hotel prices.

Toscana-Tofanelli, Via Garibaldi, Castello 1650–1653 (tel. 5235722). Near the Arsenal in Castello. From Pier 18 on the Piazzale Roma-Lido service cross the Rio di S. Giuseppe and walk down Viale Garibaldi into Via Garibaldi.

Villa Rosa, Calle della Misericordia, Cannaregio 388 (tel. 716569). Also some singles at 28,500L (£13.25; $23). Other singles and doubles at the usual price for one-star hotels. In the off-season, all room prices reduced by one-fifth. At this time, there are some doubles with bath/shower available at the normal price for doubles in a one-star hotel.

San Gallo, San Marco 1093a (tel. 5227311). Two-star hotel. Other doubles are around 61,000L (£28.50; $50).

Stella Alpina-Edelweiss, Calle Priuli, Cannaregio 99d (tel. 715179). Two-star hotel. Other doubles around 61,000L (£28.50; $50). Head left from the train station past the Church of the Barefooted and then left at Calle Priuli.

Al Veronese, Via Cappuccina 94a (tel. 926275). Other doubles are the normal price for a one-star hotel in Mestre. From Venezia-Mestre station, head right along the Via Della Giustizia, then take the left turn after Via Dante.

Montiron, Via Triestina 246, Mestre (tel. 5415068). Singles 22,500–28,500L (£10.50–13.25; $18.50–23.00). Other doubles are the normal price for a one-star hotel in Mestre.

Roberta, Via Sernaglia 21, Mestre (tel. 929355). All doubles at the price quoted above.

Trieste, Piazzale Stazione 2, Mestre (tel. 921244). Singles 23,500–28,500L (£11.00–13.25; $19–23), other doubles at the normal price for a one-star hotel in Mestre. By the station.

Vidale, Via G. Parini 2, Mestre (tel. 931968). All doubles at
the price above. Singles 28,500L (£13.25; $23).

Cheapest doubles around 43,000L (£20; $35)

Adua, Lista da Spagna, Cannaregio 233a (tel. 716184). Other
doubles at the usual price for one-star hotels. Close to the
train station. Head left into Lista da Spagna.

Rossi, Calle del Procurate, Cannaregio 262 (tel. 715164). Also
some singles at 26,500L (£12.25; $21.50). Other doubles at
the usual price for a one-star hotel.

Florida, Cannaregio 106 (tel. 715251). Two-star hotel. Also
some singles around 27,500L (£12.75; $22.50). Other singles
and doubles are considerably more expensive.

Gorizia a La Valigia, Calle dei Fabbri, San Marco 4696a (tel.
5223737). Two-star hotel. Some singles at 23,500L (£11;
$19). Other singles and doubles are considerably dearer.
Near St Mark's Square. From the Rialto Bridge head right
along the Grand Canal (past Pier 7 of the *vaporino* service)
and take the first left after crossing the Rio di S. Salvador.

Da Giacomo, Via Altinia 49, Mestre (tel. 610536). All doubles
at this price. Singles 20,500–23,500L (£9.50–11.00;
$16.50–19.00).

Dina, Via G. Parini 2/4, Mestre (tel. 5314673). Other doubles
are usual price for a one-star hotel in Mestre. Singles
24,500–28,500L (£11.50–13.25; $20–23).

Doubles around 47,500L (£22; $39)

Ai do Mori, Calle Larga San Marco, San Marco 658 (tel.
5204817). Excellent location, a few minute's walk from St
Mark's Square. Right off Mercerie, just behind the Clock
Tower.

Casa Carrettoni, Lista da Spagna, Cannaregio 130 (tel.
716231). Singles 26,500L (£12.25; $21.50). A short walk from
the train station. Head left on to Lista da Spagna.

Corona, Calle Corona 4464 (tel. 5229174).

Piccolo Fenice, San Marco 3614 (tel. 5204909).

Stefania, Fondamenta Tolentino, Santa Croce 181a (tel.

5203757). In the off-season prices are reduced by a fifth. At this time, you can get singles for 22,500L (£10.50; $18.50) and doubles with bath/shower for 52,500L (£24.50; $43). A 5-minute walk from the train station. Over the bridge, right along the Grand Canal then left before the bridge over the Rio de Tolentini. Watch out for the small lantern which marks the entry to the hotel.

Tiepolo, SS. Filippo e Giacomo, Castello 4510 (tel. 5231315). Excellent location, a short walk from St Mark's Square. Calle d. Albanesi, just past the Bridge of Sighs, leads into Campo SS. Filippo e Giacomo.

Adria, Via Cappuccina 34, Mestre (tel. 989755). See Al Veronese for directions.

Cortina, Via Piave 153, Mestre (tel. 929206). The main road heading away from Venezia-Mestre station off Via della Giustizia.

Giovanni, Via Dante 113, Mestre (tel. 926396). See Al Veronese for directions.

Johnny, Via Orlanda 223, Mestre (tel. 5415093).

La Triestina, Via Orlanda 62, Mestre (tel. 900168).

Le Perroquet, Via Orlanda 256a, Mestre (tel. 5415170).

Montepiana, Via Monte S. Michele, Mestre (tel. 926242).

Riva, Via Pescheria Vecchia 24b, Mestre (tel. 972566).

Doubles around 47,000–50,000L (£22–23; $38–41)

Al Gazzetino, Calle delle Acque, San Marco 4971 (tel. 5286523).

Al Piave-Da Mario, Ruga Giuffa, Castello 4840 (tel. 5285174). Good location. A 5-minute walk from St Mark's Square and the Rialto Bridge. From Piazza San Marco follow Mercerie to S. Zulian. From the church, head right along Calle d. Guerra and go on down Calle d. Bande to the S. Maria Formosa church. Go round the right-hand side of the church to the start of Ruga Giuffa. From the Rialto Bridge take Salizzada S. Lio to Calle d. Bande, then turn left.

Canal, Fondamenta Remedio, Castello 4422c (tel. 5228118).

Minerva e Nettuno, Lista da Spagna, Cannaregio 230 (tel. 715968). A short walk from the train station. Head left into Lista da Spagna.

Montin, Fondamenta di Borgo, Dorsoduro 1147 (tel. 5227151). From Pier 11 of the Piazzale Roma-Lido *vaporino* service, walk down past the S. Barnaba Church, then go left over Rio Malpaga after passing through the square.

Tintoretto, San Fosca, Cannaregio 2316–2317 (tel. 721522). Head left from the station on to Lista da Spagna and continue straight on until you reach S. Fosca church on Rio Terra d. Maddalena. The hotel is nearby.

Two-star hotels with some doubles around 47,000L (£22; $38)

Atlantide, Cannaregio 375a (tel. 716901). Also some singles at 23,500L (£11; $19).

Bartolomeo, Calle dell'Orso, San Marco 5494 (tel. 5235387). Also some singles at 23,000L (£10.75; $19).

Canada, San Lio, Castello 5659 (tel. 5235852). Price is for doubles with a shower/bath. Other rooms of the same type can be double the price. Near Campo S. Bartolomeo at the foot of the Rialto Bridge.

Caprera, Lista da Spagna, Cannaregio 219 (tel. 715271). Singles start from around 27,500L (£12.75; $22.50). Head left from the train station on to Lista da Spagna.

Centauro, Campo Manin, San Marco 4297a (tel. 5225832). From the Rialto Bridge, head left along the Grand Canal (past Pier 7 of the *vaporino* service) then turn left near the end of Riva d. Carbon down Calle Cavalli into Campo Manin.

Città di Milano, San Marco (tel. 5227002).

Da Bruno, San Lio, Castello 5726a (tel. 5230452). Near Campo S. Bartolomeo at the foot of the Rialto Bridge.

Hesperia, Cannaregio 459 (tel. 715251).

Lux, Castello 4541–4542 (tel. 5235767). Also some singles at 26,000L (£12; $21).

Madonna dell'Orto, Cannaregio 3499 (tel. 719955). Also some singles at 26,000L (£12; $21).

Cheapest doubles around 50,000L (£23.25; $41)

Al Gambero, Calle del Fabbri, San Marco 4687–4689 (tel. 5224384). See Hotel Gorizia a La Valigia for directions.

Al Gobbo, Campo S. Geremia, Cannaregio 312 (tel. 715001). In the off season prices fall by 20 per cent. A short walk from the train station at the end of Lista da Spagna. Head left from the exit.

Alex, Rio Terrà Frari, San Polo 2606 (tel. 5231341). Pleasant location near St Roch's (Chiesa di S Rocco). Prices are reduced by 20 per cent in the off season.

Antico Capon, Campo S. Margherita, Dorsoduro 3004/3008 (tel. 5285292). Just off the Rio di Ca' Foscari. Vaporino service to Pier 11 by the Ca' Foscari. Walk down to the S. Barnaba Church, diagonally across the square then left, right over the Rio S. Barnaba and straight on to the end of R.T. Canal then left.

Belvedere, Via Garibaldi, Castello 1636 (tel. 5285148). For directions, see Hotel Toscana Tofanelli.

Bridge, SS Filippo e Giacomo, Castello 4498 (tel. 5205287). Excellent location, close to St Mark's Square. See Hotel Tiepolo for directions.

Budapest, Corte Barozzi, San Marco 2143 (tel. 5220514).

Ca'Foscari, Calle della Frescada, Dorsuduro 3888 (tel. 5225817).

Casa Boccassini, Calle del Fumo, Cannaregio 5295 (tel. 5229892).

Casa de Stefani, Calle Traghetto S. Barnaba, Dorsuduro 2786 (tel. 5223337). Near the S. Barnaba church and the Ca' Foscari. The street running from Pier 11 of the *vaporino* service.

Casa Petrarca, Calle delle Colonne, San Marco 4386 (tel. 5200430). English speaking owner. From Riva d. Carbon, turn left up Calle d. Carbon into Campo S. Luca. Take Calle dei Fuseri on the other side of the square, second left, then first right.

Doni, S. Zaccaria, Castello 4656 (tel. 5224267). Not far from St Mark's Square. From the square go past the Bridge of

Sighs (Ponte dei Sospiri) and Pier 16 of the *vaporino* service, over the Rio del Vin, then first left to S. Zaccaria.

Galleria, Accademia, Dorsoduro 878a (tel. 5204172). Near the Accademia. Pier 12 of the *vaporino* service.

Guerrato, Calle Dietro la Scimmia, San Polo 240a (tel. 5227131).

Marte, Ponte della Guglie, Cannaregio 338 (tel. 716351). A short walk from the train station. Head left along Lista da Spagna to the Guglie bridge.

Messner, Salute, Dorsoduro 236 (tel. 522743). Near the Basilica della Salute. Pier 14 of the *vaporino* service.

Moderno, Lista da Spagna, Cannaregio 154b (tel. 716679).

Raspo de Ua, Piazza Galuppi 560 (tel. 730095).

Rio, SS Filippo e Giacomo, Castello 4356 (tel. 5234810). Good location, close to St Mark's Square. See Hotel Tiepolo for directions.

Riva, Ponte dell'Anzolo, Castello 5310 (tel. 5227034).

San Geremia, Campo San Geremia, Cannaregio 290a (tel. 716245). Near the train station. See Hotel Al Gobbo for directions.

San Samuele, Piscina S. Samuele, San Marco 3358 (tel. 5228045).

Sant'Anna, Sant'Anna, Castello 269 (tel. 5286466). Near the Arsenal. See Hotel Marin above for directions. Turn right on Via Garibaldi and follow the street into Sant'Anna.

Santa Lucia, Calle Misericordia, Cannaregio 358 (tel. 715180). Head left from the train station into Lista da Spagna, then go left.

Silva, Fondamenta Remedio, Castello 4423 (tel. 5227643).

Two-star hotels with some doubles priced around 50,000L (£23.25; $41)

Basilea, Rio Marin, Santa Croce 817 (tel. 718477). See 24 for directions.

Bucintoro, Riva degli Schiavoni 2135 (tel. 5223240).

Gallini, Calle della Verona, San Marco 3673 (tel. 5236371).

Guerrini, Cannaregio 265 (tel. 715333).

La Calcina, Zattere, Dorsoduro 780 (tel. 5206466). Prices fall
by 20 per cent off-season.

IYHF HOSTEL

'Venezia', Fondamenta di Zitelle 86, Isola della Giudecca (tel.
5238211 Fax 041–5235689). On Giudecca island. 11 p.m.
curfew. 20,000L (£9.30; $16.50). Members only, but
membership cards are sold at the hostel: 15,000L (£7;
$12.50). Waterbus 5 from the train station, or 8 from S.
Zaccaria (left along the canal as you leave St Mark's Square)
to Zitelle, then walk right. Hostel opens 6 p.m. Queue from
3 p.m. if you have not reserved in advance.

CITY HOSTELS

In the past, the city authorities have operated hostels during
the summer (mid-July to mid-Sept.). Prices and curfews similar
to those of the IYHF hostel, but the city hostels are more
conveniently located. Reservations for the city hostels are
handled by the IYHF hostel (address above). It is always
advisable to write at least one month before your date of arrival.
As there is no guarantee that any city hostels will be open in
1993 you might want to give the IYHF hostel as an alternative
in your letter.

S. Caboto, Cannaregio 1105f (tel. 716629). By the Canale di
Cannaregio, 10 minutes from the station. Head left along
Lista da Spagna to the Guglie Bridge and the Canale di
Cannaregio. The hostel is signposted from the bridge.
Various accommodation options. Cheapest of all is
throwing down a mat and a sleeping bag in the grounds;
then camping in your tent in the grounds; followed by a
night in the tents they hire out; and, lastly, dorm beds.

R. Michiel, Dorsoduro 1184 (tel. 5227227). Close to the
Accademia (waterbus 1, 2 or 34).

S. Fosca, Cannaregio 2372 (tel. 715775). A short walk from
Campo S. Fosca.

HOSTELS/DORMITORIES

Istituto Canossiane, Fondamento del Ponte Piccolo 428, Isola della Giudecca (tel. 5222157). Curfew 10.30 p.m. Dorms. Women only. Run by nuns. 14,500L (£6.75; $12). Same waterbuses as the IYHF hostel above, but get off at the Sant'Eufemia stop. Short walk to your left.

Foresteria Valdese, Castello 5170 (tel. 5286897). No curfew. B&B 18,000L (£8.50; $15) in dorms, 22,000L (£10.25; $18) er person in one of the limited number of doubles and quads. *Vaporetto* stop: S. Zaccaria. Walk away from the water to the S. Zaccaria church then head left. Go right along S. Provolo, then left over the Rio dell'Osmarin and down Ruga Giuffa into Campo S. Maria Formosa. From the right-hand side of the square follow Calle Lunga to its end. The hostel is by the bridge.

Domus Civica, Calle Chiovere & Calle Campazzo, San Polo 3082. Near the Frari church (tel. 5227139). Open June–July and Sept–mid-Oct. Curfew 11.30 p.m. Women only. Singles around 27,000L (£12.50; $22); doubles around 22,000L (£10.25; $18) per person.

Domus Covanis, Rio Terra Foscarini, Dorsoduro 912 (tel. 5287374). Open June–Sept. 11.30 p.m. curfew. Doubles 49,000L (£22.75; $40). Separate rooms for men and women in this church-run hostel.

Archie's House, Rio Terra San Leonardo, Cannaregio 1814b (tel. 720884). Open to those aged 21 and over only. 14,500–18,500L (£6.75–8.75; $12–15). Head left from the train station along Lista da Spagna, over the Guglie Bridge and into Rio Terra San Leonardo.

CAMPING

Waterbus 15 will take you to the Littorale del Cavallino, a peninsula with a string of campsites along its beach. Some charge ridiculously high prices.

Marina da Venezia, Via Hermada (tel. 966146). Open all year. 10,000–20,000L (£4.60–9.20; $8.00–16.50) per tent;

3,500–7,000L (£1.50–3.00; $3.00–5.75) p.p. depending on the time of year.

Ca' Pasqualli, Via Fausta (tel. 966110). Only slightly cheaper than the site above.

Camping Fusina, Via Moranzani, Fusina (tel. 5470055). 25,000L (£11.50; $20.50) per tent, 5000L (£2.30; $4) per person. From Mestre, bus 13 from opposite the Pam supermarket to the last stop. Last bus at 10p.m., a one-hour trip. In summer, *vaporetto* 5 to Zattere, then 16 to Fusina takes about 30 minutes. Mosquito repellant is essential.

San Nicolo, on the island of Lido (tel. 767415). Ferry to Lido, then bus A.

See also the city hostels section above.

SLEEPING ROUGH

Thieves patrol the beaches of the Lido island looking for easy targets. If you choose to sleep here, bed down beside other travellers. Even then ants and mosquitoes can make for an unpleasant night. Sleeping on the train station forecourt is illegal, and the police occasionally use water hoses to clear people away.

Verona (tel. code 045)

Tourist Offices

Ente Provinciale per il Turismo (EPT), Piazza delle Erbe 42 (tel. 30086). The administrative. Contact this office if you want information before setting off on holiday. On arrival, head for the office at Via Dietro Anfiteatro 6b, behind the Roman Arena (tel. 592828). Open Mon.–Sat. 8 a.m.–8 p.m., Sun. 9 a.m.–2 p.m. If you are arriving by car or motorbike from Milan or Venice, there is a city information office at the turn-off from the motorway.

Basic Directions

The Verona Porta Nuova train station is about 20 minutes' walk from the Piazza delle Erbe in the centre of the Old Town. Going right from the station, you arrive at the Porta Nuova, the old city gate from which the station takes its name. Turning right at this point, you can follow the road under the railway lines and down Viale Piave and Viale delle Lavoro to the Milan-Venice highway. Turning left at the Porta Nuova, you can follow Corso Porta Nuova towards the town centre. Passing through the old city walls, you arrive at Piazza Bra' with the famous Roman Arena. To the left as you enter the square, Via Roma leads off in the direction of the Castelvecchio by the River Adige. Going around the Arena, you can take Via Giuseppe Mazzini from the opposite side of Piazza Bra' into the Piazza delle Erbe. Bus 2 runs from Verona Porta Nuova to the Piazza Bra', if you want to save yourself about two thirds of the walk.

HOTELS

Cheapest singles 17,500L (£8.25; $14.50), cheapest doubles 24,500L (£11.50; $20)

Elena, Via Mastin della Scala 9 (tel. 500911). Also some doubles with bath/shower for 38,500L (£18; $31.50). Other similar rooms in this two-star hotel are around double the prices quoted.

One-star hotels. Doubles around 29,000L (£13.50; $23.50)

Borghetti, Via Val Policella 41 (tel. 941045). Singles around 18,500L (£8.50; $15).
Alla Cancellata, Via Col. Fincato 4/6 (tel. 532820). Normal rate for singles.

One-star hotels. Doubles 29,000–32,000L (£13.50–15.00; $23.50–26.00)

Catullo, Via V. Catullo 1 (tel. 8002786). Singles 17,000–21,500L (£8–10; $14.00–17.50). Left off Via Mazzini

between the Piazza Bra' and the Piazza Erbe.
Da Luigi, Via Rodigina 92 (tel. 548737).

**One-star hotels. Singles 23,500L (£11; $19), doubles
32,000–34,000L (£15–16; $26–28)**

Ciopeta, Via Teatro Filarmonico 2 (tel. 8006843).
Da Andrea, Vicoletto Cieco Disciplina 2 (tel. 32291).
Usignolo, Stradone Santa Lucia 36 (tel. 954344). No singles
    available. The main road running from Viale Piave along
    the back of the train station.

**One-star hotels. Singles 23,500L (£11; $19), doubles
34,000L (£16; $28)**

Al Castello, Via Cavour 43 (tel. 8004403). Near the
    Castelvecchio.
Romano, Via Tombetta 38 (tel. 505228). In the area behind
    Porta Nuova station, left off Viale Piave. A 5–10-minute
    walk from the station.
Rosa, Vicolo Raggiri 9 (tel. 8005693).
Santa Teresa, Via Scuderlando 87 (tel. 501508). In the area
    behind the train station. Left off Viale del Lavoro at Viale
    Agricultura, right at the end of this street into Via
    Scuderlando. A 10-minute walk from Porta Nuova.

**One-star hotels. Singles 26,000L (£12; $21), doubles
34,000L (£16; $28)**

Al Cigno, Corso Milano 26 (tel. 567716). A 15-minute walk
    from the station and town centre. Take either of the roads
    leading away from the station on the left of the exit, cross
    the canal and go left on Viale Luciano Dalcero and straight
    on down Viale Colonello Galliano, then left at Corso
    Milano.
Al Sole, Via Stanga 11 (tel. 565012).
Armando, Via Dietro Pallone 1 (tel. 8004824).
Volto Citadella, Vicolo Volto Citadella 8 (tel. 8000077).

One-star hotels. Doubles 34,000L (£16; $28), no singles

Alla Grotta, Via Bresciana 16 (tel. 564865).
La Serenissima, Viale del Lavoro 24 (tel. 501858). A
5–10-minute walk from Porta Nuova, in the area behind
the station.

**Cheapest singles with bath/shower 25,000L (£11.75;
$20.50), cheapest doubles with bath/shower 37,500L
(£17.50; $31)**

Selene, Via Bresciana 81 (tel. 8510319). Other rooms of these
types in this two-star hotel are 50 per cent dearer. No
rooms without bath/shower.

**Two-star hotels with some doubles available at around
41,000L (£19; $33.50)**

Scalzi, Via Carmelitani Scalzi 5 (tel. 590422).
Trento, Corso Porto Nuova 36 (tel. 596037).
Valverde, Via Valverde 91 (tel. 33611/31267). A 10-minute
walk from Porta Nuova. Straight on from the station,
across the gardens to the canal. Over the canal and then
virtually straight on down Via Città di Nimes into Piazza
Simone, then take Via Giberti on the right hand side of
the square into Via Valverde.

IYHF HOSTEL

Salita Fontana del Ferro 15 (tel. 590360). Curfew 11 p.m.,
extended for opera goers. 15,000L (£7; $12.50). Camping
permitted 8,000L (£3.75; $6.50). Behind the Teatro Romano,
2 miles from the station, but only 10 minutes' walk from
the town centre. Bus 2 from Verona Porta Nuovo.

DORMITORIES

Both are open to women only. Normal curfews are extended
if you are going to the opera.

Casa della Giovane, Via Pagni 7 (tel. 596880). Curfew 10.30
p.m. 14,000–23,000L (£6.50–10.75; $11.50–19.00). Higher
prices are for small rooms.
Casa della Studentessa, Via G. Trezza 16 (tel. 8005278).

CAMPING

Romeo e Giulietta, Via Bresciana 54 (tel. 989243). Open all
year. Three miles from the centre on the road to Brescia.
Castel San Pietro, Via Castel San Pietro (tel. 592037). Near
the IYHF hostel, a 10-minute walk from the centre.
Salita Fontana del Ferro 15 (tel. 590360). In the grounds of
the IYHF hostel. 8000L (£3.75; $6.50) for a solo traveller.

LUXEMBOURG
(Lëtzebuerg)

If you arrive in Luxembourg having previously visited Belgium, you will notice a similarity both in the types of accommodation on offer, and in the prices of different accommodation options. On the whole, with the exception of IYHF hostels, standards in the various types of accommodation are also on a par with those in Belgium. Prices in **hotels and pensions** start around 800LF (£13.50; $23.50) in singles, 1300LF (£21.75; $38) in doubles. A less expensive option in the more popular tourist towns such as Echternach, Vianden, Clervaux and Wiltz is the availability of **rooms in private homes**. Prices for private rooms range from 500–1000LF (£8.25–16.75; $14.50–29.50). These tend to fill quickly, so it is best to make enquiries as early in the day as possible. You can either ask about their availability at the local Tourist Office (i.e. not the National Tourist Office in the city), or approach the owner of any house advertising rooms to let (signs are usually printed in French, German, Dutch and English).

Considering their price, the facilities on offer, and the high standards of comfort and cleanliness, the Grand-Duchy's small network of **IYHF hostels** must rank among the best in Europe. All the hostels are open from mid-April to September but, at other times, different hostels are closed for anything between two days to six weeks. Curfews are normally 11 p.m. (midnight in Luxembourg). To stay at one of the hostels, a valid membership card is essential. The cost of B&B varies between 280–320LF (£4.75–5.50; $8.00–9.50), except in Luxembourg where prices range from 320–380LF (£5.50–6.50; $9.50–11.00). Other meals are available and you can cook your own food if you want, as all the hostels have kitchen facilities. Duvets (rather than the usual blanket) are supplied, but you must have a linen sheet sleeping bag – either your own, or one hired from the hostel at a cost of 100LF (£1.75; $3) – for the duration of your stay. This could be shorter than you might hope, as the maximum stay at any hostel is limited to three days, and only one day at peak periods (July and August). These rules are only enforced when the hostel is full, but it is as well to be aware of them.

Most of the main places of interest have a hostel. One notable exception is Clervaux, but here there is the choice of two of the small network of **gîtes d'étapes**. Most are open all year and prices range from 80–120LF (£1.25–2.00; $2.50–3.50).

Of the 120 or so **campsites**, only around 30 are open for the whole year. However, the vast majority are open March/April to September. The pamphlet 'Camping Grand-Duché de Luxembourg' clearly lists both opening periods and amenities. Standards do vary, but even the more basic sites are perfectly acceptable. Two people can expect to pay roughly 325LF (£5.50; $9.50) per night. All the main places of interest are covered, often with several sites. For anyone wishing to spend more than a few days in Luxembourg during the peak season (late June to August), camping is undoubtedly the best option available. Even at this time, those with only a small tent will rarely have any trouble finding a space at one of the sites in town. In the unlikely event of encountering any difficulties in the peak season, the 'Camping Guidage' service of the National Tourist Office will give advice on sites with vacancies in the area (tel. 481199 from 11 a.m. to 7.30 p.m.).

Due to the small size of the country, it is possible to visit all the places of interest on day-trips from the capital. However, accommodation prices are higher in the city and inexpensive accommodation is usually more difficult to find. Not only do many people choose to make the city a base for touring about, but it is also the arrival/departure point for Americans travelling on cheap Icelandair tickets looking for a place to spend their first or last night in Europe. Arguably, it is far more enjoyable to get out of the city and stay in the towns you visit, or, as is quite feasible, to stay in one of the smaller towns and make several day-trips from them.

Whichever option you choose, throughout most of the year you should not have much difficulty finding suitable accommodation. However, if you are travelling during the period late June to August, this happy situation alters dramatically. At these times, finding a bed of any kind in the capital, or in the smaller towns, can become very tricky. Outside of the city the two main tourist destinations are Vianden and Echternach. Because of its historic links with the House of Orange-Nassau, Vianden is thronged with Dutch tourists in summer, which makes finding a bed in a hotel, private home or the youth hostel nigh on impossible unless you arrive early in the morning. Those with a small tent should have no trouble finding a space at one of the three campsites by the River Our. Although Echternach is not quite as busy, an early arrival is still advisable unless you have fixed accommodation in advance. Again, those with tents have little to worry about as there are two campsites in Echternach, while a short walk will take you to the cheap municipal site in the German town of Echternacherbrücke on the other bank of the River Sure. There are also a number of private rooms available in Echternacherbrücke; look out for the *Zimmer frei* signs.

ADDRESSES

Luxembourg National Tourist Office	36/37 Piccadilly, London W1V 9PA (tel. 071-434 2800).
Luxembourgeois YHA	Centrale des Auberges de Jeunesse Luxembourgeoises, 18 Place d'Armes, BP 374, L–2013 Luxembourg (tel. 25588).
Camping	List available from the Luxembourg National Tourist Office in London or your capital city.
Gîtes d'Étapes	Gîtes d'Étapes de Grand-Duché de Luxembourg, Bd. Prince Henri 23, L–1724 Luxembourg (tel. 23698/472172).
	List available from the Luxembourg National Tourist Office.

Luxembourg (Lëtzebuerg)

Tourist Offices
Office National du Tourisme, Place de la Gare, Luxembourg
(tel. 481199). Open daily, from July–mid-Sept., 9 a.m.–7.30
p.m.; at other times, daily from 9 a.m.–noon and 2–6.30 p.m.
except mid-Nov.–mid-March when the office is closed
Sundays. By the Luxair terminal to the right of the train station.
There is another branch at Luxembourg-Findel airport. Both
offices provide information and services covering the whole
country.

Syndicat d'Initiative et de Tourisme de la Ville de
Luxembourg, Place d'Armes, B.P. 181, Luxembourg (tel.
22809). Open July–mid-Sept., Mon.–Fri. 9 a.m.–1 p.m. and
2–8 p.m., Sat. closes at 7 p.m., Sun. 10 a.m.–noon and 2–6
p.m.; at other times, open Mon.–Sat. 9 a.m.–1 p.m. and 2–6
p.m. Information and services for the city only. Place d'Armes
is right in the heart of the city.

HOTELS

All the hotels listed are about a 5–10-minute walk from Place
de la Gare in front of the train station, unless otherwise stated.

**Cheapest doubles around 1250LF (£21; $36.50). Singles as
shown**

Carlton, 9 rue de Strasbourg (tel. 484802/481745). Singles from
600LF (£10; $17.50). Head right past the Luxair terminal.
Rue de Strasbourg is across the road on the left.

Bristol, 11 rue de Strasbourg (tel. 485829/485830). Singles from
800LF (£13.50; $23.50). Directions Hotel Carlton above.

**Cheapest doubles around 1400LF (£23.50; $41). Singles as
shown**

Axe, 33–34 rue Joseph Junck (tel. 490953). Singles from 900LF
(£15; $26.50). The street is at the right end of Place de la
Gare.

Family, 38 avenue du X Septembre (tel. 452669). Singles start around 1000LF (£16.75; $29.50). Not central.

Cheapest doubles around 1500LF (£25; $44). Singles as shown

Le Parisien, 46 rue Ste-Zithe (tel. 492397). Singles start around 950LF (£16; $28). Right from Pl. de la Gare. At the fork left down Av. de la Liberté. Rue Ste-Zithe is left off Pl. de Paris.

Papillon, 9 rue Origer (tel. 494490). Singles from 1000LF (£16.75; $29.50). Right from Place de la Gare. At the fork right down Av. de la Gare, then left.

Paradiso, 23 rue de Strasbourg (tel. 484801/403691). Singles start around 950LF (£16; $28). Directions see Hotel Carlton, above.

Cheapest doubles around 1700LF (£28.50; $50). All rooms have baths/showers. Similar rooms are available for about the same amount at all the hotels above with the exception of Hotels Axe and Bristol.

Mertens, 16 rue de Hollerich (tel. 482638). Off to the right at the left-hand end of Place de la Gare.

New Chemin de Fer, 4 rue Joseph Junck (tel. 493528). Directions Hotel Axe above.

IYHF HOSTEL

2 rue de Fort Olisy (tel. 26889). 1 a.m. curfew, reasonably flexible. About 1½ miles from the station. Bus 9 from the station (or the airport) to the Vallée d'Alzette.

CAMPING

Luxembourg-Kockelscheur (tel. 471815). Open Easter/mid-Apr. to Oct. 2½ miles from the train station. Bus 2 from the station.

MOROCCO (Maroc)

The price of accommodation in Morocco is so low that a decent hotel room should be well within your budget. **Hotels** are divided into two main categories, classé and non-classé. The former are regulated by the National Tourist Authority, which both grades them on a scale rising from one star to five-star luxury, and fixes their prices. The one- to four-star grades are further subdivided A and B. At the lower end of the scale there is only a small variation in prices, and in the facilities offered. Even the one-star establishments offer a level of comfort and cleanliness you are unlikely to find in a non-classé hotel. As a rule, classé hotels are situated in the ville nouvelle – the new town or administrative quarters built during the French colonial period. All classé hotels are listed in the publication 'Royaume de Maroc Guide des Hôtels'.

Non-classé hotels enjoy two advantages over classé hotels: location, and, outside peak periods, price. In peak season (August, Christmas and Easter) it is not uncommon for non-classé hotels to raise their prices sharply, so that they actually exceed the price of one-star B and one-star A establishments. Non-classé hotels, which are neither listed nor regulated by the National Tourist Authority, are generally located in the medina, the old, Arab-built part of the town. Staying here, you will be close to the markets, historic buildings and the bewildering array of street performers. However, the medina, with its twisting, narrow streets, can be an intimidating place. The quality of hotels varies greatly: while some offer spotless, whitewashed rooms looking out on to a central patio, there are also a considerable number that are filthy and flea ridden. You are also far more likely to encounter problems with a poor water supply and primitive toilet facilities in the medina.

A room in the medina should cost in the region of 20–30 dh

(£1.40–2.20; $2.50–4.00). A spacious, more comfortable room in a classé hotel in the ville nouvelle might cost about 50–70 dh (£3.60–4.00; $6.50–9.00), possibly with a small extra charge for showers. At this lower end of the price scale, hot water may only be available at certain times of the day. Only during the peak season are you likely to have any problem finding a room, although any difficulties will probably be restricted to Tangier, Fez, Agadir, Rabat (in July) and, occasionally, Tetouan.

For those reaching the end of their funds, even cheaper possibilities exist. Prices at Morocco's 46 **campsites** are extremely cheap, at around 7dh (£0.50; $1) per tent, and 5dh (£0.35; $0.60) per person. On no account should you leave any valuables unattended. All the major towns have a campsite, and most also have an **IYHF hostel**. The 11 hostels differ tremendously in quality. Prices range from 10–30 dh (£0.65–1.90; $1.25–3.50; DM1.75–5.50). Anyone without a membership card is usually permitted to stay on the payment of a small supplement. All but one of the hostels are situated in the larger towns. The other, at Asni, is well worth considering as a base by those interested in hiking in the Atlas Mountains. The French Alpine Club (CAF) have a network of **refuge huts** for the use of those hiking in the Atlas.

ADDRESSES

Moroccan National Tourist Office	205 Regent Street, London W1R 7DE (tel. 071-437 0073).
Hotels	'Royaume de Maroc Guide des Hôtels'. Free from the Moroccan National Tourist Office or from any local office.
Moroccan YHA	Fédération Royale Marocaine des Auberges de Jeunes, Boulevard Okba Ben Nafii, Meknès (tel. 05–524698).
Refuge huts	Club Alpin Français, rue de la Boëtie, 75008 Paris (tel. 01 47 42 38 46).

Fez (Fès) (tel. code 06)

Tourist Offices

Office National Marocaine du Tourisme (ONMT), Place de la Résistance (tel. 623460/626297). Open Mon.–Fri. 8 a.m.–noon and 2–6 p.m., Sat. 8 a.m.–noon. At the end of Av. Hassan II, in the Immeuble Bennani. The best source of information on the city. From the train, follow rue Chenguit, go left at Place Kennedy, then turn left on to Av. Hassan II. From the CTM bus station, follow bd Mohammed V, then go right at Av. Hassan II. There are Syndicats d'Initiative on Place Mohammed V (tel. 624764) by Bab Boujeloud, the main entrance to the medina, and outside the more expensive hotels (generally open Mon.–Sat. 8 a.m.–7 p.m.).

Finding Accommodation

Fez lacks sufficient hotel accommodation of all types, which means that prices are higher than elsewhere in the country. It is best to phone ahead and try to get a reservation, as this can save you time and frustration on arrival. The best of the cheap rooms in the new town are located just to the west of bd Mohammed V, between Av. Hassan II (near the Post Office) and Av. Mohammed es Slaoui (near the CTM bus terminal). Rooms in the medina are concentrated around Bab Boujeloud.

UNCLASSIFIED HOTELS

Du Commerce, Place des Alouites, Fes el-Jdid. Across from the royal palace. The cleanest and best hotel in the medina. Singles 35 dh (£2.50; $4.50), doubles 70 dh (£5; $9), singles with a terrace 55 dh (£4; $7).

Renaissance, rue Abdekrim el-Khattabi (tel. 622193). Singles 30 dh (£2.25; $4); doubles 46 dh (£3.25; $6). Near Place Mohammed V.

Du Jardin Public, Kasbah Boujeloud 153 (tel. 633086). Singles 40 dh (£2.75; $5); doubles 66 dh (£4.75; $8.50). Considerably cleaner than other hotels in the area. Close to Bab Boujeloud down an alleyway by the Boujeloud mosque (look out for the sign pointing to the hotel).

Also situated around Bab Boujeloud are the hotels National, Erreha, Kaskade, Mauritania and Lamtani.

Regina, Av. Mohammed es Slaoui. Fine rooms. Prices are raised considerably during the summer.

Maghrib, Av. Mohammed es Slaoui. Another hotel offering good rooms, again at considerably inflated prices during the summer months.

Rex, Place de l'Atlas. No frills, but cheap and very clean.

CLASSIFIED HOTELS

Two star A:
Olympic, bd Mohammed V (tel. 624529/622403).
Two star B:
Amor, rue du Pakistan 31 (tel. 623304/622724).
Royal, rue d'Espagne 36 (tel. 624656).
Lamdaghri, Kabbour El Mangad 10 (tel. 620310).
One star A:
Kairouan, rue du Soudan 84 (tel. 623590).
Central, rue du Nador 50 (tel. 22333). Singles 55 dh (£4; $7), singles with showers 76 dh (£5.50; $9.50), singles with baths 100 dh (£7.20; $12.50); doubles with showers 84 dh (£6; $10.50), doubles with baths 100 dh (£7.20; $12.50). Very popular, so get there early. Off bd Mohammed V.
One star B:
CTM, bd Mohammed V (tel. 622811).
Excelsior, rue Larbi el-Kaghat (tel. 625602). Singles with shower 67 dh (£4.75; $8.50), doubles with shower 84 dh (£6; $10.50), double with bath 100 dh (£7.20; $12.50). Right off bd Mohammed V, three blocks up from the main Post Office.

IYHF HOSTEL

Bd Mohammed el Hansali 18 (tel. 624085). 10 p.m. curfew. 15 dh (£1.10; $2) for IYHF members, 17,50 dh (£1.25; $2.25) for non-members. IYHF membership cards available (two photos required) 75 dh (£5.25; $9.50). Roof space available when the dormitories are filled. A clean hostel with friendly staff.

CAMPING

Camping Moulay Slimane, rue Moulay Slimane (tel. 622438).

Marrakech (tel. code 04)

Tourist Offices
Office National Marocaine du Tourisme (ONMT), av Mohammed V (tel. 430258/431088/438889). At Place Abd el Moumen Benall. Open Mon.–Fri. 8.30 a.m.–noon and 2.30–6.30 p.m., Sat. 8.30 a.m.–12.30 p.m.; during Ramadan, 9 a.m.–3 p.m. only. Further down the street in the direction of the medina is the Syndicat d'Initiative at Av. Mohammed V 170 (tel. 433097). Open July–mid-Sept., Mon.–Fri. 9 a.m.–1.30 p.m. and 4–7 p.m., Sat. 9 a.m.–1.30 p.m.; at other times, Mon.–Fri. 8 a.m.–noon and 3–6 p.m., Sat. 8 a.m.–noon. Bus 1 runs along Av. Mohammed V from the Koutoubia Minaret near the Djemaâ El Fna.

UNCLASSIFIED HOTELS

Café de France, Djemaâ El Fna (tel. 43901). The centre of the medina. Relatively expensive, but the best of the unclassified hotels around the square. Double room for 90 dh (£6.50; $11.50).

De la Jeunesse, Derb Sidi Bouloukate 56 (rue de la Recette) (tel. 443631). Singles 35 dh (£2.50; $4.50), doubles 46 dh (£3.25; $6), triples 58 dh (£4.25; $7.50). Facing Hotel CTM on the Djemaâ El Fna go through the first arch to your right, then down the little street.

Hotels Afriquia, Nouzah and Eddakia are in the same street as the Hôtel de la Jeunesse above. These four establishments are the pick of the many hotels along Derb Sidi Bouloukate.

De France, Riad Zitoune el-Kedim 197 (tel. 443067). Singles 35 dh (£2.50; $4.50), doubles 50 dh (£3.50; $6.50). Recently renovated.

Chellah (tel. 441977). The Chellah is in an alley left off Zitoune el-Kedim about 50m down the street from the Hôtel de France above. Watch out for the sign pointing to the hotel.

Medina. A particularly good unclassified hotel, in an alley to the right off Zitoune el-Kedim.

Oukaimedon, Djemaâ El Fna. One of the best unclassified hotels around the square.

Near Djemaâ El Fna Hôtel des Amis and Hôtel Cecil charge around 50 dh (£3.50; $6.50) in doubles.

CLASSIFIED HOTELS

Two star A:

Al Mouatmid, Av. Mohammed V 94 (tel. 448854/448855).

Koutoubia, bd Mansour 51 Eddahbi (tel. 430921).

Les Ambassadeurs, Av. Mohammed V 2 (tel. 447159).

Ali, rue Moulay Ismail 10 (rue du Dispensaire/Place de Foucauld) (tel. 444979). Singles with shower 118 dh (£8.50; $15); doubles with shower 140 dh (£10; $17.50) with good breakfast. Extremely popular. Near Djemaâ El Fna.

Excelsior, Tarik Ibn Zaid/Ibn Aicha (tel. 431733). In the New Town.

Minaret, rue du Dispensaire 10. A relatively new and very good hotel in the medina.

Two star B:

De Foucauld, av El Mouahidine (tel. 445499). A fine hotel, but particularly good value if three or four people share one of the larger rooms.

Gallia, rue de la Recette 90 (tel. 445913).

Grand Hôtel Tazi (tel. 442152/442787). In the medina at the

corner of Av. El Mouahidine & Bab Agnaou. Singles around 115 dh (£8.20; $14.50), doubles around 140 dh (£10; $17.50).

One star A:

La Palmeraie, rue Souraya (tel. 431007). In the New Town.

CTM, Djemaâ El Fna (tel. 442325). Over the old bus station. Singles 50 dh (£3.60; $6.50); with shower 66 dh (£4.75; $8.50), doubles 64 dh (£4.60; $8), with shower 92 dh (£6.60; $11.50).

Oasis, Av. Mohammed V 50 (tel. 447179).

One star B:

Des Voyageurs, Av. Zerktouni 40 (tel. 447218).

Franco Belge, bd Zerktouni 62 (tel. 448472).

IYHF HOSTEL

Rue El Jahid, Quartier Industriel (tel. 432831/444713). Technically an IYHF card is obligatory, but non-members are usually admitted outside the peak season. 15 dh (£1.10; $2). Very clean. Lockout between 9 a.m.–noon and from 2–6 p.m. About 700m from the train station. Turn right after crossing Av. Hassan II, then take the first left and keep on going until you see the hostel on the right.

CAMPING

Camping Municipal, rue El Jahid (tel. 431707). 10 dh (£0.70; $1.25) per person, tent included. About 10 minutes' walk from the train station, on down the road from the IYHF hostel (see above for directions).

Rabat (tel. code 07)

Tourist Offices

Office National Marocaine du Tourisme (ONMT), rue el-Jazair (tel. 721252). Open July–mid-Sept, Mon.–Fri. 8 a.m.–2.30

p.m.; at other times, Mon.–Fri. 8.30 a.m.–noon and 2.30–6.30 p.m., except Ramadan, Mon.–Fri. 9 a.m.–3 p.m. A very helpful office but, unfortunately, not well located. Follow Av. Mohammed V from the train station to the Grande Essouna Mosque then go left down Av. Moulay Hassan until you see rue el-Jazair (formerly rue d'Alger) on the right. The Syndicat d'Initiative on rue Patrice Lumumba (tel. 723272) is more conveniently located. Across from the post office on Av. Mohammed V go right along rue el-Kahira for a few block. Open Mon.–Fri. 8 a.m.–7 p.m., Sat. 8 a.m.–noon.

Finding Accommodation
Accommodation can become difficult to find during July and August. At this time you might well be advised to telephone one of the classified hotels to try to make an advance reservation. Hoteliers are usually willing to hold a room to a reasonable hour if they have space available. If you arrive without a reservation, the area around the train station has a large concentration of hotels.

UNCLASSIFIED HOTELS

Marrakesh, rue Sebbahi 10 (tel. 727703). Singles 40 dh (£2.85; $5); doubles 56 dh (£4; $7). Turn right three blocks after entering the medina from Av. Mohammed V.

Also in the medina: Hôtel el Alam and Hôtel Regina. Both in rue Gebbali.

CLASSIFIED HOTELS

Two star A:
Royal, rue Amman 1 (tel. 721171/721172).
Splendid, rue de Ghazzah 24 (tel. 723283).
Des Oudaïs, bd el Alou 132 (tel. 732371). In the medina, over from the *kasbah* area. Considerably better than the other hotels in the medina.

Two star B:

Velleda, Av. Allal Ben Abdellah 106 (tel. 769531). Off Av. Mohammed V.

One star A:

Capitol, Av. Allal Ben Abdellah 34 (tel. 731236). Singles 60 dh (£4.30; $7.50); with shower 80 dh (£5.70; $10); doubles 70 dh (£5; $9); with shower 100 dh (£7.20; $12.50).

Central, rue el-Basra 2 (tel. 722131/767356). Singles 53 dh (£3.75; $7), singles with showers 63 dh (£4.50; $8), doubles 80 dh (£5.75; $10), doubles with showers 90 dh (£6.50; $11.50). To the right off Av. Mohammed V, a couple of blocks from the train station in the direction of the medina.

Gauloise, Zankat Hims 1 (tel. 723022/730573). Of the eight one-star and two-star hotels grouped at the end of Av. Mohammed V the Gauloise offers the best value for money.

Majestic, Av. Hassan II 121 (tel. 722997). The hotel fills quickly, so try to get there before noon at least.

Dahir, Av. Hassan II 429 (tel. 733026/722096).

Dakar, rue Dakar (tel. 721671).

IYHF HOSTEL

Rue Marassa, Bab El Had (tel. 725769). Just outside the medina. Members only. 20 dh (£1.40; $2.50).

CAMPING

Camping de la Plage. 5 dh (£0.35; $0.60) per tent, 10 dh (£0.70; $1.20) per person. In Salé, across the River Bou Regreg. Bus 6 leaves Av. Hassan II for Salé. Also bus 24. Get off at Bab Bou Haja, then follow the signs to the site on the beach.

Tangier (Tanger) (tel. code 09)

Tourist Offices
Office National Marocaine du Tourisme (ONMT), bd Pasteur
29 (tel, 32996). Open Mon.–Sat. 8 a.m.–2 p.m. Within walking
distance of the port, but it is more advisable to take a *petit taxi*
from the port to the office – only 4 dh (£0.30; $0.50) or so.

Trouble Spots
If you venture into the medina or the kasbah at night keep your
wits about you at all times, especially if you are on your own,
and stick to the main streets. Tourists are pestered in Tangier
to a degree unparalleled in the rest of the country. Although
this can become annoying do not adopt an aggressive manner
in trying to rid yourself of unwanted attention or you could
find yourself in serious trouble. If a dangerous situation does
develop (for whatever reason) it is up to you to extricate
yourself, as there is little chance of anyone else intervening.

Finding Accommodation
Tangier has a large number of hotels and pensions, so even
in July and August when the city becomes very busy you
should find a room without too much trouble, though you may
pay over the odds at this time of year (unclassified hotels often
up their prices in July and August, by up to 100 per cent). Local
hoteliers are generally helpful and if their own hotel is full they
will usually phone a few colleagues to see if they have vacancies
if you ask them. If you are looking for accommodation near
the port or the main train station (Gare de Ville) Zankat Salah
Eddine el-Ayoubi (previously rue de la Plage) is well supplied
with reasonably priced hotels. Walk left along Avenue
d'Espagne from the Gare de Ville, then take the first right. If
you would prefer to stay in the medina, one of the best places
to look for a room is rue Mokhtar Ahardan (formerly rue de
la Poste), just off the Petit Socco. Turn right on leaving the port
and enter the medina at rue de Cadiz. Head along the street

towards the lower gateway to the kasbah. Just before the gate turn left off rue de Cadiz and follow the steps into rue Mokhtar Ahardan.

PENSIONS/UNCLASSIFIED HOTELS

In the medina:

Pension Palace, rue Mokhtar Ahardan 2 (tel. 939248). Around 35 dh (£2.50; $4.50) p.p.

Hôtel Grand Socco (tel. 933126). On Grand Socco.

Hôtel Fuentes (tel. 934669), Hôtel Mauretania (tel. 934677) and Pension Becerra (tel. 932369). On Petit Socco.

In the new town:

Pension Miami, rue Salah Eddine el-Ayoubi 126 (tel. 932900). Singles 35 dh (£2.50; $4.50); doubles 56 dh (£4; $7), triples 90 dh (£6.50; $11.50).

El Muniria, rue Magellan.

CLASSIFIED HOTELS

Three star A:

Villa de France, rue de Hollande 143 (tel. 931475/937135). Far from being the cheapest in town, but the hotel offers a superb view over the city and immaculate rooms. Doubles 200 dh (£14.30; $25).

Two star A:

Mamora, rue Mokhtar Ahardan 19 (tel. 934105). Singles 100 dh (£7.25; $12.50), with bath 125 dh (£9; $16); doubles with shower 120 dh (£8.50; $15), doubles with bath 150 dh (£10.75; $19). The best hotel in the medina.

Anjou, rue Ibn El Banna 3 (tel. 934344/934244).

Valencia, Av. d'Espagne 72 (tel. 931714).

Marco Polo, Av. d'Espagne (tel. 938213/936087).

Miramar, Av. des F.A.R. (tel. 938948). The best of the reasonably priced hotels along the beach.

Two star B:

Astoria, rue Ahmed Chaouki 10 (tel. 937202).

Djenina, rue Grotins 8 (tel. 934759/936075).

Lutetia, Av. My Abdellah 3 (tel. 931866).

One star A:

De Paris, bd Pasteur 42 (tel. 038126/931877). Singles 50 dh (£3.60; $6.50); with shower 72 dh (£5.20; $9); doubles 66 dh (£4.70; $8.50), with shower 90 dh (£6.50; $11.50).

Panoramic Massilia, rue Marco Polo 3 (tel. 935009).

Hotel Residence Ritz, rue Soraya 1 (tel. 938074/938075).

Al Farabi, Zankat Essadia 10 (tel. 934566).

Andalucia, rue Vermeer 14 (tel. 941334).

Biaritz, Av. d'Espagne 102 (tel. 932473).

Continental, rue Dar el Baroud (tel. 931024/931143).

One star B:

Ibn Batouta, rue Magellan 8 (tel. 937170).

Olid, rue Mokhtar Ahardan 12 (tel. 931310).

Bretagne, Av. d'Espagne 92 (tel. 932339).

IYHF HOSTEL

Tanger Youth Hostel, rue El Antaki 8, Av. d'Espagne (tel. 946127). 20 dh (£1.40; $2.50) per night.

CAMPING

Miramonte (tel. 937138). Just under 2 miles west of the kasbah. Bus 1, 2 or 21 from Grand Socco. 8 dh (£0.60; $1) per tent, 5 dh (£0.35; $0.60) p.p.

Tingis (tel. 940191). Bus 15 from Grand Socco.

Camping Sahara. One mile north of train station, on the beach.

THE NETHERLANDS (Nederland)

It is a pleasure to travel in The Netherlands, not least because the Dutch are responding particularly well to the growth in independent, budget tourism. Reserving accommodation before you set off on holiday is easy. Local Tourist Offices (VVV) will book hotel rooms and B&B accommodation if you write to them in advance, though if you plan to travel around a fair bit you can save yourself the trouble of writing to individual offices by using the services of the wonderful National Reservations Centre in Leidschendam. The National Reservations Centre will book hotels, B&Bs, and even campsites all over the country for you. Campsites are reserved free of charge, though a deposit of 25 per cent may be requested for other types of accommodation, which you forfeit if you make a late cancellation. If you want to reserve a bed in an IYHF hostel all you need do is write to the hostel in Dutch, English or German, enclosing an International Reply Coupon. Try to reserve as early as possible if you want to stay in either of the IYHF hostels in Amsterdam. You can also book rooms on arrival through local Tourist Offices. Staff are generally very helpful, and fully appreciate what you mean when you say you want cheap accommodation. You need have no worries that they are trying to offer you expensive rooms when there are cheap rooms available. For a small fee, any VVV will reserve ahead for you. This is a service you might wish to use if you know you will be arriving late at your next destination, or if you are heading for Amsterdam in summer, as queues at the VVV Amsterdam Tourist Office can be horrendous at any time of day, with the cheapest rooms disappearing fast.

If you are very fortunate you may find a **hotel** or **pension** in one of the main towns with singles and doubles available for around 30 Dfl (£9.50; $16.50) per person, but these are few and far between. More likely you will pay 40 Dfl (£12.50; $22) per person and upwards for singles and doubles. The local VVV can advise you on the availability of **B&B in private homes**, which is a cheaper option than pensions or hotels. Prices range from 23–50 Dfl (£7.25–15.50; $12.50–27.50) per person, with around 28 Dfl (£8.75; $15.50) being the norm. B&B accommodation offers good value for money, as rigorous standards of cleanliness and comfort are enforced, while a traditional Dutch breakfast is a rare treat compared to the meagre offerings you get in most countries.

A similar hearty breakfast is also available at some of the country's 40–45 **IYHF hostels**. Depending on the location and the time of year B&B will cost you 22–25 Dfl (£7.00–7.75; $12–14). Full board is available at reasonable prices with meals that are good value for money. Basically, the IYHF hostels are good value all round; usually spotlessly clean, comfortable, equipped with a bar and games room, and staying open later than is usual for official hostels. Unfortunately, not all the main places of interest have an IYHF hostel in town, but those with a railpass will invariably find one in a town nearby. Hostels in the major towns are open all year. Most of the others are open from Easter to late September, but a few are open for the summer only. To stay in any IYHF hostel you must have a valid membership card.

As well as the IYHF hostels you may have the option of staying in **privately run hostels** or **youth hotels**. Both the prices and standards of these can vary dramatically. Prices can be as low as 15 Dfl (£4.75; $8.50), but on the other hand they may be as high as 40 Dfl (£12.50; $22). In most cases, when you pay 40 Dfl this gets you a single or a double, but there are some hostels which charge this price for larger rooms, representing very poor value compared to a cheap hotel. The local VVV will inform you of the whereabouts of any private hostels operating in town. It is also worth asking whether there is a local **Sleep-In**, as several towns have followed the example set by Amsterdam and established dorm hostels (sometimes open in summer only) which charge around 22 Dfl (£7; $12) for B&B.

No matter where you choose to visit you will never be far from one of the Netherlands' 2000 **campsites**. Sites are generally clean, well maintained and equipped with all the essentials. Prices for a solo traveller will normally be around 10–12 Dfl (£3.25–3.75; $5.50–6.50), but there are a few sites–primarily aimed at caravans – whose prices will bring a tear to the eye of those with a small tent. In such sites, you pay for a little hedged enclosure, designed to accommodate a caravan, plus a fee per person. For a solo traveller this is likely to amount to at least 17.50 Dfl (£5.50; $9.50).

Camping outside official sites is illegal, as is sleeping in cars, or **sleeping rough** in any public place. If you are sleeping in any public place the police are likely to wake you up and, most likely move you on, though they may press vagrancy charges if you have no money on you, so, ironically to avoid being charged with vagrancy you have to make yourself an attractive target for muggers. Just as the police are well aware of the spots in which travellers are most likely to try to bed down, so are the would-be thieves. If you try to sleep in the main train stations in Rotterdam or, especially, Amsterdam, it is likely to be touch and go whether the police get to you before the thieves do. Even worse, there is a fair chance you will be assaulted in Amsterdam Central if you are lying sleeping.

ADDRESSES

Netherlands Board of Tourism	25–28 Buckingham Gate, London SW1E 6LD (tel. 071-828 7941)
Dutch YHA	Stichting Nederlandse Jeugdherberg Centrale NJHC, Prof Tulplein 4,1018 GX Amsterdam (tel. 020–5513155).
Sleep-Ins	MAIC, Hartenstraat 16–18, Amsterdam (tel. 020–240977).
Camping	A list is available from the Netherlands Board of Tourism, complete with a form for reserving sites, which you can photocopy if you want to reserve several sites. Campsites can be reserved free of charge through the

National Reservations Centre, P O
Box 404, 2260 AK Leidschendam
(tel. 070– 3202500).

Hotels, Pensions and B&Bs
Lists for some of the main towns are available from the Netherlands Board of Tourism. Free reservations can be made through the National Reservations Centre in Leidschendam (see above). A deposit of 25 per cent may be requested, which you lose if you make a late cancellation.

Amsterdam (tel. code 020)

Tourist Offices
VVV Amsterdam Tourist Office, Postbus 3901, 1001 AS Amsterdam (tel. 6266444). Contact this office if you want information in advance.

VVV Amsterdam Tourist Office, Stationsplein 10 (tel. 6266444). Open July–Aug., daily 9 a.m.–midnight; Easter–June and Sept., same hours except Sun. closes at 9 p.m.; Oct–Easter, Mon.–Fri. 9 a.m.–6 p.m., Sat. 9 a.m.–5 p.m., Sun. 10 a.m.–1 p.m.

VVV Amsterdam Tourist Office, Leidsestraat 106. Open Easter–Sept., daily 9 a.m.–11 p.m.; Oct.–Easter, Mon.–Sat. 9 a.m.–5 p.m. Tram 1, 2 or 5 from Amsterdam Centraal.

Public Transport
The municipal transport authority (GVB) operates an integrated network of buses, trams, metro and light railway, with prices based on a zonal system. Various types of tickets are sold to visitors. Before buying any of these tickets consider carefully how much travelling you are likely to do. Most of the tourist attractions, and most of the cheap hotels and hostels are located within the central zone, much of which is easily covered on foot. Tickets covering all zones of the network are available for anything between one and nine days. Strip-tickets, once cancelled appropriately, allow you to use the system for one hour, changing as many times as you like, on all forms of public transport. You can even make a return journey. Using a strip ticket you simply cancel one more strip than the number of zones you are travelling in (e.g. travelling in the Central and Northern zones, cancel three strips). Various lengths of tickets are available. The 2-and 3-strip tickets are effectively singles. The 10- and 15-strip tickets offer better value, particularly the specially priced 15-strip ticket (actually cheaper than the 10-strip ticket, but only available at GVB counters and post offices). For details on current prices ask at the GVB information offices in the square opposite Amsterdam Centraal,

or in the Amstel station, or contact GVB head office, Prins Hendrikkade 108. The brochure 'Tourist Guide to Public Transport' clearly explains the procedures for validating tickets.

Trouble Spots

There are a few wild stories about drug-crazed gangs roaming around the city mugging tourists. Wild stories are all they are! Because of the number of tourists visiting it, the Red Light area is particularly safe, at least until the early hours of the morning although, as in the most crowded areas of all cities, pickpockets are to be found plying their trade amongst the hustle and bustle. One place you might want to avoid after dark is the Nieuwemarkt (location of the Waag), only a short walk from Oudezijds Achterburgwal in the Red Light district down Bloedstraat or Barndesteeg. Many of the casualties of the hard drug scene congregate around the square, as do those who supply them.

Basic Directions

From Stationsplein in front of Amsterdam Centraal, head across the water before crossing Prins Hendrikkade to the start of Damrak. Walking up Damrak, turning left at the end of the water takes you to Oude Brug Steeg, across Warmoesstraat and down Lange Niezel into the Red Light district. Continuing up Damrak you arrive at Dam, the large square containing the Royal Palace and the National Monument. To the right, behind the palace, Raadhuisstraat leads off across the ring of canals which encircle the town centre. Directly across Dam from Damrak is Rokin, which leads to Muntplein. The walk from Amsterdam Centraal to Dam takes about 10 minutes, that from Dam to Muntplein slightly less. Trams 4, 5, 9, 16, 24 and 25 run from the station to Muntplein.

Accommodation in Amsterdam

Of all the cities in Europe, only Rome, Paris and London receive more visitors than Amsterdam, so if you want to be sure of reasonably cheap accommodation you should reserve as far in advance as possible, particularly in summer. If you have not reserved ahead but are stopping in another Dutch town before visiting Amsterdam you can ask the local VVV to reserve ahead for you. Otherwise, try to arrive in Amsterdam as early as possible because, for obvious reasons, the cheapest accommodation goes quickly. In the sections below, directions are given for most accommodation options, often from a reference point in the Basic Directions section above. Please note that the VVV Amsterdam Tourist Office have informed us that they have received so many complaints about Hotel Van Ostade, Hotel King and Youth Hotel Aroza that they would not advise anyone to stay at these hotels. All hotels listed below have the full approval of the VVV Amsterdam Tourist Office, but do not hesitate to contact them in the unlikely event that you should have any cause for complaint.

HOTELS

Cheapest doubles around 55 Dfl (£17.25; $30)

Beurstraat, Beurstraat 7 (tel. 6263701). Without breakfast. Parallel to Damrak, right from Oude Brug Steeg.

Cheapest doubles around 65 Dfl (£20.25; $36)

Schröder, Haarlemerdijk 48b (tel. 6266272). Without breakfast. Two-night minimum stay in peak season. Right along Prins Hendrikkade, left at Singel, then right along Haarlemerstraat into Haarlemerdijk. A 5–10-minute walk from Amsterdam Centraal.

Cheapest doubles around 70 Dfl (£22; $38.50)

Pax, Radhuisstraat 37 (tel. 6249735). Without breakfast. A 10–15-minute walk from Amsterdam Centraal or take tram 13 or 17 along the street from the station.
Weber, Marnixstraat 397 (tel. 6270574). Without breakfast. Tram 1 or 2 from Amsterdam Centraal to Leidse Plein, then a few minutes' walk along Marnixstraat.

Cheapest doubles around 75 Dfl (£23.50; $41)

La Bohème, Marnixstraat 415 (tel. 6242828). Without breakfast. See Hotel Weber.

Casa Cara, Emmastraat 24 (tel. 6623135). B&B. Good value, a two-star hotel. Out by the Vondelpark. Trams 2 and 16 from Amsterdam Centraal cross the Emmastraat.

De Westertoren, Radhuisstraat 35b (tel. 6244639). B&B. See Hotel Pax.

Oosterpark, Oosterpark 72 (tel. 6930049). B&B. Metro: Weesperplein, then change to tram 6 which runs along Oosterpark. A 5–10-minute walk from Amsterdam-Muiderpoort train station. Follow Wijtenbachstraat into Oosterpark.

Amstel Boat Hotel, de Ruijterkade pier 5 (tel. 6264247). B&B. This two-star hotel is moored a short walk from the rear exit of Amsterdam Centraal.

Old Nickel, Nieuwe Brugsteeg 11 (tel. 6241912). B&B. Left along the waterside at the start of Damrak into Nieuwe Brugsteeg. A few minutes' walk from Amsterdam Centraal.

Cheapest doubles around 80 Dfl (£25; $44)

Sphinx, Weteringschans 82 (tel. 6273680). B&B. From Amsterdam Centraal tram 4 to Frederiksplein, or tram 16, 24 or 25 to Weteringplein.

Galerij, Radhuisstraat 43 (tel. 6248851). Without breakfast. See Hotel Pax.

Bema, Concertgebouwplein 19 (tel. 6791396). B&B. Tram 16 from Amsterdam Centraal.

Rokin, Rokin 73 (tel. 6267456). B&B. Two-star hotel in excellent location.

Apple Inn, Koninginneweg 93 (tel. 6627894). B&B. Two-star hotel near the Vondelpark. Tram 2 from Amsterdam Centraal runs along the street.

Aspen, Raadhuisstraat 31 (tel. 6266714). Without breakfast. See Hotel Pax.

Fox, Weteringschans 67 (tel. 6228338). B&B. Tram 16, 24 or 25 to Weteringplein.

Cheapest doubles around 85 Dfl (£26.50; $47)

Van Rooyen, Tweede Helmerstraat 6 (tel. 6184577). B&B. Tram 1, 2 or 5 to Leidse Plein from Amsterdam Centraal. Walk right along Nassaukade, past the end of 1e Helmerstraat then left on 2e Helmerstraat.

Clemens, Radhuisstraat 39 (tel. 6246089). B&B. See Hotel Pax.

Brian, Singel 69 (tel. 6244661). B&B. A 5–10-minute walk from Amsterdam Centraal. Right along Prins Hendrikkade, then left.

San Luchesio (ecumeni), Waldeck Pyrmontlaan 9 (tel. 6716861). B&B. Near the Vondelpark. Tram 2 from Amsterdam Centraal until you see Saxon-Weimar-Laan to the right off Koninginneweg. From Saxon-Weimar-Laan, right on Sophialaan, then left.

Thorbecke, Thorbeckeplein 3 (tel. 6232601). B&B.

Cheapest doubles around 90 Dfl (£28; $49)

Impala, Leidsekade 77 (tel. 6234706). From Amsterdam Centraal take tram 1, 2 or 5 to Leidse Plein.

De Leydsche Hof, Leidsegracht 14 (tel. 6232148). Without breakfast. Trams 1, 2 and 5 from Amsterdam Centraal run along Leidsestraat. Leidsegracht runs parallel to the right.

Kap, Den Texstraat 5b (tel. 6245908). B&B. Tram 16, 24 or 25 to Weteringplein from Amsterdam Centraal. Facing the canal, head right on Weteringschans, right at Weteringplantsoen, then left.

Kitty, Plantage Middenlaan 40 (tel. 6226819). B&B. Tram 9 from Amsterdam Centraal runs along the street.

Central Park West, Roemer Visscherstraat 27 (tel. 6852285). Two-star hotel near the Vondelpark. B&B. Tram 2 from Amsterdam Centraal runs past the point where Roemer Visscherstraat crosses Constantin Huygens Straat.

Wilhelmina, Koninginneweg 167–169 (tel. 6640594). Two-star

hotel near the Vondelpark. B&B. See Apple Inn.

Granada, Leidsekruisstraat 13 (tel. 6236711). B&B. From Amsterdam Centraal take tram 1, 2 or 5 along Leidsestraat to the stop over the canal (Prinsengracht) after Kerkstraat. Any of the small streets heading left will take you into Leidsekruisstraat.

Perséverance, Overtoom 78–80 (tel. 6182653). B&B. Tram 1 from Amsterdam Centraal runs along Overtoom.

International, Warmoesstraat 1–3 (tel. 6245520). Without breakfast. Right off Oude Brug Steeg. On the fringe of the Red Light district.

Cheapest doubles around 95 Dfl (£30; $52)

Ronnie, Radhuisstraat 41 (tel. 6242821). See Hotel Pax.

Amstelzicht, Amstel 104 (tel. 6236693). Two-star hotel in a good location between Muntplein and the Blauwe Brug (Blue Bridge). B&B. Tram 4 from Amsterdam Centraal runs down part of Amstel before turning off into Rembrandtsplein. From the metro stop on Waterlooplein you can take tram 9 the whole length of Amstel.

Sipermann, Roemer Visscherstraat 35 (tel. 6161866). B&B. Two-star hotel near the Vondelpark. See Hotel Central Park West.

Verdi, Wanningstraat 9 (tel. 6760073). B&B. From Amsterdam Centraal take tram 2 to the first stop after it turns off Van Baerle Straat onto Willems Parkweg. Go left down Jacob Obrecht Straat, left again at Van Bree Straat, then right.

Albert, Sarphatipark 58 (tel. 6734083). B&B. From Amsterdam Centraal take tram 2 to Constantin Huygens Straat, then change to tram 3 to the Sarphatipark.

Hegra, Herengracht 269 (tel. 6237877). B&B. Tram 13 or 17 along Raadhuisstraat to the Herengracht from Amsterdam Centraal, or a 20-minute walk.

Hemony, Hemonystraat 7 (tel. 6714241). B&B. Central location.

Museumzicht, Jan Luijken Straat 22 (tel. 6715224). B&B. Near the National Museum. Take tram 5 from Amsterdam

Centraal; the street is to the left of Van Baerle Straat.

Peters, Nicolaas Maesstraat 72 (tel. 6733454). B&B. The street crosses Van Baerle Straat shortly after tram 5 from Amsterdam Centraal passes the National Museum on Museumplein.

PRIVATE ROOMS

Enquire about the availability of private rooms at the VVV Amsterdam Tourist Office. Expect to pay around 45 Dfl (£14; $24.50) per person.

IYHF HOSTELS

'Vondelpark', Zandpad 5 (tel. 6831744). Open all year. Curfew 2 a.m. Written reservations only. Arrive early if you have not reserved. B&B 23,50 Dfl (£7.25; $13) p.p. in doubles; 20,50 Dfl (£6.50; $11.50) in dorms. From Amsterdam Centraal take tram 1, 2 or 5 to Leidseplein. Zandpad is off Stadhouderskade at the left-hand end of Leidseplein.

'Stadsdoelen', Kloveniersburgwal 97 (tel. 6246832). Open 1 Mar.–4 Nov. and 27 Dec.–2 Jan. Curfew 1.30 a.m. B&B 20,50 Dfl (£6.50; $11.50) in dorms. Between Muntplein and the Nieuwmarkt. From Muntplein follow Nieuwe Doelen Straat into Kloveniersburgwal. A 15-minute walk from Amsterdam Centraal, through the Red Light district. From Lange Niezel follow Korte Niezel, then go right at Oudezijds Achterburgwal then left at Oude Hoogstraat into Kloveniersburgwal.

CHRISTIAN HOSTELS

Both are safe, cheap, and not as rule-bound as you might imagine. 1 a.m. curfew Fri. and Sat., midnight the rest of the week. Around 15 Dfl (£4.75; $8.50) for B&B.

Eben Haëzer, Bloemstrasse 179 (tel. 6244717). Tram 13 or 17 from Amsterdam Centraal to the Marnixstraat stop. Walk back to Rozengracht, and Bloemstrasse is parallel to the left.

The Shelter, Barndesteeg 21 (tel. 6253230). A 10-minute walk from Amsterdam Centraal to the hostel in the Red Light district. From Lange Niezel follow Korte Niezel, go right on Oudezijds Achterburgwal, then left at Barndesteeg.

HOSTELS

Adam & Eva, Sarphatistraat 105 (tel. 6246206). Dorms 18 Dfl (£5.75; $10). Without breakfast. Metro: Weesperplein, then a few minutes'walk along Sarphatistraat.

Bob's Youth Hostel, Nieuwezijds Voorburgwal 92 (tel. 6230063). B&B in dorms 21 Dfl (£6.50; $11.50), slightly cheaper if you have a mattress on the floor. Good location, close to Dam, about 8 minutes' walk from Amsterdam Centraal. Right from Damrak at Oude Brugstraat, across Nieuwendijk and down Kolkstraat and Nieuwezijds Kolk into Nieuwezijds Voorburgwal. Trams 1, 2 and 5 run along the street from Amsterdam Centraal.

Keizersgracht, Keizersgracht 15 (tel. 6251364). Dorms 22 Dfl (£7; $12), doubles about 90 Dfl (£28; $49). Without breakfast. A pleasant location, about 8 minutes' walk from Amsterdam Centraal. Right along Prins Hendrikkade, left up Singel, right along Brouwersgracht to the start of Keizersgracht.

Kabul, Warmoesstraat 38–42 (tel. 6237158). No curfew. Dorms 24 Dfl (£7.50; $13), doubles from 70–90 Dfl (£22–28; $38.50–49.00). Without breakfast. In the Red Light district, 5 minutes' walk from Amsterdam Centraal. Right off Oude Brug Steeg.

Jeugdhotel Meeting Point, Warmoesstraat 14 (tel. 6277499) Dorms 26 Dfl (£8.25; $14.50). Without breakfast. See Kabul.

Hans Brinker, Kerkstraat 136 (tel. 6220687). B&B in dorms 30 Dfl (£9.50; $16.50). Doubles are more expensive than in the hotels listed above. Tram 16 from Amsterdam Centraal crosses Kerkstraat on its way down Vijzelstraat.

Zeezicht, Piet Heinkade 15 (tel. 6178706). B&B in dorms

40 Dfl (£12.50; $22). A 10-minute walk from the rear exit of Amsterdam Centraal, right along De Ruijter Kade which leads into Piet Hein Kade, or take bus 28.

Frisco Inn, Beursstraat 5 (tel. 6201610). No curfew. Dorms start at around 27 Dfl (£8.50; $15), more expensive doubles and triples are available. Just over 5 minutes' walk from Amsterdam Centraal, right at Oude Brug Steeg.

Bill's 'Happy Hours' Youth Hostel, Binnen Wieringerstraat 8 (tel. 6255259). B&B in dorms 20 Dfl (£6.25; $11). Same price per person in the hostel's one double. Off Haarlemerstraat (dir: 2) near the end of Herengracht.

Euphemia Budget Hotel, Fokke Simonszstraat 1–9 (tel. 6229045). Dorms 30 Dfl (£9.50; $16.50), doubles 85 Dfl (£26.50; $47), triples 115 Dfl (£36; $63). With breakfast. Tram 16, 24 or 25 from Amsterdam Centraal to Weteringschans. Go back over the canal (Lijnbaansgracht), then turn right.

't Ancker, De Ruijterkade 100 (tel. 6229560). Dorms 40 Dfl (£12.50; $22). Includes a buffet breakfast where you can eat as much as you like. More expensive doubles available. About 100m to the right from the rear exit from Amsterdam Centraal.

SLEEP-IN

Sleep-In Mauritskade, s'-Gravesandestraat 51 (tel. 6947444). Large dorms with mattresses on the floor. Open late June–early Sept. Also one week both at Easter and New Year. 14 Dfl (£4.50; $7.50). Hire of sheets 3 Dfl (£1; $1.75) with 25 Dfl (£7.75; $14) deposit. Beside the Oosterpark. Metro to Weesperplein, then take tram 6 along Sarphatisstraat to the Sleep-In.

HOUSEBOATS

Unless you have been informed of a good houseboat by a reliable source they are best avoided. Cleanliness is not a strong point, and many seriously breach fire regulations.

CAMPING

Zeeburg, Zuider-Ijdijk 44 (tel. 6944430). Open mid-Apr.–
Oct. 6 Dfl (£1.90; $3.50) per person with tent. Aimed at
young travellers. Live music regularly. Direct ferry from
Central Station, or tram 10, bus 22 or 37. Night bus 71 or 76.

Gaasper, Loosdrechtdreef 7 (tel. 6967326). 8.35 Dfl (£2.60;
$4.50) p.p. with tent. Metro to Gaasperplas or night bus
72. Twenty-minute trip from Central Station.

Vligenbos, Meeuwenlaan 138 (tel. 6368855). 5.50 Dfl (£1.70;
$3) p.p. with tent. From Central Station tram 1, 2 or 5 to
Leidseplein, then bus 172.

SLEEPING ROUGH

Sleeping rough is not to be recommended in Amsterdam as
a whole, and certainly not in Amsterdam Centraal train station.
Even if you are not physically attacked, it is almost guaranteed
someone will try to rob you as you sleep. If you do decide to
sleep rough, at least try to gain some extra security by bedding
down beside other travellers, rather than in some quiet spot
on your own. The most popular spots for sleeping out are the
Vondelpark, the Julianapark and the Beatrixpark. Those with
a railpass who are totally stuck but do not want to sleep rough
should put their luggage and all but a little of their money into
the left luggage office (or the lockers) and then ride the trains,
which keep up a virtually constant service between Amsterdam
and Rotterdam through the night. You will not get a lot of
sleep, but it is much safer than trying to sleep in Amsterdam
Centraal.

Delft (tel. code 015)

Tourist Offices
VVV Delft, Markt 85, 2611 GS Delft (tel. 126100). Write in
advance for information or free hotel reservations. Open

Apr.–Sept., Mon.–Fri. 9 a.m.–6 p.m., Sat. 9 a.m.–5 p.m., Sun. 11 a.m.–3 p.m.; Oct–Mar., closed Sun. The office is about 10 minutes' walk from the train station. Leaving the station, head left along the main road, turn right up Binnenwatersloot with its tree-lined canal, across Oude Delft and straight on at the top of Binnenwatersloot, left along the canal at the Wijnhaven, then right over the first bridge and straight on into the Markt. The office is at the top right-hand end of the square near the Nieuwe Kerk.

HOTELS

Cheapest doubles around 65 Dfl (£20.25; $36)

Den Dulk, Markt 61/65 (tel. 158255). Prime location.

Van Domburg, Voldersgracht 24 (tel. 123029). Also excellently located on a canal just off the Markt. Continue along the Wijnhaven (see Tourist Office above) until you see Voldersgracht on the right.

Cheapest doubles around 70 Dfl (£22; $38.50)

Parallel, Parallelweg 5–6 (tel. 126046). On the street immediately behind the train station. Head right from the station, right under the underpass and you arrive at the end of Parallelweg.

Van Leeuwen, Achterom 143 (tel. 123716). Singles the same price as doubles. About 5 minutes' walk from the centre and the train station. Take the small street opposite the station into Oude Delft then continue more or less straight on across the canals into Achterom.

Rust, Oranje Plantage 38 (tel. 126874). Singles the same price as doubles. About 10 minutes' walk from the centre, 15 minutes' walk from the station. Oranje Plantage runs between the Oostpoort and the end of Nieuwe Langendijk, the street leading out of the Markt beside the Nieuwe Kerk.

Cheapest doubles around 75 Dfl (£23.50; $41)

La Dalmacya, Markt 39 (tel. 123714).

PRIVATE ROOMS

Available from the Tourist Office. Doubles around 60 Dfl (£18.75; $33).

HOSTELS

There are no hostels in Delft. The nearest hostels (both IYHF and privately run) are in Rotterdam and the Hague, both a short rail trip from Delft.

STUDENT FLATS

Krakeelhof, Jacoba Van Beierlaan 9 (tel. 135953/146235). Open June–Aug. Singles 20 Dfl (£6.25; $11); doubles 34 Dfl (£10.60; $18.50). Prices fall by about 25 per cent if you stay more than seven days. As you leave the station turn right along Van Leeuwenhoeksingel, right at the end of the road, through the underpass, right at the first set of traffic lights, left on to Van Beierlaan, and left again over the bridge.

CAMPING

Delftse Hout (tel. 570515/130040/602323). Expensive. About 12 Dfl (£3.75; $6.50) to pitch a tent, 6 Dfl (£1.90; $3.50) p.p. In a wood about 20 minutes' walk from the town centre. From the train station, bus 60 runs every 20 minutes to the Delftse Hout entrance on Korftlaan.

The Hague (Den Haag) (tel. code 070)

Tourist Offices
The Hague Visitors & Convention Bureau, Postbus 85456, 2508

CD Den Haag (tel. 3648286). Hotels can be booked in advance through this office, either by letter or by telephone (Mon.–Fri. 8.30 a.m.–5 p.m., Sat. 9 a.m.–1 p.m.).

VVV-i, The Hague Information Office, Koningin Julianaplein (tel. 3546200). Open mid-Apr.–mid-Sept., Mon.–Sat. 9 a.m.–9 p.m., Sun. 10 a.m.–5 p.m.; at other times, Mon.–Sat. 9 a.m.–6 p.m., Sun. 10 a.m.–5 p.m. In the Babylon shopping centre, to the right of Den Haag Centraal train station.

VVV-i, Scheveningen Information Office, Gevers Deynootweg 1134. Same hours as the VVV-i above. In the Palace Promenade shopping centre.

Arriving in The Hague by Train
There are two main stations in The Hague, Den Haag Centraal and Den Haag Hollandse Spoor (usually abbreviated to Den Haag CS and Den Haag HS). Den Haag Central is the most convenient for the Tourist Office and for the tourist attractions. Paris/Brussels-Amsterdam trains stop at Hollandse Spoor only, but there are frequent connecting trains between the two stations.

Staying in The Hague
Cheap accommodation in the centre of the city is in limited supply. Most of the cheaper hotels are in Scheveningen, on the coast to the north-west of the city and the various hostels are also outside the central area. Trams link Scheveningen to The Hague.

HOTELS

Cheapest doubles around 60 Dfl (£18.75; $33)

Duinroos, Alkmaarsestraat 27, Scheveningen (tel. 3546079).

Cheapest doubles around 70 Dfl (£22; $38.50)

Aristo, Stationsweg 164–166 (tel. 3890847). A 5-minute walk down the street in front of Hollandse Spoor train station.

Meijer, Stevinstraat 62–64, Scheveningen (tel. 3558138).
Huize Rosa, Badhuisweg 41, Scheveningen (tel. 3557796).
Enak, Keizerstraat 53, Scheveningen (tel. 3556169).
Neuf, Rijswijkseweg 119 (tel. 3900748). Just under 10 minutes' walk from the Hollandse Spoor train station (Den Haag HS). Through the underpass to the right of the main exit, then down Rijswijksweg to the hotel.

Cheapest doubles around 80 Dfl (£25; $44)

Clavan, Badhuiskade 8, Scheveningen (tel. 3552844).
De Minstreel, Badhuiskade 4–5, Scheveningen (tel. 3520024).
Schuur, Badhuiskade 2 (tel. 3556583).
Jodi, Van Aerssenstraat 194–196 (tel. 3559208). Technically not in Scheveningen, but far closer to Scheveningen than the centre of The Hague.
Astoria, Stationsweg 139 (tel. 3840401). A 5-minute walk down the street in front of Hollandse Spoor station.
Empire, Keizerstraat 27a–29, Scheveningen (tel. 3505752).
Lunamare, Badhuisweg 9 (tel. 3546075).
Mont Blanc, Stevinstraat 66, Scheveningen (tel. 3559785).
De Zonnehoek, Groningestraat 19, (tel. 3541879).
El Cid, Badhuisweg 51 Scheveningen (tel. 3546667).

Cheapest doubles around 85 Dfl (£26.50; $47)

Margaretha, Geestbrugweg 18, Rijswijk (tel. 3994563).

PRIVATE ROOMS

Expect to pay around 35 Dfl (£11; $19)

These are arranged through VVV; occasionally they will not let private rooms until the hotels are full.

IYHF HOSTEL

Ockenburgh, Monsterseweg 4 (tel. 3970011). Five miles from the city centre in Kijkduin. Bus 122, 123 or 124 from Central

Station. Ask the driver for the nearest stop. A 10-minute walk, follow the signs. Midnight curfew. B&B in dorms 25 Dfl (£7.70; $14.50; DM22.25).

HOSTELS

Marion, Havenkade 3/3a, Scheveningen (tel. 3543501). Singles around 30 Dfl (£9.25; $17.50) with breakfast.

Duinrell Duinhostel, Duinrell 1, Wassenaar (tel. 01751-19314). By the camping site. Singles start around 38 Dfl (£11.90; $21).

Scheveningen, Gevers Deynootweg 2, Scheveningen (tel. 3547003). Singles around 33 Dfl (£10.30; $18), doubles around 23 Dfl (£7.20; $12.50) per person.

CAMPING

Duinhorst, Buurtweg 135, Wassenaar (tel. 3242270). Open 1 Apr.–1 Oct. 5 Dfl (£1.60; $3) p.p. and per camping site.

Duinrell, Duinrell 5, Wassenaar (tel. 01751–19212/19314). Open year round. 13,25 Dfl (£4.25; $7.50) per camping site, 2,50 Dfl (£0.80; $1.50) p.p.

Ockenburgh, Wijndaelerweg 25 (tel. 3252364). Open 3 Apr.–25 Oct. 11 Dfl (£3.50; $6) per camping site; 3,15 Dfl (£1; $1.75) p.p. Tram 3 from Den Haag Centraal.

Vlietland, Oostvlietweg 60, Leidschendam (tel. 071–612200). Open 15 Apr.–25 Oct. 17,50 Dfl (£5.50; $9.50) per camping site, 5 Dfl (£1.50; $3) p.p.

Rotterdam (tel. code 010)

Tourist Offices
Rotterdam VVV Tourist Information, Coolsingel 67, 3012 AC Rotterdam (tel. 34034065). Open Apr.–Sept., Mon.–Thurs. 9 a.m.–5.30 p.m., Sat. 9 a.m.–5 p.m. Sun. 10 a.m.–4 p.m.; Oct.–Mar., same hours except Sun. when the office is closed.

522 Cheap Sleep Guide

The head office of Rotterdam VVV Tourist Information. Information on the city and the country as a whole. Contact this office if you want to reserve hotel rooms in advance. Located near the Town Hall, a 10-minute walk from Rotterdam Centraal, left along Weena after crossing Stationsplein, then right down Coolsingel from Hofplein, or take tram 1 or the metro to Stadhuis.

Rotterdam VVV Tourist Information, Rotterdam Centraal. Branch office in the hall of the main train station. Open Mon.–Sat. 9 a.m.–10 p.m., Sun. 10 a.m.–10 p.m.

HOTELS

Doubles 47 Dfl (£14.75; $26), doubles with bath/shower 70 Dfl (£22; $38.50) for B&B

Keeldar, Virulyplein 10 (tel. 4777400). Bus 38 or 45.

Cheapest doubles around 65 Dfl (£20.25; $36) without breakfast

Bagatelle, Provenierssingel 26 (tel. 4676348). A few minutes' walk from the main train station. Leave Rotterdam Centraal by the rear exit on to Proveniersplein. Provenierssingel runs out the right hand side of the square.

Heemraad, Heemraadssingel 90 (tel. 4775461). Tram 1, 7 or 9, or a 10–15 minute walk from Rotterdam Centraal. From Stationsplein head right along Weena and Beukelsdijk, then left at Heemradssingel.

Cheapest doubles around 70 Dfl (£22; $38.50)

Metropole, Nieuwe Binnenweg 13a (tel. 4360319). Overnight price includes breakfast. A 15-minute walk from Rotterdam Centraal. Head directly across Stationsplein and keep going until you see Nieuwe Binnenweg on the right at the end of Westersingel. Metro: Eendrachtsplein leaves a short walk along Nieuwe Binnenweg from the square, or you can take tram 5 or 6.

Rox-Inn, s'-Gravendijkwal 14 (tel. 4366109). Without breakfast. Tram 1, 7 or 9, or a 15-minute walk from Rotterdam Centraal. Head straight from the exit across Stationsplein and down Kruisplein. Turn right at West-Kruiskade, and keep on going until you see s'-Gravendijkwal on the left.

Cheapest doubles around 75 Dfl (£23.50; $41)

De Gunst, Brielselaan 190–192 (tel. 4850940). Metro: Maashaven, then tram 2.

Cheapest doubles around 80 Dfl (£25; $44)

Traverse, s'-Gravendijkwal 70–72 (tel. 4365050). B&B. Tram 6 or 9, or bus 32, or a 20-minute walk from Rotterdam Centraal. Follow the directions for the Rox-Inn, above.

Bienvenue, Spoorsingel 24 (tel. 4669394). Overnight price includes breakfast. A few minutes' walk from Rotterdam Centraal. Go out the rear exit and across Provenisplein into Spoorsingel.

Holland, Provenierssingel 7 (tel. 4653100). Without breakfast. A few minutes' walk from Rotterdam Centraal. See Bagatelle, above.

IYHF HOSTEL

Rochussenstraat 107–109 (tel. 4365763). Curfew 2 a.m. B&B 22 Dfl (£7; $12). Metro or tram 4 to Dijkzigt on Rochussenstraat, or a 20-minute walk from Rotterdam Centraal. Across Stationsplein and straight on to Eendrachtsplein from which Rochussenstraat runs off to the right.

CAMPING

Kanaalweg 84 (tel. 4159772). Bus 33.

524 Cheap Sleep Guide

Utrecht (tel. code 030)

Tourist Office
VVV Utrecht, Vredenburg 90 (tel. 34034085). Open Mon.–Fri.
9 a.m.–6 p.m., Sat. 9 a.m.–4 p.m. Accommodation service,
town plans and leaflets with suggested walking tours. When
closed, information and accommodation listings are available
from the vending machine outside the office. To reach the office
in the Muziekcenter from Utrecht Centraal Station you have
to negotiate your way through the Hoog Catherine shopping
complex (watch out for signs pointing to the VVV).

HOTELS
There is a dire shortage of cheap hotels in the city.

Cheapest doubles around 75 Dfl (£23.50; $41)

Pension Van Ooyen, Dantelaan 117 (tel. 938190). From
Utrecht Centraal Station take bus 4 dir. Kanaleiland to
Everard Meijsterlaan.

Cheapest doubles around 80 Dfl (£25; $44)

Hotel Ouwi, F.C. Donderstraat 12 (tel. 716303). From Utrecht
Centraal take bus 4 dir. Wilhelminapark to F.C.
Donderstraat.

Cheapest doubles around 85 Dfl (£26.50; $47)

Parkhotel, Tolsteegsingel 34 (tel. 516712). From Utrecht
Centraal take bus 2 dir. Kanaleiland to Ledig Erf.

B&Bs
Local Bed & Breakfast accommodation can be booked through
the VVV Utrecht. Prices start around 35 Dfl (£10.75; $19) per
person.

IYHF HOSTEL

Rhijnauwenslaan 14, Bunnik (tel. 03405–61277). 12.30 a.m.
curfew. 23 Dfl (£7; $12.50). Bus 40 from Utrecht Centraal
stops about 5 minutes' walk away from this excellent hostel
set in the countryside outside Utrecht (ask the driver for
the Jeugdherberg).

CAMPING

De Berekuil, Ariënslaan 5–7 (tel. 713870). Open Apr.–Oct.
5 Dfl (£1.50; $3) per tent and per person. Within walking
distance of the town centre. Bus 57 from Utrecht Centraal
Station to the Veemarkt.

NORWAY (Norge)

Not surprisingly, cheap accommodation options are severely limited in Norway, reputedly the most expensive country in mainland Europe. Even if the prices below seem affordable to you, remember that you are also going to spend a considerable amount of money simply feeding yourself. As the Norwegian Tourist Board admit, 'Hotel accommodation in Norway is not cheap.' This is a bit of an understatement, as even in summer when **hotels** reduce their prices, it is rare to find prices lower than 250kr (£22.70; $40) for singles, 400kr (£36.40; $64) for doubles. The only consolations are the excellent standards, and the chance of gorging yourself on the buffet breakfast. A room in a small **boarding house**, known as a *pensjonat* or *hospit* is cheaper, but you can still expect to pay at least 170kr (£15.50; $27) for a single, 280kr (£25.50; $45) for a double, without breakfast. These are usually available in the more popular tourist towns.

More affordable is a room in a private home, at 100–160kr (£9.10–14.50; $16.00–25.50) for singles and 180–220kr (£16.40–20.00; $29–35) for doubles, without breakfast. These have to be booked through the local Tourist Office, which charges a fee of 15kr (£1.40; $2.50; DM4). Unfortunately, private rooms may be difficult to find outside the larger towns, and may also have a specified minimum stay.

There are around 90 **IYHF hostels** around the country, with convenient clusters in the western fjords, the popular hiking areas of the centre, and in the vicinity of Oslo. Standards are unquestionably excellent, but prices are high. Overnight fees start at around 60kr (£5.50; $9.50), but are normally around 90–120kr (£8.20–11.00; $14.50–19.00). However, prices can be as high as 140–160kr (£12.70–14.50; $22.50–25.50) in some hostels. One slight consolation is that a substantial buffet breakfast is included in the overnight price at most hostels charging over 130kr (£11.80; $21). It is advisable to have an IYHF card, otherwise you will have to pay an extra 25kr (£2.25; $4), assuming you are admitted to the hostel. Only a few hostels operate throughout the year. Most open from June to September only; some for even shorter periods.

Groups of three to seven travellers planning to stay in the same area for a while might consider hiring a chalet. **Chalets** (*hytte*) are let by the week only and prices vary from 60–140kr (£5.50–12.70; $9.50–22.50) per person per night. In the peak period of late June to mid-August expect to pay about 90–100kr (£8.20–9.00; $14.50–16.00) p.p. per night. At other times prices fall, so that in May, or September to December, chalets are let out for perhaps two thirds of the peak-season price. Most chalets are located in rural areas, ideal for hiking and fishing, but if you can find one with a train station nearby, it can make a good base for touring about. Just occasionally, a chalet can be found in the suburbs of the main towns.

There are some 1300 **campsites**, rated with from one to three stars according to the facilities available. High standards are assured, but there are no fixed prices, and charges can vary considerably. Most charge 50–60kr (£4.50–5.50; $8.00–9.50) for a tent, with a fee of 5–10kr (£0.45–0.90; $0.80–1.60) per occupant. Sites do not accept reservations, but these are not necessary in any case, and while the FICC camping carnet is valid, it is not essential. An increasing number of sites offer self-catering chalets for rent, with one-night stays possible. Sleeping between four and six people, these chalets have fully equipped kitchens and prices range from 250–350kr (£23–32; $40–56) per night. All the sites, complete with addresses, telephone numbers, facilities and opening times are listed in the brochure 'Camping in Norway', published annually by the Norwegian Tourist Board. Prices are not listed because they are set later in the year.

As in neighbouring Sweden and Finland, the right to **camp rough** is written into the law, with certain restrictions. You are allowed to camp for two days on any uncultivated land or open area without asking permission, provided you pitch your tent at least 150 metres away from the nearest habitations. Between 15 April and 15 September, avoid setting fires in open fields or woodland areas. Do not leave litter lying around. Wherever you may be camping or sleeping rough, it is likely to get very cold at night, even during the summer, so a good sleeping bag and tent with a flysheet is recommended. Nor is there any time of the year that is particularly free of rain (Bergen especially is renowned for its wet weather). It is also advisable to have a good mosquito repellant.

Anyone heading out into the countryside who would prefer a roof over their head should contact the Norwegian Mountain Touring Association for a list of the simple **mountain huts** they operate throughout the country. Open at Easter, and from late June to early September, these huts cost 50–120kr (£4.50–11.00; $8–19) per night. Non-members pay an additional 50kr (£4.50; $8) surcharge. Mountain huts can provide an alternative to hostelling, or act as a supplement in areas where there are no hostels. In the Lofoten Islands, it is possible to rent old fishermen's cabins (*rorbuer*). These were once the temporary homes of fishermen from other parts of the country who needed a base during the winter. Most have been modernized; some come equipped with a shower and toilet, while others still lack running water. One-night stays are possible in some cabins. Advance booking of 'rorbuer' is essential.

ADDRESSES

Norwegian Tourist Board	Charles House, 5–11 Lower Regent Street, London SW1Y 4LR (tel. 071-839 6255).
Norwegian YHA	Norske Vandrerhjem, Dronningensgate 26, N–0154 Oslo 1 (tel. 02– 421410).
'Hytte' (Chalets)	Den Norske Hytteformidling, Kierschowsgate 7, Boks 3207 Sagene, N–0405 Oslo 4 (tel. 02–356710).
	Fjordhytter, Jan Smrgsgate 11, 5011 Bergen (tel. 05–232080).
'Rorbuer'	Lofoten Reiselivslag, Boks 210, N–8301 Svolvaer (tel. (0)88– 71053).

Mountain huts	Den Norske Turistforening, Stortinsgate 28, Oslo 1.
Camping	Norges Campingplassforbund, Dronningensgate 10–12, N–0152 Oslo 1 (tel. 02–421203).

Bergen (tel. code 05)

Tourist Offices
Bergen Reiselivslag, Slottsgt. 1, 5003 Bergen (tel. 313860).
Contact the Bergen Tourist Board if you want information on
the city in advance.

Turistinformasjon (tel. 321480). From the train and bus
stations on Strømgaten, walk left and right respectively before
turning down Kaigaten and then along Starvhusgaten to the
pavilion on Torgalmenning (a 10-minute walk). Open
May–Sept., Mon.–Sat. 8.30 a.m.–9.00 p.m., Sun. 10 a.m.–7
p.m.; Oct.–Apr., Mon.–Fri. 10 a.m.–3 p.m.

HOTELS

Steens Frokosthotel, Parkveien 22 (tel. 326993). Expect to pay
around 500kr (£46; $80) in doubles.

PENSIONS/GUESTHOUSES

Fagerheim Pensjonat, Kalvedalsveien 49A (tel. 310172).
Singles around 200kr (£18.50; $32); doubles around
280–330kr (£26–30; $45–53).
Mrs Bernstens, Klosteret 16 (tel. 233502). Doubles around
320kr (£29; $51).
Myklebust Pensjonat, Rosenbergsgt. 19 (tel. 311328). Doubles
from around 380kr (£35; $61).

PRIVATE ROOMS

Available at the Tourist Office. Singles 160–190kr
(£14.50–17.50; $26–31); doubles 260–320kr (£23.60–29.00;
$41–51). Commission of 15kr (£1.40; $2.50) for one person,
20kr (£1.75; $3.50) for two people.

IYHF HOSTEL

Montana, Johan Blyttsveien 30 (tel. 292900). Open 10 May–30
Sept. 140kr (£12.75; $22.50) for IYHF members. Best

reserved ahead. The IYHF Information Office at Strandgaten 4 (tel. 326880) will inform you whether there are beds available. Strandgaten runs off Torgalmenning. The hostel is 2½ miles from the town centre, roughly halfway up Mt Ulriken. Take bus 4 from the head post office (right off Kaigaten/Starvhusgaten) to Lægdene.

HOSTELS

KFUM (YMCA) Interpoint Bergen, Kalfarveien 77 (tel. 318125; KFUM head office). Open 1 July–15 Aug. Mattresses on the floor, 75kr (£7.25; $13). From the bus and train stations walk right along Strømgaten, and then right along Kalfarveien. A 10-minute walk from the town centre. The location of the hostel may be different in 1993. If so, the KFUM head office will inform you of the new location.

Intermission, Kalfarveien 8 (tel. 313275). Open mid-June–mid-Aug. Mixed dorm 90kr (£8.25; $14.50). See the hostel immediately above for directions.

Vågenes, J.L. Mowinckelsvej (tel. 161101) 110kr (£10; $17.50) p.p. for doubles with kitchen facilities, mattresses on the floor, 85kr (£7.75; $13.50). Call ahead. A 10-minute trip on bus 19.

Bergen Interpoint, Kalfarveien 77, turn right out of the station and walk along Kalfarveien for 10 minutes.

CAMPING

Bergenshallen, Vilhelm Bjerknesveien 24 (tel. 270180). Open 24 July–10 Aug. 50kr (£4.50; $8) per tent and all occupants. Bus 3 from Strandgaten (see Tourist Offices above).

Lone (tel. 240820). Not cheap. Far from the centre.

FREELANCE CAMPING

Provided you follow the normal rules you can pick your spot. Camping on top of Mt Fløyen is popular. To reach the top it is a one-hour walk by a well-maintained path, or a funicular ride costing 26kr (£2.40; $4) (half price for students).

Oslo   (tel. code 02)

Tourist Offices

Oslo Tourist Board, Rådhuset, N-0037 Oslo 1 (tel. 334386).
Contact this office to reserve hotels, pensions or guesthouses
in advance. The Tourist Board operates two Tourist Information
offices in the city where you can obtain information or book
accommodation on arrival.

Turistinformasjon Rådhusplassen (tel. 830050). Open
June–mid-Aug., Mon.–Fri. 9 a.m.–4.30 p.m.; weekends, 9
a.m.–2.30 p.m.; at other times, Mon.–Fri. 9 a.m.–4.30 p.m.,
except Dec.--Feb. when the offices closes at 4 p.m.

Turistinformasjon Centralstasjon. Open daily 8 a.m.–11 p.m.

USE IT, Trafikanten (tel. 172728). Open mid-June–late Aug.,
Mon.–Fri. 7 a.m.–5 p.m., Sat. 9 a.m.–2 p.m. Lists of the
cheapest accommodation possibilities in the city. In front of
Oslo Sentral.

HOTELS

Expect to pay around 500kr (£46; $80) for doubles

Gyldenløve, Bogstadveien 20 (tel. 601090). Price valid mid-
  June–mid-Aug. only. Tram 1 from the National Theatre.
Majorstuen, Bogstadveien 64 (tel. 693495). Price applies late
  June–early Aug. only. Metro to Majorstuen, or tram 1, 2
  or 11 from the National Theatre.
Munch, Munchsgatan 5 (tel. 424275). Price applies year
  round. Centrally located.

PENSIONS/GUESTHOUSES

Bella Vista, Årrundveien 11b (tel. 654588). Singles around
  230kr (£21; $37), doubles around 430kr (£39; $69).
Cochs Pensjonat, Parkveien 25 (tel 604386). Doubles start
  around 400kr (£36.50; $64), triples around 430kr (£39; $69)
  and quads around 480kr (£44; $77). Beside the royal park,

at the corner of Hegdehaugsveien. The entrance is on Hegdehaugsveien.

Ellingsens Pensjonat, Holtegte 25 (tel. 600359). Singles around 190kr (£17.50; $31); doubles around 300kr (£27.50; $48). Tram 1 to the Uranienborg Church from the National Theatre.

Lindes Pensjonat, Ths. Heftyesgt 41 (tel. 5553782). Tram 2 to Frogner Plass from the National Theatre.

Oslo Sjømannshjemmet, Fred Olsen Gate 2/Tollbugata (tel. 412005). Singles around 260kr (£23.50; $42); doubles around 310kr (£28; $49) p.p. Central location, near the harbour.

St Katarinahjemmet, Majorstuveien 21b (tel. 601370). Open mid-June–mid-Aug. Run by nuns. Doubles around 320kr (£29; $51) p.p. Tram 1 from the National Theatre to Valkyrie Plass.

Holtekilen Sommerhotell, Micheletsveien 55 (tel. 533853). Open 1 June–20 Aug. Singles around 245kr (£22.30; $39), doubles 350kr (£31.80; $56).

PRIVATE ROOMS

Innkvartering in the Central Station book rooms with a two-day min. stay Singles are in short supply 160kr (£14.50; $25.50); doubles 270kr (£24.50; $43). Commission 20kr (£1.80; $3).

IYHF HOSTELS

Haraldsheim, Haraldsheimveien 4 (tel. 222965). No curfew. B&B 150kr (£13.75; $24) for IYHF members, 180kr (£16.50; $29) for non-members from May–Sept. At other times, these prices are increased slightly. Tram 1 or 7 from Storgata to the Sinsen terminus, or a local train to Grefsen.

Pan, Sognsveien 218 (tel. 237640). Open 1 June–20 Aug. No curfew. B&B 160kr (£14.50; $25.50) for IYHF members, 190kr (£17.50; $30.50) for non-members. Tram 13 to the Kringsjå station from National Theatre, then over the lines and downhill for about 500m.

534 Cheap Sleep Guide

HOSTELS

KFUM (YMCA), Møllergata (tel. 421066). Open July –Aug. Midnight curfew. 75kr (£7.25; $13) for a mattress on the floor. About 500m from Oslo Sentral, just past the cathedral (hostel entrance on Grubbegata).

Holtekilen Sommerhotell, Micheletsveien 55 (tel. 533853). Open 1 June–20 Aug. Dorms 135kr (£12.30; $21.50).

IYHF HOSTELS NEARBY

Drammen Vandrerhjem, Korsvegen 62, Drammen (tel. 03-822189). Open late June–mid-Aug. 80kr (£7.25; $13). Trains run frequently between Oslo Sentral and Drammen (30-minute journey). From the station in Drammen take the bus to Lijordet.

CAMPING

Bogstad, Ankerveien 117 (tel. 507680). Open year round. Chalets for rent. Around 400kr (£36.50; $64) per night. Bus 41 from the National Theatre to Bogstad.

Ekeberg, Ekebergveien 65 (tel. 198568). Open June–Aug. 70kr (£6.50; $11) to pitch a tent. No charge per person. Two miles from the centre. Bus 24 or 72 from Oslo Sentral, or bus 72 from the National Theatre.

Stubljan, Hvervbukta (tel. 264289). Open June–Aug. Bus 75 from Oslo Sentral to Ingierstrand.

FREELANCE CAMPING

You can pitch a tent in the woods to the north of Oslo, provided you stay clear of public areas. Take the metro to Sognsvann.

Stavanger (tel. code 04)

Tourist Office
Turistinformasjon, Jernbaneveien 3, P.O. Box 11, 4001

Stavanger (tel. 535100). Turn left down Jernbaneveien from the train and bus stations. Open June–Aug., 8.30 a.m.–4.00 p.m.; Sept–May., Mon.–Fri. 8.30 a.m.–4 p.m.; Sat. 9 a.m.–1 p.m.

HOTELS

Commandor, Valberggt. 9 (tel. 528000). Doubles around 280–500kr (£25.50–46.00; $45–80) from June–Aug. In the centre of the old town.

Mosvangen Parkhotel, Henrik Ibsensgate 21 (tel. 870977). Doubles start around 420kr (£38; $67) from mid-June–late Aug.

PENSIONS/GUESTHOUSES

Gjestehuset Phønix, Lagårdsveien 47 (tel. 520437). Doubles around 360kr (£33; $57) from mid-June–mid-Aug. Right at the opposite end of Jernbaneveien from the Tourist Office.

Bergeland Gjestgiveri, Vujedaksgata 1a (tel. 534110). B&B around 220kr (£20; $35) per person.

Melands Gjestgiveri, Nedre Holmeg. 2 (tel. 523821). Around 410kr (£37.50; $65) for doubles from mid-June–Aug. In the centre of the old town.

Paradis Hospits, Lyder Sagensgt. 26 (tel. 529655).

Rogalandsheimen, Muségata 18 (tel. 520188).

Skogstuen Hospits, Stasjonsveien 26 (tel. 585117).

Øglænd Hospits, Jens Zetlitzgt. 25 (tel. 520832). The street begins near the Tourist Office.

IYHF HOSTEL

Mosvangen YH, Henrik Ibsensgate 21 (tel. 870977). Open June–Aug. 120kr (£11; $19) for IYHF members, 150kr (£13.50; $24) for non-members, without breakfast. Double rooms are available. Bus 78 from the train station, or a half hour walk. Kannikgata (near the station) leads into Madlaveien. Left off Madlaveien along the E18, then follow the cycle path round.

CAMPING

Mosvangen, Henrik Ibsensgate 21 (tel. 870977). Open 29 May–1 Sept. 60kr (£5.50; $9.50) per tent and all its occupants. Cabins available. Located by Lake Mosvatn, beside the IYHF hostel (see above for directions).

Ølberg, Ølberg Havnevei (tel. 667170). Open May–Aug. Cabins for rent. Farther out than the Mosvangen site.

Trondheim (tel. code 07)

Tourist Office

Trondheim Reiselivslag, P.O. Box 2102, 7001 Trondheim. Contact the Tourist Board at this address if you want information on the city in advance. On arrival go to their Turistinformasjon on the Market Square (Torvet) (tel. 527201). Open June–mid-Aug., Mon.–Fri. 8.30 a.m.–8 p.m., Sat. 8.30 a.m.–6 p.m., Sun. 10 a.m.–6 p.m.; rest of the year, Mon.–Fri. 9 a.m.–4 p.m., Sat. 9 a.m.–1 p.m. The main bus station is close to Torvet. From the train station head straight ahead from the exit, then turn right at the end of Søndregate.

HOTELS

Trondheim, Kongensgt. 15 (tel. 527030). Doubles around 460kr (£42; $73) from late June–early Aug. Kongensgt. runs out of Torvet.

Singsaker Sommerhotell, Rogertsgate 1 (tel. 520092). Open mid-June–mid-Aug. Singles around 220kr (£20; $35), doubles around 330kr (£30; $52), with breakfast. About 15 minutes' walk from the train station. Head straight down Søndregate, left at the end of the street, then right along Kjøpmannsgt, over the Nidelva by the Old Town Bridge (Bybrua) and straight on.

PENSIONS/GUESTHOUSES

Lade Pensjonat, Jarleveien 44 (tel. 931855/920200).
Linde Pensjonat, Kongensgt 40 (tel. 513218). The street runs
out of Torvet.

PRIVATE ROOMS

Available from the Tourist Office. Singles around 165kr (£15;
$26) doubles around 280kr (£25.50; $45), plus a 20kr (£1.75;
$3.50) commission.

IYHF HOSTEL

Trondheim Vandrerhjem, Weidemannsv. 41 (tel. 530490)
140kr (£12.75; $22.50) for IYHF members, 170kr (£15.50;
$27) for non-members. Bus 63 or a 20-minute walk from
the train station. Head straight on from the exit down
Søndregate, left at the junction with Olav Tryggvasonsgt,
and over the Nidelva by the Bakke bru, left along
Innherredsveien past the Bakke kirke, right at Nonnegt.
then left along Weidemannsv.

HOSTELS

Singsaker Sommerhotell, Rogertsgate 1 (tel. 520092).
Mattresses on the floor 110kr (£10; $17.50). See the entry
in Hotels section above for directions.

CAMPING

Sandmoen (tel. 886135) 60kr (£5.50; $9.50) per tent. No
charge per person. About 5 miles out of Trondheim. Bus
44 or 45 to Sandbakken.

FREELANCE CAMPING

Not permitted in the area around Trondheim.

POLAND (Polska)

In common with the other countries of the former Soviet bloc, Poland has recently been receiving unprecedented numbers of tourists. With the obvious exception of the old DDR, none of the other new democracies has coped so admirably with the influx as Poland. In contrast to Czechoslovakia and Hungary, good quality tourist information is available in most of the main towns and, at least in 1992, finding reasonably priced accommodation was relatively straightforward. As long as you arrived in town when the local Tourist Office or accommodation agency was open, you were virtually guaranteed a cheap night's accommodation, even in the two most popular tourist destinations, Warsaw and Cracow. With the lifting of visa restrictions for many European nationalities this happy situation may change: visa fees of £20 ($35) were probably a deterrent to railpass holders who might otherwise have visited Poland for a few days.

It is difficult to say anything specific about Polish **hotels**, other than that the standards of cleanliness and comfort are fine. Previously ORBIS, like most other East European state tourist organizations, tried to push Westerners into the most expensive hotels and were loath to admit even the existence of the cheapest hotels, which were not meant to admit Western guests in any case. Now that these hotels can open their doors freely there are some great bargains to be found. Although in Warsaw you will struggle to find doubles for under £20 ($35), elsewhere there are some excellent hotels offering doubles for as little as £8–10 ($14.0–17.50). Even in Cracow there are several hotels offering singles for £5.50–7.00 ($9.50–12.50). While it is possible to turn up in as popular a destination as Cracow in mid-August and find a room in one of the cheaper hotels, it is advisable to try and reserve ahead, preferably in writing (use German if you can) a month or so in advance.

An organization called PTTK run a network of cheap hotels known as '**Dom Turysty**', '**Dom Wycieczkowy**', offering accommodation in singles, doubles, triples, quads and eight-bed dormitories. The local PTTK or Tourist Office will inform you of the whereabouts of any such hotels operating in the locality. The prices of PTTK hotels vary substantially across the country: whereas in Lublin you can get a single for around £3 ($5.50), the same amount will only get you a bed in a four-or eight-bed room in Warsaw. The larger rooms are very popular with visiting groups, which may mean that the rather cramped triples, doubles and singles are the only option available to you. In the more expensive Dom Turysty/Dom Wycieczkowy these probably represent poor value for money, especially as Dom Turysty/Dom Wycieczkowy are frequently very noisy. In such cases, you would probably be better off spending a similar amount or a little bit more on a private room.

It is the widespread availability of **private rooms** that has helped Poland avoid a dire accommodation shortage. In most well-visited towns, private rooms can be arranged through the Biuro Zakwaterowania (and occasionally by other organizations). Prices are generally very low, with singles available for under £4 ($7) in destinations as popular as Danzig and Poznan. Even in Warsaw you can find singles for around £5.50 ($9.50), with rooms in Cracow being the most expensive, at around £7.70 ($13.50) for singles, £10.90 ($19) for doubles. Payment is to the booking agency rather than to your host. It is not uncommon to be approached by locals offering **rooms,** particularly in the vicinity of the train stations and Tourist Offices. These rooms are normally clean, and safe for you and your belongings. As a rule, prices are a bit lower than rooms fixed up through the local Biuro. The one problem you might have with such offers is the location of the rooms. Try to find out if they are centrally located, or, at the very least, well served by public transport. If you are not specifically asked to pay in hard currency you can often obtain a reduction on the asking price by offering to do so (Deutschmarks and US dollars are especially welcome).

During the university/college summer holidays (July to Aug./mid-Sept.) the student travel organization ALMATUR runs 'International Student Hostels' in **vacant student flats.** Accommodation is usually in two-or four-bed rooms. While rooms are supposedly only available to holders of the ISIC/IUS card who are aged under 35, this rule is rarely enforced if there is space. There is very little chance of simply turning up and finding a bed in the hostels in Cracow, Danzig or Warsaw, and this is likely to become the case in other cities as well. Possibly your only chance of getting a bed on arrival is to head for the local ALMATUR office early in the morning and enquire if there are any beds available (the office is invariably much easier to reach than the hostel as the latter tends to be situated out from the centre). **International Student Hostels** can be reserved in advance using ALMATUR vouchers, and with these reservations you can reserve a bed until 2 p.m., but thereafter reservations are invalid. It is probably worth making the effort to reserve International Student Hostels in this manner, at least in the main cities, because although initially you pay a bit more this way, you are still getting reasonable value for money as the hostels are by and large very comfortable, and a good place to meet other travellers. Moreover, you will save yourself time looking for accommodation on arrival, and perhaps save yourself money as well.

The Polish affiliate of the IYHF, the **Polish Federation of Youth Hostels** (PTSM), runs a network of 1500 hostels covering all the main places of interest. A comprehensive list of Polish hostels is available from PTSM, but the abbreviated list in the IYHF handbook covers the towns that you are most likely to visit. Again, hostels in the main towns should be reserved in advance, preferably by means of a reservation card. At all hostels priority is given to school children and students, but there is no maximum age limit. All hostels have a 10 p.m. curfew, but you must arrive before 9 p.m. Prices are very low, with dormitory accommodation ranging in price from £1.00–2.50 ($1.75–4.50). Unfortunately, standards are also low, hostels tend to be very crowded, and facilities are rudimentary, while standards of cleanliness at many hostels leave a lot to be desired.

The camping season runs from April/May to September/October. There are **campsites** in all the places you are likely to visit. Polish campsites are certainly cheap, with prices for an overnight stay rarely rising above £2.50 ($4.50) for a solo traveller. Although facilities at some sites can be very basic, prices are generally set accordingly, so you seldom have cause to grumble about lack of value for money. On the contrary, you are likely to find sites which are real bargains: very clean, well maintained and efficiently run. At many sites it is possible to hire bungalows sleeping two to four people. Average prices work out at around £4 ($7), assuming all the beds are taken. Otherwise you can usually expect to be charged extra to cover the empty bed space. The first-class publication *Campingi w Polsce* lists details of all the sites, and shows their locations on a map. Copies are available from main bookstores, or from PZMot (the National Automobile Club). ALMATUR also operates a chain of sites in summer. Any of their local offices will supply you with a list. A few of the IYHF hostels also allow camping in their grounds, but this is not usually permitted.

Tourist Information

In contrast to the other countries of the former Soviet Bloc, good quality tourist information is available for most of the main towns of interest. The detailed street plan (sometimes indexed) entitled 'Poland: A Tourist Map of . . .' is available for many of the main tourist attractions. These plans, which are sold for a nominal fee, are actually superior to much of the tourist information on offer in Western Europe. The major local sights are numbered on the plan, with a basic historical background provided. The one difficulty in the past has been that local offices have occasionally run out of these plans. For that reason alone, you might want to invest in a good guidebook to the country before setting off on holiday. However, if you are travelling extensively in Poland, a good guidebook is highly recommended, preferably one that offers detailed coverage of the public transport system.

ADDRESSES

Polish National Tourist Office	82 Mortimer Street, London W1N 7DE (tel. 071-6362217/6374971)
Hostels	ALMATUR, ul Ordynacka 9, 00364 Warszawa (tel. 262356). Polskie Towarzystwo Schronisk Mlodziezowych, ul Chocimska 28, 00791 Warszawa (tel. 498354/498128).
Camping	Polska Federacja Campingu i Caravaningu,ul Króléwska 27a, Warszawa. PZMot, ul. Krucza 6/14, Warszawa (tel. 290467/293541).

Breslau (Wrocław) (tel. code 071)

Tourist Offices

At the time of writing, Breslau had no main 'it' office similar
to those in the other main cities. ORBIS, Rynek 45 (tel.
447946/447679/444109) is the best office for general tourist
information. Open Apr.–Sept., Mon.–Sat. 8 a.m.–5 p.m.;
Oct.–Mar., same hours but closed on Sat. A small Tourist
Information operates at Rynek 38 (tel. 443111), open Mon.–Sat.
10 a.m.–4 p.m. English-speaking staff are rare, so whether it
is worth a visit depends on how much Polish or German you
know. The Biuro Ustug Turystycznych, ul. Piłsudskiego 98 (tel.
444101), open Mon.–Fri. 9 a.m.–5 p.m. and the first Sat. each
month 9 a.m.–2 p.m., may be of some help, while students
can obtain assistance at the ALMATUR office at ul. Tadeusza
Kościuszki 34 (tel. 443003). If you can get a copy, the
publication 'A Tourist Map of Wroclaw' is indexed and has
basic background information on the main places of historical
interest, which are marked on the plan.

Basic Directions

Arriving in Breslau by train, your most likely point of arrival
is Wrocław Głowny, which is about a mile to the south of the
Rynek. A new main bus terminal is being constructed on ul.
Sucha to the rear of the Wrocław Głowny which will replace
the station at pl. Konstytucji 3 Maja, to the right across ul.
Małachowskiego from Wrocław Głowny. Most trains from
Jelenia Góra, and some from Legnica and Głogów arrive at
Wrocław Świebodzki, to the left of the junction of ul.
Piłsudskiego and Podwale, from which Wrocław Głowny is
easily reached on foot by following the inner ring road round
to the right from Swiebodzki. Trains from Łódź, Trzebnica and
Oleśnica arrive at Wrocław Nadodrze on pl. Staszica, about
1¼ miles north of the centre.

Walking from Wrocław Głowny to the Rynek there are two
routes which are easy to follow. Across from the main exit is
the inner ring road, at this point ul. Skiego, with ul.

Małachowskiego along to the right. Diagonally left from the main exit of Wrocław Głowny, the main street running away from the station is ul. Kołłataja. Going straight ahead you eventually arrive at pl. Dominikański with the imposing barn-like structure of St Adalbert's Church. By the church you can turn left along ul. Wita Stwosza which leads into the Rynek. Alternatively, walk left along ul. Piłsudskiego past the end of ul. Stawowa (take this street if you want the ALMATUR office), before turning right at the crossroads up into Tadeusza Kościuszki square. Going straight on across the square, you can follow Świdnicka across ul. Kazimierza Wielkiego into the Rynek.

From Wrocław Świebodzki head left along Podwale to pl. Dominikański from which either ul. Św. Mikołaja or Ruska on the right will take you to the Rynek. From Wrocław Nadodrze tram 0 or 1 run to the centre. If you want to walk, follow ul. Trzebnicka right from the station, then ul. Łokietka and cross the River Oder (Odra) by the Most Uniwersytecki. Head right along Grodzka following the river, then just before the next bridge turn left down Ordrzańska which takes you into the Rynek.

HOTELS

The cheapest hotels in Breslau are all situated well out from the centre, but there are a number of hotels in and around the centre which fall within the budget category.

Cheapest hotels

Zeglarz, ul. Władysława Reymonta 4 (tel. 212996). Near the Wrocław Nadodrze train station (the street runs off pl. Staszica on tram route 14.

Oficerski, ul. Adama Prchnika 130 (tel. 603303). Far out in the south-west of the city. Trams 13, 14 and 20 pass close by the hotel.

Ślask (tel. 611611). Far out to the west of the city, located in a park close to ul. Oporowska. Trams 1, 4, 5, 13, 16, 18 or 20.

DOSiR, ul. Wejherowska 2 (tel. 550198). Sports hotel, out to the west, near the terminus of bus 127.

Nauczycielski, ul. Nauczycielska 2 (tel. 229268). About 20–25 minutes' walk from the centre off Marii Skłodowskiej-Curie beyond the Most Grunwaldzki. Trams 0, 1, 2, 10 or 12.

Singles around £4.25 ($7.50), singles with baths around £5.50 ($9.50), doubles around £7 ($12.50), doubles with baths around £9 ($16). By Wrocław Głowny unless otherwise stated

Odra, ul. Stawowa 13 (tel. 37560/45447).

Piast, ul. Piłsudskiego 98 (tel. 30033).

Polonia, ul. Piłsudskiego 66 (tel. 31021).

Europejski, ul. Piłsudskiego 88 (tel. 31071).

Grand, ul. Piłsudskiego 100 (tel. 36071).

Dom Kultury, ul. Kazimierza Wielkiego 45 (tel. 443866). A short walk from the Rynek. Rooms at this hotel are a bit cheaper than the prices quoted above.

Singles around £7.50 ($13), doubles around £8.50–10.75 ($15–18)

Olimp, ul. Wita Stwosza 22/23 (tel. 442751). Operated by the Polytechnic Institute, a short walk from the Rynek.

PRIVATE ROOMS

Available from the Biuro Ustug Turystycznych, ul Piłsudskiego 98 (tel. 444101). See Tourist Offices for opening hours. Across the street from Wrocław Głowny. Singles £5.75 ($10), doubles £6.80–8.60 ($12–15).

PTTK DOM TURYSTY

ul. Karola Szajnochy 11 (tel. 443073). Close to the Rynek. Walking from Wrocław Głowny turn left along ul. Kazimierza Wielkiego from Świdnicka, right at ul.

Gepperta, then left into ul. Karoly Szajnochy. Ul Gepperta continues into pl. Solny, which adjoins the Rynek.

IYHF HOSTELS

ul. Kołłataja 20 (tel. 38856). £0.90 ($1.50) for under 26s, £2.25 ($4) otherwise. Near Wrocław Głowny.

ul. Na Grobli 30 (tel. 37402). Close to the Oder, 2 miles from Wrocław Głowny and the centre. No convenient tram service. Ask for directions at one of the Tourist Offices.

INTERNATIONAL STUDENT HOSTELS

ALMATUR (see Tourist Offices) will inform you of any hostels operating in the city in 1993.

CAMPING

ul. Ignacego Paderewskiego 35 (tel. 484651). Chalets available. The better of the two sites. Further out, but easier to reach. The site is close to the Olympic Stadium, left off ul. Adama Mickiewicza. Trams 16 and 17 pass close by.

ul. Na Grobli (tel. 34442). Chalets available. Near the IYHF hostel in ul. Na Grobli, by the Oder. Two miles from Wrocław Głowny and the city centre. Difficult to reach by public transport.

Cracow (Kraków) (tel. code 012)

Tourist Office
Centralny Ośrodek Informacji Turystycznej, ul. Pawia 8, 31-016 Kraków (tel. 220471/226091). Open Mon.–Fri. 8 a.m.–4 p.m., Sat. 8 a.m.–noon. Arguably the best Tourist Office in the country. Knowledgeable and helpful staff. A good source of books, maps and general information on the city and its

surroundings. 'A Tourist Map of Cracow' costs little to buy
and is a good basic guide to the city.

Basic Directions
The main bus station is beside the main train station, Kraków
Głowny, which is likely to be still undergoing reconstruction
during 1993. When you finally make your way through the
market stalls in front of the stations, you arrive on ul. Pawia.
Crossing the street and heading left, you pass the Tourist Office
and the Hotel Warszawski before arriving at the junction of
ul. Pawia with ul. Basztowa (right), ul. Westerplatte (more or
less straight ahead) and ul. Lubicz (left). Turning right on ul.
Basztowa you pass the information booth for the tram network
on the left, and then, again on the left, the end of ul. Szpitalna.
Next on the left is the Barbican (Barbakan). Turning left through
the Barbican and going straight ahead you can follow
Floriańska into Rynek Głowny, the market square at the heart
of the city. The walk from the train station to Rynek Głowny
takes around 10 minutes. If, instead of turning left at the
Barbican, you continue along ul. Basztowa the next main street
on the left is ul. Sławkowska, which also leads into Rynek
Głowny. On the right at this point, is ul. Długa. By the junction
of ul. Długa and ul. Basztowa is a small mini-market, which
opens daily and keeps long hours.

Finding Accommodation
Over the past few years, Cracow has (understandably) become
exceptionally popular, especially during the period mid-June
to August. If you are travelling at this time it makes sense to
try and reserve accommodation as far in advance as possible.
Wawel Tourist, ul. Pawia 6 (inside the Hotel Warszawski)
books hotels in advance, or on arrival. Write to the office or
telephone 221509 to reserve in advance (tel. 229370 or call in
person for same-day bookings). Even in peak season, you
should be able to get a private room if you arrive while the
Biuro Zakwaterowania is open, though the later in the day you
arrive the less likely you are to get a reasonably located room,
or one of the cheaper rooms.

HOTELS

Singles around £5.50 ($9.50), doubles around £7 ($12.50), triples around £8.75 ($15.50)

Holiday Hotel Mercury al. 29, Listopada 48a (tel. 118826). Operated by the students of the Kraków Academy of Economics. Bus 105 or 129 from Krakw Głowny.

Singles around £6 ($10.50), doubles around £9.50 ($16.50), triples around £10.50 ($18.50) if available

Student Hotel Zaczek, ul. Karasia (tel 331914). Triples. Near the Biblioteka Jagiellońska on al. Zygmunta Krasińskiego. Tram 15 crosses this street before heading along al. 3 Maja. Either walk right along ul. Krasińskiego then left or walk right along ul. Oleandry from al. 3 Maja into ul. Karasia.

Wisła, ul. Reymonta 22 (tel. 334922). Near the Wisła Kraków football stadium (one of Poland's best teams over the years). Bus 144 stops nearby. Alternatively, you can take tram 15 along al. 3 Maja to the Cichy Kacik terminus, followed by a short walk along ul. D. Chodowieckiego into wł. Reymonta.

Korona, ul. Pstrowskiego 9/15 (tel. 666511). On the fringe of the wartime Jewish ghetto.

Singles around £8 ($14), singles with baths/showers around £10.25 ($18), doubles around £11 ($19), doubles with baths/showers around £14.75 ($26)

Warszawski, ul. Pawia 6 (tel. 220622).
Europeijski, ul. Lubicz 5 (tel. 220911).
Saski, ul. Sławkowska 3 (tel. 214222).
Polonia, ul. Basztowa 25 (tel. 221661). Triples around £14.25 ($25), triples with bath/shower £17 ($30), quads £17.50 ($31).

Singles around £10.50 ($18.50), doubles around £14.50 ($25), doubles with baths/shower £18 ($31.50). Price includes breakfast

Pollera, ul. Szpitalna 30 (tel. 221044). Fine location, a 5-minute walk from both Kraków Główny and the Rynek Główny.

PRIVATE ROOMS

Biuro Zakwaterowania, ul. Pawia 8 (tel. 221921). Open Mon.–Fri. 7a.m.–9p.m.; Sat. 1–6p.m. Singles £7.70 ($13.50), singles with bath £9.50 ($16.50), doubles £10.90 ($19), doubles with bath £14 ($24.50).

PTTK DOM TURYSTY

Westerplatte 15–16 (tel. 229566) Eight-bed dorms £2.75 ($5) per person, singles £7.50–12.00 ($13.50–21.00), doubles £12–15 ($21.00–26.50), doubles with bath £18 ($31.50). Good location, near the main Post Office, within easy walking distance of the town centre and the bus and train stations.

IYHF HOSTELS

ul. Oleandry 4 (tel. 338822/338920). Open all year. Doubles £4 ($7) per person, three-to five-bed rooms £3 ($5.50), sixteen-bed dorms. £2 ($3.50). Tram 15 along al. 3 Maja, until you see ul. Oleandry, the first street on the right. The hostel is a 10–15-minute walk from the centre.
ul Kościuszki 88 (tel. 221951). Open all year. Tram 1, 2 or 6.
ul Złotej Kielni 1 (tel. 372441). Open 1 July–26 Aug.

INTERNATIONAL STUDENT HOSTEL

ALMATUR, Rynek Główny 7–8 (tel. 215130). ALMATUR will inform you of the current location, as it changes almost annually. Open July–mid-Sept.

CAMPING

Krak, ul. Radzikowskiego 99 (tel. 372122). Category I site. Open May–Sept. £2.10 ($3.75) p.p., tent included. Far from town centre. Tram 8 or 12 to Fizyków, or bus 208. Krakowania, ul. Zywiecka Boczna (tel. 664191). A good category II site, cheaper and quieter than Krak. £1.60 ($2.75) p.p., tent included. Take tram 19 to the Borek Fałecki terminus along Zakopiańska from ul. Basztowa (or any tram to Łagiewniki, then change to tram 19). From the terminus, head in the direction of the housing estate to the right, then take the path which leads away to the right. You will see the site as you walk along this path. Left at the end of the path. Register at the motel.

Częstochowa (tel. code 034)

Tourist Office
Informacji Turystycznej ('it'), al. Najświetszej Marii Panny 65, 42-200 Częstochowa (tel. 41360) In the underpass at the junction of al. Najświetszej with ul. Pułaskiego, near Jasna Góra.

Basic Directions
The train and bus stations are both located about two miles from the Jasna Góra monastery. From the bus station, head right along al. Wolności; from the train station, go straight ahead then right along the same road to the junction with al. Najświetszej Marii Panny. Turn left at this point and then head straight on to Jasna Góra.

Finding Accommodation
The constant influx of pilgrims to Częstochowa means that accommodation can be difficult to find on arrival at any time, with the task becoming virtually impossible at the time of major pilgrimages and religious festivals. It is advisable to make

finding a bed your first priority on arrival so that if there is nothing suitable available you can check times for moving on to another town (Cracow is 2–3 hours away by train, Opole about the same). Those with a railpass can always take a night train out of Częstochowa if they cannot find a place to stay (trains leave for a variety of destinations). If you want to reserve a couchette or sleeper you will find ORBIS at al. Najświetszej Marii Panny 40/42 (tel. 47987).

HOTELS

Two hotels near the train station are relatively cheap. The better of the two is the May, ul. Katedralna 18 (tel. 43391); the other is the Centralny, ul. Piłsudskiego 9 (tel. 44076).

PRIVATE ROOMS

At the time of writing there was no information available on the letting of private rooms in Częstochowa, but you might as well enquire at ORBIS, al. Najświetszej Marii Panny 40/42 (tel. 47987) if you are passing, or at the Tourist Office.

IYHF HOSTEL

ul Wacławy Marek 12 (tel. 31296). Far from the train and bus stations on the other side of town from Jasna Góra.

INTERNATIONAL STUDENT HOSTELS

Details of any such hostels operating in the city in 1993 will be available from ALMATUR, ul. Zawadzkiego 29 (tel. 54106).

PILGRIM HOSTELS

Dom Pielgrzyma. The hostel is by the car park, directly behind Jasna Góra as you approach the monastery from al. Najświetszej Marii Panny.

Dom Rekolekcyjny. Near St Barbara's Church. From the end of al. Najświetszej Marii Panny head left along ul. Pułaskiego, turn right down ul. Sw. Kazimierza, then left at ul. Sw. Barbary.

CAMPING

To the rear of Jasna Góra. At the end of al. Najświetszej Marii Panny turn right along ul. Pułaskiego, then right again along ul. 7. Kamienic down the side of the park. After passing ul. Klasztorna on the right the road bends away to the left to become ul. ks. Augustyna Kordeckiego. Take the first right from this street, then go left along Oleńki.

Danzig (Gdańsk) (tel. code 058)

Tourist Offices

Gdański Ośrodek Informacji Turystycznej, ul. Heweliusza 27, 80-890 Gdańsk (tel. 316637/314355). The head office of the Tourist Board and the main 'it' point. Open Mon.–Sat. 8 a.m.–4 p.m. Good range of maps and guides and a knowledgeable staff who do their best to answer any enquiries. A short walk from the main train station.

ALMATUR, Długi Targ 11/13 (3rd floor, to the rear) (tel. 317801/312403). Open Mon.–Fri. 9 a.m.–3 p.m. Limited range of publications, but again the staff are very helpful if you have any questions. Near the Town Hall.

Gdańsk Dworzec Głowny to Długi Targ

Gdańsk Dworzec Głowny, the main train station, and the main bus station behind it, are both within 10–15 minutes' walk of Długi Targ, the centre of Danzig's Old Town. From the train station take the underpass to the other side of Podwale Grodzkie. Two streets run off Podwale Grodzkie opposite Gdańsk Dworzec Głowny: ul. Heweliusza and ul. Elżbietańska. Turning right along Podwale Grodzkie then left along ul. Wały Jagiellonskie and straight on, you arrive at the old Upland Gate (Brama Złota) into Ulica Kługa, which opens out into Długi Targ by the imposing Town Hall.

The Tri-City
Danzig, Sopot and Gdynia combine to make up a conurbation often referred to as the Tri-City (population around ¾ million). Travelling around the conurbation is relatively easy. Trams run within but do not cross the boundaries of the three constituent parts of the Tri-City. Buses do run between the different parts, as do frequent local trains. The most important local stations between Gdańsk Dworzec Głowny and Gdynia Dworzec Głowny are Gdańsk-Wrzeszcz, Gdańsk-Zaspa, Gdańsk-Oliwa and Sopot. The journey time from Gdańsk Dworzec Głowny to Gdynia Dworzec Głowny by local train is around 25–30 minutes, but there are frequent express trains which make the trip in about half that time.

Finding Accommodation
Hotels and hostel accommodation are best reserved in advance if you are arriving in Danzig during the summer, especially in July and August. Not only are increasing numbers of visitors coming to see the historic Old Town but the beaches of Danzig and Sopot are the most popular in Poland, which ensures that hotels and hostels in the Tri-City are frequently filled to capacity during the summer.

HOTELS

Expect to pay around £6.25–7.50 ($11–13) for singles, £9.75–12.75 ($17.00–22.50) for doubles, and £12.00–18.50 ($21–32) for doubles with a shower bath

Jantar, Długi Targ 19 (tel. 316241). Also triples with showers around £16 ($28.50).
Piast, ul. Piastowska 199/201 (tel. 530928).
Żabianka, ul. Dickmana 15 (tel. 522772).
Dom Harcerza, ul. Zam Urami 2/10 (tel. 313621).

Mesa, ul. Waly Jagelliońskie 36 (tel. 318052).
OPO, ul. Wiejska 1 (tel. 524636).
Students' Home, ul. Polanki 65 (tel. 524212).
Pensjonat Irena, ul. Chopina 36 (tel. 512074). In Sopot.
Pensjonat Maryla, ul. Sepia 22 (tel. 510034). In Sopot.
Antracyt, ul. Korzeniowskiego 19d (tel. 206811). In Gdynia.
Miastral, ul. Ejsmonda 2 (tel. 221542). In Gdynia.

PRIVATE ROOMS

Singles around £3 ($5.25), doubles around £5 ($9)

Available in Danzig at ul. Elżbietańska 10–11 (tel. 319444/
338840), in Sopot at ul. Dworcowa 4 (tel. 512617), and in
Gdynia at ul. Dworcowa 7 (tel. 218265). The offices in Sopot
and Gdynia are down the street from the train stations. In
summer, there are usually locals offering rooms outside the
office in Danzig.

DOM TURYSTY

ul. Zamkowa Góra 25 (tel. 518011). In Sopot/Sopot Kamienny
Potok.

IYHF HOSTELS

ul. Smoluchowskiego 11 (tel. 323820). £2.50 ($4.50) for dorms.
In Gdańsk-Wrzeszcz, about one mile from Gdańsk
Dworzec Główny. From the train station, take tram 2, 8,
12, 13 or 14 as far as al. Zwyciestwa, from which the hostel
is only a short walk.
ul. Wałowa 21 (tel. 312313). 10 p.m. curfew. £2.50 ($4.50)
for dorms. Smaller rooms are available. A 10-minute walk
from Gdańsk Dworzec Główny station. Turn left off
Heweliusza along Rajska, and then right at Wałowa.
ul. Legionów 11 (tel. 414108) 10 p.m. curfew. £2.50 ($4.50)
for dorms. No showers. In Gdańsk-Wrzeszcz. Tram 2, 4,

7, 8 or 14, or a 10-minute walk from Gdańsk-Wrzeszcz train
station.

Grunwaldzka 238/240 (tel. 411660). In a sports centre in
Gdańsk-Wrzeszcz, near the boundary with the suburb of
Oliwa. Tram 2, 4, 7, 8 or 14. The closest train station to
the hostel is Gdańsk-Zaspa.

ul. Karpia 1 (tel. 318219). Open July–Aug. only. On the
northern fringe of the Old Town, beside the canal.

ul. Morska 108c (tel. 270005). In Gdynia, close to the Gdynia-
Grabowek train station. Tram 22, 25, 26 or 30, or bus 109,
125 or 141.

INTERNATIONAL STUDENT HOSTEL

No hostel operated in Danzig in 1992, but ALMATUR will
inform you of the latest situation.

HOSTELS

YMCA, ul. Zeromskiego 26, Gdynia (tel. 203115). Open 15
June–31 Aug. £4 ($7). In the town centre, about 10
minutes' walk from Gdynia Dworzec Głowny.

CAMPING

Gdańsk-Jelitkowo, ul. Jelitkowska (tel. 532731). Open
June–mid-Sept. £2 ($3.50) p.p. tent included. Bungalows
around £10.50 ($18.50) per night. Clean, well-maintained
site. Tram 6 from Gdańsk Dworzec Głowny to the
Jelitkowo terminus, past the pond and out on to the main
road, then left along to the site entrance.

Gdańsk-Brzeźno, ul. Gen. Hallera 234 (tel. 566531). Open
mid-May–Oct. Tram 7, 13 or 15, or bus 124 or 148 all stop
reasonably close to the site.

Gdańsk-Sobieszewo-Orle, ul. Lazurowa 5 (tel. 380739). Well
out to the east of the centre. Bus 112 runs by the site.

Lublin (tel. code 081)

Tourist Office

Informacji Turystycznej ('it'), ul. Krakowskie Przedmieście 78, 20-101 Lublin (tel. 24412). Open Mon.–Fri. 9 a.m.–5 p.m., Sat. 10 a.m.–2 p.m. Well supplied with maps and other information. Exceptionally helpful staff. Bus/trolleybus 50 and 150 from the train station. From the bus station walk right along the main road (al. Tysiaclecia, left up ul. Lubartowska into pl. Łokietka, then right along ul. Krakowskie Przedmieście.

HOTELS

Lublinianka, ul. Krakowskie Przedmieście 56 (tel. 24261). Singles around £5.50 ($10), singles with bath around £7.50 ($13.50), doubles around £9.50 ($16.50), doubles with bath around £19 ($33). Good central location, between pl. Łokietka and the Tourist Office.

Motel PZM, ul. B. Prusa 8 (tel. 34232). Singles £8–11 ($14–19), doubles with bath £18 ($31.50). Operated by the Polish Automobile Association. A well-run hotel with pleasant rooms. From the bus station go right along the main road (al. Tysiaclecia), then right at ul. B. Prusa. From pl. Łokietka go down ul. Lubartowska, left along al. Tysiaclecia, then right.

ZNP Dom Noclegowy, ul. Akademicka 4 (tel. 38285). Singles £3.50 ($6), doubles with bath £6 ($10.50). Primarily for teachers and lecturers, the hotel admits other guests when space is available (most likely outside term-time). By the Marie Skłodowskiej-Curie university. From the train station take trolleybus 150 along ul. Krakowskie Przedmieście into al. Racławickie to the junction with ul. Łopacińskiego. Walk down the latter, go left at the end of the street, then almost immediately right down ul. Akademicka.

PRIVATE ROOMS

At the time of writing there was no agency booking private rooms in Lublin, but you can ask at the Tourist Office if they are aware of any new developments.

PTTK DOM WYCIECZKOWY

ul. Krakowskie Przedmieście 29 (tel. 22102). Singles £3.25–5.25 ($5.50–9.50), doubles £4.25–7.00 ($7.50–12.50), triples £6.75–8.00 ($11.50–14.00). Prices per person are very low in the four-bed dormitories. Excellent location, a short distance along ul. Krakowskie Przedmieście from pl. Łokietka.

IYHF HOSTELS

ul. Długosza 6a (tel. 30628). Seniors pay around £2.10 ($4), juniors slightly less. Non-members pay slightly more than the senior price if there is space available. Kitchen facilities. Run by a very friendly and helpful staff. Usually you can camp in the hostel garden. Trolleybus 160 from the train station or ul. Krakowskie Przedmieście. Just after ul. Krakowskie Przedmieście runs into al. Racławickie you will see a large park (Ogrd Saski) on the right. al. Długosa is off al. Racławickie to the right at the end of the park.

CAMPING

There are several sites in Lublin, details of which are available from the Tourist Office, as well as the directions how to get to the sites. One site is at ul. Stawinkowska 46 (tel. 32231). Bungalows available. From ul. Krakowskie Przedmieście take bus 18 (ask the Tourist Office for exact directions if you can). If you turn up late in the evening with your tent at the IYHF hostel it is unlikely you will be turned away.

Cheap Sleep Guide

Olsztyn (tel. code 089)

Tourist Office
Tourist Information Centre, Wysoka Brama, 10-039 Olsztyn (tel. 272738). A good range of information on the town, and on the surrounding area. Just along the street from the High Gate (Wysoka Brama).

PRIVATE ROOMS

Enquire at the reception desk of the Hotel Nad Lyna, al. Wojska Polskiego 14 (tel. 266401).

PTTK DOM TURYSTY

Wysoka Brama (tel. 273675). Located in the Gothic High Gate.

IYHF HOSTELS

ul. Kopernika 45 (tel. 274062). Open year round. Between the main train and bus stations and the town centre, near the junction of ul. Kopernika with ul. Adama Mickiewicza.
ul. Ketrzynskiego 6 (tel. 335045). Open July–Aug. only.

INTERNATIONAL STUDENT HOSTELS

During the summer, ALMATUR operate hostels in the student accommodation at the Agricultural College in the suburb of Kortowo. The ALMATUR office is located at the college (tel. 278653). The Tourist Office will probably be willing to check out the availability of beds at the hostels for you.

CAMPING

PTTK operate a site by Lake Krzywe, open from May–Sept.

Poznań (tel. code 061)

Tourist Office

Informacji Turystycznej ('it'), Stary Rynek 59, 61-772 Poznań (tel. 526156). Open Mon.–Fri. 9 a.m.–4 p.m., Sat. 9 a.m.–2 p.m. A well organized office with a wide range of information and maps. 'A Tourist Guide to Poznań' costs little to buy yet contains a good street map of the central area and basic details on the main historic sites which are marked on the map. The staff are helpful and will do their best to answer any questions you have.

Basic Directions

The main train station (Poznań Głowny) is about 15–20 minutes' walk from the Stary Rynek at the heart of the old town. The main bus station is about 500m from Poznań Głowny, to the right along ul. Towarowa. Trams 5 and 21 run from the main exit of the train station (between platforms 1 and 4) and the city centre. To walk the simplest way is to head away from the train station past the taxi ranks and straight on down Dworcowa onto ul. Świety Wojciech (you can take a shortcut through the Karola Marcinkowskiego park). Follow ul. Czerwonej Armii to the right until you see al. Karola Marcinkowskiego on the left. Go down this street, and then turn left between the Hotel Bazar and the National Museum and then go straight ahead, on down ul. Padarewskiego into the Stary Rynek.

HOTELS

Because of the Poznań Trade Fair, hotel prices in Poznań are relatively high by Polish standards. The cheapest hotels are all out from the centre.

Olimpia, ul. Warmińska 1 (tel. 45821/415025). Tram 9 or 11.

Naramowice, ul. Naramowicka 150 (tel. 2006612). In the suburb of Naramowice. Bus 67 or 105.

POSiR, ul. Marcina Chwiałkowskiego 34 (tel. 330511). A sports hotel located just outside the city centre.

Near the centre of the old town are three three-star hotels at which you can expect to pay around £10.50 ($18.50) for singles, £17 ($30) for singles with a bath, £12 ($21) for doubles, and £18 ($32) for doubles with a bath.

Poznański, al. Karola Marcinkowskiego 22 (tel. 528121).

Wielkopolska, ul. Sw. Wojciech 67 (tel. 527631).

Lech, ul. Sw. Wojciech 75 (tel. 6660512).

PRIVATE ROOMS

There is a Biuro Zakwaterowania at ul. Głogowska 16 (tel. 60313), across the road from the side entrance to Poznań Głowny. Open Mon.–Fri. 9 a.m.–7 p.m., Sat. 9 a.m.–3 p.m. Around £3.50 ($6) per person. In the past, the office has displayed reluctance to book rooms on a short-term basis. The ORBIS office in the Hotel Poznań at pl. Henryka Dabrowskiego 1 (tel. 331811) has no such qualms. Singles around £5.75 ($10) doubles around £6.80–8.60 ($12–15). The hotel overlooks the Henryka Dabrowskiego park, not far from the bus station, about 10 minutes' walk from Poznań Głowny. A short distance from the main exit, head right along ul. Towarowa. Go left at the first main junction, then turn right immediately after passing ul. Kosciuszki on the left.

PTTK DOM TURYSTY

Stary Rynek 91 (tel. 528893). Singles around £8.75 ($15.50), singles with bath around £10.50 ($18.50), doubles around £14 ($24.50), doubles with bath around £15.50 ($27), triples around £17.50 ($31). Prices per person in the eight-bed dorms are very low if you are lucky enough to get a bed. The location of the Dom Turysty cannot be bettered.

IYHF HOSTELS

ul. Berwińiskiego 2/3 (tel. 663680). A 5–10-minute walk from Poznań Głowny. Leave the station by the side exit on to ul. Głogowska, go left and then keep on going until you see ul. Berwińskiego on the right.

ul. Niepodległości 32/40 (tel. 56706). About 15–20 minutes'
walk from Poznań Głowny. More convenient to the city
centre than the hostel above. From Poznań Głowny head
right along Dworcowa onto ul. Czernowej Armii, go right
a short distance and then left along al. Niepodległości. The
hostel is along a corridor on the top floor of the building.

ul. Trybunalska 17 (tel. 673340). Far from the centre, but
trams 1, 3, 6, 13 and 15 all pass close to the hostel.

ul. Jesionowa 14 (tel. 321412). Close to the Debiec suburban
train station.

ul. Głuszyna 127. This hostel has the largest capacity of the
five, but rather frustratingly is both inconveniently located
and lacking a telephone. To get there, take a local train
to Starołeka, then bus 58 from the station.

INTERNATIONAL STUDENT HOSTELS

ALMATUR, al. Aleksandra Fredry 7 (tel. 523645) will have
details of where any hostels may be operating in 1993, as the
locations vary from year to year.

CAMPING

Both the campsites are about 5½ miles from the city centre.
Bungalows are available at both sites.

Strzeszynek, ul. Koszalińska 15 (tel. 47224). Pleasantly
located by a lake in the north-west of Poznań. Bus 95.

Ławica, ul. Wichrowa 100 (tel. 43225). On the western fringe
of the city. Bus 122 takes a long route to the site.

Stettin (Szczecin) (tel. code 091)

Tourist Office

In the past, Informacji Turystycznej ('it') operated at al.
Jednosci Narodwej 50 (tel. 42832). This office was particularly

well supplied with information on the city and the rest of Pomerania. Unfortunately, information from the Polish Tourist Information Centre in Warsaw suggests this office is closed at the time of writing. Whether it will reopen in 1993 (or whether a new office will open) is unclear. As things stand, your most likely source of information is ORBIS at pl. Zwyciestwa 1 (tel. 35808). 'A Tourist Map of Szczecin' provides a good basic guide to the city.

Basic Directions
The city centre is a 10–15-minute walk from the main train station (Szczecin Głowny), or the bus station nearby. From Szczecin Głowny, walk along ks. Świetopełka, turn left up Dworcowa, then right at the top of this street. After a short distance you will see the baroque Harbour Gate on your left. Pl. Zwyciestwa is on the other side of the Harbour Gate (Brama Portowa). If, instead of turning left at the Harbour Gate, you continue straight ahead along al. Niepodległości you reach the site of the old 'it' office, near the junction with pl. Żołnierza Polskiego.

HOTELS

The two cheapest hotels are both sports hotels located out from the city centre. The most conveniently sited is the Pogon, ul. Twardowskiego 12 (tel. 72878), near the Pogon Szczecin football stadium, a 5-minute walk from Szczecin-Turzyn train station. The Wojewdzki Dom Sportu, ul. Unisławy (tel. 222856) is far from the centre. Reasonably priced rooms are available at three hotels in the central area. Cheapest of these is the Pomorski, by the Harbour Gate at Brama Portowa 4 (tel. 36051). The Piast, pl. Zwyciestwa 3 (tel. 3071) is slightly more expensive than the Brama Portowa. The Gryf, al. Wojska Polskiego 49 (tel. 34035) is a little bit dearer than the Piast but is definitely the choice hotel amongst the three centrally located hotels listed here. Al. Wojske Polskiego runs off pl. Zywciestwa.

PRIVATE ROOMS

Enquire at ORBIS on pl. Zywciestwa as to whether there is an agency in Stettin letting private rooms.

PTTK DOM TURYSTY

Pl. Batorego 2 (tel. 45833). Near the main bus and train stations, off ul. Korzeniowskie which runs parallel to ks. Swietopetka.

IYHF HOSTELS

ul. Unisławy 26 (tel. 232566). Open all year. The hostel is on the top floor of a school. Not central. Tram 2 or 3 to pl. Kilińskiego.
ul. Grodzka 22 (tel. 89424). Open July–Aug. Central location.
ul. Reymonta 23 (tel. 73032). Open July–Aug.

INTERNATIONAL STUDENT HOSTELS

Locations of the hostels change regularly. ALMATUR, ul. Wawrzyniaka 7 (tel. 233678) will inform you of the latest details.

CAMPING

PTTK Camping, ul. Przestrzenna 24, Szczecin-Dabie (tel. 613264). Open May–Sept. Bungalows available. Two miles from the city centre. Easily reached from the Szczecin-Dabie train station.
ul. Szosa Stargardzka 45 (tel. 621288)

Toruń (tel. code 056)

Tourist Office
At the time of writing, the best source of information on accommodation possibilities and on the town in general is the

helpful PTTK office at pl. Rapackiego 2 (tel. 24926). Open
Mon.–Fri. 8 a.m.–4.30 p.m., weekends 10 a.m.–1 p.m. The
ORBIS office at ul. Żeglarska 31 (just off Rynek Staromiejskie)
(tel. 22553) can provide you with brochures on the town. Open
Mon.–Fri. 9 a.m.–5 p.m., Sat. 9 a.m.–2 p.m.

Basic Directions
Most trains stop at the main station (Toruń Głowny), about
2 miles from the centre, across the River Vistula (Wisła). Buses
12 and 22 maintain a frequent service between the bus terminal
near the station and the city centre. Buy tickets before boarding
from the kiosk by the bus stop. Get off the bus shortly after
crossing the Vistula when you see the old city gate on the right.
The PTTK office is close to the gate. The main bus station on
ul. Dabrowskiego is within easy walking distance of the old
town (Stare Miasto).

HOTELS

Trzy Korony, ul. Stary Rynek 21 (tel. 26031). Singles around
£4.50 ($7.50), doubles around £8.75 ($15.50). Communal
bathrooms. On the fringe of Rynek Staromiejskie, looking
out on to the Town Hall.

Wileński, ul. Mostowa 15 (tel. 25024). Singles around £5.50
($9.50), doubles around £8.75 ($15.50). A considerable step
up in quality from the Trzy Korony. Best reserved ahead.
Follow ul. Szeroka from Rynek Staromiejskie, then turn
right down ul. Mostowa.

Polonia, ul. Szosa Chełmińska (near pl. Teatrainy) (tel.
23028). Singles around £8 ($14), doubles around £7
($12.50), triples around £8.50–9.50 ($15.00–16.50). A short
walk along ul. Chełmińska from Rynek Staromiejskie.

Wodnik, Bulwar Filadelfijski. Singles around £7.50 ($13),
doubles around £13.50 ($24).

Zajazd Starapolski, ul. Żeglarska 12/14 (tel. 26061/26063).
Singles around £11.50 ($20), doubles around £17 ($30). The
street runs out of Rynek Staromiejskie down to the Vistula.

Kosmos, ul. Ks. J. Popiełuszki 2 (tel. 28900). Singles around
£13 ($23), doubles around £19.50 ($34).

PRIVATE ROOMS

Book through the office at Rynek Staromiejskie 20.

PTTK DOM WYCIECZKOWY

ul. Legionów 24. Singles around £3.50 ($6), doubles around
£7.50 ($13.50), triples around £9.75 ($17), quads around
£12 ($21). A fair distance north of the city centre. From pl.
Rapackiego take bus 10 to the third stop to reach the hostel.
Before making the trip enquire whether space is available
at the PTTK office on pl. Rapackiego (tel. 24926).

IYHF HOSTELS

Until 1991, Toruń had two PTSM hostels, one of which was
one of the most unusual in Europe, being located in a medieval
tower on ul. Podmurna. This hostel was closed 1991–92, but
it is worth checking with the IYHF handbook or the local PTTK
office to see if it has reopened as its central location contrasted
sharply with the other hostel which is 2 miles from the centre.
ul. Rudacka 15 (tel. 27242). Around £1.75 ($3) per night. Take
bus 13 from the centre; the hostel is one stop beyond the
main train station.

INTERNATIONAL STUDENT HOSTELS

During the summer, university accommodation is converted
into temporary hostels. The ALMATUR office (tel. 20470)
located near the university at ul. Gargarina 21 will provide
details.

CAMPING

Tramp, ul. Kujawska 14. Open May–Sept. Bungalows

available. The site is located about 600m from the main train station.

Warsaw (Warszawa) (tel. code 02 or 022)

Tourist Offices

Centrum Informacji Turystycznej, pl. Zamkowy 1–13 (tel. 6351881). Open daily 10 a.m.–6 p.m. Although the 'it' office does not book accommodation, it does sell a very useful guide listing all the htoels and accommodation offices. Around £1.75 ($3). The staff are highly competent in dealing with the usual requests for information and do their best to answer more obscure questions. The office faces the castle. Take bus 128 from al. Jerozolimskie or bus 150 from ul. Świetokrzyska (see Around Warszawa Centralna below). Both stop near the castle at the foot of the Ślasko-Dabrowski bridge. Buy tickets at a *Ruch* kiosk and cancel both ends on the bus.

ORBIS. At the junction of Marzałkowska and Krlewska. Queues at this office are frequently very long. Information is also available at the 'it' points in ORBIS hotels.

'it', Okecie airport and Warszawa Centralna train station. Long queues are the norm at these two very basic information points.

Around Warszawa Centralna

The main road running past the main train station is al. Jerozolimskie. Opposite the station are the IOT terminal and the multi-storey Hotel Marriott. Facing these buildings al. Jerozolimskie runs right towards pl. Artura Zawiszy, and then on to the Zachodnia train station and the main bus station. Going left, the street crosses Emilii Plater and Marszałkowska before continuing straight on Most Ks. Józefa Poniatowskiego which crosses the river Wisła. Going left up Emilii Plater from al. Jerozolimskie takes you round the back of the Palac Kultury and onto ul. Świetokrzyska.

Left Luggage
There are two left luggage offices in Warszawa Centralna. Lines are long during the summer and the staff procede at a leisurely pace. You may find the office you are queuing at closing for a break which precipitates a rush towards the other office. Although there are lockers it is highly unlikely you will find one free. Queues at Warszawa-Wschodnia are rarely long, so if your train runs through to Wschodnia (many trains to Warsaw do), leave your luggage at that station. Trains run at least every 10 minutes between Wschodnia and Warszawa-Śródmieście, across Emilii Plater from Warszawa Centralna.

HOTELS

Expect to pay around £7–11 ($12.50–19.00) for singles, £9–13 ($15.50–23.00) for singles with bath/shower, from £10 ($17.50) for doubles, and around £17–22 ($29.50–38.00) for doubles with bath/shower

ZNP (Teachers' Hotel), Wybrzeże Kościuszki 33 (tel. 262600). Admits non-teachers when space permits. Prices are at the lower end of the scales quoted above. Take bus 102 from Swietokrzyska along ul. Tamka. The hotel is down by the River Wisła.

Pensjonat Stegny, ul. Idzikowskiego 4 (tel. 422768). Far out, on the road to Wilanow Palace.

Skra, ul. Wawelska 5 (tel. 225100). In the Ochota suburb beside the Skra stadium. See Camping Gromada for buses and directions to the stadium.

Orzel, ul. Podskarbińska 11/15 (tel. 105060). In the Praga suburb. Bus 102 or 115.

Druh, ul. Niemcewicza 17 (tel. 6590011). Trams 7, 8, 9 or 25.

Sokrates, ul. Smyczkowa 9 (tel. 133889/439551) Around the top of the price range quoted above. Overnight price includes breakfast.

Harctur, ul. Niemcewicza 17 (tel. 6590011). Triples £17 ($29.50), quads £17.50–21.00 ($31–37). Doubles with bath/shower are at the bottom of the price range quoted above. No doubles, and no singles of any kind. The street is off ul. Raszyńska. Within walking distance of Warszawa Centralna. See Camping Gromada for directions or take bus 136, 175 or 512.

Dom Chłopa, pl. Postańców (tel. 279251). No doubles without a bath. Prices at the top of the range quoted above. Located between Nowy Świat and the Palc Kultury.

PRIVATE ROOMS

Syrena, ul. Krucza 17 (tel. 287540/257201). Open 8 a.m.–8 p.m. Singles around £5.40 ($9.50), doubles around £7.70 ($13.50). Right off al. Jerozolimskie after Marsałkowska.

Romeo and Juliet, Emilii Plater 30 (third floor) (tel. 292993). Doubles around £22 ($38). Payment in hard currency only. US dollars preferred. Centrally located rooms.

PTTK DOM TURYSTY

Krakowskie Przedmieście 4/6 (tel. 263011). Singles £7.50 ($13.50), singles with bath £10 ($17.50), doubles £6.25 ($11) per person, doubles with bath £8.50 ($15) p.p., triples £3.75 ($6.50) p.p., and quads £3.25 ($6) p.p. Best reserved in advance. Well located, near the university. Within walking distance of Warszawa Centralna and the Old Town. From Centralna, head right along Świetokrzyska to the start of Krakowskie Przedmieście. Otherwise take bus 175 heading along al. Jerozolimskie towards the river to the Uniwersytet stop.

IYHF HOSTELS

ul. Karolkowa 53a (tel. 328829). 11 p.m. curfew. £3.75 ($6.50) per person in quads, £2.50 ($4.50) in dorms. Clean, but not central. Out in the Wola suburb. From al. Jerozolimskie take tram 24 to al. Świerczewskiego, close to the Wola shopping centre.

ul. Smolna 30 (tel. 278952). 10 p.m. curfew. £2 ($3.50) for

dorms. Well located, off Nowy Świat, opposite the National Museum on al. Jerozolimskie. Within walking distance of Warszawa Centralna. Follow al. Jerozolimskie towards the Wisła, turn left down Nowy Świat at the Rondo Charles de Gaulle, then right almost immediately along ul. Smolna. Alternatively take tram 7, 9, 22 , 24 or 25, or bus 158 or 175 heading along al. Jerozolimskie towards the river. A final option is to take a train from Warszawa-Śródmieście (across Emilii Plater from Warszawa Centralna) to Warszawa Powiśle near the National Museum (frequent trains, a 5-minute trip).

INTERNATIONAL STUDENT HOSTEL

Wackacyjny, ul. Kickiego 12 (tel. 100985/100981) £6 ($10.50)
ALMATUR, ul. Kopernika 23 (tel. 263512). ALMATUR office open Mon.–Fri. 8.30a.m.–8p.m., Sat. 10a.m.–6p.m., Sun. 10a.m.–3p.m. Restricted hours Sept.–June, Mon.–Fri. 9a.m.–3p.m. Even when the student hostels are not open ALMATUR may help students to find reasonably priced accommodation.

CAMPING

Expect to pay around £1.75 ($3) p.p. including tent

Gromada, ul. Żwirki i Wigury (tel. 254391). Twin-bedded bungalows £4.75 ($8.50) per night. Bus 136, 175, 188 or 512 heading along al. Jerozolimskie towards pl. Artura Zawiszy. A 25-minute walk from Warszawa Centralna. Left at pl. Zawiszy down Raszyńska, across Filtrowa and on down ul. A. Krzyckiego onto Wawelska. Żwirki i Wigury runs down the right-hand side of the Skra stadium complex.
PTTK Camping, ul. Połczyńska 6a (tel. 366716). In the suburb of Wola. Bus 105.
Wisła, u. Bitwy Warszawskiej 1920 (tel. 233748). A short distance south of the bus station and Warszawa Zachodnia train station. Bus 154, 167, 173 or 191.

570 Cheap Sleep Guide

Zakopane (tel. code 0165)

Tourist Offices
Tatry, ul. Kościuszki 7. The main information office for
Zakopane and its surroundings.
PTTK, ul. Krupówki 37. A good selection of maps and
guidebooks, plus information on the mountain refuges
operated by PTTK in the area (the vast majority of local
refuges are run either by PTTK or ALMATUR). The Biuro
Obsługi Ruchu Turystycznego, ul. Krupówki 12 also has
information on refuges. ORBIS, ul. Krupówki 22 (tel. 4609)
books trains, buses and local excurstions, and hotels and
private rooms.

HOTELS

Słoneczny, ul. Słoneczny 2a (tel. 66253). A student hotel run
by Juventur. Singles £4.75 ($8.50), singles with a bath £8
($14), doubles £9.50 ($16.50). doubles with a bath £15.50
($27). Prices include breakfast. The hotel is between the
train station and the centre of town.
Gazda, ul. Zaruskiego 2 (tel. 5011). Singles £6.70–9.50
($11.50–16.50), singles with a bath £11–12 ($19.50–21.00),
doubles with a bath £16.50 ($29). Without breakfast.
Rooms at the Morskie Oko, Krupówki 30 (tel 5076), the
Imperial, ul. Balzera 1 (tel. 4021), and the Warszawianka,
Jagiellońska 7 (tel. 3261) are similar in price to those of the
Gazda. Expect to pay around £11.20–13.30 ($19.50–23.50)
for doubles.

PRIVATE ROOMS

Biuro Zakwaterowania, ul. Kościuszki 7 (tel. 4000). Singles
£1.75–2.75 ($3.00–4.50), doubles £3.25–4.25 ($5.50–7.50).
ORBIS, ul. Krupówki 37 (tel. 4609) £2.75 ($4.50) per person.

PTTK DOM WYCIECZKOWY

ul. Zaruskiego 5 (tel. 3281/3282). Singles with a bath £5 ($9), doubles with a bath £4.60–5.30 ($8.00–9.50) per person, larger rooms £1.40–1.75 ($2.50–3.00) p.p. Near the Post Office.

IYHF HOSTEL

ul. Nowotarska 45 (tel. 4203). £2–4 ($3.50–7.00). From the train and bus stations, head towards the centre, go right along ul. Chramcówki, then left.

CAMPING

Pod Krokiwa, ul. Żeromskiego (tel. 2256). Open May–Aug. Opposite the foot of the ski jump.

PORTUGAL

By northern European standards accommodation is cheap here, and there are plenty of possibilities open to budget travellers. In most places it should be quite easy to find somewhere cheap to stay, but it can be difficult on the Algarve in peak season, where it is advisable to write or telephone ahead as early as possible, for any type of accommodation.

Inexpensive and convenient options are pensions and cheap hotels. These are graded and priced by the municipal authority, albeit in a manner which at times seems quite arbitrary. Location does not affect the price, so you have the bonus of being able to stay in the town centre, or near the train station, without having to pay extra for the privilege. **Hotels** are rated from one star up to five stars, with the less expensive *pensoes* and *residencias* graded from one up to three stars. In general, three-star pensions and one-star hotels are roughly similar in price. However, it is quite possible to pay more for a very poor one-star hotel than for a comfortable three-star pension, and vice versa. Prices in one-star hotels/three-star pensions range from 2400 to 7000$ (£10–29; $17.50–51.00) for singles, 4000–8500$ (£16.70–35.40; $29–62) per person for doubles. In the lower-rated pensions, singles cost around 1500–2200$ (£6.25–9.25; $11–16), doubles around 2500–3500$ (£10.50–14.50; $18.50–25.50).

In the smaller towns, seaside resorts, and areas particularly popular with tourists, **rooms in private homes** (*quartos* or *dormidas*) can be both less expensive and more comfortable than pensions. Private rooms are sometimes offered to travellers at bus and train stations. Such offers may be worth considering as private rooms are generally more difficult to find than pensions. Local Tourist Offices have lists of private rooms available in the locality. Alternatively, simply enquire at any house with a sign in the window advertising private rooms (signs are frequently written in several languages).

Hostelling can be a cheap way to see much of the country, but, especially during the peak periods, you may not feel it is worth the added effort, considering the restrictions hostelling imposes. However, hostelling can be a more attractive option in the off-season, as the hostels offer an excellent opportunity to meet other travellers, especially outside Lisbon and Oporto. There are 19 IYHF hostels and most of the main places of interest have a hostel of some sort, or can be reached on a day-trip from the nearest hostel. Standards at the hostels are high, and prices are very reasonable. Depending on the standard of the hostel, the age of the user and the time of year, the overnight charge for B&B and sheets varies from 800–1450$ (£3.30–6.00; $6–11). Hostels are open to IYHF members only, but it is possible to buy a membership card at the hostels, though the 2400$ (£10; $17.50) fee is roughly twice what under 25s pay to join one of the British associations in advance. Unless the warden agrees to you staying longer, you are limited to three consecutive nights in any hostel. Curfews (midnight, 1 May–30 Sept.; 11.30 p.m., at other times) can be a real nuisance, since bars and clubs stay open late, many football matches kick off at 9 p.m., and cinemas often show late films in English. The peak periods for the hostels are June to September, around Christmas, and Holy Week. At these times, it is advisable to write or phone ahead to reserve a bed. As the hostel in Oporto is pitifully small considering the numbers who visit the town, to have a chance of getting a bed at any time of year you will either have to write in advance, or arrive at the hostel or phone ahead between 9.00–10.30 a.m.

In contrast to Mediterranean countries, **camping** is well worth considering in Portugal. Sites tend to be more conveniently located in and around the main towns than in Greece, Italy or neighbouring Spain. Portuguese sites are seldom more than three miles out from the town centre, and usually have a direct bus link. Nor will you have problems carrying around your tent as left luggage stores are available at all train stations. Camping is a great way to meet the locals as the Portuguese themselves are enthusiastic campers. The relative unpopularity of camping with budget travellers is due to the widespread availability of other cheap accommodation, and nothing to do with the standard of the campsites, which is actually quite high. There are 97 official sites, graded from one star up to four stars, many of which require a Camping Carnet. All the sites have the basic, essential facilities – most even have a café and a supermarket – so bearing in mind the facilities available, prices are very reasonable. Even at some of the more expensive sites around Lisbon and on the Algarve charges are unlikely to exceed 500$ (£2.10; $3.70), with around 350$ (£1.50; $2.50) per tent and per person being the norm elsewhere. **Camping outside official sites** is permitted with the consent of the landowner, but is not allowed in towns, at any spot less than one kilometre from a beach, or from an official site, or in the vicinity of a reservoir.

Note: Over the least few years the Portuguese telephone system has been undergoing a process of modernization. Whilst every effort has been made to ensure that telephone numbers and codes quoted below were correct at the time of writing, they may well have altered by 1993 (several sections of the 1992 guide were affected in this way). If you find you are getting no response after trying several numbers, contact the Tourist Office or the Post Office for assistance.

ADDRESSES

Portuguese National Tourist Office	22–25a Sackville Street, London W1X 1DE (tel. 071 494 1441).
Portuguese YHA	Assoçiaão de Utentes das Pousadas de Juventude, Rua Andrade Corvo No 46, 1000 Lisboa (tel. 3511–571054).
Camping	Federaçao Portuguesa de Campismo, Rua Voz de Operario, Lisboa (tel. 01–862350).
	Orbitur, Av. Almirante Gago Coutinho 25d, Lisboa. Orbitur operates 15 sites

Camping (continued)	which are amongst the best managed, but also the most expensive, in Portugal. A free list of the 97 official sites, 'Portugal Camping', is available from the Portuguese National Tourist Office, and from local Tourist Offices.

Cascais (tel. code 01)

Tourist Office
Turismo, Avenida Dom Carlos I (tel. 4868204).

Finding Accommodation
During the summer, finding cheap accommodation can be difficult. There are relatively few pensions in Cascais, so consider any reasonable offers of a private room made by locals at the train station.

PENSIONS

One-star:
  Avanida, Rua da Palmeira 14–1 (tel. 4864417).
Two-star:
  Le Biarritz, Avda do Ultramar (tel. 482216).
Three-star:
  Casa Lena, Avda do Ultramar 329 (tel. 4868743).
  Italia, Rua do Poo Novo 1 (tel. 480151).
  Palma, Avda Valbom 15 (tel. 480257).

CAMPING

  Parque de Campismo do Guincho, Guincho, Areia (tel. 4851014). About 4½ miles from Cascais. Orbitur site, open year round.

Coimbra (tel. code 039)

Tourist Office
Posto de Turismo, Largo Portagem (tel. 23886). Open Apr.–Sept., Mon.–Fri. 9 a.m.–7 p.m., weekends 9 a.m.–12.20 p.m. and 2.00–5.30 p.m.; Oct.–Mar., Mon.–Fri. 9 a.m.–6 p.m., Sat. 10 a.m.–1 p.m. A short walk from Coimbra A train

station. Follow the main road (Avenida Emidio Navarro) with the Mondego river on your right until you see the office.

Arriving By Train
Most long-distance trains stop at the Coimbra B station on the outskirts of the town, about 2 miles from the centre. From Coimbra B, there are frequent connecting trains to the centrally situated Coimbra A.

Finding Accommodation
The area around Coimbra A has the least expensive accommodation in town, particularly Rua da Sota and the streets running off it. While this is not the most attractive of areas, the pensions are generally perfectly acceptable and safe.

HOTELS

Expect to pay around 2500–4000$ (£10.40–16.70; $18–29) for doubles

Vitoria, Rua da Sota 9 (tel. 24049).

Lorvanese, Rua da Sota 27.

Sota, Rua da Sota 41.

Flor de Coimbra, Rua da Poo 8. Good inexpensive meals available to residents. Singles around 1500$ (£6.25; $11).

Residencia Luis Atenas, Avda Fernão de Magalhães 68 (tel. 26412). Singles around 2750$ (£11.50; $20), doubles around 3850$ (£16; $28), triples around 5500$ (£23; $40) with breakfast. The avenue running away to the left from the station.

Residencial Internacional de Coimbra, Avda Fernão de Magalhães (opposite the train station) (tel. 25503). Doubles around 2600$ (£10.80; $19). Prices per person are lower in triples and quads.

Aviz, Avda Fernão Magalhães 64 (tel. 23718).

Residencial Larbelo, Largo da Portagem (tel. 29092).

Rivoli, Praça do Comercio. Three-star pension. Doubles around 3800$ (£15.80; $28).

Gouveia, Rua João de Rouão 21. Not central, but close to the station.

Jardim, Avda Emidio Navarro 65. Two-star pension. The street runs alongside the river.

Parque, Avda Emidio Navarro 42. Two-star pension. Doubles around 3200$ (£13.30; $23.50), doubles with bath around 3800$ (£15.80; $28).

Diogo, Praça da República 18–2. In the university area.

Antunes, Rua Castro Matoso (tel. 23048). University quarter, beneath the aqueduct. Advance reservation advised.

IYHF HOSTEL

Rua Henriques Seco 12–14 (tel. 22955). Excellent hostel. B&B 1200$ (£5; $9). Close to the Parque de Santa Cruz. From Coimbra A take bus 7, 8, 29 or 46 to Praça República. From the square, walk up Rua Lourenço de Almeida Azevdo along the side of the park until you see Rua Henriques Seco.

CAMPING

Parque de Campismo Municipal de Coimbra, Praça 25 de Abril (tel. 712997). 500$ (£2.10; $3.50) per tent, including person.

Estoril (tel. code 01)

Tourist Office
Turismo, Arcadas do Parque (tel. 4680204).

Finding Accommodation
Finding a cheap bed in a pension can be very difficult during the summer, so if you are approached by locals letting private rooms it might be worth giving serious consideration to any reasonable offer.

HOTELS

Two-star:
  Chique do Estoril, Avda Marginal 60 (tel. 4680393).
  Costa, Rua da Olivena 2–1&2 (tel. 4681699).
  Maryluz, R. Maestro Lacerda 13 r/c 1 & 2 (tel. 4682740).

Three-star:
  Casa Londres, Avda Fausto Figueiredo 7 (tel. 4681541).
  Continental, Rua Joaquim dos Santos 2 (tel. 4680050).
  Smart, Rua José Viana 3 (tel. 4682164).
  São Cristvão, Estrada Marginal (tel. 4680913).

Évora (tel. code 066)

Tourist Office
Turismo, Praça do Giraldo 73. Open June–Sept., Mon.–Fri.
9 a.m.–7 p.m., weekends 9 a.m.–12.30 p.m. and 2.00–5.30
p.m.; Oct.–May., Mon.–Fri. 9 a.m.–6 p.m., weekends 9
a.m.–12.30 p.m. and 2.00–5.30 p.m. The office is on the town's
main square, about 15 minutes' walk from the train station (no
buses). Follow Rua de Baronha from the train station, then
straight on when the street runs into Rua da República.

HOTELS

Évora is a particularly popular destination, with the result that
hotel prices in peak season are higher than usual (prices fall
by 10–20 per cent in the off-season). The vast majority of the
cheaper hotels are located within a radius of about ½ mile from
Praça do Giraldo.

  Os Manuéis, Rua do Raimundo 35a (tel. 22861). Singles 2200$
    (£9.35; $16.50), doubles from 3300$ (£13.75; £24). The street
    runs off Praça do Giraldo.
  Casa Portalegre, Travessa do Barão 18. Another (relatively)

cheap establishment close to Praça do Giraldo, in a street off Rua do Raimundo.

O Eborense, Larga da Misericordia 1 (tel. 22031). B&B in doubles from 5500$ (£23; $40). Off Rua da República, close to Praça do Giraldo.

Giraldo, Rua Meroadores (tel. 25833). Singles from 2850$ (£12; $21), doubles from 4200$ (£16.75; $29). Prices per room fall by around 1000$ (£4.25; $7.50) in winter. Two blocks from Praça do Giraldo.

Policarpo, Rua da Freira de Baixo 16 (tel. 22424). B&B in doubles from 4000$ (£16.75; $29). Near the cathedral.

PRIVATE ROOMS

The Tourist Office book rooms in locals' homes on an irregular basis. Enquire as to whether rooms (*quartos*) are available.

IYHF HOSTEL

Rua de Corredoura 32 (tel. 25043). One of the best hostels in the country. Located near the temple. Closed in 1992. Check with the Tourist Office or the IYHF handbook to see if it has reopened.

CAMPING

Parque de Campismo Évora (tel. 25190) Orbitur site. 320$ (£1.35; $2.50) per tent, 380$ (£1.60; $3) p.p. The site is off Estrada das Alcáçovas, about 2½ miles from the centre, served by just one bus each day. From Praça do Giraldo walk down Rua Raimundo then turn along Estrada das Alcáçovas at the end of the street.

Faro (tel. 089)

Tourist Office
Turismo, Rua da Misericordia 8. By the harbour. Open daily
9 a.m.–7/8 p.m.

Finding Accommodation
During the summer, cheap accommodation can be difficult to
find in Faro unless you look early in the day. Many people only
stay one night in Faro (before flying out or after flying in) so
if you can start your search early you have a fair chance of
benefiting from this turnover of visitors. The Tourist Office will
supply you with a list of pensions, but leave it up to you to
phone around or call in person. The best streets in which to
look for pensions are Filipe Alistão, Alportel, Conselheiro
Bivar, Infante Dom Henrique and Vasco da Gama. Not only
are beds difficult to find in July and August, but, in response
to the high level of demand, hoteliers often increase their
prices. At the very height of the season, private rooms may
be your best option.

HOTELS

**Expect to pay from 1750–2500$ (£7.30–10.50; $13.00–18.50)
for singles, 2500–3200$ (£10.50–13.30; $18.50–23.50) for
doubles**

One-star:
  Mirense, Rua Capitão Mor (tel. 22687).
  Nunes, Rua Horta Machado (tel. 27876).
Two-star:
  S. Filipe, Rua Infante Dom Henrique (tel. 24182).
  Dany, Rua Filipe Alistão 62 (tel. 24791). Recommended.
  Delfim, Rua da Alportel (tel. 22578).
  Carminho, Rua da Alportel (tel. 23709).
  Dina, Rua Teofilo Braga (tel. 23897).
  Emilia, Rua Teixeira Guedes (tel. 823852).

Madalena, Rua Conselheiro Bivar (tel. 27284). One of the best.

Novo Lar, Rua Infante Dom Henrique.

Tivoli, Praça Alexandre Herculano (tel. 28541).

Tinita, Rua do Alportel (tel. 25040).

Three-star:

Algarve, Rua D. Francisco Gomes (tel. 823346).

Condado, Rua Gonçalo Barreto (tel. 22081/22082).

Yorque, Rua de Berlim (tel. 23973).

Lumena, Praça Alexandre Herculano (tel. 801990).

Rest. O Faraó, Largo da Madalena (tel. 823356).

Marim, Rua Gonçalo Barreto (tel. 824063).

Oceano, Travessa Ivens (tel. 823349).

Afonso III, Rua Gomes Freire (tel. 27042/27054).

Solar do Alto, Rua de Berlim (tel. 22091).

Samé, Rua do Bocage (tel. 24375/23370).

Residencial Galo, Rua Filipe Alistão 41 (tel. 26435). Doubles around 3200$ (£13.30; $23.50).

PRIVATE ROOMS

The Tourist Office have a good supply of rooms, some well located, others less so. In peak season, take what you get. As is the case throughout the Algarve during the summer, touts frequently offer rooms at the bus and train stations. Expect to pay 2000–3000$ (£8.30–12.50; $14.50–22.00) for doubles.

CAMPING

Parque de Campismo Municipal da Ilha de Faro, Ilha de Faro (tel. 24876). Year-round site. Often full. Very crowded in summer. Camping Carnet required. Bus 16 from the airport or town centre to Praia de Faro. May–Sept. bus runs twice hourly from 7.30a.m.–8p.m., hourly the rest of the year. Infrequent service at weekends.

Lisbon (Lisboa) (tel. code 01)

Tourist Offices

Turismo, Palácio da Foz, Praça dos Restauradores (tel. 3463314/3463643). Open Mon.–Sat. 9 a.m.–8 p.m., Sun. 10 a.m.–6 p.m. The office distributes a simple plan of the city and lists of accommodation. Branch offices operate at the Santa Apolónia station, open Mon.–Sat. 9 a.m.–7 p.m., and at the airport, open daily round-the-clock. Both the branch offices can be very busy so you might prefer to just head to the main office.

Arriving and Basic Directions

Most long-distance trains arrive at the Lisboa Santa Apolónia station, by the River Tajus (Rio Tejo), just over 15 minutes' walk from the Tourist Office. Bus 9 or 9A from the side of the station by the Tajus will take you to Praça dos Restauradores. To walk, simply keep the river on your left and go straight on until you see the broad expanse of Praça do Comércio with the statue of Dom José I on your right, off Terreiro do Paco. Diagonally right across this square is the start of Rua do Ouro, which you can follow into Praça Dom Pedro IV, commonly known as Rossio (the streets to the right of Rua do Ouro are laid out on a grid pattern, an area known as the Baixa). At the far end of Praça Dom Pedro IV is the National Theatre. Going right from Praça Dom Pedro IV leads you into Praça de Figueira. Turning left from the National Theatre brings you to the Rossio train station (services to Queluz and Sintra) at the foot of Praça dos Restauradores. On the left as you walk up Praça dos Restauradores is the Elevador da Gloria which provides an easy means of reaching the Bairro Alto. Stretching away towards the statue of the Marqués de Pombal is Avenida da Liberdada, a continuation of Praça dos Restauradores.

Arriving by train the other two stations are within easy reach of the centre. Trains from the Algarve and the south terminate at the Barreiro train station across the Tajus, from which there are frequent services to the terminal on Terreiro do Paco, a short walk from Praça do Comércio. The Cais do Sodré station

by the Tajus on Praça Duque da Terceira handles traffic from
Cascais, Estoril and Oeiras (if you want to visit Bélem, you can
take a local train from this station). Walking away from Cais
do Sodre with the river on your right you reach Praça do
Commércio after about 5 minutes' walk. Heading away from
the river out of Praca Duque da Terceira, Rua do Alecrim leads
into Rua da Misericordia which subsequently leads into Rua
S. Pedro de Alcantara near the upper terminus of the Elevador
da Gloria, by the Port Wine Institute.

The terminal for buses of the state-run Rodoviária Nacional
is on Avenida Casal Ribiero, close to Praça Saldanha, and lined
to Praça dos Restauradores by buses 1, 21, 32 and 36. Arriving
at the airport, you can take bus 44 or 45 to Avenida da
Liberdade, or the quicker *linha verde* (green line express). At
around 300$ (£1.25/$2.25) the trip on the *linha verde* costs
roughly twice that of the normal service buses. Unless taxi
prices have risen dramatically, three people can save money
by taking the taxi to the Baixa in preference to using the *linha
verde*.

Trouble Spots

Although prostitutes use some of the cheapest hotels around
the Rossio station, this area is not really the red light district
of the city. The crowds of people in this part of town mean
it is quite safe for women to walk around in until the early
hours of the morning. More dangerous (for women especially)
are the Bairro Alto (which contains the red light district) and
Mouraria (around the castle); quarters which many travellers
head for to try and escape the noise and bustle of Rossio.
Women are advised not to walk alone in these parts of town
after dusk.

Finding Accommodation

At most times of the year finding a cheap room near Rossio
should be quite easy: singles 2000–2500$ (£8.25–10.50;
$14.50–18.50); doubles 3200–3600$ (£13.50–15.00;
$23.50–26.50). There are cheaper pensions, but some of the
rooms are likely to have quite a turnover of occupants (about

every half hour). Nevertheless, most of these cheaper pensions are perfectly safe. As a rule, prices are slightly higher in the streets on either side of Avenida da Liberdade, and higher again (though still affordable) on Avenida da Liberdade itself. Because of their location, pensions on Avenida da Liberdade fill quickly; those in the streets off the avenue are more likely to have space. In the summer months, however, you may have difficulty finding accommodation at the prices quoted above as the amount of rooms available just manages to satisfy demand. Singles become very scarce as owners often put an extra bed in the room during peak season. The best advice is to start looking for a room as early as possible. If you arrive in the afternoon be prepared to take something slightly more expensive, and then look around early next morning. If you are willing to pay 5000–6000$ (£21–25; $36.50–44.00) for a double the main Tourist Office will find rooms in this price range free of charge.

HOTELS

Rossio area:

Ibérica, Praça da Figueira 10–2 (tel. 865781). Doubles around 3300$ (£13.75; $24) with breakfast.

Londres, Rossio/Praça Dom Pedro IV 53–1 (tel. 346 2203).

Coimbra e Madrid, Praça de Figueira 3–3&4 (tel. 321 760).

Evora, Rossio/Praça Dom Pedro IV 59–2 (tel. 346 7666).

Do Sul, Rossio/Praça Dom Pedro IV 59–2 (tel. 814 7253).

Beira Minho, Praça de Figueira 6–2 (tel. 3461846). B&B. All rooms have baths. Singles around 3800$ (£15.80; $28), doubles around 4400$ (£18.30; $32).

Baixa – the lower town; a roughly rectangular area stretching from Praça Dom Pedro IV & Praça de Figueira down to Praça do Comercio:

Rossio, Rua dos Sapateiros 173–2 (tel. 3427204). Doubles around 3800$ (£15.80; $28). Just off Praça Dom Pedro IV.

Arco Bandeira, Rua Arco Bandeira 226–4 (tel. 3423478).

Around 5400$ (£22.50; $40) for doubles. Not cheap, but a
very comfortable pension. Just off Rossio.
Moderna, Rua dos Correiros 205–4 (tel. 3460818). Doubles
around 4400$ (£18.25; $32). Clean rooms.
Angoche, Rua dos Douradores 121–4 (tel. 870711). Doubles
around 3300$ (£13.75; $24). Very clean.
Bom Conforto, Rua dos Douradores 83–3 (tel. 878 328).
Norte, Rua dos Douradores 159–1&2 (tel. 878941).
Santiago, Rua dos Douradores 222–3 (tel. 874353).
Prata, Rua da Prata 71–3 (tel. 3468908). Reasonably priced
and very good. Singles from around 2750$ (£11.50; $20),
doubles from 3100$ (£13; $22.50). Rooms with baths are
about 10 per cent more expensive.
Galiza, Rua do Crucifixio 50–5 (tel. 328430).

Around São Jorge castle and close to the Alfama:
São João da Praça, Rua São João da Praça 97 (tel. 862591).
Cheap and high quality.
Ninho das Aguias, Rua Costa do Castelo 74 (tel. 862151).
Slightly more expensive than the prices quoted above, but
an excellent pension set in a garden. Doubles start around
3800$ (£15.80; $28). Highly recommended (unfortunately,
by all guidebooks, it seems).

To the west of the Baixa, around San Roque and the Rossio
railway station:
Estacio Central, Calçada do Carmo 17–21 (tel. 323308). Behind
the train station.
Henriques, Calçada do Carmo 37–11 (tel. 326886).
Do Duque, Calçada do Duque 53 (tel. 3463444). Inexpensive
and very clean.

To the west of the Baixa, between the Trinidad Theatre and
Chiado Church and the river:
Hotel Borges, Rua Garrett 108 (tel. 361953). Doubles with
bath start around 6500$ (£27; $47.50) in this two-star hotel.
Close to the Chiado Church.
Hotel Bragança, Rua Alecrim 12–1 (tel. 327061/321114). One-

star hotel within easy walking distance of the Cais do Sodré train station.

Bairro Alto:

Globo, Rua do Texeira 37 (tel. 3462279). Doubles around 3800$ (£15.80; $28). An excellent pension). Close to the upper terminus of the Elevador da Gloria.

Between Praça dos Restauradores and the statue of the Marqués de Pombal. L. Avenida da Liberdade is the main road running between the two. Rua das Portas de Santo Antao is parallel to the right off Liberdade as you walk up from Rossio. From the Elevador da Gloria, Rua da Gloria runs parallel to Liberdade on the left as you walk up from Rossio. Praça Alegria can be reached by turning left off Liberdade after Rua Conceicao da Gloria. Rua da Alegria runs out of Praça da Alegria.

D. Maria II, Rua Portas de Santo Antao 9–3 (tel. 371128). Large, well-kept rooms. Doubles around 3300$ (£13.75; $24).

Iris, Rua da Gloria 2a–1 (tel. 323157). Doubles around 3300$ (£13.75; $24). A simple pension, but highly recommended for women travelling on their own.

Pembo, Avda da Liberdade 11–3 (tel. 325010). Singles 1750–2250$ (£7.30–9.40; $13–16.50), doubles with bath 2750–3300$ (£11.50–13.75; $20–24).

Mucaba, Avda da Liberdade 53–2 (tel. 346567).

Lis, Avda da Liberdade 180 (tel. 521084).

Dom Sancho I, Avda da Liberdade 202–3&5 (tel. 548648).

Ritz, Avda da Liberdade 240–4 (tel. 521084).

Mansarde, Avda da Liberdade 141–5 (tel. 372963).

Do Sul, Avda da Liberdade 53 (tel. 3465647).

Modelo, Rua das Portas de Santo Antão 12 (tel. 327041).

Flor de Baixa, Rua das Portas de Santo Antão 81–2 (tel. 323153). Good value.

Floroscente, Rua das Portas de Santo Antão 99 (tel. 326609). Large capacity with some very cheap rooms. Singles and doubles start around 2250$ (£9.40; $16.50).

Monumental, Rua da Gloria 21 (tel. 3469807).

Milanesa, Rua da Alegria 25–2 (tel. 3466456).
Sevilha, Praça da Alegria 11–2&3 (tel. 369579).
Alegria, Praça da Alegria 12–1 (tel. 3475522).
Solar, Praça da Alegria 12–2 (tel. 322608).
Dos Restauradores, Praça dos Restauradores 13–4.
Imperial, Praça dos Restauradores 79 (tel. 320166).

Avenida Almirante Reis. A main thoroughfare beginning at
Lg. Martin Moniz, close to Praa de Figueira:
Almirante Reis, Avda Almirante Reis 98–2 (tel. 823773).
  Doubles around 5000$ (£20.80; $36.50).

IYHF HOSTELS

Rua Andrade Corvo 46 (tel. 532696). Metro: Picoas. Bus 1
or 45 from Rossio or Cais do Sodré. Twenty-minute walk
from the centre, off Avda Fontes Pereira de Melo, in the
area beyond the Pombal statue. Phone ahead to check if
this hostel is open in 1993.
Lisboa-Catalazete, Estrada Marginal, OEIRAS (tel. 2430638).
11.30 p.m. curfew. A good hostel, but with a relatively
small capacity, so phone ahead to check on the availability
of beds. Frequent trains from Cais do Sodré; a 20-minute
trip. On leaving the station, go through the underpass, to
the right beneath the Praia sign. Look for the sign pointing
out the way to the hostels. It's about three quarters of a
mile and well signposted.

CAMPING

Parque de Campismo Municipal de Lisboa Monsanto (tel.
704413/708384). Open all year round. 150$ (£0.60; $1) per
tent, 550$ (£2.30; $4) per person. Bus 14 runs from Praça
de Figueira.
Parque de Campismo Municipal de Oeiras, Rua de S. Pedro
do Areeiro (tel. 2430330). Train from Cais do Sodré to
Oeiras. Open May–Oct.

There are six sites on the Costa da Caparica. Ask the Tourist

Office which metro and/or bus you should take for the different sites. Open all year round unless indicated:

Costa da Caparica, Estrada da Trafaria (tel. 2900661). Orbitur site. Bungalows available. From Praça de Espanha a bus runs right to the site, or take the metro to Palhava.

Um Lugar ao Sol, Estrada da Trafaria (tel. 2901592).

Costa Velha, Estrada da Trafaria (tel. 2900100/2900374).

C. do Concelho de Almada, Praia da Sade (tel. 2901862).

Costa Nova, Estrada da Costa Nova (tel. 2903078). Closed Jan.

Piedense, Praia da Mata (tel. 2902004).

Oporto (Porto) (tel. code 02)

Tourist Office
Turismo, Rua Clube dos Fenianos 25 (tel. 312740). Open June–Sept., Mon.–Fri. 9 a.m.–7 p.m., Sat. 9 a.m.–2 p.m., Sun. 10 a.m.–2 p.m.; Oct.–May., Mon.–Fri. 9 a.m.–12.30 p.m. and 2.00–5.30 p.m., Sat. 9 a.m.–4 p.m. From São Bento train station follow Avenida dos Aliados to the Town Hall, from which the Tourist Office is over to the left.

Arriving by Train
Your most likely point of arrival is Porto Campanha, which is quite a distance from the city centre. Rather than start walking you should wait for a connection to the São Bento station in the heart of the city (you will rarely have to wait over 20 minutes, the trip takes 5 minutes). A few trains arrive at the Trinidad station by the Trinidad Church, just to the rear of the Town Hall.

Finding Accommodation
Most of the city's pensions are on and around Avenida dos Aliados, particularly on the western side of Aliados (on the left as you walk up the street towards the Town Hall). You should be able to find a single for around 1800–2500$

(£7.50–10.50; $13.00–18.50) or a double for around 2800–3800$ (£11.75–16.00; $20–28) without too much difficulty at most times of year, but because many pensions have undergone renovation in recent years and consequently upped their prices, you may have to settle for something a little more expensive during July and August. The cheapest rooms in the city are to be found along Rua do Loureiro, close to São Bento train station, but this is the red-light area of Oporto.

PENSIONS

Estoril, Rua de Cedofeita 193 (tel. 2002751). Doubles around 3300$ (£13.75; $24). Very smart rooms. From the western side of Aliados, near the Tourist Office, follow Rua Fabrica into Praça Carlos Alberto. Rua do Cedofeita runs from the right hand end of this square.

San Marino, Praça Carlos Alberto 59 (tel. 325499). Doubles with breakfast around 4000$ (£16.75; $29). See the Estoril, above, for directions.

Pão-de-Azucar, Rua do Almada 262 (tel. 2002425). Three-star pension. Doubles with private bathrooms around 5000$ (£21; $36.50). Rua do Almada is parallel to Aliados, immediately to the west.

Astoria, Rua Arnaldo Gama 56 (tel. 2008175). In a quiet area of town to the rear of the city wall. Very popular, so reserve ahead.

Monumental, Avda dos Aliados 151–4 (tel. 23964). Large rooms, good value.

Next door to Monumental, above the Bel Arte, there is another good pension. Unfortunately, this pension is nameless.

Norte, Rua Fernando Tomás 579 (tel. 2003503). East off Aliados from the Trinidad church. The pension is at the junction with Rua Santa Catarina.

Vera Cruz, Rua da Ramalho Ortigão 14 (tel. 323396). B&B. Doubles 5700$ (£23.75; $41.50). Doubles with baths are only slightly dearer. The street off Aliados before the Tourist Office.

Dos Aliados, Rua Elisio de Melo 27 (tel. 24853). B&B. Doubles 4800$ (£20; $35). Off Aliados.

Novo Mundo, Rua Conde de Vizela 92 (tel. 25403). West of Aliados. Off Rua Clerigos, the street going up the hill to the Clerigos Tower from São Bento station.

União, Rua Conde de Vizela 62 (tel. 23078).

Duas Naçães, Praça Guilherme Gomes Fernandes 59 (tel. 26807). Along Rua Carmelitas from the Clerigos Tower. See the Novo Mundo, above.

Grand Oceano, Rua da Fabrica 45 (tel. 382447). Joins Aliados on the west side near the Tourist Office.

Franco, Praça Parada de Leitão 41 (tel. 381201). To the west of Aliados.

D'Ouro, Praça Parada de Leitão 41 (tel. 381201).

Nobreza, Rua do Breyner 6 (tel. 312409). Rundown and not the cleanest of places. Rua do Breyner is on the left as you walk up Cedofeita from Praça Carlos Alberto. See the Estoril, above.

Porto Rico, Rua do Almada 262 (tel. 922425). See the Pão-de-Azucar, above.

Europa, Rua do Almada 398 (tel. 26971). Two-star pension. See the Pão-de-Azucar, above.

Moderna, Rua Estacão 74 (tel. 571280). A short walk from Porto Campanha train station.

Continental, Rua Mousinho da Silveira 14 (tel. 320355). West of Aliados, close to the São Bento station.

Madariz, Rua Cimo da Vila. Very cheap pension, close to the São Bento station.

IYHF HOSTEL

Rua Rodrigues Lobo 98 (tel. 65535). Very small and usually full by midday. Curfew midnight. Twenty-minute walk from the town centre. Bus 3, 19, 20 or 52 from Praça da Liberdade (at the foot of Avda dos Aliados) runs to nearby Rua Júlio Dinis.

STUDENT ACCOMMODATION

Colegio de Gaia, Rua Padua Correia 166, Vila Nova de Gaia (tel. 304007). On the other side of the River Douro from Porto. Frequent train connections, as well as local buses.

CAMPING

Parque de Campismo da Prelada, Rua Monte dos Burgos (tel. 812616). Open all year. Around 300$ (£1.25; $2.50) per tent, 375$ (£1.60; $3) per person. Bus 6 from Praça da Liberdade; bus 9 from Bolhao (last bus 9 p.m.); bus 50 from Cordoaria. Closest site to the town centre, but 3 miles from the beach.

There are three sites in Vila Nova da Guia, closer to the beaches than Prelada. Ask the Tourist Office about the local bus service to these sites:

Salguieros-Canidelo (tel. 7810500). Open May–Sept.

Madalena, Lugar da Marinha (tel. 714162). Open June– Sept. Bus 50 from Rua Mouz, near Porto Sao Bento train station.

Marisol, Rua Alto das Chaquedas 82, Canidelo (tel. 715942).

Sintra (tel. code 01)

Tourist Office
Turismo, Praça República 19 (tel. 2931157).

Finding Accommodation
Finding a bed in a pension can be a problem during the summer unless you arrive early in the day as the local pensions fill quickly at this time of year, so a private room is probably your best option if you want to stay in Sintra. Trains from Lisbon's Rossio station take only 50 minutes to reach Sintra, so you might want to consider visiting the town on a day-trip from the capital to save yourself the trouble of finding a room.

PENSIONS

Cyntia Café. From the station, head away from the town centre along Avda Dr. Miguel Bombarda until you see the pension.

Nova Sintra, Largo Alfonso de Albuquerque 25 (tel. 9230220). Further along from the Cyntia Café through Largo D. Manuel I.

Familiar. Past the Nova Sintra. About 10 minutes' walk from the station.

Casa Adelaide, Avda Guilherme Gomes Fernandes 11–1 (tel. 9230873). Near the Town Hall, roughly halfway between the train station and the Palácio Real.

Bristol. Close to the Palácio Real.

Economica. One of the cheapest. Near the Palácio Real.

PRIVATE ROOMS

The Tourist Office books rooms at reasonable rates. Rooms are frequently touted by locals at the train station.

CAMPING

No really convenient site.

Capuchos convent is over 6 miles from Sintra. The nearest bus stop is about 3 miles from the site, with most of the remaining walk uphill.

Parque de Campismo Praia Grande (tel. 9290581/9291834) is situated on the coast 7½ miles from Sintra, and 2½ miles from Colares. Open year round. Ask the Tourist Office for details of the bus service. The bus stops only 50m from the site.

ROMANIA

In an effort to bolster Romania's economy, the Ceausescu regime followed a policy of consistently devaluing its hard currencies; by some 90 per cent from 1975 to 1989. This policy had a profound effect on the tourist industry, rendering most accommodation options comparable in price to their Scandinavian equivalents. Hotel prices were one striking example of this development: classified deluxe, Category I or II, in 1989 the cheapest double in a Category II hotel in Bucharest cost £50 ($88). Outside Bucharest, a similar room costs £40 ($70). Some sanity has now returned to the pricing structure and, although this does not mean that there are any bargains to be had, at least a night in one of the cheaper hotels will not ruin your budget for days, as was the case previously.

A number of Category II **hotels** in Bucharest now offer singles for around £17 ($30), doubles for around £25 ($45). Outside the capital you can look for a 20–25 per cent reduction on these prices for similar accommodation. *All hotel bills must be settled in hard currency.* If these prices seem attractive to you, bear in mind that either you will have to be very fortunate to get one of these rooms on arrival, or you will have to book well in advance. During the peak season (mid-June to mid-September), hotels are frequently booked to near capacity by East European groups. You may be lucky enough to get one of the remaining places, or find space caused by a late cancellation, but do not expect too much help from the National Tourist Organization (ONT) in your quest for a cheap hotel room. ONT supply hotel lists and book hotels, but old habits die hard and, especially in Bucharest, you may find they devote much of their energy to persuading you to stay in a more expensive hotel. Expect to be told that the cheaper hotels are full. If you are not pressed for time, you can try some of the hotels in person. It is a sad fact that the staff at hotel reception desks often only remember about vacant rooms on production of a bribe in hard currency. Whether you will want to make such an offer will depend on how desperate you are. Athough it is possible to make hotel reservations through various private organizations in the UK before departure, they, like ONT, are not always too receptive to enquiries regarding the cheaper hotels.

The letting of private homes was legalized in 1990. Previously Romanians were liable to severe punishment if they were found to have given lodgings to foreigners. Nowadays **rooms in private homes** offer budget travellers a way to avoid paying over the odds in hotels, and the efforts involved in trying to book a hostel bed. Many Romanians are keen to let rooms to earn some extra money and, as the problems besetting the country deter many people from visiting Romania, there is a plentiful supply of rooms available. Private rooms can usually be booked through ONT, and occasionally through private agencies. Prices are around £6.80 ($12) per person in Bucharest, £5.70 ($10) elsewhere. *Once again payment has to be made in hard currency.* Rooms offered by locals are much cheaper – rarely will their asking price reach £2.80 ($5) p.p., and usually it will be considerably less.

Do not be immediately suspicious of anyone offering you a room for free. This is quite a common practice. Your host may well expect some favour in return, such as exchanging money at a rate favourable to all concerned; that is, above the official rate but below the black market norm (this is still illegal). If you do decide to take up an offer of private accommodation, keep an eye on your valuables, or leave them at the station.

Youth hostels are controlled by the Romanian youth and student organization CATT (Compania Autonomă de Turismpentru Tineret – the Independent Youth Tourism Company). Like other East European tourist organizations, CATT have a marked preference for dealing with groups rather than individuals. Most of the beds at the majority of youth hostels are reserved months in advance by school and youth groups. This puts the onus on you to book well ahead of your time of arrival, a major task considering the difficulties of dealing with CATT. Incredibly, when hostels have plenty of space, many simply choose to shut their doors until the next group arrives. In the later years of the Ceausescu regime the cost of CATT youth hostels spiralled dramatically. Prices remain inflated even today at around £5–9 ($9–16).

During the university and college summer holidays, CATT lets out **student accommodation** (*caminul de studenti*) in towns with a sizeable student population. As with youth hostels, these lodgings are frequently filled up by vacationing groups. If you do manage to get a bed, expect to pay in the region of £3.40–4.30 ($6.00–7.50). Many towns and university rectorates maintain a surplus capacity of student accommodation, specifically for the use of visiting foreign students. Prices are exceptionally low, at around £1.40–2.80 ($2.50–5.00). Such accommodation offers an excellent opportunity to meet Romanian students. You may receive offers from Romanian, African or Asian students to share their rooms. Probably the only favour they will be looking for is the chance to speak to you.

There are well over 100 **campsites,** most of which are listed on the map *Popasuri Turistice* (text in French). A solo traveller should pay no more than £1.70 ($3) to pitch a tent for one night. Cabins are available at most sites, with charges of around £2.90 ($5) per person being the norm though, unfortunately, these are usually full in summer. Sites are sometimes located a good distance out of town, and occasionally are none too easy to reach by public transport. Your main complaint may be the quality of the sites. Facilities are very basic, and the toilets and washrooms can be really atrocious. **Camping rough** is technically illegal, but there are few places you are likely to have any trouble once you get out into the countryside. The authorities outside the towns often ignore freelance campers, as long as you do not light fires, leave litter, or damage the natural habitat. Occasionally, you may be sent on your way, but it is very rare for the statutory fine to be imposed.

In the countryside, there are well in excess of 100 '*cabanas*', simple accommodations for hikers and walkers, many of which are in the more mountainous parts of the country. A booklet 'Invitation to the Carpathians', shows the locations of many cabanas, plus suggested itineraries. An overnight stay costs around £3.50 ($6). By law, cabanas are debarred from refusing entry to any hiker or climber, but it still might be sensible to reserve ahead, either through ONT, or through the Regional Tourist Office. Overnight stays are also possible at a number of **monasteries**, but it can be very difficult to gain entrance. An approach has to be made first to ONT, who will do their utmost to convince you to stay in a hotel instead. Persistence is essential on your part, but there is still no guarantee of success.

If you cannot find a bed in town, and face a night sleeping rough, do not attempt to bed down in the town, but rather head for the **train station waiting room.** If you are disturbed by the police explain that you are taking a train early in the morning. The chances are that you will have a few Romanians for company in the waiting room as this is quite a common practice amongst people setting off on an early morning train. Try to leave your pack in the left luggage store as theft is quite common.

As there are several long overnight train journeys in Romania it is possible to spend a few **nights on the train.** Trains are usually packed so there is little chance of you getting stretched out in a compartment, but booking a couchette gives you the chance of a good night's sleep. Prices vary according to the length of the journey, but are low by Western standards. However, couchettes have to be booked four to seven days in advance, either at an ONT office, or through a CFR (Romanian Railways) office in town (not at the station). The problem with sleeping on overnight trains is that there is a high incidence of theft from travellers on such trains.

Tourist Information
The quality of tourist information available locally is often very poor, with stocks of pamphlets etc. liable to become exhausted long before the end of the main tourist season. If you know which places you will be visiting, it is worth asking at any office

whether they have any information on those destinations, as
it is not unknown for information on town A to be available
in town B when it is no longer available in town A. At the time
of writing, the best guides to the sights were several old East
European guides. While the information on accommodation
in these guides is out of date, they provide a good, basic guide
to the places of interest (you should also be wary of any
information regarding times of buses/trains contained in these
guides).

ADDRESSES

Romanian National Tourist Office	17 Nottingham Street, London W1M 3RD (tel. 071 224 3692).
Hotels	booked in the UK by: Thomas Cook, VIP Travel, 42 North Audley Street, London, W1Y 2DU (tel. 071–499 4221) (or your local Thomas Cook agent). Any branch of American Express. Romanian Holidays, 54 Pembroke Road, London, W8 6NX (tel. 071–602 7093) (London only) or through the Romanian National Tourist Office.
Youth and student hostels	CATT, Onesti 6–8, Bucuresti (tel. 140566). CATT, 7–15 Str. Mandeleev, Bucuresti (tel. 144200).

Brasov (tel. code 21)

Tourist Office
ONT. In the lobby of the Hotel Aro Palace on Bd Revolucion. Maps of the town and the surrounding area. Open daily 8 a.m.–6 p.m. Bus 4 from the train station to Bd Revolucion, or a 20-minute walk.

Accommodation Agencies
Postăvrul, 9 Eroilor Blvd (tel. 42840).
  Cristianul, 1 Toamnei Str. (tel. 87110).

HOTELS

For information on hotel accommodation contact Postăvrul or Cristianul.
  Aro Sport, Str. Maiakovski. The cheapest hotel in town. Doubles around £25 ($44). To the rear of the Hotel Aro Palace.

PRIVATE ROOMS

Rooms range in price from £2.75–4.25 ($5–12). Book through Postăvrul or Cristianul. ONT seem to have stopped dealing in private rooms, but there is no harm in asking if you are collecting information.

STUDENT ACCOMMODATION

Dorm rooms available year round, at about £1.30 ($2.50) for those with student ID. Enquire at the Rector's Office, University of Braşov. Open Mon.–Fri. 10a.m.–5p.m. Just along Bd Revolucion from the Hotel Aro Palace.

CAMPING

  Zimbrul. On the road to the mountain resort of Poiana-

Braşov. From Parc Central bus 20. Bus 4 links the train station to Parc Central.

Dîrste. Roughly 4½ miles from the town centre, close to the motorway to Bucharest. From the Parc Central, bus 17 until it leaves Calea Bucureştilor. From here a 10-minute walk parallel to the motorway, then under the train tracks and across the river.

Bucharest (Bucereşti) (tel. code 0)

HOTELS

Expect to pay £11.50–15.00 ($20–26) for singles, £18.00–25 ($31.50–44.00) for doubles

Near the Gara de Nord:
Bucegi, Str. Witing 2 (tel. 495120).
Dunărea, Calea Griviţei 140.
Griviţa, Calea Griviţei 130 (tel. 505380).
Oltenia, Calea Griviţei. Cheapest of the three hotels listed on this street.
Marna, Str. Buzeşti.

More centrally located:
Opera, Str. Brezoianu 37.
Muntenia, Str. Academiei 21 (tel. 146010).
Cişmigiu, Bd Gheorghiu-Dej 18 (tel. 147410).
Carpaţi, Str. Matei Millo 16 (tel. 157690).

Most people arrive at the Gara de Nord. Beside the ONT office in the train station there is a board listing all the hotels in the city, with their addresses and telephone numbers.

PRIVATE ROOMS

Available through ONT main office at Bd Magheru (tel.

145160). £6.25 ($11) p.p. Mon.–Sat. 8 a.m.–8 p.m., Sun. 8 a.m.–2 p.m.

HOSTELS/STUDENT DORMS

Expect to pay around £8 ($14) for singles, £14.75 ($26) for doubles

CATT are at Str. Mendeleev 7–15 (tel. 144200). Open Mon.–Fri. 8a.m.–5p.m. Generally unwilling to help independent travellers. You might have better luck approaching hostels/dorms in person.

N. Bălescu Agronomical Institute. Close to the Coresi Pringint House (the former Casa Scînteii, reached by bus 131. Open 1 July–31 Aug.

Institutul Politechnic. Near the Grozăveşti metro stop. Open 1 July–31 Aug.

Most of the Arab, African and Asian students remain at the colleges during the summer vacation. They will probably be able to tell you where to make enquiries about staying the night. They may even offer to let you share their room. At other times, Romanian students may extend the same hospitality.

CAMPING

Bănasea. Twin-bedded bungalows are available, £2.80–8.50 ($5–15). From Gara de Nord, bus 205 or trolleybus 81 (also trolleybus 82 from Piaţa Victoriei) to Bănasea airport. Bus 149 runs to the site (Sundays bus 348). Bus 148 lets you off about 10 minutes' walk from the site. Fine during the day, but the road is unlit at night.

Constanţa (tel. code 16)

Affordable accommodation in Constanţa is limited so you may have to stay in one of the resorts nearby. Two of the easiest to reach are Mamaia and Eforie Nord, 3 3/4 miles north and 6 1/4 miles south respectively. Trolleybus 41 from the station in Constanţa will take you to Mamaia, and trolleybus 11 runs from the Sud bus station to Eforie Nord. Ask the ONT office in Constanţa about the availability of rooms in the cheap hotels in Mamaia or Eforie Nord, or of bungalows at the campsites.

Accommodation Agencies

ONT, Bd Tomis 46, Constanţa. Open Mon.–Sat. 8 a.m.–6 p.m., Sun. 9 a.m.–1 p.m. In the past, this office has been staffed by unhelpful non-English speakers. If this is still the case, try asking the English-speaking staff in the Hotel Continental (tel. 15660) at the intersection of Bd Tomis and Bd Republicii for advice on accommodation possibilities.

CATT, Bd Tomis 20–24, Constanţa (tel. 16624).

ONT, Hotel Perla, Mamaia (tel. 31670). Also in the Bucureşti B hotel (tel. 31152/31179).

Eforie Nord Tourist Office, Bd Republicii 13 (tel. 41351).

HOTELS

Constanţa – ask ONT about rooms in the hotels below, or at other hotels:

Expect to pay £6.25–7.50 ($11–13) for singles, £9.20–12.00 ($16–21) for doubles

Victoria, Bd Republicii.
Constanţa, Bd Tomis 46. Above the Tourist Office.

Mamaia Nord:
The Tourist Office lets rooms in those hotels which have not been block-booked by travel operators. Amongst the cheapest in town are the Favorit and the Paloma. There are a number of others which are only slightly more expensive, such as the Apollo, Select, and the Caraiman I and II.

Eforie Nord:
Much the same system as in Mamaia. Hotel beds start at

around £6.25 ($11), so state that you are looking for a bed around that price (quote the $11 figure).

PRIVATE ROOMS

Enquire about their availability at any of the Tourist Offices.

HOSTELS

CATT control the letting of dormitory accommodation during the summer, but are more accustomed to dealing with groups.

CAMPING

No sites in Constanţa. Just north of Mamaia is Turist, while another three miles further on is Hanul Piraţilor. There are two sites in Eforie Nord: the Şincai and the Meduza. In July and August, the sites are invariably overcrowded. All four sites have bungalows for hire and in summer these bungalows are very popular, but try to make reservations at the Tourist Offices before going to the sites and consider yourself fortunate if you are successful.

Sibiu (Sibiu/Hermannstadt)

(tel. code 24)

The cheapest hotel is the Impăratul Romanilor, just off Piaţa Republicii on Str. N. Balcescu. Cheaper lodgings are available at the inn on Calea Dumbravii: from the bus station (adjacent to the train station on Piaţa Garii) take the bus to Pădurea Dumbrava and you'll find the inn located next to the campsite, on the left as you travel down Calea Dumbravii. For private rooms in Sibiu or the neighbouring villages contact ONT. From Piaţa Republicii walk down Str. N. Balcescu until you see the ONT office. CATT are located at Str. Kornhauser 4, close to the ONT office. CATT operate a student hotel in town, where reasonable doubles with a shower cost around £23 ($40). In summer, you can also ask them about any cheaper accommodation which might be available in student dormitories.

Sighişoara (tel. code 23)

HOTELS

Steaua, Str. Gheorghiu-Dej. Affordable singles and doubles.

PRIVATE ROOMS

Enquire at ONT on Str. Gheorghiu-Dej.

CAMPING

There is a site on top of the hill to the rear of the train station and bungalows are also available there. From the station, walk right along Str. Liberati until you see the tunnel going under the tracks on your right. As you emerge on to Str. Primaverii go right and watch out for the path leading to the site. The Hula Danes site is located about 2½ miles from town along the road to Mediaş. Hula Danes also has bungalows for hire.

SLOVENIA

The information included in the Llubljana section below has not been updated since the 1992 edition. For information regarding the various accommodation possibilities in Slovenia refer to the final chapter of this guide for the introduction which accompanied the Yugoslavian section of the 1992 edition of this book.

Llubljana (tel. code 061)

HOTELS

Cheapest singles around £7 ($13; DM20), doubles around £5.25 ($9.75; DM15) p.p.

Grandovec Inn (tel. 666350/666449).

Cheapest doubles around £9.25 ($17.75; DM27) p.p.

Park Hotel, Tabor 9 (tel. 316777). Also triples.
Primraku Hotel (tel. 223412).
Zajčja Dobrava Inn (tel. 442108).
Dom učencev Tabor, Vidovdanska 7 (tel. 321067). Ask the
  Tourist Office if this hotel has re-opened.

Cheapest doubles around £11.25 ($21.25; DM32.50) p.p.

Ilirija Hotel (tel. 551162).
Pension Lieber (tel. 374080).

PRIVATE ROOMS

Turistično-Informacijski center, Titova II (tel. 215412/224222).
Price p.p. in doubles: Category I £5.35 ($10.25; DM15.50).
Category II £4.50 ($8.50; DM13). Category III £3.80 ($7.20;
DM11). Singles range from £5 to £6 ($9.50–11.50;
DM14.50–17.50). Same price year round, but there's a limited
supply of rooms.

IYHF HOSTEL

Bežigrad, Kardeljeva ploščad 28 (tel. 312185/321897). Open
25 June–28 Aug. For information contact Mladi turist,
Celovška 49, Llubljana. Bus 6 from Titova Cesta to Stadion.
Walk a short distance, then go right on to Dimičeva, then
left.

HOSTELS

Zvezni Center, Kardeljeva ploščad 27 (tel. 342626). £7 ($13.25; DM20.25), price includes sheets and showers.

Dijaški Dom Ivana Cankarja, Poljanska 26–28 (tel. 318948). Bus 11 from the train station. Alternatively, walk down Resljeva, then go left on Poljanska. Take the path between nos. 24 and 26. At the foot of the path go left.

Ask the Turistično-Informacijski center at Titova II (tel. 215412/224222) about the current location of the International Student Hostel as it tends to change annually. Open from July–Sept. They will also book you doubles in student residences at £7 ($13.25; DM20.25) p.p.

CAMPING

Ježica, Titova Cesta 260a (tel. 372901). Bus 6 from the train station. £2.10 ($4; DM6) per tent and p.p. Also twin-bedded bungalows with showers, £11.20 ($21.25; DM32.50) p.p.

SPAIN (España)

Although prices have risen substantially over the past decade Spain still offers the budget traveller a plentiful supply of some of the least expensive accommodation possibilities in Europe. Virtually all the various types of accommodation are inspected and categorized by the Secretaria de Estado de Turismo. If you are looking for your own room there is quite an array of officially categorized lodgings to choose from (for the sake of convenience, these are grouped together under the heading **pensions** in the city sections below). The intricacies of the rating system detailed below are intended as a rough guide. For the reasons given, do not treat them as hard and fast rules. Least expensive of all the officially categorized accommodations are *fondas*, denoted by a white 'F' on a square blue sign. Next up the scale are *casas de huespedes* (blue sign with white CH), followed by *pensiónes* (P), graded from one up to three stars. Then come *hospedajes*, infrequently seen in the country as a whole, but common in Santiago do Compostela. At this lower end of the market there is little point expecting anything other than basic facilities, but standards of cleanliness are usually perfectly acceptable. *Hostal-residencias* (HR) and *hostales* (H), both graded from one up to three stars, are a bit more expensive, while at the pinnacle of the rating system are *hoteles* (H) and *hotel-residencias* (HR), graded from one up to five stars. The appendage *residencia* indicates that no meals, other than (perhaps) breakfast, are served at the establishment; otherwise a *hostal-residencia* or *hotel-residencia* is similar in every respect to a comparably rated *hostal* or *hotel*.

As a rule the singles in any establishment cost around 60–70 per cent of the price of comparable doubles. By law, guests can request that an extra bed be included in a room. This should add no more than 35 per cent to the cost of a double and no more than 60 per cent to the cost of a single. The Secretaria de Estado de Turismo not only categorizes establishments but also sets maximum prices for their rooms, according to the facilities available. By law these prices have to be displayed on the door of the room. With certain agreed and stipulated exceptions, it is illegal for owners to charge more than the stated price. The more usual exceptions are the peak season (usually July and August) and, in Seville, during Holy Week and the April Fair, when prices can be raised quite legally. Some owners choose to offer their rooms below the official price, though this can create the impression that the whole system is a bit of a shambles; for example, you can pay more for a room in a *casa de huespedes* than for a similar room in a better category of accommodation such as a *pensión* or *hostal-residencia*. During the quieter period of the year (October to early March) there is scope for bargaining with owners who have not already voluntarily dropped their prices. Understandings can be reached fairly easily with owners who know there are plenty of rooms available just down the street.

Even in peak season there are rooms available in all the types of accommodations mentioned above which fall into the budget category. Your interest in *hoteles* and *hotel-residencias* however is likely to be confined to the bottom ranking, as prices for a basic one-star double start at around 3400–3800ptas (£18.90–21.00; $33–37). A comparable room in a *three-star hostel* or *hostal-residencia* is usually similar in price, though they can be considerably more expensive. In other types of accommodation singles in the price range 900–2000ptas (£5–11; $9.00–19.50) are widely available, as are doubles for 1600–3500ptas (£8.90–19.50; $15.50–34.00). You are more likely to find rooms at the lower end of these price scales outside the main resorts and the more popular tourist towns. On average you can expect to pay around 1500ptas (£8.30; $14.50) for singles, 2300ptas (£12.80; $22.50) for doubles in the main tourist destinations. Although there are some very cheap rooms available in popular places such as Madrid, Barcelona and the Andalucian cities, these tend to fill early in the day during the peak season. Phoning ahead is difficult unless you speak

Spanish as very few owners speak any other language (signs outside their establishment claiming otherwise are often just a ruse to attract your attention), and in any case, owners seldom accept reservations made by phone. At best, phoning ahead will let you ascertain whether rooms are available, but do not be surprised if they have been filled by the time you arrive in person. One consolation is that there are generally a host of other accommodation possibilities in the same street, or even in the same building.

Now and again you may also see *camas* (beds), *camas y comidas* (bed and board), or *habitaciones* (rooms) advertised in bars or private homes. These can work out the least expensive accommodation option of all, with the possible bonus of good, cheap meals thrown in. As always, have a look at the room before making a firm acceptance. Again, there is probably nothing to be lost by trying to haggle the price down a bit, except in the peak periods when owners can afford to be choosy, and may just send you packing.

Hostelling is not a particularly good option in Spain as a whole. There are about 150 hostels of vastly differing quality, at which IYHF cards are obligatory. Most of the main places of interest are covered, with several notable exceptions, such as Salamanca and Santiago de Compostela. Only about 20 hostels remain open all year round, with many operating from July to September only. This means that outside these months hostel accommodation is lacking in a number of places of considerable interest. Even during the period from July to mid-September independent travellers may not be able to get into the temporary hostels in places such as León, Segovia and Avila, as they are frequently filled by school and youth groups.

However, hostelling is not to be dismissed as a way of seeing the main cities, with the possible exception of Seville (with a very small hostel for so popular a city, which is usually full of local students). The question is whether prices, curfews, lack of security and the fact hostels are rarely centrally located make hostelling worthwhile. The normal hostel curfew of 10.30p.m. in winter and 11.30p.m. in summer is extended to 1–2a.m. in Madrid, Barcelona and San Sebastian (no curfew at Madrid

'Richard Schirrmann' but the hostel is a long way from the centre if you miss the last metro). Even a 1a.m. curfew is a bit early for anyone wanting to enjoy the nightlife of the cities, where things do not really begin to get going until around midnight. Charges for an overnight stay at most hostels are 700ptas (£3.90; $7) for under 26s, 830ptas (£4.60; $8) for seniors. Breakfast adds about 150–200ptas (£0.85–1.10; $1.50–2.00) to these prices. For two people travelling together, it might well be worth paying a little extra for the security of a room in one of the cheap lodgings mentioned above, plus the freedom to come and go as you wish.

Camping is not a great option either, and probably not worth considering unless you plan to travel extensively outside the main towns. Sites are frequently situated far from the town centre, and ill served by public transport. In effect, this can impose a curfew more restrictive than at any hostel. If you are keen on camping, at least the standards at the government-regulated sites are quite high, and although rating makes little difference to price, the facilities at the Class 1 sites do tend to be better than at the lesser-rated sites. Even in the sites serving the main towns you should pay no more than 400ptas (£2.25; $4) per person and per tent. However, to this you can add the cost of getting to the site, and, as security is a problem, the cost of leaving your luggage at the train or bus station, usually 150ptas (£0.85; $1.50).

Camping outside the official campgrounds is possible, provided the consent of the landowner is obtained. However, tents must not be pitched in a town; close to roads, military bases or reservoirs; in a dry river bed which may be subject to flooding; or within 1 kilometre of any official site. Camping on publicly owned land is prohibited by some local authorities.

Throughout most of the year the weather will present few problems for those **sleeping out,** but the Guardia Civil make a habit of patrolling areas which are popular and will wake up anybody they discover. Only if you are very short of money will they charge you with vagrancy. This leaves you with the same dilemma as in Belgium or the Netherlands: namely, staying within the law makes you an attractive target for muggers. Basically, sleeping out is foolhardy, especially in the cities and coastal resorts. If you are attacked it is likely to be by an organized gang, who may well become vicious if you try to resist (and sometimes even if you do not).

In the remote mountain regions, a network of cheap **refuges** with bunk-bedded dormitories and basic cooking facilities is maintained by the Federacion Español de Montañismo. It may also be possible to stay in some **monasteries** in the more isolated areas. As the number of inhabitants have fallen, some monasteries have taken to letting vacant cells for about 400ptas (£2.25; $4) per night in order to supplement monastic income. Many admit visitors of either sex. Some, especially in Galicia, Catalonia, and Majorca, are located in spectacular settings. It is possible simply to enquire about staying the night on arrival, but as there may be no one about it is advisable to contact the local Tourist Office first. They will arrange a time for you to show up at the monastery.

ADDRESSES

Spanish Tourist Office	57 St James's Street, London SW1A (tel. 071 499 0901)
Spanish YHA	Red Española de Albergues Juveniles, José Ortega y Gasset 71, Madrid 28006 (tel. 91–3477700).
Camping	Federacion Española de Empresarios de Campings, Gran Via 88, Madrid 28013 (tel. 91–2423168).
	ANCE, Principe De Vergara 85, 2 Ocha, 28006 Madrid. Maps and information on the official campsites from the above. A map is also available on request from the Spanish Tourist Office.
Mountain refuges	Federacion Español de Montañismo, Calle Alberto Aguiler 3, Madrid 15 (tel. 91–4451382).

Barcelona (tel. code 93)

Tourist Offices

Oficina de Turismo e Información. Various locations throughout the city.

Barcelona Sants train station (tel. 2505224). Open daily 7.30 a.m.–10.30 p.m.

Barcelona Termino train station (tel. 3192791). Open Mon.–Sat. 8.30 a.m.–9 p.m.

Placa Sant Jaume (tel. 3182525). Open Mon.–Fri. 9 a.m.–9 p.m., Sat. 9 a.m.–2 p.m. In the Gothic Quarter. Metro: Jaume I, then follow Jaume I.

Monumento a Colón, Porta de la Pau (tel. 3025224). Open Mon.–Fri. 9.30 a.m.–1.30 p.m. and 4.30–8.30 p.m. Metro: Drassanes, then a short walk down to the Columbus monument on the waterfront.

Gran Via Corts Catalanes 658 (tel. 3017443). Open Mon.–Fri. 9 a.m.–1.30 p.m. and 4–7 p.m. Information on all of Spain. Metro: Passeig de Gràcia.

Airport (tel. 3255829). Open daily 8 a.m.–8 p.m., except Sun. (morning only).

Barcelona Information. Round the clock information service (tel. 010). English speakers available.

Street Names

All street signs in Barcelona give the Catalan and Spanish versions of the street's name. The Catalan version is used in most of the addresses below.

Trouble Spots

The Placa Reial is best avoided after 10–11 p.m., as is the area around the docks at the foot of the Ramblas (by the Columbus monument). During the daytime the crowds which throng the Ramblas provide an attractive working environment for pickpockets and petty thieves, so be especially careful with your valuables.

PENSIONS

Cheapest doubles around 950ptas (£5.25; $9.50)

1 Unin, Unión 14 (tel. 3181581).
2 La Paz, Argentera 37 (tel. 3194408). Metro: Jaume I. The street is left off Via Laietana heading towards the waterfront.

Cheapest doubles around 1400–1600ptas (£7.75–9.00; $13.50–15.50)

3 Call, Arc de Sant Ramn de Call 4 (tel. 3021123). Metro: Jaume I. Along Jaume I and through the square until you see Sant Domenc del Call on the right. From this street, Call on the left takes you into the square.
4 Río, Sant Pau 119 (tel. 2410651). In the area between Av. del Paral-lel and the Ramblas. Metro: Paral-lel. Go right at the junction of Paral-lel and Ronda de Sant Pau.
5 Figueras, Pasaje San Pablo/Sant Pau 2 (tel. 2550594).
6 Galerias Malda, Pino 5 (tel. 3173002).
7 Romea, Junta do Comercio 21 (tel. 3180299). Metro: Jaume I, then follow Princesa.

Cheapest doubles around 1800–2000ptas (£10–11; $17.50–19.50)

8 Sant Pancrás, Merced 4 (tel 3022426). Metro: Barceloneta. Head left along the main road PG de Colom towards the Columbus monument, then right at Marquet.
9 Iglesias, Nou de la Rambla (tel. 3188534). Metro: Liceu. Right off the Ramblas, walking down towards the port.
10 Morato, Sant Ramn 29 (tel. 2423669).
11 Plaza, Fontanella 18 (tel. 3010139). Between Plaça Catalunya and Plaça del Bisbe Urquinaona. Metro: Urquinaona or Catalunya.

Cheapest doubles around 2200ptas (£12.25; $21.50)

12 Alhambra, Jonqueres 13 (tel. 3171924). Metro:

Urquinaona. Jonqueres runs out of Urquinaona square
to the right of Trafalgar.

13 Asunción, Rambla de Catalunya 42 (tel. 3012869). Metro:
Catalunya. A few blocks down the street from Plaça
Catalunya.

14 Catalunya, Plaça Catalunya 4 (tel. 3015389). Metro:
Catalunya.

15 Alberdi, Menéndez e Pelayo 95 (tel. 2173025).

16 El Cantón, Nou de Sant Francesc 40 (tel. 3173019). Metro:
Drassanes. Walk down towards the Columbus
monument, left along J.A. Clave, then left.

17 Coral, Calella 1 (tel. 3023120).

18 Florinda, Montserrat 13 (tel. 3022053). Metro: Drassanes.
Off the Ramblas near the stop is Madalena, from which
Montserrat runs off to the right.

19 Lis, Paseo de San Gervásio 71 (tel. 2115088).

20 Meridiana, Avda Meridiana 2 (tel. 3095125). Near the Parc
de la Ciutadella. Metro: Marina.

21 New York, Gignas 6 (tel. 3150304). Metro: Barceloneta.
Head away from the port, across the main road and take
the street to the left of Laietana into Gignas.

22 Nilo, J Anselmo Clave 17 (tel. 3179044). See 16. Outside
the period July–Aug. the price falls by about 10 per cent.

23 Le Parisien, Rambla de Sant Josep 114 (tel. 2318519).
Metro: Liceu. Walk towards the Plaa Catalunya.

24 El Rocío, Cadena 1 (tel. 2423594). See 4. Cadena is left
off Sant Pau.

Cheapest doubles around 2400ptas (£13.50; $23.50)

25 Mediterráneo, Rambla de Catalunya 106 (tel. 2150900).
Metro: Provença. A few minutes' walk along Rossello
brings you to Rambla de Catalunya and the hotel.

26 Ballestero, Manuel Sancho 2 (tel. 3495053).

27 Lepanto, Rauric 10 (tel. 3020081). Metro: Liceu. Near the
station Boqueria heads off the Ramblas (opposite
Hospital). Rauric is right off Boqueria.

28 La Lonja, PG d'Isabel II 14 (tel. 3193032). Metro:

616 Cheap Sleep Guide

Barceloneta. On the main road opposite the port. From Sept–June prices are about 20 per cent cheaper.

29 Marmo, Gignas 25 (tel. 3154208). See 21.
30 Noya, Rambla de Canaletas 133 (tel. 3014831). Just off Plaça Catalunya. Metro: Catalunya.Sept.–June prices fall by around 20 per cent.
31 Victoria, Comtal 9 (tel. 3174597). Metro: Urquinaona. Follow Laietana from the square, then right.

Cheapest doubles around 2600ptas (£14.50; $25.50)

32 Dali, Boqueria 12 (tel. 3185580). See 27.
33 Canaletas, Rambla de Canaletas 133 (tel. 3015660). See 30.
34 Joventut, Junta de Comercio 12 (tel. 3018499). See 7.
35 Calella, Calella 1/Pral 2 (tel. 3176841).
36 Layetana, Pl. Ramón Berenguer el Grand 2 (tel. 3192012). Off Via Laietana. Metro: Jaume I. Head up Via Laietana away from the port.

Cheapest doubles around 2800ptas (£15.50; $27.50)

37 Esmeralda, Via Laietana 42 (tel. 3199500). Metro: Jaume I.
38 Barcelona, Roser 40 (tel. 2425075). Metro: Paral-lel. Roser runs off Paral-lel near the station towards the hills.
39 Levante, Bajada San Miguel 2 (tel. 3179565).
40 Navarro, Fontanella 16 (tel. 3012496). See 11.
41 Santcarlo, Plaça de Urquinaona 5 (tel. 3024125). Metro: Urquinaona. From Oct.–May rooms are about 20 per cent cheaper.

Cheapest doubles around 3000ptas (£16.75; $29)

42 Lloret, Rambla de Canaletas 125 (tel. 3173366). See 30.
43 Sans, Antonio de Campmany 82 (tel. 3313700).
44 Comercio, Nueva de Zurbano 7 (tel. 3187374).
45 Palacios, Gran Via Corts Catalanes 629 Bis (tel. 3013792). Metro: Passeig de Gràcia. A short walk from the exit on Corts Catalanes.
46 Roma, Plaça Reial 11 (tel. 3020366). Metro: Liceu. Right

off the Ramblas as you head down to the Columbus monument.

47 Conde Guell, Comte d'Urgell 32–34 (tel. 2400257). Metro: Urgell (closest) or Hospital Clinic.

48 Cervantes, Cervantes 6 (tel. 3025168). Metro: Liceu. Near the station Boqueria heads off the Ramblas (opposite Hospital). At the end of Boqueria turn right, go straight on across Ferran and on down Avinyo into Cervantes.

49 Colón, Aragó 281 (tel. 2154700). Metro: Passeig de Gràcia (exit on to Aragó).

50 La Hípica, General Castanos 2 (tel. 3151392). Metro: Barceloneta. From Pas de Sota take Muralla. General Castanos is on the opposite side of Plaça del Palau. From Termino station head left on Av. del Marqués de l'Argentera then left again.

51 Nuevo Colón, Avda. Marqués de la Argentera 19 (tel. 3195077). See 50. One street further up Plaça del Palau from General Castanos.

52 Zurbano, Zurbano 8 (tel. 3177200).

53 Vergara, Bergara 5 (tel. 3173035). Off Plaa Catalunya. Metro: Catalunya.

Cheapest doubles around 3300ptas (£18.50; $32)

54 Goya, Pau Claris 74 (tel. 3022565). Metro; Urquinaona or Passeig de Gràcia (exit onto Via de Corts Catalanes).

55 Lider, Rambla de Catalunya 84 (tel. 2155065). Metro: Passeig de Gràcia (exit onto Arag). Short walk to Rambla de Catalunya.

56 45, Tallers 45 (tel. 3027061). Tallers runs out off Plaça de la Universitat to the left of Sant Antoni. Metro: Universitat.

57 Alcazar, Via Laietana 145 (tel. 2153868). Metro: Passeig de Gràcia (exit onto Arag). Short walk to Via Laietana.

58 Dos Reinos, Trafalgar 39 (tel. 3173077). See 12.

59 Fontanella, Via Laietana 71 (tel. 3175943). Metro: Urquinaona. Via Laietana runs out of the square.

60 Mayoral, Plaça Reial 2 (tel. 3179534). See 36.

61   Mont Thabor, Ramblas 86 (tel. 3179404). Close to Plaça
     Catalunya. Metro: Catalunya.

62   Opera, Sant Pau 20 (tel. 3188201) Metro: Liceu. Sant Pau
     runs off the Ramblas near the station, one street closer
     to the port than Hospital.

63   La Palmera, Jerusalem 30 (tel. 3170997). By the 'La
     Boqueria' market, also known as the Mercat de Sant
     Josep, off Rambla de Sant Josep. Metro: Liceu.

64   Pereira, Diputacio 346 (tel. 2451981). Metro: Universitat.
     Walk up Aribau from Plaça de la Universitat, then right.

65   Lleida, Corsega 201 (tel. 4300122). Metro: Hospital Clinic.
     Follow Comte d'Urgell one block (ascending street
     numbers) then right two blocks on Corsega.

66   Barcino, Jonqueres 12 (tel. 3019020). See 12.

Cheapest doubles around 3600ptas (£20; $35)

67   River, Sant Pau 15 (tel. 3189493). See 62.

68   Ribagorza, Trafalgar 39 (tel. 3024069). See 12.

69   Cisneros, Aribau 54 (tel. 2541800). See 64.

70   Felipe II, Mallorca 329 (tel. 2587758). Metro: Provença.
     From Provença turn left down Girona onto Mallorca.

71   París, Corsega 236 (tel. 2182375). See 65. One block
     further along Corsega.

IYHF HOSTELS

Hostal de Joves, Passeig Pujades 29 (tel. 3003104). Midnight
curfew. By the Parc de la Ciutadella. Only 300m from the
Termino station. Right on leaving the station, left on PG
de Picasso, then right. Metro: Arc de Triomf on Line 1.
From Barcelona Sants take Line 3 to Espana to change to
Line 1.

'Mare de Deu de Montserrat', Passeig de Nostra Senyora del
Coll 41–51 (tel. 3210004). Curfew 1 a.m. A 25-minute trip
from the centre. Bus 28 from Plaça de Catalunya (Metro:
Catalunya). Although the other two permanent hostels are
very good, this is a particularly pleasant hostel to stay in.

'Pere Tarres', Numancia 149–151 (tel. 4102309). Numancia runs from Barcelona Sants station in the opposite direction from Tarragona. The hostel is a 15-minute walk along the street. Two metro stops are slightly closer: Les Corts and Maria Cristina. From Les Corts follow Trav. de les Corts (ascending street numbers) then left on to Numancia. From Maria Cristina follow Av. Diagonal (descending street numbers), then right onto Numancia. About the same distance as from Les Corts, but there is an El Corte Ingles department store near Maria Cristina if you want to buy food. The hostel is within easy walking distance of the two football grounds, the Sarri of Espanol and the awesome Nou Camp of FC Barcelona.

'Studio', Duquesa d'Orleans 58 (tel. 2050961). Open 1 July–30 Sept.

CAMPING

Cala-Gogo-El Prat (tel.3794600). Open Mar.–Nov. 500ptas (£2.75; $5) per person, tent included. By the beach in Prat de Llobregat, five miles from the city. Take bus 605 from Plaça de Espanya to the terminus in Prat, then change to bus 604 to the beach.

El Toro Bravo (tel. 6581250). Open year round. 475ptas (£2.60; $4.75) per tent and per person. In Vildecans, slightly further out than the site above. Bus L93 from Plaça de la Universitat, or bus L90 from Plaça Goya.

Filipinas (tel. 6582895). Open year round. Same prices as the El Toro Bravo. Also in Vildecans. Buses as above.

La Ballena Alegre (tel. 6580504). Open mid-May–Sept. The third site in Vildecans; considerably more expensive than the other two. 750ptas (£4.25; $7.50) per tent, 400ptas (£2.25; $4) per person.

Barcino, Laureano Miro 50 (tel. 3728501). Open year round. 500ptas (£2.75; $5) per tent and per person. In Esplugues de Llobregat, the closest site to the city. Accessible by bus CO or BI from Plaça de Catalunya.

Córdoba (tel. code 957)

Tourist Offices

Oficina de Turismo de la Junta de Andalucía, Torrijos 10 (Palacio de Congresos), 14003 Cordoba (tel. 471235). Open Mon.–Fri. 9.30 a.m.–2.00 p.m. and 5–7 p.m., Sat. 10 a.m.–1 p.m in summer; Mon.–Fri. 9.30 a.m.–2.00 p.m. and 3.30–5.30 p.m., Sat. 10 a.m.–1 p.m. in winter. Well supplied with information on the city and the region.

Oficina Municipal de Turismo, Plaza Judá Levi (tel. 290740). Open Mon.–Fri. 8 a.m.–3 p.m. A useful source of information on the city.

Basic Directions

The two Tourist Offices are close to the Mezquita, the focal point of the old city, a 20-minute walk away from the train station on Avenida de América. For anyone unfamiliar with the city, finding the way from the train station through the labyrinthine old town to the Mezquita can be a tortuous experience (it is worth trying to get the free plan 'Cordoba Guia Practica' from the Spanish Tourist Office in advance). The route described below, while not the shortest, at least has the advantage of being relatively straightforward. Take the main road (Avda. de Cervantes) running away from the train station slightly to the right across Avda. de América, and then continue on down Paseo de la Victoria. Turn left along Lope de Hoces heading towards the Trinidad Church, then right down Tejón y Marn. Go across Fernandez into Almanzor and continue straight ahead to the junction with Deanes. Head right along Deanes (at which point Plaza Judá Levi is off to your right) and then left down Medina y Core to the Mezquita. Torrijos runs down the side of the Mezquita towards the Triurfo de San Rafael and Puerta del Puente.

Finding Accommodation

The best area to look for cheap accommodation in Córdoba is the Judería, the old Jewish quarter between Plaza de las

Tendillas and the River Guadalquivir. Within this district the streets to the east of the Mezquita (the opposite side of the Mezquita from Torrijos) are particularly good places to look, with Rey Heredia having the largest concentration of cheap accommodation in the city.

PENSIONS

Cheapest doubles around 2200ptas (£12.25; $21.50)

Mari, Pimentera 6–8 (tel. 479575).

Nieves, La Cara 12 (tel. 475139).

La Milagrosa II, Rey Heredia 12 (tel. 473317). Close to the Mezquita. On the opposite side of the Mezquita from Medina y Core Encarnación leads into Rey Heredia.

Perales, Avda de los Mozrabes 13 (tel. 230325). Head right along Avda de América from the train station and the street is off to the left after Avda de Cervantes.

Rey Heredia, Rey Heredia 26 (tel. 474182). See La Milagrosa.

Trinidad, Corregidor Luis de la Cerda 58 (tel. 487905). The street begins at the foot of Torrijos, near the Triunfo de San Rafael and the Puerta del Puente.

Cheapest doubles around 2550ptas (£14.60; $25.25)

El Portillo, Cabezas 2 (tel. 472091). Off the right-hand end of Rey Heredia if you join the latter from Encarnación (see La Milagrosa).

El León, Céspedes 6 (tel. 473021). The street runs from the Mezquita, along the tower.

Maestre, Romero Barros 16 (tel. 475395). Go left from the foot of Torrijos and follow Ronda de Isasa along the river. Turn left at Cruz Rastro and continue up San Fernando, then turn right along Romero Barros.

Cheapest doubles around 2750ptas (£15.70; $27.25)

Las Tendillas, Jesús y Maria 1 (tel. 223029). From the train station head left, then turn right and follow Avda del Gran

Capitán to its end. Go left along Conde Gondomar into Plaza de las Tendillas, then right to the start of Jesús y Maria.

Alhaken, Alhaken II 10 (tel. 471593). Left off Avda de Cervantes.

Martinez Rücker, Martinez Rücker 14 (tel. 473561). Off Magistral Glez Frances, the street running down the opposite side of the Mezquita from Torrijos.

Mary II, Horno de Porras 6 (tel. 479545).

El Alcazar, San Basilio 2 (tel. 202561). From the foot of Torrijos turn right along Amador de los Rios, cross the gardens and take Caballerizas Reales, turn left up M. Rao, then left into San Basilio.

Cheapest doubles around 3100ptas (£17.70; $31)

Lucano, Lucano 1 (tel. 476098). Lucano is to the right at the junction of Cruz Rastro and San Fernando (see Maestre).

La Alegra, Menéndez Pelayo 1 (tel. 470504). Right off Avda del Gran Capitán (see 10), opposite Gongora.

Almanzor, Corregidor Luis de la Cerda 10 (tel. 485400). See Trinidad.

El Cisne Verde, Pintor Greco 6 (tel. 294360).

Esmerelda, Lucano 16 (tel. 474354). See Lucano.

Cheapest doubles around 3300ptas (£18.50; $32)

Magdalena, Muñices 25 (tel. 483753). The price is for doubles with baths.

Cheapest doubles around 3500ptas (£20; $35)

Antonio Machado, Buen Pastor 4 (tel. 296259). From the end of Tejón y Marín turn left along Fernandez and continue more or less straight ahead until you see Buen Pastor on the right.

Luis de Góngora, Horno de la Trinidad 7 (tel. 295399). Price is for doubles with baths. Off Plaza de la Trinidad by the Trinidad Church.

IYHF HOSTEL

Residencia Juvenil Cordoba, Plaza Judá Leví (tel. 290166). IYHF members under 26 pay 750ptas (£4.20; $7.50), those aged 26 and over 950ptas (£5.25; $9.50). Excellent hostel, opened as recently as 1990. Fine location, a couple of blocks from the Mezquita.

CAMPING

Campamento Municipal, Avda del Brillante 50 (tel. 472000/275048). Buses every 10 minutes to/from the city centre. 380ptas (£2.10; $3.50) per tent and per person. Grade I site, open year round.

Cerca de Lagartijo (tel. 250426). Situated 2 miles out on the Madrid-Cádiz road. 290ptas (£1.60; $3) per tent and per person. Grade II site, open 1 June–30 Sept.

Granada (tel. code 958)

Tourist Offices

Oficina de Turismo de la Junta Andalucía, Calle Liberos 2, 18001 Granada (tel. 225990/221022). Open Mon.–Fri. 10 a.m.–1.00 p.m. and 4–7 p.m., Sat. 10 a.m.–1 p.m. Knowledgeable and helpful staff. Details of bus services and the relevant timetables are displayed on the walls of the office along with a wide range of other useful information. From Gran Vía de Colón turn right down Cárcel de Baja along the north side of the cathedral, then head left along the western façade of the cathedral and straight on. Libreros runs away to the right.

Oficina de Turismo del Patronato Provincial de Turismo, Plaza Mariana Pineda 10 (tel. 226688). Open Mon.–Fri. 10.00 a.m.–1.30 p.m. and 4.30–7.00 p.m., Sat. 10 a.m.–1 p.m. From Puerta Real follow Angel Ganivet into Plaza Mariana Pineda.

624 Cheap Sleep Guide

Basic Directions

The train station is linked to the town centre by buses 4, 5, 9 or 11, but it is only 15 minutes on foot if you want to walk. From the station, go straight ahead down Avenida de Andaluces then turn right along Avenida de la Constitución. Continue straight on until you see Gran Vía de Colón running away to the right. This street leads right into the heart of old Granada, passing the cathedral before arriving at Plaza Isabel la Católica. Turning left from this square along Calle Reyes Católicos you pass through Plaza Nueva before arriving at Plaza Santa Ana, from which Cuesta de Gomérez runs up to the Alhambra. Following Calle Reyes Católicos to the right from Plaza Isabel la Católica you pass Plaza del Carmen on the left before arriving at Puerta Real. Angel Ganivet leads off to the left from Puerta Real, while Calle Recogidas runs virtually straight on from Reyes Católicos down to Camino de Ronda.

Near the end of Avenida de la Constitución, Calle San Juan de Dios leads off to the right, passing the Church of San Juan de Dios before running into Gran Capitán which ends at Plaza Gran Capitán. Turning left of Gran Capitán along Calle de la Duquesa takes you into Plaza Trinidad. At this point, Tablas runs away to the right, while on the other side of Plaza Trinidad Los Mesones and Alhóndiga both head off in the direction of Puerta Real.

Turning left from the train station along Calle del Halcón, then left under the tracks and left again, brings you to the start of Camino de Ronda. The main bus station is at Camino de Ronda 97 by the Glorieta Arabial. Bus 11 will get you to the city centre, but it is only about 10 minutes away on foot. From Camino de Ronda follow Hurtado then go straight on down Obispo and Tablas into Plaza Trinidad. Across the square take Capuchinas or Sillera into Pescadería and head right into Plaza Bib-Ramla. Calle Liberos and the Tourist Office are across this square.

Finding Accommodation

As a rule you should not have much trouble finding a bed in Granada. Two streets near the station are particularly well supplied with cheap rooms: Avenida Andaluces and, a bit further away, Calle San Juan de Dios. The small streets on either side of Gran Vía de Colón are also worth investigating. In the town centre, the streets around Plaza Nueva (Cuesta de Gomérez in particular) and Plaza del Carman (especially Calle de Navas which runs off the square) have a more than adequate number of cheap establishments at most times of year, as has the area around Plaza Trinidad. The exceptions to this happy situation are the very peak of the summer season and the period immediately before and during Holy Week. Whereas at the former time you will invariably find something with a bit of effort, looking for accommodation around Easter can be an intensely frustrating experience as the Andalusian cities receive a huge influx of visitors at this time. The shortage of hotel space during this period is illustrated by the appearance of touts offering private rooms at the bus and train stations. Provided that the price and location are acceptable there is little reason to worry about accepting an offer as regards personal safety – though you might want to leave any valuables at left luggage.

PENSIONS

Doubles around 1200ptas (£6.75; $12)

Terminus, Avda Andaluces 10–1 (tel. 201423).

Doubles around 1350ptas (£7.50; $13)

Castil, Darrillo Magdalena 1 (tel. 259507).

Doubles around 1750ptas (£9.75; $17)

Savoy, Avda Dr. Olriz 4–4 (tel. 270847). Across Avda de la Constitución from Avda de Andaluces.
Yale, Santos 2 (tel. 279592). Turn right off Gran Vía de Colón down Boquerón Almona, then left.

Cheapest doubles around 1950–2100ptas (£10.75–11.75; $19.00–20.50)

Mesones, Mesones 44 (tel. 263244).

Gomérez, Cuesta Gomérez 10 (tel. 224437).

Navarro Ramos, Cuesta de Gomérez 21 (tel. 221876).

Lis, Recogidas 14 (tel. 264933).

Meridiano, Angulo 9 (tel. 262981).

San José de la Montaña, San José Baja 19 (tel. 252490).

Cheapest doubles 2300ptas (£12.75; $22.50)

California, Cuesta de Gomérez 37 (tel. 224056).

Duquesa, Duquesa 10 (tel. 279603).

El Hidalgo, Horno de Espadero 8 (tel. 263384).

Turin, Ancha de Capuhinos 16 (tel. 200311). Follow Avda Andaluces, then go straight down Avda del Dr. Olriz into Ancha de Capuchinos.

Venecia, Cuesta Gomérez 2 (tel. 223987).

Sevioca, Avda Dr Olriz 12 (tel. 202366). See Savoy.

Landazuri, Cuesta de Gomérez 24 (tel. 221406).

Andalucia, Campo Verde 5–1 (tel. 261909). Near Puerta Real. Follow Mesones until you see Campo Verde on the right.

Cheapest doubles 2400–2550ptas (£13.50–14.50; $23.50–25.50)

Acapulco, San Juan de Dios 57 (tel. 271313).

Colonial, Joaquín Costa 5 (tel. 227673). Near the cathedral turn left off Gran Vía de Colón down Cetti Meriem then right.

Londres, Gran Vía de Colón 29 (tel. 278034).

Martínez, San Pedro Mártir 34 (tel. 228793). From Puerta Real follow Acera del Casino and head straight on across Plaza del Campillo and Plaza Bitaubin to San Pedro Mártir.

Muñoz, Mesones 53 (tel. 263819).

Romero, Sillería de Mesones (tel. 266079). Off Plaza Trinidad.

Zacatín, Ermita 11 (tel. 22115).

Florida, Principe 13 (tel. 223757).

Gran Vía, Gran Vía de Colón 17 (tel. 279212).

Los Montes, Arteaga 3 (tel. 277930). Left off Gran Vía de
Colón.

Olimpia, Alvaro de Bazán 6 (tel. 278238). The street crosses
Gran Vía de Colón.

San Antón, San Antón 51 (tel. 262365). Off Recogidas close
to Puerta Real.

San Jerónimo, San Jerónimo 12 (tel. 275040). The street runs
from Plaza Universidad. Turn right off Gran Vía de Colón
down Marqués de Falces and go straight ahead until you
reach Plaza Universidad, then go left.

Veracruz, San Antón 39 (tel. 262770). See San Anton.

**Cheapest doubles around 2650–2850ptas (£14.75–15.75;
$26–28)**

Fabiola, Angel Ganivet 5 (tel. 223572).

Mario, Cardenal Mendoza 15 (tel. 201427). Left off San Juan
de Dios.

La Redonda, Camino de Ronda 84 (tel. 254477). Near the
main bus station.

Sevilla, Fábrica Vieja 18 (tel. 278513). Off Tablas near Plaza
Trinidad. From Alhóndiga turn right down Mlaga and keep
going until you see Fábrica Vieja on the left.

Gran Capitan, Plaza Gran Capitan 4 (tel. 272124).

Granada-Ronda, Sócrates 12 (tel. 280099). Off Camino de
Ronda by the Glorieta Arabial and the main bus station.

Princesa, San Matias 2 (tel. 229381). From Plaza Isabel la
Catolica go through Plaza Descalzas into Plaza San Juan
de la Cruz. San Matias is off to the right. From Puerta Real
follow Angel Ganivet into Plaza Mariana Pineda then go
left.

Regibel, Caballerizas 6 (tel. 274226).

Roma, Navas 1 (tel. 226277). Off Plaza del Carmen.

Valencia, Alhóndiga 9 (tel. 264412).

Viena, Hospital de Santa Ana 2 (tel. 221859). The street runs
between Cuesta de Gomérez and Plaza Santa Ana.

Vista Nevada, Dr. Guirao Gea 6 (tel. 271506). Right off Avda
del Dr. Olóriz. See Savoy.

Yuca, Moral de la Magdalena 38 (tel. 266735). From Alhóndiga turn right down Calle de la Gracia, left along Puentezelas then right.

Guirardo, Recogidas 6 (tel. 262872).

Miriam, Camino de Ronda 147 (tel. 200321).

San Joaquín, Mano de Hierro 14 (tel. 282879). Left off San Juan de Dios near the church.

Cheapest doubles around 3100ptas (£17.25; $30)

Granadina, Párraga 7 (tel. 256714). From Alhondiga turn right down Calle de la Gracia then left. Párraga runs from Calle de la Gracia to join Recogidas near Puerta Real.

Atenas, Gran Vía de Colón 38–1 (tel. 278750).

Cónsul, San Antón 34 (tel. 259857). See San Antón.

Las Nieves, Sierpe Baja 5 (tel. 265311). The street runs between Mesones and Alhóndiga.

Matilde, Puentezelas 46 (tel. 263429). Follow Carril del Picon from Plaza Gran Capitán into Puentezelas or walk down Tablas from Plaza Trinidad then go left at the end of the street.

La Milogrosa, Santa Teresa 15 (tel. 254414). Off Plaza Trinidad, parallel to Tablas.

Cheapest doubles around 3300ptas (£18.50; $32)

Nuevas Naciones, Plaza Triviño 1 (tel. 270503).

Britz, Cuesta Gomérez 1 (tel. 223652).

Los Girasoles, Cardenal Mendoza 48–50 (tel. 280725). See Mario.

Las Cumbres, Cardenal Mendoza 4 (tel. 291222). See Mario.

Lisboa, Plaza del Carmen 27 (tel. 221413/221414).

España, Peñón de la Mata 8 (tel. 280529).

Cheapest doubles around 3500ptas (£19.50; $34)

Loren, Alvaro de Bazán 2 (tel. 276500). See Olimpia.

Sonia, Gran Vía de Colón 38–3 (tel. 206116/283809).

Miami, Camino Purchil 1 (tel. 259708). Off Camino de Ronda by the main bus station.

Cheapest doubles around 3850ptas (£21.50; $38)

Paris, San Antón 3 (tel. 263622). See San Antón.

IYHF HOSTEL

Camino de Ronda 171 (tel. 272638). Not far from the station. Turn left as you leave, left under the tracks. This takes you to the start of Camino de Ronda.

HOSTELS

Albergue Juvenil de Viznar, Camino de Fuente Nueva (tel. 490307).

CAMPING

There are a number of sites in and around Granada, all of which charge 325–425ptas (£1.80–2.50; $3–4) per person and per tent:

Sierra Nevada, Avda de Madrid 107 (tel. 270956). Grade 1 site, open 15 Mar.–15 Oct. Bus 3.

El Ultimo, Camino Huetor Vega 22 (tel. 123069). Grade 2 site, open all year.

Maria Eugenia, Carretera de Malaga (tel. 200606). Grade 2 site, open all year.

Los Alamos, Carretera Jerez-Cartagena (tel. 275743). Grade 2 site, open 1 Apr.–30 Oct.

Madrid (tel. code 910)

Tourist Offices
Información turistica Oficina Nacional. Various locations. The

head office is in the Torre de Madrid at Plaza de España 1 (tel. 5412325). Metro: Plaza de España. Branch offices operate in the Chamartin train station (tel. 3159976) and near the international arrivals desk at Barajas airport (tel. 2058656).

Información turistica Oficina Nacional, Plaza Mayor 3 (tel. 2665477). Metro: Sol. Along Calle Mayor from Puerto del Sol.

The municipal office will provide you with tourist information about the city, the national offices with information about Madrid and the country as a whole. None of the offices will book rooms, though they will offer advice on accommodation. A private agency called Brujula will book rooms (office in the underground bus terminal at Plaza de Colon. Metro: Colon).

Trouble Spots

While Fuencarral and Hortaleza are safe places to stay, you should be wary of the nearby Chuecca quarter (right of Hortaleza as you walk up from Gran Vía). This area, around Plaza de Chuecca including Reina, Utantas, San Marcos and the streets in between, is the gay and hard drugs centre of Madrid. Although there is plenty of cheap accommodation in this area (including some listed below), this part of town should be a last resort if you are looking for somewhere to stay.

Finding a Place to Stay

Madrid has a more than adequate supply of cheap rooms, even in summer. The hotels section below offers numerous possibilities which you can telephone to see if they have rooms available. However, occasionally you may find the room has been filled by the time you arrive. Do not get upset, because you should have little trouble finding a similarly priced room in the same street, or even the same building. If you would prefer simply to head off in search of a room, some areas are particularly good to look in. Gran Vía, the main thoroughfare, has an excellent supply of rooms, but prices are generally higher than elsewhere in the city. Prices are noticeably lower in the streets leading off Gran Vía. Amongst these Hortaleza and Fuencarral (metro: Gran Vía) and San Bernardo (metro: Noviciado) are especially well supplied with cheap places to stay. The cheapest part of town to stay in is between the Atocha train station and Puerta del Sol. Some of the cheapest establishments around Puerta del Sol are used by prostitutes, which, although the hotels are usually safe enough, hardly makes for a peaceful night. Whichever way you set about looking for a room, read the section on Trouble Spots above before you begin.

PENSIONS

Cheapest doubles around 550–650ptas (£3.00–3.75; $5.50–6.50)

1 González, San Marcos 28 (no telephone). San Marcos runs between Hortaleza and Barquillo, both off Gran Vía. Metro: Gran Vía or Banco.

2 Elorriaga, San Marcos 18 (tel. 2212212). See 1.

Cheapest doubles around 1050–1250ptas (£5.75–7.00; $10–12)

3 Bañezana, Cruz 26 (tel. 2213134). Follow Espoz y Mina from Puerta del Sol. Metro: Sol.

4 Marcos, San Marcos 24 (tel. 2315095). See 1.

5 Campos, Infantas 32 (tel. 2323013). Infantas runs between Hortaleza and Barquillo, both of which are off Gran Vía. Metro: Gran Vía or Banco.

6 Santa Ana, Plaza Santa Ana 1 (tel. 5213058). Metro: Sevilla or Sol. From Sevilla walk down Calle Sevilla, across Carrera de San Jerónimo, then down Príncipe. From Sol follow Carrera de San Jerónimo, then right at Príncipe.

7 Corros, Atocha 28 (tel. 2390025). The street leading from Atocha train station towards Plaza Mayor. Metro: Atocha or Antón Martín.

632 Cheap Sleep Guide

Cheapest doubles around 1300–1550ptas (£7.25–8.50; $12.50–15.00)

8 Suiza Española, Carrera de San Jerónimo 32 (tel. 4296814). Metro: Sol or Sevilla. San Jerónimo runs out of Puerta del Sol. From Sevilla Calle Sevilla leads down to San Jerónimo.

9 Iserte, Fuencarral 16 (tel. 2315212). Off Gran Vía. Metro: Gran Vía.

10 Josefina, Gran Vía 44 (tel. 5218131). Metro: Plaza de España.

11 Las Nieves, Infantas 26 (tel. 2228001). See 5.

12 Recoletos, Recoletos 14 (tel. 4310673). Metro: Colon. Off to the left as you walk along Paseo de Recoletos.

13 Santo Domingo, Cuesta Santo Domingo 22 (tel. 2471158). Off Plaza Santo Domingo. Metro: Santo Domingo.

14 Vives, Barquillo 25 (tel. 2325263). Off Gran Vía. Metro: Banco.

Cheapest doubles around 1600–1750ptas (£8.75–9.75; $15.50–17.00)

15 La Noyesa, Aduana 16 (tel. 5313844). Aduana runs between Montera (off Puerta del Sol) and Peligros (off Alcala). Metro: Sol or Sevilla.

16 Fernando, Flora 3 (tel. 2419118). Off Arenal near Plaza de Isabel II. Metro: Opera.

17 Juli, Juan Alvarez Menzibal 44 (tel. 2413094). Three blocks off Princesa down Evaristo San Miguel. Metro: Ventura Rodriguez (closest) or Argüelles.

18 Nuestra Señora del Camino, Fuencarral 39 (tel. 5228481). Metro: Tribunal (closest) or Gran Vía. Fuencarral is off Gran Vía.

19 Peral, Cruz 26 (tel. 2320052). See 3.

20 Rios, Juan Alvarez Menzibal (tel. 2485156). See 17.

21 Valdeorresa, Fuencarral 41 (tel. 2327897). See 18.

22 Del Valle, Príncipe 11 (tel. 4295935).

Cheapest doubles around 1800–2000ptas (£10–11; $17.50–19.50)

23 Marimart, Puerta del Sol 14 (tel. 5229815). Metro: Sol.
24 Miño, Arenal 16 (tel. 5315079). Arenal runs out of Puerta del Sol towards the opera. Metro: Sol.
25 Mori, Plaza de las Cortés 3 (tel. 4297208). Metro: Banco. Walk down Marqués de Cubas, then across Carrera de San Jerónimo.
26 Portugal, Flora 4 (tel. 2487626). See 16.
27 El Burgalés, Isabel la Católica 17 (tel. 2472233). Off Plaza de Santo Domingo. Metro: Santo Domingo.
28 Nuestra Señora de las Mercedes, Mayor 9 (tel. 2665612). The street runs from Puerta del Sol to the Palacio Real. Metro: Sol.
29 Sol, Puerta del Sol 9 (tel. 2321516). Metro: Sol.
30 Universal, Carrera de San Jerónimo 32 (tel. 4296779). See 8.

Cheapest doubles around 2050–2200ptas (£11.50–12.25; $20.00–21.50)

31 Covadonga, Magdalena 17 (tel. 2305017). Metro: Antón Martín. The street runs out of Plaza Antón Martín.
32 Delfina, Gran Vía 12 (tel. 5226423). Metro: Banco or Gran Vía.
33 Felipe V, Gran Vía 15 (tel. 5226143). See 32.
34 Guerra, Carrera San Jerónimo 3 (tel. 5225577). Metro: Sol. The street runs out of Puerta del Sol.
35 Lorenzo, Infantas 26 (tel. 5213057). See 5.
36 Odesa, Horteleza 38 (tel. 5210338). Off Gran Vía. Metro: Gran Vía or Chueca.
37 Riosol, Mayor 5 (tel. 5323142). See 28.
38 Bilbao, San Bartolomé 7 (tel. 5310839). Off Infantas. See 5.
39 Faustino, Cruz 33 (tel. 5329098). See 3.
40 Jeyma, Arenal 24 (tel. 2487793). See 24.
41 Las Murallas, Fuencarral 23 (tel. 2321063). Off Gran Vía. Metro: Gran Vía or Tribunal.
42 Río Navia, Infantas 13 (tel. 5323050). See 5.
43 Santa Fé, Cruz 6 (tel. 5216180). See 3.

44 Sol y Mina, Espoz y Mina 8 (tel. 2321311). See 3.

Cheapest doubles around 2200–2400ptas (£12.25–13.50; $21.50–23.50)

45 Don José, Gran Vía 38 (tel. 2321385). See 10.

46 Excelsior, Gran Vía 50 (tel. 2473400). See 10.

47 Laredo, Arenal 15 (tel. 2482423). See 24.

48 Alcoriza, Gran Vía 20 (tel. 5213308). Metro: Gran Vía or Banco.

49 Breogán, Fuencarral 25 (tel. 5228153). See 41.

50 Mairu, Espejo 2 (tel. 2473088). Very good, but also very popular. Off Plaza de Isabel II, to the right of the steps leading down into Escalinata. Metro: Opera.

51 Mondragón, Carrera San Jerónimo 32 (tel. 4296816). See 8.

52 El Pinar, San Bartolemé 2 (tel. 5310134). Off Infantas. See 5.

53 Quintana, Tetun 19 (tel. 5318676). Metro: Sol. Take Carmen (near the El Corte Inglés department store) out of Puerta del Sol, then right.

54 Río, Cruz 26 (tel. 2319177). See 3.

55 Villagarcia, Fuencarral 10 (tel. 5220585). See 9.

56 Xucar, Magdalena 28 (tel. 2281226). See 31.

Cheapest doubles 2450–2650ptas (£13.75–14.75; $24–26)

57 America, Hortaleza 19 (tel. 5226448). Off Gran Vía. Metro: Gran Vía.

58 Miami, Gran Vía 44 (tel. 5211464). See 10.

59 La Perla Asturiana, Plaza de Santa Cruz 3 (tel. 2664600). By the Church of the Holy Cross (Iglesia de Santa Cruz). Metro: Sol. Follow Mayor from Puerta del Sol, then left down Esparteros towards the church.

60 Splendid, Gran Vía 15 (tel. 5224737). See 32.

61 Vasco, Infantas 3 (tel. 5224632). See 5.

62 Alonso, Espoz y Mina 17 (tel. 2915679). See 3.

63 Conchita, Preciados 33 (tel. 5224923). Metro: Callao or Sol. The street runs out of Puerta del Sol (near the El Corte

Inglés department store) to Plaza de Callao (off Gran Vía).
64 Cosmopólitan, Puerta del Sol 9 (tel. 5226651). Metro: Sol.
65 Cruz Sol, Plaza Santa Cruz 6 (tel. 2327197). Metro: Sol.
66 Fuente Mar, Magdalena 29 (tel. 2281922) See 31.
67 Madrid Centro, Carrera de San Jerónimo 32 (tel. 4296813). See 8.

Cheapest doubles 2700–2850ptas (£15–16; $26–28)

68 Numancia, Magdalena 8 (tel. 4686876). See 31.
69 Jamic, Plaza de las Cortes 4 (tel. 4290068). See 25.
70 Aranza, San Bartolemé 7 (tel. 5311165). Off Infantas. See 5.
71 Margarita, Gran Vía 50 (tel. 2473549). See 10.
72 Regional, Príncipe 18 (tel. 5223373). See 6.
73 Villar, Príncipe 18 (tel. 5316600). See 6.
74 Abril, Fuencarral 39 (tel. 5315338). See 18.
75 Berti, Hortaleza 7 (tel. 5223760). See 57.
76 Capricho, Infantas 30 (tel. 5323517). See 5.
77 El Hostal, San Bernardo 55 (tel. 5321649). Off Gran Vía. Metro: Noviciado.
78 Leonés, Nuñez de Arce 14 (tel. 5310889). Off Plaza de Santa Ana. See 6.
79 Pérez, Juan Alvarez Menzibal 44–3 (tel. 5419190). See 17.
80 Valer, Cruz 33 (tel. 5226219). See 3.
81 Infantas la Vega, Infantas 30 (tel. 5210673). See 5.
82 Rodriguez, Núñez de Arce 9 (tel. 5224431). Off Plaza de Santa Ana. See 6.

UNIVERSITY ACCOMMODATION

Available to those wishing to stay five days or more. Ask the Tourist Office for details.

IYHF HOSTELS

Calle Santa Cruz de Marcenado 28 (tel. 2474532). Very high risk of theft. Consider leaving your pack at the station.

Things have even been known to go missing from the lock-up at the reception. Metro: Arguelles.

'Richard Schirrmann', Casa de Campo (tel. 4635699). A pleasant hostel, with a well run lock-up at the reception. No curfew, but far from the centre if you miss the last metro. Set in a large park within easy walking distance of the Lago and Batan metro stops. From Lago the shortest route is to turn left on leaving the station and follow the dirt track along the side of the wire fence. At times the path is enclosed by bushes and trees, so you may feel wary of walking along it, particularly in the evening when the path is unlit. However, by following the well-lit footpath by the roadside to the left at all times you will arrive at the hostel.

CAMPING

Osuna, Avda de Logroño (tel. 7410510). 350ptas (£2; $3.50) per tent and per person. Ten miles out of the city beside the Ajalvir to Vicalvaro road. Metro to Canillejas, then bus 105.

Madrid, Iglesia de los Dominicos (tel. 2022835). Same prices as Osuna. Located just off the N–II, the main road to Barcelona. Metro to Plaza de Castilla, followed by bus 129.

Málaga (tel. code 952)

Tourist Offices

Oficinas de Turismo de la Junta de Andalucía. The head office is at Pasaje de Chinitas 4, 29016 Malaga (tel. 213445/228948). Open Mon.–Fri. 9 a.m.–2.00 p.m., Sat. 9 a.m.–1 p.m. Pasaje de Chinitas is just off Plaza de la Constitución. Branch offices operate at Málaga airport (tel. 230488), and outside the main train station (Málaga Principal) on the Explanada de la Estación.

Oficinas Municipales de Turismo. One office is in the Area Municipal de Turismo at Cister 11–1 (tel. 227907), the other is at the bus station on Paseo de los Tilos (tel. 350061 ext. 260).

Basic Directions

The main bus and train stations are close to each other on the opposite side of the Guadalmedina river from the historic centre of the city. From Málaga Principal (the main train station) head left from the exit until you reach Paseo de los Tilos. The bus station is a short walk up this street to your left. Bus 3 links both stations to the centre. Otherwise it is a 15–20-minute walk. To get to the town centre from Málaga Principal walk to the far right-hand end of the square in front of the station (Explanada de la Estación) and then follow either of the small streets which lead on to Cuarteles. Head left along this street until you reach the Rio Guadalmedina, then cross the river by the Puente Tetun to the left of the tall Post Office building. The bridge leads into Alameda Principal. By the end of the bridge Alameda de Colón runs away to the right. Continuing down Alameda Principal you pass San Lorenzo (one street beyond Alameda de Colón) then Tomás de Heredia (on the right) before arriving at the junction with Córdoba (right) and Puerta del Mar (left) just before the statue of the Marqués de Larios. By the station, the street called Marqués de Larios runs left off Alameda Principal into Plaza de la Constitución. Going on along Alameda Principal past the statue the next major street on the left is Molina Lario, which leads up to the cathedral and then on to Plaza Siglo. Just past the cathedral the turning on the right takes you into Cister.

Finding Accommodation

The streets to the north of Alameda Principal (left as you come from the train station) are well supplied with cheap rooms but the quality of the establishments varies considerably, so make a point of checking rooms out before you agree to take them. As a rule, you get what you pay for, so it is probably best to go for a moderately priced room. Streets which are especially well endowed with cheap lodgings include Calle Martínez, Calle Bolsa and Calle San Augustín. Martínez runs between Puerta del Mar and Marqués de Larios. From Marqués de Larios you can turn right down J. Diaz into Bolsa, while San Augustín is reached by going round the cathedral.

Trouble Spots

Although Málaga has sufficient points of interest to merit a visit, many travellers' only reason for being in the city is that they have taken advantage of cheap flights into Málaga airport. The city is one of the most dangerous in Spain. In common with other cities suffering high levels of unemployment, petty theft is a problem. More worrying is the high level of violent assault, possibly associated with the relatively severe drug problems of the city. It is not unknown for travellers to be mugged en route from the train station to the Tourist Office. The best advice is to leave your pack in left luggage if you are going to the Tourist Office, or going looking for accommodation, or to take only a toilet bag, towel and change of clothes if you are heading for a hotel. Sleeping in Málaga station is sheer folly, no matter what you may have heard to the contrary. Incidences of travellers being threatened at knife point and forced to hand over their valuables are regrettably common. Moreover, even if you give up your belongings without a struggle, assailants may still inflict serious injury on their victims.

PENSIONS

Cheapest doubles around 1750ptas (£9.75; $17)

Hostal Galicia, Ayala 5 (tel. 313842). Walk right from the train station exit then down Fortuny into Ayala.

Cheapest doubles around 2000ptas (£11; $19.50)

Córdoba, Bolsa 9–11 (tel. 214469). From Marqués de Larios turn right down J. Diaz into Bolsa.
Hostal Lampaerez, Calle Santa Maria 6 (tel. 219484).
Hostal Torres, Sevilla 40 (tel. 270024).

Cheapest doubles around 2400–2650ptas (£13.50–14.75; $23.50–26.00)

Viena, Strachan 3 (tel. 224095). Right of Marqués de Larios.

Las Antillas, Heroes de Sostoa 31 (tel. 314388). Go right from the train station exit, then right again along Heroes de Sostoa.

Hostal Magaña, Rio 11 (tel. 354308).

Cheapest doubles around 2850ptas (£15.75; $28)

Casa Vasca, Avda Dr. Galvez Cinanchero 14 (tel. 305794).
Estela, Pasaje de Campos 15 (tel. 223031).
La Palma, Martinez 7 (tel. 226772). Between Puerta del Mar and Marqués de Larios.
La Paloma, Barcenillas 6 (tel. 256879).
Las Tres Rosas, Heroes de Sostao (tel. 333266). See Las Antillas, above.
El Ruedo, Trinidad Grund 3 (tel. 215820).

Cheapest doubles around 3100ptas (£17.50; $30)

Chinitas, Pasaje de Chinitas 2 (tel. 214683). Off Plaza de la Constitución, beside the main Tourist Office.

Cheapest doubles around 3300ptas (£18.50; $32)

Acapulco, Explanada Estación, Edif. Terminal 3 (tel. 318988).
Hostal Aurora, Muro de Puerta Nueva 1 (tel. 224004).
Hostal Castilla, Córdoba 7 (tel. 218635).
Hostal Guerrero, Córdoba 7 (tel. 218635).

Cheapest doubles around 3500ptas (£19.50; $34)

El Cenachero, Barroso 5 (tel. 224088). Turn left off Alameda de Colón.

Cheapest doubles around 3800ptas (£21; $37)

Mar y Cielo, San Juan de Dios 1 (tel. 216445).
Buenos Aires, Bolsa 12 (tel. 218935). See the Córdoba above.
Lalo, Mármoles 24 (tel. 305294).
Hostal Maly, Casas de Campos 5 (tel. 211974).

Cheapest doubles around 4000ptas (£22.50; $39)

Hostal Cisneros, Cisneros 7 (tel. 212633). After crossing the Puente Tetuán follow the river to the left until you see the Cisneros on the right.

CAMPING

Balneario del Carmen, Avda Juan Sebastian Ekano. Open year round. 350ptas (£2; $3.50) for a small tent, 450ptas (£2.50; $4.50) per person. Two miles out on the road to El Palo. Bus 11.

Salamanca (tel. code 923)

Tourist Offices
Oficina de Turismo de la Communidad de Castilla y Leon, Gran Vía 39–41, 37071 Salamanca (tel. 268571). Open Mon.–Fri. 9.30 a.m.–2.00 p.m. and 4.30–7.00 p.m., Sat. 10 a.m.–2 p.m., Sun. 11 a.m.–2.00 p.m. Good source of information on the city, and the region. Free plan of Salamanca and a list of local accommodation.

Oficina Municipal de Turismo, Plaza Mayor 10 (tel. 218342). Open Mon.–Fri. 10 a.m.–1.30 p.m. and 5–7 p.m., Sat. 10 a.m.–2 p.m., Sun. 11 a.m.–2 p.m. A basic information service. Fine if you have a few simple questions you want answered.

Basic Directions
The train station and bus station are on opposite sides of the town, both about 15–20 minutes' walk from the centre. From both stations you can catch a bus to Plaza del Mercado which adjoins Plaza Mayor. To walk from the train station, head left along Paseo de la Estación to Plaza de España and the ring road which circles the historic centre. Almost directly opposite Paseo de la Estación across the junction is Azafranal. Take this road and go straight ahead till you arrive at Plaza Mayor. Just to the left of Azafranal at the junction with the ring road is Calle

de España, otherwise known as Gran Vía. From the bus station follow Avenida Filiberto Villalobos down to the ring road. Crossing over directly ahead is Ramon y Cajal. At the end of this street turn left, then right up Prior to Plaza Mayor.

Finding Accommodation

Prices for accommodation are relatively low by Spanish standards. If you have travelled around the country a bit you should notice that you get a higher standard of accommodation for your money here. It is just as well that higher quality accommodation is within the reach of the budget traveller as rooms disappear fast in July and August. Then, just as you might expect things to improve, the September fiesta makes finding a room even more difficult. At these times, you are likely to be approached at the train station with offers of accommodation in local houses. If you are wary of accepting such offers, ask at the tourist offices if they have a list of rooms available in private houses that are occupied by students during the university year (ask about casas particulares).

Outside these times of year you should be able to fix yourself up with a cheap bed easily. The small streets in the area around Plaza Mayor have a large supply of fondas, casas de huespedes and cheap hostales, particularly Meléndez, which runs from the church at San Martín down to the seminary (La Clerca).

PENSIONS

Cheapest doubles around 1400ptas (£7.75; $13.50)

Cristo de los Milagros, Cristo de los Milagros 6 (tel. 261127). Off Azafranal near the ring road.

Cheapest doubles around 1550ptas (£8.75; $15)

Internacional, Avda de Mirat 15 (tel. 262799). Right along the ring road from the end of Paseo de la Estación.
Los Charros, Pollo Martín (tel. 252204).
Africa, Tejares 5–7 (tel. 232325).

Cheapest doubles around 1750ptas (£9.75; $17)

Peña de Francia, San Pablo 96 (tel. 216687).
Salamanca, Avda S. Augustín 23 (tel. 252208).

Cheapest doubles around 1975ptas (£11; $19.50)

La Liebre, Perdón 5 (tel. 217261).
Santander, Varillas 17 & 19–1 (tel. 211961).
Barez, Meléndez 19 (tel. 217495).

Cheapest doubles around 2100ptas (£11.75; $20.50)

Lisboa, Meléndez 1–2 (tel. 214333).
Europa, Eras 3 (tel. 221844).
Barragués, Plaza de España 12 (tel. 263433).

Cheapest doubles around 2300ptas (£12.75; $22.50)

Feli, Libreros 58 (tel. 216010).
Marina, Doctrinos 4 (tel. 216569).
Mary, Doctrinos 4 (tel. 218638).
Las Vegas, Meléndez 13–1 (tel. 218749).
Currican I, Los Hidalgos 8–12 (tel. 220159). The Currican II
   at Hidalgos 2–6 has the same rates and same owner.
Libano, Paseo San Vicente 16 (tel. 264350). Left at the end
   of Avda F. Villalobos as you walk from the bus station.

Cheapest doubles around 2450ptas (£13.75; $24)

Estefania, Jesús 3 (tel. 217372).
Emma, Paseo San Vicente 16 & 18–1 (tel. 264303). See the
   Libano for directions.

Cheapest doubles around 2575ptas (£14.50; $25)

Carabela, Paseo de Canalejas 10–12 (tel. 260708). Head left
   from the end of Paseo de la Estación when you reach the
   ring road walking from the train station.
Laguna, Consuelo 19 (tel. 218706).
Los Angeles, Plaza Mayor 10 (tel. 218166).

Hostería de la Universidad, Traviesa 1–3 (tel. 215302).
Albacete, Caleros 3 (tel. 218480).

Cheapest doubles around 2750ptas (£15.50; $27)

Marly, Plaza de España 12 (tel. 263432).
València, Paseo San Antonio 5 (tel. 269864).
Madrid, Toro 1 (tel. 214296). The street runs from the ring road (right of Azafranal as you walk from the train station) down to Plaza Mayor.
Las Rías, Pozo Amarillo 17 (tel. 213339).

Cheapest doubles around 2975ptas (£16.50; $29)

Uría, Garca Moreno 1 (tel. 223054).

Cheapest doubles around 3275ptas (£18.25; $32).

Gabriel y Galán, Plaza Gabriel y Galán 3–5 (tel. 221316).
Oriental, Azafranal 13 (tel. 212115).
Mindanao, Paseo San Vicente 2 (tel. 263080). See the Libano, above, for directions.
Alianza II, Plaza de las Carmelitas 13 (tel. 267706).
Alianza III, Avda Villamyor 2 (tel. 268360). Same management as the Alianza II.
Tormes, Rua Mayor 20 (tel. 219683). The street is just off Plaza Mayor, running from the church of San Martín down past the Casa de las Conchas.
La Castellana, Zamora 1–3 (tel. 212120).

Cheapest doubles around 3300ptas (£18.50; $32)

Virginia, Paseo de la Estación 109 (Escalera D–1) (tel. 241016).
Hispánico, Avda Italia 21 (tel. 226286).

Cheapest doubles around 3500ptas (£19.50; $34)

Goya, Avda Alemania 58–62 (tel. 267886). Head left from the bus station from the end of Avda F. Villalobos onto Avda Alemania.
Torio, Maria Auxiliadora 13 (tel. 226601).

PRIVATE ROOMS

Casas particulares are the cheapest accommodation possibility, other than camping. During the university year many local people let rooms to students. Outside term-time these rooms are available to visitors. Ask about availability of casas particulares at the Tourist Offices.

CAMPING

There are several campsites a few miles outside the city. The Tourist Offices will inform you as to the relevant bus services.

Regio (tel. 200250). Open year round. 390ptas (£2.25; $4) per small tent, 440ptas (£2.50; $4.50) per person. In Santa Marta de Tormes, 2½ miles out on the road to Madrid.

Don Quijote (tel. 257504). Open 20 Jan.–10 Dec. 300ptas (£1.70; $3) per small tent, 350ptas (£2; $3.50) per person. In Cabrerizos, 2½ miles out on the road to Aldealengua.

San Sebastian (Donostia/San Sebastián) (tel. code 943)

Tourist Offices
Eusko Jaurlaritza, Kultura Eta Turismo Saila, Gipuzkoako Lurralde Ordezkaritza, Miramar, s/n. 20004 Donostia. Contact this office if you want information on the city in advance. On arrival, go to the Tourist Office the Basque government operate in the city.

Turismo Bulegoak, Kalea Reina Regente (ground floor of the Victoria Eugenia Theatre) (tel. 426282). Open Mon.–Fri. 9 a.m.–1.30 p.m. and 4–7 p.m., Sat. 9 a.m.–1 p.m. Turn right after crossing the Maria Cristina bridge and follow the River Urumea to the second bridge (Zurriola) at which point Kalea Reina Regente runs left.

Basic Directions

From the train station, walk towards the River Urumea, cross the Maria Cristina bridge, and head straight on into Plaza Bilbo. From Plaza Bilbo, Kalea Bergara (Vergara) and Kalea Getaria run to the right, crossing Kalea San Martin and Kalea San Martzial before arriving at Hiribidea Askatasunaren (Avda de la Libertad). Walking right a little you can then turn left down Kalea Okendo (Oquendo) which runs as far as the junction of Boulevard Zumardia (Alameda del Boulevard) and Kalea Reina Regente. Going straight across this junction you can follow Kalea Aldamar down to the coast. If instead of turning right at Plaza Bilbo you head more or less straight on down Kalea Alfonso VIII you arrive at the Cathedral of the Good Shepherd (Artzai Onaren), crossing Kalea Hondarribia (Fuenterrabia) on the way. On the other side of the cathedral, opposite Alfonso VIII, is Kalea San Bartolome. If on leaving the train station you turn right down the side of the station you can follow Pasealekua Frantzia (Paseo de Francia) to its junction with Kalea Iztueta. Heading right you can then turn left down Kalea Iparragirre, right along Kalea S. Esnaola, and then left down Kalea Aita J.M. Larroka to reach Plaza Katalunia (Plaza de Cataluña).

Street Names

In the accommodation listings below the Basque version of the street name is used. In most cases this bears sufficient resemblance to the Spanish version to be easily identified on street maps printed in Spanish. Where this is not the case, the Spanish version is bracketed. Be sure to read Basic Directions above.

Finding Accommodation

Donostia is immensely popular during the summer months, so you may experience some difficulty in finding cheap accommodation. Prices are high in the peak season (June/July–Sept.) so do not expect to find a double for under 2000ptas per person outside a *fonda* or *casa de huespedes*. As a rule, prices are higher in the Old Town between Boulevard

Zumardia and Urgull. The area around the cathedral has a particularly good supply of (by local standards) cheap rooms. Kalea Urdaneta, Kalea San Bartolemé and Kalea Loiola are especially good streets to look in. The streets around Plaza Katalunia are also a good place to look for relatively inexpensive lodgings. If you are visiting Donostia outside the peak season you should have no trouble finding suitable accommodation at a reasonable price as the cost of rooms often falls substantially. Considering that standards of different types of accommodation in the city are comparatively high, this means you invariably get good value for money if you arrive in the off-season.

FONDAS

Donostia, Hondarrabia 19–3 (third floor) (tel. 422157).

Garate, Triunfo 8 (tel. 461571). The street runs from San Bartolome across San Martin.

Vicandi, Iparragirre 1 (tel. 270795).

Goi-Argi, S. Esnaola 13 (tel. 278802).

Garcia, Soraluze 6 (tel. 427236).

CASAS DE HUESPEDES

Aldazabal, San Martin 36–5 (tel. 420094).

Ezkurra, Hiribidea Ametzagaina 5 (tel. 273594). From the train station head left until you reach Pasealekua Duke de Mandas. Head right but take the left fork in the road to reach Egia. Follow the main road round until you see Ametzagaina on the left.

La Parisien, Urdaneta 6 (tel. 464312). After crossing the Maria Cristina Bridge watch out for Kalea Prim heading left to the start of Urdaneta. The street passes by the cathedral.

Ricardo, San Bartoleme 21&23–3 (tel. 461374).

Lau Aizeta, Lau Haizeta (Alza) (tel. 352445). Out from the centre in Intxaurrondo.

ONE-STAR PENSIONES

Amaiur, Abuztuaren 31 44–2 (31 de Agosto) (tel. 429654). Abuztuaren 31 is a continuation of Soraluze. Left off Aldamar.

Amalur, San Martin 43–2 (tel. 460861).

Añorga, Easo 12–1 (tel. 467945). The street crosses San Bartolome.

Aralar, Easo 12–2 (tel. 470410). See Anorga.

Aristizabal, Alfonso VIII 6 (tel. 421323). Open July–Sept. only.

Boulevard, Boulevard Zumardia 24–1 (tel. 429405)

Donostia, Hondarribia 19–3 (tel. 422157). Open July–Sept. only.

Josefina, Easo 12 (tel. 461956). Open July–Sept. only. See Anorga.

Kaia, Portu 12–2 (tel. 431342). Walk left along Boulevard Zumardia, right up San Jeronimo into Konstituzio Enparantza, and then go left along Portu.

Larrea, Narrika 21–1 (tel. 422694). Walk left along Boulevard Zumardia, then right.

San Jeronimo, San Jeronimo 25 (tel. 281689). See Kaia.

San Lorenzo, San Lorenzo 2–1 (tel. 425516). Doubles with shower/bath 4500ptas (£25; $44) from late June–Sept. At other times prices fall to around 2800ptas (£15.50; $27.50). Singles 1150ptas (£6.50; $11.50) in the off-season. Walk left along Boulevard Zumardia, right up San Juan, then left.

San Martin, San Martn 10–1 (tel. 428714).

Urkia, Urbieta 12 (tel. 424436). The street crosses San Bartolome.

Urgull, Esterlines 10–3 (tel. 430047). Walk left along Boulevard Zumardia, right up Narrika, then left.

TWO-STAR PENSIONES

Alemana, San Martin 53 (tel. 464881). Mid-June–Oct. 4600ptas (£25.50; $45) for doubles. At other times around 3600ptas (£20; $35) for the same rooms

Donostiarra, San Martin 6 (tel. 426167)

La Concha, San Martin 51 (tel. 450389). Doubles 4600ptas (£25.50; $45) year round.

La Perla, Loiola (tel. 428123). Late June–Oct. doubles with shower and WC 4300ptas (£24; $42). At other times the same rooms cost around 3300ptas (£18.50; $32).

Lorea, Boulevard Zumardia 16–1 (tel. 427258)

Maite, Hiribidea Madrid 19–1B (tel. 470715). Out from the centre, on the way to Anoeta. Take a bus dir: Amara-Anoeta from Brbieta (the street crosses San Bartolome), or a walk from the centre. Turn left down Prim at Plaza Bilbo and head straight on until you reach Plaza Pio XII, then go left down Hiribidea Madrid at the fork in the road.

HOSTALES AND HOSTAL-RESIDENCIAS

Easo, San Bartoleme 24 (tel. 466892). June–Oct. doubles start around 4250ptas (£23.50; $41.50). At other times prices fall to around 3650ptas (£20.50; $35.50).

Lasa, Bergara 15 (tel. 423052). June–Sept. doubles start around 4250ptas (£23.50; $41.50). Oct.–Dec. prices fall to around 3850ptas (£21.50; $37.50), and at other times to around 3650ptas (£20.50; $35.50).

Comercio, Urdaneta 24 (tel. 464414). July–Sept. doubles start around 4250ptas (£23.50; $41.50), at other times around 3650ptas (£20.50; $35.50).

Ozcáriz, Hondarrabia 8–2&3 (tel. 425306). June–Sept. doubles start around 4150ptas (£23; $41). Only a slight fall in the off-season.

Fernando, Enparantza Gipuzkoako 2 (Plaza de Guipuzcoa) (tel. 425575). June–Sept. doubles start around 4850ptas (£27; $47), at other times around 3650ptas (£20.50; $35.50). From Bergara cross Hiribidea Askatasunaren into Idiakez, which leads into the square.

Isla, Pasealekeu Mirakontxa 17 (tel. 464897). Doubles start around 4600ptas (£25.50; $45) year round. Pleasant location near the Kontxa beach. Follow San Martin to its end.

Alameda, Boulevard Zumardia 23 (tel. 421687). Doubles start around 4600ptas (£25.50; $45) year round.

PRIVATE ROOMS

In the past, a list of private rooms (*casas particulares*) has been available from the Tourist Office.

IYHF HOSTELS

'Anoeta', Ciudad Deportiva Anoeta (tel. 452970). 2 a.m. curfew. Check the IYHF handbook to see if this hostel is open in 1993. A 20-minute walk from the town centre. From Urbieta (the street crosses San Bartolome) take the bus dir: Amara-Anoeta.

Parque Ulia, s/n (tel. 471546/293751/452970).

CAMPING

Igueldo (tel. 214502). Open May–Sept. 375ptas (£2.10; $3.50) per person. Price includes tent. Located about 3 miles west of the town centre on the landward side of Monte Igueldo. The Barrio de Igueldo bus 16 from Boulevard Zumardia will get you there, but the service is poor. Only 13 buses per day Mon.–Sat.; five buses on Sun. Last bus from town 10 p.m.

SLEEPING ROUGH

Although sleeping on the beach is technically illegal the police invariably turn a blind eye during the peak season. If you are sleeping out, bed down beside other people to give you some extra security, and leave your pack and valuables at the train station.

Seville (Sevilla) (tel. code 95)

Tourist Offices

Oficina de Turismo de la Junta de Andalucía, Avenida de la Constitución 21, 41004 Sevilla (tel. 4221404). Open Mon.–Fri. 9.30 a.m.–7.30 p.m., Sat. 9.30 a.m.–2 p.m. A good source of information on the city and the region. Well-informed and helpful staff. Centrally located. A branch office operates at San Pablo airport (tel. 4255046).

Oficina Municipal de Turismo, Edificio Costurero de la Reina, Paseo de las Delicias 9 (tel. 4234465). Friendly staff, but the office is less well stocked with pamphlets and is on the edge of the old city. By the Guadalquivir river, a short distance from the Glorieta de los Marineros Voluntarios and the Puente del Generalsmo.

Arriving in Seville

All mainline trains now stop at the recently opened Estación de Santa Justa, about 30 minutes' walk from the Tourist Offices. The main bus station on Plaza de San Sebastian (just off Menéndez Pelayo) is much closer to the centre; about 10 minutes' walk from the Tourist Offices. From the bus station walk down on to Menéndez Pelayo and head left a short distance until you reach Plaza Don Juan de Austria. At this point you can head straight down to the Glorieta de los Marineros Voluntarios by following Avda del Cid and then Avda de Maria Luisa. Turning right from Plaza Don Juan de Austria you can walk down San Fernando to the Puerta de Jerez, from which the Tourist Office on Avda de la Constitución is just a minute's walk to the left. From the Santa Justa train station you can take bus 70 to the main bus station. The airport bus EA also picks up near Santa Justa and lets you off at Puerta de Jerez, but the service is less frequent than bus 70.

Finding Accommodation

Only during Holy Week (the week leading up to Easter) and around the time of the April Fair are you likely to have difficulty finding cheap accommodation in Seville. At these times not only do large numbers of visitors converge on the city, but room prices can be raised quite legally, sometimes by as much as 70–100 per cent. Otherwise, even during July and August, there are enough cheap beds to go round. That said, finding a room is not quite as easy as it used to be, thanks to the opening of the Santa Justa station and the closure of the Plaza de Armas (Córdoba) station. The area around the old Plaza de Armas station on the western fringe of the old city has a large supply of cheap lodgings, especially San Eloy, which probably has more fondas and casas de huespedes than any other street in the city. In contrast, the streets around Santa Justa are relatively bare of cheap lodgings, so it is no longer really possible to find a cheap bed within 10–15 minutes of getting off the train. The other area with a good supply of relatively cheap lodgings is the Barrio Santa Cruz, in the heart of the old city around the Giralda. Although rooms here are slightly more expensive than around the old train station, their location cannot be matched and they are now easier to reach from the main train station.

Pension Prices
In 1992, the city played host to EXPO '92, and confidently expected to receive 40 million visitors. Accommodation prices rose sharply in 1992, and although they will fall back to more normal levels in 1993 there is no way of knowing at the time of writing what individual pensions will be charging. In many cases what was a cheap pension in 1991 will still be a cheap pension in 1993, and similarly so for moderately priced establishments. However, many pensions were extensively modernized in preparation for 1992, so their prices may bear no relation to what they might have been in the past. Use the following information as a rough guide only.

CHEAP AND MODERATELY PRICED PENSIONS IN 1992

Cheapest doubles around 1700ptas (£9.50; $16.50)

Estoríl, Gravina 78 (tel. 4225095). Close to the Museo de Bellas Artes, in the area around the old Plaza de Armas station.

Cheapest doubles around 2650ptas (£14.75; $26)

San Pancracio, Cruces 9, (tel. 4413104).
Gravina, Gravina 46 (tel. 4216414). See Estoril.

Cheapest doubles around 3175ptas (£17.75; $31)

Casa Manolo, Don Fadrique 5 (tel. 4370293).
La Francesa, Juán Rabadán 28 (tel. 4383107).
Gran Plaza, Gran Plaza 4 (tel. 4631598).
Alvertos, Cervantes 4 (tel. 385710).
Casa Saez, Plaza Curtidores 6 (tel. 4416753).
Jerez, Rastro 2 (tel. 4420560).
Monsalves, Monsalves 29 (tel. 4216853).
San Esteban, San Esteban 8 (tel. 4222549).
Triano Manolo, Antillano Campos 17 (tel. 4333079).
Romero, Gravina 21 (tel. 4211353). See Estoril.

Cheapest doubles around 3300ptas (£18.50; $32)

Espadafor, Avda Cruz Campo 23 (tel. 4573866).

Cheapest doubles around 3700ptas (£20.50; $36)

Arquelles, Alhóndiga 58 (tel. 4214455).
Arenal, Anton de la Cerda 8 (tel. 4226177).
Pino Lordelo, Quintana 29 (tel. 4387905). In 1991, the cheapest doubles in this hostal cost 2500ptas.
La Posada, Relator 49 (tel. 4374768).

Cheapest doubles around 4775ptas (£26.50; $47)

Goya, Mateos Gagos 31 (tel. 4211170). The street runs off Plaza Virgen de los Reyes by the cathedral and the Giralda. In 1991, the cheapest doubles in this hotel cost 2200ptas.
Archeros, Archeros 23 (tel. 4418465).

Pino, Tarifa 6 (tel. 4212810). Near the old Plaza de Armas station, close to the Iglesia de San Andres.

Marco de la Giralda, Abades 30 (tel. 4228324). From Plaza Virgin de los Reyes by the Giralda follow Mateos Gago until you see Abades on the left.

Cheapest doubles around 5300ptas (£29.50; $52)

La Muralla, Macarena 52 (tel. 4371049). In 1991, the cheapest doubles at this hostal cost 3000ptas.

Capitol, Zaragoza 66 (tel. 4212441). From the town hall (Ayuntamiento) on Avda de la Constitución turn down Madrid, which leads into Zaragoza. In 1991, the cheapest doubles at this hostal-residencia cost 1900ptas.

Los Gabrieles, Plaza de la Legión 2 (tel. 4223307). Off Marqués de Paradas, one block from Gravina. See Estoril.

Monreal, Rodrigo Caro 8 (tel. 4214166). From Plaza Virgen de los Reyes by the Giralda, follow Mateos Gago until you see Rodrigo Caro on the right.

Rivero, Bailén 67 (tel. 4216231). Close to the Iglesia de la Magdalena, in the area near the old Plaza de Armas station.

Toledo, Santa Teresa 15 (tel. 4215335).

MODERATELY PRICED PENSIONS IN 1991

Cheapest doubles around 2500ptas (£13.75; $24.50)

Bonanza, Sales y Ferre 12 (tel. 4228614).

Cheapest doubles around 2750ptas (£15.50; $27)

Londres, San Pedro Mártir 1 (tel. 4212896).
Central, Zaragoza 18 (tel. 4217660). See Capitol.

Cheapest doubles around 2850ptas (£16; $28)

Suiza, Méndez Nez 16 (tel. 4220813).

Cheapest doubles around 3200ptas (£18; $31)

Nuevo Suizo, Azafaifo 7 (tel. 4229147).
Duque, Trajano 15 (tel. 4387011).

IYHF HOSTEL

Albergue Juvenil Fernando el Santo, Isaac Peral 2 (tel.
4613150). No curfew. Generally filled to near capacity with
local students. IYHF members aged under 26 pay around
750ptas (£4.25; $7.50), those aged 26 and over about
950ptas (£5.25; $9.50). Roughly 1½ miles from the city
centre. Bus 34. For up-to-date information contact the
English-speaking Inturjoven (tel. 4225171).

CAMPING

Buses to the three sites below depart from the main bus station
on Plaza de San Sebastian.

Sevilla (tel. 4514379). Grade 2 site, open all year. 1992 prices
were 490ptas (£2.75; $5) per tent and per person, a large
increase on the previous year (expect them to fall back in
line with the other two sites). Six miles out on the road
to Madrid. The bus service to Empresa Casal runs more
or less hourly from 7 a.m.–9.30 p.m. Take the bus as far
as Carmona.

Villsom (tel. 4720828). Grade 2 site, open year round. 1992
prices were 350ptas (£2; $3.50) per tent and per person.
In Dos Hermanos, 11 miles out on the road to Cádiz. The
Los Amarillos bus runs about every 45 minutes from 6.30
a.m.–midnight.

Club de Campo (tel. 4720250). Grade 1 site, open year round.
1992 prices were 350ptas (£2; $3.50) per tent and per
person. In Dos Hermanos, 10 miles out on the road to Dos
Hermanas. Same bus as for Villsom above.

Toledo (tel. code 925)

Tourist Offices
Junta de Communidades de Castilla-La Mancha, Oficina de
Turismo, Puerta de Bisagra, 45003 Toledo (tel. 220843). Open
Mon.–Fri. 9 a.m.–2 p.m. and 4–6 p.m., Sat. 9 a.m.–1.30 p.m.
A 15-minute walk from the train station. One of the local buses
stops near the office. A basic information booth operates on
the main square (Plaza Zocodover), again a 15 minute walk
from the train station or bus 5 or 6 to the terminus.

Basic Directions
If you know you will be arriving in Toledo when the Tourist
Office is closed, try to get a plan of some description before
you arrive, either from the Spanish Tourist Office in London
(or your capital city), or from another branch in Spain, as the
old part of the town is a maze of small streets. Arriving at the
train station, head right along the main road in front of the
station. Before long you get a first glimpse of the old city rising
above the Rio Tajo. Go right where the road forks, cross the
river and go straight ahead to arrive at the Puerta Bisagra. Head
left along Paseo de la Rosa at the fork in the road you arrive
at the Alcantara gate and bridge. Cross the river and then make
your way up the steps to the left. Going straight on from the
top of the steps will take you to Plaza Zocodover. Take
Comercio from the square and continue straight ahead for the
Cathedral and the start of Trinidad. This street leads down to
the junction of Rojas, San Tome, San Salvador and Santa
Ursula by the church of San Tome.

PENSIONS

La Belvisea, Cuesta del Can 7 (tel. 220067). 850ptas (£4.75;
$8.50) per person in singles or doubles. From Zocodover
follow Cuesta de Carlos V up the side of the Alcazar.
Continue down the small street at the end of Carlos V, then
turn left into Plaza Seco. Cross this small square and keep

going until you reach San Justo. Turn left, then right almost immediately and you are in Cuesta del Can.

Maria Soledad, Soledad 1 (tel. 223287). Singles around 1100ptas (£6; $11), doubles around 1750ptas (£9.75; $17). Not easy to find. At the end of Cuesta Carlos V (see La Belvisena above) turn left and then take the small street on the right. Alternatively, you can follow the directions for La Belvisena to Plaza Seco and walk up Soledad from there.

Lumbreras, Juan Labrador 7 (tel. 221571). Singles around 1500ptas (£8.50; $14.50), doubles around 2100ptas (£11.75; $20.50). From Zocodover follow Barrio Rey to the Magdalena church. Juan Labrador is one of several streets which starts on the other side of the church.

Segovia, Recoletos 2 (tel. 211124). Doubles around 2100ptas (£11.75; $20.50). Off Silleria, which runs out of Zocodover.

Nuncio Viejo, Nuncio Viejo 19 (tel. 228178). Doubles 2300–2650ptas (£12.75–14.75; $22.50–26.00). Close to the cathedral. The street runs away to the right near the start of Trinidad.

Labrador, Juan Labrador 16 (tel. 222620). Singles around 2050ptas (£11.50; $20), doubles around 2450–2900ptas (£13.75–16.00; $24–28). See Lumbreras above for directions.

Hostal Descalzos, Descalzos 32 (tel. 222888). Singles around 2050ptas (£11.50; $20), doubles start around 3300ptas (£18.50; $32). Jan.–mid-Mar. prices are reduced by one sixth. A short way along Santa Ursula from the end of Trinidad turn right down Taller del Moro. Go left at the end of the street and follow the street to the right of Calle San Cristobal and Paseo de San Cristobal.

Hostal Esperanza, Covarrubias 2 (tel. 227859). Doubles start around 3380ptas (£19; $33).

Los Guerreros, Avda Reconquista 8 (tel. 211807). Doubles start around 4350ptas (£24.50; $43). Mid-Oct.–mid-Apr. the price falls by about 15 per cent. Outside the Old Town. Continue on beyond the Puerta Nueva de Bisagra then head right at the main intersection.

UNIVERSITY ACCOMMODATION

For information contact the Oficina de Información Juvenil in Trinidad.

IYHF HOSTEL

'San Servando', Castillo de San Servando (tel. 224554). Midnight/12.30 a.m. curfew. Juniors pay slightly above the normal price for a Spanish hostel. Those aged 26 and over can expect to pay around 1200ptas (£6.75; $12). The hostel is in a castle overlooking the Old Town. Foreign guests are usually housed in the adjoining annex, as the castle is normally full of local students. A 15-minute walk from the train station by the simplest route. Walk towards the Alcantara gate, then just before the gate, turn sharp left up the hill.

CAMPING

Circo Romano, Circa Romano (tel. 220442). Around 375ptas (£2.10; $3.50) per tent and per person. Not a particularly good site. On the outskirts of the old town, off Carretera de Carlos III. Carretera de Carlos III begins at the major intersection beyond the Puerta Nueva de Bisagra.

El Greco (tel. 210090). Around 375ptas (£2.10; $3.50) per tent and per person. Far superior to the Circo Romano site. Splendid view of the old town. A mile out on the road to Madrid (N-401).

València (tel. code 96)

Tourist Offices
Oficina de Turismo, Calle de la Paz 46 (tel. 3522897/3524000). Open Mon.–Fri. 10 a.m.–2.00 p.m. and 4–8 p.m., Sat. 10 a.m.–2 p.m. Free reservation of hotel rooms for personal callers

when the office is open or over the phone 9 a.m.–9 p.m. daily.

Oficina Municipal de Turismo, Plaza del Ayuntamiento 1 (tel. 3510417). Open Mon.–Fri. 9 a.m.–1.30 p.m. and 4.30–7.00 p.m., Sat. 9 a.m.–1 p.m. Follow Avda Marqués de Sotelo from opposite the train station exit to Plaza del Ayuntamiento.

There are another two more basic information points, one in the main train station, the other at the airport.

PENSIONS

Cheapest doubles around 1150ptas (£6.50; $11.50)

España, Embajador Vich 5 (tel. 3529342).

Cheapest doubles around 1650ptas (£9.25; $16)

Hospedera del Pilar, Mercado 19 (tel. 3316600).
En Llop, En Llop 2 (tel. 3517335).
El Rincón, Carda 11 (tel. 3316083).

Cheapest doubles around 2100ptas (£11.75; $20.50)

Hostal el Cid, Cerrajeros 13 (tel. 3322323).
Carrasco, Buenos Aires 61 (tel. 3415527).

Cheapest doubles around 2300ptas (£12.75; $22.50)

Puerto, J J Sister 6 (tel. 3233376).

Cheapest doubles around 2450ptas (£13.75; $24)

Boluda, Bailén 10 (tel. 3529761). July–Sept. the price rises to around 3300ptas (£18.50; $32).

Cheapest doubles around 2550ptas (£14.25; $25)

San Andrés, Matemático Marzal 3 (tel. 3529755).
Castelar, Ribera 1 (tel. 3513199).

Cheapest doubles around 2900ptas (£16; $28)

San Vicente, San Vicente 57 (tel. 3527061).

Cheapest doubles around 3050ptas (£17; $30)

Alicante, Ribera 8 (tel. 3512296).
Don Pelayo, Pelayo 7 (tel. 3521135).
Granero, Martinez Cubelis 4 (tel. 3512548).
Moratín, Moratín 15 (tel. 3521220).

Cheapest doubles around 3250ptas (£18; $32)

La Palmera, Julio Antonio 1 (tel. 3423816).
Lyon, Jativa 10 (tel. 3517247).
Venecia, En Llop 5 (tel. 3524267).

Cheapest doubles around 3500ptas (£19.50; $34)

Europa, Ribera 4 (tel. 3520000). A one-star hotel. Good value
for money.
La Pepica, Avda de Neptuno 2 (tel. 3714111). A one-star
hotel-residencia, close to the beach. Also good value for
money.

IYHF HOSTEL

Colegio Mayor 'La Paz', Avda del Puerto 69 (tel. 3617459).
Open July–Sept. Midnight curfew. Bus 19 from Plaza del
Ayuntamiento (follow Avda Marqués de Sotelo from
opposite the train station to reach Plaza del Ayuntamiento).

CAMPING

There is no site close to the city centre, but there are two grade-
one sites easily reached by bus from the Puerta del Mar by the
Glorieta Park.
El Saler (tel. 3670411). Open year round. Six miles out of the
city on a pleasant beach.
El Palmar (tel. 1610853). Open June–Sept. Ten miles from
València near La Albufera.

SWEDEN (Sverige)

As with the other Scandinavian countries, the best advice to the budget traveller in Sweden is to prepare for hostelling and camping. While many **hotels** cut their prices substantially during the summer, even this, unfortunately, does not bring them into our accommodation price range, as you can still expect to pay from 250kr (£24; $42.50) in singles, and 400kr (£39; $68) in doubles. Very occasionally, you may find hotels or *pensionat* outside the main cities which charge 170–210kr (£16.50–20.50; $29–36) in singles, 200–320kr (£19.30–31.00; $34–54) in doubles all year round. If this is within your budget, enquire at the local Tourist Office about the cheapest hotels in town. Tourist Offices will also book **private rooms** for you where these are available, costing around 150kr (£14.50; $25.50) for singles, 250kr (£24; $42.50) in doubles or larger rooms. In villages and small towns look out for the 'Rum' sign, because approaching the owner directly will save you paying the 50kr (£4.80; $8.50) booking fee charged by the Tourist Offices.

Most towns that you are likely to visit will have an IYHF hostel. Of the 280 IYHF hostels in Sweden, about 130 stay open all year round, others open only during the main tourist season (June to late August). Most of the hostels are located in the southern and central regions of the country. There are three grades of hostel: the lowest grade has cold running water only, but these are few and far between; the intermediate-grade hostels have hot running water and hot showers. By far the most common are the superior-grade hostels, which usually have hot running water in small bedrooms, hot showers, and various other special facilities. Prices vary from 76–90kr (£7.35–8.70; $13–15). Non-members are charged an extra 35kr (£3.40; $6). Outside the main towns superior-grade hostels are very popular with families, so no matter where you are heading, it makes sense to book a bed in advance. If you expect to arrive after 6 p.m. you should inform the hostel, otherwise your reservation will not be held beyond that time. In university towns, it is often possible to find a bed in a student hostel during the summer. The local Tourist Office will advise you about the availability of such accommodation.

Almost every town or village of any size has a **campsite,** and quite often you will have a choice of sites. There are some 750 sites officially approved and classified by the Swedish Tourist Board and these account for most of the sites. Approved sites are rated from one star up to three stars. A one-star site has everything you would expect, while three-star sites tend to offer a whole range of facilities you will rarely use, if at all. Most sites operate with all their facilities between June and September, while in those which are also open in April and May, certain supplementary facilities may not be available. The Tourist Board boasts that the overnight charge for a family is one of the lowest in Europe, and this is hard to refute. But, as the fee for a tent is the relatively high 70–80kr (£6.75–7.75; $12.00–13.50), and some sites also make a nominal charge per person, this means that solo travellers do not benefit from the pricing system, whereas three or four people sharing a tent certainly do. There are very few sites at which a camping pass is not required, so unless you have an International Camping Carnet you will be obliged to buy a Swedish camping pass at the first site you visit, which costs 43kr (£4.20; $7.50) and is valid for the rest of the camping season. There are also 4500 cabins for rent, spread over 350 sites. Cabins sleep between two and six people, are usually equipped with a kitchen and their overnight charges vary from 70–100kr (£6.75–9.75; $12–17) per person.

Under the ancient law of Allmannsratt it is possible to **camp for free,** with certain restrictions. It is permissible to erect a tent for a day and a night on land that is not used for farming, providing you are some distance from habitations. You must obtain the consent of the landowner before pitching your tent near any dwelling place or if you are camping in a group. Avoid setting any potentially dangerous fires, and make sure you leave no rubbish behind on your departure. In more sparsely populated areas, such as the mountains, it is perfectly acceptable to stay longer than a day and a night. As with neighbouring Norway, the two problems facing campers are the cold nights and mosquitoes, so prepare yourself accordingly.

The Swedish YHA operates two other types of accommodation in the mountains. **Mountain centres** can be expensive, with the cost of a bed ranging from 70 to 350kr (£6.75–33.25; $12.75–63.25). **Mountain huts,** however, offer relatively cheap beds for around 75kr (£7.25; $13.50), in areas where any accommodation can be hard to find. These huts are normally sited far from either roads or railways, so they are likely to appeal only to those planning on doing some hiking.

ADDRESSES

Swedish Tourist Board	29–31 Oxford Street (5th Floor), London W1R 1RE (tel. 071 437 5816)
Camping	Stanfords, 12–14 Long Acre, London, WC2 (tel. 071–236 1321) sell a comprehensive list. The Swedish Tourist Board supplies shorter lists free of charge.
Student hostels	SFS, Kungsgatan 4, Box 7144, Stockholm (tel. 08–234 515). For accommodation in Stockholm.
	SFS-Serviceverksahmet, Drottninggatan 89, 113 60 Stockholm (tel. 08–340180).
Swedish YHA	Svenska Turistföreningen (STF), Box 25, 101 20 Stockholm.
	Information Office, Drottninggaten 31–33, Stockholm (tel. 08–7903100).
Mountain huts and mountain centres	Contact the Swedish YHA Information Office.

Gothenburg (Göteborg) (tel. code 031)

Tourist Offices
Göteborg's Turistbyrå, Kungsportsplatsen 2, 411 Göteborg (tel.
100740). Open daily in summer, 9 a.m.–8 p.m., at other times,
10 a.m.–8 p.m. A 10-minute walk from the train station. From
the Brunnsparken by Drottningtorget head left down stra
Larmgatan. A branch office operates in the Nordstan Shopping
Centre, about 200m from the train station of Nils Ericsonsgatan
(open Mon.–Fri. 9.30 a.m.–6 p.m., Sat. 9.30 a.m.–3 p.m.

HOTELS

Cheapest doubles around 450kr (£44; $76)

Savoy, Andra Lònggatan 23 (tel. 124960). 15–20 minutes'
walk from the railway station. Price applies 20 June–25
Aug. only.

Cheapest doubles around 500kr (£48; $85)

Royal, Drottninggatan 67 (tel. 806100). Price applies from
mid-June to mid-Aug. A few minutes' walk from the train
station.

PRIVATE ROOMS

Either of the city Tourist Offices will make bookings. Expect
to pay from 200kr (£19.50; $34) in doubles and larger rooms.
A commission of 25kr (£2.40; $4.50) is charged.

IYHF HOSTELS

Studenthemmet Ostkupan, Mejerigatan 2 (tel.
254761/401050). Open June–26 Aug. 90Dkr (£8.75; $15.50).
About 2 miles from the city centre. Tram 5 to St
Sigfridsplan, then bus 62 or 64 to Gräddgatan.

Alternatively tram 1, 3 or 6 from the station to Redberg, then change to bus 62.

Vandrarhem Partille, Landvettervägen 433, Partille (tel. 446163). 90Dkr (£8.75; $15.50). About 10 miles from the centre. Bus 513 from Central Station to Åstebo. Ask the Tourist Office about directions to the hostel from Partille train station if you want to save some cash.

Torrekulla turistation, Kållered (tel. 951495). 90Dkr (£8.75; $15.50) for IYHF members, 35kr (£3.40; $6) supplement for non-members. Eight miles from the centre in a nature reserve. Bus 730 from Central Station.

HOSTELS

Nordengården, Stockholmsgatan 16 (tel. 196631). Open all year. 75kr (£7.25; $13) per night in dorms, 40kr (£3.85; $7) sleeping on a mattress with your own sleeping bag, 40kr (£3.85; $7) to hire sheets. Best reserved in advance. More centrally located than the IYHF hostels. Tram 1 or 3 to Stockholmsgatan, or tram 6 to Radbergsplatsen.

M/S Seaside, Packhuskajen (tel. 136467). Beds in the cabins of this ship moored about 300m from the train station cost around 180kr (£17.50; $30.50).

KFUK/KFUM (YMCA/YWCA), Garverigatan 2 (tel. 803962). Open 12 July–16 Aug. Midnight curfew. 75kr (£7.25; $13). A 15-minute walk from Central Station, or tram 1, 3 or 6 to Svingeln.

CAMPING

Kärralund (tel. 252761). From Brunnsparken, a few minutes' walk from the train station, take tram 5 dir: Torp to Welandergatan. Near the beach. Fills quickly and is expensive for solo travellers at 110kr (£9.25; $17.50) per tent and all occupants.

Gielas, Järnvägsgatan 111, Arvidsjaur (tel. 0980-13420) 80kr (£ ; $) for a tent and all its occupants. chalets available: twin bedded 175kr (£ ; $), 4-bedded 450kr (£ ; $), 5-bedded

500kr (£ ; $), 6-bedded 540kr (£ ; $). An 800m walk along Järnvägsgatan from the train station in Arvidsjaur.

Delsjö Camping (tel. 252909). A 20-minute walk from the nearest train station.

Valhalla Idrottsplats (tel. 204185).

Kiruna (tel. code 0980)

Tourist Office
Hjalmar Lundbohmsvagen 42 (tel. 18880). Open mid-June–mid-Aug., Mon.–Sat. 9 a.m.–8 p.m., Sun. noon–8 p.m.; rest of the year, Mon.–Fri. 10 a.m.–4 p.m.

PRIVATE ROOMS

Available from the Tourist Office. Expect to pay 160kr (£15.50; $27) p.p. No commission is charged.

Gult Hus (tel. 11451). This organization lets both second homes and the houses of locals away on holiday. They will pick you up at the train station for free. Singles and doubles both cost around 160kr £15.50; $27) p.p., but renting a three-, four-or five-bed apartment works out at around 100kr (£9.75; $17) p.p. per night.

IYHF HOSTELS

Standstigen, c/o Tyyne Isaksson, Brytar 9 (tel. 17195/12784). Open 13 June–31 Aug. 76kr (£7; $13) for IYHF members, non-members pay a 35kr (£3.40; $6) supplement.

CAMPING

Radhusbyn Ripan (tel. 13100). Just over a mile from the train station. 75kr (£7.25; $13) per tent and all occupants. Cabins sleeping four are available for around 560kr (£54; $95).

Stockholm (tel. code 08)

Tourist Offices

Stockholm Information Service, Box 7542, Kungstradgarden/ Hamgatan, 103 93 Stockholm (tel. 7892000). Open mid-June–late Aug., Mon.–Fri. 8.30 a.m.–6 p.m., weekends 8.30 a.m.–5 p.m.; rest of the year, Mon.–Fri. 9 a.m.–5 p.m., weekends 9 a.m.–2 p.m. In the Sverigehuset in the Kingstradgarden on Hamngatan. T-bana (underground): Kungstradgarden.

Hotellcentralen (tel. 240880). In Stockholm Central train station. Open June–Aug., daily 8 a.m.–9 p.m.; May and Sept., 9 a.m.–7 p.m., at other times 9 a.m.–5 p.m.

Accommodation Agencies

From June to August, finding somewhere reasonably cheap to stay in Stockholm can be difficult. If you have not booked ahead consider using the services of the Tourist Offices for a hostel bed. The charge for this service is 12kr (£1.15; $2). The Tourist Offices will also find you a hotel room for about 25kr (£2.40; $4.50), but hopefully you will not be reduced to this option as even the cheapest hotels are outside the budget-travel category.

Hotelljänst, Vasagatan 15–17 (tel. 104437/104457/104467). Open Mon.–Fri. 9 a.m.–5 p.m. Accommodation found free of charge, provided you stay at least two days. Close to Central Station.

Allrum, Wallingatan 34 (tel. 213789/213790). Open Mon.–Fri. 9 a.m.–5 p.m. Specializes in finding private rooms and apartments. No commission, but a 5-day minimum stay.

Caretaker, Vasagatan 15–17 (tel. 202545).

HOTELS

Many hotels lower their prices in summer. At other times, prices can be much higher.

Cheapest doubles around 350kr (£34; $59)

Residens, Kungsgatan 50 (tel. 233540). Price applies 23 June–6 Aug. only. Good location, about 8 minutes' walk from Central Station.

Cheapest doubles around 450kr (£43.50; $76)

Jerum, Studentbacken 21 (tel. 6635380). Price applies 1 June–31 Aug. only.
Pensionat Oden, Odengatan 38/2 (tel. 6124349).
Gustavsvikshemmet, Västmannagatan 15 (tel. 214450). Year round price. Ten-minute walk from Central Station.

Cheapest doubles around 500kr (£48.50; $85)

Gustav Wasa, Västmannagatan 61 (tel. 343801). Price applies year round. Ten-minute walk from Central Station. T-bana: Odenplan.
Sana, Upplandsgatan 6 (tel. 203982). Price applies 15 June–15 Aug. only. Near Central Station.

PRIVATE ROOMS

Book at either of the Tourist Offices, or through Allrum, Hotelljänst or Caretaker. Expect to pay from 150kr (£14.50; $25.50) for singles, and from 250kr (£24.20; $42.50) in doubles, plus commission if you book through either of the Tourist Offices.

IYHF HOSTELS

'Af Chapman', Skeppsholmen (tel. 6795015/103715). A fully rigged, late nineteenth-century sailing ship. Reserve about three months in advance, or turn up really early. 1 a.m. curfew. 90kr (£8.70; $15.50) for IYHF members; 125kr (£12; $21) for non-members.
Långholmen, Kronohäktet (tel. 6680510). No curfew. Same

prices as the 'Af Chapman'. On Långholmen Island. T-bana (metro): Hornstull.

Zinken, Zinkensväg 20 (tel. 6685786). No curfew. Same prices as the 'Af Chapman'. T-bana: Zinkensdamm, then right on to Hornsgatan. Follow the street to no. 103, then go left down the steps at the hostel sign.

Skeppsholmen, Västra Brobänken (tel. 6795017). In the Hantverkshuset, close to the 'Af Chapman'. Same prices as the 'Af Chapman'.

Botkyrka, Eriksbergsskolan, Tre Källors väg 8, Norsborg (tel. 0753–62105). Open 22 June–7 Aug.

Grävlingsberg, Drottningv. 15 (tel. 7478288). Open May–mid-Oct. 76kr (£7.35; $13) for IYHF members, 111kr (£10.75; $19) for non-members. 12½ miles from the centre. Bus 421 from Stockholm-Slussen train station.

HOSTELS

Sleep Inn, Döbelnsgatan 56 (tel. 6123118). Open mid June–Aug. 1 a.m. curfew. Mattresses on the floor 85kr (£8.20; $14.50). If you do not have a sleeping bag, sheets are available for hire at 20kr (£2; $3.50). Reception open 7 a.m.–1 p.m. and 4 p.m.–1 a.m. T-bana: Rådmandgatan, or bus 52 from Stockholm Central to the stop across from the Hard Rock Cafe. From the bus stop follow Surbrunnsgatan to the crossroads and head left.

Kista InterRail Points KFUM (YMCA), Jyllandsgatan 16 (tel. 7526456). Open 20 July–16 Aug. Midnight curfew. 75kr (£7.25; $13). T-bana line 11 dir: Akalla to Kista. Leave the station by the Sorogatan exit.

Frescati, Professorsslingan 13–15 (tel. 159434). Student accommodation converted into a hostel from June–Aug. Doubles 350kr (£34; $59). Singles around 250kr (£24; $42.50). T-bana: Universitetet.

Columbus Hotell-Vandrarhjem, Tjärhovsgatan 11 (tel. 6441717). No curfew and 24-hour reception. Two- to six-bedded rooms. 110kr (£11.60; $19). T-bana: Medborgarplatsen.

Gustaf af Klint, Stadsgårdskajen 153 (tel. 6404077). In an old navy ship. 24-hour reception. 120kr (£11.60; $19). T-bana: Odenplan.

CAMPING

Bredäng (tel. 977071). Open all year. Expensive. Six miles out on Lake Mälaren. T-bana: Bredang (line 13 or 15). Ten-minute walk signposted from the station.

Ångby (tel. 370420). Open all year. Also on Lake Mälaren. T-bana: Angbyplan (line 17 or 18).

Flaten (tel. 7730100). Open May–Sept. Bus 401 from Slussen.

Uppsala (tel. code 018)

Tourist Offices

Turistinformation Uppsala, St Persgatan 4 (tel. 117500). Open June–Aug., Mon.–Fri. 9 a.m.–7 p.m., Sat. 9 a.m.–2 p.m.; May and Sept., closes 6 p.m. Mon.–Fri.; rest of the year, Mon.–Fri. 10 a.m.–6 p.m., Sat. 10 a.m.–2 p.m. From the train station, head right along Kungsgatan until you see St Persgatan on the left.

Turistinformation Uppsala, Domkyrkoplan (tel. 161880). By the cathedral, in the castle complex. This office is open Saturday afternoons and Sunday when the other office is closed.

HOTELS

Cheapest doubles around 480kr (£46; $81).

Hotell Årsta Gård, Jordgubbsgatan 14 (tel. 253500). From the Town Hall (Stadshuset) on Kungsgatan, just to the right from the train station, take bus 19 (day) or bus 52 (evening). The bus stops a short distance from the hotel.

IYHF HOSTEL

Sunnersta herrgård, Sunnerstavägen 24 (tel. 324220). IYHF members pay 83kr (£8; $14), non-members 118kr (£11.40; $20). From Dragarbrunnsgatan, not far from St Persgatan, bus 20 as far as Herrgardsvagen. After 6.20p.m. and at weekends take bus 50 instead. Short walk from the bus stop.

HOSTEL

Uppsala KFUM-KFUK (YMCA-YWCA), Torbjörnsgatan 2 (tel. 156300/276635). Open 29 July–9 Sept. 75kr (£7.25; $13). Twenty minutes from the town centre. Bus 10 from Stora Torget. After 6.20p.m. bus 50 from Dragarbrunnsgatan.

CAMPING

Fyris (tel. 232333). Down by the river. Open all year. 70kr (£6.75; $12) for a tent and all occupants. Four-bedded cabins are available: 545kr (£53; $92) for the superior grade.

SWITZERLAND (Helvetia)

Despite being widely regarded as one of the most expensive countries in Europe, it is quite possible both to eat well, and to sleep cheaply in Switzerland. **Hotels** are likely to be outside your budget, and probably only to be considered in emergencies. The cheapest hotels cost 30–35SFr (£12.20–14.30; $21.50–25.00) in singles, 55SFr (£22.50; $39.50) in doubles, but such prices are rare. More typical for the lower end of the hotel market are charges of 40–45SFr (£16.30–18.40; $28.50–32.50) in singles, 65–75SFr (£26.50–30.60; $46.50–53.50) in doubles. In country areas, B&Bs or private rooms can be more reasonable but, in the main, your choice is between hostelling or camping. In some ways, this is quite fortuitous because both of these give you the opportunity of meeting other travellers, and also vastly increase your chances of meeting young Swiss holidaymakers. In a country where the cost of a night out can limit your visits to pubs and clubs, these opportunities to make friends can be invaluable.

There are about 100 **IYHF hostels,** the vast majority of which are open to members only. While hostels in the larger towns may admit non-members (not Lucerne), this tends to incur an extra charge of 7SFr (£2.80; $5). In the main towns, hostels are open all year, except perhaps for a couple of weeks around Christmas and the New Year. Elsewhere, hostels shut for differing periods, from a few weeks to several months, at no specific time of the year. In the larger cities a midnight or 1 a.m. curfew is normal in summer, but you can expect a 10 p.m. closing time at the others. Prices vary according to the grading of the hostel: the top-rated ones cost up to 18SFr (£7.30; $13), mid-range hostels up to 15SFr (£6.10; $11), and the lower grade up to 11SFr (£4.50; $8). Facilities in the lower-grade hostels tend to be quite basic, but are perfectly adequate. In the top-rated hostels you will have no access to kitchen facilities, though these are available in many of the lesser-rated establishments. Except in the main towns, where a three-night maximum stay operates in summer, there is no limit to how long you can stay at any hostel. During the summer it is advisable to reserve hostels in the larger towns, either by letter or by phoning ahead. If you find a hostel full, you might consider staying in one in a nearby town if you have a railcard, rather than having to pay for a room in a hotel.

There is no shortage of campsites; around 1200 in all. Unfortunately, there are three camping organizations, which makes advance planning slightly more complicated. Swiss campgrounds rank amongst the best Europe has to offer, being particularly clean and well run. Prices can vary quite substantially, starting at around 4SFr (£1.60; $3) per tent and per person, but rising to the 10SFr (£4.10; $7) per tent, 6SFr (£2.50; $4.50) charged at one site in Interlaken. On average a solo traveller might expect to pay around 8–10SFr (£3.20–4.10; $6–7) per night. One drawback to camping is that some of the large towns have no central or easily reached site, such as Berne. In other places, however, you may have a choice between two, or more, sites. In such cases, try to find out the prices of the different sites, as there can be quite a difference (one site in Interlaken works out at 7SFr (£2.80; $5) per night, more expensive for solo travellers than two other sites in town). Some campsites also offer dormitory accommodation. The local Tourist Office will advise you on the availability of such accommodation.

Tourist Offices will also have information on whether you can **camp rough** in the area. Most cantons allow freelance camping on uncultivated land, but the permission of the landowner is required on privately owned land. Camping in public places or along the roadside is expressly forbidden. Sleeping rough is not illegal, and is generally accepted in the parks of the larger towns. Whether you camp or sleep rough a good quality sleeping bag is recommended as it gets very cold at night, even in summer, and especially in the more mountainous areas. Hikers and climbers might wish to take

advantage of the chain of **mountain refuges** run by the Swiss
Alpine Club.

ADDRESSES

Swiss National Tourist Office	Swiss Centre, 1 New Coventry Street, London W1V 8EE (tel. 071 734 1921)
Hotels	Swiss Hotels Association, Montbijoustrasse 130, 3001 Bern (tel. 031–507111).
B&Bs	Bed and Breakfast Club, Case Postale 2231, 1110 Morges 2 (tel. 021–8023385).
Swiss YHA	Schweizerischer Bund für Jugendherbergen, Postfach, 3001 Bern (tel. 031–245503). List available from the Swiss National Tourist Office.
Camping	Schweizerischer Camping und Caravanning-Verband, Habsburgerstrasse 35, 6000 Luzern 4 (tel. 041–234822). Guides available from the Swiss National Tourist Office. They will tell you the latest price. Expect to pay around £4.
	Touring-Club der Schweiz Division Camping, 9 rue Pierre Fatio, 1211 Genève 3 (tel. 022--7371212).
	Verband Schweizerischer Campings, Im Sydefadeli 40, 8037 Zurich. (tel. 01–2725713). Guides available, as for Schweizerischer, above.
Mountain huts	Schweizer Alpine Club (SAC), Helvetiaplatz 4, 3005 Bern (tel. 031–433611).

Basle (Basel) (tel. code 061)

Tourist Offices

City-Information and Hotel Reservation. In Basel SBB train station (tel. 2713684). Open May–Sept., Mon.–Fri. 8.30 a.m.–7 p.m., Sat. 8.30 a.m.–12.30 p.m. and 1.30 p.m.–6 p.m., Sun. 10 a.m.–2 p.m.; Oct.–Nov. and Mar.–Apr., closed Sun.; Dec.–Feb., open only 8.30 a.m.–12.30 p.m. on Sat.

Basel Hotelreservation, Messeplatz 7, 4021 Basel (tel. 6917700). A short walk down Rosentalstrasse from Basel Bad Bhf. Open Mon.–Fri. 8 a.m.–noon and 1 p.m.–5 p.m.

Offizielles Verkehrsbüro Basel, Blumenrain 2/Schifflände, 4001 Basel (tel. 2615050). Open Mon.–Fri. 8.30 a.m.–6 p.m., Sat. 8.30 a.m.–1 p.m. A short walk along the Rhine from the Mittlere Rheinbrücke. Tram 8 from Basel SBB.

HOTELS

Steinenschanze, Steinengraben 69 (tel. 2724573). Students with ISIC pay 38SFr (£15.50; $27) for B&B in singles or doubles for the first three nights. Walk left on leaving Basel SBB, turn right downhill at Steinertorberg until it joins the main road on the right. Follow the main road to the hotel.

Cheapest doubles around 85SFr (£34.70; $61)

Hecht am Rhein, Rheingasse 8 (tel. 6810788). Tram 8 from in front of Basel SBB. Rheingasse is on the right, a short distance after the tram crosses the Rhine.

St Gotthard, Centralbahnstrasse 13 (tel. 2715250). The street running along the front of Basel SBB.

Cheapest doubles around 95SFr (£39; $68)

Steinenschanze, Steinengraben 69 (tel. 2724573). Normal price paid by non-students. See above for directions.

Klingental Garni, Klingental 20 (tel. 6816248). Same

directions as for the Hecht am Rhein, above, but look for
Untere Rheingasse on the right. This street leads into
Klingental.

Stadthof, Gerbergasse 84 (tel. 2618711). Walk left from Basel
SBB, then left on to Margarethenstrasse, where you can
catch tram 16 to Gerbergasse.

Bristol, Centralbahnstrasse 15 (tel. 2713822). The street
running along the front of Basel SBB.

Rochat VCH, Petersgraben 23 (tel. 2618140). Bus 37 from
Basel SBB.

If you are not keen on hostelling or camping and would prefer
a hotel room but cannot afford the prices quoted above consider
staying over the border in Germany or France where rooms
are cheaper. Local trains run from Basel Bad Bhf (tram 2 from
Basel SBB) to a number of small German towns where you
should be able to find a room for DM30 (£10.50; $18.50) per
person. Rheinfelden is a particularly pleasant place to stay. The
Rhine divides the town in two, one part German, the other
part Swiss. Regular trains from Bâle SNCF (adjoining Basel
SBB) make the 40-minute trip to Mulhouse in France. Trains
from Paris, Calais, Ostend, Luxembourg and Strasbourg stop
in Mulhouse before reaching Basle. The Office du Tourisme
in Mulhouse is at 9, avenue de Maréchal Foch (tel.
(0)89-456831). From the train station, head straight across the
river down av. Auguste Wicky, right at rue 17 Novembre, then
left into av. Foch. Mulhouse is well worth a visit in its own
right.

IYHF HOSTEL

St Alban Kirchrain 10 (tel. 2720572). Dorms 21SFr (£8.60;
$15). Singles and doubles 25SFr (£10.20; $18) per person.
1 a.m. curfew during the summer, midnight the rest of the
year. Five minutes' walk from the town centre, 15 minutes
from Basel SBB. From Centralbahnplatz in front of Basel
SBB follow Aeschengraben away from the station, turn
right along St Alban Anlage, left down St Alban-Talstrasse

by the St Alban Tor (an old city gatetower), then left again
at St Alban-Berg which leads into St Alban-Kirchrain. By
tram, take tram 1 from Centralbahnplatz to Aeschenplatz
(the first stop), then tram 3 to the stop by the St Alban-Tor.

CAMPING

Six miles out of Basle along Highway 18 is the town of Reinach,
which has the cheapest site in the area. 'Wahldort' (tel.
7116429). Open Mar.–Oct. However, those with a railpass
would probably be better making their way to the site in
Muttenz.

IYHF HOSTELS NEARBY

Route de Bâle 185, Delemont (tel. 066–222054). Regular
trains, half-hour trip.

Steinenweg 40, Lörrach (Germany) (tel. 07621–47040). Ten-
minute trip on the regular service from Basel Bad station.
Trains from Basel SBB heading for Germany stop at Basel
Bad. The station is about 15–20 minutes' walk across the
Rhine from the town centre.

37 rue de l'Illberg, Mulhouse (France) (tel. 89426328). Near
the university, 1½ miles from the train station. From the
town centre, bus 2 to Coteaux or bus 1 to Hericourt. For
further information on Mulhouse see the hotels section,
above.

Berne (Bern) (tel. code 031)

Tourist Offices

Verkehrsverein Bern, Offizielles Verkehrs- und
Kongressbüro, Im Bahnhof, Postfach, 3001, Bern (tel.
227676). Open in summer, Mon.–Sat. 8 a.m.–8.30 p.m.,
Sun. 9 a.m.–8.30 p.m.; in winter, Mon.–Sat. 8 a.m.–6.30
p.m., Sun. 10 a.m.–5 p.m. In the train station.

HOTELS

Cheapest doubles around 90SFr (£37; $65)

Bahnhof-Süd, Bümplizstrasse 189 (tel. 565111). Bus 13. Nearest train station Bern-Bümpliz.

Hospiz sur Heimat, Gerichtigkeitgasse 1 (tel. 220436). Bus 12, or a 15-minute walk from the train station through the Old Town. From Bahnhofplatz head down Spitalgasse, Marktgasse and Kramgasse into Gerichtigkeitgasse.

National, Hirschengraben 24 (tel. 251988). A 5-minute walk from the train station. Head right along Bubenbergplatz, then left on to Hirschengraben.

Marthahaus Garni, Wyttenbachstrasse 22a (tel. 424135). Bus 20, or a 15-minute walk from the train station. From Bahnhofplatz follow Bollwerk, cross the River Aare by the Lorrainebrücke, turn right down Schanzlihalde, then left.

Alpenblick, Kasernenstrasse 29 (tel. 424255). Tram 9.

GUESTHOUSES

More affordable than the city's hotels are guesthouses in neighbouring towns which you can book through the Tourist Office. Prices are normally in the range 26–35SFr (£10.20–14.30; $18–25) per person. If you have a railpass you can easily travel to any of the small towns nearby which have a train station. Otherwise you will have to take into account the cost of getting to the guesthouse.

IYHF HOSTEL

'Jugendhaus', Weihergasse 4 (tel. 226316). ??SFr (£ ; $) Midnight curfew. A 10–15-minute walk from the train station. From Bahnhofplatz cross Bubenbergplatz then go along Schauplatzgasse until you reach Bundesplatz with the Swiss Parliament. Look for the sign near the Parliament pointing down the steps to the hostel.

CAMPING

Eichholz, Strandweg 49 (tel. 542602). 3SFr (£1.20; $2) per tent, 4SFr (£1.60; $3) p.p. Also twin-bedded rooms 12SFr (£4.90; $8.50), plus 4SFr (£1.60; $3) p.p. Tram 9 to Wabern, the end of the line.

Eymatt (tel. 361007). Around 9,80SFr (£4; $7) for one person with a tent. From the train station take the postal bus dir. Bern-Hinterkappelen to Eymatt.

IYHF HOSTELS NEARBY

Rue de l'Hôpital 2, Fribourg (tel. 037–231916). 21SFr (£8.60; $15). From the train station follow Av. de la Gare from Pl. de la Gare, along rue de Ramont into Pl. Georges Python from which rue de l'Hôpital runs off to the left. Take the first right off Av. de la Gare for the Tourist Office on Grands Places (tel. 037-813175). Fribourg is an attractive and interesting old town on the train line between Geneva and Berne. Linked to Berne by frequent Inter-city trains, a half-hour trip.

Geneva (Genève) (tel. code 022)

Tourist Offices

Office du Tourisme de Genève, Casa Postale 440, 1211 Geneve 11. The administrative office. Contact this office for information or to book.

Office du Tourisme de Genève, Gare de Cornavin (tel. 7385200). In the main train station. Open June–Sept., Mon.–Fri. 8 a.m.–8 p.m., weekends 8 a.m.–6 p.m.; at other times, Mon.–Sat. 9 a.m.–6 p.m.

Arriving in Geneva

The main train station in Geneva is the Gare de Cornavin, which receives trains from Spain, Italy, Nice and Paris, as well

as from all over Switzerland. Coming from Chamonix or
Annecy (via La Roche-sur-Foron) you arrive at the Gare des
Eaux-Vives. There is no connecting train service between the
stations, but you can easily get between them by bus. The
simplest way to get from Eaux-Vives to Cornavin is to walk
down Av. de la Gare, turn right down Route de Chêne, then
right again at Av. Pictet-de-Rochemont which leads into Pl.
des Eaux-Vives, from which you can take bus 9 to Cornavin.
Alternatively, walk left a short distance up Route de Chêne
to the bus stop, then take bus 12 to Pl. Bel-Air, from which
you can take bus 1, 4 or 5 to Cornavin. If you fly into Cointrin
Airport there are trains about every six minutes to Cornavin
(railpasses valid).

Public Transport
The city's integrated transport network is operated by
Transports Publics Genèvois (TPG). Various types of ticket are
available to visitors. At every stop there is a vending machine
where you can buy a single ticket allowing you to use the
network within the city for one hour, changing as often as you
like, and even returning to your point of departure. A variation
on this is a cheaper ticket valid only for journeys up to three
stops, with which you can make a return journey within thirty
minutes. You can save yourself money by buying either of
these tickets in blocks of six or twelve (details of the nearest
sales point are posted at the stop). If you want to head out
into the country network (réseau régional) tickets are sold by
bus conductors. Day tickets for the complete network (town
and country) are available from the agents listed at public
transport stops. You can also buy 2-day and 3-day tickets, but
only from TPG at the Cornavin and (Rond-Point de) Rive bus
stations.

Basic Directions
From Pl. de Cornavin in front of the train station Rue des Alpes
runs from the left-hand end of the square down to Lake
Geneva (Lac Léman). At the right-hand end of the square rue
du Mont-Blanc leads to the Pont du Mont-Blanc which crosses

the River Rhône just as it flows out of the lake. Going straight
ahead you arrive at Pl. du Port from which Pl. Longmalle and
then rue de la Fontaine lead into the picturesque Pl. du Bourg-
de-Four, in the heart of the Old Town, beneath the cathedral.
The walk from Cornavin to Pl. du Bourg-de-Four takes 10–15
minutes. A slightly longer route to the same destination (15–20
minutes) is to follow rue de Cornavin from the right side of
Pl. de Cornavin, then go left down rue de Coutance to the
Rhône. Crossing the river you arrive at Pl. Bel-Air, from which
rue de la Monnaie leads into rue de la Cité, then Grand-Rue,
and finally rue de l'Hôtel de Ville, which runs downhill into
Pl. du Bourg-de-Four.

HOTELS

If you want a hotel room but cannot afford the prices quoted
below, those with railpasses can stay in the French town of
Bellegarde, a half-hour train trip from Cornavin.

Cheapest doubles around 60SFr (£24.50; $43)

1. Hôtel de la Cloche, rue de la Cloche 6 (tel. 7329481).
   About 10 minutes' walk from Cornavin. Left off rue des
   Alpes along rue Philippe-Plantamour at place des Alpes,
   then right at rue Cloche.
2. Pension de la Servette, rue de la Prairie 31 (tel. 7340230).
   A 10-minute walk from Gare de Cornavin. From the rear
   exit head left, diagonally right at rue de la Pepinière,
   across rue de la Servette and into rue de Lyon, then first
   right up rue de Jura into rue de la Prairie. Bus 6 or 26
   from Cornavin run along rue Voltaire, stopping at one
   end of rue de la Prairie, while buses 3, 10 and 15 run
   along rue de la Servette passing the other end of the
   street.

Cheapest doubles around 70SFr (£28.60; $50)

3. Hôtel Pâquis Fleuri, rue des Pâquis 23 (tel. 7313453).
   About 8 minutes' walk from Cornavin, left off rue des

Alpes at place des Alpes. Bus 1 dir: Wilson from Cornavin runs along the street.

4. Hôtel Saint Victor, Rue Lefort 1 (tel. 461718). Bus 8 from Cornavin to Florissant then a short walk, back to Bd des Tranchées, from which any of the small streets on the opposite side of the road will take you into rue Lefort.

5. Centre Saint Boniface, av. du Mail 14 (tel. 3218844). Bus 1, 4, or 44 from Cornavin to place du Cirque, or a 15-minute walk. Right from Cornavin along bd James-Fazy to the Rhône. Cross the river and go straight on, along bd Georges-Favon to place du Cirque, then right on the other side of the square down Av. du Mail.

Cheapest doubles around 75SFr (£30.60; $54)

6. Hôtel Le Prince, rue des Voisins 16 (tel. 298544/298545). Triples available. The street crosses bd du Pont d'Arve. Bus 1 from Cornavin runs along bd du Pont d'Arve.

7. Hôtel Luserna, Av. Luserna 12 (tel. 441600/3441600). A 20-minute walk from Cornavin. Right down rue de la Servette (see 2), left at Av. Wendt, right at Av. Luserna. Buses 3, 10 and 15 from Cornavin stop at Servette Ecole, just before Av. Wendt.

Cheapest doubles around 80SFr (£32.70; $57)

8. Hôtel Beau Site, place du Cirque 3 (tel. 281008/3281008). Triples around 95SFr (£39; $68), quads around 110SFr (£45; $79). A 15-minute walk from Cornavin or a direct bus (see 5).

9. Hôtel du Lac, rue des Eaux-Vives 15 (tel. 7354580). Slightly cheaper per person in triples. Bus 9 from Cornavin to Pl. des Eaux-Vives, then a short walk along rue des Eaux-Vives. A 15–20-minute walk from Cornavin. Left along Quai Général Guisan after crossing the Pont du Mont-Blanc and straight on along rue Versonnex into Pl. des Eaux-Vives.

10. Rio, place Isaac Mercier 1 (tel. 7323264). Around 90SFr

(£36.80; $64) for triples. A few minutes' walk from Cornavin, right along bd James Fazy into Pl. Isaac Mercier.

Cheapest doubles around 85SFr (£34.70; $61)

11. Pension Ravier, rue Argand 2 (tel. 7383773). Five minutes from Cornavin. Right along bd James Fazy, then left.
12. Hôtel Saint Gervais, rue des Corps-Saints 20 (tel. 7324572). Five minutes from Cornavin. The street is a continuation of rue Cornavin.
13. Hôtel des Tourelles, bd James Fazy 2 (tel. 7324423). Around 100SFr (£41; $72) for triples. About 100m to the right of Cornavin.

IYHF HOSTEL

14. Nouvelle Auberge de Jeunesse, rue Rothschild 28–30 (tel. 7326260). Midnight curfew in summer, 11 p.m. at other times. IYHF members pay 18SFr (£7.50; $13) in dorms. 70SFr (£28.60; $50) for doubles with shower and WC. Overnight price includes breakfast. About 8 minutes' walk from Cornavin, left along rue de Lausanne, then right.

HOSTELS/FOYERS/STUDENT ACCOMMODATION

15. Armée du Salut, Ch. Galiffe 4 (tel. 449121). 11 p.m. curfew. B&B in dorms 12SFr (£4.90; $8.50). A 10-minute walk from Cornavin. Left from the rear exit, following the tracks all the way, across rue de la Servette and along rue de Malatrex until you see ch. Galiffe on the right.
16. Armée du Salut, rue de l'Industrie 14 (tel. 7336438). Women only. Curfew 10.30/11.00 p.m. Dorms 14–17SFr (£5.70–7.00; $10–12) without breakfast. Just over 5 minutes' walk from Cornavin. Left from the rear exit,

right up rue des Grottes until you see rue de l'Industrie on the left.

17. Home St-Pierre, cour St-Pierre 4 (tel. 3103707). Women only. No curfew. Dorms start at around 14SFr (£5.70; $10), triples around 50SFr (£20.50; $36), doubles around 40SFr (£16.30; $29) and singles around 25SFr (£10.20; $18). Breakfast included. Excellent location by the Cathedral. Just over 15 minutes' walk from Cornavin. From Grand-Rue take rue du Puits St-Pierre, then right towards the cathedral. From rue de l'Hôtel-de-Ville take Pl. de la Taconnerie. Bus 3 or 5 from Cornavin to Croix Rouge, then walk back to Pl. du Bourg-de-Four.

18. Cité Universitaire, av. Miremont 46 (tel. 3462355). Curfew 10 p.m. Dorms 15SFr (£6.15; $11), doubles start around 45SFr (£18.40; $32), singles around 31SFr (£12.70; $22) without breakfast. From place de 22 Cantons by Cornavin station take bus 3 to the Crêts de Champel terminus.

19. Centre St-Boniface, Av. du Mail 14 (tel. 3218844). Dorms 18–27SFr (£7.35–11.00; $13.00–19.50) for B&B. See 5.

20. Maison International Etudiants, rue Daniel-Colladon 2 (tel. 292034). B&B in singles 29–35SFr (£11.80–14.30; $21–25). Near the Reformation Monument. Bus 5 from Cornavin to Croix Rouge. A 15–20-minute walk from Cornavin. From Pl. du Bourg-de-Four follow rue St-Léger, first right, then first left.

21. Bureau logements université, rue de Candolle 4 (tel. 7057720). Singles 29–35SFr (£11.80–14.30; $21–25) with breakfast. Three-day minimum stay. See 18.

22. Evangelische Stadtmission, rue Bergalonne 7 (tel. 3212611). Curfew 11 p.m. B&B in dorms 22–25SFr (£9.00–10.20; $16–18). Triples 85–100SFr (£34.70–40.80; $61–72), doubles 70–80SFr (£28.50–32.70; $50–57), singles 42–50SFr (£17.20–20.50; $30–36). Bus 1, 4 or 44 from Cornavin to to Ecole-Médecine (rue Bergalonne is to the rear of the Musée d'Ethnographie), or a 15–20-minute walk. Rue Bergalonne runs right off av. du Mail (see 5).

23. Centre Masaryk, av. de la Paix 11 (tel. 7330772). 11 p.m. curfew. B&B in dorms 25SFr (£10.20; $18). Triples 90SFr (£36.75; $65), doubles 65SFr (£26.50; $47). Singles 38SFr (£15.50; $27). Near the Palace of the United Nations. Bus 5 or 8 from Cornavin to the Nations terminus, or a 20-minute walk. From the rear exit of Cornavin head to the right and follow rue de Montbrilliant to av. de France and place Nations. Go right along av. de la Paix from Pl. des Nations.

24. Foyer l'Accueil, rue Alcide-Jentzer 8 (tel. 3209277). 55SFr (£22.50; $40) for doubles, 33SFr (£13.50; $23.50) for singles with breakfast. Bus 1 por 5 to Hôpital. Walk back onto bd de la Cluse, head left, then left again at rue Alcide-Jentzer by the maternity clinic.

25. Foyer St-Justin, rue du Prieuré 15–17 (tel. 7311135). Singles 30–43SFr (£12.25–17.50; $21.50–31.00) without breakfast. A 5-minute walk from Cornavin, left along rue de Lausanne, then right.

26. Centre Universitaire Zofingien, rue des Voisins 6 (tel. 291140/295113). With breakfast. Triples 95SFr (£39; $68), in doubles 78SFr (£31.80; $56), in singles 51SFr (£20.80; $36.50). During the university year only.

27. Centre Universitaire Protestant, Av. du Mail 2 (tel. 296245). Singles 43SFr (£17.50; $31) without breakfast. See 5.

28. Hôtel le Grenil, av. Ste-Clotilde 7 (tel. 3283055). B&B in dorms 27SFr (£11; $19.50). Prices in triples and doubles are higher than in the hotels listed above.

29. Residence Universitaire Internationale, rue des Pâquis 63 (tel. 7325606). Singles 30–40SFr (£12.25–16.25; $21.50–28.50), doubles 42–52SFr (£17–21; $30–37). See 3.

30. YMCA Geneva, 9 av. Ste-Clotide (tel. 3216313).

CAMPING

Sylvabelle, Chemin de Conches 10 (tel. 3470603). Two miles out, the closest site to the city centre. Bus 8 from Cornavin dir: Vernier

Pointe-à-la-Bise (tel. 7521296). Open Apr.–Sept. About 5 miles out from the centre, close to Lake Geneva. From Cornavin take bus 9 to Rive, then change to bus E.

D'Hermance, Chemin des Glerrêts (tel. 7511483). Open Apr.–Sept. About 10 miles out from the city centre, close to Lake Geneva. Bus 9 from Cornavin to Rive, then take bus E to the terminus.

Lausanne (tel. code 021)

Tourist Offices

Office du Tourisme et des Congrès, av. de Rhodania 2, Case postale 248, 1000 Lausanne 6 (tel. 6177321, or tel. 6171427 for general tourist information). Open Easter–mid-Oct., Mon.–Sat. 8 a.m.–7 p.m., Sun. 9 a.m.–noon and 1 p.m.–6 p.m. At other times, closes Mon.–Fri. at 6 p.m., open Sat. 8.30 a.m.–noon and 1–5 p.m., closed Sunday. In Ouchy. From the train station take the metro to the end of the line. The office is about 100m from the metro stop.

Office du Tourisme et des Congrès. Branch office in the train station.

HOTELS

Cheapest doubles around 70SFr (£28.60; $50)

Hôtel du Marché, Pré-du-Marché 42 (tel. 379900). Near Pl. de la Riponne.

Auberge de Rivaz (tel. 9461055). In Rivaz, 8 miles out of Lausanne.

Cheapest doubles around 90SFr (£37; $65)

Hôtel d'Angleterre, Ouchy (tel. 6172111). Lakeside location. Take the metro from the train station to the last stop.

Hôtel Près-Lac, Av. Général Guisan 16 (tel. 284901).

IYHF HOSTEL

Chemin du Muguet 1, Lausanne-Ouchy (tel. 265782). 18SFr (£7.35; $13). Take bus 1 dir: La Maladière to the La Batelière stop, from which the hostel is signposted.

HOSTELS/DORMITORIES

Prés de Vidy, Chemin du Bois de Vaux (tel. 242479). Further out of town on the same bus route as the IYHF hostel.
Foyer la Croisée, av. Marc Dufour 15 (tel. 204231).

CAMPING

Camping de Vidy-Lausanne, Chemin du Camping 3 (tel. 242031). High quality lakeside site. 4–8SFr (£1.60–3.20; $3–6) per tent, 6 SFr (£2.50; $4.50) p.p.

Lucerne (Luzern) (tel. code 041)

Tourist Offices

Tourist Information, Frankenstrasse 1 (tel. 517171). Open Mon.–Fri. 8 a.m.–6 p.m., Sat. and public holidays 9 a.m.–5 p.m. Leaving the train station head left down the side of the station, Frankenstrasse is to the right off Zentralstrasse.
Hotel Information (tel. 235244). In the train station.

HOTELS

Cheapest doubles around 75SFr (£30.60; $54)

Hotel Schlüssel, Franziskanerplatz 12 (tel. 231061). Bus 2, 9 or 18, or a ten minutes walk from the train station. Head left along the River Reuss, past the Jesuit Church, then left into Franziskanerplatz.

Doubles around 78SFr (£31.80; $56)

Hotel Linde, Metzgerrainie 3 (tel. 513193). Singles around 40SFr (£16.25; $28.50). Excellent location in the Old Town, a 10–15-minute walk from the train station. Head left along the waterfront, then cross the bridge after the Jesuit Church into Kramgasse. Metzgerrainie is on the right.

Cheapest doubles around 88SFr (£36; $63)

SSR Touristenhotel, St Karliquai 12 (tel. 512474). Bus 2, 9 or 18, or a 15-minute walk from the train station. From Kramgasse (directions see Hotel Linde, above) go left through Muhlenplatz and back towards the River Reuss and St Karliquai.

Hotel Villa Maria, Haldenstrasse 36 (tel. 312119). Overlooks the lake. A 25-minute walk from the train station (follow the directions for Camping Lido, below), or take bus 2 to the stop near the Hotel Europe.

DORMS

Available at the SSR Touristenhotel, but more expensive than those of the IYHF hostel. See also Camping Lido.

IYHF HOSTEL

Am Rotsee, Sedelstrasse 12 (tel. 368800). 23SFr (£9.40; $16.50). Midnight curfew. Not central. A 30-minute walk from the train station. Bus 18 to Goplismoos/Friedental leaves you with a couple of minutes' walk. Last bus 7.30 p.m. The more frequent bus 1 to Schlossberg leaves you a 10-minute walk down Friedentalstrasse. Reception opens 4 p.m., and 1½ hour queues are not uncommon during the summer, with no guarantee of getting in. If possible arrive early, fill in a form and leave it with your IYHF card in the box provided, then go back when the queue is likely to have disappeared, or at any time before reception closes at 10 p.m.

CAMPING

Lido, Lidostrasse (tel. 312146). Near the beach and the lake. Thirty-minute walk from the train station, over the Seebrücke, then right along the lakeside. Bus 2 to Verkehrshaus. 2.50SFr (£1; $2) per tent, 5SFr (£2.10; $4) p.p. Also dorms 14SFr (£5.85; $11). Cheapest in town. Site open Apr.–Oct.

Steinbachried (tel. 473558). Bus 20 for a 20-minute trip to Horw Rank. 4SFr (£1.65; $3.25) per tent, 5SFr (£2.10; $4) p.p. Open Apr.–Sept.

IYHF HOSTELS NEARBY

Allmendstrasse 8, Sportstadion 'Herti', Zug (tel. 042–215354). Frequent trains, 30-minute trip.

Zürich (tel. code 01)

Tourist Office

Offizielles Verkehrsbüro Zürich, Bahnhofplatz 15, 8023 Zürich (Hauptbahnhof) (tel. 2111131 for hotel reservations; tel. 2114000 for general information). Open Mar.–Oct., Mon.–Fri. 8 a.m.–10 p.m., weekends 9 a.m.–6 p.m.; Nov.–Feb., closes 8 p.m. Mon.–Thurs., closed at weekends.

Trouble Spots

In recent years, the city authorities operated a controversial needle exchange in one of the city's parks. It has been claimed that this attracted drug users from all over the country (and even from Germany) to the city. In late 1991, the authorities halted the scheme and closed the park. The result was that addicts began to gather on the city's streets, particularly around the main train station. Although there have been no reports of violence around the station at the time of writing, the sight

itself is harrowing (particularly as drugs are injected quite
openly), and you are likely to be pestered for money.

HOTELS

Doubles around 56SFr (£23; $40)

Hinterer Sternen, Freieckgasse 7 (tel. 2513268). A 10-minute
walk from Zürich Hbf. Cross the river Limmat, right along
Limmatquai, then up Ramistrasse at Bellevueplatz. Or take
tram 4, 5, 8 or 15 to Bellevueplatz.

Cheapest doubles around 65SFr (£26.50; $46.50)

Justinusheim, Freudenbergstrasse 146 (tel. 3613806). Singles
around 33SFr (£13.50; $23.50). Tram 9 or 10 to the junction
of Winterthurerstrasse and Langensteinerstrasse, then bus
39 to Freudenbergerstrasse. You can also catch bus 39 from
the terminus of trams 5 and 6 near the zoo, though this
is a longer journey.

Cheapest doubles around 75SFr (£30.60; $53.50)

Dufour, Seefeldstrasse 188 (tel. 553655). Trams 2 and 4 pass
the hotel.
Regina, Hohlstrasse 18 (tel. 2426550). A 10-minute walk from
Zürich Hbf. Diagonally right across Bahnhofplatz, along
Gessnerallee, right over the Gessnerbrücke, left along the
River Sihl, then right down Zeughausstrasse.

Cheapest doubles around 85SFr (£34.70; $61)

Italia, Zeughausstrasse 61 (tel. 2410555). A 10-minute walk
from Zürich Hbf. See Hotel Regina above.

Cheapest doubles around 90SFr (£36.75; $65)

St Georges, Weberstrasse 11 (tel. 211144). Just over 10
minutes' walk from Zürich Hbf. Diagonally right across
Bahnhofplatz, along Gessnerallee, right over

Gessnerbrücke then left along the River Sihl until you see
Webergasse on the right after the second bridge.

Splendid, Rosengasse 5 (tel. 2525850). A 5-minute walk from
Zürich Hbf. Cross the River Limmat by the
Bahnhofsbrücke, then right along the Limmatquai until
you see Rosengasse on the left after Mühlegasse.

Seefeld, Seehofstrasse 11 (tel. 2522570). Tram 4 along
Seefeldstrasse until you see Seehofstrasse on the right after
the tram turns off Ramistrasse along Theaterstrasse, or a
15 minute walk from Zürich Hbf. Follow the directions for
Hotel Hinterer Stern to Ramistrasse, then turn right along
Theaterstrasse and keep going until you see Seehofstrasse
on the right.

Vorderer Sternen, Bellevueplatz (tel. 2514949). A 10-minute
walk from Zürich Hbf. See Hotel Hinterer Sternen for
directions.

IYHF HOSTEL

Mutschellenstrasse 114, Zürich-Wollishofen (tel. 4823544). 1
a.m. curfew. Tram 7 to Morgental, then a well-signposted
5-minute walk. There is a local train station, Zürich-
Wollishofen, if you have a railpass and want to save some
money on transport.

DORMITORY ACCOMMODATION

Hotel Martahaus, Zähringerstrasse 36 (tel. 2514550). Six-bed
dorms 28SFr (£11.50; $20). Doubles around 95SFr (£39;
$68). A 5-minute walk from Zürich Hbf. Cross the River
Limmat by Bahnhofsbrücke. Limmatquai runs away to the
right along the river. Zähringerstrasse runs parallel to the
Limmatquai, two streets back from the river.

Foyer Hottingen, Hottingerstrasse 31 (tel. 2619315). Dorms
28SFr (£11.50; $20). Doubles around 95SFr (£39; $68). This
one-star hotel run by nuns is open to women, married
couples and families only. Tram 3 to Hottingerplatz from
Bahnhofplatz.

CAMPING

'Seebucht', Seestrasse 559, Zürich-Wollishofen (tel. 4821612). Excellent site on the Zürichsee. Local train to Zürich-Wollishofen, then a 10-minute walk.

IYHF HOSTELS NEARBY

Kanalstrasse 7, Baden (tel. 056–261796). Open 16 Mar.–23 Dec. Frequent trains, a half-hour trip.

Allmendstrasse 8, Sportstadion 'Herti', Zug (tel. 042–215354). Frequent trains, a 45-minute trip.

Cevi-Zentrum, Stockerstrasse 18, Horgen (tel. 01-7258934/ 7253104). Open 27 July–30 Aug. 23SFr (£9.40; $16.50). About 500m from the train station in Horgen. Trains run thrice hourly from Zürich Hbf.

TURKEY (Türkiye)

As a rule, budget travellers will seldom encounter any difficulty finding suitably priced accommodation in Turkey, with the notable exceptions of the coastal resorts and the capital at the height of the summer season. While Ankara is not really a tourist town (and is correspondingly short on budget accommodation), it seems to attract many travellers on the basis of its status as the national capital. Otherwise, it is usually quite simple to find a place to stay for about £1.75–3.00 ($3.00–5.50) per person along the Aegean coast, £1.50–3.00 ($2.50–5.50) along its Mediterranean counterpart, or from £1.25–2.75 ($2–5) per person in the east of the country.

In any town with a reasonable tourist trade you will have the option of staying at one of the **hotels** which are registered with the Ministry of Tourism. These hotels are rated from one star up to five stars. Standards of cleanliness and comfort are rigorously enforced by the authorities, so it is highly unlikely that you will ever have cause for complaint if you stay at one of these hotels. In hotels registered with the Ministry of Tourism you can expect to pay from £10–20 ($17.50–35.00) for a double in a one-star hotel, rising to £12–24 ($21–42) in Istanbul. The cost of a double in a two-star hotel starts around £17 ($30), again being slightly higher in Istanbul.

The quality of hotels licensed by the local authorities varies widely. As is the case in most countries, there are always a few hotels where standards of cleanliness can leave a lot to be desired (most often in the larger cities), so make a point of checking rooms before agreeing to take them. If you are not satisfied, simply take your custom elsewhere. The vast majority of locally licensed hotels are perfectly acceptable, with some almost on a par with one-star hotels, so you should have no trouble finding acceptable and similarly priced accommodation nearby. Locally licensed hotels are usually a good bit cheaper than those registered with the Ministry of Tourism; expect to pay in the region of £2.80–4.60 ($5–8) per person in singles or doubles.

During the peak season, it is not unusual for hotel touts to approach travellers at bus and train stations, and at ferry terminals. Where there are several touts trying to attract custom, there is a fair chance of bargaining them down from their initial asking price. Nor is there anything to be lost by haggling with hoteliers if the price seems to be on the high side. In the off-season, it is quite normal for hoteliers to drop their prices by up to 25 per cent.

An excellent alternative to hotel accommodation is a **guesthouse**, known as a *pansiyon*, or in ski resorts as an *oberj*. Guesthouses are plentiful throughout the country, often small family-run establishments providing good-value meals. A few guesthouses are registered with the Ministry of Tourism. The standard of accommodation in these establishments is uniformly high. Doubles cost £8–20 ($14–35), depending on the facilities available. At other guesthouses you can expect to pay from £1.50–4.00 ($2.50–7.00) per person in singles or doubles. As with locally licensed hotels, check rooms at unregistered guesthouses before making a firm acceptance, just in case you have been unlucky enough to come across a rogue establishment where standards are less than acceptable. Another cheap accommodation option are private rooms, though these are much less common than guesthouses. Look out for the sign 'Oda Var' indicating rooms are available (sometimes also advertised in German: 'Zimmer frei'). Prices for private rooms are unlikely to be above £2.50 ($4.50) per person.

There are 45 **youth hostels** in Turkey, only one of which is affiliated to the IYHF. Some student residences also serve as hostels (mainly during the months July and August, though some operate all year round). Normally a student ID card guarantees entrance to a hostel, but it makes sense to have an IYHF card as, for some strange reason, even some of the non-affiliated hostels sometimes ask for an IYHF card.

Camping is popular in Turkey, and the number of sites is growing annually. Campsites are generally open from April/May to October. Although facilities are still on the whole exceptionally basic, you nevertheless get reasonable value for money as prices are normally around £1 ($1.75) per person (tent included) for an overnight stay. At the network of BP mocamps, prices are around £2 ($3.50) per person per night, again including tent (a 20 per cent surcharge is added in July and August). Some campers have cast doubt upon whether BP mocamps offer good value for money. In truth, you might wonder how BP mocamps can justify charging twice as much as most other sites in Turkey, but on a European scale it is fair to say that they do offer reasonable value for money. Unless you are going to be travelling widely outside the main towns, it may not be worth taking a tent: the sites serving the cities can be inconveniently located far out of town, and not always well served by public transport. In the cities, your best bet for finding a convenient place to pitch a tent can be to make enquiries as to any hotels which allow camping in their garden for a small charge.

Freelance camping is not illegal, but it is very rarely practised, except in the remoter areas. In the east, where official sites are few and far between, it is best to choose a location, and then ask the permission of the locals to pitch your tent. If nothing else, this is likely to prevent any possible misfortune arising out of camping in a military area. Anyone (girls especially) worried about camping out in the country but who, for any reason, get stranded outside the towns, should note that petrol stations will rarely object to you pitching your tent close to the station, so affording you that little extra security. If you set up a tent in a town you can expect to be disturbed by the police. Their concern is more likely to be for your safety than anything else. Street crime and petty theft are remarkably low in Turkey, but it is inviting trouble to camp or **sleep rough** in the larger towns, Istanbul especially. It is safe to say that of those travellers who do encounter serious trouble in Turkey, the vast majority have been sleeping rough or camping rough in the cities.

ADDRESSES

Turkish Information
Office

Gençtur

First Floor 170/173 Piccadilly, London
W1V 9DB (tel. 071 734681)

Yerebatan Caddesi 15, 3 Sultanahmet,
33410 Istanbul (tel. 01 5136150/
5136151). Information on youth and
student travel and accommodation
possibilities.

Ankara (tel. code 04)

Tourist Offices

The administrative office is at Gazi Mustafa Kemal Bulvar. 121,
Demirtepe. Contact this office if you want information on the
city in advance. The main information office (tel.
2301911/2317380), Gazi Mustafa Kemal Bulvarı 33 is by the
Maltepe mosque. Open in peak season, Mon.–Fri. 8.30
a.m.–6.30 p.m., weekends 8.30 a.m.–5.00 p.m.; at other times,
Mon.–Fri. 8.30 a.m.–6.30 p.m. only. Two offices operate in
the city centre: one at Istanbul Caddesi 4 (tel. 3112247/3106818),
by the Cumhriyet Museum in Ulus (same hours as the main
office), the other at the Atatürk Cultural Centre off Kâzim
Karabekir Caddesi. Another branch office is located at the
international terminal of Esenboğa airport.

Basic Directions

Ankara's train station is about 10 minutes' walk from Ulus
Meydanı in the centre of the old town, straight down
Cumhuriyet Bulvarı opposite the station. About 750m down
the street is the Cumhuriyet Museum, with one of the branches
of the Tourist Office nearby. Three important streets lead out
of Ulus Meydanı. Left from the end of Cumhuriyet Bulvarı is
Çankırı Cad. Hisarparki Cad. is across the square and to the
right, while a sharp right takes you onto Atatürk Bulvarı.

The bus station is about 400m from the train station, left along
Hipodrum Cad. near the junction with Kâzim Karabakir Cad.
Turning right up the latter, after a short distance you will see
the Atatürk Cultural Centre on your left; turning right Kâzim
Karabakir Cad. leads under the rail lines to Tandob Meydanı,
from which Gazi Mustafa Kemal Bulvarı runs off to the left.
Gazi Mustafa Kemal Bulvarı can also be reached by going
straight ahead from the rear exit of the train station. Whichever
of these two ways you arrive on Gazi Mustafa Kemal Bulvarı,
head left along the street to reach the Maltepe Mosque and
the main Tourist Information Office.

Talat Paşa Cad. heads right from the train station, towards

the Samanpazari and Dörtyol districts. About 800m along the
street is the crossroads with Atatürk Bulvarı. Going right
Atatürk Bulvarı leads down into the modern part of the city,
passing thorugh the Kizilay district (around the junction with
Gazi Mustafa Kemal Bulvarı), going right you can follow
Atatürk Bulvarı up past the Opera and the post office to Ulus
Meydanı. A further 200m along Talat Paşa Cad. on the left, is
the junction with Denizciler Cad., which runs into Anafartalar
Cad., the latter continuing on its junction with Hisarparki Cad.,
a short walk from Ulus Meydanı. Another 200m along Talat
Paş Cad. you can turn left up Hasircilar Sok and follow the
street as it bends round, crossing Denizciler Cad. and passing
the Gazi Lisesi before joining Atatürk Bulvarı near the Opera.
A short distance beyond the junction of Talat Paş Cad. and
Hasircilar Cad. you can turn left to reach the junction of
Anafartalar Cad. and Ulucanlar Cad.

Finding Accommodation
The largest concentration of cheap hotels are located in the
streets off Atatürk Bulvarı between the Opera and Ulus
Meydanı. Hotels in this area have the advantage of being
centrally located, and close to both the bus and train stations.
There are also plenty of cheap hotels along this stretch of
Atatürk Bulvarı, but street noise is a major problem afflicting
these establishments. Although less conveniently located for
the centre of the old city (but still within easy walking distance),
Gazi Mustafa Kemal Bulvarı and the Maltepe district contain
a good supply of cheap hotels. The Kizilay district (1½ miles
from the centre) is also well supplied with cheap and
moderately priced hotels, the standards of which generally
surpass similarly priced accommodation elsewhere.

HOTELS

Locally licensed hotels

Pinar, Hisar Cad. 14 (tel. 3118951). Doubles with shower
£4.60 ($8), singles £2.30 ($4). Ulus district.

Babil, Gazi Mustafa Kemal Bulvarı 66 (tel. 2317877). Singles £5.20 ($9), doubles £9.20 ($16).

Buhara, Sanayi Cad. 13 (tel. 3245245/3245246). Singles £4.60 ($8), doubles with bath £9.20 ($16). Good value for money. Ulus district.

Sıpahı, Itfaiye Meydanı, Kosova Sok 1 (tel. 3240235/3240236). Singles £4 ($7), doubles £5.20 ($9). Simple, clean rooms. Recommended. Across from the Opera, take the road leading off Atatürk Bulvarı to the junction of Derman Sok and Kosova Sok.

Hisar, Hisarparki Cad. 6 (tel. 311988/3108128). Singles £3.40 ($6), doubles £6.30 ($11). Particularly good. Ulus district.

Zümrüt Palas, Posta Cad. 16 (tel. 3103210/3103211). Singles £4 ($7), singles with bath £5.70 ($10), doubles £6.30 ($11), doubles with bath £7.40 ($13). One of the best hotels listed here.

Çoruh, Denizciler Cad. 47 (tel. 3124113/3124114). Singles £4 ($7), doubles with shower £8 ($14).

Suna, Çankırı Cad., Soğukkuyu Sok 6 (tel. 3115465). Singles with bath £5.70 ($10), doubles with bath £8 ($14). Ulus district. off Çankırı Cad. near the Olimpiyat Otel.

Avrupa, Posta Cad., Susam Sok 9 (tel. 3114300). Singles and doubles £2.80 ($5) per person. Ulus district.

Devran, Opera (Itfaiye) Meydanı (tel. 3110485/3110486). Singles £5.70 ($10), doubles £7.40 ($13). All rooms have baths. Small rooms, but clean and comfortable. Recommended.

Erden, Itfaiye Meydanı (tel. 3243191/3243192). Singles and doubles £4.30 ($7.50) per person, singles and doubles with baths £5.20 ($9) per person.

Kösk, Denizciler Cad. 56 (tel. 3245228/3245229). Singles with bath £5.20 ($9), doubles with bath £8 ($14).

Mithat, Itfaiye Meydanı, Tavus Sok 2 (tel. 3115410/3115651). Singles with bath £5.70 ($10), doubles with bath £9.70 ($17).

Oba, Posta Cad. 9 (tel. 3124128/3124129). Singles with bath £5.70 ($10), doubles with bath £8 ($14). Ulus district.

Santral Palas, Denizciler Cad., Dibek Sok (tel.

3125577/3126588). £4.60 ($8) per person in singles and doubles with bath.

Uğur Palas, Itfaiye Meydanı Sanayi Cad. 54.

Ertan, Selanik Cad. 70 (tel. 1184038). Singles £5.70 ($10), doubles £9.20 ($16). Kizilay district, at the junction of Atatürk Bulvarı and Gazi Mustafa Kemal Bulvarı, follow the street opposite Gazi Mustafa Kemal until it is crossed by Selanik Cad.

Turan Palas, Çankırı Cad., Beşik Sok 3 (tel. 3125225/3125226). Singles £3.40 ($6), doubles £6.30 ($11). Ulus district.

Savaş, Altan Sok 3 (tel. 3242113). Singles £4 ($7), doubles £6.90 ($12). Off Anafartalar Cad.

Beyrut Palas, Denizciler Cad. 11 (tel. 3108407). Singles £4.60 ($8), singles with bath £5.20 ($9), doubles £6.90 ($12), doubles with bath £9.20 ($16).

Esen Palas, Hükümet Cad. 22 (tel. 3112747). Singles £3.40 ($6), doubles £6.60 ($11.50). Ulus district. Near the Column of Julian (Jülyanüs Sütunu), left off Hisarparki Cad., a short walk from Ulus Meydanı.

Pamukkale, Hükümet Cad. 18 (tel. 3117812). Singles £3.40 ($6), doubles £6.60 ($11.50). Ulus district. See the Esen Palas above, for directions.

Tarabya, Itfaiye Meydanı, Kosova Sok 9 (tel. 3119552). Singles £2.80 ($5), doubles £4.60 ($8). Dull, but acceptable rooms. See the Sıpahı, above, for directions.

Ucler, Itfaiye Meydanı, Kosova Sok 7. Singles £2.80 ($5), doubles £4.60 ($8). See the Sıpahı, above, for directions.

One-star hotels. Expect to pay from £12 ($21) in doubles

Anit, Gazi Mustafa Bulvarı 111 (tel. 2292144/2317880). Singles £14.30 ($25), doubles £20 ($35). All rooms with baths

As, Rüzgarli Sok 4 (tel. 3103998/3103999). Singles £8.60 ($15), singles with bath £11.40 ($20), doubles £12.60 ($22), doubles with bath £14.30 ($25). Ulus district.

Safir, Denizciler Cad. 34 (tel. 3241194). Singles and doubles £8.60 ($15) per person.

Paris, Denizciler Cad. 14 (tel. 3241283/3241284/3241285).

Efes, Denizciler Cad. 12 (tel. 324311/324312). Singles with bath £11 ($19), doubles with bath £16 ($28).

Ergen, Karanfil Sok 48 (tel. 1175906). Singles £10.30 ($18), doubles £14.30 ($25). Kizilav district. At the junction of Atatürk Bulvarı and Gazi Mustafa Kemal Bulvarı follow the road opposite Gazi Mustafa Kemal, then turn right almost immediately down Karanfil Sok.

Bulduk, Sanayi Cad. 26 (tel. 3104915). Singles £6.90 ($12), doubles £11.40 ($20). Ulus district.

Terminal, Hipodrum Cad. (tel. 3104949). Singles £6.90 ($12), singles with bath £8 ($14), doubles £10.30 ($18), doubles with bath £12 ($21). Near the bus station.

Öztürk, Talat Paşa Bul. 57 (tel. 3125186/3125187). Samanpazari district.

Hanecioğlu, Ulucanlar Cad. 68 (tel. 3202572).

Koyunlu, Ulucanlar Cad. 35 (tel. 3104900).

Tac, Çankırı Cad. 35 (tel. 3243195). Ulus district.

Saral, Işiklar Cad. (tel. 3103488).

Olimpiyat, Rüzgarli Eşdost Sok 18 (tel. 3243088). Ulus district.

Sembol, Sümer Sokak 28 (tel. 2318222). Singles £11.40 ($20), doubles with bath £17.20 ($30). Off Gazi Mustafa Kemal Bulvarı between the Maltepe Mosque and the junction with Atatürk Bulvarı.

Medine, Istanbul Cad. 14 (tel. 3091381/3091382/3091383). The street runs left off Cumhuriyet Bulvarı by the Cumhuriyet Museum, crossing Kâzim Karabakir Cad. after about 500m.

Yenibahar, Çankırı Cad. 25 (tel. 3104895). Singles £8.60 ($15), doubles £14.30 ($25). Ulus district.

Elhamra, Ismetpaşa Mah. Çankırı Cad. (tel. 3104885). Ulus district.

Two-star hotels

Başyazicioğlu, Çankırı Cad. 27 (tel. 3103935). Singles £9.70 ($17), doubles £17.20 ($30). Ulus district.

Akman, Opera Meydanı, Tavus Sok 6 (tel. 3244140). Singles with bath £10.30 ($18), doubles with bath £14.30 ($25).

Barinak, Koç Yurdu Yani Onur Sok 25 (tel. 2318040). Singles
with bath £14.30 ($25), doubles with bath £20 ($35). The
street runs off Gazi Mustafa Kemal Bulvarı.

Erşan, Meşrutiyet Cad. 13 (tel. 1184092). Singles with bath
£14.30 ($25), doubles with bath £20 ($35). Kizilay district.
Off Atatürk Bulvarı, about 400m beyond the junction with
Gazi Mustafa Kemal Bulvarı.

YOUTH HOSTELS

Cumhuriyet Öğrenci Yurdu Cebeci, Siyasal Bilgiler Fakultesi
Arkasi (tel. 3193634). Open 1 July–31 Aug.

CAMPING

Altinok (tel. 3414406/3417291). 12½ miles out on the road to
Istanbul.

Antalya (tel. code 31)

Tourist Office
Turizm Danişma Bürosu, Cumhuriyet Cad. (tel. 111747). Open
Mon.–Fri. 8.00 a.m.–5.30 p.m., weekends 9 a.m.–5 p.m. The
office distributes small plans of the city, and lists of local
accommodation registered with the Ministry of Tourism, but
no lists of locally licensed accommodation. As you walk along
Cumhuriyet Cad. from Kazim zalp Cad. the office is about
250m beyond the Atatürk statue, set back a little off the right-
hand side of Cumhuriyet Cad. (beside the THY office).

Telephone Code
Antalya recently changed from a telephone code of 311
followed by a five-figure number to a code of 31 followed by
a six figure number. In any instance where you see a five-figure
number given for Antalya, insert the figure 1 before the number
given.

Basic Directions

Walking down Kazim Özalp Cad. (also known as Sarampol) from the bus station you arrive at the junction with Cumhuriyet Cad., at which point you should turn right to reach the Tourist Office on Cumhuriyet Cad. Going left you come to the crossroads with Ismet Paşa Cad. (left) and Atatürk Bulvarı (right). ABout 150m along Atatürk Bulvarı you pass the end of Hidirlik Sok on your right, then about 300m further on you reach Hadrian's Gate, through which is the start of Hesapçı Sok. This street leads down to the clifftop Hıdırlık Tower. Continuing down Atatürk Bulvarı you reach the Karaalioğlu Park. Going left along the park's edge and then straight ahead Ofuz Ağustos Cad. leads down to the coast, and the main street running along the coast, Lara Cad.

Finding Accommodation

Over the past decade, many townhouses in the old town (Kaleiçi – the area roughly bounded by Cumhuriyet Cad. and Atatürk Bulvarı) have been converted into guesthouses. Hıdırlık Sok and Hesapçı Sok are particularly well supplied with guesthouses. There is a cluster of cheap hotels around the bus station, but this area is much noisier than the old town.

GUESTHOUSES

Locally licensed guesthouses

Adler Pansiyon, Barbaros Mahalle, Cıvelek Sok 46 (tel. 117818). £3.40 ($6) in singles or doubles. Cıvelek Sok runs between (and roughly parallel to) Hıdırlık Sok and Hesapçı Sok.

Saltur Pansiyon, Hesapçı Sok 67 (tel. 176238). Singles £6.80–9.20 ($12–16). Near the Hıdırlık Tower.

Pansiyon Falez, Hıdırlık Sok 48 (tel. 170985) Singles £4.60 ($8), doubles £8 ($14). Breakfast included.

Tunay Pansiyon, 7 Mermerli Sok (tel. 124677). Singles £3.20 ($5.50), doubles £5.70 ($10). From the Clock Tower by the junction of Kazim Özalp Cad. and Cumhuriyet Cad. walk

towards the coast, and then look for the signs leading up
to the guesthouse.

Aksoy Pansiyon, Kocatepe Sok 39 (tel. 126549). Doubles
£6.90 ($12). Just around the corner from the Adler, above.

Atelya Pansiyon, Cıvelek Sok 21 (tel. 116416). Singles with
bath £8 ($14), doubles with bath £13.70 ($24). Breakfast
included. See the Adler, above.

Sabah Pansiyon, Hesapçı Sok 60a (tel. 175345). Singles £5.70
($10), doubles £9.20 ($16). Breakfast included.

The Garden, Hesapçı Sok 44 (tel. 110816). Singles £4.60 ($8),
doubles £8 ($14). Most rooms have a shower. Breakfast
included. Across from the Truncated Minaret (Kesik
Minare).

Hadriyanus Pansiyon, Zeytin Çıkmazı 4 (tel. 112313). Singles
with bath £6.90 ($12), doubles with bath £10.30 ($18).
Breakfast included. Off Hıdırlık Sok.

Erken Pansiyon, Hıdırlık Sok 5 (tel. 176092). Singles with
bath £6.90 ($12), doubles with bath £12.60 ($22). Breakfast
included.

Dedkonak Pansiyon, Hıdırlık Sok 11 (tel. 175170). Singles
with bath £6.90 ($12), doubles with bath £10.30 ($18).
Breakfast included.

Mini Orient, Cıvelek Sok 30 (tel. 124417). Singles with bath
£10.30 ($18), doubles with bath £14.30 ($25). Breakfast
included. See the Adler above.

Guesthouses registered with the Ministry of Tourism

Ak-Asya, Yeni Kapı Fırın Sok 5 (tel. 111404).

Holland, Lara Yolu, Bannaklar 2049 Sok 17 (tel.
126528/231389).

Altun, Iskele Cad. 10/Kaleiçi Mev 10 (tel. 116624).

Gözde, Kazim Özalp Cad., 106 Sok 3/C (tel. 128656).

Anadolu, Gençlik Mah. 1311 Sok 18 (tel. 125938).

Türel, Çağlayan Mah. 2055 Sok 39 (tel. 231382/120433).

Ozkavak, Cıvelek Sok 6 (tel. 127055). See the Adler above.

Frankfurt, Hıdırlık Sok 25 (tel. 176224).

Abad, Hesapçı Sok 52 (tel. 176662).

HOTELS

Locally licensed hotels

Sargin, 459 Sok 3 (tel. 111408). Singles £3.40 ($6), doubles £5.70 ($10). Off Kazim Özalp Cad.

Kaya, 459 Sok 12 (tel. 111391). Singles £4 ($7), doubles £6.90 ($12). Off Kazim Özalp Cad.

Kumluca 457 Sok 21 (tel. 111123). Singles £3.40 ($6), doubles £5.70 ($12). Between Kazim Özalp Cad. and Ismet Paşa Cad.

One-star hotels

Büyük, Cumhuriyet Cad. 57 (tel. 111499).

Perge, Karaali Park Yani 1311 Sok (tel. 123600). By the coast at the Karaalioglu Park.

Aras, Hüsnü Karakaş Cad. (tel. 118695). Off Atatürk Bulvarı, close to the junction with Cumhuriyet Cad.

Duru, Lara Cad. 150 Demircikara Cad. (tel. 118636).

CAMPING

Camping Bambus, Lara Yolu (tel. 215263). By the beach at the Bambus Motel, 2 miles out of town along the road to Lara. Although the site is expensive by Turkish standards, the facilities available are of a good standard. Freelance camping within Antalya itself is not to be recommended.

Ephesus (Efes)

The ruins of the city of Ephesus, one-time Roman capital of Asia Minor, are only 10 miles from Kuşadasi, so it is quite possible to stay there and visit Ephesus on a day trip. If you would prefer to stay closer to Ephesus, or to stay for a few days, then there are plenty of cheap places to stay in the village of

Selçuk (tel. code 5451), about a mile from the ruins. The Tourist Office in Selçuk is at Atatürk Mah., Agora Çarşisi 35 (tel. 1945/2712/1328), across from the bus station. Open daily in the summer, 8.30 a.m.–6.30 p.m.; in winter, Mon.–Fri. 9.00 a.m.–5.30 p.m.

GUESTHOUSES

Locally licensed guesthouses. Expect to pay around £2.50 ($4.50) per person

Barim, Turgutreis Sok 34 Muze Arkasi Sok (tel. 1923). Off Turgutreis Sok, the street to the rear of the Ephesus Museum.

Kirhan, Turgutreis Sok 7 (tel. 2257). Behind the Ephesus Museum.

Star, Atatürk mah. Ova Sok 22 (tel. 3858). Rooms with baths £2.50 ($5.50) per person. Close to the Kirhan.

Australian, Zafer mah. Durak Sok 20/A (tel. 1050). Signposted from the rear of the Ephesus Museum.

Ilyada, Miltner Sok 17 (tel. 3278).

Deniz, Sefa Sok 9 (tel. 1741).

Suzan, Kallinger Cad. 46 (tel. 3471). Along the street heading towards the Isa Bey Camii.

Amazon, Serin Sok 8 (tel. 3215). About 200m from the Isa Bey Camii.

Artemis, Zafer mah. Atilla Sok 5 (tel. 1862).

Blue, Isa Bey mah. Eski Izmir Cad. (tel. 3646).

Çakiroğlu, Atatürk mah. Kubilay Sok 9 (tel. 2582).

Isa Bey, Isa Bey mah, Serin Sok 2. Close to the Isa Bey Camii.

Öztürk, Fevzipaşa Cad. 2 (tel. 1937). Close to the main square.

Galaxi, Atatürk mah. Atatürk Cad. 21. (tel. 1304).

Evin, Isa Bey mah. Meydan Sok 37 (tel. 1261).

Taşkin, Isa Bey mah. Meydan Sok 21 (tel. 2171).

Sevil, Atatürk mah. Turgutreis Sok (tel. 2340).

Saray, Atatürk mah. Kubilay Sok (tel. 3820).

Buket, Isa Bey mah. Atatürk Cad. 6 (tel. 2378).

Ferah, Atatürk mah. Karanfil Sok 5/A (tel. 3814).
Gezer, Ikinci Spor Sok 9 (tel. 2010).
Akbulut, Ikinci Spor Sok 4.
Mengi, Ikinci Spor Sok 8.
Önder, Ikinci Spor Sok 7.
Hasan Ağa, Atatürk mah. Koçak Sok.

HOTELS

Locally licensed hotels

Akay, Atatürk Mah. Serin Sok 3 (tel. 3009/3172). £5.70 ($10),
per person in singles or doubles with bath. About 200m
from the Isa Bey Camii.

Aksoy, Isa Bey Mah. Cengiz Topel Cad. (tel. 1040). £5.70
($10), per person in singles or doubles with bath. By the
aqueduct.

Subası, Cengiz Topel Cad. 10 (tel. 1359). £5.70 ($10) per
person in singles or doubles with bath. Opposite the post
office (PTT).

Hasan Ağa, Koçak Sok. (tel. 1317).
Ürkmez, Isa Bey Mah. Cengiz Topel Cad. (tel. 1312).
Artemis, Atatürk mah. 2 Pazaryeri Sok (tel. 1191).
Karahan, Atatürk Mah. 1 Okul Sok. (tel. 3294).
Atlanta, Atatürk 2ci Pazaryeri (tel. 2883).
Güneş, Kuşadasi Cad. (tel. 1229).
Güven, 1002 Sok 9 (tel. 1294).
Gazi, Istasyon Meydanı (tel. 1467).

One-star hotels

Katibim, Atatürk Cad. 5 Spor Sok 1 (tel. 2498).
Tusan Motel (tel. 1060). Along the road to Ephesus.

CAMPING

Tusan Motel. Just off the road to Ephesus.

Blue Moon Camping. By Pamucak beach, 5½ miles from
Selçuk.

İstanbul (tel. code 01)

Tourist Offices

The administrative office is at Beyoğlu Meşrutiyet Caddesi 57/6.
Contact this office if you want information on the city in
advance. On arrival, head for one of the several offices the
Tourist Board operates in the city. Arriving by train from
Europe, the most conveniently located office is at Divanyolu
Cad. 3 (tel. 5224903), in the Sultanahmet district (open daily
9 a.m.–5 p.m.). The offices at the Karaköy ferry terminal (tel.
1495776) and at Atatürk airport (tel. 5737399/5734136) keep the
same hours as the Sultanahmet office. Another office operates
in the Hilton Hotel Arcade, off Cumhuriyet Cad., in the
Harbiye district (tel. 1330592).

Basic Directions

Trains from Europe arrive at the train station in Sirkeci, a short
distance from the main sights in the Sultanahmet district.
Going left from the exit of the station you cross two main roads
before arriving at the junction with Aşirefendi Caddesi (right)
and Ebussuut Caddesi (left). Go straight across and follow the
winding Ankara Caddesi into Yerebatan Caddesi. Go right and
follow the street down to the magnificent Aya Sofya Church.
The Tourist Office is just a short walk to the left at the start
of Divan Yolu Caddesi. The walk from the train station to the
Tourist Office takes about 10 minutes. Divan Yolu Cad. runs
into Yeniçeriler Cad. which subsequently becomes Ordu
Caddesi. The Lâleli Mosque, about halfway along Ordu Cad.
is about 20 minutes' walk from the Tourist Office. Many of the
Tourist Board registered hotels listed below are in the streets
of Ordu Cad. around the mosque. Entering Ordu Cad. from
Yeniçeriler Cad. Herikzadeler Sok runs right off Ordu Cad. one
block before the mosque. Fethibey Cad. runs right at the Lâleli

Mosque, Koska Cad. goes left over the road. One block on from
Koska Cad. is Lâleli Cad. Another block further on is the
crossroads at which Aksaray Cad. goes left, while Gentürk
Cad. heads right. One block from Gentürk Cad., near the end
of Ordu Cad., Yeşiltulumba Sok. runs off to the right. Turning
left at the end of Fethibey Cad. the first street on your right
is Fevziye Cad. Mesihpaşa Cad. crosses Koska Cad., Lâleli
Cad., and Aksaray Cad. two blocks down from Ordu Cad.
Azimkar Sok runs parallel to Mesihpaşa Cad. another block
further on.

Finding Accommodation
Due to its proximity to the major sights, the Sultanahmet
district is a particularly popular place to stay. Fortunately, the
area has the largest concentration of cheap rooms in the city,
so outside peak season you are virtually assured a room here.
Although there are few one-star hotels in the district, the
standard of locally licensed accommodation is generally fine,
but check thoroughly before accepting a room as there are some
very poor establishments in Sultanahmet. There is quite a
choice of one-star hotels in the Lâleli and Aksaray districts (a
20-minute walk from Sultanahmet), as well as a host of hotels
licensed by the municipal authorities. Standards at locally
licensed hotels in these areas are more consistent than in
Sultanahmet: while there are few of the very good
establishments that can be found in Sultanahmet, there are also
relatively fewer unacceptable accommodations.

LOCALLY LICENSED HOTELS AND GUESTHOUSES

Sultanahmet district:
  Hippodrome Pansiyon, Üçler Sok 9 (tel. 5160902). Singles
    £5.70 ($10), doubles £6.90 ($12), triples £9.20 ($16). A short
    walk from the Hippodrome.
  Hacıbey Pansiyon, Özbekler Sokak. Singles £2.30 ($4),
    doubles £4 ($7). Close to the Sokullu Mehmet Paşa

Mosque, about 200m from the Hippodrome.

Optimist Pansiyon. Singles £6.30 ($11), doubles £8 ($14). Breakfast included. Contact the Optimist Guesthouse (see below) and the staff will take you to the *pansiyon*.

Side Pansiyon, Utangaç Sok 20 (tel. 5128175). Doubles £6.90 ($12), triples and dorms £2.90 ($5) per person.

Hotel Park, Utangaç Sok 26 (tel. 5223964). Singles £4.60 ($8), singles with shower £9.70 ($17), doubles £6.90 ($12), doubles with shower £11.40 ($20).

Hotel Anadolu, Salkim Söğüt Sok 3 (tel. 5120135). £5.20 ($9) per person. Off Yerebatan Cad.

Optimist Guesthouse, Hippodrome (tel. 5162398). Singles £9.20 ($16), singles with bath £14.90 ($26), doubles £12.60 ($22), doubles with bath £18.30 ($32). Spotlessly clean, with superb views from the roof. Understandably popular, so advance reservation is recommended.

Berk Guesthouse, Kutluğun Sok 27 (tel. 5110737). Doubles with bath £18.30 ($32). The street runs from the rear of the Sultan Ahmet mosque to the walls of the Topkapı Palace.

Hotel Antique, Küçük Ayasofya Cad., Oğul Sok 17 (tel. 5164936/5160997). Doubles with bath £15.50 ($27). Looking at the Sultan Ahmet mosque from the Hippodrome, Küçük Ayasofya Cad. runs from the rear of the mosque, to the right.

Elit Hotel, Salkim Söğüt Sok 14 (tel. 5115179/5190466). Doubles with bath & WC £13.70 ($24). Dorms £4 ($7). Off Yerebatan Cad.

Hotel Merih, Zeynep Sultan Camii Sok 25 (tel. 5228522). Singles £5.20 ($9), doubles £6.30 ($11), and dorms £3.40 ($6). The street runs off Alemdar Cad., which is off Yerebatan Cad. by Aya Sofya.

Hotel Ema, Salkim Söğüt Sok 18. Singles £8 ($14), doubles with bath £13.70 ($24). Dorms £3.70 ($6.50). Roof space £2 ($3.50). Off Yerebatan Cad.

Hotel Klotfarer, Klotfarer Cad. 22 (tel 5284850). Singles with shower £8 ($14), doubles with shower £12 ($21). Left off Divan Yolu as you walk from Aya Sofya and the Hippodrome.

Lâleli and Aksaray districts:

Hotel Mine Pansiyon, Gençtürk Cad. 54 (tel. 5112375). Singles £5.20 ($9), doubles £8 ($14). Four-bedroom flats £20.60 ($36).

Hotel Burak, Fethibey Cad., Ağa Yokusu 1 (tel. 5118679/5227904). Singles £10.30 ($18), doubles £6 ($28).

Hotel Neşet, Harikzadeler Sok 23 (tel. 5267412/5224474). Singles £8.60 ($15), doubles £13.70 ($24).

Hotel Kul, Büyük Reşit Paşa Cad., Zeynep Kamil Sok 27 (tel. 5260127/5282892). Singles with shower £9.20 ($16), doubles with shower £13.70 ($24).

Hotel La Mirajz, Fethibey Cad. 28 (tel. 5112445). Singles £9.70 ($17), doubles £10.30–13.70 ($18–24). Another hotel of that name at the same location is considerably more expensive.

ONE-STAR HOTELS

Expect to pay from £12 ($21) in doubles

Around the Sirkeci train station:

Ağan, Saffetinpaş Sok 6 (tel. 5278550).

Eriş, Istasyon Arkasi 9 (tel. 5278950). The street runs down the side of the station.

Yaşmak, Ebussuut Cad. 18 (tel. 5263155).

Sultanahmet district:

Alzer, At Meydanı 72 (tel. 5166262). By the Hippodrome.

Lâleli and Aksaray districts:

Nobel, Aksaray Cad. 23 (tel. 5220617).

Okey, Fethibey Cad. 65 (tel. 5112162).

Uzay, Şair Fitnat Sok 20 (tel. 5268776). Off Ordu Cad., near Koska Cad.

Tanin, Mesihpaşa Cad. 60 (tel. 5138336).

Selim, Koska Cad. 39 (tel. 5119377).

Side Koska Cad. 33 (tel. 5267178).

Ensar, Yeşiltulumba Sok 39 (tel. 5206135).

Florida, Fevziye Cad. 38 (tel. 5281021).

Karakaş, Gençtürk Cad. 55 (tel. 5265343).

Karatay, Saitefendi Sok 42 (tel. 5265692).
Oran, Harikzadeler Sok 40 (tel. 5285813).
Babaman, Lâleli Cad. 19 (tel. 5268238).
Geçit, Aksaray Cad. 5 (tel. 5278839).
Tebriz, Muratpaşa Sülüklü Sok (tel. 5244135).
Nazar, Ordu Cad. Yeşiltulumba Sok 17 (tel. 5268060).
Pamukkale, Ordu Cad. Selimpaşa Sok 8 (tel. 5276793).
Tahran, Mehmet Lütfişekerci Sok 21 (tel. 5214650).
Bariş, Küçüklanga Cad. 15 (tel. 5254288).
Aygün, Azimkar Sok 95 (tel. 5284986).
Delta, Azimkar Sok 3 (tel. 5114855).
Cevher, Mesihpaşa Cad. 66 (tel. 5111782/5209669). Singles
£9.70 ($17), doubles £16 ($28).
Rio, Saitefendi Sok 20 (tel. 5222860). Off Aksaray Cad.
Urol, Yenikapı Fabrika Sok 7 (tel. 5272672).
Yilmaz, Valide Cami Sok 79 (tel. 5867400).

TWO-STAR HOTELS

Cidde, Aksaray Cad. 10 (tel. 5224211/5224212/5224213).
Singles £9.70 ($17), doubles £15.40 ($27). An extra bed can
be added to a room at a cost of £4 ($7).

IYHF HOSTEL

Yücelt Youth Hostel, Caferiya Sok 6/1 (tel. 5136150). Doubles
£9.20 ($16); dorms £3.40 ($6). IYHF membership
compulsory, but cards are sold at the hostel for £6.90 ($12).
Best reserved in advance. The street runs from the foot of
Yerebatan Cad. along the side of Aya Sofya.

HOSTELS

Hotel Büyükayasofya, Caferiya Sok 5 (tel. 5222981). £5.70
($10) per person in rooms with showers, £4.60 ($8) in
rooms without. Roof space £1.40 ($2.50). Next door to the
IYHF hostel.
Topkapı Hostel, Işakpaşa Cad., Kutluğun Sok 1 (tel.

5272433). Doubles 12.60 ($22), dorms £5.20 ($9). Roof space £3.70 ($6.50). The street runs from the rear of the Sultan Ahmet mosque to the walls of the Topkapı Palace.

True Blue Hostel, Akbıyık Cad. 2. Doubles £8.60 ($15). Dorms £3.40 ($6). Akbıyık Cad. runs parallel to Kutluğun Sok (see the Topkapı hostel) one block closer to the old city wall and the sea.

Orient International Youth Hostel, Akbıyık Cad. 13 (tel. 5160171/5160194). Doubles £6.90 ($12), triples £8.60 ($15). Dorms £2.30 ($4). Along the street from the True Blue Hostel, above.

Sultan Tourist Hostel, Akbıyık Cad., Terbiyik Sok 3 (tel. 5169260). Doubles £5.70 ($10), doubles with bath £11.40 ($20), triples £8 ($14). There have been complaints about this hostel from women travelling alone.

Dorms and roof space, as well as comparably priced smaller rooms, are available at several of the locally licensed hotels and guesthouses listed above.

STUDENT ACCOMMODATION

Converted into temporary hostels during July and August:

Topkapı Atatürk Öğrenci Sitesi, Londra Asfaltı, Cevizlibağ durağı (tel. 5820455/5255032/5239488/5250280). Topkapı district.

Kadırga Öğrenci Yurdu, Sahsuvar Mah. Cömertler Sok (tel. 5282480/5282481). In the Kumkapı district.

Ortaköy Kiz Öğrenci Yurdu, Palanga Cad. 20 (tel. 1600184/1601035/1617376). In the Ortaköy district.

CAMPING

Londra Mokamp, Eski Londra Asfaltı, Bakırköy (tel. 5594200/5594201/5594202). Very crowded site, about three quarters of a mile from the airport. Linked to Aksaray by buses and dolmuses.

Ataköy Tatil Köyü, Rauf Orbay Cad., Ataköy (tel. 5596000

– 6 lines). Close to the airport, between the main road and
the Marmara Sea.

Yeşilyurt (tel. 5738408/5744230). By the Marmara Sea, close
to the village of Yeşilköy.

Kervansaray Kartaltepe Mokamp, Çobançeşme Mev.,
Bakırköy (tel. 5754721).

Florya Truistik Tesisleri, Florya (tel. 5740000). About 15 miles
from the city centre. Local trains run from Eminönü and
Ataköy to Florya station, 500m from the site. From the
Topkapı bus station there is a dolmus service to Florya,
while bus 73 runs from Taksim to Florya.

Izmir (tel. code 051)

Tourist Offices

The main information office is at Gaziosmanpaşa Bulvarı 1/C
(tel. 142147/199278). Open daily June–Oct., 8.30 a.m.–7.30
p.m.; Nov.–May, Mon.–Sat. 8.30 a.m.–5.30 p.m. If you arrive
by ferry there is an office at Alsancak Harbour (tel.
631600/631263), while the administrative office is between the
harbour and the Alsancak train station at Atatürk Cad. 418.
A fourth office operates at the Adnan Menderes airport (tel.
512626/511950/511081).

Basic Directions

There are two main train stations in Izmir, the Alsancak station
which serves the ferry terminal, and the Basmane station
serving the city centre. Anafartalar Cad. runs across the front
of the Basmane station. Directly across Anafartalar Cad. from
the station is Fevzipaşa Bulvarı, which leads straight to the
Aegean. Heading right from the train station about 200m you
reach 9 Eylül Meydanı, from which Gazi Bulvarı runs left down
to the shore. Following Anafartalar Cad. left from the station,
after about 300m the street turns sharp right to run parallel
to Fevzipasa Bulvarı as far as the junction with Gaziosmanpaş
Bulvarı. Thereafter Anafartalar Cad. follows a circuitous route

towards the coast and Konak Meydanı (a major local bus and dolmus terminal). Gaziosmanpaşa Bulvarı runs straight across Anafartalar Cad. Fevzipaşa Bulvarı and Gazi Bulvarı. Across the junction with Gazi Bulvarı the street heads diagonally down to the shore and Cumhuriyet Meydanı. The main Tourist Information Office is by the Büyük Efes Hotel and the THY office on the stretch of Gaziosmanpaş Bulvarı between Gazi Bulvarı and Cumhuriyet Meydanı.

The city's main bus station is by the Atatürk stadium, about 1½ miles from the Basmane train station and the city centre. Buses 50, 51 and 52 (red-and-white) run from the bus station to Konak Meydanı, but these buses are few and far between. A more frequent service to the city centre is provided by the blue-and-white minibuses marked Çankaya-Mersinli, which stop on Gazi Bulvarı about 250m from 9 Eylül Meydanı.

Finding Accommodation

With the exception of Izmir's annual fair (late August to mid-September) when you will toil to find a room in any price category, there are usually more than enough cheap beds to go round. Most of the cheaper hotels are in the Akinci area (also known as Yenigün), roughly the district bounded by Anafatraler Cad., Gaziosmanpaşa Bulvarı and Gazi Bulvarı. As a rule, hotels in the streets between Fevzipaşa Bulvarı and Gazi Bulvarı are of a better standard than those between Fevzipaşa Bulvarı and Anafartalar Cad., with only a minimal difference in price. The average standard of locally licensed accommodation is probably the lowest in the hotels lining (and just off) 1294 Sok and 1296 Sok.

GUESTHOUSES

Registered with the Ministry of Tourism

Imperial Pansiyon, 1296 Sok, 54 (tel. 149771). Turn left off Fevzipasa Bulvarı along 1295 Sok, then right on to 1296 Sok.

LOCALLY LICENSED HOTELS

Gümüş Palas, 1299 Sok 12 (tel. 134153). Small but clean. Doubles £5.20 ($9). No shower in the hotel.

Olimpiyat, 945 Sok 2 (tel. 251269). Doubles £7.40 ($13). Off Anafartalar Cad. after the street bends sharp right.

Saray, Anafartalar Cad. 635 (tel. 136946). Singles £4 ($7), doubles £5.20 ($9). Within easy walking distance of Basmane train station.

Yıldız Palas, 1296 Sok 50 (tel. 251518). Doubles £6.90 ($12). One of the good hotels on 1296 Sok. Turn left off Fevzipaşa Bulvarı along 1295 Sok, then right into 1296 Sok.

Bakıklı, 1296 Sok 18 (tel. 142560). Doubles £5.20 ($9). Another reasonable hotel on 1296 Sok. See the Yıldız Palas above for directions.

Özcan, 1368 Sok 3 (tel. 135052). Singles £5.70 ($10), doubles £9.20 ($16), doubles with bath £10.30 ($18). 1368 Sok runs right off Fevzipaşa Bulvarı, a short walk from the train station.

Güzel Izmir, 1368 Sok 8 (tel. 135069/146693). Doubles with bath £10.90 ($19). See the Özcan above.

Nil, Fevzipaşa Bulvarı 155 (tel. 135228). Doubles with shower £10.90 ($19).

Yeni Park, 1368 Sok 6 (tel. 135231). Doubles £10.30 ($18). See the Özcan, above.

Bilen Palas, 1369 Sok 68 (tel. 139246). Singles £4.60 ($8), doubles £6.90 ($12). Off 9 Eylül Meydanı, between Anafartalar Cad. and Gazi Bulvarı.

Işık, 1364 Sok 11 (tel. 131029). Doubles with bath £10.30 ($18). Right off Fevzipaşa Bulvarı.

Bayburt, 1370 Sok 1 (tel. 122013). Doubles with bath £11.40 ($20). From Fevzipaşa Bulvarı turn right along 1361 Sok, then left down 1369 Sok. Almost immediately 1369 Sok is crossed by 1370 Sok: the hotel is at the junction of the two.

Efes, Gaziosmanpaşa Bulvarı 48 (tel. 147276). Doubles with shower £9.20 ($16).

Atlas, Şair Eşref Bulvarı 1 (tel. 144265). Doubles with shower £10.90 ($19). At the junction of Gaziosmanpaşa Bulvarı,

Gazi Bulvarı and Şair Eşref Bulvarı.

Meseret, Anafartalar Cad. 66 (tel. 255533). Doubles £7.40 ($13). Close to Konak Meydanı.

Ankara Palas (tel. 142850/137969). Doubles with bath £12 ($21). By the elevated walkway near Konak Meydanı.

ONE-STAR HOTEL

Babadan, Gaziomanpaşa Bulvarı 50 (tel. 139640). Doubles with bath £17.20 ($30).

YOUTH HOSTELS

Atatürk Öğrenci Yurdu, 1888 Sok 4, Inciraltı (tel. 152980/152981/152856). Open 1 July–31 Aug.

CAMPING

Lervamsarau Inciraltı Mocamp, Balcova (tel. 154760). Closed during the winter months. 7½ miles out from the centre.

Kuşadası (tel. code 636)

Tourist Office

Turizm Danisma Burosu, Iskele Meydanı (tel. 11103/16295). Open July–Aug., 7.30 a.m.–8.00 p.m. daily; May–June and Sept.–Oct., 8 a.m.–6 p.m. daily; Nov.–Apr., Mon.–Fri. 8.30 a.m.–5.30 p.m. The office distributes a list of around 300 local hotels and guesthouses, and a decent plan of the town. Across from the ferry terminal.

Telephone Code

Kuşadası recently changed from a telephone code of 6361 followed by a four-figure number to a code of 636 followed by a five-figure number (the figure 1 dropped from the code being added to the start of all existing numbers). In any instance where you see a four-figure number given for Kuşadası, insert the figure 1 before the number.

Finding Accommodation

Outside the peak months of July and August, finding a cheap room in Kuşadası is usually quite simple. Several streets within easy walking distance of the Tourist Office are particularly well supplied with reasonably priced accommodation: Kıbrıs Cad., Yıldırım Cad., Aslanlar Cad., and Bezirgan Sok. Following the street leading away from the ferry terminal (Liman Cad.), turn right at the end of the street and then left to reach Kıbrıs Cad. Aslanlar Cad. crosses the other end of Kıbrıs Cad. Going left at this point, Aslanlar Cad. runs into Yıldırım Cad.; going right Bezirgan Cad. is off to the right after a short distance. From the coast road running right from the ferry terminal, a set of steps between the Shell petrol station and the Odin Restaurant lead up to Bezirgan Sok.

GUESTHOUSES

Locally licensed guesthouses

Su Pansiyon, Arslanlar Cad. 13 (tel. 11453). £3.40 ($6) per person in singles or doubles. Breakfast included.

Cennet Pansiyon, Yayla Sok 1. Doubles with bath £7.40 ($13). Breakfast included. At the junction with Yıldırım Cad.

Dinç Pansiyon, Mercan Sok (tel. 14249). Doubles £5.70 ($10). Breakfast included. Mercan Sok is off Bezirgan Sok.

Şanli, Bezirgan Sok 13 (tel. 13028). Doubles £7.40 ($13). Breakfast included.

Işikli Pansiyon, Aslanlar Cad. 22. £3.20 ($5.50) per person.

Özhan, Kıbrıs Cad. 5 (tel. 12932). Singles £3.70 ($6.50), doubles with bath £7.40 ($13).

Safak (tel. 11764). £3.20 ($5.50) per person. A block further up the hill from Su Pansiyon (see above)

Enişte Pansiyon, Bezirgan Sok (tel. 12171).

Hasgül Pansiyon, Bezirgan Sok (tel. 13641).

King Pansiyon, Bezirgan Sok (tel. 13128).
Seçkin, Yıldırım Cad. 35 (tel. 14735). Doubles with bath £7.40 ($13). Breakfast included.
Golden Bed, Aslanlar Cad., Uğurlu Çikmazi 4 (tel. 18708). Doubles with bath £7.40 ($13). Breakfast included.

Guesthouses registered with the Ministry of Tourism

Bahar, Cephane Sok 12 (tel. 11191).
Grup, Istiklal Cad. 3 (tel. 11230).
Özer, Istiklal Cad. 11A (tel. 11138).
Çi-Dem, Istiklal Cad. 9 (tel. 11895).
Yunus, Istiklal Cad. 7 (tel. 12268).
Nil, Ismet Inönu Bulvarı 59 (tel. 13134).

HOTELS

Locally licensed hotels

Rose, Aslanlar Cad., Aydınlık Sok 7 (tel. 11111). Singles £5.20 ($9), doubles £9.20 ($16). Beds on the roof £2.50 ($4.50). Right at the junction with Kıbrıs Cad.
Kalyon, Kıbrıs Cad. 7 (tel. 13346). Singles £10.30 ($18) doubles with bath £14.30 ($25). Breakfast included.
Panorama, Kıbrıs Cad. 14 (tel. 14671). Singles £10.30 ($18), doubles with bath £14.30 ($25). Breakfast included.
Dülger, Yıldırım Cad. (tel. 15769). Doubles £11.40 ($20). Close to the bazaar.
Konak, Yıldırım Cad. 55 (tel. 16318). Doubles £12.60 ($22). Breakfast included.

One-star hotel

Atadan, Ismet Inönu Bulvarı (tel. 11679).

CAMPING

Camping Önder (tel. 2413) and Camping Yat (tel. 1333) are

located close by each other on Atatürk Bulvarı about 1½ miles
out of town on the road to Seluk (behind the yacht marina).
Three-bed bungalows are available at both sites.

UNITED KINGDOM

If, as is probable, London is your first stop in the UK, you might well wonder just how long your budget will survive, given that hostels cost £10–16 ($17.50–28.00), B&B is rarely available for under £17 ($30) and the Tourist Information Centre charges a staggering £5 ($9) to find rooms that are well outside the budget category – the comparable service in Paris charges 15FF (£1.60; $2.75). And although you may find some comfort in the knowledge that things improve once you get outside the English capital, a trip to the UK is likely to put some strain on your budget, as there is a shortage of accommodation possibilities under £10 ($17.50) per night.

Bed and breakfast accommodation in guesthouses and B&Bs is available throughout the UK, with prices starting at around £11–12 ($19–21). In most towns, including popular destinations such as Edinburgh and York, you should be able to find a bed in the £11–13 ($19–23) price range without much difficulty, except at the height of the season or during special events. However, in some of the more popular small cities, such as Bath and Oxford, you can consider yourself lucky if you find a bed for under £15 ($26.50).

Tourist Information Centres distribute free lists of local guesthouses and B&Bs, so unless the town is very busy you can normally find a bed quite easily by trying a few telephone numbers from the brochure. However, there is not much point in doing this if the office operates a free local room-finding service. Many offices run a system whereby you pay a deposit (not a commission) at the office, which is then deducted from your final bill. A few offices do charge for finding a room, normally £1.50–2.50 ($2.50–4.50). One really useful service provided by Tourist Information Centres is the Book-a-Bed-Ahead facility, which costs £2.50 ($4.50). This service lets you make a reservation at your next destination, and can save you a great deal of time, aggravation and even money, especially if you are heading for a town where you anticipate trouble in finding cheap accommodation, such as Edinburgh during its festival, York at weekends, or London at any time.

The IYHF hostel network in the UK is extensive, although there are several important gaps: notably some of the larger English cities such as Birmingham, Leeds, Manchester and Liverpool. There are three **youth hostel** associations in the UK: the Youth Hostels Association of England and Wales, the Youth Hostel Association of Northern Ireland, and the Scottish Youth Hostels Association. Curfews are normally 11 p.m. in England and Wales (later in London – some London hostels have no curfew), 11.30 p.m. in Northern Ireland and 11.45 p.m. in Scotland (2 a.m. in Glasgow, Edinburgh, Aberdeen and Inverness).

Prices vary according to the standard of facilities and the age of the user. At the Scottish and Northern Irish hostels those aged over 18 and over are referred to as 'seniors', whereas in England and Wales 'seniors' are those aged 21 and over, while visitors aged 16 to 20 are classed as 'juniors'. In the Northern Irish hostels, seniors pay around £6.75 ($12) during the peak season (May to September), except at the Belfast hostel which charges around £8.75 ($15.50). The most expensive hostels in Scotland, those in the cities and Inverness, charge around £7.00–7.75 ($12.50–13.50) for seniors, but normally seniors pay £5.00–5.80 ($9–10). Prices tend to be higher in English and Welsh hostels. Seniors normally pay £5.25–7.75 ($9.00–13.50), but there are also a fair number of hostels which charge £8–12 ($14–21) and the London hostels charge from £11–17 ($19–30) (a small peak-season supplement of around £0.50 ($1) is added at many English and Welsh hostels in July and August).

Advance booking of hostels in the main places of interest is advisable from May to September and around Easter, preferably in writing, with payment enclosed. Telephone reservations are accepted on the day, but you must turn up by 6 p.m. to claim your bed. At the time of writing, hostels in 26 popular destinations in England and Wales are part of a Book-A-Bed-Ahead scheme for which a £1 ($1.75) fee is charged (the An Oige hostels in Dublin are also included in the network). Full details are available at hostels or in the Youth Hostels Association of England and Wales handbook. A similar system operates at 20 of the most visited Scottish hostels. Beds reserved through the Book-A-Bed-Ahead system can be claimed up until 10 p.m.

There are a number of independent hostels in the main places of interest. Standards are generally on a par with the local IYHF hostels, prices are generally slightly higher. The YMCA and YWCA operate hostels in several cities in which accommodation is usually in singles or doubles. However, prices can be as high as for bed and breakfast accommodation. During the Easter and summer vacations (normally mid-March to mid-April and July to early September) many universities let rooms (mostly singles) in student residences. The universities are primarily concerned with attracting visiting groups, so to be sure of a place you will have to book well in advance. Overnight prices are generally in the £16–21 ($28–49) price range. If there are any spare beds available some universities will let rooms on the day for around £10 ($17.50) to students with ID. If there are a number of you travelling together, renting a furnished student flat from a university is better value. The Tourist Information Centre will inform you about individuals and organizations letting self-catering accommodation in the locality. The one hitch to renting a flat may be an insistence on a minimum stay of up to one week, although this is not always the case.

There are campsites in, or just outside most of the main places of interest (Glasgow is a notable exception). Standards, and prices, vary dramatically but, short of sleeping rough, **camping** is the best option for keeping accommodation costs low. That said, you may still be bemused by the cost of camping in the UK. In comparison to other European countries, prices are high. In popular tourist destinations it is not unusual for a solo traveller to pay £7–8 ($12.50–14.00) for an overnight stay. Elsewhere it is unusual for prices to rise above £5 ($12.50–14.00) for an overnight stay. In smaller towns and villages, which have a minimal tourist trade, local farmers will usually let you pitch a tent on their land if you ask permission first. In the more remote areas, there will seldom be any objection to your camping rough, provided you do not leave litter lying about, or set any potentially dangerous fires. As the nights can be very cold in the hilly parts of the country, a good-quality sleeping bag is essential, especially in the Scottish Highlands (anyone visiting the Highlands in summer would also be well advised to invest in an effective insect repellant). The one main drawback to camping is the damp climate, so be sure that your tent really is waterproof.

ADDRESSES

National Tourist Boards
: English Tourist Board, Thames Tower, Black's Road, Hammersmith, London W6 9EL. Enquiries in writing only.
Northern Ireland Tourist Board, St Anne's Court, 59 North Street, Belfast, BT1 2DS (tel. 0232–231221)
Northern Ireland Tourist Board, 11 Berkeley Street, London W1X 5AD (tel. 071 493 0601)
Scottish Tourist Board, 23 Ravelston Terrace, Edinburgh EH4 3EU (tel. 031 930 8661)
Bwrdd Croeso Cymru (Welsh Tourist Board), Ty Brunel, 2 Ffordd Fitzalan, Caerdydd CF2 1UY (tel. 0222–499909)

IYHF hostels
: Youth Hostels Association of England and Wales, Trevelyan House, 8 St Stephen's Hill, St Albans, Hertfordshire, AL1 2DY (tel. 0727–55215).
Youth Hostel Association of Northern Ireland, 56 Bradbury Place, Belfast, BT7 1RU (tel. 0232–324733).
Scottish Youth Hostels Association, 7 Glebe Crescent, Stirling, FK8 2JA (tel. 0786–51181).

724 Cheap Sleep Guide

Bath (tel. code 0225)

Tourist Office
Tourist Information Centre, The Colonnades, Bath Street (tel. 462831). Open June–Sept., Mon.–Sat. 9.30 a.m.–7.00 p.m., Sun. 10 a.m.–6 p.m.; Oct.–May., Mon.–Sat. 9.30 a.m.–5.00 p.m. The small city plan sold at the office is useful for sightseeing and for finding your way to accommodation. £0.25 ($0.50). Free local accommodation service. You pay a 10 per cent deposit at the office, which is subtracted from your final bill. Book-A-Bed-Ahead service available.

Finding Accommodation
The popularity of the town, especially with more affluent, middle-aged tourists, means that prices in local B&Bs are slightly higher than normal. You can expect to pay about £14–15 ($24.50–26.50) per person to share a room in one of the cheaper establishments.

Finding a bed in one of the cheaper B&Bs can be difficult in summer as the city attracts large numbers of visitors. At this time of year, you are as well heading straight for the Tourist Information Centre and asking them for the cheapest B&B available. If you arrive early in the morning there are a few areas of the city you can look in before the office opens, all within 15 minutes' walk of the bus and train stations (see Basic Directions below). The best area to look is around Pulteney Road, as this has the highest concentration of the cheaper B&Bs. After that the area around Wells Road is probably just slightly better than that around the start of Upper Bristol Road.

Basic Directions
The bus station and the main train station (Bath Spa) are located almost right next to each other at the junctions of Manvers Street and Dorchester Street. The Tourist Office is just over 5 minutes' walk from the stations. From the train station, go left along Dorchester Street, turn right down Newark Street past the bus station, left at Henry Street, right along Stall

Street, then left on to Bath Street. The Tourist Information Centre is on the ground floor of The Colonnades shopping centre.

To reach Pulteney Road from the train station head along Manvers Street and then Pierrepoint Street, before turning right along North Parade. Going straight ahead along North Parade Road brings you into Pulteney Road. Pulteney Gardens, Pulteney Avenue and Pulteney Terrace are all along to the right from this point. Pulteney Gardens takes you into Lime Grove, another good street in which to look for B&Bs. Turning left along Pulteney Road, you arrive at the roundabout and the start of Raby Place. Continuing on down Pulteney Road to the end and then turning left you reach the end of Great Pulteney Street, which also has a fair supply of B&Bs. The quickest way to Great Pulteney Street from the train station is to continue right along Pierrepont Street, walk across Orange Grove and along Grand Parade, then turn right at Argyle Street. Going straight ahead you come to Great Pulteney Street.

Heading left from the train station along Dorchester Street, you can turn left off Broad Quay across the Churchill Bridge to the start of Wells Road (A367). Continuing along Broad Quay, then Green Park Road and subsequently Charles Street, you reach the junction with Monmouth Place and Monmouth Street. Heading left at the junction, Monmouth Place leads into Crescent Gardens, which in turn leads into Upper Bristol Road.

GUESTHOUSES AND B&Bs

Doubles from £22 ($38.50)

Wellsway Guest House, 51 Wellsway (tel. 423434). Fifteen minutes' walk from the train station. Wellsway is a continuation of Wells Road.

16 Bloomfield Road, Bear Flat (tel. 337804). A 15-minute walk from the train station. Right off the A367.

Doubles from £25 ($44)

Athelney Guest House, 5 Marlborough Lane (tel. 312031).

Just under 15 minutes' walk from the train station, right off the Upper Bristol Road.

Old Mill Lodge, Tollbridge Road (tel. 858476). By the River Avon, 1½ miles from the city centre.

Doubles from £26 ($45.50)

The Terrace Guest House, 3 Pulteney Terrace (tel. 316578).

Arney Guest House, 99 Wells Road (tel. 310020).

Sovereign Guest House, 38 St. James' Park (tel. 338162). Within 10–15 minutes' walk of the city centre.

Avon Guest House, 160 Newbridge Road (tel. 423866). In the Lower Weston Area of town. Bus 17 to Upper Weston from the bus station runs along the street.

The Shearns, Prior House, 3 Marlborough Lane (tel. 313587). See Athelney Guest House.

Doubles from £27 ($47.50)

2 Crescent Gardens (tel. 331186).

Membland Guest House, 7 Pulteney Terrace (tel. 336712).

Cherry Tree Villa, 7 Newbridge Hill (tel. 331671). About 1 mile from the town centre, right from Upper Bristol Road. Bus 17 from the bus station.

Arosa Guest House, 124 Lower Oldfield Park (tel. 425778). About 15 minutes' walk from the train station. Cross the Churchill Bridge and head right along the Lower Bristol Road, then left at Lower Oldfield Park.

Abbey Rise, 97 Wells Road (tel. 312031).

Doubles from £28 ($49)

Kinlet Guest House, 99 Wellsway (tel. 420268). See Wellsway Guest House.

Doubles from £29 ($51)

Sampford, 11 Oldfield Road (tel. 310053). A 10–15-minute walk from the train station, right off Wells Road.

Mardon Guest House, 1 Pulteney Terrace (tel. 311624).

Sheridan Guest House, 95 Wellsway (tel. 429562). See Wellsway Guest House.

The Albany Guest House, 24 Crescent Gardens (tel. 313339).

Astor House, 14 Oldfield Road (tel. 429134). See Sampford.

Baileys, 46 Crescent Gardens (tel. 333594).

Ashley House, 8 Pulteney Gardens (tel. 425027).

Abode, 7 Widcombe Crescent (tel. 422726). A 10–15-minute walk from the station. After crossing the Churchill Bridge follow Claverton Street. Widcombe Hill is on the left as the main road bends away to the right.

Toad Hall Guest House, 6 Lime Grove (tel. 423254/312853).

Doubles from £30 ($52.50)

Elgin Villa, 6 Marlborough Lane (tel. 424557) See Athelney Guest House.

Doubles from £31 ($54.50)

Smith's, 47 Crescent Gardens (tel. 422382).

Lynwood Guest House, 6–7 Pulteney Gardens (tel. 426410).

Holly Villa Guest House, 14 Pulteney Gardens (tel. 310331).

Waltons' Guest House, 17 Crescent Gardens (tel. 426528).

Mrs Guy, 14 Raby Place (tel. 465120).

The Georgian Guest House, 34 Henrietta Street (tel. 424103). From Grand Parade follow Argyle Street across the River Avon into Laura Place, then head left.

Crescent Guest House, 21 Crescent Gardens (tel. 425945).

Joanna House, 5 Pulteney Avenue (tel. 335246).

Milton House Guest House, 75 Wellsway (tel. 335632) See Wellsway Guest House.

The White Guest House, 23 Pulteney Gardens (tel. 426075).

Alderney Guest House, 3 Pulteney Road (tel. 312365).

IYHF HOSTEL

Bath Youth Hostel, Bathwick Hill (tel. 465674). Juniors £6.30 ($11), seniors £7.60 ($13.50). In July and August, a supplement of £0.50 ($1) is added to these prices. A

15–20-minute walk from the train station. From the roundabout on Pulteney Road by St Mary's Church turn down Raby Place, which becomes George Street and then Bathwick Hill. Badgerline bus 18 from the bus station.

HOSTELS

YMCA International House, Broad Street Place (tel. 60471). Open to men and women. No curfew. Dorms around £9.75 ($17), doubles around £11.50 ($20) per person, singles £12.75 ($22.50). Very popular, so reserve in writing well in advance. About 300m from the Tourist Office.

CAMPING

Newton Mill Touring Centre, Newton Street Loe (tel. 333909). The site charges an extortionate £6.75 ($12) per tent, £3.50 ($6) per person. Three miles from the centre. Bus 5 from the bus station to Newton Road (every 12 minutes).

IYHF HOSTELS NEARBY

Bristol International YHA Centre, Hayman House, 64 Prince Street, Bristol (tel. 0272–221659). Two- to six-bed rooms. Juniors £10 ($17.50), seniors £12.25 ($21.50). About 8 minutes' walk from Bristol Temple Meads train station. Bristol is 14 miles from Bath and the two towns are linked by frequent trains.

Belfast (tel. code 0232)

Tourist Office
Northern Ireland Tourist Board, St Anne's Court, 59 North Street, Belfast BT1 1ND. Head office of the Tourist Board. Very helpful if you want information to help you plan your trip. On

arrival, head for their Tourist Information Centre at the same
address (tel. 246609). Open June–Sept., Mon.–Fri. 9 a.m.–5.15
p.m., Sat. 9 a.m.–2 p.m.; Oct.–May., closed on Sat. Courteous
and knowledgeable staff. Room-finding service £0.50 ($1) fee.
The office distributes a good map, complete with bus routes,
and a pamphlet detailing an enjoyable walking tour of the city.
From Central Railway Station go left along East Bridge Street,
right at Victoria Street, left along Chichester Street into
Donegall Square, then right along Donegall Place and straight
on down Royal Avenue into North Street.

Finding Accommodation
No matter when you arrive in Belfast you should be able to
fix yourself up with suitable accommodation without too much
difficulty. The bulk of the accommodation possibilites are about
2 miles south of the centre, around the Botanic Gardens and
the university, along or just off the Lisburn Road and Malone
Road. There is also a reasonable supply of B&Bs to the east
of the River Lagan, around Belmont Road and Upper
Newtonards Road.

Public Transport
Although most of the accommodation is out from the centre,
regular buses run all over the city. Most buses depart from
Donegall Square, or from the streets off the square. To get to
the area around the Botanic Gardens and the university take
bus 69, 71, 84 or 85 from the City Hall on Donegall Square.
Bus 16 runs along Upper Newtonards Road, while Belmont
Road is served by buses 20, 22 and 23. Those with a railpass
staying around the Botanic Gardens area can save on bus fares
by taking a train to the Botanic Rail Station or the City Hospital
station. The Adelaide, Balmoral and Finaghy stations may be
useful if you are staying around Lisburn Road and Malone
Road.

Trouble Spots
Do not be deterred from visiting Northern Ireland because of
fears about your safety. Tourists have nothing to worry about,

either in or outside the capital, provided they are sensible. A bonus is that the incidence of petty crime is actually considerably lower than in mainland Britain. Another plus point is that there are few places in the United Kingdom where visitors are as warmly received by the local people as in Belfast. For obvious reasons, you should avoid talking about politics, religion and Irish history. Young males from mainland Britain should make sure they cannot be mistaken for off-duty soldiers if they are planning to travel around a bit (avoid really short haircuts and shave irregularly is the advice many soldiers give).

GUESTHOUSES AND B&Bs

Prices quoted below are for a double room with breakfast. Singles generally cost slightly more than half the price of a double room.

Around £25 ($44)

East Sheen House, 81 Eglantine Avenue (tel. 667149). Singles half the price of doubles. The street runs between the Lisburn Road and Malone Road, near the start of the latter.

Around £26 ($45.50)

Innisfail, 16 The Green (tel. 610044). Singles half the price of doubles.

Around £27 ($47.50)

James House, 55 Oakland Avenue (tel. 650374). East of the Lagan.
Lucy's Lodge, 72 Salisbury Avenue (tel. 776036). Singles half the price of doubles.
Marine House, 30 Eglantine Avenue (tel. 666828).

Around £28 ($49)

Liserin Guest House, 17 Eglantine Avenue (tel. 660769). See East Sheen House.

Aisling House, 7 Taunton Avenue (tel. 771529). Off the Antrim Road. Buses 2 and 45 run along the Antrim Road.

Mrs E. MacNamara, 7 Fortwilliam Park (tel. 779904). Off the Antrim Road, see Aisling House.

Around £29 ($51)

Dun-Roamin, 170 Upper Newtonards Road (tel. 659902).

Around £30 ($52.50)

Eglantine Guest House, 21 Eglantine Avenue (tel. 660769).

Ben Eadan Cottage, 9 Thorburn Road (tel. 777764). Off the Antrim Road. See Aisling House.

Bowdens, 17 Sandford Avenue (tel. 652213). Singles half the price of doubles.

Drumragh, 647 Antrim Road (tel. 773063). See Aisling House.

The Eagles, 131 Upper Newtonards Road (tel. 673607). Singles half the price of doubles.

The George, 9 Eglantine Avenue (tel. 683212). Singles half the price of doubles. See East Sheen House.

Harberton Lodge, 1 Harberton Avenue (tel. 666263). Singles half the price of doubles. University/Malone Road area.

Maramtha, 398 Ravenhill Road (tel. 645814). Singles half the price of doubles. Buses 78 and 79 run along Ravenhill Road.

Around £31 ($54.50)

Helga Lodge, 7 Cromwell Road (tel. 324820). Off Botanic Avenue, near the Botanic Rail Station. Bus 83 or 85 from Donegall Square.

Around £32 ($58.50)

Botanic Lodge Guest House, 87 Botanic Avenue (tel. 327682/247439). See Helga Lodge.

Pearl Court Guest House, 11 Malone Road (tel. 666145). Singles half the price of doubles.

Crecora, 114 Upper Newtonards Road (tel. 658257). Singles half the price of doubles.

Harveys, 192 Belmont Road (tel. 652320). Singles half the price of doubles.

STUDENT RESIDENCES

Queen's Elms, Queen's University, 78 Malone Road (tel. 381608). Open mid-June–mid-Sept. No curfew. Singles £10 ($17.50), doubles £14 ($24.50). Student discount of around 20 per cent on these prices. Bus 71 from Donegall Square East. The closest rail station is Adelaide.

Ulster People's College, 30 Adelaide Park (tel. 665161/381368). Open year round. £13 ($23) per person in singles or doubles. Close to the Queen's Elms residence above. Adelaide Park runs between Malone Road and Lisburn Road.

IYHF HOSTEL

Belfast International Youth Hostel, 'Ardmore', 11 Saintfield Road (tel. 647865). Closes for a couple of weeks around the Christmas/New Year period. Open all day during the summer. July and Aug. £8.50 ($15) for seniors. Around £7.50 ($13) at other times. Two miles from the centre on the Newcastle road. From the City Hall on Donegall Square East take bus 38 or 84 and ask the driver to stop at the hostel. A new hostel will be operating in Belfast in 1993. Contact the Youth Hostel of Northern Ireland or the Tourist Information Centre for details, or consult the IYHF handbook.

HOSTELS

YWCA, Queen Mary's Hall, 70 Fitzwilliam Street (tel. 240439). Singles £12.50 ($22), doubles £24 ($42). Fitzwilliam Street runs between the Lisburn Road and University Road, joining the latter opposite the university. The hostel is just off Lisburn Road. Bus 59 runs along the Lisburn

Road. The closest rail station is City Hospital, just over 5
minutes' walk away.

YWCA, Wellesley House, 3/5 Malone Road (tel. 240439).
Singles £13.50 ($24), doubles £24 ($42). Close to the other
YWCA hostel. Take bus 71 from Donegall Square East.

YMCA Interpoint, 12 Wellington Place (tel. 327231). Bus/walk
to Belfast City Hall, about 500 metres further on.

CAMPING

Belvoir Forest. The closest site to the city, 3 miles from the
centre off the A504. The site is operated by the Forest
Service. A permit is required to use all Forest Service sites.
A casual permit is valid for anything between two days
and two weeks. Annual permits are also sold. Forest
Service, Dundonald House (Room 34), Belfast BT4 3SB (tel.
650111 ext. 456).

Cambridge (tel. code 0223)

Tourist Office

Tourist Information Centre, Wheeler Street (tel. 322640). Open
Mar.–Oct., Mon.–Sat. 9 a.m.–6 p.m., Sun. 10.30 a.m.–3.30
p.m.; Nov.–Feb., Mon.–Fri. 9.00 a.m.–5.30 p.m., Sat. 9
a.m.–5 p.m. Room-finding service for £1 ($1.75) fee. The office
sells a list of local accommodation for £0.30 ($0.50), a copy of
which is displayed in the office window. Book-A-Bed-Ahead
service available.

Basic Directions

The train station is just under 20 minutes' walk from the centre.
Head down Station Road, turn right at the end of the street
along Hills Road (A604), and keep going straight ahead until
you see Downing Street running left off St Andrew's Street.
Turning right off Downing Street along Corn Exchange Street
takes you into Wheeler Street. Buses 1, 5 and 9 link the train

station with the centre. The Drummer Street bus station is right in the heart of the city. From the station, the lane running down the side of Christ's College brings you out on to the main street opposite the Post Office. Cross the road, head right, and then take the lane on your left to reach Wheeler Street.

Finding Accommodation

Cambridge has a plentiful supply of rooms, so only during the peak season (late June to the end of August) are you likely to have some difficulty finding a room, at which time it is advisable to try to reserve a bed in advance. Tenison Street, near the train station, is a good place to look for one of the cheaper B&Bs at any time of year. Outside university term-time in and around Jesus Lane, near Jesus College is another good area to look in. Many of the establishments in this part of town are only open to visitors during the university vacations (mid-June–end Sept., and possibly Easter and Christmas), because they are filled with students during the university year.

GUESTHOUSES AND B&Bs

Doubles from around £24 ($42)

Lyngamore Guest House, 35/37 Chesterton Road (tel. 312369).

Doubles from around £25 ($44)

Tenison Towers Guest House, 148 Tenison Road (tel. 63924).
Mrs C. McCann, 40 Warkworth Street (tel. 314098). University vacations only.
Mrs H. Barr, 25 Worts Causeway (tel. 245391).
Acorn Guest House, 154 Chesterton Road (tel. 353888).
Mr J. Antony, 4 Huntingdon Road (tel. 357444).

Doubles from around £26 ($45.50)

The Milton Guest House, 63 Milton Road (tel. 311625).
European Centre Guest House, 94 Milton Road (tel. 357474).

Mrs P. Droy, El Shaddai, 41 Warkworth Street (tel. 327978). University vacations only.

Doubles from around £27 ($47.50)

Lovell Lodge Guest House, 365 Milton Road (tel. 425478).
Railway Lodge, 150 Tenison Road (tel. 467688).
All Seasons Guest House, 219 Chesterton Road (tel. 353386).
Mrs M. Saunders, 145 Gwydir Street (tel. 356615).
Arbury Lodge Guest House, 82 Arbury Road (tel. 64319).
Mrs A. Bartram, 18 Covent Garden (tel. 323340).
Green End Guest House, 70 Green End Road (tel. 420433).
Mrs S. Bradshaw, Mowbray House, 153 Mowbray Road (tel. 411051).
Abbey Guest House, 588 Newmarket Road (tel. 241427).
Mr & Mrs M. Dixon, Windy Ridge, 4 Worts' Causeway (tel. 246783).

Doubles around £28 ($49)

Mrs J. Norman, 27 New Square (tel. 355613).

Doubles from around £28 ($49)

Mrs R. Tempest-Holt, 44 Natal Road (tel. 249003).
Mrs M. Spence, St Mark's Vicarage, Barton Road (tel. 63339).
Mr S. Brown, 40 Lensfield Road (tel. 62839). University vacations only.
Mrs H. Rowell, 39 Trumpington Street (tel. 355439). University vacations only.

Doubles around £29 ($51)

Mrs M.E. Lockwood, 'Alfriston', 7 Harvey Goodwin Avenue (tel. 359351).

Doubles from around £29 ($51)

Antwerp Guest House, 36 Brookfields, Mill Road (tel. 247690).

Mrs M. Anderson, Norman Cross, 175 Hills Road (tel. 411959).

Southampton Guest House, 7 Elizabeth Way (tel. 357780).

Benson House, 24 Huntingdon Road (tel. 311594).

De Freville House, 166 Chesterton Road (tel. 354933).

Doubles around £31 ($54.50)

Mr & Mrs Dow, Hazelwood, 58 Maids Causeway (tel. 322450).

Mrs S. Payne, 16 Eltisley Avenue (tel. 328996).

Mrs J. Diaper, 22–24 Portugal Street (tel. 357769). University vacations only.

Mr & Mrs Holmes, 6 Portugal Street (tel. 67845). University vacations only.

Doubles from around £31 ($54.50)

Belle Vue Guest House, 33 Chesterton Road (tel. 351859).

Warkworth Guest House, Warkworth Terrace (tel. 63682).

Mrs S. Cook, 7 Brookfields, Mill Road (tel. 211259).

Bon Accord House, 20 St Margaret's Square (off Cherry Hinton Road) (tel. 246568/411188).

IYHF HOSTEL

Cambridge Youth Hostel, 97 Tenison Road (tel. 354601). Open year round. Mostly four- to seven-bed rooms. Described by the YHA England and Wales as one of their busiest hostels, so try to reserve well in advance. Juniors £7.50 ($13), seniors £8.90 ($15.50). In July and Aug., a supplement of £0.60 ($1) is added to these prices. A few minutes' walk from the train station, right along Tenison Road from Station Road.

HOSTEL

Cambridge YMCA, Queen Anne House, Gonville Place (tel.

356998). Open to men and women. B&B from £15.25–18.75 ($26.50–33.00).

CAMPING

There is no shortage of sites in the Cambridge area (16 in all). Details of these sites are contained in the list sold by the Tourist Information Centre for a nominal fee.

Camping & Caravan Club, Cabbage Moor, Cambridge Road, Great Shelford (tel. 841185). Open Apr.–Oct. Peak season (24–30 May and 21 June–29 Aug) £4.20 ($7.50) per person; at other times, £3.75 ($6.50) per person. Three miles south of town. Follow the A10 and turn left along the A1031.

Highfield Farm Camping Site, Long Road, Comberton (tel. 262308). Open Apr.–Oct. £6.25 ($11) for a small tent in July and August, £5.25 ($9) at other times. Four miles from town, on the B1046 (turn off the A603 at Barton). Bus 118 or 119 from the Drummer Street bus station.

Edinburgh (Dun Eid Eann)

(tel. code 031)

Tourist Offices
Edinburgh & Scotland Information Centre, 3 Princes Street (tel. 5571700). Open daily, 8.30 a.m.–9.00 p.m. July–Aug.; daily, 8.30 a.m.–8.00 p.m. May–June and Sept.; April, Mon.–Sat. 9 a.m.–6 p.m., Sun. 11 a.m.–6 p.m.; Oct.–Mar., Mon.–Sat. 9 a.m.–6 p.m. Book-A-Bed-Ahead and local accommodation services. £2.50 ($4.50) fee for finding rooms in local guesthouses and B&Bs; the only town in Scotland charging for this service (see Finding Accommodation below). You pay 10 per cent of the bill at the office as a deposit, and the remaining 90 per cent to the proprietor. Free lists of local guesthouses and B&Bs, and hostels. The staff will check the availability of beds in local hostels, but cannot make bookings. Good range of information

on the city. Very helpful staff. Set back off Princes Street, by the Waverly Steps, right above the Waverley Market shopping centre.

Tourist Information Desk, Edinburgh International Airport (tel. 3332167). Open Apr.–Oct., Mon.–Sat. 8.30 a.m.–9.30 p.m., Sun. 9.30 a.m.–9.30 p.m.; Nov.–Mar., Mon.–Fri. 9 a.m.–6 p.m., weekends 9 a.m.–5 p.m. Opposite Gate 5 in the main hall.

Basic Directions

All trains to Edinburgh stop at the main Waverley station, just off Princes Street. With the exception of express services running on the East Coast line (through Newcastle and Berwick-upon-Tweed) all trains also pass through the Haymarket station, just over one mile from the Waverley Station along Princes Street, Shandwick Place and West Maitland Street. To reach the Tourist Office from the Waverley station either go up the Waverley Steps (beginning near platforms 1 and 19) and turn left at the top, or go out of the rear exit used by taxis, turn right up Waverley Bridge towards Princes Street, then right again across the pedestrian concourse. Some long-distance coaches drop passengers on Waverley Bridge, but most use the nearby St Andrew's Square Bus Station. From the bus station, walk out on to the open space of St Andrew's Square, turn left and follow South St Andrew's Street on to Princes Street, at which point the Tourist Office is diagonally left across the street. The shuttle buses which serve the airport run from/to Waverley train station or Waverley Bridge.

Standing with your back to the Tourist Office, the east end of Princes Street is about 100m to your right. Running right from the end of Princes Street at that point is a series of streets known locally as The Bridges. Walking along to the west end of Princes Street you can continue more or less straight ahead along Shandwich Place and West Maitland Street to the Haymarket, or turn left up Lothian Road. Lothian Road is roughly one mile from Waverley train station and St Andrew's Square bus station, 1/3 mile from the Haymarket station.

Public Transport

Most of the cheaper guesthouses and B&Bs are at least 20–25 minutes' walk from the centre. There are a variety of bus companies operating within the city, but the most comprehensive service is provided by the maroon-and-white buses of Lothian Region Transport (LRT). Information on their services can be obtained by telephoning 220411, or from the information office behind the Sheriff Court on St Giles' Street (open normal office hours). If all you want is information on bus routes you can save a lot of time by visiting this office rather than the Tourist Office. From Princes Street walk down Waverley Bridge past the train station, turn right up Market Street, climb the set of stairs on your left, and the office is to the left at the top of the stairs. When using LRT buses remember that no change is given, so have plenty of coins ready.

Finding Accommodation

Despite the fact that the Scottish capital has more guesthouses and B&Bs than any other city in the UK save London, plus a relatively large hostel capacity in peak season, you will toil to find a bed in a hostel or one of the cheaper guesthouses or B&Bs if you arrive without reservations during the annual Edinburgh Festival (a three-week period in August). If you are arriving from another Scottish town at this time it is a good idea to try and fix up one of the cheaper B&Bs in advance using the Book-A-Bed-Ahead service; you pay roughly the same fee as the local Tourist Office charges to find a bed, but will avoid the queues, which can be horrendous. Otherwise, the chances are that you will just have to see what the local Tourist Office can find for you on arrival. There is a free accommodation service in the Waverley train station (by platforms 1 and 19) but they have a limited supply of rooms, while phoning around on your own during the Festival period can be both soul-destroying and expensive. If you arrive without reservations and find all the affordable accommodations gone, those with railpasses might consider staying in the surrounding counties of Eastlothian, Midlothian and West Lothian for your first night, while trying to make a reservation in the city for subsequent nights (see the Staying Around Edinburgh section, below). Fortunately, the accommodation situation improves dramatically outside the Festival period: even in July it is not too difficult to find one of the cheaper beds, provided you arrive reasonably early in the day. The exception is in the week leading up to one of the Five Nations' rugby internationals (played around the turn of the year), when hordes of visiting fans descend on the city. The situation is at its worst when the Welsh are the visitors, as they not only fill up the cheaper accommodation in the capital but in most of the towns within thirty miles south and east of the city. If you want to look for guesthouses and B&Bs on your own, particularly good areas to search in are Bruntsfield, and Newington/Mayfield (between the Royal Commonwealth Pool and the Cameron Toll shopping centre). LRT buses running up Lothian Road will take you into Bruntsfield, while those heading up The Bridges will take you into Newington/Mayfield.

Trouble Spots

If you are staying in Bruntsfield, Newington or Mayfield, the tree-lined park known as the Meadows can be a useful short cut to the centre if you are on foot. The Meadows should, however, be avoided after dark. In recent years there have been a number of rapes here and numerous instances of women being subjected to severe sexual harassment. Unprovoked assaults on men by gangs of youths have also become regrettably common over the last few years.

GUESTHOUSES AND B&Bs

Prices quoted for the guesthouses and B&Bs below are minimum and maximum prices per person for Bed & Breakfast, based on two people sharing a room. Prices frequently vary with the season, and are usually at their height during the Edinburgh Festival. Whereas most guesthouses are open year round, B&Bs generally open from May to September. Exceptions to these rules are noted in the listings below.

GUESTHOUSES

From £11–16 ($19–28)

Armadillo Guest House, 5 Upper Gilmore Place (tel. 2294669).

From £11–17 ($19–30)

Lorne Villa Guest House, 9 East Mayfield (tel. 6677159).

From £11–19 ($19–33)

Cree Guest House, 77 Mayfield Road (tel. 6672524).

From £11–20 ($19–35)

Kingsview Guest House, 28 Gilmore Place (tel. 2298004).

From £11–21 ($19–37)

Dargil Guest House, 16 Mayfield Gardens (tel. 6676177).

From £12–15 ($21–26)

Waverley House, 75 Viewforth (tel. 2298627).
Appleton House, 15 Leamington Terrace (tel. 2293059).
Leamington Guest House, 57 Leamington Terrace (tel. 2283879).
Quendale Guest House, 32 Craigmillar Park (tel. 6673171).

From £12–17 ($21–30)

Sharon Guest House, 1 Kilmaurs Terrace (tel. 6672002).

From £12–18 ($21.00–31.50)

Highland Park Guest House, 16 Kilmaurs Terrace (tel. 6679204).
Sherwood Guest House, 42 Minto Street (tel. 6671200).

From £12–19 ($21–33)

Cafe Royal Guest House, 5 West Register Street (tel. 5566894).

From £12–20 ($21–35)

Averon Guest House, 44 Gilmore Place (tel. 2299932).

From £13–16 ($23–28)

Ardmor Guest House, 74 Pilrig Street (tel. 5544944).
Allan Lodge Guest House, 37 Queens Crescent (tel. 6682947).
Devon House, 2 Pitville Street (tel. 6696067).
Dunard Guest House, 16 Hartington Place (tel. 2296848).
Edinburgh Thistle Guest House, 10 East Hermitage Place (tel. 5548457).
Hillview Guest House, 92 Dalkeith Road (tel. 6671523).
Torivane, 1 Morton Street (tel. 6691648). Open Mar.–Oct.

From £13–17 ($23–30)

Dalwin Lodge Guest House, 75 Mayfield Road (tel. 6672294).
Glenesk Guest House, 39 Liberton Brae (tel. 6641529).
Hopetoun Guest House, 15 Mayfield Road (tel. 6677691).
Joppa Turrets Guest House, 1 Lower Joppa (tel. 6695906).
Maple Leaf Guest House, 23 Pilrig Street (tel. 5547692).

From £13–19 ($23–33)

Falcon Crest, 70 South Trinity Road (tel. 5525294).
Highfield Guest House, 83 Mayfield Road (tel. 6678717).
Tankard Guest House, 40 East Claremont Street (tel. 5564218).
Tiree Guest House, 26 Craigmillar Park (tel. 6677477).
Valentine Guest House, 19 Gilmore Place (tel. 2295622).

B&Bs

£11 ($19)

Mrs J. Ferguson, 20 Restalrig Gardens (tel. 6613762).

£12 ($21)

Mrs M. Melrose, 26 Dudley Avenue (tel. 5541915). Open June–Sept.

From £11–13 ($19–23)

Sylvia Cranston, 17 McDonald Road (tel. 5578367).
Catherine Duncan, 68 Willowbrae Avenue (tel. 6612699). Open Aug.–Sept.
Carol Glover, 13 Lismore Crescent (tel. 6611186).
Mrs A. Hamilton, 6 Cambridge Gardens (tel. 5543113).
Mr and Mrs Irvine, 116 Greenbank Crescent (tel. 4479454).
Mrs H. McKue, 1 Moat St. (tel. 4438020).
Kathryn H. Robertson, 12 Swanston Avenue (tel. 4451103).

From £11–15 ($19–26)

Rachel G. Argo, 61 Lothian Road (tel. 2294054).
Angela Burnett, Roxzannah, 11 Bernard Terrace (tel. 6678933).
Mrs Monica M. Fallon, 5 Cameron Park (tel. 6673857).
Mrs S. Sadol, Harrist, 33 Straiton Place (tel. 6573160).
M.A. Urquhart, The Rowans, 34 Liberton Brae (tel. 6581980).

From £11–16 ($19–28)

Mr Lawrence Essien, The Hedges, 19 Hillside Crescent (tel. 5581481).
Mr J. McConnachie, Ben Aven, 3 Shandon Road (tel. 3378839).
E.C. Simpson, 17 Crawfurd Road (tel. 6671191).

From £12–13 ($21–23)

Mrs Mary Coutts, Meadowplace House, 1 Meadowplace Road (tel. 3348459).
Mrs M. Fitzgerald, 10 Lauriston Gardens (tel. 2293848).

Barbara Mallen, 33 Belgrave Road (tel. 3345721).
Mrs M. Vance, 21 Murieston Crescent (tel. 3377108).

From £12–14 ($21.00–24.50)

J. Ruth Hutchison, 38 Hope Terrace (tel. 4477627).
Elizabeth F. Smith, 36 Farrer Terrace (tel. 6691262). Open
Apr.–Sept.
Mrs R.C. Torrance, 15 Viewforth Terrace (tel. 2291776).

From £12–15 ($21–26)

A.M. Royden, Coigach, 5 Polwarth Grove (tel. 3379866).

£13 ($23)

Mrs L. Birnie, 8 Kilmaurs Road (tel. 6678998).
Mrs E. McTighe, 4 Coinyie House Close (tel. 5563399).

From £13–14 ($23.00–24.50)

Mary Campbell, Star Villa, 36 Gilmore Place (tel. 2294991).
Mr & Mrs O'Donnell, 5 Sciennes Road (tel. 6677634).

From £13–15 ($23–26)

Alison Albuisson, 7 Sciennes Road (tel. 6677437). Open
July–Sept.
Elizabeth Banigan, 5 Viewforth Terrace (tel. 2296698). Open
June–Sept.
Mrs E.M. Bradu, 32 Grange Road (tel. 6674795). Open
June–Sept.
Mrs Sheila Crichton, The Garth, 10 Silverknowles Bank (tel.
3363478).
Mary Downing, 11 Johnston Terrace (tel. 2266689).
Mrs A. Egan, 157 Craiglea Drive (tel. 4471580).
Mrs D. Fulton, 3 Brunton Place (tel. 5560459).
Alexia Graham, 18 Moston Terrace (tel. 6673466). Open
June–Sept.

Mrs N.L. Jameson, Aros House, 1 Salisbury Place (tel. 6671585).

Mr Philip Lugton, 29 Leamington Terrace (tel. 2297033). Open year round.

E Manson, Doocote House, 15 Moat Street (tel. 4435455).

Mrs S.M. McKie, The Haven, 74 Glasgow Road (tel. 3394712). Open year round.

Mrs U. McLean, 7 Crawfurd Road (tel. 6672283).

Mrs. S.J. McLennan, Airdenair, 29 Kilmaurs Road (tel. 6682336).

From £13–16 ($23–28)

Maria Boyle, Villa Maria, 6A Mayfield Gardens (tel. 6677730).

Lynn Cooper, 24 Gilmore Place (tel. 2282136).

FURNISHED FLATS WITH KITCHEN FACILITIES

Old Town Flat, Kings Stables Road. One flat sleeping four, right under the castle at the foot of the Grassmarket. Available year round. Min. stay one week. From £90–260 ($160–450) per week. Bookings to: Mr John N. Watson, 20 Grange Road, Edinburgh, EH9 1UJ (tel. 6675269).

Linton Court Apartments. Available year round. Forty flats sleeping one to seven. No minimum stay. Weekly rates from £155–435 ($270–760). Bookings to W.G. Hay, Murieston Road, Edinburgh, EH11 2JJ (tel. 3374040).

Lauriston Self-Catering Flats. Four flats sleeping three to five people. Close to Edinburgh University, a 5-minute walk from the centre. Available year round. Min. stay one week. Weekly rates from £125–185 ($220–320). Bookings to: John M. Forbes, 10B Lauriston Park (tel. 2290513).

West End Apartments. Available year round. Five flats sleeping two to six people. Min. stay two nights. From £150–440 ($260–770) per week. Bookings to: Brian Mathieson, 2 Learmouth Terrace, Edinburgh, EH4 1PQ (tel. 3320717/5567520).

STUDENT RESIDENCES

Prices in local student residences are expensive, although if there are any beds which have not been pre-booked by groups, they may be let out to students with ID for about half the normal price.

Pollock Halls of Residence (University of Edinburgh), 18 Holyrood Park Road (tel. 6671971). Open for four weeks in the period Mar.–Apr. and July–early Sept. B&B from £16.50–25.00 ($29–44). By the Royal Commonwealth Pool.

Melvin House, 3 Rothesay Terrace (tel. 2206715). Open year round. B&B from £20–23 ($35–40). Down Palmerston Place from West Maitland Street, then right along Rothesay Place.

IYHF HOSTELS

18 Eglinton Crescent (tel. 3371120). Curfew 2 a.m. £7 ($12.50). Best reserved in advance with payment during peak period July–Sept. A 20-minute walk from the Waverley train station but only 5 minutes from the Haymarket station. From West Maitland Street, turn down Palmerston Place and watch for Eglinton Crescent on your left. Buses 3, 4, 12, 13, 22, 26, 28, 31, 33 and 34 run along Princes St to Palmerston Place.

7 Bruntsfield Crescent (tel. 4472994). Curfew 2 a.m. Check in from 11.30 a.m. (no earlier). £7.75 ($13.50). Again book well in advance during the peak season. About 30 minutes' walk from either train station. Buses 11, 15, 16 and 17 run down Lothian Road into Bruntsfield.

HOSTELS

Belford Youth Hostel, 6/8 Douglas Gardens (tel. 2256209). Within a church, choose between sleeping in the Great Hall or a private room. A lovely new hostel with great facilities. Free bus from train or bus station. Advance booking recommended. Open 24 hours. No rules worth mentioning. £6.95 nightly. Breakfast £1. Laundry available. From Princes Street go to Queensferry Street, bear left to Belford Road. Hostel is at intersection with Douglas Gardens.

High Street Hostel, 8 Blackfriars St. (tel. 5573984). Open to British students and foreign visitors only. £7 ($12.50). Advance bookings are accepted if accompanied by the cost of the first night's stay. Free luggage storage. Turn left down the High Street from the Bridges, then right down Blackfriars Street. From Waverley train station, go out the exit the taxis use, then left up Waverley Bridge. At the mini-roundabout go uphill on Cockburn Street, then turn left down the High Street to the junction with The Bridges. Go straight ahead, then turn right at Blackfriars Street.

Cowgate Tourist Hostel, 112 The Cowgate (tel. 226 2153). Open during the Edinburgh Festival. Singles from £10 ($17.50), doubles from £18 ($31.50). If you go right down Blackfriars Street (see the High Street Hostel) you arrive in the Cowgate.

Christian Alliance Frances Kinnaird Hostel, 14 Coates Crescent (tel. 2253608). Open year round. Midnight curfew, extended to 1.30 a.m. at festival time. Women, married couples and children only. Singles from £18 ($31.50), doubles from £12 ($21) per person. Free luggage storage. A five-minute walk from Haymarket Station, left off West Maitland Street two streets after Palmerston Place. A 15-minute walk from Waverley, or bus 3, 4, 12, 13, 22, 26, 28, 31, 33 or 34 along Princes Street ot Palmerston Place. Walking from the Waverley, Coates Crescent is the right turning off Shandwick Place after Stafford Street.

CAMPING

Muirhouse Caravan Park, Marine Drive, Silverknowes (tel. 312 6874). Open Apr.–Oct. Two sharing a tent pay £6 ($10.50). Bus 14. Do not walk through the nearby Muirhouse or Pilton housing schemes: much of Edinburgh's reputation as the heroin and AIDS capital of

Europe was built around these areas and unprovoked assaults are common.

Little France Caravan Park, 219 Old Dalkeith Road (tel. 666 2326). Two people sharing a tent pay £7 ($12.50). LRT bus 33, 82, or 89 from The Bridges.

Mortonhall Park Caravan Park, 38 Mortonhall Gate, Frogston Road East (tel. 664 1533). Two people sharing a tent pay £8 ($14). LRT buses 11, 81 or 81B run from Princes St to Mortonhall.

STAYING AROUND EDINBURGH

Linlithgow (tel. code 0506), the county town of West Lothian is one of the oldest royal burghs of Scotland, and was, for a time, the summer residence of the Scottish royal family. The ruins of the royal palace by the loch are testimony to the town's past importance. Eighteen miles from Edinburgh, Linlithgow is a short train journey away on the lines to Glasgow, Falkirk and Stirling (not all trains stop at Linlithgow, but the service is frequent). There are also frequent Midland Scottish buses (blue and white) from St Andrew's Square bus station and/or Princes Street. The train station is just off one end of the High Street. The Tourist Information Centre (tel. 844600) in the Burgh Halls at The Cross is set back off the High Street (on the right walking from the train station or as the bus passes through town).

South Queensferry (tel. code as for Edinburgh), is another ancient royal burgh, traditionally part of West Lothian, but now (technically) part of the City of Edinburgh. The town has an attractive main street, but most visitors come for the views of the Forth road and rail bridges. About 8 miles from Edinburgh, the town is served by frequent buses from St Andrew's Square bus station and/or George Street (parallel to Princes Street). There are also regular train services to the neighbouring town of Dalmeny, a 10–15-minute walk from South Queensferry.

The coastal town of **Musselburgh** (tel. code as for Edinburgh) is 5 miles from the city centre. The town's main attraction is its racecourse, though its town hall provides evidence of the links between this part of Scotland and the Netherlands. The capital is a 10-minute trip away by hourly trains. The station is on the outskirts of the town, a 15-minute walk from the centre. There is also a frequent bus service from Edinburgh. LRT buses 26,44, 85 and 86 from Princes Street run through Musselburgh to Wallyford and Tranent, while Lowland and Eastern Scottish buses from St Andrew's Square/St Andrew's Square bus station to North Berwick, Dunbar, Haddington and Pencaitland usually stop in Musselburgh (only a few express buses such as the X08 or X13 do not – ask the driver). From June to September, a Tourist Information Centre (tel. 6656597) operates in the Brunton Hall (buses stop right outside).

North Berwick (tel. code 0620), 25 miles from Edinburgh, is another of Scotland's oldest royal burghs. Nowadays North Berwick is a pleasant seaside town, but its former strategic importance is shown by the impressive ruins of Tantallon Castle a short distance along the coast. Hourly trains make the 30-minute trip from Haymarket and Waverley stations. The bus journey from the capital is long and expensive. The Tourist Information Centre is on Quality Street (tel. 2197).

Twenty-eight miles from Edinburgh is the old fishing town of **Dunbar** (tel. code 0368), now a quiet seaside resort, and the sunniest town in Scotland. Travelling by bus from Edinburgh is expensive and takes over an hour, but Dunbar is just over 20 minutes' away by train on the line to Newcastle-upon-Tyne and London King's Cross (not all trains stop in Dunbar). The train station is only 5 minutes' walk from the Tourist Information Centre at 143 High Street (tel. 63353).

Prices quoted for the guesthouses and B&Bs below are per person based on two people sharing a room.

From £11 ($19)

Mrs M. Findlay, 43 Clarendon Crescent, Linlithgow (tel. 842574). Open year round.

From £11–13 ($19–23)

Mrs Craven, 19 Bridge Street, Musselburgh (tel. 6656560). Open year round. By the River Esk.

From £11-14 ($19.00-24.50)

Mrs P. Swanston, Chestnut Lodge, 2a Ware Road, North
Berwick (tel. 4256). Open year round.

From £12 ($21)

Mrs B. Douglas, Melville House, 103a North High Street,
Musselburgh (tel. 6655187). Open Apr.-Oct. In the
Fisherrow part of town, along the main street as the bus
enters Musselburgh.

Mrs C. Douglas, 5 Craighall Terrace, Musselburgh (tel.
6654294). Open June-Oct. Close to the racecourse.

Mrs Mackay, 16 Craighall Terrace, Musselburgh (tel.
6655641). Open year round. Close to the racecourse.

Mrs Moffat, Arden House, 26 Linkfield Road, Musselburgh
(tel. 6650663). Open Apr.-Oct. Overlooking the
racecourse.

Mrs Mooney, 137 Barons Hill Avenue, Linlithgow (tel.
843903). Open Apr.-Oct.

Mrs H. Sherratt, 23 Merker Terrace, Linlithgow (tel. 845213).
Open Apr.-Oct.

From £12-13 ($21-23)

Mrs I. Brown, 14 Marine Parade, North Berwick (tel. 2063).
Open year round.

From £12-14 ($21.00-24.50)

Mrs Clyne, The Shieling, 14 Mayville Park, Dunbar (tel.
62983). Open May-Sept.

Mrs McGowan, 23 Linkfield Road, Musselburgh (tel.
6657436). By the racecourse.

From £13 ($23)

Marine Guest House, Marine Road, Dunbar (tel. 63315).
Open year round.

Mrs J. M. Aitken, 18 Woodside Gardens, Musselburgh (tel.

6653170/6653344). Open year round. Close to the racecourse.

Miss Mitchell, Craigesk, 10 Albert Terrace, Musselburgh (tel. 6653344/6653170). Open year round. Overlooking the racecourse.

Mrs Duns, Windrow, 20 Marmion Road, North Berwick (tel. 2066). Open Apr.–Sept.

Mrs McNeill, 3 Kirk Potts, North Berwick (tel. 2594). Open May–Sept.

Anne M. Watt, 130 Baron's Hill Avenue, Linlithgow (tel. 842866). Open year round.

From £13–14 ($23.00–24.50)

Crachan Guest House, East Links Road, Dunbar (tel. 63006). Open year round.

Mrs R. Lumsden, 26 Dundas Avenue, North Berwick (tel. 2651). Open Apr.–Sept.

£14 ($24.50)

Mrs N. Smith, St Mary's House, 18 Kirkliston Road, South Queensferry (tel. 3312550). Open Apr.–Sept.

Exeter (tel. code 0392)

Tourist Office
Tourist Information Centre, Civic Centre, Paris Street (tel. 265700). Open Mon.–Fri. 9 a.m.–5 p.m., Sat. 9 a.m.–1 p.m. and 2–5 p.m. Local accommodation service and Book-A-Bed-Ahead. The office provides free lists of local accommodation.

Basic Directions
Exeter St David's (the main train station) is just under 1 mile from the city centre, just off the A377 to north Devon. Going straight ahead from the station, cross the A377 and then follow the path on the opposite side of the road to its end. Across

the road at this point is the start of Howell Road (a street with
a fair supply of B&Bs), while turning right at this point takes
you up into St David's Hill (the street with the highest
concentration of B&Bs in the city). Walk a short distance down
Howell Road then turn right at the junction with the New
North Road. At the Clock Tower, New North Road heads left
around the rear of the castle. Continuing straight ahead past
the Clock Tower you can follow Queen Street past Exeter
Central train station and the Arts Centre before reaching the
junction with the High Street. Go left, then at the end of the
High Street turn right to reach the Tourist Information Centre
in Paris Street. The bus and coach station is right opposite the
Tourist Information Centre.

GUESTHOUSES AND B&Bs

From £10–11 ($17.50–19.00) per person

The Old Mill, Mill Lane, Alphington (tel. 5977). One mile
from the city centre. Enter through Brookfield Gardens.

From £11 ($19) per person

Highbury, 89 St David's Hill (tel. 70549).
Mr & Mrs Pearmain, 12 Devonshire Place (tel. 58147) A
10-minute walk from the city centre.

From £12 ($21) per person

St David's Lodge, 65 St David's Hill (tel. 51613).

From £13 ($23) per person

Mr & Mrs La Pla, 64 Collins Road (tel. 50266). Non smokers
only.
Cyrnea, 73 Howell Road (tel. 438386).
Mead's Guest House, 2 St David's Hill (tel. 74886).
Janbri Guest House, 102 Alphington Road (tel. 77346).
Rhonas, 15 Blackall Road (tel. 77791). Close to the centre.
Off the New North Road, near the castle.

Dunmore Hotel, 22 Blackall Road (tel. 431643. See Rhonas, immediately above.

Telstar Hotel, 77 St David's Hill (tel. 42466).

Fort William Guest House, 75 St David's Hill (tel. 438495).

Viburnum House, 80 Topsham Road (tel. 76344).

From £14–16 ($24.50–28.00) per person

The Helliers Guest House, 37 Heavitree Road (tel. 436277). Close to the Tourist Information Centre, across the roundabout at the end of Paris Street.

IYHF HOSTEL

Exeter YH, 47–49 Countess Wear Road (tel. 873329). Juniors £6.30 ($11), seniors £7.60 ($13.50). Supplement of £0.50 ($1) in July and August. Two miles from the centre in the direction of Topsham. From the High Street, take bus K or T to Countess Wear Post Office, and then walk along Exe Vale Road.

CAMPING

Hill Pond, Sidmouth Road (tel. 32483).

Glasgow (Glas Chu) (tel. code 041)

Tourist Offices

Tourist Information Centre, 35 St Vincent Place (tel. 2044400). Open June–Sept., Mon.–Sat. 9 a.m.–9 p.m., Sun. 10 a.m.–6 p.m.; Easter–May., Mon.–Sat. 9 a.m.–7 p.m., Sun. 10 a.m.–6 p.m.; Oct.–Easter, Mon.–Sat. 9 a.m.–6 p.m. Free local accommodation service. Lists of local accommodation. Book-A-Bed-Ahead service available. The office is just off George Square, a short walk from both Queen Street train station and the Buchanan Street bus station, and about 10 minutes' walk from Glasgow Central railway station.

Tourist Information Desk, Glasgow Airport (tel. 8484440)

Finding Accommodation

Glasgow has become increasingly popular in recent years, partly due to a vigorous advertising campaign aimed at altering the popular perception of Glasgow as an uninteresting and violent city, and partly due to the opening in the mid-1980s of the exceptional Burrell Collection. Both of these factors contributed to the city being crowned 'European City of Culture' in 1990, which brought in even larger numbers of visitors. Unfortunately, the supply of accommodation possibilities has failed to keep pace with the increasing demand. Although the hiatus of 1990 has now passed, you are still likely to encounter difficulties in finding a bed during the summer months (August especially). At this time of year, there is little point phoning guesthouses and B&Bs yourself, since the Tourist Information Centre provides an efficient and free room-finding service. Most of the cheaper accommodation is at least 20 minutes' walk from the centre, so you are probably going to have to use local buses or the underground to get to them. Railpass holders can save money if there is a local rail station close to their lodgings: ask the owner or the Tourist Information Centre.

Trouble Spots

In the 1980s, with Glasgow still unjustifiably blighted by a reputation for violence earned decades before, much effort and money were invested in a public relations campaign which did much to dispel the popular image of Glasgow as a violent city. Then, only on the days of Rangers v Celtic football matches (usually Saturday, occasionally Sunday or Wednesday) were tourists likely to be caught up in trouble in the city centre. To some Scots (and Irish, and even English), these games are an excuse for the venting of old religious bigotries. Trouble in the city centre in the immediate aftermath of a match is not uncommon, particularly at bus and train stations, and in the bars nearby, with sporadic outbreaks of trouble possible at night as well. At other times, tourists genuinely had nothing to fear in Glasgow; a bonus being that (with the possible exception of Belfast) in no other large city in the UK are visitors so warmly received by the locals. Tragically, however, at the time of writing there is good reason for anyone to be wary of a night out in Glasgow. Since early 1992 there has been a huge upsurge in late night violence both inside and outside the city centre, which is all the more worrying because so many of the serious assaults seem to be totally unprovoked.

GUESTHOUSES AND B&Bs

The prices quoted below are minimum and maximum prices per person for Bed & Breakfast based on two people sharing a room. In a few cases, singles are available at the same price; more commonly, you can expect to pay another £1–2 ($1.75–3.50). Unless stated otherwise, the establishments below are open all year round.

From £11–13 ($19–23)

Mrs M. Williamson, 15 Kintillo Drive (tel. 9591874). Open May–Sept. Off Queen Margaret Drive, near the Botanic Gardens.

From £12–13 ($21–23)

Mrs J. Freebairn-Smith, 14 Prospect Avenue (tel. 6415055). Same price for singles. Off the Glasgow Road in Cambuslang.

Mrs C. McArdle, 171 Mount Annan Drive (tel. 6320671). Same price for singles. Ten minutes' walk from King's Park train station. Off the Aikenhead Road towards Hampden Park (home of Queen's Park Football Club and the Scottish national team, and occasionally a concert venue).

£13 ($23)

Mrs C. Allan, 25 Stamperland Avenue (tel. 5442757). Same price for singles.

Browns Guest House, 2 Onslow Drive (tel. 5446797). In Dennistoun, a short walk from Duke Street.

Linby Guest House, 29 Carmyle Avenue (tel. 7630684). Same price for singles. In Carmyle.

Mrs M. Prior, 24 Jedburgh Avenue (tel. 6477970). In Rutherglen.

From £13–14 ($23.00–24.50)

Mrs E. Anderson, 3 King Edward Road (tel. 9548033). Open Apr.–Sept. Same price for singles. Near the Gartnavel Royal Hospital. A short walk from Anniesland train station.

Mrs K. Boyle, 49 Kingsknowe Drive (tel. 6478464). In Rutherglen.

Mrs M. Coyle, 18 Arnhall Place (tel. 8826642). Open Apr.–Sept. Off the Paisley Road West in Cardonald.

From £13–15 ($23–26)

Mrs I. Campbell, 12 Regent Park Square (tel. 4230727). Open Apr.–Sept. No singles. Close to the Pollokshaws Road and the Queen's Park. Short walk from Pollokshields (West) train station.

Mrs J. Cunningham, 160 Wedderlea Drive (tel. 8824384). Off the Paisley Road West in Cardonald.

Mr & Mrs J. Shearer, 2 Avdie Place (tel. 6320644). Same price for singles. Off Propecthill Road, near Hampden Park.

Symington Guest House, 26 Circus Drive (tel. 5561431). Close to the centre. In the area to the rear of the cathedral between Duke Street and Alexandra Parade.

White Pillars Guest House, 385 Hamilton Road (tel. 7731170). No singles. In Uddingston.

£14 ($24.50)

Mrs J. Forsyth, 3 Blairbeth Terrace (tel. 6344399). Open Apr.–Oct. Same price for singles. A few minutes' walk from Burnside train station.

Mrs F. Robertson, 201 Old Castle Road (tel. 6370263). Open Mar.–Sept.

Alamo Guest House, 46 Gray Street (tel. 3392395). By Kelvingrove Park.

Mrs M. Hendry, Redtops, 248 Wedderlea Drive (tel. 8837186). Off the Paisley Road West in Cardonald.

Mrs J. McArthur, 62 Mill Street (tel. 5500270). Open Apr.–Sept. The price is for B&B in the owner's one single. By the River Clyde at one end of Glasgow Green.

Mrs D. McEwen, 36 Dorchester Avenue (tel. 3396076). Open Apr.–Sept. Off the Great Western Road beyond the Botanic Gardens.

Mrs J.T. McLeod, 4 Islay Avenue (tel. 6344689). Open Apr.–Sept. In Rutherglen.

From £14–15 ($24.50–26.00)

Mrs I. Adey, 4 Holyrood Crescent (tel. 3348390). Open Apr.–Sept.

From £14–16 ($24.50–28.00)

Mr R. Bruce, 24 Greenock Avenue (tel. 6370608). Singles similarly priced. Off the Clarkston Road.

Mrs M. McAdam, 33 Finlay Drive (tel. 5561975). In Dennistoun, just off Duke Street.

£15 ($26)

Mr & Mrs J. Demarco, 5 Erskine Avenue (tel. 4276205). Open Apr.–Sept. Same price for singles. In Pollokshields.

Mrs J. B. Malcolm, 157 Camphill Avenue (tel. 6323133). In Giffnock.

From £15–16 ($26–28)

Mr G. Beattie, 18 Walmer Crescent (tel. 4275231). Same price for singles. Off the Paisley Road, just before the junction with Emiston Drive. Close to Ibrox Park, home of Rangers, Scotland's most successful football team.

Craigielea House, 35 Westercraigs (tel. 5543446). Singles similarly priced. Just off Duke Street in Dennistoun.

Craigpark Guest House, 33 Circus Drive (tel. 5544160). Close to the centre. In the area to the rear of the cathedral between Duke Street and Alexandra Parade.

Mr & Mrs P. Michael, 8 Marlborough Avenue (tel. 3345651). Open Apr.–Sept. Same price for singles. Off the Crow Road, near the Victoria Park. Just under 10 minutes' walk from Hyndland train station.

FURNISHED FLATS

University of Strathclyde, Forbes Hall, Rottenrow East (tel. 5534148). 20 flats sleeping 4–6 people. Available June–Sept. Weekly rates from £225–275 ($395–480). Right in the heart of the city.

University of Strathclyde, Garnett Hall, Cathedral Street (tel. 5534148). 24 flats sleeping 4–6 people. Available June–Sept. Weekly rates from £225–275 ($395–480). City centre location.

University of Glasgow, McLay Hall, 18 Park Terrace (tel. 3325056). 160 rooms sleeping 1–3 persons. Available around Easter, and from July–Sept. No minimum stay. Weekly rates up to £65 ($115). By Kelvingrove Park.

University of Glasgow, Kelvinhaugh Street Flats, Kelvinhaugh Street (tel. 3305385). 30 flats sleeping 5 people. Available July–Sept. Three night minimum stay. Weekly rates from £285–300 ($500–525). Close to the Kelvingrove Park and the Art Gallery.

YMCA Glasgow, Branston Court, 95 Panmure Street (tel. 9452526). 7 flats sleeping 4–6 people. Available Apr.–Oct. No minimum stay. Weekly rates from £145–190 ($255–335).

YMCA Aparthotel, David Naismith Court, 33 Petershill Drive (tel. 5586166). 50 flats sleeping 4–6 people. Open June–Sept. Weekly rates from £165–200 ($290–350).

STUDENT RESIDENCES

Rooms in local student residences are expensive. The University of Glasgow charges £22 ($39) per person for B&B in singles and doubles. With a few exceptions, similar rates are charged in the University of Strathclyde halls listed below. If you have a student ID it may be worth phoning the halls on arrival to see if any spare rooms might be let at a reduction. The University of Strathclyde halls have the advantage of being located right in the city centre.

University of Strathclyde, (tel. 5534148–central office).

Baird hall, 460 Sauchiehall Street. Open year round. Usual rate for singles, around £18 ($31.50) per person in doubles.

Forbes Hall, Rottenrow East. Open June–Sept. Singles only.

Garnett Hall, Cathedral Street. Open June–Sept. Singles only

Murray Hall, Collins Street. Open Mar.–Apr. and July–Sept. Singles only

Clyde Hall, 318 Clyde Street. Open June–Sept. Singles from £22–29 ($39–51), usual rate for doubles.

University of Glasgow

Keith Hall, 10–13 Botanic Crescent (tel. 9451636). Open Mar.–Apr. and July–Sept. Singles and doubles. By the Botanic Gardens.

Queen Margaret Hall, 55 Bellshaugh Road (tel. 3342192). Open Mar.–Apr. and July–Sept. Singles and doubles. Off the Great Western Road, by the Botanic Gardens.

Horselethill House, 7 Horselethill Road (tel. 3399943). Open Mar.–Apr. and July–Sept. Singles and doubles. Off the Great Western Road, near the Botanic Gardens.

Dalrymple Hall, 22 Belhaven Terrace West (tel. 3395271). Open Mar.–Apr. and July–Sept. Singles and doubles. Off the Great Western Road, near the Botanic Gardens.

Wolfson Hall, Garscube Estate, Maryhill Road (tel. 9465252). Open Mar.–Apr. and July–Sept. Singles and doubles.

IYHF HOSTEL

7/8 Park Terrace (tel. 3323004). Curfew 2 a.m. Opened last year. Mainly two-, three- and four-bed rooms, with some six- and eight-bed dorms. Around £7.50 ($13). Advance reservation advised in summer. By the Kelvingrove Park. At Charing Cross, turn off Sauchiehall Street up Woodlands Terrace (site of the old hostel) then turn left along Lynedoch Street into Park Terrace.

HOSTELS

Glasgow Central Tourist Hostel, Balmanno Building, 81 Rottenrow East (tel. 5522401). Open in summer only. Right in the centre of the city.

Brown's Hostel, 1 Woodlands Drive, flat 3/1 (tel. 3321618). Small capacity. £8.50 ($15). Near the Kelvinbridge metro station.

CAMPING

There was no conveniently located campsite operating in 1992. Contact the Tourist Information Centre for up-to-date information.

Inverness (Inbhir Nis)   (tel. code 0463)

Tourist Office
The Inverness, Loch Ness and Nairn Tourist Board, 23 Church Street, Inverness IV1 1EZ (tel. 234353). Open in summer, Mon.–Sat. 9.00 a.m.–8.30 p.m., Sun. 9 a.m.–6 p.m.; at other times, the office shuts at 5.30 p.m. Mon.–Fri. and is closed at weekends. Beds in local B&Bs registered with the office are booked free of charge. Book-A-Bed-Ahead service available. Five minutes' walk from the bus and train stations.

Basic Directions

The bus and train stations are both just off Academy Street. Any of the small streets on the other side of Academy Street will take you down into Church Street. The Tourist Office is at the left-hand end of Church Street. Following School Lane from Academy Street (head right from the train station) you arrive at the River Ness. The footbridge takes you into Huntly Street on the opposite bank of the river. Turning left and then right up Greig Street brings you into Kenneth Street. Straight across Kenneth Street from Greig Street is Fairfield Road. Walking right from the stations along Academy Street you join Chapel Street. Friars Bridge runs left from the roundabout at the end of Chapel Street to the far end of Kenneth Street. Walking left from the stations along Academy Street the road bends away to the left into Eastgate. Across the road at the bend the small Inglis Street leads down into the High Street. Turning left at this point leads you into Crown Road. Near the junction of the High Street and Crown Road Kingsmills Road runs off to the right. Along Kingsmills Road, just past the junction with Hill Street Southside Road leads off to the right, passing the end of Argyle Street and then crossing the Old Edinburgh Road before joining Culduthel Road. Across the High Street from Inglis Street the set of steps leads down to Ardconnel Terrace (left) and Ardconnel Street (right). Turning right down the High Street from the foot of Inglis Street, the street runs into Bridge Street, at which point Castle Street runs off to the left into Culduthel Road by the start of the Old Edinburgh Road. Continuing on down Bridge Street you can cross the river by the Ness Bridge into Young Street and then Tomnahurich Street, passing the opposite end of Kenneth Street from Friars Bridge on the way.

Finding Accommodation

Throughout most of the year you should have little trouble finding a room in one of the places listed below. The exception is the summer months when finding lodgings is not easy. At this time of year, unless you arrive before the Tourist Office opens, there is not much point in looking on your own. Not only is it difficult to find an unregistered guesthouse or B&B with space, but there is no guarantee that their rooms will be cheaper than those on the Tourist Office book. If you want to look for a room on your own, then Kenneth Street, Argyle Street and the Old Edinburgh Road are best supplied with relatively cheap lodgings. If your train or bus is scheduled to arrive in Inverness in the late afternoon it is probably wise to have accommodation pre-booked through the Scottish Tourist Board's Book-A-Bed-Ahead scheme, as poor rail services and heavy traffic on the roads can mean your arrival will be a lot later than you planned.

GUESTHOUSES (Tourist Office registered)

Singles and doubles around £11.50 ($20) per person

Eskdale House, 48 Greig Street (tel. 240933). A 10-minute walk from the stations.

Singles and doubles around £12.50 ($22) per person

Rozean Guest House, 44 Crown Drive (tel. 239001). A 10-minute walk from the stations. An extension of Crown Road.

Singles and doubles around £12–13 ($21–23) per person

Ivanhoe Guest House, 48 Lochalsh Road (tel. 223020). A 10-minute walk from the stations. From Friars Bridge turn right along Abban Street (by the junction with Huntly Place) into Lochalsh Road.

Singles and doubles £12–14 ($21.00–24.50) per person

Glen Fruin Guest House, 50 Fairfield Road (tel. 712623). A 10–15-minute walk from the stations.
Ardnacoille Guest House, 1a Annfield Road (tel. 233451). A 15-minute walk from the stations. Left off Old Edinburgh Road near the junction with Southside Road.

Singles and doubles £13 ($23) per person unless shown otherwise

Cedar Villa Guest House, 33 Kenneth Street (tel. 230477). A 10-minute walk from the stations.

Leinster Lodge Guest House, 27 Southside Road (tel. 233311). A 10–15-minute walk from the stations.

Crown Hotel, 19 Ardconnel Street (tel. 231135). Singles around £15 ($26.50). A 5–10-minute walk from the stations.

B&Bs (Tourist Office registered)

Singles and doubles £9–11 ($16.00–19.50) per person

Mrs C. McQueen, 80 Telford Road (tel. 240502). A 10-minute walk from the stations. From Friars Bridge turn right along Abban Street (by the junction with Huntly Place) and head straight on until you reach Telford Road.

Singles and doubles around £10 ($17.50) per person

Mrs A. Buchan, 1 Cuthbert Road (tel. 237924). Quite far from the centre, off the Old Perth Road beyond the golf course. For a small fee to cover the petrol the owner will provide you with transport.

Singles and doubles £10–11 ($17.50–19.50) per person

Mrs A. MacDonald, 31 Clachnaharry Road (tel. 235954). Overlooking the Caledonian Canal, about 20 minutes' walk from the stations. At the end of Friars Bridge turn right along Telford Street and onto Clachnarry Road.

Doubles £10–12 ($17.50–21.00) per person, singles as shown

Mrs I. Fraser, 3 Ballifeary Lane (tel. 232028). Singles similarly priced. A 15–20-minute walk from the stations. Cross the Ness Bridge, turn left along the riverside and follow the Ness Walk until you see Ballifeary Lane on the right.

Mrs Zandra MacDonald, 5 Muirfield Gardens (tel. 238114).

No singles. A 15–20-minute walk from the stations. Turn left off Culduthel Road at Sunnybank Road and follow the street round into Muirfield Gardens.

Mrs A. MacKinnon, 6 Broadstone Park (tel. 221506). Singles £11–14 ($19.50–24.50). A 10-minute walk from the stations, left off the Kingsmills Road.

Doubles around £11 ($19.50) per person

Mrs Boynton, 12 Annfield Road (tel. 233188). No singles. A 15-minute walk from the stations, left off the Old Edinburgh Road by the junction with Southside Road.

Mrs MacCuish, 5 Drumblair Crescent (tel. 231104). No singles. Well out from the centre, a 20–25-minute walk from the stations. Off the B862 to Dores. From the foot of Bridge Street turn left along Castle Road, and continue straight ahead along Haugh Road and Island Bank Road until you see Drumblair Crescent to the left off Dores Road.

Mrs MacCuish, 50 Argyle Street (tel. 235150). Singles similarly priced. A 10-minute walk from the stations.

Singles and doubles from £11 ($19.50) per person

Mrs M. Green, 64 Telford Street (tel. 235780). A 10–15-minute walk from the stations, left at the end of Friars Bridge.

Singles and doubles £11–12 ($19.50–21.00) per person

Mr Eric MacFall, 10a Ballifeary Road (tel. 234363). About 15 minutes' walk from the stations. Cross the Ness Bridge, turn left along the riverside and follow the Ness Walk. Turn right up Bishop's Road, then left at Ballifeary Road.

Mr L.P. Cook, 9 Fairfield Road (tel. 232058). A 10-minute walk from the stations.

Doubles around £11–13 ($19.50–23.00) per person

Mrs H. MacGregor, 9 Sunnybank Avenue (tel. 233835).

Singles similarly priced. A 15-minute walk from the stations, left off Culduthel Road.

Mrs I. M. Matheson, 81 Kenneth Street (tel. 240519). No singles.

Mrs F. Thompson, 4 Glenurqhart Road (tel. 221660). Singles from £12 ($21). About 15 minutes' walk from the stations. The street is a continuation of Tomnahurich Street.

Doubles around £12 ($21) per person

Mrs M.J. Cameron, 9 Aultnaskiach Avenue (tel. 235400). Singles similarly priced. A 15-minute walk from the stations, right off Culduthel Road.

Mrs Mactaggart, 1 Ross Avenue (tel. 236356). No singles. Just over 10 minutes' walk from the stations. The street runs between the Friars Bridge end of Kenneth Street and Fairfield Road.

IYHF HOSTEL

1 Old Edinburgh Road (tel. 231771). Open year round except 5 Jan.–1 Feb. 2 a.m. curfew. Latest check in 11.30 p.m. Advance booking essential at Easter and during July and August. A 10-minute walk from the stations. Follow Castle Street from the High Street.

HOSTELS

Inverness Student Hotel, 8 Culduthel Road (tel. 236556). Open year round. 2.30 a.m. curfew. Telephone reservations not accepted unless made by Edinburgh's High Street Hostel, but phoning ahead will allow you to check out the availability of beds. A ten minute walk from the stations. Follow Castle Street from the High Street.

CAMPING

In summer sites are frequently filled with caravans.

Bught Caravan and Camping Site (tel. 236920). Open
  Apr.–Oct. Cheap municipal site near the Bught Park and
  the Ness Islands. From around £2.20 ($4) per person. The
  closest site to the town centre, about 20–25 minutes' walk
  from the stations off the main road (A22) to Loch Ness and
  Fort William. Turn left off Glenurqhart road (a continuation
  of Tomnahurich Street) at Bught Drive. On the Craig
  Dunain bus route.

Torvean Caravan Park, Glenurqhart Road (tel. 220582). Open
  Easter–Oct. From £6.50 ($11.50). Only slightly further out
  than the Bught Caravan and Camping site, on the other
  side of the Caledonian Canal.

Scaniport Caravan and Camping Site (tel. 046375–351). Open
  Easter–Sept. Around £3.50 (£6.50). A small site about 5
  miles out from Inverness, off the B862 to Dores.

The Lake District

Carlisle (tel. code 0228)

This town, with a population of just over 100,000, is a gateway
to the Lake District. There are trains to and from Glasgow,
Edinburgh, Newcastle, and the south of England. Trains run
from Carlisle to Oxenholme, and from there a branch line takes
you to Windermere, in the heart of the Lake District. The
Tourist Information Centre in the Old Town Hall on Green
Market (tel. 512444) books rooms in the city and throughout
Cumbria. This service is effectively free. Although you pay a
10 per cent deposit at the office, this is subtracted from your
final bill. Book-A-Bed-Ahead service also available.

B&Bs

Expect to pay from £12 ($21) in local B&Bs

Mrs Thompson, 19 Aglionby St. (tel. 24566). Around £13.50 ($23.50). From the train station right along Botchergate, then left along Tait St, which runs into Aglionby St.

IYHF HOSTEL

Carlisle Youth Hostel, Etterby House, Etterby (tel. 23934). Juniors £5.30 ($9.50), seniors £6.50 ($11.50). Bus 62 from the City Centre to the Red Fern Inn, then walk down Etterby Road.

Keswick   (tel. code 07687)

Thirty-four miles from Carlisle, and 12 miles from Grasmere. The Tourist Information Centre in the Moot Hall on the Market Square (tel. 72645) books local accommodation free of charge. Book-A-Bed-Ahead service available.

B&Bs

Bridgedale, 101 Main St. (tel. 73914). £9 ($16) without breakfast. By the bus station.

Mr and Mrs Nixon, Grassmoor, 10 Blencathra St. (tel. 74008). £13 ($23). Price falls by around 20 per cent in the off-season.

Mrs Walker, 15 Acorn St. (tel. 74165). £13 ($23).

Mrs Peill, White House, 15 Ambleside Road (tel. 73176). Around £12.50 ($22).

IYHF HOSTELS

Keswick YH, Station Road (tel. 72484). Off the Market Place, down towards the River Greta.

Derwentwater YH, Barrow House, Borrowdale (tel. 77246). Two miles out. Hourly Borrowdale bus CMS 79 to Seatoller.

CAMPING

Castlerigg Hall (tel. 72437). One mile out of town to the south-east.
Dalebottom Holiday Park (tel. 72176). Two miles south-east. More expensive than Castlerigg Hall.

Cockermouth (tel. code 0900)

Twenty-five miles from Carlisle, 13 miles from Keswick, and 10 miles from Buttermere. The Tourist Information Centre in the Riverside Car Park on Market Street (tel. 822634) offers a local accommodation service and Book-A-Bed-Ahead.

IYHF HOSTEL

Cockermouth YH, Double Mills (tel. 822561). Nearest train station: Workington, 8 miles away. Local buses.

Buttermere (tel. code 07687)

Eight and a half miles from Keswick, 10 miles from Cockermouth. There is no Tourist Information Centre in the village.

IYHF HOSTELS

King George VI Memorial Hostel, Buttermere (tel. 70245).
Honister House YH (tel. 77267). Four miles from Buttermere. At the top of the beautiful Honister Pass.

Black Sail YH, Black Sail Hut. No telephone in this remote YH. Located one mile up the Green Gable Hill, 3½ miles from Buttermere. To book write well in advance to the hostel at Ennerdale, Cleator, Cumbria, CA23 3AY.

Ennerdale YH, Cat Crag, Ennerdale (tel. 0946–861237). Three miles or 7 miles from Buttermere over the hills, depending on whether you go via Red Pike or Scarth Gap respectively; 18 miles away by road.

Westwater YH, Wasdale Hall, Seascale (tel. 09046–222). Eleven miles from Buttermere by mountain path; 7–8 miles from Black Sail, Ennerdale and Honister Hause, again by mountain paths.

Boot

IYHF HOSTEL

Eskdale YH (tel. 09403–219). One mile from Boot village; 1/4 mile from the Woolpack Inn; 1½ miles from the Ravenglass to Eskdale steam railway. Seven miles from Wastwater YH and 10 miles from Black Sail and Coniston (Copper-mines) by mountain paths.

Grasmere (tel. code 09665)

About 5½ miles from Ambleside and 12 miles from Keswick. In summer, a Tourist Information Centre operates on the Redbank Road (tel. 245) providing a local accommodation service and a Book-A-Bed-Ahead facility.

B&Bs

Prices in the village's B&B are slightly higher than is normal for the Lake District, with few rooms available for under £14 ($24.50) per person.

IYHF HOSTELS

Butharlyp How YH (tel. 316). Just outside the village. A few minutes' walk along the road to Easedale. The hostel is on your right.

Thorney How YH (tel. 591). About a mile out. Follow the road to Easedale for about three quarters of a mile. You will see the hostel signposted.

High Close (Langdale) YH, High Close, Loughrigg (tel. 09667–313). Two miles from Grasmere, 4 miles from Ambleside.

Elterwater YH (tel. 09667–245). Three and a half miles from Grasmere and Ambleside. One mile from High Close (Langdale) YH. Close to Langdale Pike.

Ambleside (tel. code 05394)

About 5½ miles from Grasmere, 6 miles from Hawkshead, 4 miles from Windermere. The Tourist Information Centre in the Old Courthouse on Church Street (tel. 32582) books local accommodation free of charge. You pay 10 per cent of the bill at the office as a deposit and the remainder to the proprietor. Book-A-Bed-Ahead service also available.

B&Bs

Prices start around £12 ($21). Try Church Street or the Compston Road. The road leading out to Windermere, Lake Road, is particularly well supplied with B&Bs.

Mr and Mrs Richardson, 3 Cambridge Villas, Church St. (tel. 32307). By the Tourist Information Centre.

Raaesbec, Fair View Road (tel. 33844).

Thorneyfield, Compston Road (tel. 32464). More expensive. Prices start at around £16 ($28).

IYHF HOSTELS

Ambleside YH, Waterhead (tel. 32304). By Lake Windermere. Juniors £7 ($12.50), seniors £8.10 ($14) in July and Aug.

HOSTELS

YWCA, Old Lake Road (tel. 32340). Open to men and women. Dorms and smaller rooms from £11 ($19.50).

CAMPING

Low Wray (tel. 32810). Three and a half miles from town, on the road to Hawkshead. The bus to Hawkshead stops nearby.

Windermere and Bowness

(tel. code 09662)

Four miles from Ambleside and 9 miles from Hawkshead (by ferry). Another of the major gateways to the Lake District, thanks to the town's train station. Windermere's Tourist Information Centre is in Victoria Street (tel. 6499), close to the railway station. The office books local accommodation for free: a 10 per cent deposit is paid at the office, the remainder to the owner. Book-A-Bed-Ahead service also available. In summer, similar services are available at the Bowness Tourist Information Centre in Glebe Road (tel. 2895).

B&Bs

Prices in local B&Bs start around £11–12 ($19.50–21.00)

Mr and Mrs Austin, 'Lingmore', 7 High St. (tel. 4947). One of the cheapest. £11 ($19.50).

Mrs Graham, Brendan Chase Guest House, College Road (tel. 5638). Around £12 ($21).

Kirkwood, Prince's Road (tel. 3907). From around £14.50 ($25.50). The owners will pick you up from the train station. Down the main road to Bowness.

IYHF HOSTEL

Windermere YH, High Cross, Bridge Lane, Troutbeck (tel. 3543). Juniors £5.60 ($10), seniors £6.80 ($12). Troutbeck village is 2 miles to the north of Windermere, off the A591. The bus to Ambleside stops in Troutbeck Bridge, about 10 minutes' walk from the hostel.

CAMPING

Park Cliffe, Birks Road (tel. 05395–31344). Open May–Oct. Off the A592 to the north of Windermere (dir. Patterdale and Penrith).

Limefitt Park (tel. 05394–32300). Mixed couples and families only. More expensive than the site above. On the A592 4½ miles south of Bowness.

Hawkshead

Five and a half miles from Ambleside, 11 miles from Grasmere, 9 miles from Windermere (by ferry). In summer, the Tourist Information Centre (tel. 09666–525) in the main car park offers a local accommodation service and a Book-A-Bed-Ahead facility.

IYHF HOSTEL

Hawkshead YH, Esthwaite House (tel. 05394–36293/ 09666–293).

Coniston (tel. code 05394)

Hawkshead 5 miles away, Ambleside 6 miles, Elterwater 5 miles by mountain path, Windermere 11 miles. In summer, a local accommodation service and Book-A-Bed-Ahead is available at the Tourist Information Centre, 16 Yewdale Road (tel. 41533).

IYHF HOSTELS

Coniston YH, Holly How, Far End (tel. 41323). Juniors £5.60 ($10), seniors £6.80 ($12). Just outside Coniston village on the road to Ambleside.

Coniston Coppermines YH, Coppermines House (tel. 41261). Juniors £5.20 ($9), seniors £6.40 ($11.50). 1¼ miles from the village at the top of the Coppermines Valley.

Patterdale

Ambleside 10 miles away, Grasmere 9 miles by mountain path.

IYHF HOSTEL

Patterdale YH, Goldrill House (tel. 07684–82394).

Glenridding

Patterdale 2½ miles away, Thirlmere 4 miles by path, Grasmere 8 miles by path, Keswick 10 miles by path, Ambleside 12 miles.

IYHF HOSTEL

Helvellyn YH, Greenside, Glenridding (tel. 07684–82269). Same price as Patterdale. Near Ullswater. Three miles from Aira Force, the highest waterfall in the Lake District.

Thirlmere

Keswick 5 miles away, Grasmere 7 miles, Helvellyn 4 miles over the hills by path.

IYHF HOSTEL

Thirlmere YH, The Old School, Stanah Cross (tel. 05874–286).

Kendal (tel. code 0539)

Eleven miles from Windermere, Kendal's train station and its proximity to the M6, mean it is likely to be on your route if you are coming from the south. The Tourist Information Centre is in the Town Hall on Highgate (tel. 725758). Local accommodation and Book-A-Bed-Ahead services available.

IYHF HOSTEL

Kendal YH, Highgate (tel. 724066).

London (tel. code 071 or 081 – use the 071 prefix unless shown otherwise)

Tourist Offices

London Tourist Board, 26 Grosvenor Gardens, London SW1 0DU. Write to this office for information on the city in advance. For help with making reservations, write to the Accommodation Services department at the same address, at least six weeks before you plan to arrive.

There are seven/eight Tourist Information Centres operating in Central London, according to the time of year. All these offices will book accommodation in London for a hefty £5 ($9) commission. There are also eleven Tourist Information Centres operating in Outer London, mostly operated by the London Boroughs, with the aid of the London Tourist Board. An accommodation service is only available at the offices in Greenwich, Harrow, Richmond, and at Heathrow Airport.

Victoria Station Forecourt (tel. 7303488; 8248844 for accommodation). Open Mon.–Sat. 8 a.m.–7 p.m., Sun. 8 a.m.–4 p.m. Book-A-Bed-Ahead service available.

Liverpool Street Underground station, Liverpool Street (tel. 7303488; 8248844 for accommodation). Open Mon.–Sat. 9.00 a.m.–4.30 p.m., Sun. 8.30 a.m.–3.30 p.m. (extended hours in the summer season). Book-A-Bed-Ahead service available.

Selfridges, Oxford Street (Basement Services Arcade, Duke Street Entrance) (tel. 7303488; 8248844 for accommodation). Open during store hours.

British Travel Centre, 12 Regent Street, Piccadilly Circus (tel. 7303400; 9300572 for accommodation). Open May–Sept. Mon.–Fri. 9.00 a.m.–6.30 p.m., weekends 10 a.m.–4 p.m. Book-A-Bed-Ahead service available.

Harrods, Knightsbridge (Basement Banking Hall)

Tower of London, West Gate. Open during the summer only.

Clerkenwell Heritage Centre, 33 St John's Square (tel. 2501039). Book-A-Bed-Ahead service available.

Bloomsbury Tourist Information Centre, 35–36 Woburn Place (tel. 5804599). Book-A-Bed-Ahead service available.

Heathrow Terminals 1, 2, 3 Underground Station Concourse, Heathrow Airport (tel. 7303488; 8248844 for accommodation). Open daily 8.30 a.m.–4.30 p.m. Book-A-Bed-Ahead service available.

Greenwhich Tourist Information Centre, 46 Greenwich Church Street (tel. 081–8586376).

Harrow Tourist Information Centre, Civic Centre, Station Road (tel. 081–4241103/4241102).

Richmond Tourist Information Centre, Old Town Hall, Whittaker Avenue (tel. 081–9409125).

Finding Accommodation

There is a serious shortage of cheap places to stay in London throughout most of the year, but especially in the summer. If you plan to arrive during the summer months, it is advisable to book a bed as far in advance as you possibly can as you will struggle to find a place in a hostel, hall of residence, or one of the cheaper guesthouses or hotels on arrival. Outside the IYHF hostels and a few independent hostels it is difficult to find a bed for under £15 ($22.75). You can expect to pay from £20 ($35) for a single in a guesthouse, with doubles rarely available for under £30 ($53). There are cheaper guesthouses, but they are invariably filled with homeless families, temporarily boarded by the Department of Social Security.

HOTELS & GUESTHOUSES

The cheapest singles at the establishments listed below are generally around two thirds of the price of the cheapest doubles. All hotels and guesthouses listed are in Central London, unless stated otherwise.

Doubles from £22–29 ($38.50–51.00)

Europa Hotel, 60–62 Anson Road (tel. 6075935). North London. Underground: Tufnell Park (Northern Line)

Eric House, 328 Green Lanes (tel. 081 8006125). North
London. Underground: Manor House (Piccadilly line).

Doubles from £22.00–37.50 ($38.50–66.00)

Colliers Hotel, 97 Warwick Way (tel. 8346931/8280210).
Underground: Victoria (Circle, District and Victoria lines).
BR mainline station.

Doubles from £22–40 ($38.50–70.00)

Hyde Park Rooms Hotel, 137 Sussex Gardens, Hyde Park
(tel. 7230225/7230965). Underground: Paddington (Circle,
District, Bakerloo and Hammersmith & City lines). BR
mainline station.

Doubles from £22–42 ($38.50–74.00)

Ms Julie Samuel, 37 Stokenchurch Street (off New Kings
Road) (tel. 3710230). Underground: Fulham Broadway
(District line).

Doubles from £24–40 ($42–70)

Janus Hotel, 26 Hazlitt Road (tel. 6036915/6033119).
Underground: Kensington (Olympia) (District line).

Doubles from £25.50–27.50 ($45–48)

Pearl Hotel, 40 West Cromwell Road, Earl's Court (tel.
3739610/8352007). Underground: Earl's Court (District and
Piccadilly lines).

Doubles from £25.50–31.00 ($45–54)

Grangewood Lodge Hotel, 104 Clova Road, Forest Gate (tel.
081–5340637). East London. Close to British Rail's Forest
Gate station.

Doubles from £26.50–33.00 ($46–58)

Rasool Court Hotel, 19–21 Penywern Road, Earl's Court (tel. 3738900/3734893). Underground: Earl's Court (District and Piccadilly lines).

Doubles from £26.50–40.00 ($46–70)

Sass House Hotel, 10 & 11 Craven Terrace (tel. 2622325). Underground: Paddington (Circle, District, Bakerloo and Hammersmith & City lines). BR mainline station.

Doubles from £27.50–38.50 ($48–67)

Charlotte Guest House & Restaurant, 221 West End Lane, West Hampstead (tel. 7946476). North London. Underground: West Hampstead (Jubilee line).

Doubles from £28.50–46.00 ($50–81)

Westpoint Hotel, 170–172 Sussex Gardens (tel. 4020281). Underground: Paddington (Circle, District, Bakerloo and Hammersmith & City lines). BR mainline station.

Doubles from £28.50–50.00 ($50–88)

Merlyn Court Hotel, 2 Barkston Gardens (tel. 3701640). Underground: Earl's Court (District and Piccadilly lines).
Abbey Court Hotel, 174 Sussex Gardens (tel. 4020704). Underground: Paddington (Circle, District, Bakerloo and Hammersmith & City lines). BR mainline station.

Doubles from £28.50–55.00 ($50–96)

Kensbridge Hotel, 31 Elvaston Place (tel. 5896265). Underground: Gloucester Road (Circle, District and Piccadilly lines).
Nevern Hotel, 29–31 Nevern Place (tel. 2448366/2448367). Underground: Earl's Court (District and Piccadilly lines).

Doubles from £30–33 ($53–58)

Hotel Strand Continental, 143 The Strand (tel. 8364880). Underground: Charing Cross (Jubilee, Northern and Bakerloo lines). BR mainline station.

Doubles from £31–39 ($54–68)

James Lodge, 116 Barry Road, Dulwich (tel. 081 6937744). South East London. Close to Crystal Palace stadium. Closest rail station is British Rail's East Dulwich.

Sara Hotel, 15 Eardley Crescent (tel. 2449500). Triples from £40 ($70). Underground: Earl's Court (District and Piccadilly lines).

Doubles from £31–41 ($54–72)

Dillons Hotel, 21 Belsize Park, Hampstead (tel. 7943360). North London. Underground: Belsize Park (Northern Line)

Doubles from £31–44 ($54–77)

Stanley House Hotel, 19–21 Belgrave Road (tel. 8345042/8347292). Underground: Victoria (Circle, District and Victoria lines). BR mainline station.

Windsor House, 12 Penywern Road (tel. 3739087). Underground: Earl's Court (District and Piccadilly lines).

Doubles from £33 ($58)

Hyde Park House, 48 St Petersburgh Place (tel. 2299652). Underground: Queensway (Central line).

Doubles from £33–40 ($58–70)

Melbourne House, 79 Belgrave Road (tel. 8283516). Underground: Victoria (Circle, District and Victoria lines). BR mainline station.

St George's Hotel, 25 Belgrave Road (tel. 8282961/8283605). Underground: Victoria (Circle, District and Victoria lines). BR mainline station.

Half Moon Hotel, 10 Earl's Court Square (tel. 3739956/3732900). Underground: Earl's Court (District and Piccadilly lines).

Manor Hotel, 23 Nevern Place (tel. 3706018/3704164). Underground: Earl's Court (District and Piccadilly lines).

Acton Hill Guest House, 311 Uxbridge Road (tel. 081–9922553). West London. Underground: Acton Town (Piccadilly and District lines).

Doubles from £33–44 ($58–77)

Astoria Hotel, 39 St George's Drive (tel. 8341965). Underground: Victoria (Circle, District and Victoria lines). BR mainline station.

Belgrave House Hotel, 28–32 Belgrave Road (tel. 8281563/8348620). Underground: Victoria (Circle, District and Victoria lines). BR mainline station.

Doubles from £33–46 ($58–81)

Luna House Hotel, 47 Belgrave Road (tel. 8345897). Underground: Victoria (Circle, District and Victoria lines). BR mainline station.

Simone House Hotel, 49 Belgrave Road (tel. 8282474). Underground: Victoria (Circle, District and Victoria lines). BR mainline station.

Doubles from £33–50 ($58–88)

Moss Hall Hotel, 10–11 Moss Hall Crescent, Finchley (tel. 081–4456980). North London. Underground: West Finchley (Northern Line).

Doubles from £33–56 ($58–98)

Claremont Hotel, 154 High Street, Wealdstone, Harrow (tel. 081–4272738). North London. Underground: Harrow & Wealdstone (Bakerloo line). The underground service operates at peak hours only. At other times you have to catch a British Rail train.

White Lodge Hotel, 1 Church Lane, Hornsey (tel. 081–3489765). North London. Underground: Turnpike Lane (Piccadilly line).

Doubles from £35–38 ($61–67)

B&B Flatlets, 64 Holland Road (tel. 2299233). Underground: Holland Park (Central line).

Andrews Hotel, 12 Westbourne Street, Hyde Park (tel. 7235365/7234514). Underground: Lancaster Gate (Central line).

Doubles from £35–42 ($61–74)

Acton Grange Guest House, 317 Uxbridge Road, Acton (tel. 081–9920586). West London. Underground: Acton Town (District and Piccadilly lines).

Doubles from £35–44 ($61–77)

Ruddimans Hotel, 160–162 Sussex Gardens (tel. 7231026). Underground: Paddington (Circle, District, Bakerloo and Hammersmith & City lines). BR mainline station.

Doubles from £35–46 ($61–81)

Dalmacia Hotel, 71 Shepherds Bush Road, Hammersmith (tel. 6032887/0831–309692). West London. Underground: Hammersmith (District, Piccadilly and Hammersmith & City lines)

Doubles from £36–43 ($63–75)

St David's Hotel, 16 Norfolk Square, Hyde Park (tel. 7233856/4029061). Underground: Paddington (Circle, District, Bakerloo and Hammersmith & City lines). BR mainline station.

Doubles from £36–60 ($63–105)

Gower House Hotel, 57 Gower Street (tel. 6364685). Underground: Goodge Street (Northern line).

Doubles from £37.50–40.00 ($66–70)

York House Hotel, 28 Philbeach Gardens (tel. 3737519/3737579). Underground: Earl's Court (District and Piccadilly lines).

More House, 53 Cromwell Road, South Kensington (tel. 5842040/5842039). Underground: Gloucester Road (Circle, District and Piccadilly lines).

Doubles from £37.50–44.00 ($66–77)

Balmoral House Hotel, 156 Sussex Gardens (tel. 7237445/7234925). Underground: Paddington (Circle, District, Bakerloo and Hammersmith & City lines). BR mainline station.

St Athan's Hotel, 20 Tavistock Place, Russell Square (tel. 8379140/8379627). Underground: Russell Square (Piccadilly line).

Doubles from £37.50–50.00 ($66–88)

Melita House Hotel, 35 Charlwood Street (tel. 8283516). Underground: Victoria (Circle, District and Victoria lines). BR mainline station.

Doubles from £37.50–53.00 ($66–93)

Albro House Hotel, 155 Sussex Gardens (tel. 7242931). Underground: Paddington (Circle, District, Bakerloo and Hammersmith & City lines). BR mainline station.

Doubles £38.50 ($68)

Brookside Hotel, 32 Brook Avenue, Wembley Park (tel.

081–9040019/9085336). Underground: Wembley Park (Metropolitan and Jubilee lines).

Doubles from £38.50 ($68)

Magnolia Hotel, 104–105 Oakley Street, Chelsea (tel. 3520187). Underground: Sloane Square (District and Circle lines)

Holly House Hotel, 20 Hugh Street (tel. 8345671). Underground: Victoria (Circle, District and Victoria lines). BR mainline station.

Kirness Hotel, 29 Belgrave Road (tel. 8340030). Underground: Victoria (Circle, District and Victoria lines). BR mainline station.

Falcon Hotel, 11 Norfolk Square (tel. 7238603). Underground: Paddington (Circle, District, Bakerloo and Hammersmith & City lines). BR mainline station.

Chumleigh Lodge Hotel, 226–228 Nether Street, Finchley (tel. 081–3461614). North London. Underground: West Finchley (Northern line).

Arran House Hotel, 77 Gower Street (tel. 6362186/6371140). Underground: Goodge Street (Northern line) or Euston Square (Circle and Hammersmith & City lines)

Glynne Court Hotel, 41 Great Cumberland Place (tel. 2624344/7243384). Underground: Marble Arch (Central line).

Kenwood House Hotel, 114 Gloucester Place (tel. 9353473/9359455/4865007). Underground: Baker Street (Circle, Bakerloo, Jubilee, Metropolitan and Hammersmith & City lines).

Rhodes House Hotel, 195 Sussex Gardens (tel. 2625617/2620537). Underground: Paddington (Circle, District, Bakerloo and Hammersmith & City lines). BR mainline station.

Rilux House, 1 Lodge Road (tel. 081–2030933). North London. Underground: Hendon Central (Northern line).

Regency House Hotel, 71 Gower Street (tel. 637 1804). Underground: Euston (Northern, Piccadilly and Victoria lines). BR mainline station.

Doubles around £40 ($70)

Keren Hotel, 14 Highbury New Park, Islington (tel. 2261035). Singles half the price of doubles. North London. Underground: Highbury & Islington (Piccadilly line)

Oxford House, 92 Cambridge St. (tel. 8346467). Underground: Victoria (Circle, District and Victoria lines). BR mainline station.

Doubles from £40 ($70)

Apollo Hotel, 64 Queensborough Terrace (tel. 7273066/2295180). Underground: Bayswater (Circle and District lines)

Bedford/Cosmo House Hotel, 27 Bloomsbury Square (tel. 6364661/6360577). Underground: Holborn (Central and Piccadilly lines).

Gower Hotel, 129 Sussex Gardens (tel. 2622262). Underground: Paddington (Circle, District, Bakerloo and Hammersmith & City lines). BR mainline station.

Linden House Hotel, 4–6 Sussex Place (tel. 7239853/2620804). Underground: Paddington (Circle, District, Bakerloo and Hammersmith & City lines). BR mainline station.

Doubles around £42 ($74)

Easton Hotel, 36–40 Belgrave Road (tel. 8345938). Underground: Victoria (Circle, District and Victoria lines). BR mainline station.

Queens Hotel, 5–7 Queens Avenue, Muswell Hill (tel. 081–8834384/830722). North London. Underground: East Finchley and Highgate (both stations on the Northern line).

Doubles from £42 ($74)

Chester House, 134 Ebury Street (tel. 7303632). Underground: Victoria (Circle, District and Victoria lines). BR mainline station.

Cosmo/Bedford House Hotel, 1 Bloomsbury Place (tel. 6360577). Underground: Holborn (Central and Piccadilly lines).

Hammersmith Hotel, 186 Hammersmith Grove (tel. 081–7430820). West London. Underground: Hammersmith (District, Piccadilly and Hammersmith & City lines)

Tudor Court & Gallenco Hotel, 10–12 Norfolk Square (tel. 7236553/7235157). Underground: Paddington (Circle, District, Bakerloo and Hammersmith & City lines). BR mainline station.

Olympic House Hotel, 138–140 Sussex Gardens (tel. 2623782). Underground: Paddington (Circle, District, Bakerloo and Hammersmith & City lines). BR mainline station.

Barclay Court Private Hotel, 12–14 Hafer Street (tel. 071–2285272/081–6738301). South West-London. BR train from Victoria to Clapham Junction.

Demetriou Guest House, 9 Strathmore Gardens (tel. 2296709). Underground: Notting Hill Gate (Central, District and Circle lines)

London House Hotel, 80 Kensington Gardens Square (tel. 7270696). Underground: Bayswater (District and Circle lines).

Garden Court Hotel, 30–31 Kensington Gardens Square (tel. 2292553). Underground: Bayswater (District and Circle lines).

Beaver Hotel, 57–59 Philbeach Gardens (tel. 3734553). Underground: Earl's Court (District and Piccadilly lines).

Concord Hotel, 155–157 Cromwell Road (tel. 3704151). Underground: Earl's Court (District and Piccadilly lines).

Doubles around £44 ($77)

Glenville Hotel, 4 & 5 Belgrove Street, King's Cross (tel. 2785836). Underground: Kings Cross (Northern, Piccadilly, Victoria, Circle and Metropolitan lines). BR mainline station.

Doubles from £44 ($77)

Foubert's Hotel, 162–166 Chiswick High Road (tel. 081–9945202/9956743). West London. Underground: Turnham Green (District line).

Lonsdale Hotel, 9–10 Bedford Place, Bloomsbury (tel. 6361812/5809902). Underground: Holborn (Central and Piccadilly lines).

Cardiff Hotel, 5–9 Norfolk Square (tel. 7239068/7233513/7234500). Underground: Paddington (Circle, District, Bakerloo and Hammersmith & City lines). BR mainline station.

Oliver Plaza Hotel, 33 Trebovir Road (tel. 3737183/3732058/3737184). Underground: Earl's Court (District and Piccadilly lines).

Somerset House Hotel, 6 Dorset Square (tel. 7230741). Underground: Baker Street (Circle, Bakerloo, Jubilee, Metropolitan and Hammersmith & City lines)

St Peter's Hotel, 407–411 Goldhawk Road (tel. 081–7414239). West London. Underground: Stamford Brook (District line).

Crescent Hotel, 49–50 Cartwright Gardens (tel. 3871515). Underground: Russell Square (Piccadilly line).

Lancaster Court Hotel, 202–204 Sussex Gardens (tel. 4028438/4026369). Underground: Lancaster Gate (Central line) or Underground: Paddington (Circle, District, Bakerloo and Hammersmith & City lines). BR mainline station.

Centaur Hotel, 21 Avonmore Road (tel. 6023857/6035973). Underground: West Kensington (District and Piccadilly lines).

Hotel Slavia, 2 Pembridge Square (tel. 7271316/2290803). Underground: Notting Hill Gate (Central line).

Manor Court Chambers Hotel, 7 Clanricarde Gardens (tel. 7923361/2292875). Underground: Notting Hill Gate (Central line).

Central Hotel, 35 Hoop Lane, Golders Green (tel. 081–4585636). North London. Underground: Golders Green (Northern line).

Mrs Josephine Clements, 17 Madeley Road (tel. 081–9985222). West London. Underground: Ealing Broadway (Central and District lines)

Premier West Hotel, 28–34 Glenthorne Road (tel. 081–7486181). Underground: Hammersmith (District, Piccadilly, Hammersmith & City lines).

Bickenhall Hotel, 119 Gloucester Place (tel. 9353401). Underground: Baker Street (Circle, Bakerloo, Jubilee, Metropolitan and Hammersmith & City lines)

PRIVATE ROOMS

Alma Tourist Services, 10 Fairway, West Wimbledon (tel 081–5423771). Rooms available in South-West and Central London. Minimum stay of two nights. Singles from £17.50 ($31), doubles from £28 ($49). With breakfast.

Anglo World Travel Limited, 18 Ogle Street (tel 4363601). Office open Mon.–Fri. 9.00 a.m.–5.30 p.m. Rooms available in the suburbs of Harrow, Wembley, Streatham and Bromley. Minimum stay of 3 nights. Reservations taken in advance or on the day. Full payment required with advance bookings. Singles from £17.50 ($31), doubles from £26 ($46). With breakfast.

Best London Homes, 126 Lower Richmond Road (tel 081–7809045). Rooms available in Central London, Chelsea, Fulham, Kensington, Bayswater and South and West London. No minimum stay, but a surcharge is added for stays of less than three nights. Reservations taken in advance or on the day. Deposit of 25 per cent required with advance bookings. Singles from £14.50 ($25.50), doubles from £28 ($49). With breakfast.

Capital Homes, 200 Chase Side (tel. 081–4407535); at weekends and evenings 081–4417378). Rooms available in North, North-west and South London. Minimum stay of two nights. Reservations taken in advance or on the day. Payment for the first night required with advance bookings. Singles from £16.50 ($29), doubles from £28 ($49). With breakfast.

Host and Guest Service, The Studio, 635 Kings Road (tel. 7315340/7365645). Office open Mon.–Fri. 9.00 a.m.–5.30 p.m. Rooms available in Greater London. Minimum stay of three nights. Advance and same day reservations. Full payment is required with advance bookings. Singles from £14 ($24.50), doubles from £24 ($42). With breakfast.

In London, London House, Suite 409, 19 Old Court Place (tel. 3760405/3761070). Office open 9.30 a.m.–6.00 p.m. Rooms available in Central, North-west and South-east London. Minimum stay of two nights. Singles from £17.50 ($31), doubles from £31 ($54). With breakfast.

Le Weekend London West, Ealing Broadway (tel. 081–9980413). Office open daily 7.30 a.m.–9.30 p.m. Rooms available in West London. Singles from £17.50 ($31), doubles from £34 ($60). With breakfast.

London Homestead Services, Coombe Wood Road, Kingston-Upon-Thames, Surrey (tel 081–9494455). Rooms available in Central London, and in the suburbs. Minimum stay of three nights. Advance and same day reservations. Deposit of 25 per cent required with advance bookings. Singles from £16.50 ($29), doubles from £28 ($49). With breakfast.

Central London Accommodations, P.O. Box 2623, London W14 0EF (tel. 6029668). Minimum stay of three nights. B&B from £14.50 ($25.50) per person.

IYHF HOSTELS

London's IYHF hostels are frequently filled to capacity around Easter, and from June to September, so advance reservation is highly recommended. If the hostel you write to is full on the dates you want, they will automatically transfer your booking to any other hostel with space available, unless you state otherwise. Full information on London's hostels is available from: YHA London Regional Office, 8 St Stephen's Hill, St Albans, Herts AL1 2DY (tel. 0727–55215).

Carter Lane YH, 36 Carter Lane (tel. 2364965). Open year

round. No curfew. Juniors £15 ($26.50), seniors £17 ($30). About 300m from St Paul's underground station (Central line) and Blackfriars underground (Circle and District lines) and BR station.

Earl's Court YH, 38 Bolton Gardens (tel. 3737083). Open year round. Apr.–Sept. Juniors £14 ($24.50), seniors £15 ($26.50). Prices fall by £1 ($1.75) at other times of the year. 300m from Earl's Court underground station (District and Piccadilly lines), off the Earl's Court Road.

Hampstead Heath YH, 4 Wellgarth Road (tel. 081–4589054). Open year round. Apr.–Sept. Juniors £13.50 ($23.50), seniors £14.50 ($25.50). Prices fall by £0.50 ($0.90) at other times. About 400m from the Golders Green underground station (Northern line), off North End Road.

Highgate Village YH, 84 Highgate West Hill (tel. 081–3401831). Open year round. Juniors £9.60 ($17), Seniors £11.30 ($20). The Archway underground station (Northern line) is about 10 minutes' walk away. Walk past the Whittington Hospital, then turn left off Highgate Hill down South Grove into Highgate West Hill.

Holland House YH/King George VI Memorial YH, Holland Walk, Kensington (tel. 9370748). Open year round. Apr.–Sept. Juniors £14.50 ($25.50), seniors £16.50 ($29). Prices fall by £0.50 ($0.90) at other times of the year. About 400m from both the Holland Park underground station (Circle and District lines) and the High Street Kensington underground station (District and Circle). Holland Walk cuts through Holland Park between Holland Park Avenue and Kensington High Street.

Oxford Street YH, 14 Noel Street (tel. 7341618). Open year round. No curfew. Groups are not admitted to this hostel. Apr.–Sept. Juniors £15.50 ($27), seniors £17.50 ($31). At other times, prices fall by £0.50 ($0.90). Around 400m from both the Oxford Circus (Central, Bakerloo and Victoria lines) and Tottenham Court Road (Central and Northern lines) underground stations. From Oxford Street, turn down Poland Street or Berwick Street.

Rotherhithe YH, Island Yard, Salter Road (tel. 2322114).

Open year round. Juniors £15 ($26.50), seniors £17 ($30). 300m from Rotherhithe underground station on the East London line. Join the East London line at Whitechapel (District and Metropolitan lines). Bus P105 from Waterloo BR station runs straight to the hostel.

HOSTELS/STUDENT RESIDENCES

Astor College, 99 Charlotte Street (tel. 5807262/5807263/ 5807264). Singles and doubles. £14.50–19.50 ($25.50–34.00). Underground: Goodge Street (Northern Line).

Bryanston Residence, 16 Bryanston Square (tel. 4028608/7963889). Singles, doubles and larger rooms. B&B from £11–22 ($19.50–39.00) Weekly rates offer a small reduction. Underground: Marble Arch (Central line).

Carr-Saunders Hall, 18–24 Fitzroy St. (tel. 5806338). Open Mar.–Apr. and July–Sept. Singles and doubles. B&B from £16–20 ($28–35). Underground: Goodge Street (Northern line).

Goldsmid House, 36 North Row (Oxford Street) (tel. 4938911/6292977). Open June–Sept. Singles and doubles. £11–20 ($19.50–35.00). Underground: Marble Arch (Central line). For advance reservations contact: Reservations Dept, EST (Goldsmid House), 34–36 South Street, Lancing, West Sussex BN15 8AG (tel. 0903–753555).

International Students House, 229 Great Portland Street (tel. 6313223). Singles, doubles and larger rooms. £13.50–23.00 ($23.50–40.00) for B&B. Underground: Great Portland Street (Circle and Hammersmith & City lines).

Allen Hall Summer Hostel, Allen Hall, 28 Beaufort Street (tel. 3511296/3511297). Open July–Aug. Singles and doubles. B&B from £20 ($35). Underground: Sloane Square (Circle and District lines).

Anne Elizabeth House Hotel, 30 Collingham Place. (tel. 3704821). Doubles and larger rooms. B&B from £8.50–20.00 ($15–35). Underground: Earl's Court (District and Piccadilly lines).

Crofton Hotel, 13–16 Queen's Gate (tel. 5847201). Singles, doubles and larger rooms. £11–33 ($19.50–58.00). Underground: Gloucester Road (Circle, District and Piccadilly lines).

Culture Link International Student Residence, 161 Old Brompton Road (tel. 3736061). Singles, doubles and larger rooms. Underground: West Brompton (District line).

Curzon House Hotel, 58 Courtfield Gardens (tel. 3736745). Singles, doubles and larger rooms. £11.00–17.50 ($19.50–31.00) for B&B. Underground: Earl's Court (District and Piccadilly lines).

Queen Alexandra's House, Bremner Road, Kensington Gore (tel. 5893635). Open July–Aug. Women only. Singles and doubles. B&B from £22 ($39). Underground: South Kensington (Circle, District and Piccadilly lines).

Queensberry Court, 7–11 Queensberry Place, South Kensington (tel. 5893693). Singles, doubles and larger rooms. B&B from £17–33 ($30–58). Full board £100–200 ($175–350) per week. Underground: South Kensington (Circle, District and Piccadilly lines).

Hotel Saint Simeon, 38 Harrington Gardens (tel. 3730505/3704708). Doubles and larger rooms. £9–12 ($16–21). Full board £65–92 ($115–160) per week. Underground: Gloucester Road (Circle, District and Piccadilly lines).

Holland Park Independent Hostel, 31 Holland Park Gardens (tel. 6023369). Triples and larger rooms. £9.50–11.00 ($16.50–19.00). Underground: Holland Park (Central line).

Palace Court Hotel, 12–14 Pembridge Square (tel. 7274412). Singles, doubles and larger rooms. £8–18 ($14–32). Underground: Bayswater (Circle and District lines).

C/E/I International Youth Hotel, 61 Chepstow Place, Notting Hill Gate (tel. 2218134). Singles, doubles and larger rooms. £12–24 ($21–42). Underground: Bayswater (Circle and District lines).

Glendale Hotel, 8 Devonshire Terrace (tel. 2621770). Singles, doubles and larger rooms. £9.50–12.50 ($16.50–22.00) for B&B. Underground: Paddington (Circle, District, Bakerloo and Hammersmith & City lines). BR mainline station.

Lords Hotel, 20–22 Leinster Square (tel. 2298877). Singles, doubles and larger rooms. B&B from £14–42 ($24–74). Underground: Bayswater (Circle and District lines).

Ifor Evans Hall/Max Rayne House, 109 Camden Road (tel. 4859377). Open Mar.–Apr. and June–Sept. Singles and doubles. B&B from £21–34 ($37–60). Underground: Camden Town (Northern line)

John Adams Hall, 15–23 Endsleigh Street (tel. 3874086/3074796). Open Dec.–Jan., Mar.–Apr. and June–Sept. Singles and doubles. B&B from £20–22 ($35–39). Underground: Russell Square (Piccadilly line) or Euston (Northern and Victoria lines). BR mainline station.

Passfield Hall, 1 Endsleigh Place (tel. 3877743/3873584). Open Mar.–Apr. and July–Sept. Singles, doubles and larger rooms. B&B from £17.50–21.00 ($31–37). Underground: Euston (Northern and Victoria lines)

Regent's College, Inner Circle, Regents Park (tel. 4877483). Open Dec.–Jan. and May–Sept. Singles, doubles and larger rooms. £20.50–33.00 ($36–58). Underground: Baker Street (Jubilee, Northern, Metropolitan, Bakerloo and Hammersmith & City lines).

Repton House Hotel, 31 Bedford Place (tel. 6367045). Doubles and larger rooms. B&B from £12.50–28.00 ($22–49). Full board £75–180 ($130–315) per week. Underground: Russell Square (Piccadilly line).

Rosebery Avenue Hall, 90 Rosebery Avenue (tel. 2783251). Open Mar.–Apr. and June–Sept. Singles and doubles. B&B from £18.50–28.00 ($32–49). Underground: Angel (Northern line).

Queen Mary & Westfield College Halls of Residence, 98–110 High Road, South Woodford (tel. 081–5049282). Open Mar.–Apr. and July–Sept. Singles and doubles. B&B £17 ($30). Underground: South Woodford (Central line).

Finsbury Hall, City University, Bastwick Street (tel. 2514961). Open Mar.–Apr. and July–Sept. Singles and doubles. B&B from £19.50–21.50 ($34–38). Underground: Barbican (Circle and Metropolitan lines).

Kent House, 325 Green Lanes (tel. 081–80208000/8029070). Singles, doubles and larger rooms. £8.50–17.00 ($15–30). Reduced rates in the off-season. Underground: Manor House (Piccadilly line).

Northampton Hall, City University, Bunhill Row (tel. 6282953). Open Mar.–Apr. and July–Sept. Singles and doubles. B&B from £20–33 ($35–58). Underground: Old Street (Northern line).

Polytechnic of North London, James Leicester Hall, Market Road (tel. 6073250). Open April, and July–Sept. B&B in singles from £18–20 ($32–35). Underground: Caledonian Road (Piccadilly line).

Polytechnic of North London, Tufnell Park Hall, Huddleston Road (tel. 6073250). Open Mar.–Apr., and July–Sept. B&B in singles from £18–20 ($32–35). Underground: Tufnell Park (Northern line).

Waynefleet House, 5 Lynton Road, Kilburn (tel. 6256839). Doubles and larger rooms. £8.50–15.00 ($15–26). Full board from £60–115 ($105–200) per week. Underground: Queens Park (Bakerloo line).

Driscoll House Hotel, 172 New Kent Road (tel. 7034175). Full board £150 ($265) per week. Underground: Elephant & Castle (Bakerloo and Northern lines).

King George's House YMCA, 40–46 Stockwell Road, Stockwell (tel. 2747861). Singles, doubles and larger rooms. B&B from £15.50 ($27). The hostel is primarily aimed at long-term guests. Underground: Stockwell (Piccadilly and Northern lines).

Milo Guest House, 52 Ritherdon Road, Balham (tel. 081–6713683/7677225). Singles, doubles and larger rooms. From £7.50 ($13). Underground: Tooting Bec (Northern line). For advance bookings contact: Ms H. Milo, 'Kismet', Poynders Road, Clapham Park, London SW4 8PS (tel. 081–6713683).

Tent City, Old Oak Common Lane, East Acton (tel. 081–7435708). Open June–Sept. Simple accommodation under several large marquees. 448 beds. £5.50 ($9.50) per night. Underground: East Acton (Central line).

CAMPING

Lea Valley Campsite, Sewarstone Road, Chingford (tel. 081–5295689). Open Easter–Oct. £4.50 ($8) per person per night (tent included). 12 miles from the centre. British Rail train from Liverpool Street to Chingford, then take bus 505 or 379, both of which stop about 800m from the site. Alternatively, take the underground (Victoria line) to Walthamstow Central, then bus 505 or 215 to Chingford, 800m from the site. In peak season, bus 215 runs right to the site.

Pickett's Lock Sport & Leisure Centre, Pickett's Lock Lane, Edmonton (tel. 081–3456666). Open year round. Minimum pitch fee of £6 ($10.50), so this is what solo travellers must pay. £4.50 ($8) per person. Ten miles from the centre. British Rail train from Liverpool Street to Lower Edmonton, then bus W8. Alternatively take the underground (Victoria line) to Seven Sisters, then take a BR train to Lower Edmonton, followed by bus W8.

Tent City, Old Oak Common Lane, East Acton (tel. 081–7499074). Open June–Aug. Six miles from the centre. £5.50 ($9.50) per person (tent included). Similarly priced dormitory accommodation available. Underground: East Acton (Central line). Bus 12 or 52A.

Abbey Wood, Federation Road, Abbey Wood (tel. 081–3102233). Open year round. Twelve miles from the centre. Peak season (18 May–31 Aug.) £3.50 ($6) per person (tent included). £3 ($5.50) in the off-season. British Rail train from Charing Cross to Abbey Wood.

Crystal Palace Caravan Club Site, Crystal Palace Parade (tel. 081–7787155). Open year round. Twelve miles from the centre. Peak season (18 May–31 Aug.) £3.50 ($6) per person (tent included), £3 ($5.50) in the off-season. British Rail train from Victoria to Crystal Palace. Buses 2A, 3 and 3A stop close to the site.

Eastway Cycle Circuit and Campsite, Temple Mills Lane, Stratford (tel. 081–5346085). Open Mar.–Oct. Four miles from the centre. £4.50 ($8) per person (tent included). One

mile from Leyton underground station (Central line).
Hackney Camping, Millfields Road (tel. 081–9857656). Open
18 June–25 Aug. £4.50 ($8) per person (tent included). Bus
38 stops at Clapton Pond, from which you can walk along
Millfields Road to the site. Bus 22A stops in Mandeville
Street, from which you can cross the canal to the site.

SLEEPING ROUGH

It is not possible to sleep in the train stations, nor is it safe to
sleep in the surrounding areas. Sleeping rough is not to be
advised in London as a whole, but if you must sleep rough,
at least try to bed down beside other people (other travellers,
preferably). The embankment at Westminster Bridge, or Hyde
Park, are the most obvious places to try.

Manchester (tel.code 061)

Tourist Office
Tourist Information Centre, Town Hall Extension, Lloyd Street
(tel. 2343157/2343158). Rooms found in local accommodations
for £1 ($1.75) fee. Book-A-Bed-Ahead service also available.

Finding Accommodation
Local B&Bs start around £12–13 ($21–23), but it is very difficult
to find a centrally located B&B at those prices. The most
reasonable terms for B&B in the city centre are offered by some
of the pubs along Chapel Street. Apart from these, you are
going to have to base yourself outside the centre. One of the
better areas to look is the Chorlton district of the city, a
15–20-minute trip from the centre by bus 85, 86, 102 or 103.

B&Bs

The Black Lion, 65 Chapel Street (tel. 8341974). Around £15
($26.50).

Mrs McMahon, 7 The Meade (tel. 8812714). £13 ($23). Four miles out from the centre. Bus 47, 82, 86 or 87 to Beech Road. From Beech Road turn left along Claude Road, left again onto North Meads, which subsequently becomes The Meade.

STUDENT RESIDENCES

University of Manchester, Wolton Hall (tel. 2247244). Mainly singles, with only a limited number of doubles. B&B £16 ($28). Highly popular with groups. Buses 40–46 and bus 49 to Owens Park.

HOSTELS

YMCA, 20 Mount Street (tel. 8345907). Exceptionally busy hostel. Close to the Town Hall.

Oxford (tel. code 0865)

Tourist Office
Tourist Information Centre, St Aldate's (tel. 726871). Open Mon.–Sat. 9.00 a.m.–5.30 p.m., Sun. 1–4 p.m. A small charge is made for the town map listing the opening hours of the university colleges and local museums. There is a huge charge of £4 ($7) for the room-finding service. During the summer, long queues are the norm. St Aldate's Street begins at the Carfax Tower in the centre of the town. Any time after the office closes up until 10 p.m. you can obtain free help with finding accommodation by phoning Mrs Downes, Secretary of the Oxford Association of Hotels and Guesthouses (tel. 241326/250511). Book-A-Bed-Ahead service available.

Finding Accommodation
Rooms (especially singles) can be at a premium in July and August in Oxford, so try to book a bed in advance if possible.

You may be asked to send a deposit to confirm a booking. Local guesthouses and B&Bs are more expensive than normal, which means you will struggle to find a double room for under £15 ($26.50) per person. The least expensive B&Bs are on Iffley Road (nos. 200–240), on Cowley Road (nos. 250–350), and on Abingdon Road.

GUESTHOUSES AND B&Bs

The prices quoted below are based on two people sharing a double. Expect to pay a further 15–20 per cent for a single.

B&B from £13 ($23) per person

Windrush Guest House, 11 Iffley Road (tel. 247933).

B&B from £14 ($24.50) per person

Brenal Guest House, 307 Iffley Road (tel. 721561).

B&B from £15 ($26.50) per person

Pine Castle Guest House, 290 Iffley Road (tel. 241497/727230).
Hansa Guest House, 192 Iffley Road (tel. 249757).
Bronte Guest House, 282 Iffley Road (tel. 244594).
Southfields, 240 Abingdon Road (tel. 244357).
Beaumont Guest House, 234 Abingdon Road (tel. 241767).
Micklewood, 331 Cowley Road (tel. 247328).

B&B from £16 ($28) per person

Bravalla Guest House, 242 Iffley Road (tel. 241326/250511).
The Athena, 253 Cowley Road (tel. 243124).
Acorn Guest House, 260 Iffley Road (tel. 247998).
Shannon Guest House, 329 Cowley Road (tel. 247558).
Ascot Guest House, 283 Iffley Road (tel. 240259/727669).
Adams Guest House, 302 Banbury Road, Summertown (tel. 56118).
Burren Guest House, 374 Banbury Road (tel. 513513).
Newton House, 82–84 Abingdon Road (tel. 240561).
Lakeside Guest House, 118 Abingdon Road (tel. 244725).

B&B from £17 ($30) per person

St Michael's Guest House, 26 St Michael Street (tel. 242101).
The Whitehouse, 315 Iffley Road (tel. 244524).
Five Mile View, 528 Banbury Road (tel. 58747).
Becket House, 5 Becket Street (tel. 724675).
The Ridings, 280 Abingdon Road (tel. 248364).
Greengables, 326 Abingdon Road (tel. 725870).
White House View, 9 White House Road (tel. 721626).
Gables' Guest House, 6 Cumnor Hill, Botley (tel. 862153).
Conifer Lodge, 159 Eynsham Road, Botley (tel. 862280).

B&B from £18 ($31.50) per person

Westminster Guest House, 350 Iffley Road (tel. 250924).
Earlmont Guest House, 324 Cowley Road (tel. 240236).

IYHF HOSTEL

Oxford Youth Hostel, Jack Straw's Lane (tel. 62997). Open
daily 1 Feb.–28 Dec. Juniors £6.30 ($11), seniors £7.60
($13.50). About two miles from the city centre. Frequent
minibus service (every 15–20 minutes until 10.30 p.m.)
from the Job Centre (near the Tourist Information Office)
or from Queen's College.

HOSTELS

YMCA, Alexandra Residential Club, 133 Woodstock Road
(tel. 52021). Women aged over 16 only. 2 a.m. curfew (2.30
a.m. Fri. and Sat.) Three night maximum stay. Around
£6.50 ($11.50) for one night, £12 ($21) for two nights, and
£16 ($28) for three nights. About a mile from the centre.
Bus 60 or 60A.

CAMPING

Oxford Camping International, 426 Abingdon Road (tel.
246551). Open year round. Around £7 ($12.50) for a tent

and two adults. One and a half miles from the centre, to the rear of the Texaco petrol station.

Cassington Mill Caravan Site, Eynsham Road, Cassington (tel. 881081). Open Apr.–Oct. Around £6 ($10.50) for a tent and two occupants. Four miles out of town, off the A40 to Cheltenham. Bus 90 from the bus station.

Stratford-upon-Avon (tel. code 0789)

TOURIST OFFICE
Tourist Information Centre, Bridgefoot (tel. 293127/294466). Open Apr.–Oct., Mon.–Sat. 9.00 a.m.–5.30 p.m.; Nov.–Mar., Mon.–Sat. 10.30 a.m.–4.30 p.m. Room-finding service. After office hours an accommodation list is displayed. Book-A-Bed-Ahead service available.

Guide Friday, Civic Hall, 14 Rother Street (tel. 294466). Limited range of information. In the past, this office has operated a room-finding service but at an extortionate £3 ($5.50) fee.

Finding Accommodation
Even though the town has a large number of B&Bs considering its size, rooms (especially singles) are in short supply from late June to early September. At these times, try to book lodgings at least one week in advance. The best area to look for B&Bs is around Evesham Road, Evesham Place and Grove Road. To get there go down Alcester Road from the train station, then right on to Grove Road. This road runs into Evesham Place, which subsequently becomes Evesham Road. Across the river, the Shipston Road also has quite a concentration of B&Bs.

GUESTHOUSES AND B&Bs

Doubles from around £23 ($40)

Bradbourne Guest House, 44 Shipston Road (tel. 204178).

Kawartha House, 39 Grove Road (tel. 204469).
Amelia Linhill Guesthouse, 35 Evesham Place (tel. 292879).

Doubles from around £24 ($42)

Clomendy Guest House, 157 Evesham Road (tel. 266957).

Doubles around £25 ($44)

34 Banbury Road (tel. 269714).

Doubles from £25–27 ($44–47)

Bronhill House, 260 Alcester Road (tel. 299169).

Doubles from £25–29 ($44–51)

Field View, 35 Banbury Road (tel. 292694).

Doubles from around £26 ($45.50)

Compton House, 22 Shipston Road (tel. 205646).
Green Gables, 47 Banbury Road (tel. 205557).
Salamander Guest House, 40 Grove Road (tel. 205728/297843).
Barbette, 165 Evesham Road (tel. 297822).
Stretton House, 38 Grove Road (tel. 268647).

Doubles from £27–29 ($47–51)

Moonlight Bed & Breakfast, 144 Alcester Road (tel. 298213).
Naini Tal Guest House, 63A Evesham Road (tel. 204956).

Doubles from £27 ($47)

Courtland Hotel, 12 Guild Street (tel. 292401).
The Croft, 49 Shipston Road (tel. 293419).
Arden Park Hotel, 6 Arden Street (tel. 296072).

Doubles from £29–31 ($51–54)

Cherangani, 61 Maidenhead Road (tel. 292655).

Doubles from around £29 ($51)

Aberfoyle Guesthouse, 3 Evesham Place (tel. 295703).
Newlands, 7 Broad Walk (tel. 298449).
Chadwyns, 6 Broad Walk (tel. 269077).
Parkfield, 3 Broad Walk (tel. 293313).
Woodstock Guest House, 30 Grove Road (tel. 299881).

Doubles from £30–33 ($52.50–58.00)

Brett House, 8 Broad Walk (tel. 266374).

Doubles around £31 ($54)

Winterbourne Guest House, 2 St Gregory's Road (tel. 292207).

Doubles from around £31 ($54)

Nando's, 18–19 Evesham Place (tel. 204907).

IYHF HOSTEL

Stratford-upon-Avon YH, Hemmingford House, Wellesbourne Road, Alveston (tel. 297093). Open mid-Jan.–mid-Dec. Juniors £6.80 ($12), seniors £8 ($14). Reserve well in advance. About 2 miles from the centre of town: walk along the B4086 to Alveston, or take the hourly 518 bus from the Travel Shop (at the junction of Guild Street and Warwick Road) or from the bus station.

CAMPING

Elms, Tiddington Road (tel. 292312). Open Apr.–Oct. £3.50 ($6) per tent, £2 ($3.50) per person. On the B4056, a mile north-east of the centre.

Dodwell Park, Evesham Road (tel. 204957). Open year round. Similar prices to the site above. Two miles out from the centre on the A439.

Wales (Cymru/Wales)

Aberystwyth (tel. code 0970)

Tourist Office

Tourist Information Centre, Terrace Road (tel. 612125). Open year round. Local accommodation service and Book-A-Bed-Ahead.

GUESTHOUSES AND B&Bs

The greatest concentration of guesthouses and B&Bs are along South Marine Terrace and Rheidol Terrace.

Myrddin, Rheidol Terrace (tel. 612799). Singles and doubles from £12 ($21) per person.

Yr Hafod, South Marine Terrace (tel. 617579). Singles and doubles from £15 ($26.50) per person.

IYHF HOSTEL

The closest IYHF Hostel is 8 miles away in Borth, a town linked to Aberystwyth by train and bus.

Borth YH, Morlais (tel. 0970–871498). Juniors £6 ($10.50), seniors £7.30 ($13).

Betws-y-Coed (tel. code 0690)

Tourist Office

Tourist Information Centre, Royal Oak Stables (tel. 710426). Open in the summer season only. Local accommodation service and Book-A-Bed-Ahead. Information on the Snowdonia National Park and nearby Swallow Falls.

GUESTHOUSES AND B&Bs

Glan Llugy, Holyhead Road (tel. 710592). Singles from £13 ($23), doubles from £24 ($42).

Mount Pleasant, Holyhead Road (tel. 710502). Singles from £13 ($23), doubles from £24 ($42).

Bryn Llewely, Holyhead Road (tel. 710601). Singles and doubles from £13 ($23) per person.

IYHF HOSTELS

There is no IYHF hostel in Betws-y-Coed, but the Capel Curig and Lledr Valley Hostels are only 5 and 6 miles away respectively. A mountain path links these two hostels (a 5-mile walk).

Lledr Valley YH, Lledr House, Pont-y-Pant, Dolwyddelan (tel. 06906–202). Juniors £5.60 ($10), seniors £6.80 ($12). The hostel is located on the main road linking Betws-y-Coed to Ffestiniog (A470).

Capel Curig YH, Plas Curig, Capel Curig (tel. 06904–225). Juniors £6 ($10.50), seniors £7.30 ($13). A supplement of £0.40 ($0.70) is added to these prices in July and August. By the garage in Capel Curig, a village on the main road (A5) between Betws-y-Coed and Bangor.

Blaenau Ffestiniog (tel. code 0766)

Tourist Office
Tourist Information Centre, Isallt, High Street (tel. 830360). Open in summer only. Local accommodation service and Book-A-Bed-Ahead.

GUESTHOUSES AND B&Bs

Affalon, Manod Road (tel. 830468). Singles and doubles from £12 ($21) per person.

IYHF HOSTEL

There is no IYHF Hostel in Blaenau Ffestiniog itself, but there may still be a hostel in the neighbouring village of Llan Ffestiniog, 1½ miles from Blaenau Ffestiniog. At the time of writing, this hostel was up for sale. Check with the Tourist Office or the Youth Hostels Association of England and Wales for up-to-date information.

Ffestiniog YH, Caerblaidd, Llan Ffestiniog (tel. 762765). Juniors £5.20 ($9), seniors £6.40 ($11.50).

Caernarfon (tel. code 0286)

Tourist Office
Tourist Information Centre, Oriel Pendeitsh, Castle Street (tel. 672232). Open year round, 10 a.m.–5.30 p.m. daily. Local accommodation service and Book-A-Bed-Ahead available.

GUESTHOUSES AND B&Bs

Mrs Hughes, Victoria Road (tel. 76229). Around £12 ($21) per person in singles and doubles.

Wallasea Guest House, 21 Segontium Terrace (tel. 3564). Singles from £14 ($24.50), doubles from £27 ($47.50).

Menai View Hotel, North Road (tel. 4602). Singles from £15 ($26.50), doubles from £27 ($47.50).

Gorffwysfa Private Hotel, St David's Road (tel. 2647). Singles around £17 ($30), doubles around £28 ($49).

Tal Menai, Bognor Road (tel. 2160). Singles from £15.50 ($27), doubles from £29 ($51).

IYHF HOSTELS

There is no IYHF hostel in Caernarfon. The Llanberis and Bangor youth hostels are 8 and 12 miles away respectively.

Llanberis YH, Llwyn Celyn (tel. 0286–870280). Juniors £6 ($10.50), seniors £7.30 ($13). Llanberis is on the A4086

between Caernarfon and Betws-y-Coed. Bus Gwynedd 88
from Caernarfon. The hostel is just outside the village.
Bangor YH, Tan-y-Bryn (tel. 0248–353516). Juniors £6
($10.50), seniors £7.30 ($13). Frequent bus services run
between Caernarfon and Bangor.

CAMPING

Cadnant Valley Park, Llanberis Road (tel. 3196). Around
£5.75 ($10) for a solo traveller.

Cardiff (Caerdydd/Cardiff)
(tel. code 0222)

Tourist Office
Tourist Information Centre, 8–14 Bridge Street (tel. 227281).
Open year round 9 a.m.–7 p.m. daily, except in winter, when
the office is closed on Sundays. Local accommodation service
and Book-A-Bed-Ahead available. Free guide to the city's
sights.

Finding Accommodation
Usually you will have few problems fixing yourself up with
suitable accommodation in the Welsh capital. The one
exception is if you arrive in the week leading up to one of the
Five Nations rugby internationals, when the city is swamped
by visiting fans. Fortunately, these games take place around
the turn of the year, a time when there are few other visitors
to the city.

GUESTHOUSES AND B&Bs

The Bed and Breakfast, 2 Shirley Road, Roath (tel. 462843).
Singles and doubles from £11 ($19.50) per person.
Y Dderwen Deg, 57 Ninian Road, Roath Park (tel. 481001).
Singles and doubles from around £13 ($23) per person.

806 Cheap Sleep Guide

Ty Gwyn, 5–7 Dyfrig Street (off Cathedral Road) (tel. 239785). Singles from £14 ($24.50), doubles from £26 ($46).

Plas-y-Bryn, 93 Fairwater Road, Llandaff (tel. 561717). Singles from £14 ($24.50), doubles from £26 ($46).

Austins Hotel, 11 Coldstream Terrace (tel. 377148). Singles from £15 ($25), doubles from £28 ($47.50). Great location, 400m from the castle.

Bon Maison, 39 Plasturron Gardens, Pontcanna (tel. 383660). Singles from £16 ($28), doubles from £28 ($49).

Albany Guest House, 191/193 Albany Road, Roath (tel. 494121). Singles from £17 ($30), doubles from £28 ($49).

IYHF HOSTEL

Cardiff YH, 2 Wedal Road, Roath Park (tel. 462303). Reception does not open until 3 p.m. Juniors £6.80 ($12), seniors £8 ($14). Two miles from the city centre, near the Roath Park Lake at the junction of Wedal Road and Lake Road West. Bus 80 or 82 from the centre.

HOSTELS

YWCA, Newport Road (tel. 497379). Women only. Singles £8.50 ($15).

YMCA, The Walk, Roath Park (tel. 489101). Men only.

Conwy (tel. code 0492)

Tourist Office
Conwy Castle Visitor Centre (tel. 592248). The Tourist Information service operates in summer only. Local accommodation service and Book-A-Bed-Ahead.

GUESTHOUSES AND B&Bs

Llys Gwilym Guest House, 5 Mountain Road, Cadnant Park

(tel. 592351). Singles from £13 ($23), doubles from £25
($44).

Bryn Derwen, Woodlands (tel. 596134). Singles from £11.50
($20), doubles from £26 ($46).

Henllys Farm, Llechwedd (tel. 593269). Singles and doubles
from £13 ($23) per person. The farmhouse is only 1½ miles
from the town.

Pen-y-Bryn, 28 High Street, Lancaster Square (tel. 596445).
Doubles from £28 ($49).

IYHF HOSTELS

There is no IYHF hostel in Conwy, but there is a hostel just
outside the popular beach resort of Colwyn Bay, only 4 miles
from Conwy, and served by frequent buses and trains.

Colwyn Bay YH, Foxhill, Nant-y-Glyn (tel. 0492–530627).
Juniors £5.20 ($9), seniors £6.40 ($11.50). In July and
August, a supplement of £0.50 ($1) is added to these prices.

Llangollen (tel. code 0978)

Tourist Office
Tourist Information Centre, Town Hall, Castle Street (tel.
860828). Open year round. Local accommodation service and
Book-A-Bed-Ahead. Well supplied with information on the
surrounding area.

Finding Accommodation
With the exception of early July, when the town plays host
to the annual international Eisteddfod, finding a bed in
Llangollen is usually straightforward. For information in
advance on accommodation possibilities during the Eisteddfod,
contact: International Eisteddfod Office, Llangollen, Clwyd
LL20 8NG (tel. 860236).

GUESTHOUSES AND B&Bs

Dinbren House, Dinbren Road (tel. 860593). Singles and doubles from £14 ($24.50) per person.

Glanafon Guest House, Abbey Road (tel. 860725). Singles and doubles from £14 ($24.50) per person.

IYHF HOSTEL

Llangollen YH, Tyndwr Hall, Tyndwr Road (tel. 860330). Juniors £6.30 ($11), seniors £7.60 ($13.50). One and a half miles from the town. The Crosville bus to Chester passes the hostel, but the service is infrequent.

St David's (Tyddewi/St David's)
(tel. code 0437)

Tourist Office

Information on the town, the surrounding area and on accommodation possibilites available from the National Park Information Centre (tel. 720392).

GUESTHOUSES AND B&Bs

The Mount, 66 New Street (tel. 720276). Doubles from £24 ($42)

Ty Olaf, Mount Gardens (tel. 720885). Singles and doubles from £12.50 ($22) per person.

Y Gorlan, 77 Nun Street (tel. 720037). Singles and doubles from £13.50 ($24) per person.

IYHF HOSTELS

St David's YH, Llaethdy (tel. 720435). Juniors £4.80 ($8.50), seniors £6 ($10.50). In July and August a supplement of £0.75 ($1.50) is added to these prices. Two miles from the town.

York (tel. code 0904)

Tourist Office

There are three official City of York Tourist Information Centres in the city. The main office is close to York Minster in the De Grey Rooms on Exhibition Square (opposite the Art Gallery) (tel. 621756). Branch offices operate in the train station (tel. 643700) and in the Askham Bar Visitor Centre on the Tadcaster Road (tel. 701888). Opening hours are Mon.–Sat. 9 a.m.–8 p.m., Sun. 2–5 p.m. from June–Sept.; Mon.–Sat. 9 a.m.–5 p.m. from Oct.–May. All the offices are well supplied with information on the city. A local room-finding service is provided which is effectively free; you pay a 10 per cent deposit at the office, which is subtracted from your final bill at the B&B. Outside office hours an accommodation list is displayed at the office on Exhibition Square. Book-A-Bed-Ahead service available.

Finding Accommodation

Finding a cheap place to stay in York during the summer can be very difficult. At this time, even campsites are best reserved in advance. The city is also highly popular with visitors taking weekend breaks, so try to arrive in midweek if possible. B&Bs start at around £11–12 ($19.50–21.00), but the cheapest establishments fill early in the day. If you arrive in York when the Tourist Information Centres are open there is little point in looking around on your own. This is true even in the summer when the long queues can be off putting. However, if you get into town early in the morning during the summer there are a few areas which are worth looking in if you want a B&B. The Bootham area of the city, the Haxby Road, Bishopthorpe Road and the streets off Scarcroft Road are all well stocked with B&Bs and within easy walking distance of the bus and train stations.

Basic Directions

The bus and train stations are both within 10 minutes' walk

of the city centre. Leaving the train station, follow Station Road away to the left past the Royal Station Hotel. Station Road runs right to the River Ouse, passing the end of Rougier Street (site of the main bus station) on the way. Crossing the Ouse by the Lendal Bridge you can follow Museum Street and then Duncombe Place to the junction with High Petergate, a few yards from the Minster. Turning left down St Leonard's Place from the end of Museum Street takes you to Exhibition Square, as does heading left along High Petergate from the end of Duncombe Place.

Two of the best places to look for a B&B are easily reached from Exhibition Square. The street known as Bootham runs out of the square. On the other side of the railway line Bootham becomes Clifton. The streets on either side of Bootham and Clifton have a very good supply of B&Bs. Following Gillygate and then Clarence Street from Exhibition Square brings you to a fork in the road at which point the Haxby Road is to the right.

To reach the Mount area of the city, head right from the train station exit along Queen Street. At the first crossroads head right along Blossom Street, which leads into The Mount. The Scarcroft Road is off to the left. If instead of turning right down Blossom Street you continue straight on from Queen Street along Nunnery Lane, you arrive at the start of the Bishopthorpe Road. Bishopthorpe Road can also be reached by walking down Scarcroft Road.

GUESTHOUSES AND B&Bs

The cheapest singles at the guesthouses and B&Bs listed below are normally around 50–60% of the cost of the cheapest doubles.

Doubles from £13–18 ($23–32). No singles.

1   Aaron Guest House, 42 Bootham Crescent, Bootham (tel. 625927). About 15 minutes' walk from the train station.

Follow Bootham, then take the second right beyond the railway line.

Doubles around £21 ($37)

2 South View Guest House, 114 Acomb Road (tel. 796512). Just over 10 minutes' walk from the train station. From Blossom Street turn right down Holgate Road then left at Acomb Road.

Doubles from around £21 ($37)

3 Dalescroft Guest House, 10 Southlands Road (tel. 626801). Right off the Bishopthorpe Road, about ten minutes' walk from the train station.
4 Southland's Guest House, 69 Nunmill Street, South Bank (tel. 631203). A 10-minute walk from the train station. From the Bishopthorpe Road turn right along Scarcroft Road then take the first left.
5 Brontë House, 22 Grosvenor Terrace, Bootham (tel. 621066). About 15 minutes' walk from the train station. Follow Bootham, then take the first right beyond the railway line.
6 Burton Villa, 22 Haxby Road (tel. 626364). About 15 minutes' walk from the train station.

Doubles from around £22 ($39)

7 Acorn Guest House, 1 Southlands Road (tel. 620081). See 3.

Doubles from around £23 ($40)

8 Birchfield Guest House, 2 Nunthorpe Avenue (tel. 636395). About ten minutes' walk from the train statino. Turn left off Blossom Street/The Mount along Scarcroft Road, then right at Nunthorpe Avenue.
9 Bishopgarth Guest House, 3 Southlands Road (tel. 635220). See 3.

10 Clifton View Guest House, 118 Clifton (tel. 625047).
About 15 minutes' walk from the train station.

11 Queen Anne's Guest House, 24 Queen Anne's Road,
Bootham (tel. 629389). About 15 minutes' walk from the
train station. Follow Bootham then take the second left
beyond the railway line.

12 Staymore Guest House, 2 Southlands Road (tel. 626935).
See 3.

13 York Lodge Guest House, 64 Bootham Crescent, Bootham
(tel. 654289). See 1.

Doubles from around £25 ($44)

14 Heworth Guest House, 126 East Parade, Heworth (tel.
426384).

15 Bridge House, 181 Haxby Road (tel. 636161).

16 Green Guest House, 31 Bewlay Street (tel. 652509). About
10 minutes' walk from the train station, left off the
Bishopthorpe Road.

17 Romley Guest House, 2 Millfield Road (tel. 652822). A
10-minute walk from the train station. Right off the
Scarcroft Road immediately after Nunthorpe Avenue.
See 8.

18 Greenside, 124 Clifton (tel. 623631). About 15 minutes'
walk from the train station.

19 Alemar Guest House, 19 Queen Anne's Road, Bootham
(tel. 652367). See 11.

20 Bank House, 9 Southlands Road (tel. 627803). See 3.

21 Grange Lodge, 52 Bootham Crescent, Bootham (tel.
621137). See 1.

22 Healey Grange Guest House, Malton Road (tel. 415700).

23 St Raphael Guest House, 44 Queen Anne's Road,
Bootham (tel. 645028). See 11.

24 Minster View Guest House, 2 Grosvenor Terrace,
Bootham (tel. 655034). See 5.

25 The Limes, 135 Fulford Road (tel. 624548).

Doubles from around £26 ($46)

26 Arnot House, 17 Grosvenor Terrace, Bootham (tel. 641966). See 5.

27 Tree Tops, 21 St Mary's, Bootham (tel. 658053). A 10-minute walk from the train station, left off Bootham.

28 Ashwood Place, 19 Nunthorpe Avenue (tel. 623412). See 8.

29 Sycamore Guest House, Sycamore Place, Bootham (tel. 658053). About 15 minutes' walk from the train station. Follow Bootham and take the first left beyond the railway line. Follow Bootham Terrace until you see Sycamore Place on the right.

30 Claremont Guest House, 18 Claremont Terrace, Gillygate (tel. 625158). Good location close to the centre. From Exhibition Square follow Gillygate and then turn left at Claremont Terrace.

Doubles around £27 ($47)

31 Brookside Guest House, 73 Huntingdon Road (tel. 633575).

Doubles from around £27 ($47)

32 Hillcrest Guest House, 110 Bishopthorpe Road (tel. 653160).

33 Stanley Guest House, Stanley Street (tel. 637111). On the right, a short distance down the Haxby Road.

34 Martin's Guest House, 5 Longfield Terrace, Bootham (634551). A 15-minute walk from the train station. Follow Bootham and take the first left beyond the railway line. Longfield Terrace is an extension of Bootham Terrace.

35 Jubilee Guest House, 120 Haxby Road (tel. 620566).

36 Holmlea Guest House, 6–7 Southlands Road (tel. 621010). See 3.

37 Mont Clare Guest House, 32 Claremont Terrace, Gillygate (tel. 627054). Well located, close to the centre. See 30.

38 Alcuin Lodge, 15 Sycamore Place, Bootham (tel. 632222). See 29.

39 Craig-y-Don, 3 Grosvenor Terrace, Bootham (tel. 637186). See 5.

40 Gleneagles Lodge Guest House, 27 Nunthorpe Avenue (tel. 637000). See 8.

41 Brentwood, 54 Bootham Crescent, Bootham (tel. 636419). See 1.

42 The Hollies, 141 Fulford Road (tel. 634279).

Doubles around £29 ($51)

43 Blakeney Hotel, 180 Stockton Lane (tel. 422786).

44 Linden Lodge, 6 Nunthorpe Avenue (tel. 620107). See 8.

Doubles from around £29 ($51)

45 Clifton Guest House, 127 Clifton (tel. 634031). About 15 minutes' walk from the train station.

46 Crossways Guest House, 23 Wiggington Road (tel. 637250). Follow Gillygate and then Clarence Street from Exhibition Square to the fork in the road. The Wiggingon Road is to the left.

47 Eastons, 90 Bishopthorpe Road (tel. 625546).

48 Regency House, 7 South Parade (tel. 633053). About 5 minutes' walk from the train station, left off Blossom Street.

49 Dairy Whole Food Guest House, 3 Scarcroft Road (tel. 639367). See 8.

50 Park View Guest House, 34 Grosvenor Terrace, Bootham (tel. 620437). See 5.

51 Jubilee Cottage Guest House, 23 Barbican Road (tel. 624013) A 15–20-minute walk from the train station. From Nunnery Lane go left along Price's Lane. Turn left along Bishopgate Street, cross the Ouse by the Skeldergate Bridge and continue straight ahead to the junction with Tower Street. Follow the latter right into Fishergate. Turn left off Fishergate down Paragon Street, which runs into Barbican Road.

52 Airden House, 1 St Mary's, Bootham (tel. 638915). See 27.

53 Barrington House, 15 Nunthorpe Avenue (tel. 634539). See 8.

54 River View Hotel, 1 Marlborough Villas, Marlborough Grove (tel. 626826). A 20-minute walk from the train station. Marlborough Grove is to the right off Fishergate. See 50.

55 Nunmill House, 85 Bishopthorpe Road (tel. 634047).

SELF-CATERING ACCOMMODATION

Bishophill Holidays, 5 Kyme Street. House sleeping up to six people. High season price from around £170–260 ($300–450) per week. Low season price from around £100–160 ($175–280) per week. The house is about 5 minutes' walk from the train station, off Victor Street, which runs off Nunnery Lane. For bookings contact Mrs L.A. Shimmin, 49 Moorgate, Acomb, York, Y02 4HP (tel. 796118).

Abba House, 42 Hambleton Terrace. House sleeping up to six people. High season rates from £220–260 ($380–450), low season rates from £140–210 ($250–370). Hambleton Terrace is off the Haxby Road, about 10 minutes' walk from the city centre. For bookings contact Mrs A.M. Paterson, 14 Sycamore Terrace, Bootham York, Y03 7DN (tel. 630750).

UNIVERSITY ACCOMMODATION

Fairfax House, University of York, 98 Heslington Road (tel. 432095). Open Mar.–Apr. and July–Sept. Singles from £12–16 ($21–28).

IYHF HOSTEL

Peter Rowntree Memorial Hostel, Haverford, Water End, Clifton (tel. 653147). Curfew 11.30 p.m. Juniors £8 ($14), seniors £9.50 ($17). The hostel is about a mile from the train station and the town centre, close to the River Ouse. Water End runs left off Clifton. From the train station head left along Station Road, turn left at Station Rise and then follow Leeman Road to the left past the National Railway Museum. At the end of Kingsland Terrace turn left and follow Salisbury Terrace and then Salisbury Road on to Water End. Turn right and cross over the Ouse to get to the hostel.

HOSTELS

York Youth Hotel, 11–13 Bishophill Senior Road (tel. 625904). Singles £13–17 ($23–30) doubles £11–15 ($19.50–26.50), dorms £9 ($16). About 5 minutes' walk from train station. At the end of Queen Street turn left along Micklegate, then right on to Trinity Lane which leads into Bishophill Senior.

Maxwell's Hotel, 54 Walmgate (tel. 624048). Singles and doubles £12–15 ($21.00–26.50) per person. From the end of Duncombe Place turn right along High Petergate and go straight ahead until you reach Walmgate.

The New Racecourse Centre. Singles, doubles and dorms. The booking office is at 5 High Petergate (tel. 636553). The accommodation is in the racing stables at Dringhouses on the outskirts of the city.

IYHF HOSTELS NEARBY

Malton Youth Hostel, Derwent Bank, York Road, Malton (tel. 0653–692077). In a picturesque small town about 20 miles from York. The hostel is just over 10 minutes' walk from the train station in Malton. Juniors £5.20 ($9), seniors £6.40 ($11.50).

Beverley Friary Youth Hostel, The Friary, Friars' Lane, Beverley (tel. 0482–881751). In a historic market town with a beautiful minster, 30 miles from York. Juniors £5.20 ($9), seniors £6.40 ($11.50).

CAMPING

Caravan Club Site, Terry Avenue (tel. 0203–694995). Around £4 ($7) per person. The only site within the city. In summer, the site is often filled to capacity, so reserve as far ahead as you can. A 10–15-minute walk from the train station. Follow Nunnery Lane and when the road forks go left along Price's Lane. Cross Bishopsgate Street and follow Clemnthorpe down to the River Ouse. The site is along to the right.

Bishopthorpe (tel. 704442). Open Easter–Sept. Around £4 ($7) for one person and tent. Not much more expensive for four sharing a tent as the price per person is low. By the river in Bishopthorpe, 3 miles out on the A64 towards Tadcaster and Leeds. Bus 14, 15 or 15A.

Post Office Site (tel. 706288). Open Apr.–Oct. Similar price for a solo traveller to the Bishopthorpe site. Also by the river, one mile further out on the A64 than the Bishopthorpe site. Any Acaster Malbis bus will get you to the site.

Poplar Farm (tel. 706548). Not far from the Post Office Site, but more expensive. Same buses as for the Post Office site. Also the Sykes' bus, which runs every two hours from Skeldergate.

'YUGOSLAVIA'

Note: The information below has not been updated since 1992.

Over the last decade the Yugoslav government raised the price of accommodation in an effort to earn hard currency to support its flagging economy. This has not (yet) resulted in a situation similar to that which prevailed in Romania, as most accommodation possibilities are still within the range of the budget traveller, but accommodation is no longer dirt cheap.

During the camping season (April to October) a tent can be a useful standby as you may encounter difficulties finding a cheap bed in some of the larger cities such as Belgrade, Zagreb and Llubljana, and also in the coastal towns and resorts, especially Split and Dubrovnik. Accommodation possibilities can be just as restricted in the off-season when the campgrounds are closed and the availability of private rooms declines dramatically. One notable exception to the general rule is Sarajevo. In summer you should have little difficulty finding suitable accommodation here but expect difficulties in winter as Sarajevo is a major winter sports centre.

The local travel agencies will find rooms for you in hotels or private rooms, but, as these are in business to make money, they invariably try to push you towards concerns they control. If you feel they are paying little attention to your requests (especially as regards price) try to see if one of the other agencies will offer you a more acceptable deal. As well as local and regional organizations, such as Dubrovnikturist and Dalmacijaturist, there are others which operate throughout the country such as Kompas, Atlas, Putnik, Generalturist and Inex.

Hotels are graded L (de luxe), and then in descending order from A to D. There are some B- and C-class hotels in the major cities where doubles are available for around £10 ($19; DM29) p.p. but on the whole hotels are probably well outside your price range. Pensions, rated from third up to first class, are more affordable, but be wary of staying more than three days, as, after this period, pensions and hotels can legally make full-board obligatory, pushing the price up sharply. Inns are establishments which fail to meet the minimum requirements laid down for hotels and pensions: they are a good budget option with B&B in doubles from £4.50 ($8.50; DM13) per person, but are difficult to find.

More readily available, and starting from around the same price, are **rooms in private homes** (*sobe*). There is a good supply of rooms along the coast, and in the more popular tourist destinations of Macedonia, Montenegro, Serbia and the Julian Alps. Wherever you go the supply of singles is very limited, and even where singles do exist, prices approach those of doubles, so solo travellers may want to find someone to share with. Rooms are graded downwards from Category I to III. In peak season (July and Aug.) prices range from £3.50 to £10.00 ($6.75–19.00; DM10–29) p.p. for doubles depending on classification and location. At other times prices for the most expensive rooms fall to £7.50 ($14.50; DM22) p.p. for doubles.

It is possible to find rooms on your own: look out for the 'sobe' sign, or a sign showing a stylized bed, or, especially in the northern areas popular with Austrian and German holidaymakers, a sign inscribed 'Zimmer'. Occasionally the owner may ask you to go into town and book the room at an agency because owners can be duty bound to do this in order that the agencies know where rooms are available. In the larger, more popular towns you are probably better to head for an agency rather than search on your own, especially during the peak season. When booking through an agency you will find that they generally add a surcharge of up to 30 per cent for stays of less than four days. In the popular coastal towns travellers are often approached at bus and train stations, and at ferry terminals, by locals offering rooms. These are no great bargains, as the asking price will normally be on a par with prices at the local agencies, but the bonus for you is the convenience of getting a room virtually on arrival and unless there is a high ratio of travellers to touts they can usually be talked down from their initial asking price, but do not expect anything more than a 20–25 per cent reduction. Have a look at the room before committing yourself. If the room is not nearby leave your pack at the station while you go and have a look.

There are about 40 **IYHF hostels** in 'Yugoslavia', covering many of the major places of interest, with the notable exceptions of Split and Mostar. In theory IYHF cards are obligatory, but most hostels will settle for adding a small surcharge for non-members. Very few hostels remain open all year round, while in peak season you will struggle to find a bed unless you have reserved in advance. Hostels are not particularly good value for money, costing between £3.10 and £6.20 ($6–12; DM9–18). Not only are inflexible early curfews common, but also many hostels are not clean and lack hot running water.

A more pleasant alternative, and not much more expensive, are studentski domovi, or **student dormitories**, which are converted into hostels during July and August. They are aimed particularly at young Yugoslav holidaymakers and their popularity means that they are often full, but they are still well worth enquiring about. Try to reserve ahead where possible. Studentski domovi cost around £4.25–5.25 ($8–10; DM12.25–15.25) for B&B in small rooms. Unlike the IYHF hostels studentski domovi do offer good value for money. They can be found in most towns with a university, notably Llubljana, Zagreb, Split, Sarajevo and Skopje. The youth and travel organization Yugotours-Narom operate several International Youth Centres, including one in Dubrovnik. For more information on these centres, and to make reservations, contact the head office of Yugotours-Narom.

There are few of the towns of major interest that do not have a **campsite**. There are roughly 300 official sites, with concentrations along the coast, and in the Slovene mountains. Sites open for varying periods of time during the camping season and as a rule they are large, and frequently crowded. Most are equipped with leisure facilities and shops, the latter of which can be a godsend as they are often open when the local shops are closed. Camping is inexpensive, usually costing a solo traveller from £2.75 to £3.75 ($5.25–7.25; DM8–11). Occasionally this can rise to £4.50 ($8.50; DM13) in exceptionally popular places such as Dubrovnik. Camping rough is strictly illegal unless you have been granted a permit by the local authority. The authorities invariably take strong action against anyone caught flouting the law by imposing hefty fines. The same applies to anyone caught sleeping rough, especially in town parks, or along the beaches of the Adriatic.

ADDRESSES

Yugoslav YHA	Ferijalni savez Jugoslavije, Mose Pijade 12/V, 11000 Beograd (tel.011–339802).
International Youth Centres	Yugotours-Narom, Dure Dakoviča 31, 11000 Beograd (tel. 011–764622).
Youth hostels, travel, and International Youth Travel	Accommodation Centre, FSJ/FSH, Trg žrtava fasizma 13, 41000 Zagreb (tel. 041–415038).
	International Information Centre, FS Srbija, Mladost-turist-Beograd, Terazije 3, Beograd (tel. 011–322131).
Camping	Maps and lists of organizations booking private rooms are available from the National Tourist Office in London or your capital city.

Index

Hitch-hiker's Guide to Europe 1993

Ken Welsh

The new 14th edition of the Hitch-hiker's Bible completely updated for 1993.

British Isles ● Western Europe ● Eastern Europe ● Scandinavia ● Iceland ● Morocco ● Tunisia ● Algeria ● Turkey ● Middle East

An invaluable guide for anyone wanting to travel cheaply in Europe including over two hundred letters full of tips on cheap travelling from Europe's toughest hitchers!

Packed with inside info on:

- Survival
- Hitching tactics
- Routes
- What to see
- Where to sleep
- Where to eat
- Sex and drugs on the road
- Black markets
- Emergencies
- Roughing it
- Travel philosophy
- Language

'Practically researched . . . colossal fun to read'   *Observer*

THEY WERE RIGHT!

Fontana

Europe by Train 1993

Katie Wood and George McDonald

The bestselling classic, recommended by EUROTRAIN

Europe by Train is still the best value and most comprehensive book on the market for eurorailers. It contains all the essential, practical information required by students and those on a tight budget:

- Maximizing the benefits of rail passes
- Train networks and station facilities
- The best routes
- Local transport
- What to see
- Where to sleep
- What to eat
- Where the nightlife is

In addition to being fully revised and updated for 1993, this year's new edition of *Europe by Train* includes even more information on eastern Europe, plus details of all new passes and tickets.

'Excellent . . . a reliable guide to the systems of all European countries'   *Independent*

Fontana

On the Waterfront in France 1993

Telegraph Magazine Guide to Hotels, Restaurants and Cafés

Edited by Gill Charlton

On the Waterfront in France is the definitive guide to eating, drinking and sleeping beside the sea and on the banks of lakes, rivers and canals throughout France. It contains detailed descriptions of over 600 waterside hotels, guesthouses, restaurants and cafés, each one personally inspected by our team of researchers.

- More than 350 family-run hotels and restaurants, including many converted watermills, and over 30 château-hotels and private châteaux
- Good value, seaside hotels, perfect for family holidays, from Brittany to the French Riviera
- Special emphasis on places to stay and eat in the Loire Valley and along the Dordogne and Lot rivers
- Seductive waterside restaurants off the autoroutes, with directions on how to reach them

This guide also contains useful information on sightseeing, good sandy beaches, boat trips and many sporting opportunities including fishing, cycling, canoeing and riding. With maps to help you on your way, *On the Waterfront in France* will prove an invaluable travelling companion – whatever your budget.

Fontana

The Family Welcome Guide 1993

Malcolm Hamer and Jill Foster

The *Family Welcome Guide* is the only comprehensive and authoritative guide to the best hotels, self-catering accommodation, pubs, restaurants and places to visit for parents and children.

Over 600 establishments are listed, with maps to help you locate them. Every one extends a friendly welcome to all the family, and provides the essential basic services: hotels with cots, high chairs, a free baby-listening service; pubs with separate family rooms; and restaurants with high chairs and special menus for children. If you are planning some sightseeing, this guide will help you pick the museums, stately homes, wildlife and theme parks with the best facilities for families.

Whether you are planning a meal or day out, a journey or a holiday, don't leave home without it!

'The entries in the guide are informative, practical and bear the stamp of honest, down-to-earth assessment.' *Observer*

'An essential handbook for anyone planning a family outing.'
Parents Magazine

Fontana

Fontana Non-Fiction

Fontana is a leading paperback publisher of non-fiction. Below are some recent titles.

☐ EUROPE BY TRAIN Katie Wood & George McDonald £7.99
☐ CHEAP SLEEP GUIDE TO EUROPE Katie Wood £7.99
☐ ON THE WATERFRONT IN BRITAIN 1993 Alice Hart-Davis £8.99
☐ ON THE WATERFRONT IN FRANCE 1993 Gill Charlton £8.99
☐ HITCH-HIKER'S GUIDE TO EUROPE 1993 Ken Welsh £5.99
☐ FAMILY WELCOME GUIDE Malcolm Hamer & Jill Foster £5.99
☐ OBSESSIVE TRAVELLER David Dale £4.50

You can buy Fontana Paperbacks at your local bookshops or newsagents. Or you can order them from Fontana, Cash Sales Department, Box 29, Douglas, Isle of Man. Please send a cheque, postal or money order (not currency) worth the price plus 24p per book for postage (maximum postage required is £3.00 for orders within the UK).

NAME (Block letters)_____

ADDRESS_____

_____

While every effort is made to keep prices low, it is sometimes necessary to increase them at short notice. Fontana Paperbacks reserve the right to show new retail prices on covers which may differ from those previously advertised in the text or elsewhere.